Data Analytics & Visualization

ALL-IN-ONE

by Jack Hyman; Luca Massaron;
Paul McFedries; John Paul Mueller;
Lillian Pierson; Jonathan Reichental, PhD;
Joseph Schmuller; Alan Simon;
and Allen G. Taylor

for
dummies®
A Wiley Brand

Data Analytics & Visualization All-in-One For Dummies®

Published by: **John Wiley & Sons, Inc.**, 111 River Street, Hoboken, NJ 07030-5774, www.wiley.com

Copyright © 2024 by John Wiley & Sons, Inc., Hoboken, New Jersey

Media and software compilation copyright © 2024 by John Wiley & Sons, Inc. All rights reserved.

Published simultaneously in Canada

For general information on our other products and services, please contact our Customer Care Department within the U.S. at 877-762-2974, outside the U.S. at 317-572-3993, or fax 317-572-4002. For technical support, please visit https://hub.wiley.com/community/support/dummies.

Wiley publishes in a variety of print and electronic formats and by print-on-demand. Some material included with standard print versions of this book may not be included in e-books or in print-on-demand. If this book refers to media such as a CD or DVD that is not included in the version you purchased, you may download this material at http://booksupport.wiley.com. For more information about Wiley products, visit www.wiley.com.

Library of Congress Control Number: 2024932207

ISBN 978-1-394-24409-6 (pbk); ISBN 978-1-394-24411-9 (ePDF); ISBN 978-1-394-24410-2 (epub)

SKY10068233_022624

Contents at a Glance

Table of Contents

Introduction

Everywhere you go in the business world, you are likely to encounter executives who make decisions driven by tidbits of raw data that together tell a meaningful story. In fact, in our everyday worlds, websites and mobile apps express data using powerful visualizations to explain complex numbers and concepts, not extensive written passages anymore. The phrase "a picture speaks a thousand words" rings true in the world of data analytics and visualization, and for good reason.

Data analytics and visualization allow anyone to turn raw data into meaningful stories and insights. You, as the analyst, act as the detective. Instead of having to solve a mystery with clues, you are provided datasets that, if provided with enough clarity, can answer complex questions using trend and pattern analysis. If you review a dataset enough, you'll inevitably have an ah-ha moment in your interpretation quest, but if the dataset can be presented visually, you can accelerate your understanding like a racecar going from 0 to 100 miles per hour in seconds.

Data analytics and visualization help you uncover creative ways to showcase data in a manner that is both informative and engaging. Data often starts out as nothing more than a bunch of jumbled numbers; turning those numbers into a story that can influence decisions and drive change is incredibly powerful. Global enterprises rely on folks who have the skills you are about to embark on in this book as a way to determine business strategies, make corporate decisions, and influence change. If you are ready to learn these skills, you are in for a treat with this book.

About This Book

If you've picked up this book, you might be on a quest to piece together a whole lot of terms being thrown around in the information economy regarding data, the most precious tool in the information economy. Data is a business asset that sits at the intersection of many disciplines; the resultant product from data can be methodologies, processes, algorithms, and system outputs. To the end user though, the end game is extracting knowledge and insights from the byproducts of data, and taking action upon review.

Book 1 covers the foundational aspects of the data analytics and visualization lifecycle that every user must understand to be proficient as an analytics and visualization savvy. Books 2 and 3 focus on the two leading tools in the enterprise business intelligence market used to perform complex data analytics and visualization tasks; Microsoft Power BI and Tableau. Books 4 through 6 cover the key programming languages used by both proprietary and open-source data analytics and visualization platforms to extract, assess, and visualize data at scale when commercial off-the-shelf enterprise business platforms are unavailable.

This book uses the following technical conventions:

>> Bold text means that you're meant to type the text just as it appears in the book. The exception is when you're working through a steps list: Because each step is bold, the text to type is not bold.

>> Web addresses and programming code appear in monofont. If you're reading a digital version of this book on a device connected to the Internet, note that you can click the web address to visit that website, like this: `www.dummies.com`.

>> For command sequences in software, this book uses the command arrow. Here's an example that uses Microsoft Word: Click the Office button and then choose Page Layout⇨Margins⇨Narrow to decrease the default margin setting.

If you don't think the book contains any conventions that need to be spelled out in this section, discuss omitting conventions information with your editor.

To make the content more accessible, we divided it into 6 books:

>> **Book 1, "Learning Data Analytics & Visualization Foundations."**

Book 1 introduces terms and fundamental concepts. You learn about big data, data lakes, and data science, and you see how you can apply visualization tools to create meaningful stories based on data you collect.

>> **Book 2, "Using Power BI for Data Analysis & Visualization."**

Book 2 covers Microsoft Power BI, a data analysis and visualization tool used by many large organizations. This book illustrates how you can use Power BI to make sense of structured, unstructured, and semi-structured data, and develop robust business analytics outputs for your organization.

>> **Book 3, "Using Tableau for Data Analysis & Visualization."**

Book 3 covers Tableau, a data analysis and visualization tool favored by researchers and educational institutions. In this book, you discover how to prepare data and present your findings using Tableau's storytelling and visualization features. You also see how to collaborate and publish your work with Tableau Cloud.

>> **Book 4, "Extracting Information with SQL."**

Book 4 describes SQL and the relational database model. You discover how SQL is a powerful tool that nonprogrammers can use to write complex queries to get the most out of their data, and more.

>> **Book 5, "Performing Statistical Data Analysis & Visualization with R Programming."**

Book 5 introduces the open-source R programming language. You see how you can use R to perform statistical data analysis, data visualization, and other data science tasks.

>> **Book 6, "Applying Python Programming to Data Science."**

Book 6 describes how Python is used as a data science and visualization tool. The book includes a "crash course" on MatPlotLib.

Foolish Assumptions

To get the most out of this book, you need the following:

>> **Access to the Internet:** This may sound a bit obvious. Even with the Desktop client, an Internet connection is required in order to access datasets from the Internet.

>> **A meaningful dataset:** A meaningful dataset includes at least 300 to 400 records containing a minimum of five or six columns' worth of data.

Icons Used in This Book

Throughout this book, icons in the margins highlight certain types of valuable information that call out for your attention. Here are the icons you'll encounter and a brief description of each.

Best Practice icons highlight points of common knowledge among seasoned professionals in the data industry. If you don't want to look like a complete newbie, follow the well-worn advice described in these paragraphs.

Tips point out shortcuts or essential suggestions that you can use to do things quicker, faster, and more efficiently.

Consider these small suggestions that are quite helpful. Remember icons are like signs on the road to suggest a potential better route.

The Technical Stuff icon marks information of a highly technical nature that you can normally skip over. When appropriate, these paragraphs also suggest specialized resources you may find helpful down the road.

The Warning icon makes you aware of a common issue or product challenge many users face. Don't fret, but *do* take note when you see this icon.

Beyond the Book

In addition to the abundance of information and guidance related to data analysis and visualization provided in this book, you get access to even more help and information online at *Dummies.com*. Check out this book's online Cheat Sheet. Just go to *www.dummies.com* and search for "Data Analysis & Visualization All-in-One For Dummies Cheat Sheet."

Where to Go from Here

The book has three core themes: foundational concepts, tools, and programming languages.

If you want to learn the essential data analytics and visualization concepts, including learning the lingo of the land, head to Book 1.

If you're looking to get up to speed on Microsoft's Enterprise BI tools, head to Book 2. Tableau, a tool used for Enterprise BI but heavily leveraged in communities where data is regulated such as banking, healthcare, insurance, and government, head to Book 3.

The underpinning for data analytics and visualization is SQL, a querying language. To get a crash course on SQL, which is necessary for any proprietary or open-source data analytics and visualization platform, head to Book 4.

Finally, Books 5 and 6 are an introduction to two popular open-source programming languages, R and Python. Both languages can be configured for use with Power BI and Tableau, but are more commonly used with open-source (free) platforms like Jupyter Notebook and Anaconda to conceive data analytics outputs and visualizations. Unlike Power BI and Tableau, open-source tools leveraging programming languages are used in academic settings or by analysts requiring technologies that are data intensive.

1

Learning Data Analytics & Visualizations Foundations

Contents at a Glance

IN THIS CHAPTER

» **Understanding the different types of data**

» **Managing large datasets with business intelligence tools**

» **Recognizing the importance of data analytics**

» **Appreciating the role of data management**

» **Presenting data analytics visually**

Chapter **1**

Exploring Definitions and Roles

ata is everywhere — literally. From the moment you awaken until the time you sleep, some system somewhere collects data on your behalf. Even as you sleep, data is being generated that correlates to some aspect of your life. What is done with this data is often the proverbial 64-million-dollar question. Does the data make sense? Does it have any sort of structure? Is the dataset so voluminous that finding what you're looking for is like finding a needle in a haystack? Or is it more like you can't even find what you need unless you have a special tool to help you navigate?

The answer to that last question is an emphatic yes, and that's where data analytics and business intelligence join the party. And let's be honest: The party can be overwhelming if data is consistently generating something on your behalf.

This chapter discusses the different types of data you may encounter when you begin working with data. It introduces the key terminology you should become familiar with upfront. You learn a few key concepts to give you a head start working with business intelligence, and you get the "what's what" of business intelligence tools and techniques.

What Is Data, Really?

Ask a hundred people in a room what the definition of data is and you may receive one hundred different answers. Why is that? Because, in the world of business, data means a lot of different things to a lot of different people. So, let's try to get a streamlined response. Data contains facts. Sometimes, the facts make sense; sometimes, they're meaningless unless you add a bit of context.

The facts can sometimes be quantities, characters, symbols, or a combination of sorts that come together when collecting information. The information allows people — and more importantly, businesses — to make sense of the facts that, unless brought together, make absolutely no sense whatsoever.

When you have an information system full of business data, you also must have a set of unique data identifiers you can use so that, when searched, it's easy to make sense of the data in the form of a transaction. Examples of transactions might include the number of jobs completed, inquiries processed, income received, and expenses incurred.

The list can go on and on. To gain insight into business interactions and conduct analyses, your information system must have relevant and timely data that is of the highest quality.

REMEMBER

Data isn't the same as information. *Data* is the raw facts. That means you should think of data in terms of the individual fields or columns of data you may find in a relational database or perhaps the loose document (tagged with some descriptors called *metadata*) stored in a document repository. On their own, these items are unlikely to make much sense to you or a business. And that's perfectly okay — sometimes. *Information* is the collective body of all those data parts that result in the factoids making logical sense.

Working with structured data

Have you ever opened a database or spreadsheet and noticed that data is bound to specific columns or rows? For example, would you ever find a United States zip code containing letters of the alphabet? Or, perhaps when you think of a first name, middle initial, and last name, you notice that you always find letters in those specific fields. Another example is when you're limited to the number of characters you can input into a field. Think of Y as Yes; N is for No. Anything else is irrelevant.

This type of data is called *structured data*. When you evaluate structured data, you notice that it conforms to a tabular format, meaning that each column and row must maintain an interrelationship. Because each column has a representative name that adheres to a predefined data model, your ability to analyze the data should be straightforward.

If you're using Power BI (covered in Book 2) or Tableau (covered in Book 3), you notice that structured data conform to a formal specification of tables with rows and columns, commonly referred to as a *data schema*. In Figure 1-1, you find an example of structured data as it appears in a Microsoft Excel spreadsheet.

FIGURE 1-1:
An example of
structured data.

	A	B	C	D	E	F	G	H
1	Employee ID	First Name	Last Name	Birth Date	Email Address	Mobile Number	Department	Office Location
2	123-45-453	Joe	Smith	1/3/2000	joe.smith@dataco.com	555.421.9051	Data Management	Seattle
3	123-45-459	Bob	Jones	2/14/1974	bob.jones@dataco.com	555.429.9082	Data Management	Seattle
4	123-49-907	Jane	Richards	3/15/1978	jane.richards@dataco.com	555.904.2852	Data Management	Seattle
5	190-90-223	Sally	Frank	2/28/1967	sally.frank@dataco.com	555.229.1804	Accounting	Atlanta
6	229-29-004	Emma	Donaldson	10/21/2002	emma.donaldson@dataco.com	555.867.5309	Marketing	San Francisco

Looking at unstructured data

Unstructured data is ambiguous, having no rhyme, reason, or consistency whatsoever. Pretend that you're looking at a batch of photos or videos. Are there explicit data points that one can associate with a video or photo? Perhaps, because the file itself may consist of a structure and be made of some metadata. However, the byproduct itself — the represented depiction — is unique. The data isn't replicable; therefore, it's unstructured. That's why any video, audio, photo, or text file is considered unstructured data. Products such as Power BI and Tableau offer limited support for unstructured data.

Adding semi-structured data to the mix

Semi-structured data does have some formality, but it isn't stored in a relational system and it has no set format. Fields containing the data are by no means neatly organized into strategically placed tables, rows, or columns. Instead, semi-structured data contains tags that make the data easier to organize in some form of hierarchy. Nonrelational data systems or NoSQL databases are best associated with semi-structured data, where the programmatic code, often serialized, is driven by the technical requirements. There is no hard-and-fast coding practice.

For the business intelligence developer utilizing semi-structured languages, serialized programming practices can assist in writing sophisticated code. Whether the goal is to write data to a file, send a data snippet to another system, or parse the data to be translatable for structured consumption, semi-structured data does have the potential for business intelligence systems. A semi-structured dataset has great potential if the serialized language can communicate and speak the same language.

Discovering Business Intelligence

Many IT vendors define business intelligence differently. They put their spin on the term by injecting their tool lingo into the definition. For example, if you were to go to a Microsoft website, you'd be sure to find a page or two that would have a pure definition of business intelligence, but you'd also find a gazillion pages detailing how you can apply Power BI or Excel-based solutions to every conceivable business problem.

So, let's avoid the vendor websites and stick with a no-frills definition of *business intelligence:* Simply put, business intelligence (BI) is what businesses use in order to be in a position where they can analyze current as well as historical data. Throughout the process of data analysis, the hope is that an organization will be able to uncover the insights needed to make the right decisions for the business's future. By using a combination of available tools, an organization can process large datasets across multiple data sources in order to come up with findings that can then be presented to upper management. Using the enterprise BI tool, for example, interested parties can produce visualizations via reports, dashboards, and KPIs as a way to ground their growth strategies in the world of facts.

REMEMBER

Not so very long ago, businesses had to do many tasks manually. BI tools now save the day by reducing the effort to complete mundane tasks. You can take four actions right now to transform raw data into readily accessible data:

» **Collect and transform your data:** When using multiple data sources, BI tools allow you to extract, transform, and load (ETL) data from structured and unstructured sources. When that process is complete, you can then store the data in a central repository so that an application can analyze and query the data.

» **Analyze data to discover trends:** The term *data analysis* can mean many things, from data discovery to data mining. The business objective, however, is all the same: It all boils down to the size of the dataset, the automation process, and the objective for pattern analysis. BI often provides users with a variety of modeling and analytics tools. Some come equipped with visualization options, and others have data modeling and analytics solutions for exploratory, descriptive, predictive, statistical, and even cognitive evaluation analysis. All these tools help users explore data — past, present, and future.

» **Use visualization options in order to provide data clarity:** You may have lots of data stored in one or more repositories. Querying the data to be understood and shared among users and groups is the actual value of business intelligence tools. Visualization options often include reporting, dashboards, charts, graphics, mapping, key performance indicators, and — yes — datasets.

>> **Taking action and making decisions:** The process culminates with all the data at your fingertips to make actionable decisions. Companies act by taking insights across a dataset. They parse through data in chunks, reviewing small subsets of data and potentially making significant decisions. That's why companies embrace business intelligence — because with its help, they can quickly reduce inefficiency, correct problems, and adapt the business to support market conditions.

Understanding Data Analytics

Raw data is largely useless. If you've ever briefly glanced at a large data set that has columns and rows of numbers, it quickly becomes clear that not much can be gleaned from it.

In order to make sense of data, you have to apply specific tools and techniques. The process of examining data to produce answers or find conclusions is called *data analytics*. Data analysts take a formal and disciplined approach to data analytics. This step is necessary for any individual or organization seeking to make good decisions.

The process of data analytics varies depending on resources and context, but generally follows the steps outlined in Figure 1-2. These steps commence after the problem and questions have been identified.

FIGURE 1-2: Basics steps in data analysis.

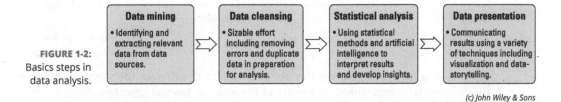

(c) John Wiley & Sons

Data analytics has four primary types. Figure 1-3 illustrates the relative complexity and value of each type.

>> **Descriptive:** Existing data sets of historical data are accessed, and analysis is performed to determine what the data tells stakeholders about the performance of a key performance indicator (KPI) or other business objective. It is insight on past performance.

>> **Diagnostic:** As the term suggests, this analysis tries to glean the answer from the data as to why something happened. It uses descriptive analysis to look at the cause.

>> **Predictive:** In this approach, the analyst uses techniques to determine what may occur in the future. It applies tools and techniques to historical data and trends to predict the likelihood of certain outcomes.

>> **Prescriptive:** This analysis focuses on what action should be taken. In combination with predictive analytics, prescriptive techniques provide estimates on the probabilities of a variety of future outcomes.

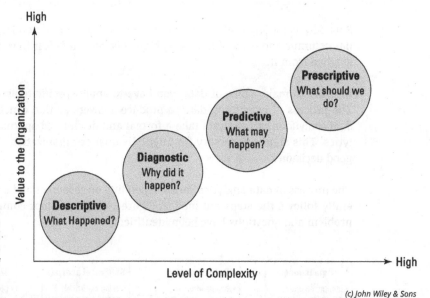

FIGURE 1-3:
The relative complexity and business value of four types of analytics.

(c) John Wiley & Sons

REMEMBER

Data analytics involves the use of a variety of software tools depending on the needs, complexities, and skills of the analyst. Beyond your favorite spreadsheet program, which can deliver a lot of capabilities, data analysts use products such as R, Python, Tableau, Power BI, QlikView, and others.

If your organization is big enough and has the budget, one or more data analysts is certainly a minimum requirement for serious analytics. With that said, every organization should now consider some basic data analytic skills for most staff. In a data-centric, digital world, having data science as a growing business competency may be as important as basic word processing and email skills.

Exploring Data Management

WARNING

No, data management is not the same as data governance. But they work closely together to deliver results in the use of enterprise data.

Data governance concerns itself with, for example, defining the roles, policies, controls, and processes for increasing the quality and value of organizational data.

Data management is the implementation of data governance. Without data management, data governance is just wishful thinking. To get value from data, there must be execution.

At some level, all organizations implement data management. If you collect and store data, technically you're managing that data. What matters in data management is the degree of sophistication that is applied to managing the value and quality of data sets. If it's on the low side, data may be a bottleneck rather than an advantage. Poor data management often results in data silos across an organization, security and compliance issues, errors in data sets, and an overall low confidence in the quality of data.

Who would choose to make decisions based on bad data?

On the other hand, good data management can result in more success in the marketplace. When data is handled and treated as a valuable enterprise asset, insights are richer and timelier, operations run smoother, and team members have what they need to make more informed decisions. Well-executed data management can translate to reduced data security breaches and lower compliance, regulatory, and privacy issues.

Data management processes involve the collection, storage, organization, maintenance, and analytics of an organization's data. It includes the architecture of technology systems such that data can flow across the enterprise and be accessed whenever and by whom it is approved for use. Additionally, responsibilities will likely include such areas as data standardization, encryption, and archiving.

Technology team members have elevated roles in all these activities, but all business stakeholders have some level of data responsibilities, such as compliance with data policies and realizing data value.

Diving into Data Analysis

Data analysis is the application of tools and techniques to organize, study, reach conclusions, and sometimes make predictions about a specific collection of information.

For example, a sales manager might use data analysis to study the sales history of a product, determine the overall trend, and produce a forecast of future sales. A scientist might use data analysis to study experimental findings and determine the statistical significance of the results. A family might use data analysis to find the maximum mortgage it can afford or how much it must put aside each month to finance retirement or the kids' education.

Cooking raw data

The point of data analysis is to understand information on some deeper, more meaningful level. By definition, *raw data* is a mere collection of facts that by themselves tell you little or nothing of any importance. To gain some understanding of the data, you must manipulate the data in some meaningful way. The purpose of manipulating data can be something as simple as finding the sum or average of a column of numbers or as complex as employing a full-scale regression analysis to determine the underlying trend of a range of values. Both are examples of data analysis, and Excel offers several tools — from the straightforward to the sophisticated — to meet even the most demanding needs.

Dealing with data

The *data* part of *data analysis* is a collection of numbers, dates, and text that represents the raw information you have to work with. In Excel, this data resides inside a worksheet, which makes the data available for you to apply Excel's satisfyingly large array of data-analysis tools.

Most data-analysis projects involve large amounts of data, and the fastest and most accurate way to get that data onto a worksheet is to import it from a non-Excel data source. In the simplest scenario, you can copy the data from a text file, a Word table, or an Access datasheet and then paste it into a worksheet. However, most business and scientific data is stored in large databases, so Excel offers tools to import the data you need into your worksheet. (See Book 1, Chapter 4.)

After you have your data in the worksheet, you can use the data as is to apply many data-analysis techniques. However, if you convert the range into a *table*, Excel treats the data as a simple database and enables you to apply a number of database-specific analysis techniques to the table.

Building data models

In many cases, you perform data analysis on worksheet values by organizing those values into a *data model,* a collection of cells designed as a worksheet version of some real-world concept or scenario. The model includes not only the raw data but also one or more cells that represent some analysis of the data. For example, a mortgage amortization model would have the mortgage data — interest rate, principal, and term — and cells that calculate the payment, principal, and interest over the term. For such calculations, you use formulas and Excel's built-in worksheet functions.

Performing what-if analysis

One of the most common data-analysis techniques is *what-if analysis,* for which you set up worksheet models to analyze hypothetical situations. The "what-if" part means that these situations usually come in the form of a question: "What happens to the monthly payment if the interest rate goes up by 2 percent?" "What will the sales be if you increase the advertising budget by 10 percent?" Excel offers four what-if analysis tools: data tables, Goal Seek, Solver, and scenarios.

Visualizing Data

Raw data that is transformed into useful information can only go so far. Assume for a moment that you were able to aggregate ten data sources whose total record count exceeded 5 million records. As a data analyst, your job was to try to explain to your target audience what the demographics study dataset incorporates among the 5 million records. How easy would that be? It's not simple to articulate unless you can summarize the data cohesively using some data visualization.

Data visualizations are graphical representations of information and data. Suppose you can access visual elements such as charts, graphs, maps, and tables that can concisely synthesize what those millions of records include. In that case, you are effectively using data visualization tools to provide an accessible platform to address trends, patterns, and outliers within data.

TIP

For those who are enamored with big data, the use of data visualization tools helps users analyze massive amounts of data quickly by applying data-driven decisions using graphical representations rather than requiring users to parse through lines of text one by one.

Chapter **2**

Delving into Big Data

P eople create and use data all the time. We usually take it for granted. It's part of our daily personal and business vernacular. As with many things, your definition of data probably differs from someone else's definition of the same. In fact, your (or their) definition may not even be entirely accurate. We tend to take data for granted and perhaps neglect to ensure we're all on the same page when discussing it.

For example, your colleague may ask you to gather *data* on a topic. Seems straight-forward. But might they actually be asking you to gather *information* instead? They're different things. If you gather data and then produce it for them, they're going to be disappointed when their expectation was information.

This chapter helps get everyone on the same page with regard to data. First you see how data is typically used as part of day-to-day business functions, and then in the rest of the chapter, you get the scoop on big data and how organizations can get the most from it today.

Identifying the Roles of Data

To fully appreciate the value that data brings to every organization, it's worth exploring the many ways that data shows up on a day-to-day basis. Recognizing the incredible diversity of data use and the exposure it has across all business functions reinforces its importance. It's critical to ensure that data is high quality, secure, compliant, and accessible to the right people at the right time.

Data isn't something that just concerns the data analytics team or the information technology department. It's also not something that is limited to decision-makers and leaders.

Operations

Business operations concern themselves with a diverse set of activities to run the day-to-day needs and drive the mission of an organization. Each business has different needs, and operational functions reflect these specific requirements. Some core functions show up in almost every organization. Consider payroll, order management, and marketing. At the same time, some operational support won't be required. Not every organization needs its own IT organization, or if it's a service business, it may not have a warehouse.

REMEMBER

Operations run on and are powered by a variety of data and information sources. They also create a lot of both.

The performance of operations is often easily quantified by data. For example, in a human resources (HR) function, they'll want to know how many openings there are, how long openings are taking to fill, and who is accepting offers. There's a multitude of data points to quantify the answers so that relevant decisions can be made.

In HR, data is also created by the activities of the function. For example, candidates enter data when they apply for a position, data is entered when evaluating an applicant, and all along the way, the supporting systems log a variety of automated data, such as time, date, and how long an application took to complete online.

In this HR example, and frankly, in any other operations teams explored, data is abundantly created as a result of and in support of functions.

Operations use data to make decisions, to enable systems to run, and to deliver data to internal and external entities. For example, a regional sales team will deliver their monthly results to headquarters to be presented to vice presidents or the C-suite.

Many data functions in support operations are automated. For example, a warehouse inventory system may automatically generate a replenishment order when stock drops to a certain level. Consider all the notifications that systems generate based on triggers. Who hasn't received an email notifying them that they haven't submitted their time and expense report?

REMEMBER

As you'll notice in almost all data scenarios, there are skilled people, dedicated processes, and various technologies partially or wholly focused on handling operational data.

Strategy

Every organization has a strategy, whether it's articulated overtly or not. At the organizational level, this is about creating a plan that supports objectives and goals. It's essentially about understanding the challenges to delivering on the organization's purpose and then agreeing on the proposed solutions to those challenges. Strategy can also be adopted at the department and division levels, but the intent is the same: understand the journey ahead and make a plan.

Strategy leads to implementation and requires the support of operations to realize its goals. In this way, strategy and operations are two sides of the same coin. Done right, a data-driven strategy delivered with operational excellence can be a winning ticket.

Creating a strategy typically comes down to a core set of activities. It begins with an analysis of the environment followed by some conclusions on what has been gathered. Finally, a plan is developed, driven by some form of guiding principles. These principles may be derived from the nature of the work, the values of the founders, or some other factors.

TIP

Deeply tied to all these steps is the availability of good quality data that can be processed and analyzed and then turned into actionable insights.

Certainly, data and information won't be the only mechanisms in which the plan will be constructed. There must be room for other perspectives, including the strength of belief that people with experience bring to the discussion. The right mix of data and non-data sources must be considered. Too much of one or the other may not deliver expected results.

A best practice for strategy development is to consider it an ongoing process. This doesn't mean updating the strategy every month — that is a recipe for chaos — but it may mean revisiting the strategy every six months and tweaking it as necessary. Revisions to strategy should be guided by new data, which can mean new knowledge and new insights. While a regular process of strategy revisions is encouraged, new information that suddenly presents itself can trigger an impromptu update.

In the 21st century, organizations need to react quickly to environmental conditions to survive. Data will form the backbone of your response system.

Decision-making

It's generally accepted in business that the highest form of value derived from data is the ability to make better informed decisions. The volume and quality of data available today has no precedent in history. Let's just say it as it is: we're spoiled.

Without even creating a single unit of raw data, there's a universe of existing data and information at our fingertips. In addition, increasing numbers of easy-to-use analysis capabilities and tools are democratizing access to insight.

Popular consumer search engines such as Google and Bing have transformed how we make decisions. Doctors, for example, now deal with patients who are more informed about their symptoms and their causes. It's a mixed blessing. Some of the information has reduced unnecessary clinic visits, but it's also created a headache for physicians when the information their patients have consumed is incorrect.

Within organizations, access to abundant data and information has resulted in quicker, more timely, and better-quality business decisions. For example, executives can understand their strengths, weaknesses, opportunities, and threats closer to real time. For most, gone are the days of waiting until the end of the fiscal quarter to get the good or bad news. Even if the information is tentative in the interim, it's vastly better than being in the dark until it may be too late.

While there's little surprise that data-driven decision-making is a fundamental business competency, it all hinges on decision-makers getting access to quality data at the right time. Abundant and out-of-date data are not synonymous with data value. Bad data may be worse than no data. Bad data processed into information and then used as the basis for decisions will result in failure. The outcome of decisions based on bad data could range from a minor mistake to job termination right up to the closing of the business.

Measuring

Organizations are in a continuous state of measurement, whether it's overt or tacit. Every observed unit of data contributes to building a picture of the business. The often-used adage, *what gets measured gets managed*, is generally applicable. That said, some things are hard to measure and not everything gets measured.

The aspiration for every leader is that they have the information they need when they need it. You might not always think of it this way, but that information is going to be derived from data that is a result of some form of measurement.

TIP

Data measurements can be quantitative or qualitative. Quantitative data is most often described in numerical terms, whereas qualitative data is descriptive and expressed in terms of language.

My favorite way of distinguishing the two is described as follows: When asked to describe a journey in a plane, a person could answer it quantitatively. For example, the flight leveled off at 35,000 feet and traveled at a speed of 514 mph. Another person who asked the same question could answer it qualitatively by saying the flight wasn't bumpy and the meals were tasty. Regardless, the data and information tell a story that, depending on the audience, will have meaning. It might be worthless, but meaningful.

REMEMBER

The type of information desired directly correlates to the measurement approach. This is going to inform your choices of at least what, when, where, and how data is captured. A general rule is only to capture and measure what matters. Some may argue that capturing data now to measure later has value even if there isn't a good case yet. That may be true, but be careful with your limited resources and the potential costs.

Monitoring

Monitoring is an ongoing process of collecting and evaluating the performance of, say, a project, process, system, or other item of interest. Often the results collected are compared against some existing values or desired targets. For example, a machine on a factory floor may be expected to produce 100 widgets per hour. You engage in some manner of monitoring to inform whether this expectation is being met. Across a wide range of activities, monitoring also helps to ensure the continuity, stability, and reliability of that being supervised.

REMEMBER

Involved in monitoring is the data produced by the thing being evaluated. It's also the data that is produced as a product of monitoring. For example, the deviation from the expected result.

The data is produced through monitoring feeds reports, real-time systems, and software-based dashboards. A monitor can tell you how much power is left in your smartphone, whether an employee is spending all their time on social media, or if through predictive maintenance, a production line is about to fail.

Monitoring is another process that converts data into insight and as such, exists as a mechanism to guide decisions. It's probably not lost on you that the role of data in measurement and monitoring often go together. Intuitively, you know you have to measure something that you want to monitor. The takeaway here is not the obvious relationship they have, but the fact that data is a type of connective tissue that binds business functions. This interdependence requires oversight and controls, as stakeholders often have different responsibilities and permissions. For example, the people responsible for providing measurement data on processes may belong to an entirely different team from those who have to monitor and report on the measurement data. Those that take action may again belong to an entirely different department in the organization.

This is not the only way to think about monitoring in the context of data. Data monitoring is also the process of evaluating the quality of data and determining if it is fit for purpose. To achieve this, it requires processes, technologies, and benchmarks. Data monitoring begins with establishing data quality metrics and then measuring results over time on a continuous basis. Data quality monitoring metrics may include areas such as completeness and accuracy.

TIP

By continuously monitoring the quality of the data in your organization, opportunities and issues may be revealed on time. Then, if deemed appropriate, actions can be prioritized.

Insight management

Data forms the building blocks of many business functions. In support of decision-making — arguably its most important value — data is the source for almost all insight. As a basic definition, business insight is sometimes referred to as information that can make a difference.

WARNING

It's not enough to simply collect lots of data and expect that insight will suddenly emerge. There must be an attendant management process. Thus, insight management means ensuring that data and information are capable of delivering insight.

Insight management begins with gathering and analyzing data from different sources. To determine what data to process, those responsible for insight management must deeply understand the organization's information needs. They must be knowledgeable about what data has value. In addition, these analysts must know how information flows across the organization and who it must reach.

With the data gathered and processed, analytics will be applied — this is the interpretation of the data and its implications.

Finally, insight management involves designing and creating the most effective manner to communicate any findings. For different audiences, different mechanisms may be required. This is seldom a one-size-fits-all. Some people will want an executive summary while others may want the painful details. You'll know whether your organization's insight communications are working if those who receive it can make decisions that align with the goals of the organization.

TIP

For insight to be most valuable, it must be the right information, at the right time, in the right format, for the right people. This is no simple task.

As you've probably guessed, there's a strong overlap between insight management and knowledge management. For simplicity, you can think of knowledge management as the organizational support structures and tools to enable insight to be available to employees for whatever reason they need it.

Reporting

Perhaps the most obvious manifestation of data and information management in any organization is the use of reports. Creating, delivering, receiving, and acting on reports are fundamental functions of any organization. Some say they are the backbone of every business. That sounds overly glamorous, but it does speak to the importance of reporting and reports.

The content of a report, which can be summarized or detailed, contains data and information in a structured manner. For example, an expenditure report would provide a basic overview of the purpose of the report and then support it with relevant information. That could include a list of all expenditures for a department over a certain period or it could just be a total amount. It will depend on the audience and purpose of the report. Including visuals is a recommended approach to present such data.

For example, a chart, considered a visual form of storytelling, is a way to present data so that it can be interpreted more quickly. With so much data and complexity in today's business environment, data storytelling is growing as both a business requirement and an in-demand business skill.

The report may discuss the findings and will conclude with a summary and sometimes a set of recommendations.

REMEMBER

Reports are typically online or physical presentations of data and information on some aspect of an organization. For example, a written and printed report may show all the sales of a particular product or service during a specific period. Sometimes a report is given verbally in person or via a live or recorded video. Whatever the format — and that's less important today as long as it achieves its objective — a report is developed for a particular audience with a specific purpose.

With so many uses of data and information, the purpose of reporting is largely about improved decision-making. With the right information, in the right format, at the right time, business leaders are empowered to make better decisions, solve problems, and communicate plans and policies.

WARNING

While reports do empower leaders and give them more tools, they don't guarantee the right decisions. Knowing something is not the equivalent of making the right choices at the right time.

Other roles for data

Earlier sections of this chapter present some of the most visible uses of data in organizations today. Listing every conceivable way that data is used is not possible, but following is a short list of some other important areas that shouldn't be overlooked.

>> **Artificial intelligence (AI):** Data is considered the fuel of AI. It requires a high volume of good data (the more, the better!). With huge quantities of quality data, the outcomes of AI improve. It's from the data that AI learns patterns, identifies relationships, and determines probabilities. In addition, AI is being used to improve the quality and use of data in organizations.

>> **Problem solving:** Acknowledging the close association with decision-making, it's worth calling out problem solving as a distinctive use of data. Data plays a role in how a problem is defined, determining what solutions are available, evaluating which solution to use, and measuring the success or failure of the solution that is chosen and applied.

>> **Data reuse:** While we collect and use data for a specific primary purpose, data is often reused for entirely different reasons. Data that has been collected, used, and stored can be retrieved and used by a different team

at another time — assuming they have permission, including access and legal rights (notable controls within data governance). For example, the sales team in an organization will collect your name and address in order to fulfil an order. Later, that same data set may be used by the marketing team to create awareness about other products and services. These are two different teams with different goals using the same data. Data reuse can be considered a positive given that it reduces data collection duplication and increases the value of data to an organization, but it must be managed with care so that it doesn't break any data use rules. (**Note:** High-value shared data sets are called master data; in data governance, they are subject to master data management.)

DEFINING BIG DATA AND THE BIG THREE V

BEST PRACTICE

If companies want to stay competitive, they must be proficient and adept at infusing data insights into their processes, products, as well as their growth and management strategies. This means that business leaders must understand big data and know how to work with it.

Big data is a term that characterizes data that exceeds the processing capacity of conventional database systems because it's too big, it moves too fast, or it lacks the structural requirements of traditional database architectures.

Three characteristics — also called "the three Vs" — define big data: volume, velocity, and variety. Because the three Vs of big data are continually expanding, newer, more innovative data technologies must continuously be developed to manage big data problems.

In a situation where you're required to adopt a big data solution to overcome a problem that's caused by your data's velocity, volume, or variety, you have moved past the realm of regular data — you have a big data problem on your hands.

Before investing in any sort of technology solution, business leaders must *always* assess the current state of their organization, select an optimal use case, and thoroughly evaluate competing alternatives, all before even considering whether a purchase should be made. This process is so vital to the success of data science that *Data Science For Dummies*, 3rd Edition, covers the topic at length.

TECHNICAL STUFF

OVERHYPING BIG DATA

Unfortunately, the term *big data* was so overhyped across industries that countless business leaders made misguided impulse purchases. In a nutshell, they didn't do their homework before purchasing expensive products and services, such as Hadoop clusters, that ultimately failed to deliver on vendors' promises, and the entire industry suffered for it.

Hadoop is a data processing platform designed to boil down big data into smaller datasets that are more manageable for data scientists to analyze. Hadoop is, and was, powerful at satisfying one requirement: batch-processing and storing large volumes of data. That's great if your situation requires precisely this type of capability, but the fact is that technology is never a one-size-fits-all sort of thing.

Unfortunately, in almost all cases, business leaders bought into Hadoop before evaluating whether it was an appropriate choice. Vendors sold Hadoop and made lots of money. Most of those projects failed. Most Hadoop vendors went out of business. Corporations got burned on investing in data projects, and the data industry got a bad rap.

For any data professional who worked in the field between 2012 and 2015, the term *big data* represents a blight on the industry.

Grappling with data volume

The lower limit of big data volume starts as low as 1 terabyte, and it has no upper limit. If your organization owns at least 1 terabyte of data, that data technically qualifies as big data.

WARNING

In its raw form, most big data is *low value* — in other words, the value-to-data-quantity ratio is low in raw big data. Big data is composed of huge numbers of very small transactions that come in a variety of formats. These incremental components of big data produce true value only after they're aggregated and analyzed. Roughly speaking, data engineers have the job of aggregating it, and data scientists have the job of analyzing it.

Handling data velocity

A lot of big data is created by using automated processes and instrumentation nowadays, and because data storage costs are relatively inexpensive, system velocity is often the limiting factor. Keep in mind that big data is low-value. Consequently, you need systems that are able to ingest a lot of it, in short order, to generate timely and valuable insights.

In engineering terms, *data velocity* is data volume per unit time. Big data enters an average system at velocities ranging between 30 kilobytes (K) per second to as much as 30 *gigabytes* (GB) per second. Latency is a characteristic of all data systems, and it quantifies the system's delay in moving data after it has been instructed to do so. Many data-engineered systems are required to have latency less than 100 milliseconds, measured from the time the data is created to the time the system responds.

Throughput is a characteristic that describes a system's capacity for work per unit time. Throughput requirements can easily be as high as 1,000 messages per second in big data systems! High-velocity, real-time moving data presents an obstacle to timely decision-making. The capabilities of data-handling and data-processing technologies often limit data velocities.

Tools that intake data into a system — otherwise known as data ingestion tools — come in a variety of flavors. Some of the more popular ones are described in the following list:

>> **Apache Sqoop:** You can use this data transference tool to quickly transfer data back-and-forth between a relational data system and the *Hadoop distributed file system (HDFS)* — it uses clusters of commodity servers to store big data. HDFS makes big data handling and storage financially feasible by distributing storage tasks across clusters of inexpensive commodity servers.

>> **Apache Kafka:** This distributed messaging system acts as a message broker whereby messages can quickly be pushed onto and pulled from HDFS. You can use Kafka to consolidate and facilitate the data calls and pushes that consumers make to and from the HDFS.

>> **Apache Flume:** This distributed system primarily handles log and event data. You can use it to transfer massive quantities of unstructured data to and from the HDFS.

Dealing with data variety

Big data gets even more complicated when you add unstructured and semi-structured data to structured data sources. This *high-variety* data comes from a multitude of sources and most notably, is composed of a combination of datasets with differing underlying structures (structured, unstructured, or semi-structured). Heterogeneous, high-variety data is often composed of any combination of graph data, JSON files, XML files, social media data, structured tabular data, weblog data, and data that's generated from user clicks on a web page — otherwise known as click-streams.

The terms *data lake* and *data warehouse* both describe methods of storing data; however, each term describes a different type of storage system.

BEST PRACTICE

Practitioners in the big data industry use the term *data lake* to refer to a nonhierarchical data storage system that's used to hold huge volumes of multi-structured, raw data within a flat storage architecture — in other words, a collection of records that come in uniform format and that are not cross-referenced in any way. You can read more about data lakes later in Book 1, Chapter 3.

HDFS and Azure Synapse can be used as a data lake storage repository, but you can also use the Amazon Web Services (AWS) S3 platform or other Azure Data Services — or a similar cloud storage solution — to meet the same requirements on the cloud.

Unlike a data lake, a *data warehouse* is a centralized data repository that you can use to store and access only structured data.

A more traditional data warehouse system commonly employed in business intelligence solutions is a *data mart* — a storage system (for structured data) that you can use to store one particular focus area of data belonging to only one line of business in the company.

What's All the Fuss about Data?

Data refers to collections of digitally stored units — in other words, stuff that is kept on a computing device. These units represent something meaningful when processed for a human or a computer. Single units of data are traditionally referred to as *datum* and multiple units as *data*. However, the term data is often used in singular and plural contexts. (This book uses the term data to refer to both single and multiple units of data.)

Prior to processing, data doesn't need to make sense individually or even in combination with other data. For example, data could be the word *orange* or the number 42. In the abstract and most basic form, something we call raw data, we can agree that these are both meaningless.

REMEMBER

Units of data are largely worthless until they are processed and applied. It's only then that data begins a journey that, when coupled with good governance, can be very useful. The value that data can bring to so many functions, from product development to sales, makes it an important asset.

To begin to have value, data requires effort. If we place the word *orange* in a sentence, such as "An orange is a delicious fruit," suddenly the data has meaning.

Similarly, if we say, "The t-shirt I purchased cost me $42," then the number 42 now has meaning. What we did here was process the data by means of structure and context to give it value. Put another way, we converted the data into information.

This basic action of data processing cannot be overstated, as it represents the core foundation of an industry that has ushered in our current period of rapid digital transformation. Today, the term *data processing* has been replaced with *information technology* (IT).

Figure 2-1 illustrates how you can think of data units at a basic level.

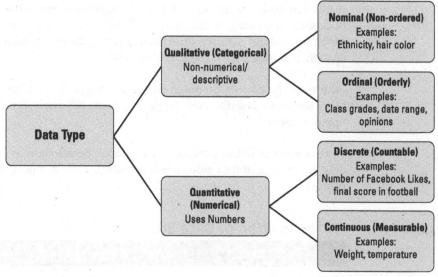

FIGURE 2-1: The qualitative and quantitative nature of data types.

(c) John Wiley & Sons

Welcome to the zettabyte era

Until a few years ago, few people needed to know what a zettabyte was. As we entered the 21st century and the volume of data being created and stored grew rapidly, we needed to break the term *zettabyte* out from its vault. A hyperconnected world accelerating in its adoption and use of digital tools has required dusting off a seldom used metric to capture the enormity of data output we were producing.

Today, we live in the zettabyte era. A zettabyte is a big number. A really big number. It's 10^{21}, or a 1 with 21 zeros after it. It looks like this: 1,000,000,000,000,000,000,000 bytes.

By 2020, we had created 44 zettabytes of data. That number continues to grow rapidly. This *datasphere* — the term used to describe all the data created — is projected to reach 100 zettabytes by 2023 and may double in 3–4 years. If you own a terabyte drive at home or at work, you'd need one billion of those drives to store just one zettabyte of data. You read that right.

Here's a simplified technical explanation of what a zettabyte is. Consider that each byte is made up of eight bits. A bit is either a 1 or 0 and represents the most basic unit of how data is stored on a computing device. Since a bit has only two states, a 1 or 0, we call it *binary*. Some time ago, computer engineers decided that 8 bits (or 1 byte) was enough to represent characters that we, as mere mortals, could understand. For example, the letter A in binary is 01000001.

It was a mutually beneficial decision. We understand the A; the computer understands the 01000001. A full word such as "hello" converted to binary reads: 01001000 01100101 01101100 01101100 01101111. Stick around with data experts long enough, and they'll have you speaking in bits.

With more data being produced in the years ahead, we'll soon begin adopting other words to describe even bigger volumes. Get ready for the yottabyte and brontobyte eras!

From a more practical perspective, this book occasionally refers to the size of data. Knowledge of data volume will be useful. Table 2-1 puts bits and bytes into context.

TABLE 2-1 **Quantification of Data Storage**

Storage Allocation	Storage Capacity
8 bits	1 byte
1024 bytes	1 kilobyte
1024 kilobytes	1 megabyte
1024 megabytes	1 gigabyte
1024 gigabytes	1 terabyte
1024 terabytes	1 petabyte
1024 petabytes	1 exabyte
1024 exabytes	1 zettabyte
1024 zettabytes	1 yottabyte
1024 yottabytes	1 brontobyte

REMEMBER

Understanding that we are in an era of vastly expanding data volume, often at the disposal of organizations, elevates the notion that managing this data well is complex and valuable.

Managing a small amount of data can have challenges, but managing data at scale is materially more challenging. If you're going to glean value from data, it has to be understood and managed in specific ways.

From data to insight

Creating, collecting, and storing data is a waste of time and money if it's being done without a clear purpose or an intent to use it in the future. You may see the logic behind collecting data even when you don't have a reason because it may have value at some point in the future, but this is the exception. Generally, an organization is on-boarding data because it's required.

WARNING

Data that is never used is about as useful as producing reports that nobody reads. The assumption is that you have data for a reason. You have your data and it's incredibly important to your organization, but it must be converted to information to have meaning.

Information is data in context. Table 2-2 explores more of the differences between data and information.

TABLE 2-2   ## The Differences Between Data and Information

Data	Information
Raw	Processed
Items such as characters, words, pictures, and numbers that have no meaning in isolation	Data that is organized and given context to have meaning
No analysis dependency	Dependent on the analysis of data
Unorganized and not dependent on context	Organized and dependent on context
Not typically useful alone	Useful alone

When we apply information coupled with broader contextual concepts, practical application, and experience, it becomes knowledge. Knowledge is actionable. In this way, knowledge really is "power."

It doesn't end there. When you take new knowledge and apply reasoning, values, and the broader universe of our knowledge and deep experiences, you get wisdom.

With wisdom, you know what to do with knowledge and can determine its contextual validity.

You could stop at knowledge, but wisdom will take you further to the ultimate destination derived from data. All wisdom includes knowledge, but not all knowledge is wisdom. Dummies books can be deep, too.

Finally, insight is an outcome that can emerge from knowledge but is best demonstrated through a combination of knowledge and wisdom. With insight, you can gain a deeper understanding of something and the skills to think or see it differently.

To summarize, consider the following:

» John Lennon is *data*.

» The fact that John Lennon is in the group, The Beatles, is *information*.

» The fact that The Beatles are looking for a record deal is *knowledge*.

» The fact that The Beatles are very talented and popular and should get a record deal is *wisdom*.

» Avoiding the decision-making processes of Decca Records is *insight*.

(The author of the preceding list is a Beatles fan. That's information.) Figure 2-2 illustrates the journey from data to insight.

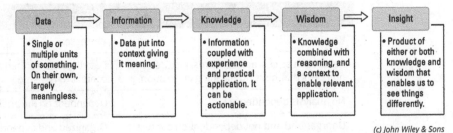

FIGURE 2-2: Data leads to insight.

(c) John Wiley & Sons

REMEMBER

It's no surprise then that data has enormous value when considering it through the lens of delivering wisdom. However, this journey from data to wisdom is full of challenges. These are significant issues that organizations struggle with every day. For example, it's not a stretch to imagine what the outcome of using bad data could be. Transforming good data into valuable information and beyond is no simple task. It requires tools, skills, and processes.

Every day, different organizations with access to the same data have different outcomes. While the best outcome can't be guaranteed no matter which processes, tools, or skills are used, good practices such as the right level of data governance can absolutely lead to better results.

Identifying Important Data Sources

Humans, machines, and sensors everywhere continually generate vast volumes of data. Typical sources include data from social media, financial transactions, health records, click-streams, log files, and the *Internet of Things* — a web of digital connections that joins together the ever-expanding array of electronic devices that consumers use in their everyday lives. Figure 2-3 shows a variety of popular big data sources.

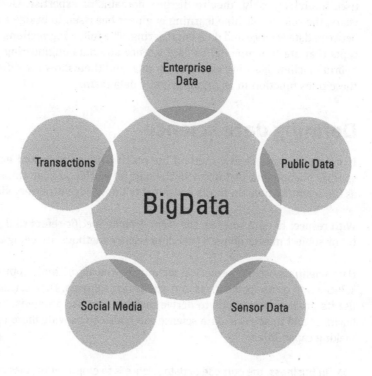

FIGURE 2-3:
Popular sources
of big data.

Role of Big Data in Data Science and Engineering

Data science, machine learning engineering, and data engineering cover different functions within the *big data paradigm* — an approach wherein huge velocities, varieties, and volumes of structured, unstructured, and semi-structured data are being captured, processed, stored, and analyzed using a set of techniques and technologies that are completely novel compared to those that were used in decades past.

All these functions are useful for deriving knowledge and actionable insights from raw data. All are essential elements for any comprehensive decision-support system and are extremely helpful when formulating robust strategies for future business growth. Although the terms *data science* and *data engineering* are often used interchangeably, they're distinct domains of expertise. Over the past five years, the role of machine learning engineer has risen to bridge a gap that exists between data science and data engineering. The following sections introduce concepts that are fundamental to data science and data engineering, as well as the hybrid machine learning engineering role, and then show the differences in how these roles function in an organization's data team.

Defining data science

If *science* is a systematic method by which people study and explain domain-specific phenomena that occur in the natural world, you can think of *data science* as the scientific domain that's dedicated to knowledge discovery via data analysis.

TECHNICAL STUFF

With respect to data science, the term *domain-specific* refers to the industry sector or subject matter domain that data science methods are being used to explore.

Data scientists use mathematical techniques and algorithmic approaches to derive solutions to complex business and scientific problems. Data science practitioners use its predictive methods to derive insights that are otherwise unattainable. In business and in science, data science methods can provide more robust decision-making capabilities:

>> **In business,** the purpose of data science is to empower businesses and organizations with the data insights they need in order to optimize organizational processes for maximum efficiency and revenue generation.

>> **In science,** data science methods are used to derive results and develop protocols for achieving the specific scientific goal at hand.

Data science is a vast and multidisciplinary field. To call yourself a true data scientist, you need to have expertise in math and statistics, computer programming, and your own domain-specific subject matter.

Using data science skills, you can do cool things like the following:

>> Use machine learning to optimize energy usage and lower corporate carbon footprints.

>> Optimize tactical strategies to achieve goals in business and science.

>> Predict for unknown contaminant levels from sparse environmental datasets.

>> Design automated theft- and fraud-prevention systems to detect anomalies and trigger alarms based on algorithmic results.

>> Craft site-recommendation engines for use in land acquisitions and real estate development.

>> Implement and interpret predictive analytics and forecasting techniques for net increases in business value.

Data scientists must have extensive and diverse quantitative expertise to be able to solve these types of problems.

TECHNICAL STUFF

Machine learning is the practice of applying algorithms to learn from — and make automated predictions from — data.

Defining machine learning engineering

A *machine learning engineer* is essentially a software engineer who is skilled enough in data science to deploy advanced data science models within the applications they build, thus bringing machine learning models into production in a live environment like a Software as a Service (SaaS) product or even just a web page. Contrary to what you may have guessed, the role of machine learning engineer is a hybrid between a data scientist and a software engineer, *not* a data engineer. A machine learning engineer is, at their core, a well-rounded software engineer with a solid foundation in machine learning and artificial intelligence. This person doesn't need to know as much data science as a data scientist but should know much more about computer science and software development than a typical data scientist.

TECHNICAL STUFF

Software as a Service (SaaS) is a term that describes cloud-hosted software services that are made available to users via the Internet. Examples of popular SaaS companies include Salesforce, Slack, HubSpot, and so many more.

Defining data engineering

If *engineering* is the practice of using science and technology to design and build systems that solve problems, you can think of *data engineering* as the engineering domain that's dedicated to building and maintaining data systems for overcoming data processing bottlenecks and data handling problems that arise from handling the high volume, velocity, and variety of big data.

Data engineers use computer science and software engineering skills to design systems for, and solve problems with handling and manipulating big datasets. Data engineers often have experience working with (and designing) real-time processing frameworks and massively parallel processing (MPP) platforms (discussed later in this chapter), as well as with RDBMSs. They generally code in Java, C++, Scala, or Python. They know how to deploy Hadoop MapReduce or Spark to handle, process, and refine big data into datasets with more manageable sizes. Simply put, with respect to data science, the purpose of data engineering is to engineer large-scale data solutions by building coherent, modular, and scalable data processing platforms from which data scientists can subsequently derive insights.

BEST PRACTICE

Most engineered systems are *built* systems — they are constructed or manufactured in the physical world. Data engineering is different, though. It involves designing, building, and implementing software solutions to problems in the data world — a world that can seem abstract when compared to the physical reality of the Golden Gate Bridge or the Aswan Dam.

Using data engineering skills, you can, for example:

>> Integrate data pipelines with the natural language processing (NLP) services that were built by data scientists at your company.

>> Build mission-critical data platforms capable of processing more than 10 billion transactions per day.

>> Tear down data silos by finally migrating your company's data from a more traditional on-premise data storage environment to a cutting-edge cloud warehouse.

>> Enhance and maintain existing data infrastructure and data pipelines.

Data engineers need solid skills in computer science, database design, and software engineering to be able to perform this type of work.

Connecting Big Data with Business Intelligence

Previous sections of this chapter discuss the foundation of data in terms of volume, velocity, and variety. This section connects the dots by adding two additional dimensions: velocity and veracity in the context of big data. Since the term *big data* is undoubtedly a catch-all buzzword. The term is meant to encompass five aspects of a business intelligence activity: data volume, data velocity, data veracity, data value, and data variety. Each of the data types that big data brings together (unstructured data, semi-structured data, and structured data) maintains some level of these five attributes:

>> **Volume:** The amount of data that exists

>> **Velocity:** The speed at which data is generated and moves

>> **Veracity:** The quality and accuracy of data available

>> **Value:** The credibility, in monetary and nonmonetary terms, that the data provides

>> **Variety:** The diversity of data types available within the dataset

Big data is paramount for business intelligence solutions such as Power BI and Tableau because businesses constantly create more data, practically by the minute. These businesses must keep up with the data deluge. A good business intelligence platform such as Tableau grows with the increasing demands; however, if the data is not maintained, your ability to handle data visualizations and the associated data sources also becomes impaired. Therefore, it's essential to implement good data hygiene and maintenance practices.

Analyzing Data with Enterprise Business Intelligence Practices

Don't get business intelligence confused with data analytics. Business intelligence platforms use data analytics as a building block to tell the complete story. A data analyst or scientist evaluates the data using the treasure trove of tools built into programs like Power BI and Tableau, from advanced statistics to predictive analytics or machine learning solutions to identify patterns and trends.

Power BI and Tableau, in particular, offers that end-to-end data analytics experience so that the analyst, scientist, and collaborator can complete the entire data life cycle, from gathering, prepping, analyzing, collaborating, and sharing data insights. Unlike its competitors, both Power BI and Tableau include a predictive AI engine, which allows users to ask questions or predict the kind of visualizations they require without manually completing the work.

Like the three-year-old child asking "Why?" all the time, as you ask more questions and the platform learns, both Power BI and Tableau build an analysis output while simultaneously learning from the output. The result is an opportunity for the system to understand why something happens and what can happen next. Business intelligence platforms take the resulting models and algorithms and break these results into actionable language insights for data mining, predictive analytics, and statistics. The final product is data analytics, the byproduct of answering a specific question (or set of questions). The collection of questions helps the organization move forward with its business agenda.

Chapter **3**

Understanding Data Lakes

Ask your favorite search engine this question: "What's a data lake?" You'll find dozens of high-level definitions that will almost certainly spur plenty of follow-up questions as you try to get your arms around the idea of a data lake.

Instead of filtering through all that varying — and even conflicting — terminology and then trying to consolidate all of it into a single comprehensive definition, just think of a data lake as the following:

> A solidly architected, logically centralized, highly scalable environment filled with different types of analytic data that are sourced from both inside and outside your

enterprise with varying latency, which will be the primary go-to destination for your organization's data-driven insights

This chapter helps make that definition more understandable by breaking it into bite-size pieces, beginning with what it means for a data lake to be solidly architected.

Rock-Solid Water

A data lake should remain viable and useful for a long time after it becomes operational. Also, you'll be continually expanding and enhancing your data lake with new types and forms of data, new underlying technologies, and support for new analytical uses.

REMEMBER

Building a data lake is more than just loading massive amounts of data into some storage location.

To support this near-constant expansion and growth, you need to ensure that your data lake is well architected and solidly engineered, which means that the data lake

>> Enforces standards and best practices for data ingestion, data storage, data transmission, and interchange among its components and data delivery to end users

>> Minimizes workarounds and temporary interfaces that have a tendency to stick around longer than planned and weaken your overall environment

>> Continues to meet your predetermined metrics and thresholds for overall technical performance, such as data loading and interchange, as well as user response time

Think about a resort that builds docks, a couple of lakeside restaurants, and other structures at various locations alongside a large lake. You wouldn't just hand out lumber, hammers, and nails to a bunch of visitors and tell them to start building without detailed blueprints and engineering diagrams. The same is true with a data lake. From the first piece of data that arrives, you need as solid a foundation as possible to help keep your data lake viable for a long time.

A Really Great Lake

You'll come across definitions and descriptions that tell you a data lake is a centralized store of data, but that definition is only partially correct.

A data lake is *logically* centralized. You can certainly think of a data lake as a single place for your data, instead of having your data scattered among different databases. But in reality, even though your data lake is logically centralized, its data is *physically* decentralized and distributed among many different underlying servers.

TECHNICAL STUFF

The data services that you use for your data lake, such as the Amazon Simple Storage Service (S3), the Microsoft Azure Data Lake Storage (ADLS), or the Hadoop Distributed File System (HDFS) manage the distribution of data among potentially numerous servers where your data is actually stored. These services hide the physical distribution from almost everyone other than those who need to manage the data at the server storage level. Instead, they present the data as being logically part of a single data lake. Figure 3-1 illustrates how logical centralization accompanies physical decentralization.

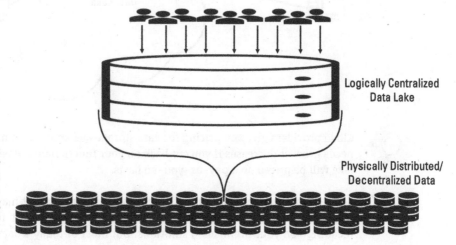

Logically Centralized Data Lake

Physically Distributed/ Decentralized Data

FIGURE 3-1: A logically centralized data lake with underlying physical decentralization.

Expanding the Data Lake

How big can your data lake get? To quote the old saying (and to answer a question with a question), how many angels can dance on the head of a pin?

Scalability is best thought of as "the ability to expand capacity, workload, and missions without having to go back to the drawing board and start all over." Your data lake will almost always be a cloud-based solution (see Figure 3-2). Cloud-based platforms give you, in theory, infinite scalability for your data lake. New servers and storage devices (discs, solid state devices, and so on) can be incorporated into your data lake on demand, and the software services manage and control these new resources along with those you're already using. Your data lake contents can then expand from hundreds of terabytes to petabytes, and then to exabytes, and then zettabytes, and even into the ginormousbyte range. (Just kidding about that last one.)

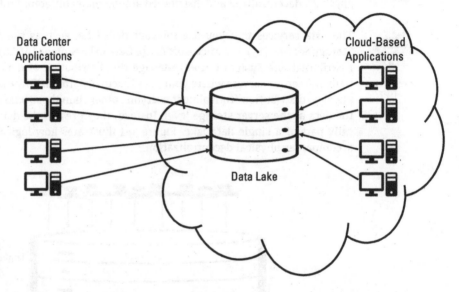

FIGURE 3-2:
Cloud-based data
lake solutions.

TIP

Cloud providers give you pricing for data storage and access that increases as your needs grow or decreases if you cut back on your functionality. Basically, your data lake will be priced on a pay-as-you-go basis.

Some of the first data lakes built in the Hadoop environment may reside in your corporate data center and be categorized as *on-prem* (short for *on-premises*, meaning "on your premises") solutions. But most of today's data lakes are built in the Amazon Web Services (AWS) or Microsoft Azure cloud environments. Given the ever-increasing popularity of cloud computing, it's highly unlikely that this trend of cloud-based data lakes will reverse for a long time, if ever.

As long as Amazon, Microsoft, and other cloud platform providers can keep expanding their existing data centers and building new ones, as well as enhancing the capabilities of their data management services, then your data lake should be able to avoid scalability issues.

TECHNICAL STUFF

A multiple-component data lake architecture further helps overcome performance and capacity constraints as your data lake grows in size and complexity, providing even greater scalability.

More Than Just the Water

Think of a data lake as being closer to a lake resort rather than just the lake — the body of water — in its natural state. If you were a real estate developer, you might buy the property that includes the lake itself, along with plenty of acreage surrounding the lake. You'd then develop the overall property by building cabins, restaurants, boat docks, and other facilities. The lake might be the centerpiece of the overall resort, but its value is dramatically enhanced by all the additional assets that you've built surrounding the lake.

REMEMBER

A data lake is an entire environment, not just a gigantic collection of data that is stored within a data service such as Amazon S3 or Microsoft ADLS.

In addition to data storage, a data lake also includes the following:

>> One or (usually) more mechanisms to move data from one part of the data lake to another.

>> A catalog or directory that helps keep track of what data is where, as well as the associated rules that apply to different groups of data; this is known as *metadata*.

>> Capabilities that help unify meanings and business rules for key data subjects that may come into the data lake from different applications and systems; this is known as *master data management*.

>> Monitoring services to track data quality and accuracy, response time when users access data, billing services to charge different organizations for their usage of the data lake, and plenty more.

Different Types of Data

If your data lake had a motto, it might be "All data are created equal."

In a data lake, data is data is data. In other words, you don't need to make special accommodations for more complex types of data than you would for simpler forms of data.

Your data lake will contain structured data, unstructured data, and semi-structured data (see Figure 3-3). To read more about each data type, see Book 1, Chapter 1.

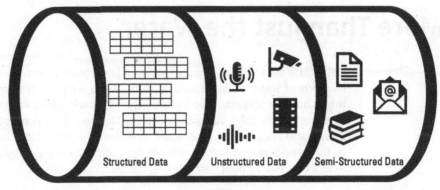

FIGURE 3-3:
Different types
of data in your
data lake.

Data Lake

In your data lake, you need to have all these types of data sitting side by side. Why? Because you'll be running analytics against the data lake that may need more than one form of data. For example, you receive and then analyze a detailed report of sales by department in a large department store during the past month.

Then, after noticing a few anomalies in the sales numbers, you pull up in-store surveillance video to analyze traffic versus sales to better understand how many customers may be looking at merchandise but deciding not to make a purchase. You can even combine structured data from scanners with your unstructured video data as part of your analysis.

If you had to go to different data storage environments for your sales results (structured data) and then the video surveillance (unstructured data), your over-all analysis is dramatically slowed down, especially if you need to integrate and cross-reference different types of data. With a data lake, all this data is sitting side by side, ready to be delivered for analysis and decision-making.

TECHNICAL STUFF

In their earliest days, relational databases only stored structured data. Later, they were extended with capabilities to store structured and unstructured data. Binary large objects (BLOBs) were a common way to store images and even video in a relational database. However, even an *object-extended* relational database doesn't make a good platform for a data lake when compared with modern data services such as Amazon S3 or Microsoft ADLS.

Different Water, Different Data

A common misconception is that you store "all your data" in your data lake. Actually, you store all or most of your *analytic* data in a data lake. Analytic data is, as you may suspect from the name, data that you're using for analytics. In contrast, you use *operational* data to run your business.

What's the difference? From one perspective, operational and analytic data are one and the same. Suppose you work for a large retailer. A customer comes into one of your stores and makes some purchases. Another customer goes onto your company's website and buys some items there. The records of those sales — which customers made the purchases, which products they bought, how many of each product, the dates of the sales, whether the sales were online or in a store, and so on — are all stored away as official records of those transactions, which are necessary for running your company's operations.

But you also want to analyze that data, right? You want to understand which products are selling the best and where. You want to understand which customers are spending the most. You have dozens or even hundreds of questions you want to ask about your customers and their purchasing activity.

REMEMBER

Here's the catch: You need to make copies of your operational data for the deep analysis that you need to undertake; and the copies of that operational data are what goes into the data lake (see Figure 3-4).

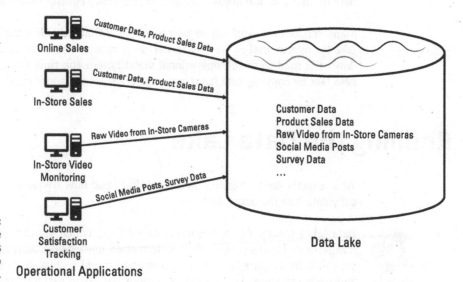

FIGURE 3-4: Source applications feeding data into your data lake.

Wait a minute! Why in the world do you need to copy data into your data lake? Why can't you just analyze the data right where it is, in the source applications and their databases?

Data lakes, at least as you need to build them today and for the foreseeable future, are a continuation of the same model that has been used for data warehousing since the early 1990s. For many technical reasons related to performance, deep analysis involving large data volumes and significant cross-referencing directly in your source applications isn't a workable solution for the bulk of your analytics.

Consequently, you need to make copies of the operational data that you want for analytical purposes and store that data in your data lake. Think of the data inside your data lake as (in used-car terminology) previously owned data that has been refurbished and is now ready for a brand-new owner.

But if you can't adequately do complex analytics directly from source applications and their databases, what about this idea: Run your applications off your data lake instead! This way, you can avoid having to copy your data, right? Unfortunately, that idea won't work, at least with today's technology.

TECHNICAL STUFF

Operational applications almost always use a relational database, which manages *concurrency control* among their users and applications. In simple terms, hundreds or even thousands of users can add new data and make changes to a relational database without interfering with each other's work and corrupting the database. A data lake, however, is built on storage technology that is optimized for retrieving data for analysis and doesn't support concurrency control for update operations.

Many vendors are working on new technology that will allow you to build a data lake for operational as well as analytical purposes. This technology is still a bit down the road from full operational viability. For the time being, you'll build a data lake by copying data from many different source applications.

Refilling the Data Lake

What exactly does "copying data" look like, and how frequently do you need to copy data into the data lake?

REMEMBER

Data lakes mostly use a technique called ELT, which stands for either *extract, transform, and load* or *extraction, transformation, and loading*. With ELT, you "blast" your data into a data lake without having to spend a great deal of time profiling and understanding the particulars of your data. You extract data (the E part of *ELT*) from its original home in a source application, and then, after that data has been transmitted to the data lake, you load the data (the L) into its initial storage location. Eventually, when it's time for you to use the data for analytical purposes, you'll need to transform the data (the T) into whatever format is needed for a specific type of analysis.

TECHNICAL STUFF

For data warehousing — the predecessor to data lakes that you're almost certainly still also using — data is copied from source applications to the data warehouse using a technique called ETL, rather than ELT. With ETL, you need to thoroughly understand the particulars of your data on its way into the data warehouse, which requires the transformation (T) to occur before the data is loaded (L) into its usable form.

With ELT, you can control the *latency*, or "freshness," of data that is brought into the data lake. Some data needed for critical, real-time analysis can be *streamed* into the data lake, which means that a copy is sent to the data lake immediately after data is created or updated within a source application. (This is referred to as a *low-latency data feed*.) You essentially push data into your data lake piece by piece immediately upon the creation of that data.

Other data may be less time-critical and can be "batched up" in a source application and then periodically transmitted in bulk to the data lake.

You can specify the latency requirements for every single data feed from every single source application.

Everyone Visits the Data Lake

Take a look around your organization today. Chances are, you have dozens or even hundreds of different places to go for reports and analytics. At one time, your company probably had the idea of building an *enterprise data warehouse* that would provide data for almost all the analytical needs across the entire company. Alas, for many reasons, you instead wound up with numerous *data marts* and other environments, very few of which work together. Even enterprise data warehouses are often accompanied by an entire portfolio of data marts in the typical organization.

Great news! The data lake will finally be that one-stop shopping place for the data to meet almost all the analytical needs across your entire enterprise.

Enterprise-scale data warehousing fell short for many different reasons, including the underlying technology platforms. Data lakes overcome those shortfalls and provide the foundation for an entirely new generation of integrated, enterprise-wide analytics.

WARNING

Even with a data lake, you'll almost certainly still have other data environments outside the data lake that support analytics. Your data lake objective should be to satisfy *almost* all your organization's analytical needs and be the go-to place for data. If a few other environments pop up here and there, that's okay. Just be careful about the overall proliferation of systems outside your data lake; otherwise, you'll wind up right back in the same highly fragmented data mess that you have today before beginning work on your data lake.

Chapter **4**

Wrapping Your Head Around Data Science

For over a decade now, *everyone* has been absolutely deluged by data. It's coming from every computer, every mobile device, every camera, and every imaginable sensor — and now it's even coming from watches and other wearable technologies. Data is generated in every social media interaction we humans make, every file we save, every picture we take, and every query we submit; data is even generated when we do something as simple as ask a favorite search engine for directions to the closest ice cream shop.

Although data immersion is nothing new, you may have noticed that the phenomenon is accelerating. Lakes, puddles, and rivers of data have turned to floods and veritable tsunamis of structured, semi-structured, and unstructured data that's streaming from almost every activity that takes place in both the digital and physical worlds. It's just an unavoidable fact of life within the information age.

Although just two decades ago no one was in a position to make much use of most of the data that's generated, the tides today have definitely turned. Specialists known as *data engineers* are constantly finding innovative and powerful new ways to capture, collate, and condense unimaginably massive volumes of data, and other specialists, known as *data scientists,* are leading change by deriving valuable and actionable insights from that data.

This chapter describes how data scientists use statistical and mathematical modeling to derive insights from data and highlights the expertise required to do so. It also covers some incredibly powerful low-code or no-code tools that help data scientists generate more profits faster from the data they're already working with without the downtime of learning to build complicated predictive models in R or Python.

Inspecting the Pieces of the Data Science Puzzle

In its truest form, data science represents the optimization of processes and resources. Data science produces *data insights* — actionable, data-informed conclusions or predictions that you can use to understand and improve your business, your investments, your health, and even your lifestyle and social life. Using data science insights is like being able to see in the dark. For any goal or pursuit you can imagine, you can find data science methods to help you predict the most direct route from where you are to where you want to be — and to anticipate every pothole in the road between both places.

To practice data science, in the true meaning of the term, you need the analytical know-how of math and statistics, the coding skills necessary to work with data, and an area of subject matter expertise. Without this expertise, you might as well call yourself a mathematician or a statistician. Similarly, a programmer without subject matter expertise and analytical know-how might better be considered a software engineer or developer, but not a data scientist.

The need for data-informed business and product strategy has been increasing exponentially for about a decade, thus forcing all business sectors and industries to adopt a data science approach. As such, different flavors of data science have emerged. The following are just a few titles under which experts of every discipline are required to know and regularly do data science: director of data science-advertising technology, digital banking product owner, clinical biostatistician, geotechnical data scientist, data scientist–geospatial and agriculture analytics, data and tech policy analyst, global channel ops–data excellence lead, and data scientist–healthcare.

Nowadays, it's almost impossible to differentiate between a proper data scientist and a subject matter expert (SME) whose success depends heavily on their ability to use data science to generate insights. Looking at a person's job title may or may not be helpful, simply because many roles are titled data scientist when they may as well be labeled data strategist or product manager, based on the actual requirements. In addition, many knowledge workers are doing daily data science and not working under the title of data scientist. It's an overhyped, often misleading label that's not always helpful if you're trying to find out what a data scientist does by looking at online job boards. To shed some light, in the following sections I spell out the key components that are part of any data science role, regardless of whether that role is assigned the data scientist label.

Collecting, querying, and consuming data

Data engineers have the job of capturing and collating large volumes of structured, unstructured, and semi structured *big data* — an outdated term that's used to describe data that exceeds the processing capacity of conventional database systems because it's too big, it moves too fast, or it lacks the structural requirements of traditional database architectures. (Find out more about big data in Book 1, Chapter 2.)

Again, data engineering tasks are separate from the work that's performed in data science, which focuses more on analysis, prediction, and visualization. Despite this distinction, whenever data scientists collect, query, and consume data during the analysis process, they perform work similar to that of the data engineer.

Although valuable insights can be generated from a single data source, often the combination of several relevant sources delivers the contextual information required to drive better data-informed decisions. A data scientist can work from several datasets that are stored in a single database, or even in several different data storage environments. At other times, source data is stored and processed on a cloud-based platform built by software and data engineers.

No matter how the data is combined or where it's stored, if you're a data scientist, you almost always have to *query* data — write commands to extract relevant datasets from data storage systems, in other words. Most of the time, you use Structured Query Language (SQL) to query data, or some incarnation of SQL proprietary to a specific tool. (The upcoming section "Getting a Handle on SQL and Relational Databases" is all about SQL, so if the acronym scares you, jump ahead to that section now.)

Whether you're using a third-party application such as Power BI or Tableau or doing custom analyses by using a programming language such as R or Python, you can choose from several universally accepted file formats:

>> **Comma-separated values (CSV):** Almost every brand of desktop and web-based analysis application accepts this file type, as do commonly used scripting languages such as Python and R.

>> **Script:** Most data scientists know how to use either the Python or R programming language to analyze and visualize data. These script files end with the extension .ply or .ipynb (Python) or .r (R).

>> **Application:** Excel is useful for quick-and-easy, spot-check analyses on small- to medium-size datasets. These application files have the .xls or .xlsx extension.

>> **Web programming:** If you're building custom, web-based data visualizations, you may be working in D3.js — or data-driven documents, a JavaScript library for data visualization. When you work in D3.js, you use data to manipulate web-based documents using .html, .svg, and .css files.

Applying mathematical modeling to data science tasks

Data science relies heavily on a practitioner's math skills (and statistics skills, as described in the following section) precisely because these are the skills needed to understand your data and its significance. These skills are also valuable in data science because you can use them to carry out predictive forecasting, decision modeling, and hypotheses testing.

REMEMBER

Mathematics uses deterministic methods to form a *quantitative* (or *numerical*) description of the world; *statistics* is a form of science that's derived from mathematics, but it focuses on using a *stochastic* (probabilities) approach and inferential methods to form a quantitative description of the world. Data scientists use mathematical methods to build decision models, generate approximations, and make predictions about the future.

This book presents advanced mathematical concepts using a plain language approach. To get detailed coverage of the many mathematical approaches that are useful when working in data science, check out Lillian Pierson's *Data Science For Dummies*, 3rd Edition (Wiley).

Deriving insights from statistical methods

In data science, statistical methods are useful for better understanding your data's significance, for validating hypotheses, for simulating scenarios, and for making predictive forecasts of future events. Advanced statistical skills are somewhat rare, even among quantitative analysts, engineers, and scientists. If you want to go places in data science, though, take some time to get up to speed in a few basic statistical methods, like linear and logistic regression, naïve Bayes classification, and time series analysis. Lillian Pierson's *Data Science For Dummies*, 3rd Edition (Wiley), covers these topics.

Coding, coding, coding — it's just part of the game

Coding is unavoidable when you're working in data science. You need to be able to write code so that you can instruct the computer in how to manipulate, analyze, and visualize your data. Programming languages such as Python and R are important for writing scripts for data manipulation, analysis, and visualization. SQL, on the other hand, is useful for data querying. Finally, the JavaScript library D3.js is often required for making cool, custom, and interactive web-based data visualizations.

Although coding is a requirement for data science, it doesn't have to be this big, scary *thing* that people make it out to be. Your coding can be as fancy and complex as you want it to be, but you can also take a rather simple approach. Although these skills are paramount to success, you can pretty easily learn enough coding to practice high-level data science. Books 4, 5, and 6 provide the basics of querying in SQL, and describe how to get started in R and Python.

Applying data science to a subject area

Statisticians once exhibited some measure of obstinacy in accepting the significance of data science. Many statisticians have cried out, "Data science is nothing new — it's just another name for what we've been doing all along!" But data science is separate, and definitely distinct, from the statistical approaches that comprise it.

Data scientists often use computer languages not used in traditional statistics and take approaches derived from the field of mathematics. But the main point of distinction between statistics and data science is the need for subject matter expertise.

Because statisticians usually have only a limited amount of expertise in fields outside of statistics, they're almost always forced to consult with a SME to verify exactly what their findings mean and to determine the best direction in which to proceed. Data scientists, on the other hand, should have a strong subject matter expertise in the area in which they're working. Data scientists generate deep insights and then use their domain-specific expertise to understand exactly what those insights mean with respect to the area in which they're working.

The following list describes a few ways in which today's knowledge workers are coupling data science skills with their respective areas of expertise in order to amplify the results they generate.

>> **Clinical informatics scientists** combine their healthcare expertise with data science skills to produce personalized healthcare treatment plans. They use healthcare informatics to predict and preempt future health problems in at-risk patients.

>> **Marketing data scientists** combine data science with marketing expertise to predict and preempt customer *churn* (the loss of customers from a product or service to that of a competitor's, in other words). They also optimize marketing strategies, build recommendation engines, and fine-tune marketing mix models.

>> **Data journalists** *scrape* websites (extract data in bulk directly from the pages on a website, in other words) for fresh data in order to discover and report the latest breaking-news stories.

>> **Directors of data science** bolster their technical project management capabilities with an added expertise in data science. Their work includes leading data projects and working to protect the profitability of the data projects for which they're responsible. They also act to ensure transparent communication between C-suite executives, business managers, and the data personnel on their team who actually do the implementation work.

>> **Data product managers** supercharge their product management capabilities with the power of data science. They use data science to generate predictive insights that better inform decision-making around product design, development, launch, and strategy. This is a classic type of data leadership role.

>> **Machine learning engineers** combine software engineering superpowers with data science skills to build predictive applications. This is a classic data implementation role.

Choosing the Best Tools for Your Data Science Strategy

Data science strategy can best be described as a technical plan that maps out each and every element required to lead data science projects that increase the profitability of a business. R and Python are often part of the plan, which may make you think that when it comes to data science strategy, Python and R are the obvious answers to this question: "Which tools do I need for my strategy to succeed?" But the obvious answer is not always the best answer. A data strategy that relies *only* on data science to improve profits from data is a limited one, cutting itself off at the pass by insisting on the use of code to monetize data.

For example, imagine that a human resources (HR) professional, without needing to write even one line of code, is able to build a software application that automatically collects applicant data, reads that data into an Applicants SQL database, and then executes an automated response to each applicant based on the manual determination of the HR personnel processing employment applications. Where appropriate, the software automatically moves candidates forward in the hiring process. This no-code application eliminates the need for manual data entry, data clean-up, email follow-up, and candidate forwarding. That's a lot of time (money, in other words) saved right there.

Do you know of any prebuilt software whose vendor could come in and configure it to create this type of system setup in-house? Yes, you probably do, but that's a lengthy, expensive, and inflexible route to take, considering that the same outcome is now possible in a no-code environment like Airtable — a collaborative, intuitive, cloud-based SQL-esque solution that acts and works like a spreadsheet and database at the same time.

No-code is a type of development platform that leverages graphical user interfaces in a way that allows coders and noncoders alike to build their software applications. If your start-up or small business has no complex data architecture, it's entirely possible to house your company's data in a no-code environment and not have to worry about integrating that data and platform with other data systems you might have.

If your company is larger and more mature, you may want to investigate *low-code* options — platforms that allow users to build applications without needing to use any code whatsoever, but that does require a small bit of code to configure on the back end to enable data integration with the rest of the company's data systems and sources. Commonly used low-code solutions are Google Forms and Microsoft Power Apps for self-service data collection and integration.

Concerning data strategy, what we're really talking about here is leveraging low-code and no-code solutions to deploy and directly monetize more of your company's data, without needing to train existing team members, or hire experienced data scientists. The idea is to equip all knowledge workers with intuitive data technologies they can use right away to start getting better results from data, without the intervention of data specialists — a true democratization of data and data monetization across the business, in other words.

Bridging the gap between no-code, low-code, SQL, and spreadsheets, SQL databases and spreadsheet applications such as Excel and Google Sheets provide just the no-code and low-code environments that knowledge workers can start using today to increase the productivity and profitability of their company's data. These technologies, covered throughout the rest of this chapter, are *very* accessible and represent great upside potential to modern businesses.

Getting a Handle on SQL and Relational Databases

Some data professionals are resistant to learning SQL because of the steep learning curve involved. They think, "I am not a coder, and the term *Structured Query Language* sure sounds like a programming language to me." In the case of SQL, though, it is *not* a programming language (see Figure 4-1). As far as the upside potential goes of learning to use SQL to query and access data, it's worth the small degree of hassle.

SQL, or *Structured Query Language,* is a standard for creating, maintaining, and securing relational databases. It's a set of rules you can use to quickly and efficiently query, update, modify, add, or remove data from large and complex databases. You use SQL rather than Python or a spreadsheet application to do these tasks because SQL is the simplest, fastest way to get the job done. It offers a plain and standardized set of core commands and methods that are easy to use when performing these particular tasks. This chapter introduces basic SQL concepts and explains how you can use SQL to do cool things like query, join, group, sort, and even text-mine structured datasets.

```
SELECT*FROM employees WHERE salary>50000 AND department=finance;
```

FIGURE 4-1:
An example
of how SQL is
human-readable.

```
SELECT    *
FROM      employees
WHERE     salary > 50000
          AND department = finance;
```

Although you can use SQL to work with structured data that resides in relational database management systems, you can't use standard SQL as a solution for handling big data. (Unfortunately, you just can't handle big data using relational database technologies.) SQL is simply a tool you can use to manipulate and edit structured data tables. It's nothing exceedingly innovative, but it can be helpful to use SQL for the data querying and manipulation tasks that often arise in the practice of data science. This introduces the basics of relational databases, SQL, and database design.

REMEMBER

Although the name Structured Query Language suggests that SQL is a programming language, don't be misled. SQL is not a programming language like R or Python. Rather, it's a language of commands and syntax that you can use to create, maintain, and search relational database systems. SQL supports a few common programming forms, like conditionals and loops, but to do anything more complex, you'd have to import your SQL query results into another programming platform and then do the more complex work there.

One fundamental characteristic of SQL is that you can use it only on structured data that sits in a relational database. SQL database management systems (DBMSs) optimize their own structure with minimal user input, which enables blazing-fast operational performance.

REMEMBER

An *index* is the lookup table. You create it in order to index, point to, and "look up" data in tables of a database. Although SQL DBMSs are known for their fast structured database querying capabilities, this speed and effectiveness are heavily dependent on good indexing. Good indexing is vital for fast data retrieval in SQL.

Similar to how different web browsers comply with, add to, and ignore different parts of the HTML standard in different ways, SQL rules are interpreted a bit differently, depending on whether you're working with open-source products or commercial vendor software applications.

TIP

Because not every SQL solution is the same, it's a good idea to know something about the benefits and drawbacks of some of the more popular SQL solutions on the market. Here are two popular open-source SQL implementations commonly used by data scientists:

>> **MySQL:** By far the most popular open-source version of SQL, MySQL offers a complete and powerful version of SQL. It's used on the back end of millions of websites.

>> **PostgreSQL:** This software adds object-oriented elements to SQL's relational language, making it popular with programmers who want to integrate SQL objects into their own platforms' object model.

As you might guess from the name, the most salient aspect of relational databases is that they're *relational* — they're composed of related tables, in other words. To illustrate the idea of a relational database, first imagine an Excel spreadsheet with rows, columns, and predefined relationships between shared columns. Then imagine having an Excel workbook with many worksheets (tables), in which every worksheet has a column with the same name as a column in one or more *other* worksheets. Because these worksheets have a shared relationship, if you use SQL you can use that shared relationship to look up data in all related worksheets. This type of relationship is illustrated in Figure 4-2.

Foreign Key

Lake Name	Max Water Depth (ft)	Average Annual Depth Change (in)
Lake Monroe	...	...
Lake Lilly	...	...
Lake Conway	...	...

Primary Key

Lake Name	Alkalinity (mEq/L)	Total Dissolved Solids (ppm)	Phosphates (u g/L)
Lake Monroe	...	...	...
Lake Lilly	...	...	...
Lake Conway	...	...	...

Foreign Key

Lake Name	Subdivision Name	Taxing District
Lake Monroe	...	...
Lake Lilly	...	...
Lake Conway	...	...

FIGURE 4-2: A relationship between data tables that share a column.

Knowing all about the keys

The *primary key* of a table is a column of values that uniquely identifies every row in that table. A good example of primary keys is the use of ISBN numbers for a table of books or employee ID numbers for a table of employees. A *foreign key* is a column in one table that matches the primary key of another and is used to link tables.

Keeping the focus on terminology, remember that proper database science often associates particular meanings to particular words, as you can see in this list:

>> **Columns,** called fields, keys, and attributes

>> **Rows,** called records

>> **Cells,** called values

The main benefits of using relational database management systems (RDBMSs, for short) is that they're fast, they have large storage and handling capacity (compared to spreadsheet applications such as Excel), and they're ideal tools to help you maintain *data integrity* — the consistency and accuracy of data in your database. If you need to make quick-and-accurate changes and updates to your datasets, you can use SQL and a RDBMS.

Let the following scenario serve as an illustration. This data table describes films and lists ratings from viewers:

id	title	genre	rating timestamp	rating
1	The Even Couple	NULL	2011-08-03 16:04:23	4
2	The Fourth Man	Drama	2014-02-19 19:17:16	5
2	The Fourth Man	Drama	2010-04-27 10:05:36	4
3	All About Adam	Drama	2011-04-05 21:21:05	4
3	All About Adam	Drama	2014-02-21 00:11:07	3
4	Dr. Yes	Thriller	NULL	

What happens if you find out that *All About Adam* is a comedy rather than a drama? If the table were in a simple spreadsheet, you'd have to open the data table, find all instances of the film, and then manually change the genre value for that record. That's not so difficult in this sample table because only two records are related to that film. But even here, if you forget to change one of these records, this inconsistency would cause a loss of data integrity, which can cause all sorts of unpredictable problems for you down the road.

In contrast, the relational database solution is simple and elegant. Instead of one table for this example, you'd have three:

```
Film    id    title
        1     The Even Couple
        2     The Fourth Man
        3     All About Adam
        4     Dr. Yes


Genre   id    genre
        2     Drama
        3     Drama
        4     Thriller


Rating  timestamp              id    rating
        2011-08-03 16:04:23    1     4
        2014-02-19 19:17:16    2     5
        2010-04-27 10:05:36    2     4
        2011-04-05 21:21:05    3     4
        2014-02-21 00:11:07    3     3
```

The primary key for the Film and Genre tables is id. The primary key for the Rating table is timestamp — because a film can have more than one rating, id is not a unique field and, consequently, it can't be used as a primary key. In this example, if you want to look up and change the genre for *All About Adam,* you'd use Film.id as the primary key and Genre.id as the foreign key. You'd simply use these keys to query the records you need to change and then apply the changes systematically. This systematic approach eliminates the risk of stray errors.

Investing Some Effort into Database Design

If you want to ensure that your database will be useful to you for the foreseeable future, you need to invest time and resources into excellent database design. If you want to create databases that offer fast performance and error-free results, your database design has to be flawless, or as flawless as you can manage. Before you enter any data into a data table, first carefully consider the tables and columns you want to include, the kinds of data those tables will hold, and the relationships you want to create between those tables.

Every hour you spend planning your database and anticipating future needs can save you countless hours down the road when your database might hold a million records. Poorly planned databases can easily turn into slow, error-ridden monstrosities — avoid them at all costs.

Keep just a few concepts in mind when you design databases:

>> Data types

>> Constraints

>> Normalization

The next few sections take a closer look at each topic.

Defining data types

When creating a data table, one of the first things you have to do is define the data type of each column. You have several data type options to choose from:

>> **Text:** If your column is to contain text values, you can classify it as a Character data type with a fixed length or a Text data type of indeterminate length.

>> **Numerical:** If your column is to hold number values, you can classify it as a Numerical data type. These can be stored as integers or floats.

>> **Date:** If your column is to hold date- or time-based values, you can designate this as a Date data type or Date-Time data type.

Text data types are handy, but they're terrible for searches. When you use a text field to do a search or select query, SQL will cause the computer to call up each of the data objects individually instead of searching and sorting through them *in memory* — in other words, processing data within the computer's memory, without actually reading and writing its computational results onto the disk.

Designing constraints properly

In the context of SQL, think of constraints as rules you use to control the type of data that can be placed in a table. As such, they're an important consideration in any database design. When you're considering adding constraints, first decide whether each column is allowed to hold a NULL value. (NULL isn't the same as blank or zero data; it indicates a total absence of data in a cell.)

Wrapping Your Head
Around Data Science

For example, if you have a table of products you're selling, you probably don't want to allow a NULL in the Price column. In the Product Description column, however, some products may have *long* descriptions, so you might allow some of the cells in this column to contain NULL values.

Within any data type, you can also constrain exactly what type of input values the column accepts. Imagine that you have a text field for Employee ID, which must contain values that are exactly two letters followed by seven numbers, like this: SD0154919. Because you don't want your database to accept a typo, you'd define a constraint that requires all values entered into the cells of the Employee ID column to have exactly two letters followed by seven numbers.

Normalizing your database

After you've defined the data types and designed constraints, you need to deal with *normalization* — structuring your database so that any changes, additions, or deletions to the data have to be made only once and won't result in anomalous, inconsistent data. There are many different degrees and types of normalization (at least seven), but a good, robust, normalized SQL database should have at least the following properties:

>> **Primary keys:** Each table has a primary key, which is a unique value for every row in that column.

>> **Nonredundancy of columns:** No two tables have the same column, unless it's the primary key of one and the foreign key of the other.

>> **No multiple dependencies:** Every column's value must depend on only one other column whose value does not in turn depend on any other column. Calculated values — values such as the total for an invoice, for example — must therefore be done on the fly for each query and should not be hard-coded into the database. This means that zip codes should be stored in a separate table because they depend on three columns — address, city, and state.

>> **Column indexes:** As you may recall, in SQL, an index is a lookup table that points to data in database tables. When you make a column index — an index of a particular column — each record in that column is assigned a unique key value indexed in a lookup table. Column indexing enables faster data retrieval from that column.

It's an excellent idea to create a column index for frequent searches or to be used as a search criterion. The column index takes up memory, but it increases your search speeds tremendously. It's easy to set up, too. Just tell your SQL DBMS to index a certain column, and then the system sets it up for you.

TIP

If you're concerned that your queries are slow, first make sure that you have all the indexes you need before trying other, perhaps more involved, trouble-shooting efforts.

>> **Subject-matter segregation:** Another feature of good database design is that each table contains data for only one kind of subject matter. This isn't exactly a normalization principle per se, but it helps to achieve a similar end.

Consider again the film rating example, from the earlier section:

```
Film    id    title
        1     The Even Couple
        2     The Fourth Man
        3     All About Adam
        4     Dr. Yes


Genre   id    genre
        2     Drama
        3     Drama
        4     Thriller


Rating  timestamp            id    rating
        2011-08-03 16:04:23  1     4
        2014-02-19 19:17:16  2     5
        2010-04-27 10:05:36  2     4
        2011-04-05 21:21:05  3     4
        2014-02-21 00:11:07  3     3
```

I could have designated `Genre` to be a separate column in the `Film` table, but it's better off in its own table because that allows for the possibility of missing data values (`NULL`s). Look at the `Film` table just shown. Film 1 has no genre assigned to it. If the `Genre` column were included in this table, then `Film 1` would have a `NULL` value there. Rather than have a column that contains a `NULL` value, it's much easier to make a separate Genre data table. The primary keys of the Genre table don't align exactly with those of the Film table, but they don't need to when you go to join them.

TIP

`NULL` values can be quite problematic when you're running a `SELECT` query. When you're querying based on the value of a particular attribute, any records that have a `NULL` value for that attribute won't be returned in the query results. Of course, these records would still exist, and they may even fall within the specified range of values you've defined for your query, but if the record has a `NULL` value, it's omitted from the query results. In this case, you're likely to miss them in your analysis.

Any data scientist worth their salt must address many challenges when dealing with either the data or the science. SQL takes some of the pressure off when you're dealing with the time-consuming tasks of storing and querying data, saving precious time and effort.

Narrowing the Focus with SQL Functions

When working with SQL commands, you use *functions* to perform tasks, and *arguments* to more narrowly specify those tasks. To query a particular set from within your data tables, for example, use the SELECT function. To combine separate tables into one, use the JOIN function. To place limits on the data that your query returns, use a WHERE argument. As indicated in the preceding section, fewer than 20 commands are commonly used in SQL. This section introduces SELECT, FROM, JOIN, WHERE, GROUP, MAX(), MIN(), COUNT(), AVG(), and HAVING.

The most common SQL command is SELECT. You can use this function to generate a list of search results based on designated criteria. To illustrate, imagine the film-rating scenario mentioned earlier in this chapter with a tiny database of movie ratings that contains the three tables Film, Genre, and Rating.

To generate a printout of all data FROM the Rating table, use the SELECT function. Any function with SELECT is called a *query*, and SELECT functions accept different arguments to narrow down or expand the data that is returned. An asterisk (*) represents a wildcard, so the asterisk in SELECT * tells the *interpreter* — the SQL component that carries out all SQL statements — to show every column in the table. You can then use the WHERE argument to limit the output to only certain values. For example, here is the complete Rating table:

```
Rating   timestamp                id    rating
         2011-08-03 16:04:23      1     4
         2014-02-19 19:17:16      2     5
         2010-04-27 10:05:36      2     4
         2011-04-05 21:21:05      3     4
         2014-02-21 00:11:07      3     3
```

If you want to limit your ratings to those made after a certain time, you'd use code like that shown in Listing 4-1.

LISTING 4-1: Using SELECT, WHERE, and DATE() to Query Data

```
SELECT * FROM Rating
WHERE Rating.timestamp >= date('2014-01-01')
```

```
timestamp            id   rating
2014-02-19 19:17:16   2    5
2014-02-21 00:11:07   3    3
```

In Listing 4-1, the DATE() function turns a string into a date that can then be compared with the timestamp column.

You can also use SQL to join columns into a new data table. Joins are made on the basis of shared (or compared) data in a particular column (or columns). You can execute a join in SQL in several ways, but the ones listed here are probably the most popular:

>> **Inner join:** The default JOIN type; returns all records that lie in the intersecting regions between the tables being queried

>> **Outer join:** Returns all records that lie outside the overlapping regions between queried data tables

>> **Full outer join:** Returns all records that lie both inside and outside the overlapping regions between queried data tables — in other words, returns all records for both tables

>> **Left join:** Returns all records that reside in the leftmost table

>> **Right join:** Returns all records that reside in the rightmost table

REMEMBER

Be sure to differentiate between an inner join and an outer join, as these functions handle missing data in different ways. As an example of a join in SQL, if you want a list of films that includes genres, you use an inner join between the Film and Genre tables to return only the results that intersect (overlap) between the two tables.

To refresh your memory, here are the two tables you're interested in:

```
Film    id   title
         1    The Even Couple
         2    The Fourth Man
         3    All About Adam
         4    Dr. Yes


Genre   id   genre
         2    Drama
         3    Drama
         4    Thriller
```

Listing 4-2 shows how you'd use an inner join to find the information you want.

LISTING 4-2:   **An Inner JOIN Function**

```
SELECT Film.id, Film.title, Genre.genre
FROM Film
JOIN Genre On Genre.id=Film.id
id     title            genre
2      The Fourth Man   Drama
3      All About Adam   Drama
4      Dr. Yes          Thriller
```

In Listing 4-2, specific columns (`Film.title` and `Genre.genre`) are named after the `SELECT` command. This avoids creating a duplicate `id` column in the table that results from the `JOIN` — one `id` from the Film table and one `id` from the Genre table. Because the default for `JOIN` is inner, and inner joins return only records that are overlapping or shared between tables, `Film 1` is omitted from the results (because of its missing `Genre` value).

If you want to return all rows, even ones with `NULL` values, simply do a full outer join, like the one shown in Listing 4-3.

LISTING 4-3:   **A Full Outer JOIN**

```
SELECT Film.id, Film.title, Genre.genre
FROM Film
FULL JOIN Genre On Genre.id=Film.id
id     title            genre
1      The Even Couple  NULL
2      The Fourth Man   Drama
3      All About Adam   Drama
4      Dr. Yes          Thriller
```

To aggregate values so that you can figure out the average rating for a film, use the `GROUP` statement. (GROUP statement commands include `MAX( )`, `MIN( )`, `COUNT( )`, or `AVG( )`.)

Listing 4-4 shows one way you can aggregate values in order to return the average rating of each film. The `SELECT` function uses the `AS` statement to rename the column to make sure it was properly labeled. The Film and Ratings tables had to be joined and, because *Dr. Yes* had no ratings and an inner join was used, that film was left out.

LISTING 4-4: **Using a GROUP Statement to Aggregate Data**

```
SELECT Film.title, AVG(rating) AS avg_rating
FROM Film
JOIN Rating On Film.id=Rating.id
GROUP BY Film.title


title           avg_rating
All About Adam  3.5
The Even Couple 4.0
The Fourth Man  4.5
```

To narrow the results even further, add a HAVING clause at the end, as shown in Listing 4-5.

LISTING 4-5: **A HAVING Clause to Narrow Results**

```
SELECT Film.title, AVG(rating) AS avg_rating
FROM Film
JOIN Rating On Film.id=Rating.id
GROUP BY Film.title
HAVING avg_rating >= 4


title           avg_rating
The Even Couple 4.0
The Fourth Man  4.5
```

The code in Listing 4-5 limits the data your query returns so that you get only records of titles that have an average rating greater than or equal to 4.

TECHNICAL STUFF

Though SQL can do some basic text mining, packages such as Natural Language Toolkit in Python (NLTK, at www.nltk.org) and General Architecture for Text Engineering (GATE, at https://gate.ac.uk) are needed in order to do anything more complex than count words and combinations of words. These more advanced packages can be used for preprocessing data in order to extract linguistic items such as parts of speech or syntactic relations, which can then be stored in a relational database for later querying.

Making Life Easier with Excel

Microsoft Excel holds a special place among data science tools. It was originally designed to act as a simple spreadsheet. Over time, however, it has become the people's choice in data analysis software. In response to user demands, Microsoft has added more and more analysis and visualization tools with every release. As Excel advances, so do its data munging and data science capabilities. (In case you're curious, *data munging* involves reformatting and rearranging data into more manageable formats that are usually required for consumption by other processing applications downstream.) As early as Excel 2013, you'll find features including easy-to-use tools for charting, PivotTables, and macros. It also supports scripting in Visual Basic so that you can design scripts to automate repeatable tasks. The newer the product, the more advanced the functionality in Microsoft Excel.

The benefit of using Excel in a data science capacity is that it offers a fast-and-easy way to get up close and personal with your data. If you want to browse every data point in your dataset, you can quickly and easily do this using Excel. Most data scientists start in Excel and eventually add other tools and platforms when they find themselves pushing against the boundaries of the tasks Excel is designed to do. Still, even the best data scientists out there keep Excel as an important tool in their tool belt. When working in data science, you might not use Excel every day, but knowing how to use it can make your job easier.

TIP

If you're using Excel spreadsheets for data analysis but finding it to be rather buggy and clunky, consider instead testing out Google Sheets — Google's cloud-based version of an Excel spreadsheet. It can be run offline on your computer, and it offers an ease-of-use and a set of collaborative features that simply aren't available within the Microsoft Office environment today. Google Sheets offers all the same functions discussed in this chapter, using all the same commands as Excel spreadsheets, but most users find Sheets to be a far more intuitive, extensible tool for data analysis, visualization, and collaboration.

REMEMBER

Although you have many different tools available to you when you want to see your data as one big forest, Excel is a great first choice when you need to look at the trees. Excel attempts to be many different things to many different kinds of users. Its functionality is well-compartmentalized in order to avoid overwhelming new users while still providing power users with the more advanced functionality they crave. The following sections show how you can use Excel to quickly get to know your data. You also see how you can use Excel PivotTables and macros to greatly simplify your data clean-up and analysis tasks.

Using Excel to quickly get to know your data

Use Excel if you're starting with an unfamiliar dataset and need patterns or trends as quickly as possible. Excel offers effective features for exactly these purposes. Its main features for a quick-and-dirty data analysis are.

>> **Filters:** Filters are useful for sorting out all records that are irrelevant to the analysis at hand.

>> **Conditional formatting:** Specify a condition, and Excel flags records that meet that condition. By using conditional formatting, you can easily detect outliers and trends in your tabular datasets.

>> **Charts:** Charts have long been used to visually detect outliers and trends in data, so charting is an integral part of almost all data science analyses.

To see how these features work in action, consider the sample dataset shown in Figure 4-3, which tracks sales figures for three employees over six months.

Salesperson	Month	Total Sales
Abbie	Jan	$ 10,144.75
Abbie	Feb	$ 29,008.52
Abbie	Mar	$ 208,187.70
Abbie	Apr	$ 21,502.13
Abbie	May	$ 23,975.73
Abbie	Jun	$ 20,172.20
Brian	Jan	$ 9,925.44
Brian	Feb	$ 9,183.93
Brian	Mar	$ 12,691.39
Brian	Apr	$ 19,521.37
Brian	May	$ 16,579.38
Brian	Jun	$ 14,161.52
Chris	Jan	$ 2,792.18
Chris	Feb	$ 5,669.46
Chris	Mar	$ 4,909.24
Chris	Apr	$ 8,731.14
Chris	May	$ 11,747.29
Chris	Jun	$ 13,856.17

FIGURE 4-3: The full dataset that tracks employee sales performance.

Filtering in Excel

To narrow your dataset view to only the data that matters for your analysis, use Excel filters to filter out irrelevant data from the data view. Simply select the data, click the Home tab's Sort & Filter button, and then choose Filter from the options that appear. A little drop-down option then appears in the header row of the selected data so that you can select the classes of records you want to have filtered from the selection. Using the Excel Filter functionality allows you to quickly and easily sort or restrict your view to only the subsets of the data that interest you the most.

Take another look at the full dataset shown in Figure 4-3. Say you want to view only data related to Abbie's sales figures. If you select all records in the Salesperson column and then activate the filter functionality (as just described), from the drop-down menu that appears you can specify that the filter should isolate only all records named Abbie, as shown in Figure 4-4. When filtered, the table is reduced from 18 rows to only 6 rows. In this particular example, that change doesn't seem so dramatic, but when you have hundreds, thousands, or even a million rows, this feature comes in very, very handy.

Salesperson	Month	Total Sales
Abbie	Jan	$10,144.75
Abbie	Feb	$29,008.52
Abbie	Mar	$208,187.70
Abbie	Apr	$21,502.13
Abbie	May	$23,975.73
Abbie	Jun	$20,172.20

FIGURE 4-4: The sales performance dataset, filtered to show only Abbie's records.

WARNING

Excel lets you store only up to 1,048,576 rows per worksheet. That said, after about 200,000 rows, data querying gets increasingly slow.

Using conditional formatting

To quickly spot outliers in your tabular data, use Excel's Conditional Formatting feature. Imagine after a data entry error that Abbie's March total sales showed $208,187.70 but was supposed to be only $20,818.77. You're not quite sure where the error is located, but you know that it must be significant because the figures seem off by about $180,000.

To quickly show such an outlier, select all records in the Total Sales column and then click the Conditional Formatting button on the Ribbon's Home tab. When the button's menu appears, choose the Data Bars option. Doing so displays the red data bar scales shown in Figure 4-5. With data bars turned on, the bar in the $208,187.70 cell is so much larger than any of the others that you can easily see the error.

Salesperson	Month	Total Sales
Abbie	Jan	$ 10,144.75
Abbie	Feb	$ 29,008.52
Abbie	Mar	$ 208,187.70
Abbie	Apr	$ 21,502.13
Abbie	May	$ 23,975.73
Abbie	Jun	$ 20,172.20
Brian	Jan	$ 9,925.44
Brian	Feb	$ 9,183.93
Brian	Mar	$ 12,691.39
Brian	Apr	$ 19,521.37
Brian	May	$ 16,579.38
Brian	Jun	$ 14,161.52
Chris	Jan	$ 2,792.18
Chris	Feb	$ 5,669.46
Chris	Mar	$ 4,909.24
Chris	Apr	$ 8,731.14
Chris	May	$ 11,747.29
Chris	Jun	$ 13,856.17

FIGURE 4-5: Spotting outliers in a tabular dataset with conditional formatting data bars.

If you want to quickly discover patterns in your tabular data, you can choose the Color Scales option (rather than the Data Bars option) from the Conditional Formatting menu. After correcting Abbie's March Total Sales figure to $20,818.77, select all cells in the Total Sales column and then activate the Color Scales version of conditional formatting. Doing so displays the result shown in Figure 4-6. From the red-white-blue heat map, you can see that Abbie has the highest sales total and that Brian has been selling more than Chris. (Okay, you can't see the red-white-blue in my black-and-white figures, but you can see the light-versus-dark contrast.) Now, if you only want to conditionally format Abbie's sales performance relative to her own total sales (but not Brian and Chris's sales), you can select only the cells for Abbie (and not the entire column).

Salesperson	Month	Total Sales
Abbie	Jan	$ 10,144.75
Abbie	Feb	$ 29,008.52
Abbie	Mar	$ 20,818.77
Abbie	Apr	$ 21,502.13
Abbie	May	$ 23,975.73
Abbie	Jun	$ 20,172.20
Brian	Jan	$ 9,925.44
Brian	Feb	$ 9,183.93
Brian	Mar	$ 12,691.39
Brian	Apr	$ 19,521.37
Brian	May	$ 16,579.38
Brian	Jun	$ 14,161.52
Chris	Jan	$ 2,792.18
Chris	Feb	$ 5,669.46
Chris	Mar	$ 4,909.24
Chris	Apr	$ 8,731.14
Chris	May	$ 11,747.29
Chris	Jun	$ 13,856.17

FIGURE 4-6: Spotting outliers in a tabular dataset with color scales.

Excel charting to visually identify outliers and trends

Excel's Charting tool gives you an incredibly easy way to visually identify both outliers and trends in your data. An XY (scatter) chart of the original dataset (refer to Figure 4-3) yields the scatterplot shown in Figure 4-7. As you can see, the outlier is overwhelmingly obvious when the data is plotted on a scatter chart.

Alternatively, if you want to visually detect trends in a dataset, you can use Excel's Line Chart feature. The data from Figure 4-6 is shown as a line chart in Figure 4-8. It's worth mentioning, the outlier was fixed in this line graph, which is what allows the Y-axis to have a more readable scale compared to Figure 4-7.

As you can clearly see from the figure, Chris's sales performance is low — last place among the three salespeople but gaining momentum. Because Chris seems to be improving, maybe management would want to wait a few months before making any firing decisions based on sales performance data.

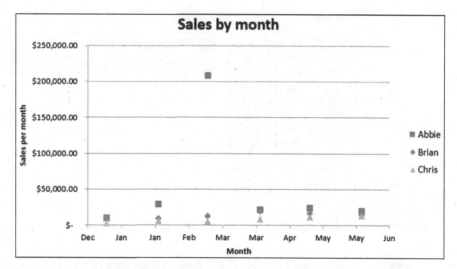

FIGURE 4-7:
Excel XY (scatter) plots provide a simple way to visually detect outliers.

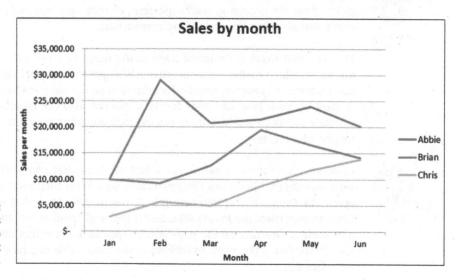

FIGURE 4-8:
Excel line charts make it easy to visually detect trends in data.

Reformatting and summarizing with PivotTables

Excel developed the PivotTable to make it easier for users to extract valuable insights from large sets of spreadsheet data. If you want to generate insights by quickly restructuring or reclassifying your data, use a PivotChart. One of the main differences between a traditional spreadsheet and a dataset is that spreadsheets tend to be wide (with a lot of columns) and datasets tend to be long (with a lot of rows). Figure 4-9 clearly shows the difference between a long dataset and a wide spreadsheet.

Long format:

Salesperson	Month	Total Sales
Abbie	Jan	$ 10,144.75
Abbie	Feb	$ 29,008.52
Abbie	Mar	$ 208,187.70
Abbie	Apr	$ 21,502.13
Abbie	May	$ 23,975.73
Abbie	Jun	$ 20,172.20
Brian	Jan	$ 9,925.44
Brian	Feb	$ 9,183.93
Brian	Mar	$ 12,691.39
Brian	Apr	$ 19,521.37
Brian	May	$ 16,579.38
Brian	Jun	$ 14,161.52
Chris	Jan	$ 2,792.18
Chris	Feb	$ 5,669.46
Chris	Mar	$ 4,909.24
Chris	Apr	$ 8,731.14
Chris	May	$ 11,747.29
Chris	Jun	$ 13,856.17

Wide format:

Salesperson	Jan	Feb	Mar	Apr	May	Jun
Abbie	$10,144.75	$29,008.52	$208,187.70	$21,502.13	$23,975.73	$20,172.20
Brian	$ 9,925.44	$ 9,183.93	$ 12,691.39	$19,521.37	$16,579.38	$14,161.52
Chris	$ 2,792.18	$ 5,669.46	$ 4,909.24	$ 8,731.14	$11,747.29	$13,856.17

FIGURE 4-9: A long dataset and a wide spreadsheet.

REMEMBER

A *PivotTable* is a table that's derived from data that sits within a spreadsheet. The pivot allows for grouping, rearrangement, display, and summary of the raw data that's stored within the underlying spreadsheet.

The way that Excel is designed leads many users to intuitively prefer the wide format — which makes sense because it's a spreadsheet application. To counter this preference, however, Excel offers the *pivot table feature* so that you can quickly convert between long and wide formats. You can also use PivotTables to quickly calculate subtotals and summary calculations on your newly formatted and rearranged data tables.

TIP

Creating PivotTables is easy: Just select all cells that comprise the table you seek to analyze. Then click the PivotTable button on the Insert tab. This action opens the Create PivotTable dialog box, where you can define where you want Excel to construct the PivotTable. Select OK, and Excel automatically generates a PivotField Interface on the page you've specified. From this interface, you can specify the fields you want to include in the PivotTable and how you want them to be laid out.

The table shown in Figure 4-10 was constructed using the long-format sales performance data shown in Figure 4-9. It's an example of the simplest possible PivotTable that can be constructed, but even at that, it automatically calculates subtotals for each column and those subtotals automatically update when you make changes to the data. What's more, PivotTables come with *PivotCharts* — data plots that automatically change when you make changes to the PivotTable filters based on the criteria you're evaluating.

FIGURE 4-10:
Creating a wide
data table from
the long dataset
via a PivotTable.

Total_Sales	Month						
Salesperson	Jan	Feb	Mar	Apr	May	Jun	Grand Total
Abbie	$10,144.75	$29,008.52	$20,818.77	$21,502.13	$23,975.73	$20,172.20	$125,622.10
Brian	$9,925.44	$9,183.93	$12,691.39	$19,521.37	$16,579.38	$14,161.52	$82,063.03
Chris	$2,792.18	$5,669.46	$4,909.24	$8,731.14	$11,747.29	$13,856.17	$47,705.48
Grand Total	$22,862.37	$43,861.91	$38,419.40	$49,754.64	$52,302.40	$48,189.89	$255,390.61

Automating Excel tasks with macros

Macros are prescribed routines written in Visual Basic for Applications (VBA). You can use macros to decrease the amount of manual processing you need to do when working with data in Excel. For example, within Excel, macros can act as a set of functions and commands that you can use to automate a wide variety of tasks. If you want to save time (and hassle) by automating Excel tasks that you routinely repeat, use macros.

To access macros, first activate Excel's Developer tab from within the Options menu on the File tab. (In other words, after opening the Options menu, choose Customize Ribbon from your choices on the left and then click to select the Developer check box in the column on the right.) Using the Developer tab, you can record a macro, import one created by someone else, or code your own in VBA.

To illustrate macros in action, imagine that you have a column of values and you want to insert an empty cell between each one of the values, as shown in Figure 4-11. Excel has no easy, out-of-the-box way to make this insertion. Using Excel macros, however, you can ask Excel to record you while you step through the process one time and then assign a key command to this recording to create the macro. After you create the macro, every time you need to repeat the same task in the future, just run the macro by pressing the key command, and the script then performs all required steps for you.

REMEMBER

Macros have an Absolute mode and a Relative mode. The Absolute mode refers to a macros routine that runs the way you recorded it — down to the spreadsheet cell positions in which the routine was recorded. Relative mode macros run the same routine you record but can be placed in whatever cell position you need within the spreadsheet.

For a more formal definition of Absolute and Relative macros, consider this:

>> **Relative:** Every action and movement you make is recorded as relative to the cell that was selected when you began the recording. When you run the macro in the future, it will run in reference to the cell that's selected, acting as though that cell were the same cell you had initially selected when you recorded the macro.

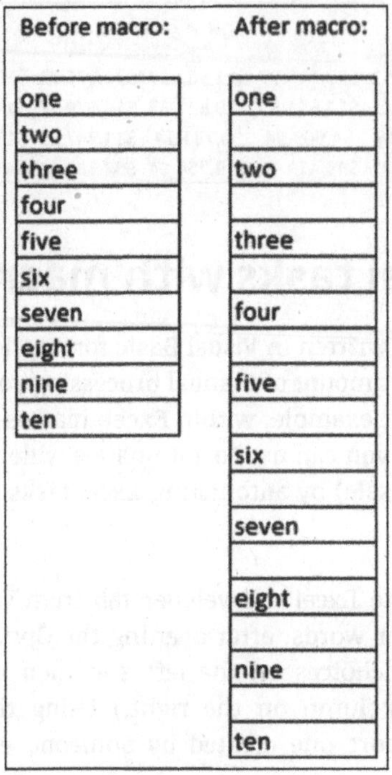

Before macro:	After macro:
one	one
two	
three	two
four	
five	three
six	
seven	four
eight	
nine	five
ten	
	six
	seven
	eight
	nine
	ten

FIGURE 4-11:
Using a macro to insert empty cells between values.

>> **Absolute:** After you start recording the macro, every action and movement you make is repeated when you run the macro in the future, and those actions or movements aren't made in any relative reference to whatever cell was active when you started recording. The macro routine is repeated exactly as you recorded it.

In the preceding example, the macro was recorded in Relative mode. This enables the macro to be run continuously, anywhere, and on top of results from any preceding macros run. Since, in this scenario, the macro recorded only one iteration of the process, if it had been recorded in Absolute mode, every time it was run, the macro would have kept adding a space between only the one and two values. In other words, it would not have operated on any cells other than the ones it was recorded on.

WARNING

Macro commands aren't entered into Excel's Undo stack. If you use a macro to change or delete data, you're stuck with that change.

TIP

Test your macros first, and save your worksheets before using them so that you can revert to the saved file if something goes wrong.

Excel power users often graduate to programming their own macros using VBA. Because VBA is a full-fledged programming language, the possibilities from pairing Excel with VBA are almost endless. Still, ask yourself this question: If you're going to invest time in learning a programming language, do you need to work within the confines of Excel's spreadsheet structure? If not, you might consider learning a scientific computing language, like R or Python. These open-source languages have a more user-friendly syntax and are much more flexible and powerful.

IN THIS CHAPTER

» Laying out the basics of data visualization and storytelling

» Choosing the perfect data visualization type for the needs of your audience

» Picking the perfect design style

» Crafting clear and powerful visual messages with the right data graphic

» Adding context

Chapter **5**

Telling Powerful Stories with Data Visualization

Any standard definition of data analytics, data science, or data visualization will specify that its purpose is to help you extract meaning and value from raw data. Finding and deriving insights from raw data is at the crux of data science, but these insights mean nothing if you don't know how to communicate your findings to others. Data visualization and storytelling are excellent means by which you can visually communicate your data's meaning. To design effective data visualizations and stories, however, you must know and truly understand the target audience and the core purpose for which you're communicating with members of that audience. You must also understand the main types of data graphics available to you, as well as the significant benefits and drawbacks of each. This chapter presents the core principles of data visualization and data storytelling design.

A *data visualization* is a visual representation that's designed for the purpose of conveying the meaning and significance of data and data insights. Because data visualizations are designed for a whole spectrum of different audiences, different purposes, and different skill levels, the first step to designing an effective data visualization is to *know your audience*. Audiences come in all shapes, forms, and sizes. For example, you might design a data visualization for the young-and-edgy readers of *Wired* magazine or convey scientific findings to a research group. Your audience might consist of board members and organizational decision-makers or a local grassroots organization.

The one thing that's consistent across all audiences, however, is the process you should follow when creating your data visualization, as spelled out here:

1. Determine the type of data visualization you will create, based on your audience and the purpose of your visualization.

2. Decide on a design style for your data visualization.

3. Choose which graphics make the most sense for your audience.

4. Test out different types of data graphics with the data, and then pick the ones that display the most clear answers.

5. Arrange your data graphics within the data visualization.

6. Where appropriate, add context to enhance the meaning of the visualization.

This chapter walks you through each and every step in sequential order.

Data Visualizations: The Big Three

Every audience is composed of a unique class of consumers, each with unique data visualization needs, so you have to clarify for whom you're designing. (See Table 5-1.) This section introduces the three main types of data visualizations and then explains how to pick the one that best meets the needs of your audience.

TABLE 5-1   **Types of Data Visualization, by Audience**

	Data Storytelling	Data Showcasing	Data Art
Audience	Less-technical business decision-makers	Data implementers, analysts, engineers, scientists, or statisticians	Idealists, dreamers, and social change-makers

Data storytelling for decision-makers

Sometimes, you have to design data visualizations for a less technical-minded audience, perhaps to help members of this audience make better-informed business decisions. The purpose of this type of visualization is to tell your audience the story behind the data. In data storytelling, the audience depends on you to make sense of the data behind the visualization and then turn useful insights into visual stories they can easily understand.

With *data storytelling*, your goal should be to use data visualization, words, and presentation skills to create a narrative that tells the story — the *meaning*, in other words — of the data insights you seek to convey. With respect to the data visualization you use within a data story, you want it to be a clutter-free, highly focused visualization that enables your audience members to quickly extract meaning without having to make much effort. These visualizations are best delivered in the form of static images, but more adept decision-makers may prefer to have an interactive dashboard they can use to do a bit of exploration and what-if modeling.

Data storytelling involves more than just data visualization design, though. You need to use words and presentation skills to communicate the data story as well. You'll want to use words sparingly within annotations on the data visualization itself. Maybe you present the data story with an accompanying slideshow, or maybe not — but you should present it with effective presentation skills.

Your presentation design should be part of the broader work you're doing concerning stakeholder management — the process of developing and maintaining the trust of those key stakeholders whom your data work is meant to support, so that you can bring your data insights to life by ensuring that they're seen, heard, and heeded in decision-making across your company.

Data showcasing for analysts

If you're designing for a crowd of data implementers, or other logical, calculating analysts, you can create data visualizations that are rather open-ended. The purpose of this type of visualization is to help audience members visually explore the data and draw their conclusions.

When using *data showcasing* techniques, your goal should be to display a lot of contextual information that supports audience members as they make their interpretations. These visualizations should include more contextual data and less conclusive focus so that people can get in, analyze the data for themselves, and then draw their conclusions. These visualizations are best delivered as static images or dynamic, interactive dashboards.

Designing data art for activists

You might design for an audience of idealists, dreamers, and change-makers. When designing for this audience, you want your data visualization to make a point! You can assume that typical audience members aren't overly analytical. What they lack in math skills, however, they more than compensate for in solid convictions.

These people look to your data visualization as a vehicle by which to make a statement. When designing for this audience, data art is the way to go. The main goal in using *data art* is to entertain, provoke, annoy, or do whatever it takes to make a loud, clear, attention-demanding statement. Data art has little to no narrative and offers no room for viewers to form their interpretations.

REMEMBER

Data science experts have an ethical responsibility always to represent data accurately. A data scientist should never distort the message of the data to fit what the audience wants to hear — not even for data art! Nontechnical audiences don't even recognize, let alone see, the possible issues.

Designing to Meet the Needs of Your Target Audience

To make a functional data visualization, you must get to know your target audience and then design precisely for their needs. But to make every design decision with your target audience in mind, you need to take a few steps to make sure that you truly understand your data visualization's target consumers.

To gain the insights you need about your audience and your purpose, follow this process:

1. **Brainstorm.**

   Think about a specific member of your audience and make as many educated guesses as you can about that person's motivations.

   TIP

   Give this (imaginary) audience member a name and a few other identifying characteristics. For example, imagine a 45-year-old divorced mother of two named Eve.

2. **Define the purpose of your visualization.**

   Narrow the purpose of the visualization by deciding exactly what action or outcome you want audience members to make as a result of the visualization.

3. **Choose a functional design.**

Review the three main data visualization types (discussed earlier in this chapter) and decide which type can best help you achieve your intended outcome.

The following sections spell out this process.

Step 1: Brainstorm (All about Eve)

To brainstorm properly, pull out a sheet of paper and picture an imaginary audience member — "Eve," for example. To create a more functional and effective data visualization, you'd want to start by answering the more important questions we could ask about Eve in order to better understand her and thus better understand and design for your target audience.

Start by forming a picture of what Eve's average day looks like — what she does when she gets out of bed in the morning, what she does over her lunch hour, and what her workplace is like. Also consider how Eve will use your visualization. These things tell you a little bit about her *psychographics* — the psychological characteristics that drive her high-level needs and wants.

To form a more comprehensive view of who Eve is and how you can best meet her needs, you can pull from the following question bank:

>> Where does Eve work? What does she do for a living?

>> What kind of technical education or experience, if any, does she have?

>> How old is Eve? Is she married? Does she have children? What does she look like? Where does she live?

>> What social, political, cause-based, or professional issues are important to Eve? What does she think of herself?

>> What problems and issues does Eve have to deal with every day?

>> How does your data visualization help solve Eve's work problems or her family problems? How does it improve her self-esteem?

>> Through what avenue will you present the visualization to Eve — for example, over the Internet or in a staff meeting?

>> What does Eve need to be able to do with your data visualization?

As possible answers to these questions, suppose that Eve is the manager of the zoning department in Irvine County. She is 45 years old and a single divorcee with two children who are about to start college. She is deeply interested in local politics and eventually wants to be on the county's board of commissioners. To achieve that position, she must get some major "oomph" on her county management résumé. Eve derives most of her feelings of self-worth from her job and her keen ability to make good management decisions for her department.

Until now, Eve has been forced to manage her department according to her gut-level intuition, backed by a few disparate business systems reports. She isn't extraordinarily analytical, but she knows enough to understand what she sees. The problem is that Eve lacks the visualization tools she needs in order to display all the relevant data she should consider. Because she has neither the time nor the skill to code something herself, she's been waiting in the lurch. Eve is excited that you'll attend next Monday's staff meeting to present data insights you've discovered that she hopes will enable her to make more effective data-driven management decisions.

Step 2: Define the purpose

After you brainstorm about the typical audience member (see the preceding section), you can much more easily pinpoint exactly what you're trying to achieve with your data visualization. Are you attempting to get consumers to feel a certain way about themselves or the world around them? Are you trying to make a statement? Are you seeking to influence organizational decision-makers to make good business decisions? Or do you simply want to lay all the data out there for all viewers to make sense of and deduce from it what they will?

Returning to the hypothetical Eve: What decisions or processes are you trying to help her achieve? Well, you'd first need to make sense of her data and uncover relevant data insights. Then you'd need to present those data insights to her in a way that she can clearly understand and use for improved decision-making. So, looking at the data — what do you see that's happening within the inner mechanics of her department? Once you've discovered some clear trends and predictions, it'd be time to use data visualization skills to guide Eve into making the most prudent and effective management choices.

Step 3: Choose the most functional visualization type for your purpose

Keep in mind that you have three main types of visualization from which to choose: data storytelling, data art, and data showcasing. Remember that, if you're designing for organizational decision-makers, you'll most likely use data story-telling to directly tell your audience what their data means with respect to their line of business. If you're designing for a social justice organization or a political campaign, data art can best make a dramatic and effective statement with your data. Lastly, if you're designing for analysts, engineers, scientists, or statisticians, stick with data showcasing so that these analytical types have plenty of room to figure things out on their own.

Back to Eve — because she's not extraordinarily analytical and because she's depending on you to help her make excellent data-driven decisions, you need to employ *data storytelling* techniques. Create either a static or interactive data visu-alization with some, but not too much, context. The visual elements of the design should tell a clear story about her business unit, such that Eve doesn't have to work through tons of complexity to get the point of what you're trying to tell her about her department.

Picking the Most Appropriate Design Style

If you're the analytical type, you might say that the only purpose of a data visualization is to convey numbers and facts via charts and graphs — no beauty or design is needed. But if you're a more artistic-minded person, you may insist that you have to *feel* something in order to truly understand it. Truth be told, a good data visualization is neither artless and dry nor completely abstract in its artistry. Rather, its beauty and design lie somewhere on the spectrum between these two extremes.

To choose the most appropriate design style, you must first consider your audi-ence (discussed earlier in this chapter) and then decide how you want them to respond to your visualization. If you're looking to entice the audience into taking a deeper, more analytical dive into the visualization, employ a design style that induces a calculating and exacting response in its viewers. But if you want your data visualization to fuel your audience's passion, use an emotionally compelling design style instead.

Inducing a calculating, exacting response

If you're designing a data visualization for corporate types, engineers, scientists, or organizational decision-makers, keep the design simple and sleek, using the data showcasing or data storytelling visualization. To induce a logical, calculat-ing feel in your audience, include a lot of bar charts, scatterplots, and line charts. Color choices here should be rather traditional and conservative. The look and feel should scream "corporate chic." (See Figure 5-1.) Visualizations of this style are meant to quickly and clearly communicate what's happening in the data — direct, concise, and to the point. The best data visualizations of this style convey an elegant look and feel.

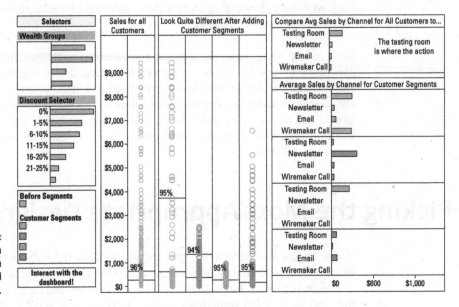

FIGURE 5-1:
This design
style conveys a
calculating and
exacting feel.

Eliciting a strong emotional response

If you're designing a data visualization to influence or persuade people, incorporate design artistry that invokes an emotional response in your target audience. These visualizations usually fall under the data art category, but an extremely creative data storytelling piece can also inspire this sort of strong emotional response. Emotionally provocative data visualizations often support the stance of one side of a social, political, or environmental issue. These data visualizations include fluid, artistic design elements that flow and meander, as shown in Figure 5-2. Additionally, rich, dramatic color choices can influence the emotions of the viewer. This style of data visualization leaves a lot of room for artistic creativity and experimentation.

TIP

Keep artistic elements relevant — and recognize when they're likely to detract from the impression you want to make, particularly when you're designing for analytical types.

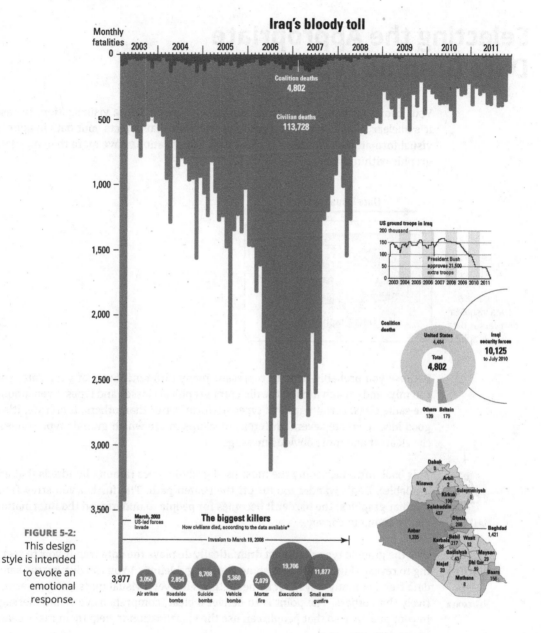

Iraq's bloody toll

Monthly fatalities

Coalition deaths
4,802

Civilian deaths
113,728

US ground troops in Iraq
200 thousand

President Bush approves 21,500 extra troops

2003 2004 2005 2006 2007 2008 2009 2010 2011

Coalition deaths

United States
4,484

Total
4,802

Iraqi security forces
10,125
to July 2010

Others
139

Britain
179

March, 2003
US-led forces invade

The biggest killers
How civilians died, according to the data available*

Invasion to March 19, 2008

3,977

| 3,050 | 2,854 | 8,708 | 5,360 | 2,079 | 19,706 | 11,877 |
| Air strikes | Roadside bombs | Suicide bombs | Vehicle bombs | Mortar fire | Executions | Small arms gunfire |

Dahuk 0
Ninawa 0
Arbil 2
Kirkuk 106
Sulaymaniyah
Salahuddin 437
Diyala 208
Anbar 1,335
Baghdad 1,421
Babil 38
Karbala 217
Wasit 52
Maysan 29
Qadisiyah 43
Najaf 33
Dhi Qar 99
Basra 156
Muthana 8

FIGURE 5-2: This design style is intended to evoke an emotional response.

Selecting the Appropriate
Data Graphic Type

Your choice of data graphic type can make or break a data visualization. In case it's unclear, a *data graphic* is a graphical element that depicts your data insight in visual format. (See Figure 5-3.) Most data visualizations have more than one data graphic within them.

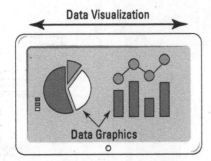

FIGURE 5-3:
Data visualiza-
tion versus data
graphics.

Because you probably need to represent many different facets of your data, you can mix-and-match among the different graphical classes and types. Even among the same class, certain graphic types perform better than others; therefore, it's a good idea to create several different mockups to see which graphic type conveys the clearest and most obvious message.

WARNING

This book introduces only the most used graphic types (among hundreds that are available). Don't wander too far off the beaten path. The further you stray from familiar graphics, the harder it becomes for people to understand the information you're trying to convey.

REMEMBER

Pick the graphic type that most dramatically displays the data trends you're seeking to reveal. (Figure 5-4 lists some general guidelines.) You can display the same data trend in many ways, but some methods deliver a visual message more effectively than others. The point is to deliver a clear, comprehensive visual message to your audience so that people can use the visualization to help them make sense of the data presented.

Among the most useful types of data graphics are standard chart graphics, comparative graphics, statistical plots, topology structures, and spatial plots and maps. The next few sections take a look at each type in turn.

Data Graphic Types	Visualization Element	Data Storytelling audience: less-technical business decision-makers	Data Showcasing audience: data implementers, analysts, engineers, scientists, or statisticians	Data Art audience: idealists, dreamers, and social change-makers
Standard Chart Graphics	Bar Chart	✓	✓	✓
	Line Chart	✓	✓	✓
	Pie Chart	✓	☐	✓
Comparative Graphics	Bubble Plots	✓	✓	✓
	Packed Circle Diagrams	☐	✓	☐
	Gantt Charts	✓	✓	☐
	Stacked Charts	☐	✓	☐
	Tree Maps	☐	✓	☐
	Word Clouds	✓	✓	✓
Statistical Plots	Histogram	☐	✓	☐
	Scatter Plot	☐	✓	☐
	Scatter Plot Matrix	☐	✓	☐
Topology Structures	Linear Topology Structures	✓	✓	✓
	Graph Models	☐	✓	✓
	Tree Network Topology	✓	✓	✓
Spatial Plots and Maps	Cloropleth	✓	✓	✓
	Point	✓	✓	✓
	Raser Surface	☐	✓	☐
Contextual Elements	Contextual Data Graphics	☐	✓	✓
	Annotations	✓	✓	☐
	Trend Lines	✓	✓	✓
	Single-Value Alerts	✓	✓	☐
	Target Trend Lines	✓	✓	☐
	Predictive Benchmarks	✓	✓	☐

FIGURE 5-4:
Types of data graphics, broken down by audience and data visualization type.

Standard chart graphics

When making data visualizations for an audience of non-analytical people, stick to standard chart graphics. The more complex your graphics, the harder it is for non-analytical people to understand them. And not all standard chart types are boring — you have quite a variety to choose from, as the following list makes clear:

>> **Area:** An area chart (shown in Figure 5-5) is a fun-yet-simple way to visually compare and contrast attribute values. You can use this type to effectively tell a visual story when you've chosen data storytelling and data showcasing. Not all area charts are 3-D like the one shown in Figure 5-5, but they all represent numerical values by the proportion of area those values consume visually on the chart.

>> **Bar:** Bar charts (see Figure 5-6) are a simple way to visually compare and contrast values of parameters in the same category. Bar charts are best for data storytelling and data showcasing.

>> **Line:** Line charts (see Figure 5-7) most commonly show changes in time-series data, but they can also plot relationships between two, or even three, parameters. Line charts are so versatile that you can use them in all data visualization design types.

>> **Pie:** Pie chart graphics (see Figure 5-8), which are among the most commonly used, provide a simple way to compare values of parameters in the same category. Their simplicity, however, can be a double-edged sword; deeply analytical people tend to scoff at them, precisely because they seem so simple, so you may want to consider omitting them from data-showcasing visualizations.

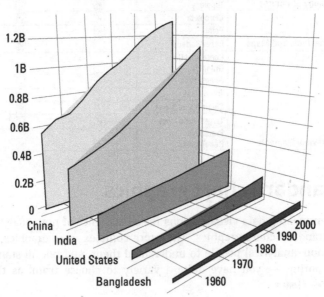

FIGURE 5-5:
An area chart in three dimensions.

Source: Adapted from Lynda.com, Python for DS

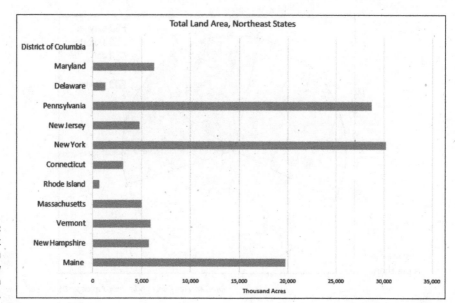

FIGURE 5-6:
A bar chart showing the area of US states by their acreage, in thousand acres.

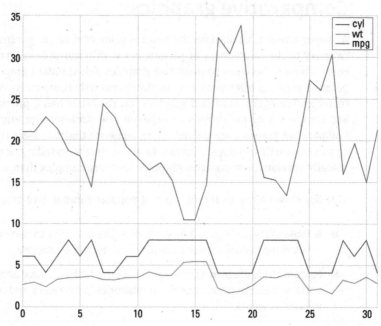

FIGURE 5-7:
A line chart.

Source: Adapted from Lynda . com, Python for DS

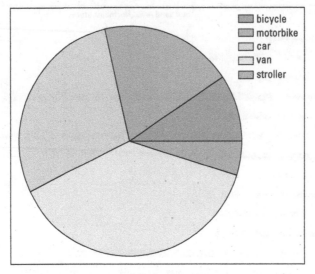

FIGURE 5-8:
A pie chart.

Source: Adapted from Lynda . com, Python for DS

Comparative graphics

A *comparative graphic* displays the relative value of multiple parameters in a shared category or the relatedness of parameters within multiple shared categories. The core difference between comparative graphics and standard graphics is that comparative graphics offer you a way to simultaneously compare more than one parameter and category. Standard graphics, on the other hand, provide a way to view and compare only the difference between one parameter of any single category. Comparative graphics are geared for an audience that's at least slightly analytical, so you can easily use these graphics in either data storytelling or data showcasing. Visually speaking, comparative graphics are more complex than standard graphics.

This list shows a few different types of popular comparative graphics:

>> **Bubble plots** (see Figure 5-9) use bubble size and color to demonstrate the relationship between three parameters of the same category.

>> **Packed circle diagrams** (see Figure 5-10) use both circle size and clustering to visualize the relationships between categories, parameters, and relative parameter values.

>> **Gantt charts** (see Figure 5-11) are bar charts that use horizontal bars to visualize scheduling requirements for project management purposes. This type of chart is useful when you're developing a plan for project delivery. It's also helpful in determining the sequence in which tasks must be completed in order to meet delivery timelines.

TIP

Choose Gantt charts for project management and scheduling.

>> **Stacked charts** (see Figure 5-12) are used to compare multiple attributes of parameters in the same category. To ensure that it doesn't become difficult to make a visual comparison, resist the urge to include too many parameters.

>> **Tree maps** aggregate parameters of like categories and then use area to show the relative size of each category compared to the whole, as shown in Figure 5-13.

>> **Word clouds** use size and color to show the relative difference in frequency of words used in a body of text, as shown in Figure 5-14. Colors are generally employed to indicate classifications of words by usage type.

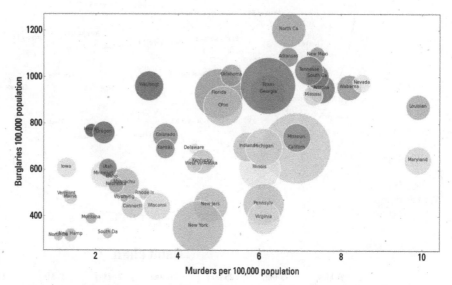

FIGURE 5-9:
A bubble chart.

Statistical plots

Statistical plots, which show the results of statistical analyses, are usually useful only to a deeply analytical audience (and aren't useful for making data art). Your statistical plot choices are described in this list:

>> **Histogram:** A diagram that plots a variable's frequency and distribution as rectangles on a chart, a histogram (see Figure 5-15) can help you quickly get a handle on the distribution and frequency of data in a dataset.

TIP

Get comfortable with histograms. You'll see a lot of them in the course of making statistical analyses.

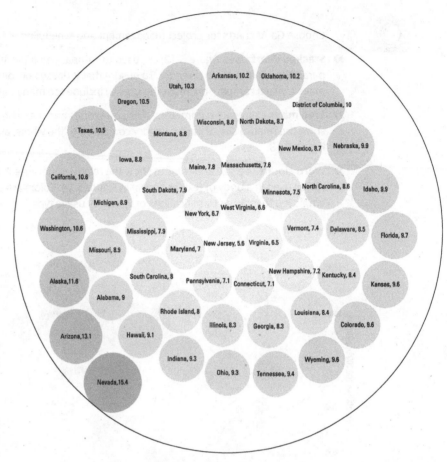

FIGURE 5-10:
A packed circle diagram.

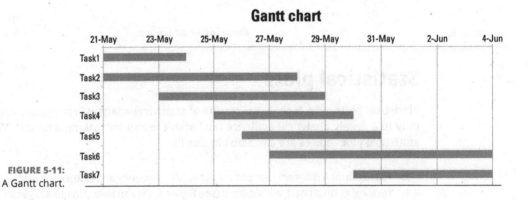

FIGURE 5-11:
A Gantt chart.

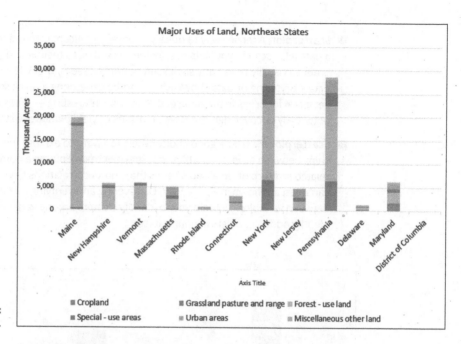

FIGURE 5-12:
A stacked chart.

FIGURE 5-13:
A tree map.

FIGURE 5-14:
A simple word
cloud.

» **Scatterplot:** A terrific way to quickly uncover significant trends and outliers in a dataset, a scatterplot plots data points according to their x- and y-values in order to visually reveal any significant patterns. (See Figure 5-16.) If you use data storytelling or data showcasing, start by generating a quick scatterplot to get a feel for areas in the dataset that may be interesting — areas that can potentially uncover significant relationships or yield persuasive stories.

» **Scatterplot matrix:** A good choice when you want to explore the relationships between several variables, a scatterplot matrix places a number of related scatterplots in a visual series that shows correlations between multiple variables, as shown in Figure 5-17. Discovering and verifying relationships between variables can help you to identify clusters among variables and identify oddball outliers in your dataset.

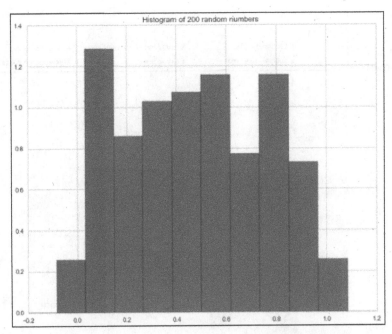

FIGURE 5-15: A histogram.

Source: Lynda.com, Python for DS

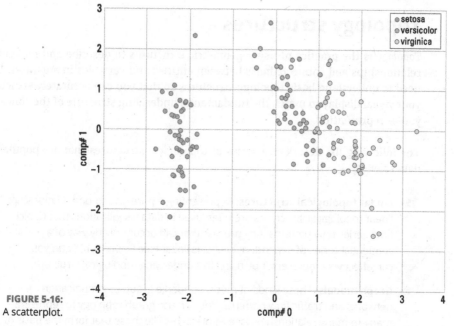

FIGURE 5-16:
A scatterplot.

Source: Adapted from Lynda.com, Python for DS

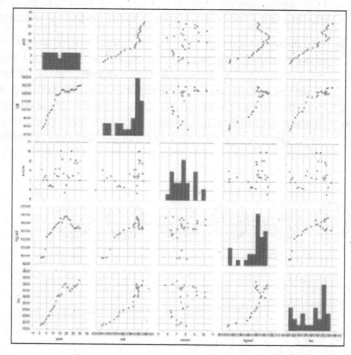

FIGURE 5-17:
A scatterplot
matrix.

Source: Adapted from Lynda.com, Python for DS

Topology structures

Topology is the practice of using geometric structures to describe and model the relationships and connectedness between entities and variables in a dataset. You need to understand basic topology structures so that you can accurately structure your visual display to match the fundamental underlying structure of the concepts you're representing.

The following list describes a series of topological structures that are popular in data science:

>> **Linear topological structures:** Representing a pure one-to-one relationship, linear topological structures are often used in data visualizations that depict time-series flow patterns. Any process that can occur only by way of a sequential series of dependent events is linear (see Figure 5-18), and you can effectively represent it by using this underlying topological structure.

>> **Graph models:** These kinds of models underlie group communication networks and traffic flow patterns. You can use graph topology to represent many-to-many relationships (see Figure 5-19), like those that form the basis of social media platforms.

In a *many-to-many* relationship structure, each variable or entity has more than one link to the other variables or entities in that same dataset.

REMEMBER

>> **Tree network topology:** This topology represents a *hierarchical* classification, where a network is distributed in top-down order — nodes act as receivers and distributors of connections, and lines represent the connections between nodes. End nodes act only as receivers and not as distributors. (See Figure 5-20.) Hierarchical classification underlies clustering and machine learning methodologies in data science. Tree network structures can represent one-to-many relationships, such as the ones that underlie a family tree or a taxonomy structure.

FIGURE 5-18:
A linear topology.

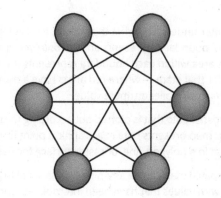

FIGURE 5-19:
A graph mesh
network
topology.

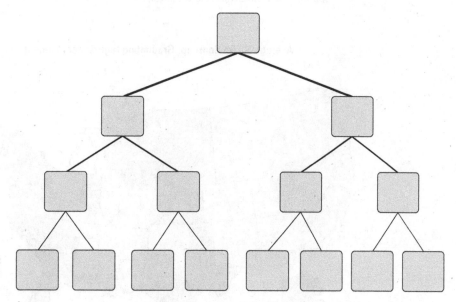

FIGURE 5-20:
A hierarchical
tree topology.

Spatial plots and maps

Spatial plots and maps are two different ways of visualizing spatial data. A *map* is just a plain figure that represents the location, shape, and size of features on the face of the earth. A *spatial plot*, which is visually more complex than a map, shows the values for — and location distribution of — a spatial feature's attributes.

The following list describes a few types of spatial plots and maps that are commonly used in data visualization:

» **Cloropleth:** Despite its fancy name, a Cloropleth map is just spatial data plotted out according to area boundary polygons rather than by point, line, or raster coverage. To better understand what this means, look at Figure 5-21. On this map, each state boundary represents an *area boundary* polygon. The color and shade of the area within each boundary represents the relative value of the attribute for that state — where red areas have a higher attribute value and blue areas have a smaller attribute value.

>> **Point:** Composed of spatial data that is plotted out according to specific point locations, a point map presents data in a graphical point format (see Figure 5-22) rather than in a polygon, line, or raster surface format.

>> **Raster surface:** This spatial map can be anything from a satellite image map to a surface coverage with values that have been interpolated from underlying spatial data points. (See Figure 5-23.)

Average SATm Score for Graduating High School Student

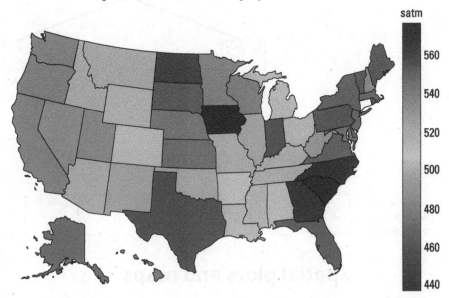

FIGURE 5-21:
A Cloropleth map.

REMEMBER

Whether you're a data visualization designer or a consumer, be aware of some common pitfalls in data visualization. Simply put, a data visualization can be misleading if it isn't constructed correctly. Common problems include pie charts that don't add up to 100 percent, bar charts with a scale that starts in a strange place, and multicolumn bar charts with vertical axes that don't match.

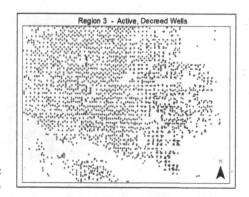

FIGURE 5-22:
A point map.

Source: Adapted from Lynda.com, Python for DS

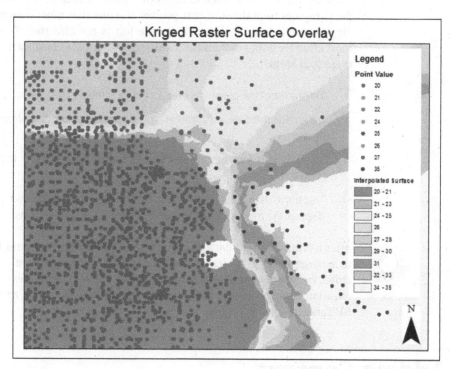

FIGURE 5-23:
A raster
surface map.

Source: Adapted from Lynda.com, Python for DS

Testing Data Graphics

Your data visualizations must convey clear and powerful visual messages. To make that happen, you have to test various data graphics and select only the most effective ones to include in the final data visualization. For example, the two data graphics shown in Figure 5-24 represent exactly the same statistic.

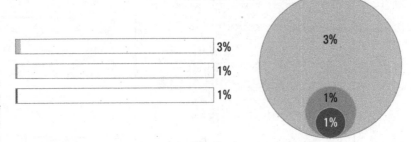

Notice how the data graphic on the right does a much better job of visually emphasizing the difference in numeric values? You should always test different data graphics to make sure that you use the one that most clearly and effectively displays your data. The graphic on the left is *not* effective. To choose only the most effective data graphics for inclusion in your data visualization, simply follow these four steps:

1. Make a list of the questions that your data is meant to answer.

2. Determine the data visualization type: data storytelling, data showcasing, or data art.

3. Select options from among appropriate data graphic types for that type of data visualization.

4. Test those data graphics with your data — see for yourself which graphic type displays the most clear and obvious answers to your questions.

TIP

After testing different data graphics and deciding what you want to use, you need to arrange those graphics within your data visualization. You can do that using either Python or R or a spreadsheet. Alternatively, you can create your data visualization using an online data visualization design tool, such as Microsoft Power BI, Tableau, or IBM Cognos.

Adding Context

Once you know exactly which data graphics you'll use, you need to decide whether and how you'll create the necessary context to add more meaning to the data visualization. Adding context helps people understand the value and relative significance of the information your data visualization conveys. Adding context to calculating, exacting data visualization styles helps to create a sense of relative perspective, but in pure data art you may consider omitting additional context. That's because, with data art, you're only trying to make a single point, and you don't want to add information that would distract from that point.

Creating context with data

In data showcasing, you should include relevant contextual data for the key metrics shown in your data visualization — in a situation where you're creating a data visualization that describes conversion rates for e-commerce sales, for example. The key metric would be represented by the percentage of users who convert to customers by making a purchase. Contextual data relevant to this metric might include shopping cart abandonment rates, the average number of sessions before a user makes a purchase, the average number of pages visited before making a purchase, or specific pages that are visited before a customer decides to convert. This sort of contextual information helps viewers understand the "why and how" behind sales conversions.

REMEMBER

Adding contextual data tends to decentralize the focus of data visualization, so add this data only in visualizations that are intended for an analytical audience. These folks are in a better position to assimilate the extra information and use it to draw their own conclusions; with other types of audiences, context is only a distraction.

Creating context with annotations

Sometimes, you can more appropriately create context by including annotations that provide a header and a small description of the context of the data shown. (See Figure 5-25.) This method of creating context is most appropriate for data storytelling or data showcasing. Good annotation is helpful to both analytical and non-analytical audiences alike.

Creating context with graphical elements

Another effective way to create context in a data visualization is to include graphical elements that convey the relative significance of the data. Such graphical elements include moving average trend lines, single-value alerts, target trend lines (as shown in Figure 5-26), and predictive benchmarks.

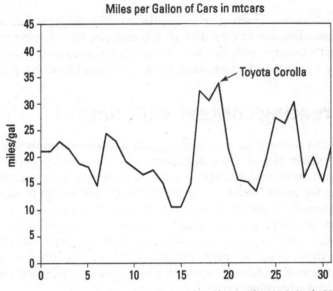

FIGURE 5-25:
Using annotation
to create context.

Source: Adapted from Lynda . com, Python for DS

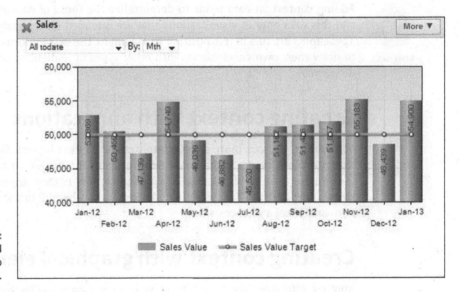

FIGURE 5-26:
Using graphical
elements to
create context.

2

Using Power BI for Data Analytics & Visualization

Contents at a Glance

IN THIS CHAPTER

» Understanding your options for
business intelligence tooling

» Familiarizing yourself with Power BI
terminology

» Understanding the licensing options
available from Microsoft

Chapter 1

Power BI Foundations

Picking out the correct version of Power BI might be like visiting the world's biggest candy store: You can choose from many alternatives with subtle nuances. The choice boils down to wants, needs, scale, and, of course, money. Some versions are free (well, sort of), and other versions can be expensive. And, of course, the most obvious difference is that some versions are desktop- or server-based, whereas others offer online-only capabilities.

If you visit the Microsoft website on any given day and search for products, you notice quite a few versions of Power BI exist. However, the Pricing page and the Products page don't necessarily match. (Thanks for the help, Microsoft!) It isn't clear whether "Free is free" or whether products are inclusive within specific Power BI versions. This chapter clears up any confusion you may have so that, moving forward, you know which product you should use.

Before moving forward with purchasing and licensing information, this chapter explores the basic capabilities of Power BI and reviews some terminology.

Looking Under the Power BI Hood

Power BI is a product that brings together many smaller, cloud-based apps and services with a specific objective: to organize, collect, manage, and analyze big datasets. Big data is a concept, where the business and data analyst will evaluate extremely large datasets, which may reveal patterns and trends relating to human behaviors and interactions not easily identifiable without the use of specific tools. A typical big data collection is often expressed in millions of records. Unlike a tool such as Microsoft Excel, Power BI can simultaneously evaluate many data sources and millions of records. The sources don't need to be structured using a spreadsheet, either. They can include unstructured and semi-structured data.

After pulling these many data sources together and processing them, Power BI can help you come up with visually compelling outputs in the form of charts, graphics, reports, dashboards, and KPIs.

As you've already read, Power BI isn't just a single source application. It has desktop, online, and mobile components.

REMEMBER

Across the Power BI platforms, you are certain at some point to encounter one (or more) of the following products:

>> **Power Query:** A data connection tool you can use to transform, combine, and enhance data across several data sources

>> **Power Pivot:** A data modeling tool

>> **Power View:** A data visualization tool you can use to generate interactive charts, graphs, maps, and visuals

>> **Power Map:** A visualization tool for creating 3D map renderings

>> **Power Q&A:** An artificial intelligence engine that allows you to ask questions and receive responses using plain language

>> **Power BI Desktop:** A free, all-in-one solution that brings together all the apps described in this list into a single graphical user interface

>> **Power BI Services:** A cloud-based user experience to collaborate and distribute products such as reports with others

The following sections explore each product's core functionality.

Posing questions with Power Query

Before Power BI became its own product line, it was originally an advanced query and data manipulation add-in for Excel circa 2010. It wasn't until around 2013 that Microsoft began to test Power BI as its own product line, with the formal launch of Power BI Desktop and Services in July 2015. One of the justifications for the switch to a dedicated product was the need for a more robust query editor. With the Excel editor, it was a single data source, whereas with Power BI's

Power Query you can extract data from numerous data sources as well as read data from relational sources, such as SQL Server Enterprise, Azure SQL Server, Oracle, MySQL, DB2, and a host of other platforms. If you're looking to extract data from unstructured, semi-structured, or application sources — such as CSV files, text files, Excel files, Word documents, SharePoint document libraries, Microsoft Exchange Server, Dynamics 365, or Outlook — Power Query makes that possible as well. And, if you have access to API services that map to specific data fields on platforms such as LinkedIn, Facebook, or Twitter, you can use Power Query to mine those platforms as well.

Whatever you have Power Query do, the procedure is always pretty much the same: It transforms the data you specify (using a graphical user interface as needed) by adding columns, rows, data types, date and time, text fields, and appropriate operators. Power Query manages this transformation by taking an extensive dataset, which is nothing more than a bunch of raw data (often disorganized and confusing to you, of course) and then creates some business sense by organizing it into tables, columns, and rows for consumption. The product produced by the Power Query output in the Editor can then be transferred to either a portable file such as Excel or something more robust, such as a Power Pivot model.

Modeling with Power Pivot

Power BI's data modeling tool is called Power Pivot. With it, you can create models, such as star schemas, calculated measures, and columns, and build complex diagrams. Power Pivot leverages another programming language called the Data Analysis eXpression Language — or DAX, for short. DAX is a formula-based language used for data analysis purposes. You soon discover that, as a language, it's chock-full of useful functions, so stay tuned.

Visualizing with Power View

The visualization engine of Power BI is Power View. The idea here is to connect to data sources, fetch and transform that data for analysis, and then have Power View present the output using one of its many visualization options. Power View gives users the ability to filter data for individual variables or an entire report. Users can slice data at the variable level or even break out elements in Power View to focus like a laser on data that may be considered anomalous.

Mapping data with Power Map

Sometimes, visualizing data requires a bit more than a Bar chart or a table. Perhaps you need a map that integrates geospatial coordinates with 3D requirements.

Suppose that you're looking to add dimensionality to your data — perhaps with the help of heat maps, by gauging the height and width of a column or basing the color used on a statistical reference. In that case, you want to consider Power BI's Power Map feature set. Another feature built into Power Map is the use of geospatial capabilities using Microsoft Bing, Microsoft's external search engine technology that includes capabilities for mapping locations. A user can highlight data using geocoordinate latitude and longitudinal data as granular as an address or as global as a country.

Interpreting data with Power Q&A

One of the biggest challenges for many users is data interpretation. Say, for example, that you've built this incredible data model using Power Pivot. Now what? Your data sample is often pretty significant in terms of size, which means that you need some way to make sense of all the data you've deployed in the model. That's why Microsoft created a natural language engine, a way to interpret text, numbers, and even speech so that users can query the data model directly.

REMEMBER

Power Q&A works directly in conjunction with Power View.

A classic example where Power Q&A can be enormously helpful would involve determining how many users have purchased a specific item at a given store location. If you want to drill down further, you could analyze a whole set of metrics — asking whether the item comes in several colors or sizes, for example, or specifying which day of the week saw the most items sold. The possibilities are endless as long as you've built your data model to accommodate the questions.

Power BI Desktop

All these Power BI platforms are great ideas, but the truly stupendous idea was bundling together Power Query, Power Pivot, Power View, and Power Q&A to form Power BI Desktop. Using Power BI Desktop, you can complete all your business intelligence activities under a single umbrella. You can also develop BI and data analysis activities far more easily. Finally, Microsoft updates Power BI Desktop features monthly, so you can always be on the BI cutting edge.

Power BI Services

Over time, the product name for Power BI Services has evolved. When the product was in beta, it was called Power BI Website. Nowadays, you often hear the product referred to as Power BI Online or Power BI Services. Whatever you call it, it functions as the Software as a Service companion to Power BI. Accessible at `https://app.powerbi.com`, Power BI Services allows users to collaborate and share their dashboards, reports, and datasets with other users from a single location.

REMEMBER

The version of Power BI you have licensed dictates your ability to share and ingest data.

Knowing Your Power BI Terminology

Whether Microsoft or another vendor creates it, every product you come across has its own terminology. It may seem like a foreign language, but if you visit a vendor's website and do a simple search, you're sure to find a glossary that spells out what all these mysterious terms mean.

Microsoft, unsurprisingly, has its own glossary for Power BI as well. (Those folks refer to terminology as *concepts*, for reasons clear only to them.). Before you proceed any further on your Power BI journey, let's establish the lay of the land. In Microsoft Power BI-speak, some concepts resonate across vendors no matter who you are. For example, all vendors have reports and dashboards as critical concepts. Now, do all other vendors adopt Microsoft's practice and call dataflows a type of workflow? Not quite. They all have their names for these specific features, although all such features generally work the same way.

TIP

Microsoft has done a pretty good job of trying to stick with mainstream names for critical concepts. Nevertheless, some of the more advanced product features specific to AI/machine learning and security adopt the rarefied lingo of Microsoft products such as Azure Active Directory or Azure Machine Learning.

Capacities

What's the first thing you think about when it comes to data? Is it the type, or is it the quantity? Or do you consider both? With Power BI, the first concept you must be familiar with is *capacities*, which are central to Power BI. Why, you ask? Capacities are the sum total of resources needed in order for you to complete any project you may create in Power BI. Resources include the storage, processor, and memory required to host and deliver the Power BI projects.

There are two types of capacity: shared and dedicated. A *shared* capacity allows you to share resources with other Microsoft end users. *Dedicated* capacities fully commit resources to you alone. Whereas shared capacity is available for both free and paying Power BI users, dedicated capacity requires a Power BI premium subscription.

Workspaces

Workspaces are a means of collaborating and sharing content with colleagues. Whether it's personal or intended for collaboration, any workspace you create is created on capacities. Think of a workspace as a container that allows you to manage the entire lifecycle of dashboards, reports, workbooks, datasets, and dataflows in the Power BI Services environment. (Figure 1-1 shows a My Workspace, a particular example of a Power BI workspace.)

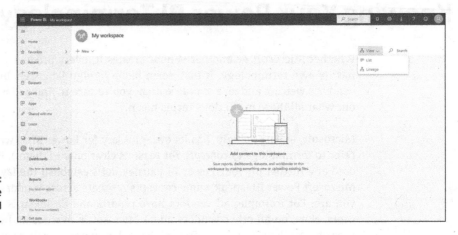

FIGURE 1-1:
My Workspace
in Power BI
Services.

REMEMBER

The My Workspace isn't the only type of workspace available. You also have the option to collaborate. If you want to collaborate, you have no choice but to upgrade to a Power BI Pro or Premium plan. Features that come with collaboration include the ability to create and publish Power BI-based dashboards, reports, workbooks, datasets, and apps with a team.

REMEMBER

Looking to upload the work you've created using Power BI Desktop? Or perhaps you need to manipulate the work online without collaborating with anyone? If the answer to either question is yes, My Workspace is all that is necessary. You only *require* the use of the Power BI Online Free License. As soon as you want to collaborate with others, you need to upgrade to a paid Pro or Premium subscription.

So now you know that your work is stored in a workspace. Next question: What happens with the data in that workspace? The answer is twofold: There is what you see as the user, and then there's what goes on behind the scenes as part of the data transformation process. Let's start with the behind-the-scenes activities.

A *dataflow* is a collection of tables that collects the datasets imported into Power BI. After the tables are created and managed in your workspace as part of Power BI Services, you can add, edit, and delete data within a dataflow. The data refresh can occur using a predefined schedule as well. Keep in mind that Power BI uses an Azure data lake, a way to store the extremely large volumes of data necessary for

Power BI to evaluate, process, and analyze data rapidly. The Azure Data Lake also helps with cleaning and transforming data quickly when the datasets are voluminous in size.

Unlike a dataflow (which, you may remember, is a collection of tables), a dataset should be treated as a single asset in your collection of data sources. Think of a dataset as a subset of data. When used with dataflows, the dataset is mapped to a managed Azure data lake. It likely includes some or all the data in the data lake. The granularity of the data varies greatly, depending on the speed and scale of the dataset available.

The analyst or developer can extract the data when building their desired output, such as a report. Sometimes, there may be a desire for multiple datasets, in which case dataflow transformation might be necessary. On the other hand, sometimes multiple datasets can leverage the same dataset housed in the Azure data lake. In this instance, little transformation is necessary.

REMEMBER

After you've manipulated the data on your own, you have to publish the data you've created in Power BI. Microsoft assumes that you intend to share the data among users. If the intent is to share a dataset, assume that a Pro or Premium license is required.

Reports

Data can be stored in a system indefinitely and remain idle. But what good is it if the data in the system isn't queried from time to time so that users like you and me can understand what the data means, right? Suppose you worked for a hospital. You needed to query the employee database to find out how many employees worked within five miles of the facility in case of an emergency. That's when, quickly (not warp speed, though), you can create a summary of your dataset, using a Power BI report. Sure, there could be a couple of hundred records or tens of thousands of records, all unique, of course, but the records are all brought together to help the hospital home in just who can be all hands on deck in case of an emergency whether it is just down the block, five miles away, or fifty miles away.

Power BI Reports translates that data into one or more pages of visualizations — Line charts, Bar charts, donuts, treemaps — you name it. You can either evaluate your data at a high level or focus on a particular data subset (if you've managed to query the dataset beforehand). You can tackle creating a report in a number of ways, from taking a dataset using a single source and creating an output from scratch to importing data from many sources. One example here would be connecting to an Excel workbook or Google Sheets document using Power View sheets. From there, Power BI takes the data from across the source and makes sense of it. The result is a report (see Figure 1-2) based on the imported data using predefined configurations established by the report author.

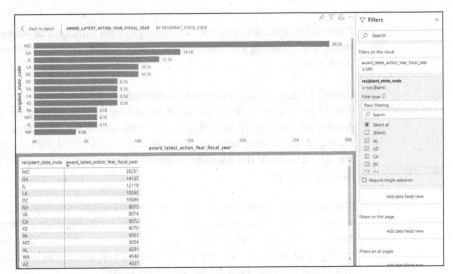

FIGURE 1-2:
A sample Power
BI report.

TIP

Power BI offers two Report view modes: Reading view and Editing view. When you open a report, it opens in Reading view. If granted Edit permissions, you can edit a report. When a report is in a workspace, any user with administrative, member, or contributor rights can edit a report.

**TECHNICAL
STUFF**

Administrative, member, or contributor access grants you access to exploring, designing, building, and sharing capabilities within Edit view. Users who access the reports created by these privileged users can interact with reports in Read-Only mode. That means they can't edit it — they can only view the output. Reports created by privileged users are accessible under a workspace's Reports tab, as shown in Figure 1-3. Each report represents a single-page visualization, which means it's based on only one dataset.

FIGURE 1-3:
The Reports
tab in Power BI
Desktop.

Dashboards

If you've had any experience with Power BI whatsoever, you already know that it's a highly visual tool. In line with its visual nature, the Power BI dashboard, also known as Canvas, brings your data story to life. If you're looking to take all the pieces of your data puzzle and capture a moment in time, you use the dashboard. Think of it as a blank canvas. As you build your reports, widgets, tiles, and key performance indicators (KPIs) over time, you pin the ones you like to the dashboard to create a single visualization. The dashboard represents the large dataset that you feel covers your topic at a glance. As such, it can help you make decisions, support you in monitoring data, or make it possible for you to drill down in your dataset by applying different visualization options.

To access a particular dashboard, you must first open a workspace. All you need to do then is click the Dashboards tab for whichever app you're working with. Keep in mind that every dashboard represents a customized view of an underlying dataset. To locate your personal dashboards, go to your My Workspaces tab (see Figure 1-4) and then choose Dashboards to see what's available.

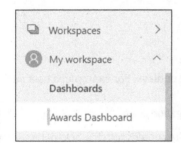

FIGURE 1-4:
Locating your
dashboards.

REMEMBER

If you own a dashboard, you have permission to edit it. Otherwise, you have only read-only access. You can share a dashboard with others, but they may not be able to save any changes. Keep in mind, however, that if you want to share a dashboard with a colleague, you need, at minimum, a Power BI Pro license. (For more on the ins and outs of licensing, see "Introducing the Power BI license options," later in this chapter.)

Navigation pane

This chapter covers a lot of the must-know concepts in Power BI, but it saves the best — the Navigation pane — for last. Why is the Navigation pane the best? Simple. All the capabilities discussed to this point in the chapter are labels found in the Navigation pane. (See Figure 1-5.) You would, for example, use the Navigation pane to complete actions to locate and move between a workspace and the various Power BI capabilities you want to use — dashboards, reports, workbooks, datasets — whatever.

FIGURE 1-5:
The Navigation pane.

Your Navigation pane options are endless. For example, a user such as yourself can

» Expand and collapse the Navigation pane.

» Open and manage your favorite content with the help of the Favorites option.

» View and open the most recently visited section of content.

Power BI Products in a Nutshell

Microsoft confuses customers by using the words *version* and *license* interchangeably. The following sections help clear up these terms before you read any further.

REMEMBER

Licensing refers to the products a customer is procuring, whereas *version* deals with where Power BI runs: on a desktop, from a server, or in the cloud. One or more Power BI products may be required to fully support deployments of Power BI. In some cases, you may require a hybrid solution of desktop *and* online versions of the product.

Introducing the Power BI license options

You can choose from four product license options: Power BI Desktop, Power BI Free, Power BI Pro, or Power BI Premium. You might be scratching your head because Microsoft also shows a few other Power BI products, including two versions of Power BI Premium as well as Power BI Mobile, Power BI Embedded, and Power BI Report Server on the Microsoft website. If you're confused, you're not alone. The good news is that some of these products are included with all three product licensing options, whereas others are specific to either the Pro or Premium version. Let's review each product license:

>> **Power BI Desktop:** The free desktop version of Power BI allows a user to author reports and data analytics inputs without publishing them to the Internet. If you want to collaborate and share your desktop output, however, you have to switch to either the Pro or Premium version.

>> **Power BI Free:** Considered the entry-level free cloud version, this version lets you author and store reports online versus the desktop. The only drawback is storage capacity, limited to 1GB, and no collaboration.

>> **Power BI Pro:** The entry-level paid version of Power BI gets you a larger storage allocation, limited to 100GB, as well as the ability to collaborate with Pro licensed users.

>> **Power BI Premium:** The enterprise paid version comes in two editions: per user and capacity. Per-user licensing is intended for those with big data aspirations who also need massive storage scale but have no global distribution requirements. Capacity is useful for an enterprise that intends to have many users. Keep in mind one catch with capacity licensing: You also need to procure Pro licenses because what you're paying for is the storage and security — Pro's killer feature.

>> **Power BI Mobile:** Intended to be a complementary product to manage reports, dashboards, and KPIs on the go, Power BI Mobile has limited, if any, authoring capabilities. Your ability to collaborate on Mobile varies depending on your license authorization.

>> **Power BI Embedded:** This version offers a way to integrate real-time reports on public- or private-facing products using the Power BI API service in Microsoft Azure,

>> **Power BI Report Server:** A server-based Power BI product intended to produce reporting output offline, its users store their reports on a server, not online. Note that you must still procure some form of Premium license, either stand-alone or using a Software Assurance subscription (an enterprise-based software plan).

Looking at Desktop versus Services options

The beauty of Software as a Service (SaaS) is that anytime a vendor such as Microsoft wants to add a new feature to a product, it can do so with little effort — a user will see the magic of the new feature instantly and will start using it. That isn't the case with downloadable software. Once an application is configured for the desktop, it's up to the end user to keep track of the updates. Vendors also update downloadable software less often. Whereas cloud-based solutions may be updated daily, a software release for a significant product happens monthly with Power BI.

Power BI Desktop is a complete authoring tool for analytics and business intelligence designers. You can download Power BI Desktop for free and install it on your local computer. The desktop version allows a user to connect to more than 70 data source types and then transform those sources into data models. You can take the reports you've created and add visuals based on the data models using Desktop. Because Power BI Desktop exists as an application, it's updated each month cumulatively with all the features and functionality made available for consumption on the Services platform.

TIP

To download a copy of the Power BI Desktop application, go to https://powerbi.microsoft.com/en-us/desktop.

Except for the Power BI Desktop and Power BI Report Server, all other versions of Power BI fall into the cloud delivery model commonly referred to as Services. Why, you ask? Because each version is delivered as Software as a Service. SaaS cloud delivery allows Microsoft to auto-update features regularly and deliver the product over the Internet using a web browser, such as Microsoft Edge, Google Chrome, or Apple Safari. In case of a technical issue, Microsoft doesn't have to wait for the end-of-the-month software release to update the code — it does so immediately. In terms of features, end users and designers can view, manipulate, and interact with reports online rather than have to rely on their desktop. Most designers who use Power BI Desktop publish their reports to the Power BI Service at some point. Suppose that you gain access to the service. In that case, you can edit reports, create visual outputs based on existing data models and datasets, and collaborate with other users requiring access to those reports, dashboards, and KPIs you've made.

Though a small number of features overlap between the Desktop and Services offerings, most users initially start with Power BI Desktop to create their reports. In Table 1-1, notice the commonalities among the Power BI features and the obvious differences. Once users finish building the reports, the Power BI Service is used to distribute the reports to others. A limited Power BI Service is offered for free; true collaboration and expanded storage require a minimum of either the Pro or Premium edition.

TABLE 1-1   **Power BI Desktop, Common, Service Features**

Power BI Desktop	Common	Power BI Services
More than 90 data sources	Reports	Limited data sources
Data transformation	Visualizations	Dashboarding
Data shaping	Security	KPI management
Data modeling	Filters	Workspaces
Measures	R visuals (big data outputs)	Sharing and collaboration
Calculated columns	Bookmarks	Hosting and storage
DAX	Q&A	Workflow/data flow
Python		Paginated reporting
Themes		Gateway management
Row Level Security creation		Row Level Security (RLS) management

Chapter **2**

The Quick Tour of Power BI

L ike a state fair judge evaluating a prize cake layered with many ingredients, Power BI requires that its users familiarize themselves with the features baked into the business intelligence (BI) solution. Virtually all users who interact with Power BI start with the Desktop version. Users can mold the data the way they want by following the old saying "Practice makes perfect" by way of ingestion and modeling. Whether you're manipulating the data to make the model just right, tackling data transformation via wrangling, or trying to create beautiful visualizations, the heavy lift is desktop-based. Seldom does the Power BI participant start using online services unless the dataset was previously created for sharing and collaboration. In this chapter, you learn the key features of Power BI Desktop and Services to know precisely when and why you need to use a specific product version.

Power BI Desktop: A Top-Down View

Power BI Desktop is the hub of all self-directed end user activities. The user installs the application on a Windows based desktop to connect to, transform, and visualize data. The data sources users can connect to aren't limited to local repositories — users can aggregate sources locally with third-party data that is structured or unstructured to create data models. The data model lets the user build a visual representation of the stored datasets. When you have many visuals, the user can derive reports or dashboards for analysis. A typical usage of Power BI Desktop is to

>> Ingest data across one or more data sources.

>> Model data to create reports and dashboards.

>> Refine, cleanse, and visualize the data by way of analysis.

>> Create reports for individual consumption.

REMEMBER

Though you can complete these activities online, the Desktop platform is purpose-built for individual user consumption or development work — it isn't intended for groups. Not until the user is ready to share the products created using Desktop do you need to expose anything to Power BI Services.

The end user gains access to three distinct views in Power BI Desktop: Report, Data, and Model. Figure 2-1 shows you the left-side navigation to find these views in Power BI Desktop. Though these features are also available in Services, feature richness for personal analysis is significantly greater in Power BI Desktop.

Each Power BI Desktop view carries out specific tasks:

>> **Report:** You can create reports and visualizations after you've ingested and modeled the data. Users spend most of their time here post-data ingestion, transformation, and modeling.

>> **Data:** You can find all data ingested, or migrated, from tables, measures, and data sources associated with reports and visualizations created here. Sources can be local to the desktop or from a third-party data source accessible over the web.

>> **Model:** Like creating a relational data model in Microsoft SQL Server, Azure SQL Server, or even Microsoft Access, you can fully manage the relationships among the structured tables you've created after you've ingested the necessary data using Power BI.

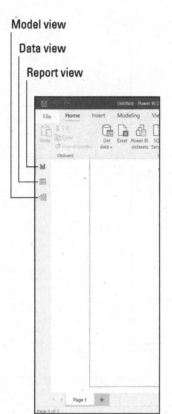

Model view

Data view

Report view

FIGURE 2-1:
Power BI Desktop
navigation.

Ingesting Data

Without data, you can't do all that much with Power BI — data truly is the main ingredient of your end-state recipe. Whether you're trying to create a chart or a dashboard or you're posing questions with Questions and Answers (Q&A), you must have data that comes from an underlying dataset. Each dataset comes from a particular data source, either found on your local desktop (if you're using Power BI Desktop) or acquired from other online data sources. These sources may be Microsoft-based applications, a third-party database, or even other application data feeds. In Power BI Desktop, you either use the Power BI Ribbon (shown in Figure 2-2) or click the Power BI Data Navigation icon (shown in Figure 2-3) to access a data source.

FIGURE 2-2:
Getting data
from the Power
BI Ribbon.

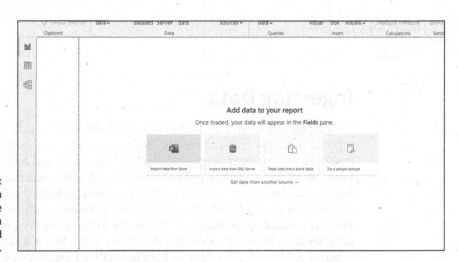

FIGURE 2-3:
Accessing a data
source using the
Data Navigation
icon and
landing page.

Files or databases?

In Power BI, you can create or import content yourself. When it comes to the type of content users can create or import, it boils down to either files or data stored in a database. A word to the wise: Files can be a bit more complicated than databases. You need to get the data, transform the data, and then import the data into a readable form. Suppose that you want to import an Excel or .cvs file that includes many data types. First, you load the data into Power BI. Then you format the data into a Power BI-ready format in conjunction with dataflows, which transforms the data to support a data model. Finally, you query the data using the Get and Transform feature in Power Query.

Now, what if the data you're trying to import isn't structured or perhaps you don't want it housed in Power BI Desktop? Your best choice is to use native Microsoft options such as OneDrive for Business. Such a choice offers the most flexibility in mapping data through application interoperability and application integration. If you prefer keeping your data on a local drive, you can do that as well.

REMEMBER

Where you store your data makes a difference when dealing with data refresh. Consider the frequency of data updates when selecting the data storage location. When the data is on your local desktop, you'll generally find better performance, even with large datasets. With shared data accessible over the Internet, you are reliant on network connectivity and other users accessing the data source. Data stored on the desktop is managed by one person — you.

TIP

You don't always have to store the data directly in Power BI Desktop. You can always use Desktop to query and load data from external sources. If you prefer to extend your data model with calculated measures or a specific relationship, consider importing the Power BI Desktop file into a Power BI Online site for easier manipulation.

Databases are a bit different from files because you connect to a live data source — sources requiring an Internet connection that are made available to either a small subset of users or to many users for consumption. This is especially true when the database is available "as a service," such as Azure SQL Database, Azure Cosmos DB, Azure Synapse Analytics, or Azure HDInsight. Because the data is live, all that a data professional must do is appropriately model the data first. Once satisfied with the intended model, the user can explore the data, manipulate the data, and create data visualizations.

TIP

If you want to explore a plethora of data sources beyond those offered by Microsoft, including open-source and third-party options, you need to utilize Power BI Desktop. Online Services offers a narrow range of options, whereas Desktop offers over 100 options for you to choose from.

WARNING

The term *data* gets thrown around a lot — you're probably already confused about data, datasets, dataflows, and even databases. When it comes to data ingestion, "dataset" and "data source" are treated the same, even though they're actually just distant relatives that support the same mission.

You create a dataset in Power BI whenever you use the Get Data feature. It's what allows you to connect and import data, including from live data sources. A dataset stores all the details about the data source and its security credentials. A data source is where all the data stored in the dataset is derived, which can be a proprietary application data source, a relational database, or a stand-alone file storage alternative such as a hard drive or file share.

Building data models

Some BI tools aren't data-model-dependent; Power BI isn't in that camp. Power BI is a data-model-based reporting tool. First, you need to understand what makes a data model unique.

These are the key characteristics of data models:

>> Tables hold meaningful data.

>> Relationships exist between the loaded tables with data.

>> Formulas, also known as *measures,* apply business rules to the raw data to extract, transform, and load data to create meaningful business insights.

You might wonder why you even need a data model. Going back to my analogy of the cake recipe from the beginning of this chapter, if you follow the recipe, it's easy to make the same cake time and time again. When the cake ingredients vary, though, inconsistency leads to data irregularity and continual rebuild efforts. And, like the cake's failure to win any culinary awards, the data needs handling and refinement. With BI solutions such as Power BI, users can streamline business issues with a data model.

To summarize, models are useful for these reasons:

>> **Reusability:** Users can solve a reporting requirement or business challenge using a formulaic approach without having to reinvent queries or rebuild datasets.

>> **Management:** Business users are in a position to manage the data on their own after models are built. Seldom is a database expert or technical professional needed to handle infrastructure requirements.

>> **Adaptive models:** You can build a logical model with minimum code. Changes are accommodative to technical and business requirements, including the use of measures (formulas) and rule sets.

Though you can find many tools on the market, including Microsoft Excel and BI-based reporting tools, not all tools offer to build data models. A BI tool not incorporating data models requires the analyst or data engineer to generate a query to fetch the data. Though many of these tools have graphical user interfaces to support query generation, you need to reinvent the process each time you use it, with little extensibility available. In Power BI, the relationships you need to keep track of are mapped out in the Model Viewer with the help of a data model. (See Figure 2-4, which models a single table named Awards.)

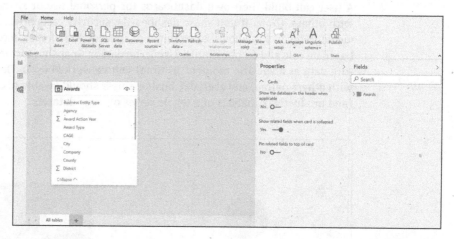

FIGURE 2-4:
Example of a data Model Viewer.

REMEMBER

You know the old saying "Reuse, reduce, recycle"? It's synonymous with the data model. A *data model* is a reusable asset that, when tweaked a little depending on the business need, can dramatically reduce development efforts and cut costs. Sometimes, you get lucky and can build new assets on top of the existing solution. At other times, recycling the asset with a few enhancements can score you the desired results.

Analyzing data

Before sharing any data with a team, you first have to carry out your own, personal data analysis using Power BI Desktop. You can conduct several forms of analysis. At the most basic level, when the data enters the system, you must review it to make sure it looks right and appears as it should. If it doesn't, you manipulate the data by cleansing it — a task often carried out by an analyst or engineer. The process often takes a while because it's quite laborious — kind of like preparing a big holiday dinner. Yet when the results are available, they're easy to read in a matter of seconds. As much as this strategy sounds like a hassle, the results are what you want to aim for in business intelligence.

Once the data source has been cleaned up and you've mapped the data into refined datasets, it's time to create the necessary visualizations. *Visualizations* are pictures that can serve as examples of your data sources — charts, maps, indicators, and gauges. You'll find these visuals in deliverables such as reports and dashboards. Even the Q&A feature in Power BI produces visuals after you ask focused questions.

You eventually want to get to a point in your use of Power BI where you can rapidly generate reports and access data using dashboards. A Power BI designer builds out dashboard visualizations, referred to as *tiles*, using data in reports and datasets. A user can build their own dashboards for personal use or share the dashboard with others. (*Note:* If you share dashboards, security credentials are tied to each visual.) Figure 2-5 shows an example of a collection of tiles across a dashboard based on role and responsibility. Using the data in Snapshot format (a way to capture data at a specific moment in time) you've worked up in Desktop or shared with others online, any everyday business user should be able to carry out a quick (and productive) analysis of a whole series of large datasets.

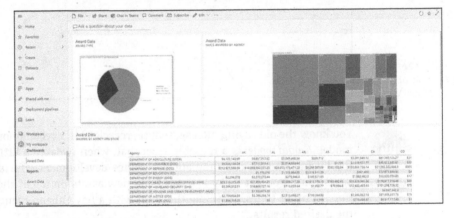

FIGURE 2-5:
A sample dashboard that aggregates many visual sources.

Creating and publishing items

You may want to learn more about Power BI by trying out the free Desktop client to tackle more complex data projects. And, at some point, you might want to post that data project on the web in a read-only format to a limited audience. And you certainly can for free. Suppose, however, that you want others to edit and collaborate with you beyond read-only support. In that case, you must pay for such features.

When you publish items from Power BI Desktop to Power BI Services, the files are workspace bound. Similarly, if you've produced any reports, they appear in Report view. Datasets migrate from the desktop with the same name, as do any reports to the workspace. The relationship is often a one-to-one relationship, with rare exceptions. (For more about importing and publishing various types of data, visualizations, and reports, see Book 2, Chapter 3.)

In Power BI Desktop, you can publish your files by choosing Publish ⇨ Publish to Power BI from the main menu or selecting Publish on the Ribbon. (See Figure 2-6 and Figure 2-7.)

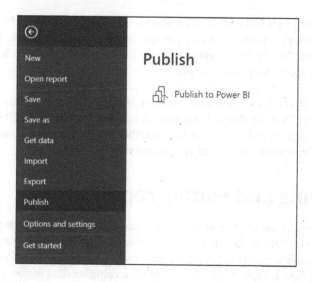

FIGURE 2-6:
Publishing items using the Power BI Desktop File menu.

FIGURE 2-7:
Publishing items using the Power BI Desktop Ribbon.

REMEMBER

When you publish an item from the Power BI Desktop to Services, you're performing the same action as using the Get Data feature. That means connecting to a data source, uploading a file from Power BI Desktop, and sending it to Services.

WARNING

Saving in Power BI Services doesn't make changes to the original Power BI Desktop file. Therefore, don't expect any updates when you or your colleagues add, delete, or change any dataset, visualization, or report.

Services: Far and Wide

Services aren't intended for a single user, whereas Desktop supports individual usage exclusively. The purpose of Services is to allow the individual user to publish data from the desktop and then share it with user groups. In a perfect Microsoft world, some users want to manipulate that data over time. The data grows, requiring either a Pro or Premium license.

REMEMBER

The Desktop user can continually update their data product, whether it is a dataset, data model, or report, after they publish it online using Power BI Services. However, Power BI Services doesn't refresh the data at the desktop level. Therefore, it's up to you to keep data in sync.

Services offers four significant product features beyond Desktop for multiuser access that Desktop doesn't support: the ability to view and edit reports, access to dashboards based on credentials, collaboration among users, and data refresh options depending on product type purchased.

Viewing and editing reports

The report lifecycle generally begins when a user sets up a dataset and builds a functional data model in Power BI Desktop. The user also crafts one or more reports. Once a report is developed, you can then publish it to Power BI Services. The workflow is typical, as refinement with complex data makes it easier to build a report deliverable offline. You can assume that you don't need an Internet connection to access the dataset.

Sometimes you might require online services access because you have large datasets from third-party applications. Everyday use cases include when you have a subscription to CRM or ERP solutions requiring data connections. Assuming that you are part of an organization and have access to a service (SaaS) app, you'll find someone in your organization whose job is to publish apps. That person generally distributes the app, granting you access to specific features and data. With Power BI Services, you connect to these apps to generate reports specific to your business needs.

REMEMBER

Though you can directly connect to data sources such as databases, files, and folders in Power BI Desktop, applications are different. You need Power BI Services to access app data.

Sharing your results

With Power BI Services, you publish your data to the Internet for a reason: You want to share with colleagues and collaborate. Once you create reports or dashboards, you can share them with users who are given Power BI Services accounts. The type of license in force dictates how the user can interact with the data, of course. Some users may be able to view only the reports and dashboards, and others may be able to collaborate fully. For you and your colleagues to manage a report or dashboard, a workspace may be established. You bundle and distribute the deliverable as an app. Once you share the dataset, it becomes the basis for a new set of dashboards or reports.

REMEMBER

A Power BI report, by default, supplies a holistic view of a dataset. It has visuals representing findings from one or more datasets. Reports may hold a single visualization or many.

Seeing why reports are valuable

The basis of a report is a single dataset, whereas a dashboard collects many reports. With reports, you get a laser-focused view of a topic. Moreover, data is static in a non-data-model-based application; such is not the case in a tool such as Power BI. The visuals are dynamic because, as the underlying data updates, so do the reports in real time. In addition, a user is free to interact with the visuals as little or as much as they want in a report. They can also use reports to filter and query in a variety of different ways within Power BI. Reports are highly interactive and even customizable based on your organizational role and responsibility.

Accessing reports from many directions

You should consider two basic scenarios when it comes to reporting access: Either you created the report yourself and imported it from Power BI Desktop or someone has shared a report with you. Any report that you imported is on your My Workspace. (See Figure 2-8.)

Within the framework of these two scenarios, access might come about as

>> Reports shared directly, for example, by email.

>> Reports shared as part of an app.

>> Reports accessible from the dashboard.

>> Recent or favorite reports, dashboards, apps, and workspaces accessible from the Services Navigation pane.

The Quick Tour of Power BI

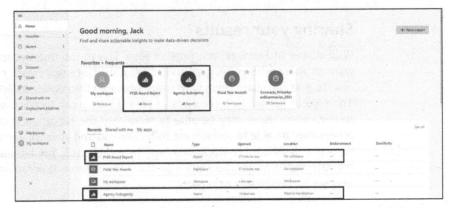

FIGURE 2-8:
Reports imported
to the workspace.

Among these options, the three most common ways users view and edit reports when collaborating are a) sharing directly, b) sharing as part of an app, and c) accessing the dashboard.

To open a report that is shared with you, follow these steps:

1. **Open Power BI Services, located at** `https://app.powerbi.com.`

2. **Select Home in the Navigation pane.**

The Home canvas appears.

3. **Click the Shared with Me icon.**

4. **Then, select a report found on the Shared with Me page.**

In Figure 2-9, you can see one dashboard and one report. The report is named FY20 Award Report. While you only see one report on the canvas, there are in fact several reports available upon clicking the Report Card. In Power BI, a single report can contain many sub-reports.

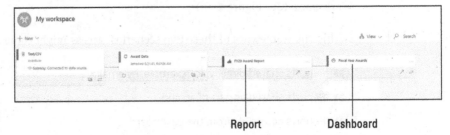

FIGURE 2-9:
Accessing
reports directly.

Report   Dashboard

The second choice is receiving an app from someone directly or accessing the app using Microsoft's AppSource. You access these apps either from the Power BI home screen or from the Apps and Shared with Me items found on the Navigation pane.

WARNING

Someone who wants to open an app must first either acquire a Power BI Pro license or have an app workspace stored in a Power BI Premium capacity. In other words, if you're looking to use apps under the free model, it isn't possible.

To access reports from an app, you need to navigate to the app source. Here's one example of how you'd do it:

1. **Point your browser to the app source's location, such as** `https://appsource.microsoft.com`**.**

2. **Select the Power Platform check box.**

3. **Using the Search box at the top of the screen, search for** *Microsoft sample Sales and Marketing***.**

4. **Click the Get it Now button.**

5. **On the new page that appears, choose Continue ⇨ Install to install the app in the Apps canvas.**

6. **Open the app in the Apps canvas or Home canvas.**

   You should see the assigned app under Apps. (See Figure 2-10.)

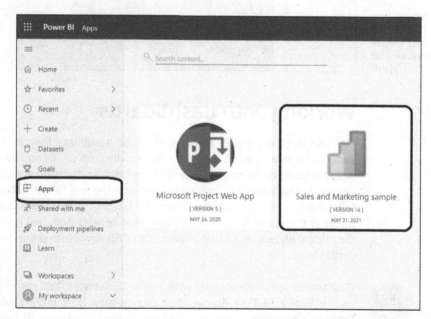

FIGURE 2-10:
Access app from
Apps menu in
Power BI.

You can also open reports from a dashboard. Most times, a tile is a snapshot of a pinned report. When you double-click the tile, a report will open. To open a report from a dashboard, follow these steps:

1. **From the dashboard, select any tile.**

   In the example (see Figure 2-11), the tile selected is NAICS Awarded By Agency using the treemap.

2. **Drill down into a more granular view of the report data by clicking on data points within a report.**

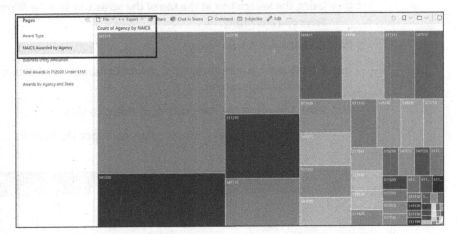

FIGURE 2-11:
Drill down from
the Power BI
dashboard for
a report.

Working with dashboards

One reason to use Power BI Services is the dashboard feature. It's all well and good to be able to work with data on the desktop on a case-by-case basis, but suppose that you want to aggregate your visualizations on a single page using a canvas. In that case, the Dashboard feature is the tool to use. A dashboard lets you tell a story from a series of visualizations — think of a dashboard as a single-page menu at the restaurant. A dashboard must be well designed because it contains the critical highlights so that a reader can drill down into related reports and view details later.

REMEMBER

Dashboards are available only with Power BI Services. You can create dashboards with a Power BI Free license, but this feature isn't integrated into Power BI Desktop. Therefore, once you build your reports in Power BI Desktop, you need to publish outputs to Power BI Services. Keep in mind that, although dashboards can be created only on a desktop-based computer, you can view and share dashboards on all device form-factors, including Power BI Mobile. When you want to create a dashboard, you need to have at least one or more reports pinned to a blank canvas. Each tile (see Figure 2-12) represents a single report based on a single dataset.

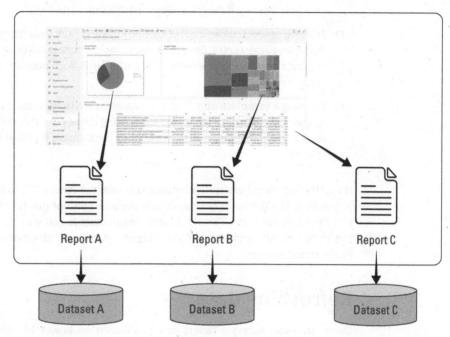

FIGURE 2-12:
Architecture of a
dashboard.

Collaborating inside Power BI Services

The transition from Power BI Desktop to Power BI Services is partially due to collaboration — you're unable to collaborate with others using Power BI Desktop. You may want to share with a small subset of users, or perhaps the group of users you're looking to share information with is distributed. Depending on the Power BI Services option you're working with, you have these options:

>> **Using workspace:** The most common way to share reports and dashboards is by using the workspace. Suppose that another user is given access to a report or dashboard. In that case, the user either views or edits the workspace area in Power BI Services.

>> **Using Microsoft Teams:** Using the Chat feature in Teams allows for collaborating on reports and dashboards with Power BI.

>> **Distributing your reports and dashboards via an app:** If your results are focused, the user can build a single app and create a working executable for sharing among other users.

>> **Embedding reports and dashboards on websites:** Sometimes, the reports and dashboards you create might be helpful for targeted public consumption on an external or internal facing website. You can create an iteration of a Power BI report or dashboard that's viewable. Any user who visits that website may view the data if they're assigned permission to do so.

>> **Printing reports:** When in doubt, you can always print your reports and distribute paper copies. Of course, each time the data is refreshed, you need to print a new copy of the report. For dashboards, each output is printed separately.

>> **Creating a template app:** If your deliverables are repetitious, distribute them so that Power BI users can access them using the Microsoft AppSource. One must assume that these items are publicly consumable for other businesses to use.

No matter which collaboration options you select, a Power BI Pro license or higher is required. The license is nonnegotiable because content needs to be implemented in a Premium capacity. Though license requirements can vary for viewing items, the ability to edit and manage the outputs mandates, at minimum, a Power BI Professional license.

Refreshing data

Every time you access a report or a dashboard on Power BI Services, you must query the data source. If there are new data points, the results are updated in the dataset as part of the visualization. Depending on the refresh requirements, one or more processes might be needed. The refresh process consists of several phases, depending on the storage operation required for the dataset. You have two concepts to consider: storage mode as well as data refresh type.

Storage modes and dataset types

Power BI offers several modes for allowing access to data in a dataset:

>> **Import mode:** Datasets are imported from the original data source into the dataset. Power BI can query the reports and dashboards submitted to the dataset and return results from the imported tables and columns. You may find this to be a snapshot copy — a dataset representing a moment in time, in other words. Each time Power BI copies the data, you can query the data to fetch the changes.

>> **DirectQuery/LiveConnect:** Two connection types that don't rely on importing data directly are DirectQuery and LiveConnect. Data results come in from the data source whenever the report or dashboard queries the dataset. Power BI

will then transform the raw data into usable datasets. Only DirectQuery mode, though, requires that Power BI not use queries using the Power Query Editor Extract Transform Load (ETL) engine. The reason for this is that the queries are processed directly using Analysis Services without having to consume resources. Data refreshes aren't required because no imports occur in the Power BI Desktop environment. Features that are still updated include tiles and reports, whereby the data updates about every hour. The schedule can be changed to accommodate business needs.

>> **Push mode:** In Push mode, there's no formal definition for a data source, so there's no requirement for a data refresh. Instead, you push the data into the dataset through an external service, which is quite common for real-time analytics processes in Power BI.

REMEMBER

Licensed users are limited to a limited number of refreshes per day for Power BI Services Free and Power BI Services Pro. If you buy Power BI Services Premium Capacity or Power BI Services Premium per User, your refresh allotment increases proportionally based on the capacity you purchased.

Chapter **3**

Prepping Data for Visualization

E nterprise software vendors such as Microsoft have built data source connectors to help organizations import data into applications such as Power BI. You quickly realize that connecting to data sources isn't necessarily the tricky part — it's often the data transformation that takes a bit of time. After you figure out which method is best to prep and load the data into Power BI, you're well on your way to analyzing and visualizing the data in your universe.

In this chapter, you discover the methods you can apply to prep and load data using Power BI Desktop and Services. Then you see how to detect anomalies and inconsistencies, check data structures and column properties, and put data statistics to use.

Getting Data from the Source

Without a data source, it's hard to use Microsoft Power BI. You can connect to your own data source or use one of the many connectors Microsoft makes available to users as part of Power BI Desktop or Services. Before you begin loading data, you must first grasp what the business requirements are for your data source. For example, is the data source local to your desktop with occasional updates? Is your data perhaps coming from a third-party data source that supplies real-time feeds? The requirements for both scenarios are vastly different.

REMEMBER

Microsoft continually adds data connectors to its Desktop and Services platform. In fact, don't be surprised to find at least one or two new connectors released monthly as part of the regular Power BI update. As a result, Power BI offers well over 100 data connectors. The most popular options include files, databases, and web services.

You can find a list of all available data sources at

https://docs.microsoft.com/en-us/power-bi/connect-data/power-
bi-data-sources

To correctly map your data in Power BI, you must determine the exact nature of the data. For example, would you use the Excel Connector if the document type were meant for an Azure SQL database? That wouldn't produce the results you're looking for as a Power BI user.

For the following steps, you can use any XLS- or CVS-based document on your hard drive that has a sufficient number of rows and columns. A reasonable number to conduct an evaluation is 500 – 1,000 records. Place the file on your desktop, and follow these steps using the filename of your file.

To connect to the C:\Desktop\<filename.xlsx> file using the Excel Connector with Power BI Desktop, follow these steps:

1. **On the Excel Home tab, click either the Excel button or the Get Data button, and then choose Excel from the drop-down menu that appears, as shown in Figure 3-1.**

2. **In the Open window, navigate to the C:\Desktop\<filename.xlsx> file, click to select it, and then click Open.**

3. **With the file open, head to the Navigator and select both check boxes on the left: Prime Awards and Sub Awards.**

   The window should now look like Figure 3-2.

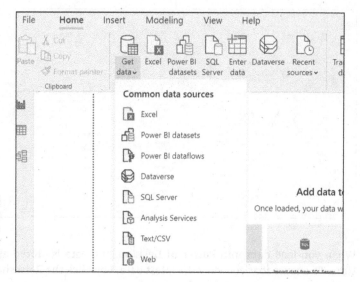

FIGURE 3-1:
Finding the
Excel Data File
Connector
in Power BI
Desktop.

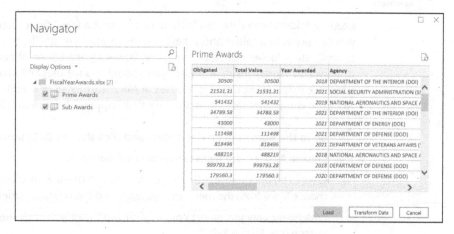

FIGURE 3-2:
Selecting data in
the Navigator.

4. **Click the Transform Data button.**

   Notice that these steps tell you to press the Load button. If you'd gone with Load, you'd have to make modifications to your dataset manually. With Transform, Power BI does the difficult work on your behalf. (The upcoming section "Cleansing, Transforming, and Loading Data" covers more about data transformation, but for now the focus is on knowing how to prepare and load data.)

   After you click Transform Data, a new interface appears called the Power Query Editor. It's what loads the data from the two Excel spreadsheet tabs you just clicked on from the previous Power BI screens. You'll find the experience to be like the one shown in Figure 3-3.

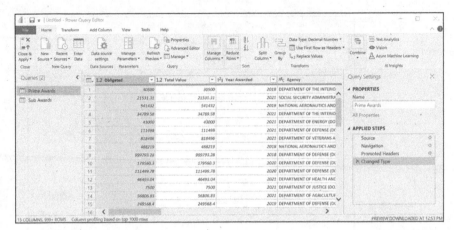

FIGURE 3-3:
Your data, loaded
into the Power
Query Editor.

REMEMBER

When you load data into Power BI Desktop, the data is stored as a snapshot in time. To ensure that you view the latest data, you click the Refresh Preview button on the home screen every so often.

Loading folders with data inside them can present a few unique challenges. Though you can point to a folder and ingest just about any type of file, it's another matter to replicate a folder structure using the Power Query Editor. When you load data in Power BI stored inside a folder, you should ensure that the same file type and structure exist. An example is a series of Microsoft Excel or Google Sheet files that would be complimentary. To make sure that happens, be sure to follow these steps:

1. **Go to the Home tab on the Ribbon and click the Get Data button.**

2. **Choose All ⇨ Folder from the menu that appears.**

   Want to try another way? Go to the Home tab on the Ribbon, click New Source, choose More from the menu that appears, and then choose Folder.

3. **Whichever way you select Folder, your next step is to click the Connect button (see Figure 3-4).**

   Pressing the Connect button enables access to a single data source.

4. **Locate the folder path specific to where you've stored files on your desktop, then browse to the location where you placed the file, similar to C:\Desktop\<filename.xlsx>.**

   The files from the folder you just selected load into a new screen, as shown in Figure 3-5.

5. **Select one or more tables that have loaded.**

6. **Once the tables have been selected, click the Combine and Transform Data button.**

   The datasets from C:\Desktop\<filename.xlsx> are now loaded into Power Query Editor.

FIGURE 3-4:
Selecting Folder
from Get Data.

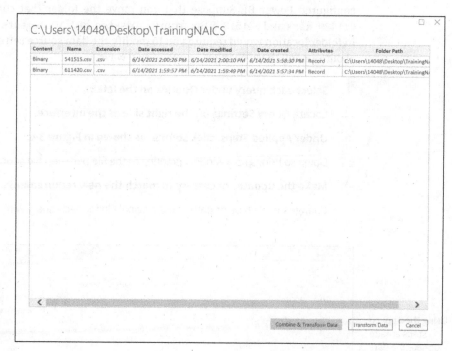

FIGURE 3-5:
Files from a
folder load into
Power BI.

TIP

The difference between the Combine and Transform Data option and the Transform Data option comes down to the file type and structure. Assuming that each file is similar and can create consistent columns, you can likely use the Combine and Transform Data option to bring everything into a single file. Otherwise, you're better served using the Transform Data option since there is usually a single file structure.

By now, you can tell you don't need to do much to load a file, folder, database, or web source into Power BI. Most users, if they can point to the file path, know the database connection and security credentials, or know the URL and associated parameters, can configure their data sources in no time. Power BI's Power Query feature automatically detects the nuances in the connection and applies the proper transformations.

Managing Data Source Settings

Commonly, your dataset requirements change over time. That means if the data source changes, so will some of the settings that were initially loaded when you configured Power BI. Suppose that you move the folder that contains the files 611420.xlsx and 54151S.xlsx from C:\Desktop to C:\Documents. Such a change in folder location would require you to modify the data source settings. You can go about making these changes in one of two ways:

1. **Select each query under Queries on the left.**

2. **Locate Query Settings on the right side of the interface.**

3. **Under Applied Steps, click Source, as shown in Figure 3-6.**

   Doing so brings up a window pointing to the file path and file source.

4. **Make the updates necessary to match the new requirements.**

   Change the file type or path of the original file for each query with this option.

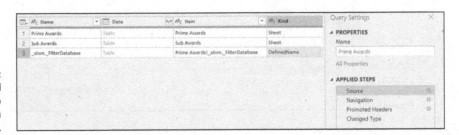

FIGURE 3-6:
Using the Applied Steps area to update the data source settings.

Though the steps outlined here may seem easy at first blush, they might become laborious because you need to make a change to each file listed for each query. That process can be pretty time-consuming, and if you have a lot of queries, you're bound to make errors, given the tedious nature of the work. That's why you want to consider an alternative option — one where you can change the source location in one fell swoop rather than tackle each query independently with this option. Follow these steps for the other method:

1. **On the Power Query Editor's Home tab, click the Data Source Settings button. (It's the one sporting a cog — see Figure 3-7.)**

   A new window opens to make the source location change.

2. **Select all files requiring a change in location by choosing Change Source.**

3. **Make the changes you want to the source location.**

4. **(Optional) Change and clear associated security credentials by selecting Edit Permissions or Clear Permissions in this interface.**

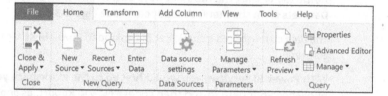

FIGURE 3-7:
The Data Source
Settings button.

Working with Shared versus Local Datasets

So far, the focus in this chapter has been on local datasets that you handle creating and managing using Power BI Desktop. After the dataset is published and shared with others — by either your workspace or a shared one — the dataset is referred to as a *shared dataset*. Unlike with Power BI Desktop, where you have to continually update the dataset on the local hard drive, a shared dataset is stored on the cloud, which means that updates are more consistent whether they're stored in your workspace or with others.

You can find many other benefits to using a shared dataset over a local dataset, including

» Consistency across reports and dashboards

>> Reduction in dataset copying due to centralization of a data source

>> The ability to create new data sources from existing sources with little effort

REMEMBER

Though you may have your own needs with a dataset, after a dataset is shared with a team, the desired outputs might be different. In that case, you may want to create a single dataset and allow the other users to develop reports and dashboards from the single dataset.

TIP

Connecting to a published dataset in Power BI Services requires a user to have Build permission. You can also be a contributing member of a shared workspace where a dataset exists. Make sure the owner of the dataset provisions your access according to your business need.

You can connect to a shared dataset using either Power BI Desktop or Power BI Services. To accomplish this action, follow these steps:

1. **Using Power BI Desktop, either click the Power BI Datasets button on the Home tab or click the tab's Get Data button and then choose Power BI Datasets from the menu that appears. (See Figure 3-8.).**

   The data is transferred from Power BI Desktop to Power BI Services for you to consume.

2. **With Power BI Services, you would first go to the workspace you've published your data to and then choose New ⇨ Report, as shown in Figure 3-9.**

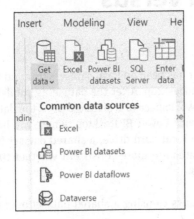

FIGURE 3-8:
Power BI datasets navigation.

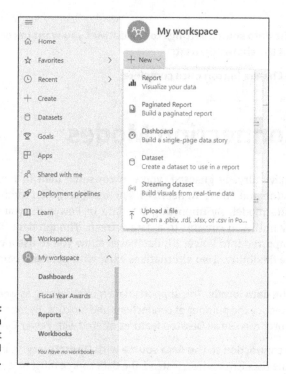

FIGURE 3-9:
Connecting to a
shared dataset
in Power BI
Services.

Whether you're using Power BI Desktop or Power BI Services, your ability to connect to a dataset without worrying about data refresh issues or version control becomes a bit easier. You also have the choice to select Save a Copy in the Power BI Service next to any report in My Workspace or a shared workspace without re-creating a dataset. This action is similar to connecting to a dataset using Power BI Desktop, because you create a report without the base data model.

WARNING

Don't be alarmed if you decide to use a shared dataset and then some buttons become inactive in Power BI Desktop. It happens because you're no longer able to make changes using Power Query Editor. As a result, the data view is also no longer visible. However, you can tell whether your dataset is shared or local by looking in the lower right corner of the Power BI Desktop interface, where you can find the name of the dataset and the user accessing the data.

If you ever need to change from a shared dataset to a local dataset, follow these steps:

1. **Click the Transform Data label.**

2. **Select the Data Source Settings option.**

Prepping Data for
Visualization

3. Modify the data source settings to the dataset you want to connect to instead of the shared dataset.

4. Click the Change button once complete.

Storage and Connection Modes

As you may have already guessed, you can consume data in many ways using Power BI Desktop and Power BI Services. The most common method is to import data into a data model. By importing the data in Power BI, you're copying the dataset locally until you commit to a data refresh. Though data files and folders can only be imported into Power BI, databases allow you to use a connection that supports more flexibility. Two alternatives exist with database connectivity:

>> **Import the data locally.** This supports data model caching as well as the ability to reduce the number of connections and lookups. By ingesting the model, a user can use all Desktop features offered with Power BI.

>> **Create a connection to the data source with DirectQuery.** With this feature, the data isn't cached. Instead, the data source must be queried each time a data call is required. Most, but not all, data sources support DirectQuery.

You can use one of two other methods. One is called Live Connection: With this method, the goal is to use the analysis services integrated with Power BI Desktop or Power BI Services. Live Connection also supports calculation-based activities that occur within a data model.

The second alternative uses composite models. Now, suppose that a user must combine both importing data and DirectQuery, or there is a requirement to connect to multiple DirectQuery connections. In that case, you apply a composite model. You face some risks, though, when dealing with model security. Suppose, for example, you open a Power BI Desktop file sent from an untrusted source. If the file contains a composite model, the information that someone retrieves from a single source using credentials from a user opening the file can be sent to another data source as part of the newly formed query. Therefore, it's vital to ensure that your data sources are correctly assigned to only those who need access to the sources.

TECHNICAL
STUFF

The four storage modes — local storage, DirectQuery, Live Connection, and composite models — have data housed in a single location. It's either local to the user or bound to some server on a network in a data center or the cloud.

Dual mode isn't a hybrid mode — instead, it allows for a table to be cached and retrieved in DirectQuery mode when necessary, applying multiple storage modalities. If another storage mode is used for another table, DirectQuery doesn't need usage. You'll find that Dual mode is beneficial when tables are similar between those imported and exclusively available using DirectQuery mode.

Data Sources Oh My!

Data can be a bit complicated at times. Admittedly, uploading a single file containing a few spreadsheets or perhaps a feed with a single stream of data to load and transform is child's play. What happens, though, when you have a dataset housed in a corporate-wide enterprise application that continually has transactions written to it? That scenario is quite different. And corporations should be concerned (for good reason) with the integration and output of business intelligence (BI) results. With Power BI, organizations don't need to worry about complex technical manipulations when it comes to their data systems or their communications with third-party data feeds. As you can see in this chapter, the integration is fluid — Power BI has the power to use a standardized connection process, no matter the connectivity requirement.

Getting data from Microsoft-based file systems

This section covers integration with Microsoft-based applications such as OneDrive for Business and SharePoint 365, both of which are Microsoft 365-based applications.

REMEMBER

When using OneDrive, you need to be logged in to Microsoft 365. As long as you're logged in, you can access files and folders as though you're accessing your local hard drive. The only difference is that your hard drive is Microsoft OneDrive. In Figure 3-10, you can see that the path to a OneDrive for Business folder is no different from the path for a standard file or folder on your hard drive.

On the other hand, SharePoint 365 offers a variety of options for document management and collaboration. The first option is to search a site collection, site, or subsite (referred to in Power BI as a SharePoint Folder). In this case, you must enter the complete SharePoint site URL. For example, if your company has an intranet, the site might be *<asite>*.sharepoint.com. An example of what you'd see after you enter a complete URL and log in with your Active Directory credentials appears in Figure 3-11.

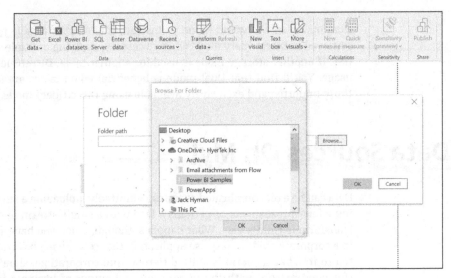

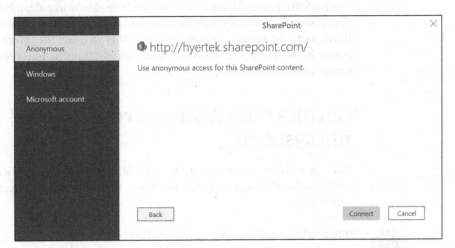

FIGURE 3-10:
OneDrive
file path.

FIGURE 3-11:
SharePoint
Folder path.

You can also collect, load, and transform one or more SharePoint lists in Power BI. (In SharePoint, a *list* looks like a simple container — kind of like an Excel spreadsheet — but acts more like a database.) Using a list lets users collect information — especially metadata — across a SharePoint site where documents might be collected. With a list, data is gathered in rows, with each row represented as a row item similar to a database or spreadsheet item. To load a SharePoint list, you must know the URL path of the SharePoint site collection, site, or subsite. Once a user is authenticated, all available lists are loaded for that person.

TIP

When you're first starting out with Power BI, you might be tempted to keep all your files on the desktop as a way to manage your data. After a while, though, dealing with numerous versions of the same dataset becomes unmanageable. That's why you should use a cloud option such as OneDrive or a SharePoint site to manage your files and datasets, reports, dashboards, and connection files. It helps keep all of it streamlined.

Working with relational data sources

Many organizations use relational databases to record transactional activity. Examples of systems that typically run relational databases are enterprise resource planning (ERP), customer relationship management (CRM), and supply chain management (SCM)-based systems. Another type of system might be an e-commerce platform. Each of these systems has one thing in common: All can benefit from having a business intelligence tool such as Power BI evaluate data by connecting with the relational database instead of extracting individual data files.

Businesses rely on solutions such as Power BI to help them monitor the state of their operations by identifying trends and helping them forecast metrics, indicators, and targets. You can start using Power BI Desktop to connect to virtually any relational database available in the cloud or on-premise on the market.

In the example shown in Figure 3-12, Power BI is connected to an Azure SQL Server, Microsoft's web-based enterprise database. Depending on your relational database solution, you have a few choices. One would be to choose the Get Data ⇨ More . . . command from the Ribbon's Home tab, then look for Database. Here you will find Microsoft-specific databases. Otherwise, if you are looking for another type of data source, choose Get Data ⇨ More . . . and look for Other. You'll find 40+ alternate database options under this section.

In this case, because the selected solution is a Microsoft Azure-based product, you can either search for the product in the Search box or click the Azure option after selecting More.

After you select the database source type under Get Data, you must enter the credentials for the relational database. In this case, you enter the following info:

>> Server name

>> Database name

>> Mode type — Import or DirectQuery

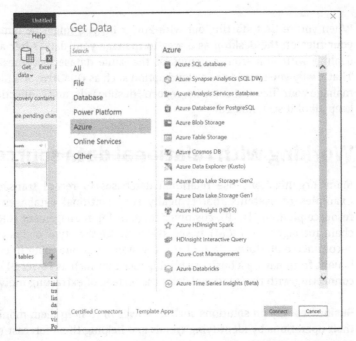

FIGURE 3-12:
Azure SQL
database
location.

Figure 3-13 gives an example with the fields correctly filled out. (You don't need to add unique command lines or SQL query statements unless you're looking for a more granular data view.)

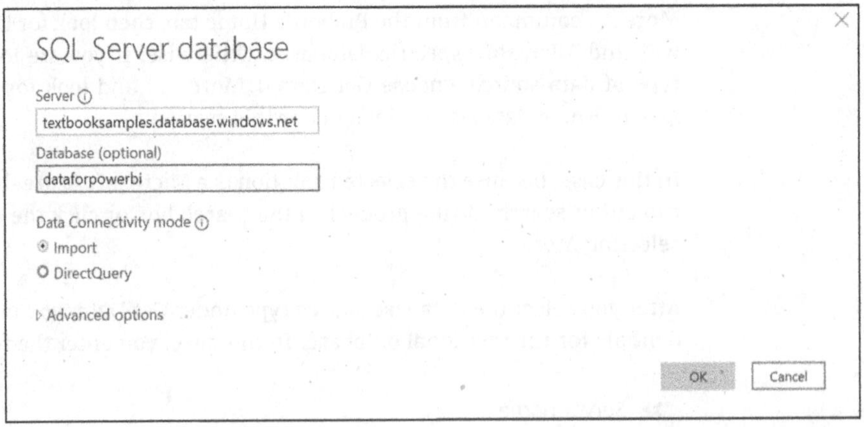

SQL Server database

Server ⓘ

textbooksamples.database.windows.net

Database (optional)

dataforpowerbi

Data Connectivity mode ⓘ
⦿ Import
◯ DirectQuery

▷ Advanced options

OK   Cancel

FIGURE 3-13:
Entry of
credentials
for relational
database.

REMEMBER

In most cases, you should select Import. The circumstances where you select DirectQuery are for large datasets. The data updates are intended for near real-time updates.

After you've entered your credentials, you're prompted to log in with your username and password using your Windows, database, or Microsoft account authentication, as shown in Figure 3-14.

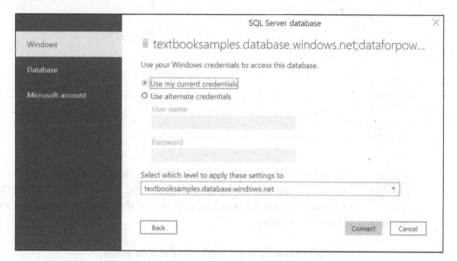

FIGURE 3-14:
Selecting the
authentication
method to
connect.

Relational databases

Connecting to the data source is often tricky because you need to make sure your database source and naming conventions are just right. However, once you get past these two facts, you often have smooth sailing — well, at least until you need to pick the data to import. Then you might become overwhelmed if the database has a lot of tables.

After you've connected the database to Power BI Desktop, the Navigator displays the data available from the data source, as shown in Figure 3-15. In this case, all data from the Azure SQL database is presented. You can select a table or one of the entities to preview the content.

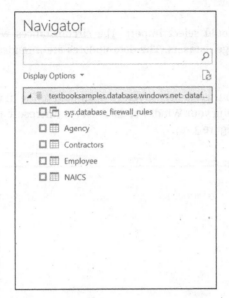

FIGURE 3-15:
Selecting the
tables from the
Navigator for
import.

REMEMBER

The data loaded into the model *must* be the correct data before moving on to the following dataset. To import data from the relational data source that you want to ingest into Power BI Desktop, and then either load or transform and load the data, follow these steps:

1. **Select one or more tables in the Navigator.**

   The data selected will be imported into Power Query Editor.

2. **Click the Load button if you're looking to automate data loading into a Power BI model based on its current state with no changes.**

3. **Click the Transform Data button if you want Power BI to execute the Power Query engine.**

   The engine performs actions such as cleaning up excessive columns, grouping data, removing errors, and promoting data quality.

Nonrelational databases

Some organizations use nonrelational databases such as Microsoft Cosmos DB or Apache Hadoop to handle their myriad of significant data challenges. What's the difference, you ask? These databases don't use tables to store their data. Data might be stored in a variety of ways in the case of nonrelational (NoSQL) data. Options run the gamut from document, key-value, wide-column, and graph. All database options provide flexible schemas and scale effortlessly with large data volumes.

Though the need still exists to authenticate to the database, the querying approach is a bit different. For example, with Microsoft Cosmos DB, the NoSQL database created by Microsoft complementary to Power BI, a user must identify the endpoint URL and the Primary key and Read-Only key so that a connection can be created to the Cosmos DB instance in the Azure portal. To connect to the Cosmos DB, follow these steps:

1. **Choose Get Data ⇨ More . . . from the Home tab in Power BI.**

2. **In the submenu that appears, locate the Azure submenu.**

3. **Click to select the Azure Cosmos DB option, as shown in Figure 3-16, allowing you to create a nonrelational database connection.**

4. **Enter the URL of the Cosmos DB in the URL field and then click OK. (See Figure 3-17.)**

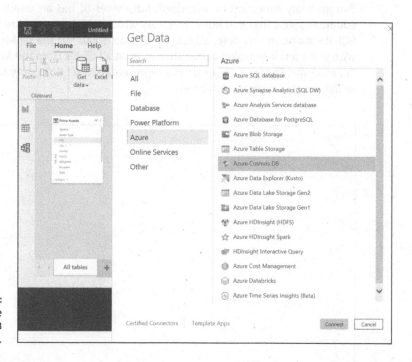

FIGURE 3-16: Selecting the Cosmos DB data source.

WARNING

When you're using a NoSQL database, you need to know the keys in order to authenticate. For Cosmos DB, you can find those keys in the Azure portal under the Cosmos DB Instance Settings, Key Link. Be sure to copy down the primary and secondary read-write keys and the primary and secondary read-only key.

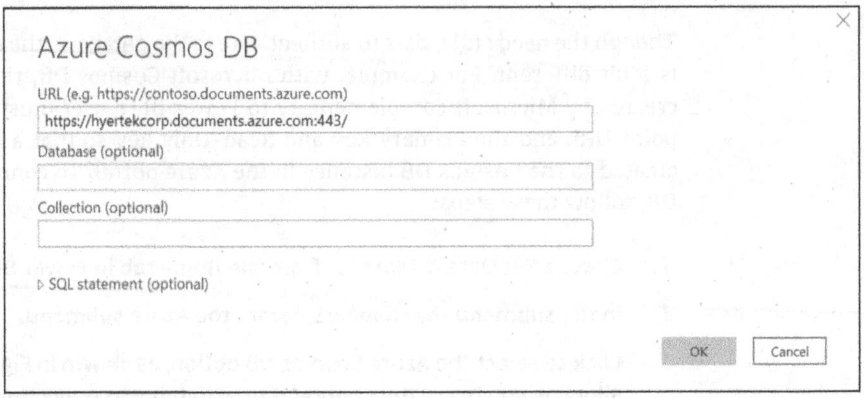

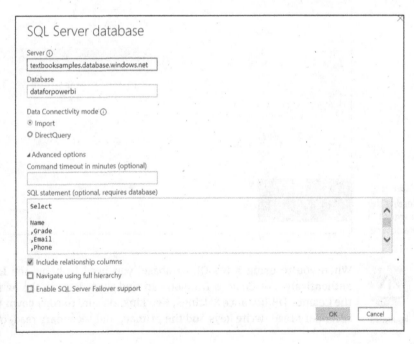

FIGURE 3-17:
Connecting to
the Cosmos DB, a
Microsoft NoSQL
database.

Using the SQL query

You probably shouldn't be surprised, but Power BI has an intelligent SQL query
editor. Suppose that you know precisely which tables you require from the Azure
SQL database. In this case, all you need to do is call out the tables in a SQL query
with just a few keystrokes rather than request all tables from the Azure SQL Server.
For example, Figure 3-18 presents a representative SELECT query for a table found
in the dataforpowerbi database.

FIGURE 3-18:
Representative
query data from
Azure SQL Server.

JSON files

JSON files don't look at all like structured data files. Why is that the case? JSON — short for JavaScript Object Notation — is a lightweight data-interchange format. Neither structured nor unstructured, the JSON file type is referred to as *semi-structured* because the file type is written by default as a key-value pair. With JSON-based records, the data must be extracted and normalized before becoming a report in Power BI. That's why you must transform the data using Power BI Desktop's Power Query Editor.

If your goal is to extract data from a JSON file, you transform the list to a table by clicking the Transform tab and selecting To Table in the Convert group. Another option is to drill down into a specific record by clicking on a record link. If you want to preview the record, click on the cell without clicking on the link. Doing so opens a data preview pane at the bottom of Power Query Editor.

Need to get a bit more in the weeds? You can click on the cog wheel next to the source step in Query Settings, which opens a window to specify advanced settings. There you can specify options such as file encoding in the File Origin drop-down list. When you are ready for show time and your JSON file is transformed, click Close and Apply to load data into the Power BI data model. In the example found in Figure 3-19, employee records have been transformed from the JSON file.

FIGURE 3-19: JSON file, transformed by the Power Query Editor.

After the Power Query Editor has transformed the file, you might still need to edit specific fields. In this example, the Country field has all null entries, so it's a prime candidate for field deletion. Such a choice is easily carried out with the help of the drop-down menu, as shown in Figure 3-20, where you can drill down and delete specific records.

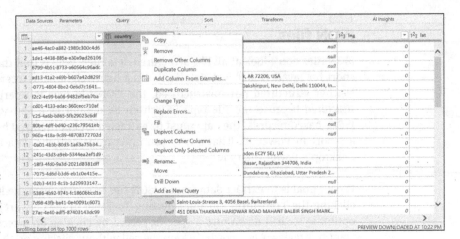

FIGURE 3-20:
Modifying a
JSON file using
the Power
Query Editor.

Online sources

Enterprise applications and third-party data feeds are widely available in Power BI. In fact, Microsoft has over 100 connectors to applications developed and managed by other vendors, including those by Adobe, Denodo, Oracle, and Salesforce, to name a few. Of course, Microsoft also supports its own enterprise application solutions, including those in the Dynamics 365, SharePoint 365, and Power Platform families. Online sources can be found across several categories using the Get Data feature in Power BI Desktop, but your best bets are under the Online Services heading or the Other heading.

The example shown in Figure 3-21 is connected to Dynamics 365 Business Central.

To connect to an online service, follow these steps:

1. **Go to Get Data from the Home tab of Power BI.**

2. **At the bottom of the Go Data menu, choose the More . . . option.**

   Selecting More provides users with more data source options.

3. **Choose Online Services from the More . . . submenu.**

   Online Services include enterprise applications, where large datasets are available (assuming user credentials are accessible).

4. **On the right side, click Dynamics 365 Business Central (see Figure 3-22).**

   Doing so allows for a connection to Microsoft's Small Business ERP Solution.

5. **At the bottom of the screen, click Connect.**

   The result is that a connection has been established to Microsoft Dynamics 365 Business Central.

FIGURE 3-21:
Connecting to
an online service
in Power BI
Desktop.

You're then asked to enter your online organizational credentials. Generally, this part is already prepopulated because it's your Single Sign-On login associated with Azure Active Directory. (Refer to Figure 3-22.)

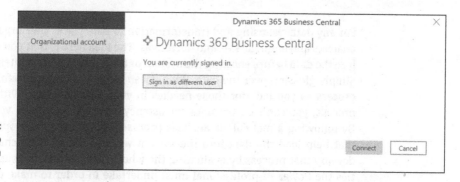

FIGURE 3-22:
Interface to
authenticate with
Online Services.

Once you authenticate a session, all data available from the database for the specific source is loaded in the Navigator pane within the Power Query Editor, as shown in Figure 3-23. Power Query transforms the data before loading it in Navigator.

Prepping Data for
Visualization

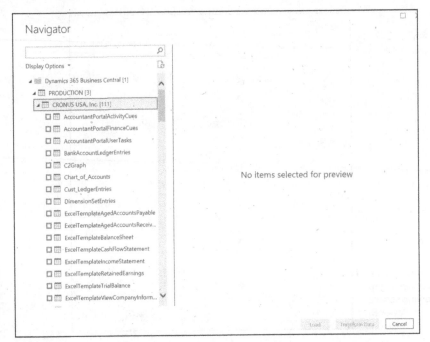

FIGURE 3-23:
Data displayed
in the Navigator
pane within
the Power
Query Editor.

Cleansing, Transforming, and Loading Your Data

For any data cleansing and transformation to take place, your organization needs analysts and engineers — and detectives. The idea here is that you must first analyze the data before entering the system or after it exists in its intended data store. Simply glossing over the data alone doesn't cut it. You need to follow a rigorous process as you look for those needles in your data haystack. Without a rigorous process, you can't ensure data consistency across all columns, values, and keys. By following a meticulous analysis process, you can engineer optimized queries that help load the data into the system without issues. This chapter helps you develop that process by evaluating the whole lifecycle and the supporting activities the Power BI professional must undertake in order to make their data shine for visualization consumption.

Detecting anomalies and inconsistencies

Anomalous data comes in many flavors. Using Power Query, you can find unusual data trends that you might be on the lookout for — even those slight ambiguities you'd have trouble catching on your own. For example, you can see how an out-of-context dollar amount or error can be traced back to missing values that skew the data results. These are all real-life scenarios that you can address using Power BI.

The easiest and most obvious way to spot errors is to look at a table in the Power Query Editor. You can evaluate the quality of each column by using the Data Preview feature. You can, among each column, review data under a header value in order to validate data, catch errors, and spot empty values. All you need to do is choose View ➪ Data Preview ➪ Column Quality from the Power Query main menu. In Figure 3-24, you notice right off the bat that the Agency column has data missing, as shown by the <1% number reported as empty. Such behavior is consistent with data anomalies.

FIGURE 3-24: Addressing column quality issues.

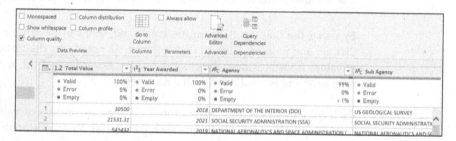

Notice that all columns except for the Agency column have 100 percent validity. In this case, that <1% means you have either a null value or mistaken data. The purpose of investigating data quality issues using Power Query is best exemplified with this sampling because all other columns show an error percentage of 0. You learn how to correct such ambiguities later in this chapter.

Checking data structures and column properties

Evaluating data goes beyond column quality. Another measurement you can use to better identify data structure issues involves *column value distribution*, which is a measure of all distinct values in the selected column as well as the percentage of rows in the table that each value represents. You enable this measurement in the Power Query Editor by choosing View ➪ Data Preview ➪ Column Distribution. In Figure 3-25, notice that the Total Value columns have a high number of distinct and unique values.

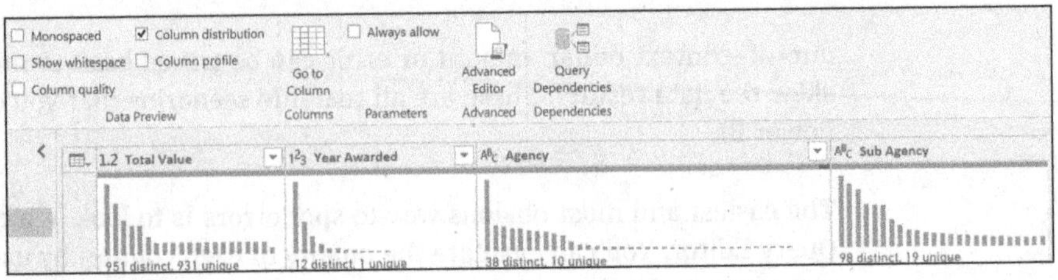

FIGURE 3-25:
A look at column
distribution.

Here's what *distinct* and *unique* are telling you:

>> **Distinct number:** The number of different values in a column when duplicates are omitted

>> **Unique number:** The number of values that occur precisely one time

By using the Column Distribution command, you can determine the number of distinct and unique values in each column. As noted, the distribution of columns of values is visible under the column header. Regardless of the analysis goal, column profiling is available for all data types.

Each column shows the shape of data — the distribution of values, say, or the frequency with which a specific data type appears. The value 2021, for example, is seen most, whereas the values for 2011 through 2020 are distributed in a proportional amount per the chart, as shown in Figure 3-25, under the Years Awarded heading.

TIP

If you want to evaluate the data outside of Power BI and the Power Query Editor, right-click the columns of choice and then select Copy Value Distribution from the menu that appears. You're supplied a list of distinct values and the number of times the data appears in the columns.

Data statistics to the rescue

Statistics can sometimes be your best friend, which is why you want to consider using them for profiling and understanding the nature of your data. To enable data preview for statistics, go to the Power Query Editor, choose View ⇨ Data Preview from its main menu, and then select the Column Quality and Column Profile checkboxes, as shown in Figure 3-26.

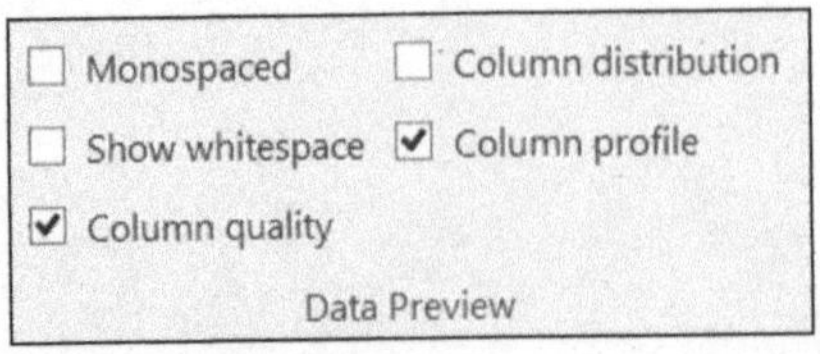

FIGURE 3-26:
Data preview
options in
the Power
Query Editor.

After enabling the features, select a column header requiring further statistical analysis. In Figure 3-27, you find the profile of the Total Value and Year Awarded columns from the Excel spreadsheet labeled Fiscal Year Awards. Notice the general-statistics panel on the bottom and then the individual column statistics. Your options aren't limited to column profile and column quality, either. You can also review data for whitespace, monospacing, and column distribution.

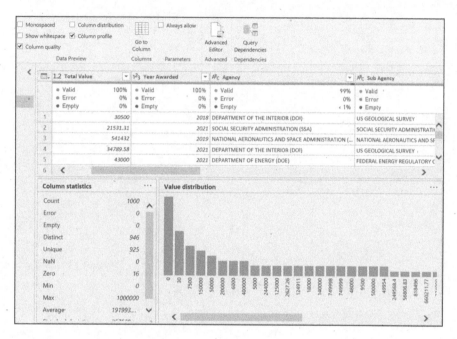

FIGURE 3-27:
Data preview of the column profile and column quality.

These are the key column statistics you can evaluate:

» Total count of value

» Number of errors

» Empty columns

» Distinct columns

» Unique values

» Minimum, maximum, and average values

» Number of zero, odd, or even values

REMEMBER

If the column has text, the statistics vary in comparison to numerical columns. With text columns, the number of empty strings and values is highlighted. In contrast, in numeric columns, you're limited to empty values alone.

Chapter **4**

Tweaking Data for Primetime

For any data cleansing and transformation to take place, your organization needs analysts and engineers — and detectives. The idea here is that you must first analyze the data before entering the system or after it exists in its intended data store. Simply glossing over the data alone doesn't cut it. You need to follow a rigorous process as you look for those needles in your data haystack. Without a rigorous process, you can't ensure data consistency across all columns, values, and keys. By following a meticulous analysis process, you can engineer optimized queries that help load the data into the system without issues. This chapter helps you develop that process by evaluating the whole lifecycle and the supporting activities the Power BI professional must undertake in order to make their data shine for visualization consumption.

Stepping through the Data Lifecycle

Data is seldom perfect. Unless you're connecting to a prepared dataset where you have limited control over what has been created for you, there's a good chance you need to do some data cleansing and data transformation before you can load anything for analysis.

Power BI offers an incredibly powerful tool to help guide you through the entire data lifecycle, emphasizing data cleansing and transformation. That tool is Power Query. Within Power Query, a user can extract, transform, and load (ETL) their data using the Get command as well as the Transform Data command. In this book, you use Power Query to connect, transform, ingest, and evaluate available data when connecting to a data source. Power Query is the infrastructure behind the Power Query Editor found in Power BI.

REMEMBER

Power Query isn't new to Power BI. In fact, the product is integral to Excel as well. Other products, in addition to Power BI and Excel, include Power Query as a means of modernizing query development using a low-code approach.

Resolving Inconsistencies

The more data you have, the more you have to be on the lookout for inconsistencies, unexpected values, null values, and other data quality issues. Power BI, with the help of Power Query, supports users with several ways to deal with inconsistencies. These include replacing values, removing rows, and completing root cause analysis.

Replacing values

Users can replace mistaken values with desired outcomes directly in the Power Query Editor interface. You would use this approach wherever errors occur in the data sources you create or import into Power BI. An example of such behavior is replacing null values with an updated, unique value. There's a catch, though, when using this technique: A user must fix the error in the source or the values during a refresh may be written over. You can access your options by right-clicking a column and then choosing an option, as shown in Figure 4-1.

To replace errors, follow these steps:

1. **Right-click a column header and choose Replace Errors from the menu that appears in the Power Query Editor.**

2. **Enter the values you want to replace in the Value box.**

3. **Click OK.**

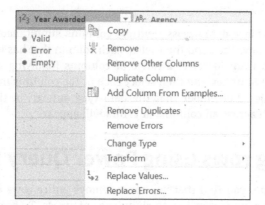

FIGURE 4-1:
Look for the
Replace Values
menu option.

Replacing values in a column follows a similar process, as shown in Figure 4-2. Follow these steps:

1. **Right-click a column header and choose Replace Value from the menu that appears in the Power Query Editor.**

2. **On the new screen that appears, fill in the Value to Find and the Replace With fields.**

3. **When you finish, click the OK button.**

Replace Values

Replace one value with another in the selected columns.

Value To Find

Replace With

OK   Cancel

FIGURE 4-2:
Replacing values.

TIP

After selecting the Replace Value menu, you're prompted to make several updates. Under Advanced, you see two options: Match Entire Cell Content and Replace Using Special Character Codes. If you try to replace text in a column, you need to match an entire cell's content. If you enable the Match Entire Cell Content option, the Power Query Editor won't replace values where the Replace With value is limited to the Value to Find value. Furthermore, suppose that you're looking to replace a unique character. In that case, you need to select the Replace Using Special Character Codes check box. Otherwise, the value isn't entered into the box.

TECHNICAL STUFF

If you want to replace data across multiple columns simultaneously, you must press the Control key (Ctrl) and then select each column that has values you want to replace. If you want to select a range of columns following a specific order instead, press the Shift key and then select each of the columns in your preferred chronological order. Remember that the data type entered in the replacement fields must match across all columns or errors will appear.

Removing rows using Power Query

From time to time, you find that you must remove entire rows of data because something in the rows is creating an abundance of errors. To remove a row, you would assume that correcting the error should be as simple as right-clicking the column and choosing Remove Errors from the contextual menu. Using this method removes only rows where known errors are present. Suppose that you prefer to remove all rows in a table that meet a particular condition that can lead to errors. In that case, you'd click the Table icon to the left of the column header, select the affected rows, and then choose Remove Errors from the menu that appears.

Digging down to the root cause

Every time an error occurs in a column, you can review the message behind the error. To review the error, select the cell in question. The error message appears in the Preview panel at the bottom of the page. Using this method enables a user to see various content types from tables, records, lists, and, of course, embedded errors.

Figure 4-3 shows that an error has been introduced after a new custom column was added to the dataset. The issue presented is a mismatch of data types. Neither a text field nor a numeric field can create a typical column value. It turns out that type conversion is often one of those root causes triggering an error message.

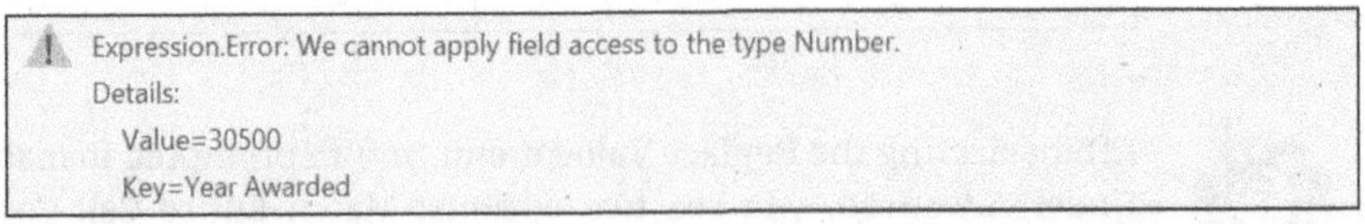

FIGURE 4-3:
An error, as presented in Power Query.

> ⚠ Expression.Error: We cannot apply field access to the type Number.
> Details:
>   Value=30500
>   Key=Year Awarded

TECHNICAL STUFF

From time to time, you may need to convert a column from one type to another (from Text to Number, for example). In Power BI, this is referred to as a *type conversion*. Most times, you make type conversion changes immediately after data is transformed using Power Query.

Evaluating and Transforming Column Data Types

Few data sources are ready for prime time. You need to shape them to be ready for use by Power BI and the Power Query Editor. (Admittedly, such behavior is more often true for files than for structured database systems, but that's beside the point.) As you work through datasets, you need to add query steps as you either add or reduce rows and column data. Even when you try to transpose column data, it should come as no surprise that evaluating and transforming data can be a complex process. This section focuses on topics that help transform data into its purest possible state. Of course, you need to perform a little bit of magic along the way.

Finding and creating appropriate keys for joins

Power BI supports users by combining data from tables in a number of different ways — but no matter which way you choose, you have to use a join in your query. (A *join* is a way to combine data from multiple tables; it brings together these tables using a common key from two or more tables.) Using Power Query Editor, you can complete this action using the Merge functionality. If you want to create relationships using a model outside of Power Query, you create implicit joins. The use of a join depends on the business requirements.

REMEMBER

Of all the many join types out there, the two you most often hear about are implicit and explicit joins. An *implicit* join performs a left outer join with a table field, pulling from another table. *Explicit* joins specify the integration of two tables. There are many benefits to using implicit joins. A key benefit is syntax because it's a useful substitute for explicit join syntax. In fact, an implicit join can appear in the same query that maintains an explicit join syntax.

TECHNICAL STUFF

Tables can be represented by one or many join statements. If a table is represented on the One side of the join, the key in the table is unique in every row. If the table is represented by the Many side of the join, not all keys are unique, which yields some duplication. As you may have guessed, the One side is represented as a primary key, and the Many side can be a foreign key. One-to-one (1:1) and many-to-many (M:M) relationships do exist at times; however, the results produced in Power Query may not be suitable; one-to-one relationship may produce a narrow result set, whereas many-to-many often produces too many results.

Here are two key terms to remember when data modeling:

>> A *relationship* is the connection between entities in a data model, which in turn reflect business rules. Relationships between entities can be either one-to-one, one-to-many, or many-to-many.

>> A *join* is a bit different in that you're setting up a relationship between two or more tables to pull data. The data is commonly mapped together using a primary key, a foreign key, or a combination, which is referred to as a *composite key*.

Consider the following information as it relates to joins and relationships:

>> **Keys for joins:** You can perform joins based on one or more columns at a time. Creating composite keys isn't a requirement to merge tables using Power Query. When you create joins in Power Query, pay particular attention to the column type. You must match the data type with one another or a join won't work.

>> **Keys for relationships:** Power BI will try its best to resolve different data types, including converting data types, if possible. Ideally, though, you should make sure that the data type in the relationship is the same when creating a join.

You can combine columns in two different ways: Create a new column or merge a column in place. To add a new merged column, first select the columns you're looking to combine and then choose Add ⇨ Column ⇨ From Text ⇨ Merge Columns from the Power Query Editor Ribbon. If you'd prefer to merge columns in place, you replace the original columns. Select the columns you want to merge and then choose Transform ⇨ Text Column ⇨ Merge Columns from the same menu.

Whether you select one of the two options, the outcome is ultimately the same. Figure 4-4 presents the Merge interface. You can combine one or more columns from Prime Awards and Sub Awards. Then, you select the type of join. The result is a new column that merges the two columns.

A final step in the process is defining separators from the Separator drop-down menu, found on the Merge interface. You can either select a predefined separator or come up with your own by choosing Custom from the menu. If you choose the latter method, you're given a choice to enter a new column name. Once you complete it, click OK.

In the example, a colon is being used as a separator. Finally, the new column is called Agency-Sub Agency, as shown in Figure 4-5.

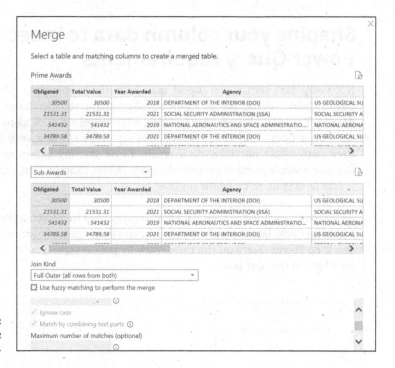

FIGURE 4-4:
The Merge
Columns option.

FIGURE 4-5:
Columns that
have been
merged.

Shaping your column data to meet Power Query requirements

Not every data source you ingest may have the proper data type. Power Query does its best to detect the data type based on characteristics found in the available dataset. For example, you may be using a US-based zip code as part of your dataset. Power Query may (incorrectly) treat zip codes starting with zeros as though they were whole numbers. As a result, those starting values get cut off. Why? Because a whole number cuts off the zero. In this example, the zip code should be a Text data type, not a whole number.

As you begin evaluating your data in columns, keep in mind that Power Query tries to convert any data it receives as one of the data types shown in Figure 4-6. You can keep Power Query on the right track by making sure you're using the correct data type in the first place.

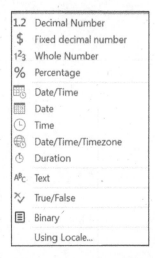

1.2	Decimal Number
$	Fixed decimal number
1²3	Whole Number
%	Percentage
	Date/Time
	Date
	Time
	Date/Time/Timezone
	Duration
ᴬᴮc	Text
	True/False
	Binary
	Using Locale...

REMEMBER

You see complex data types like functions, lists, records, and tables every so often. Keep in mind that not all data types may be available after loading data.

If you want to change the data type, you can do so by right-clicking a column header and selecting Change Type from the menu. Then select the type you want, as shown in Figure 4-7. After changing a data type once in a column, you then see a prompt asking whether you agree to change the column type and insert a step. Figure 4-8 shows an example of inserting a step.

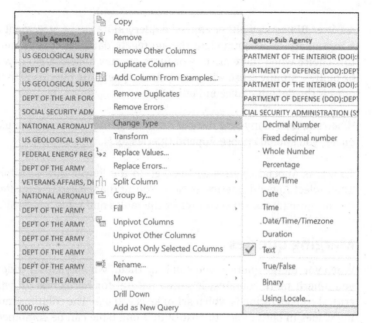

FIGURE 4-7:
Changing the
data type.

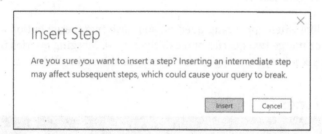

FIGURE 4-8:
Inserting a step.

Combining queries

In Power BI, you can combine queries using Power Query in one of two ways. First, you can append queries. That means you add other queries to an existing set of queries as though you're stacking the data. When you create appended queries, you often use patterns such as SQL's UNION ALL operator. On the other hand, combining queries using the merge structure is based on the supplied primary and foreign keys. You need to set up JOIN statements with Merge queries.

Appending queries

You can always make tables taller or wider. When you append, the table is taller. The reason is that your queries include the same number of columns. In some cases, the resulting tables have columns from all queries; in other instances, columns that were not present in an original query may populate in the dataset. Under these circumstances, each of the rows keeps null values.

A Power BI user can either append a query in its `as-is` statement, or it can create a new query to accommodate the aggregate data. To append queries, you make this choice when there are one or more queries to select. No new queries need to be built — simply reuse whatever exists. Appending queries without creating new ones is the default choice in Power BI.

When you take many new rows of data and string them together using the original query, you should choose Append Queries As New.

To access Append Queries as New, go to the Power Query Editor Home Ribbon. Then select Append Queries as New. You're then asked to concatenate rows from two or more tables. Once you select the tables and rows, press OK.

Merging queries

When you merge queries, you combine them, which yields a wider table. Because you inherit more columns, it's only natural for horizontal growth to occur. The critical consideration is which set of keys you use. The columns must have matching values in both tables to ensure that one table can be combined with the rows in the second table.

Much like when appending queries, you have two merge options — create a new query or merge two queries and call them new. Merging queries involves creating one of six join types using Power Query, as shown in Table 4-1.

TABLE 4-1   Join Types

Join Type	Direction
Inner	Only matching rows are visible.
Left Outer	All items in the first table appear, but only matching items from the second.
Right Outer	All items in the second table appear, but only matching items from the first.
Full Outer	All rows appear.
Left Anti	Returns all rows from the first table where a match in the second table does not exist.
Right Anti	Returns all rows from the second table where a match in the first table does not exist.

When you try to use one of these queries, you may realize that your data isn't perfect. To alleviate some of the quality concerns, Power Query supports fuzzy matching when performing merges. *Fuzzy matching* occurs when you can compare items from separate lists. A join is formed if there's a close match. You can set the matching tolerance and similarity threshold when establishing a fuzzy match. Your fuzzy matching options include those described in Table 4-2.

TABLE 4-2   **Fuzzy Matching Options**

Fuzzy Matching Option	Description
Similarity threshold	Values are from 0 to 1. When values are 0, values are said to match each other, no matter how far apart they are. With 1, you get a match only when the match is exact.
Ignore case	Treats upper- and lowercase the same.
Maximum number of matches	Limits the number of rows from the second table that matches the first, which is helpful when the result set produces multiple matches.
Match by combining text parts	Attempts to combine separate words into a single entity, looking to find matches between keys.
Transformation table	Equivalent of a to-and-from, which means there must be at least two columns.

To merge a query, follow these steps:

1. **On the Home tab of the Power Query Editor Ribbon, locate Merge Query.**

2. **Select Merge Queries, not Merge Queries As New.**

3. **Select the tables and columns you want to combine in the Merge Queries interface.**

4. **Select the key that is common to both tables.**

    Notice that the appropriate key column is highlighted.

5. **Select the type of join you want from the Join Kind drop-down list.**

6. **Click OK.**

In Figure 4-9, you can see that you're merging the Prime and Sub Awards queries. The common key selected is Obligated. The type of join kind selected is Full Outer.

Notice that a new column, Sub Awards, appears in Figure 4-10. Each row is highlighted and says Table. To view the Sub Awards data, you'd click on the Table link to drill down. When you merge two tables, you may

>> Add a new table

>> Have the table represented by hyperlinks

>> Have a double-arrow button instead of the Filter button as part of the column

   The double arrow is another filter type that allows users to search data from two or more table datasets.

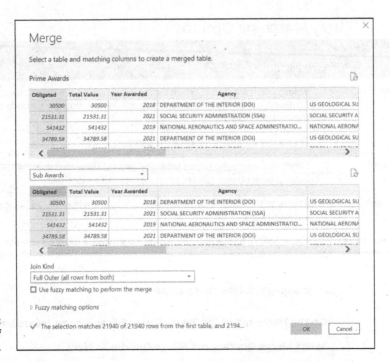

FIGURE 4-9:
An example of
merged columns.

Award Type	NAICS	Sub Awards
● Valid 100%	● Valid 100%	● Valid 100%
● Error 0%	● Error 0%	● Error 0%
● Empty 0%	● Empty 0%	● Empty 0%
PURCHASE ORDER	541511	Table
DELIVERY ORDER	541715	Table
DELIVERY ORDER	541519	Table
DELIVERY ORDER	541519	Table
DELIVERY ORDER	541519	Table
DELIVERY ORDER	541519	Table
PURCHASE ORDER	541715	Table
DELIVERY ORDER	541519	Table
DELIVERY ORDER	541611	Table
DEFINITIVE CONTRACT	541715	Table
DELIVERY ORDER	541512	Table
DEFINITIVE CONTRACT	541715	Table
PURCHASE ORDER	541715	Table
DELIVERY ORDER	541519	Table
BPA CALL	611430	Table

FIGURE 4-10:
Adding a column.

When you select any cell in the new column, a preview of the content contained in the merged table appears.

When expanding a table, you can either *expand* or *aggregate*:

>> **Expand:** Here you'd select a column from the merged table that you want to add to the current table. If the merged table has more than one matching row, the current table's row is the one duplicated.

>> **Aggregate:** If you want to combine rows without duplication in the current table, this is your best choice. Using DAX, supplying the function that's most appropriate for each column is one way to ensure that data is properly combined.

To expand a merged column using the Fiscal Awards dataset, follow these steps:

1. **In the Prime Awards query, click the double-arrow button in the newly created column.**

You see a screen that allows you to filter based on Expanded view or Aggregate view.

2. **Clear the Select All Columns check box on the Expanded Merge Columns tab.**

3. **Click to select the Agency check box and the Sub Agency check box.**

4. **Uncheck the Use Original Column Name as Prefix check box.**

5. **Click OK.**

You should now see an expanded set of columns, showing the values of both tables you just merged.

6. **Right-click the Agency Key column and select Remove Column.**

7. **Right-click the Agency.1 column and select Rename.**

8. **Rename the Agency.1 column to Agency.**

The output of what was produced after all those changes appears in Figure 4-11. There is only one Agency column and a Sub Agency column labeled Sub Agency.1

₃ NAICS		A⁸C Agency		A⁸C Sub Agency.1
● Valid	100%	● Valid	100%	● Valid
● Error	0%	● Error	0%	● Error
● Empty	0%	● Empty	0%	● Empty
	541511	DEPARTMENT OF THE INTERIOR (DOI)		US GEOLOGICAL SURVEY
	541511	DEPARTMENT OF DEFENSE (DOD)		DEPT OF THE AIR FORCE
	541715	DEPARTMENT OF THE INTERIOR (DOI)		US GEOLOGICAL SURVEY
	541715	DEPARTMENT OF DEFENSE (DOD)		DEPT OF THE AIR FORCE
	541519	SOCIAL SECURITY ADMINISTRATION (SSA)		SOCIAL SECURITY ADMINISTRATION
	541519	NATIONAL AERONAUTICS AND SPACE ADMINISTRATION (...		NATIONAL AERONAUTICS AND SPACE
	541519	DEPARTMENT OF THE INTERIOR (DOI)		US GEOLOGICAL SURVEY
	541519	DEPARTMENT OF ENERGY (DOE)		FEDERAL ENERGY REGULATORY COM
	541715	DEPARTMENT OF DEFENSE (DOD)		DEPT OF THE ARMY
	541519	DEPARTMENT OF VETERANS AFFAIRS (VA)		VETERANS AFFAIRS, DEPARTMENT OF
	541611	NATIONAL AERONAUTICS AND SPACE ADMINISTRATION (...		NATIONAL AERONAUTICS AND SPACE
	541715	DEPARTMENT OF DEFENSE (DOD)		DEPT OF THE ARMY
	541512	DEPARTMENT OF DEFENSE (DOD)		DEPT OF THE ARMY
	541715	DEPARTMENT OF DEFENSE (DOD)		DEPT OF THE ARMY
	541715	DEPARTMENT OF DEFENSE (DOD)		DEPT OF THE ARMY

FIGURE 4-11: The expanded Merged Columns example.

Configuring Queries for Data Loading

When developing a Power BI data model, users can take advantage of the fact that Microsoft gives them the ability to use Help queries. These helper tools are available by processing your model using the Get Data option and the Transform Data option. Also, when you're trying to combine files or even merge datasets, Power Query supports helper queries.

REMEMBER

Helper queries are embedded into Power BI Power Query in order to assist users in creating query strings. Rather than make the coding process complex, you can use the built-in API to simplify the most difficult parts of query development. In fact, helper queries support common terms, phrases, ranges, and geospatial functions.

Of course, you may have queries you don't need or want to load because not all data may be helpful. In this case, right-click the Queries pane and then clear the Enable Load section. When queries are already loaded, you may get errors. Otherwise, select which queries you want to omit from the load process.

One common scenario occurs when you don't want to load queries that are appended or merged with other queries. To segregate queries that should not be included, follow these steps:

1. Right-click the first query you want to omit.

2. Choose Enable Load from the menu that appears in the Queries pane.

3. Make sure each table you want to omit from the query is deselected.

4. Repeat this process for each query you don't want to load.

The result is removing unwanted entities from the data model for future querying and loading. In Figure 4-12, you can see an example of the drop-down menu to select or deselect Enable Load. Any query that's deselected isn't loaded, and it's noted by text that's italicized.

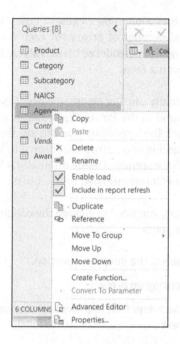

After you've modified the entities to be included in the queries, save your changes by pressing the Close & Apply button on the Ribbon's Home tab. (See Figure 4-13.)

Close & Apply

Resolving Errors During Data Import

Occasionally when you load data, you might encounter query errors in Power BI. Don't panic!

Errors come in many forms. Values alone don't cause a query to fail blatantly. Power BI lets you know the total number of errors for each query. *Error values*, or values ignored during querying, are considered blank values. Simply put, they have no text in the field — not even a zero.

To get to the bottom of what's actually causing errors in Power Query, use the View Error hyperlink, which can be found in the Power Query Editor column throwing the specified error. When you click the hyperlink, you can see the specific details related to the query. Common reasons why errors are thrown in Power Query are often linked to data conversion. For example, a value originally N/A, which is considered text, would not work in a column intended for numbers.

To correct an error such as this one, you need to change the column type. To make such a modification, follow these steps:

1. **In the Power Query Editor, select the query in question.**

2. **Right-click the column presenting an error.**

3. **Choose Change Type from the menu that appears and then change the selection from Number to Text.**

4. **Select Replace Current when the pop-up appears to validate that you want to change the column data type.**

   You have now changed the column data type from Numerical to Text. Now, alphanumeric values, not just numeric values, can be added to the column for the specific dataset. After you click the Close & Apply button for a dataset that's been corrected, the error messages disappear.

Chapter **5**

Designing and Deploying Data Models

Manipulating data after it's in Power BI is both an art and a science. Data you've imported into any application requires you to pay attention to not just your dataset but also how the data has been defined. If you learn one thing about data, you need to refine it from the get-go. That means exploiting tables, creating new hierarchies, establishing joins and relationships that make sense, and classifying the data. Of course, you want your outputs to be meaningful, so you have to pay close attention to how you arrange the data in the data model. In this chapter, you discover how to craft your data in Power BI Desktop so that you can design and deploy effective data models for visualization, reporting, and dashboards. This chapter starts out by teaching you how to design and develop a basic data model in the Power BI Desktop environment and then shows you how to publish the model to Power BI Services when you're ready for showtime.

Creating a Data Model Masterpiece

Creating visualizations requires a data model — it's just one of those things. Your data source also needs to be correct, specific, and well crafted. It's true that Power BI can do some amazing things by transforming data across multiple datasets utilizing its ETL (extract, transform, and load) framework to support development and design activity. After the data is safely in the Desktop application, though, the accessible data still needs your attention. You need to take some specific actions to prepare the data so that the model can be crafted and work as a well-oiled dataset for visualization and reporting. A well-defined dataset helps you analyze the data as well as gain prescriptive and descriptive insights.

REMEMBER

Model creation doesn't stop at data ingestion. It requires defining data types, exploiting table design, creating hierarchies, crafting joins and relationships, and classifying the data in the model.

Working with Data view and Modeling view

After importing data into the Power BI Desktop environment, your goal now is to manipulate the data so that it works the way you need it to for your models. The first stop on your journey is to explore the Data View tab and the Model View tab. The difference between the two is that the Data View tab presents all data imported into the data model. In contrast, the Model View tab is the visualization of the model based on what Power BI believes the model is at a point in time.

You are responsible for updating the model after importing the data. You can do this on either the Data View tab (by viewing all data instances) or the Model View tab (by reviewing the model itself). An example of the output on the Data View tab is shown in Figure 5-1; Figure 5-2 shows the output on the Model View tab.

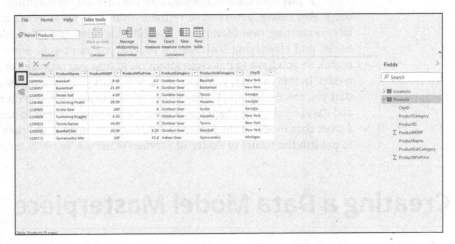

FIGURE 5-1:
The Data
View tab.

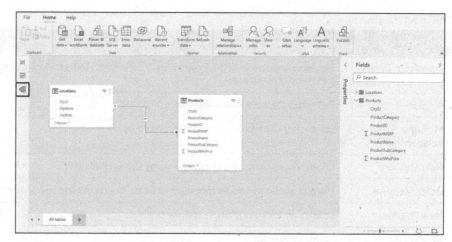

FIGURE 5-2:
The Model View tab.

The Home Ribbon for the Model view is considered the cockpit for managing many of your data actions, no matter which view you're in within the Power BI Desktop. As you can see in Figure 5-3, the Home Ribbon for the Model view is broken down into distinct areas: Data, Queries, Relationships, Calculations, Security, and Share. Each area has its own set of features, as listed in Table 5-1.

FIGURE 5-3:
The Home Ribbon in Model view.

TABLE 5-1

Buttons On the Power BI Model View Home Ribbon

Button	What It Does
Get Data	Gets data from a data source. You can choose from more than 100 data source options, both relational and nonrelational.
Excel Workbook	Gets data from an Excel file, a common Microsoft data source
Power BI Dataset	Gets data from a previously created Power BI dataset
SQL Server	Gets data from a SQL Server connection
Enter Data	Creates new tables inside Power BI
Dataverse	Connects to an environment from Power BI using a query string, including those supported by DirectQuery
Recent Sources	Allows users to access those data sources most recently created in Power BI

(continued)

TABLE 5-1 *(continued)*

Button	What It Does
Transform Data	Serves as a gateway to the Power Query Editor with tools that can be found to edit and transform datasets
Refresh	Refreshes the data in an easy way
Manage Relationships	Establishes cardinality among tables in Power BI
New Measure	Creates a new calculated measure using the Formula bar
Quick Measure	Using predefined calculations against fields, builds out the specific fields for the user
New Column	Creates a new column for a specific table
New Table	Creates a new table
Manage Roles	Determines who should be able to view specific data models
View As	Limits the dataset to specific users
Publish	Publishes the dataset to Power BI Services

The Power Query Editor shares many of the same features shown in Table 5-1, although it also has (unsurprisingly) specific features for query editing, as shown in Figure 5-4.

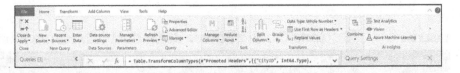

FIGURE 5-4:
The Power Query Editor Ribbon.

A noticeable difference between Model view and Power Query Editor is that Power Query Editor allows you to change the data source settings, manage parameters, configure editor parameters, configure rows and columns, group by, sort by, and handle data types. It also focuses on artificial intelligence features for text analytics. As you begin to manage the design of your datasets, you naturally want to know more about row and column management because configuring rows and columns to behave as you see fit is integral to dataset behavior. Therefore, as you probably guessed, you have a few more bells and whistles to play with under the Power Query Editor because you are manipulating queries versus model building.

Importing queries

It never hurts to practice importing one or more Excel files to establish fresh queries. Keep in mind that you can import your queries into Power BI Desktop using one of several import options. Start by using the Navigation pane on the left side of the screen to switch to Data view, where all existing tables are available. If you want to start fresh, open a new file by choosing File ⇨ New from the main menu. If, however, you want to import, follow these steps:

1. **Select the type of file or source you want to import into Power BI under Get Data.**

   Once you select your data source, the Navigator window opens, as shown in Figure 5-5.

2. **To load data, pick one or more datasets and then click the Load button.**

3. **To transform data, pick one or more datasets and then click the Transform Data button.**

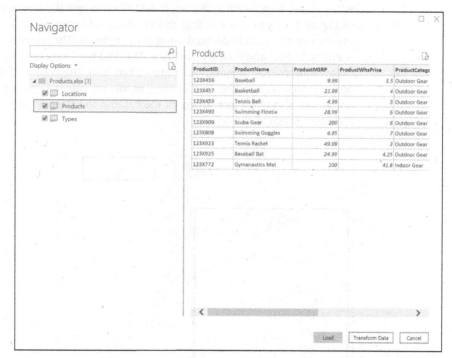

FIGURE 5-5:
The Navigator window in Data view.

REMEMBER

If you choose Load, that means the data won't be mapped to a specific data type. If you choose Transform Data, Power BI does its best to map against the proper data type based on ETL properties.

TECHNICAL STUFF

Though Data view is similar to the Power Query Editor, keep in mind that only a sample of your data is shown in the Power Query Editor, whereas all data is available in Data view after it's imported into the data model. In Data view, you're working with your entire dataset, and modifications are made live with the dashboard requirements and specifications. Both Data view and the Power Query Editor can handle the creation of calculated columns in real time, though.

After the data is loaded, you can manipulate it, add queries, add or delete columns, or manage the existing relationships between one or more tables or columns within a single table. The following sections explain in detail how to complete each of these activities.

Defining data types

When Power BI imports a dataset, it defaults to a specific data type. For example, in Figure 5-6, you can see that the Products table has several columns, two of these columns indicate decimal numbers as options. The column represented here is ProductMSRP and ProductWhsPrice. The data type may not be accurate because these columns are monetary in nature. You have the choice of decimal number or fixed decimal number. In this case, monetary values require decimal number. A user can also place formatting in the column to better represent the context of the data in each of the cells.

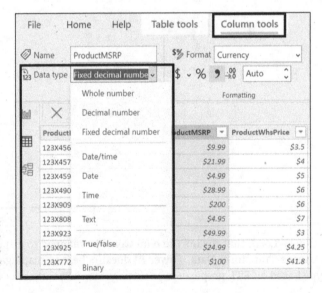

FIGURE 5-6:
Using the Column Tools tab to change the data type.

To review the data types for a given column, follow these steps.

1. **Go to Data view.**

2. **Select the column you want to review and highlight it.**

3. **Make sure you're on the Column Tools tab. (Refer to Figure 5-6).**

4. **On the Column Tools tab, check the Name property to make sure.**

5. **Check to make sure the Data Type drop-down menu (see Figure 5-7) is set to the correct data type.**

   In this case, it's set to Decimal Number.

6. **Switch the option to Fixed Decimal Number.**

7. **Using the tab's Format drop-down menu (again, see Figure 5-6), switch the option to Currency.**

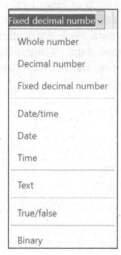

FIGURE 5-7: A list of data type options.

This process is consistent throughout Power BI for modifying data types whether you're trying to change numerical data to text or text to numeric.

Handling formatting and data type properties

Depending on whether the column is text or numeric, you can use the Format drop-down menu on the Column Tools tab to also apply specific properties to a column to ensure specific behaviors. In the preceding section, the Currency format is applied to the columns. If the column is numeric, you can also apply other behaviors, including decimal numbers, whole numbers, percentages, and scientific number formatting. (See Figure 5-8.)

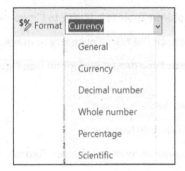

FIGURE 5-8:
Numeric
formatting
options.

Suppose you're looking to apply properties such as Measures, Geographic markers, or Mathematical Behaviors against a column. In that case, you can apply a *summarization* (a way to further evaluate data mathematically) or a data category (a way to classify geographically-based data). Summarization options for the Column Tools tab are shown in Figure 5-9, and the Data Category options are displayed in Figure 5-10.

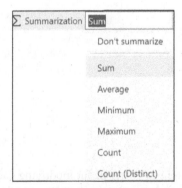

FIGURE 5-9:
The
Summarization
options on
the Column
Tools tab.

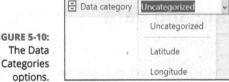

FIGURE 5-10:
The Data
Categories
options.

REMEMBER

Summarization options allow for any column of numeric data in a table to be summarized as a single value. Data Category options are applicable for Power BI mapping — latitude and longitude or degrees, in other words.

Managing tables

After you've imported a table and created a dataset, you may realize that you need to change the name of the table. Or maybe you want to delete a table. These are common actions that a data expert might perform in Power BI Desktop as they work their way through the design, development, and deployment of their data model.

Adding tables

There may be times when you need to add one or more tables to your data model after you've imported the dataset into Power BI Desktop. Perhaps you want to create an additional fact table for the transactional activity or a dimension table to support a new lookup. Both scenarios are pretty standard but, luckily, adding a table is straightforward. You'll still need to do a bit of configuration after you set the column names, though.

In any event, here's how you add a table:

1. **In Model view, click the Enter Data button on the Home tab of the Model view Ribbon, as shown in Figure 5-11.**

   The Create Table Interface appears.

2. **Enter the column names and data you want into the appropriate table cells.**

3. **Enter a table name in the Name field.**

   The table should look something like the one shown in Figure 5-12.

4. **Click Load once you are finished creating your table.**

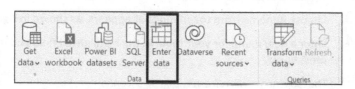

FIGURE 5-11:
The Enter
Data button.

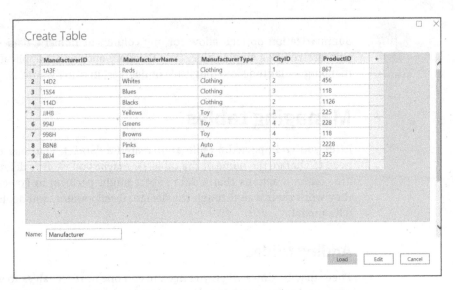

Create Table

	ManufacturerID	ManufacturerName	ManufacturerType	CityID	ProductID	+
1	1A3F	Reds	Clothing	1	867	
2	14D2	Whites	Clothing	2	456	
3	1554	Blues	Clothing	3	118	
4	114D	Blacks	Clothing	2	1126	
5	JJH8	Yellows	Toy	3	225	
6	994J	Greens	Toy	4	228	
7	998H	Browns	Toy	4	118	
8	BBN8	Pinks	Auto	2	2228	
9	88J4	Tans	Auto	3	225	
+						

Name: Manufacturer

Load   Edit   Cancel

FIGURE 5-12:
Creating a table.

The result is a brand-new table that appears as part of the data model you're able to access in Data view as well as in Model view.

Renaming tables

Renaming a table is a straightforward activity as long as no table already has the same name. With Power BI, every table in a data model must have a unique name. For example, two tables cannot have the name Product.

BEST PRACTICE

Best practices suggest that you be as descriptive as possible when naming tables within a data model. You can have a table named Product and another named Products, and although Power BI would allow you to use those names, their similarity could prove confusing for any humans working with your data model.

To rename a table in Power BI Desktop, follow these steps:

1. **In either Data view or Model view, go to the Fields pane.**

2. **Right-click the table name you want to change.**

3. **Choose Rename from the menu that appears, as shown in Figure 5-13.**

4. **Enter a new name for your table in the highlighted field and then press Enter.**

    The table name will refresh within 30 seconds.

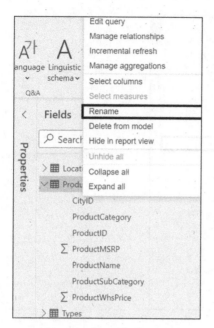

FIGURE 5-13:
Updating the
table name in
Model view.

Deleting tables

If you want to delete a table from a model, you face a few risks. If relationships are associated with the table, those relationships will break. In addition, if calculated fields are embedded within a report, those too will disappear. That said, removing a table, like moving a column, is a relatively simple process. To remove a table, follow these steps:

1. **In either Data view or Model view, go to the Fields pane.**

2. **Right-click a table to remove, and then choose Delete from Model from the menu that appears, as shown in Figure 5-14.**

   A prompt appears, asking whether you're sure you want to delete the table, as shown in Figure 5-15.

3. **Click Delete.**

   The table is deleted from the model.

Renaming and deleting columns

Renaming or deleting a column follows the same practice for renaming or deleting a table. The only caveat is that when dependencies such as key enforcements occur, deleting a column can result in potential broken relationships.

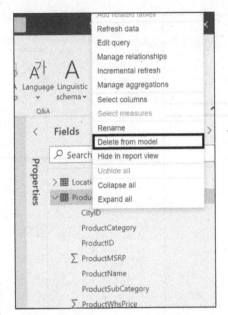

FIGURE 5-14:
Deleting a table
from the model.

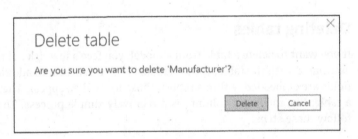

Delete table

Are you sure you want to delete 'Manufacturer'?

Delete   Cancel

FIGURE 5-15:
Asking whether
you're sure.

To rename a column, follow these steps:

1. **In either Data view or Model view, go to the Fields pane.**

2. **Right-click the column name you want to rename.**

3. **Rename the column.**

   The column name refreshes automatically.

   If relationship updates require updating, those are revised accordingly.

When the column is deleted, you'll notice that the link is broken if a relationship exists between two tables. Figure 5-16 shows Before and After views of CityID between Products and Location where the column was deleted.

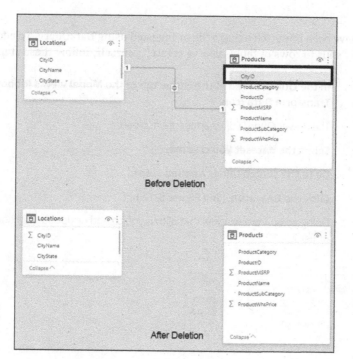

FIGURE 5-16:
Before and After
views for column
removal.

To delete a column, follow these steps:

1. **In either Data view or Model view, go to the Fields pane.**

2. **Right-click the column name, and then choose Delete from Model from
the menu that appears.**

   You're alerted that the column is about to be deleted.

3. **Press Delete.**

   The column is deleted, and the model updates automatically.

   If relationships are broken, the links between the tables are updated
   accordingly.

Adding and modifying data in tables

At times, you may want to add or modify data in an existing table. This process
is one of the less transparent ones because it requires a user to go into the Power
Query Editor to complete the action. If you've created the data within Power BI,
the process for adding or modifying is a bit more simplistic than datasets that

have been imported using a file or ingested using DataQuery. To add rows or modify cells to rows of tables you've created yourself, follow these steps:

1. **In the Queries area of the Home tab of the Model view's Ribbon, click the Transform Data icon.**

   The Power Query Editor appears onscreen.

2. **Select the dataset you created.**

3. **Go to the source under Applied Steps.**

4. **Click the Gear icon. (See Figure 5-17.)**

   Doing so opens a window that allows you to add or update additional rows or fields.

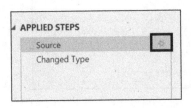

FIGURE 5-17:
The Gear icon under Applied Steps.

As you can see in Figure 5-18, the Manufacturers table has an empty field, as well as a row indicating that it should be changed.

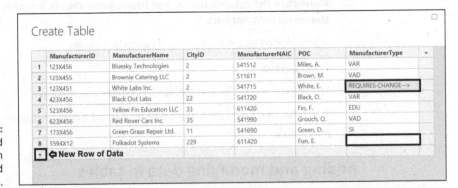

FIGURE 5-18:
The modified table with new row and changed data.

Adding and modifying data to imported, DirectQuery, and composite models

When you import or use DirectQuery and then transform the data in Power BI, your ability to add or change the data can occur only in the native data source.

There's an exception, of course: If you create custom columns or calculated columns, those are editable and managed within Power BI.

Assume that you want to make a modification to the Location table in Figure 5-19. You can add an extra three cities or states and directly change the name of one city or state in Excel. As soon as you update the file, click the Refresh icon in the Queries area of the Model view's Home Ribbon. The results are instantaneously updated, as shown in Figure 5-20.

1	1 Brooklyn	NY
2	2 Bronx	NY
3	3 Staten Island	NY
4	4 Atlanta	GA
5	5 Marietta	GA
6	6 Boise	ID
7	7 Detroit	MI

FIGURE 5-19: Before a change occurs in the Products table.

1	1 Brooklyn	NY
2	2 Bronx	NY
3	3 Staten Island	NY
4	4 Atlanta	GA
5	5 Athens	GA
6	6 Boise	ID
7	7 Detroit	MI
8	8 Chicago	IL
9	9 Denver	CO
10	10 Dallas	TX

FIGURE 5-20: Seeing the changes made in the Products table.

Managing Relationships

When two tables connect by a common bond, it often signifies that a relationship exists by way of a key. It can be a primary-primary key or a primary-foreign key relationship. In certain circumstances, a table may even be joined together in a single field. That single field can map to another table with a like-kind field, creating a lookup. This section covers the value of relationships in designing and developing the data model.

Creating automatic relationships

Power BI recognizes that when data is transformed, a relationship exists. For example, if you have two tables with a numeric data type and they're named similarly, they're considered to be in a relationship. Power BI detects these relationships as part of the ETL process. The automatic detection helps reduce the manual work that goes into identifying the relationships yourself. Also, you can reduce the risk of errors from occurring between tables.

To see how Power BI views relationships between datasets, follow these steps:

1. **Go to the Home tab of the Model view's Ribbon.**

2. **In the Relationships area, click the Manage Relationships icon.**

   Relationships that exist when the datasets are imported are automatically matched.

3. **(Optional) If you want the systems to autodetect the relationships, click the Autodetect button.**

Creating manual relationships

Sometimes the names of primary and foreign keys may not match but you know that the data between them creates a relationship. For example, LocationID and CityID might be one and the same or perhaps StateID and StateAbbreviation. All these are examples where data analysts need to manually map the relationship between two tables even though Power BI should have been able to pick up the pattern. To manually establish relationships between tables and keys, follow these steps:

1. **Go to the Home tab of the Model view's Ribbon.**

2. **In the Relationships area, click the Manage Relationships icon.**

3. **Click the New button.**

4. **The Create Relationship interface appears, as shown in Figure 5-21.**

5. **Select the two tables that are in a relationship.**

6. **Using the Cardinality and Cross-Filter Direction drop-down menus, choose the settings you want.**

7. **Press OK when you finish.**

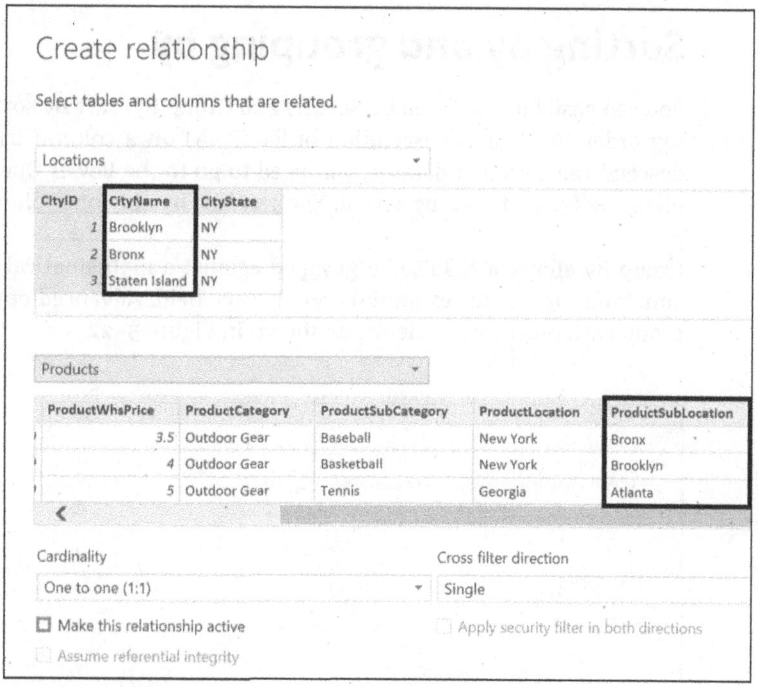

Create relationship

Select tables and columns that are related.

Locations ▼

CityID	CityName	CityState
1	Brooklyn	NY
2	Bronx	NY
3	Staten Island	NY

Products ▼

ProductWhsPrice	ProductCategory	ProductSubCategory	ProductLocation	ProductSubLocation
3.5	Outdoor Gear	Baseball	New York	Bronx
4	Outdoor Gear	Basketball	New York	Brooklyn
5	Outdoor Gear	Tennis	Georgia	Atlanta

Cardinality	Cross filter direction
One to one (1:1) ▼	Single

☐ Make this relationship active   ☐ Apply security filter in both directions

☐ Assume referential integrity

FIGURE 5-21:
The Create
Relationship
interface.

Deleting relationships

Deleting relationships occurs in one of three ways. You're either removing the field in one of the two tables that sets up the join between the two tables or using the Manage Relationships interface to disconnect the relationship the same way you created the interface. You'd uncheck the Active box. Then you'd press Delete. A warning appears, showing a break to the relationship. You'd acknowledge the relationship to be broken and then press OK.

The easiest way to break a relationship is to go to Model view and right-click the link. Choose Delete. You're prompted to acknowledge that the relationship will be broken.

Arranging Data

Arranging data in a dataset is different from what you experience when data is transformed in visualizing data. Arranging data in Power BI can be classified in a few different ways: Sort By, Group By, and Hide Data. The next few sections drill down into the specifics of each kind.

Sorting by and grouping by

You can easily be confused by Sort By and Group By. Sort By sorts data in ascending order (A–Z) and descending order (Z–A) on a column basis. To ascend or descend the data in a dataset, you need to go to the Power Query Editor to complete any form of sort-by action. You can sort by only one column at a time.

Group By allows a field to be grouped against a mathematical operation (count, sum, and means, for example) and another field. Advanced options allow you to group with one or more fields, as shown in Figure 5-22.

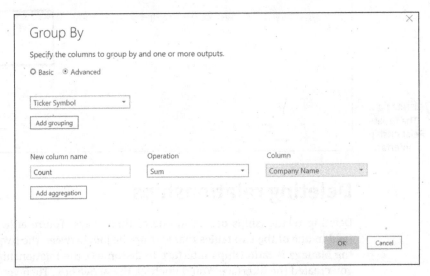

FIGURE 5-22: Grouping by capabilities.

Hiding data

At times, you may want to suppress column data from a table. Perhaps the column offers little value in the dataset when presenting results, or maybe the data adds too much complexity to the visualization. It might be that the column, when included in the dataset, actually provides inaccurate data. You might choose to hide data for any number of reasons. Hiding data, rather than deleting a column outright, ensures you can still access the data later if you need it.

To hide a column, as shown in Figure 5-23, follow these steps:

1. **In Model view, go to the table containing the column in question.**

2. **Click to select the field.**

3. **Go to the Properties pane.**

4. **Locate the Is Hidden slider.**

5. **Slide the option from No to Yes.**

   You see an eye with a line through it appear in the field, indicating that it has been hidden.

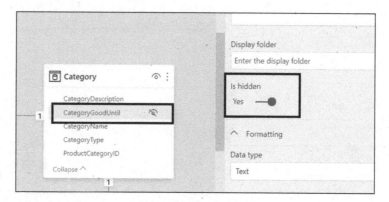

FIGURE 5-23:
Hiding data.

If at any point you want to unhide the column, simply repeat these steps, but this time slide the Is Hidden slider to No.

Publishing Data Models

When a data model is ready to be published to Power BI Services, the process is as easy as pressing a button — assuming that you've set up your online account with Microsoft's Power BI Services at https://powerbi.microsoft.com. You're asked to supply your username and the email address that logs you in to all Power Platform / Office 365 applications. Depending on the type of license you have, your model's data volume and refresh vary.

To publish your model, go to the Home Tab on the Power BI Desktop and press Publish, as shown in Figure 5-24.

FIGURE 5-24:
The Publish button for deploying the data model and reports to Power BI Services.

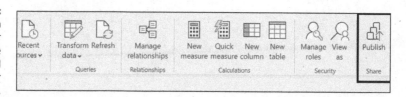

Every time you publish a new version of the data model, and for that matter, anything from Power BI Desktop to Power BI Services, you are creating a new version, hence version control is applied. To ensure consistency, make sure you use an appropriate name for the file and label each model and visualization in the Power BI Desktop output to be accurately published.

Chapter **6**

Tackling Visualization Basics in Power BI

The adage "A picture speaks a thousand words" is one of the reasons so many people use Power BI. You've imported the data, perhaps millions of records, and now you want to understand what the data says. A visualization is likely a bit easier for you or your organization to use than a large, complex dataset or a single-page report. And, of course, depending on the number of variables involved or the type of data you want to explore, having a specific type of visualization can only enhance the readability and fluency of your data experience. In this chapter, you can see how to access the visualizations and select a proper choice. To see how to configure your visualization for report creation, see Book 2, Chapter 7.

Looking at Report Fundamentals and Visualizations

There's a simple division of labor to Power BI: You use the Desktop version to create the data model and visualizations, and Services is there for you to deploy datasets, reports, and dashboards to the web. In other words, if you want to share your data, you must become familiar with Power BI Desktop as well as with the variations in Services options. That doesn't mean you can't manipulate visualizations or update them from within Services. You can, in fact, collaborate or make edits to your reports on your own. Nevertheless, the majority of your visualization manipulation occurs in Power BI Desktop, not in Power BI Services.

Creating visualizations

Assume that you have a dataset stored in Power BI Desktop, and you want to share it as a visualization. Head over to the Report tab (see Figure 6-1) by clicking the Report View tab on the left-side navigation.

FIGURE 6-1:
The Report
View icon.

At this point, you're introduced to the visualization interface, where you have the choice to drag-and-drop a visualization type from the Visualizations pane on the right side of the Visualization canvas. Figure 6-2 presents an example of Report view in Power BI Desktop, where visualization occurs.

In Report view, you can complete a number of activities associated with visualization, such as

>> Selecting a visual icon from the Visualizations pane.

>> Selecting the fields to be used in the visualization.

>> Dragging fields from the Fields pane to the canvas for visualization creation.

>> Utilizing the Ribbon to create and manage the visuals.

>> Interpreting the results of the visuals using the Q&A editor.

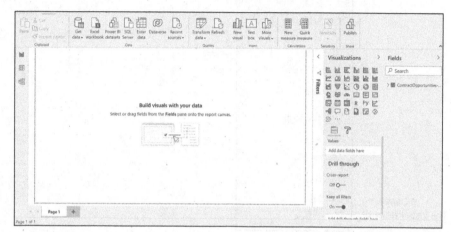

FIGURE 6-2:
Overview of
Report view in
Power BI.

To enhance one's comprehension of a report, a user can integrate text boxes, custom shapes, and images. For those looking to create multipage reports using visualizations, you have the choice to add buttons, bookmarks, and page navigation on each visualization.

Choosing a visualization

The Visualizations pane of Power BI Desktop's Report view hosts more than 20 visualization options that you can drag to the Visualization canvas. (For a description of each option, see the upcoming section, "Choosing the Best Visualization for the Job.") Each visualization requires a user to select one or more fields from the Fields pane after dragging the visual to the canvas. A user must select the check box to include the field from the Fields pane for a visual. Figure 6-3 provides an example of the Visualizations pane, and Figure 6-4 illustrates the associated Fields pane.

FIGURE 6-3:
The Visualizations
pane.

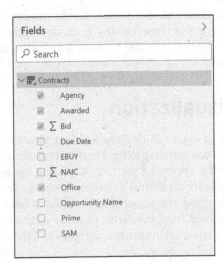

FIGURE 6-4:
The Fields pane.

TIP

Limit the number of check boxes you select, or you may create a poor visualization. Select only those variables from the Fields pane that are relevant. Use those fields that contribute to the report's specificity. Keep in mind that "The more, the merrier" isn't necessarily always the best-case scenario.

Filtering data

You will often meet the need to filter data while crafting a visualization. Every time you select a new field to incorporate into the visualization, the field appears as another value that can be filtered. Depending on the size of your dataset for a specific value, you may want to narrow the focus. For example, you've selected a value named Award as a choice. Under Award, you have five options to filter from, including Select All. Under conditions where the data is based on a category or qualitative measure, you have the choice to select which fields you prefer. (That is the case with Figure 6-5.) You'll run into instances where reducing a dataset based on a value found is always necessary. For example, if you're looking for any award data where the value is over $100,000, you'd use that as a filtering condition, as shown in Figure 6-6.

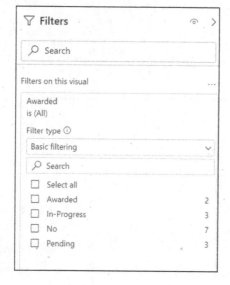

FIGURE 6-5: Filtering data based on a category.

TIP

Users can filter the data on just the specific visualization or across all visualizations by using the Filter on This Page or Filter on All Pages options within the Filter pane, as shown in Figure 6-7.

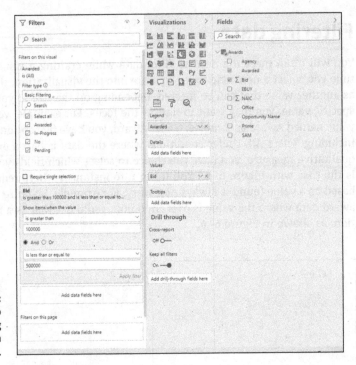

FIGURE 6-6:
Setting up
filtering
conditions with
quantitative data.

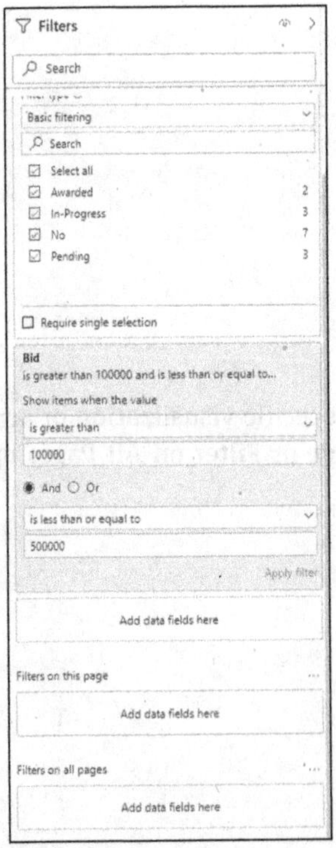

FIGURE 6-7:
The Filter on This
Page and Filter on
All Page options.

Choosing the Best Visualization for the Job

Selecting the appropriate visualization type is a critical step in creating effective and insightful Power BI reports and dashboards. When choosing a visualization, it's essential to consider the nature of your data and the story you want to convey in your presentation choices. Bar charts, Line charts, scatter plots, and treemaps are just a few examples of the diverse options available in Power BI.

BEST PRACTICE

No matter what the visualization choice, you'll want to start with a clear understanding of your audience and their needs, opting for simplicity over complexity to avoid overwhelming users. You'll then want to use color and symbolism strategically to enhance comprehension. Additionally, ensure your visualizations are interactive, allowing users to drill down into the details for a more granular view.

REMEMBER

It's crucial to maintain consistency in design across multiple reports to establish a cohesive and professional look. That means like-kind datasets should use a consistent visualization type. Regularly review and update your visualizations to keep them relevant and aligned with evolving business requirements is paramount.

Working with Bar charts and Column charts

Power BI offers several varieties of the Bar chart and Column chart. Each one allows you to summarize and compare two or more values within a focused data category. You would use a Bar chart or Column chart for comparisons because they offer a snapshot of a dataset.

Stacked Bar charts and Stacked Column charts

The Stacked Bar charts and Stacked Column charts are best used when trying to compare categories against a standard quantitative variable. The bars are proportionally displayed based on the values displayed — horizontally for Stacked Bar charts and a vertical alignment for Stacked Column charts. One axis of a chart presents a category for comparison, and the other is the focused value.

TIP

You usually begin comparing just two variables, but should you have more, Power BI supports the breakout of datasets into finer-grained details. For example, in Figure 6-8, you see a Stacked Bar chart with a single data category, Bid. A bid is then broken into segments with the value assigned to the different Award categories (No, Awarded, Pending, and In-Progress). The proportionality of the bars is the No, Awarded, Pending, and In-Progress ratio for the total bid amount (sum).

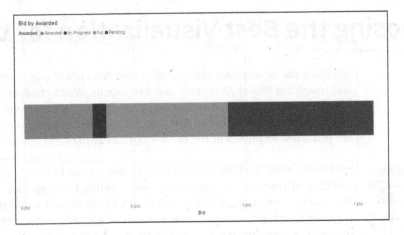

FIGURE 6-8:
A Stacked
Bar chart.

If you add a second dimension, Agency, you can see that the Stacked Bar charts are broken out even further. (See Figure 6-9.) There may be only one status with some stacked bars and several in others.

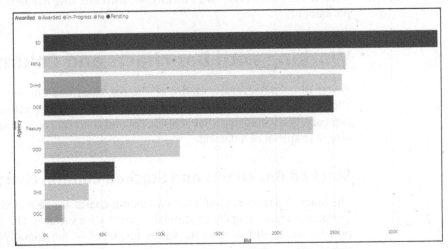

FIGURE 6-9:
Using multiple
dimensions in a
Stacked Bar chart.

A Stacked Column chart changes the direction of the data from horizontal to vertical. There is no actual difference in the summarization of data — only the visualization of the dataset. Figure 6-10 shows the same data as shown in Figure 6-8, but this time displayed vertically. The same is true for the multiple dimensions shown in Figure 6-11.

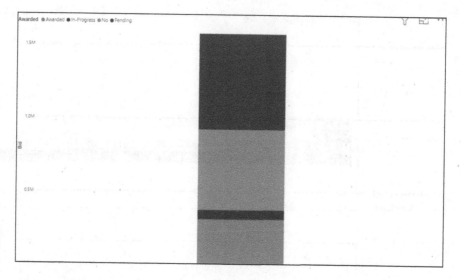

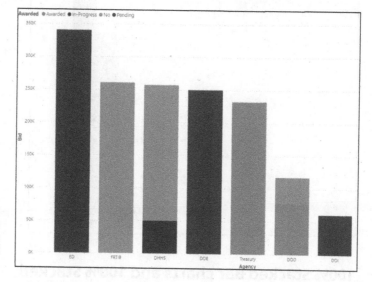

Clustered Bar charts and Clustered Column charts

Unlike Stacked Bar charts and Stacked Column charts, where the data is compressed into a single bar or column per category, the data is broken out more discretely in Clustered Bar charts and Clustered Column charts. It's easier to discern values as larger or smaller when the values are broken out in a cluster. For example, the Bid by Awarded scenario is presented in Figure 6-12 using a Clustered Bar chart and in Figure 6-13 using a Clustered Column chart. As noted by In-Progress, you notice that few opportunities are being worked on, whereas Pending has the most significant dollar volume.

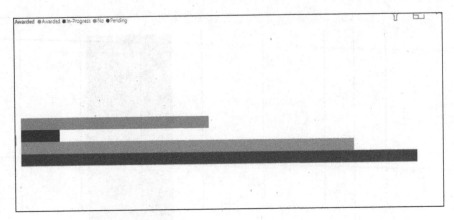

FIGURE 6-12:
A Clustered
Bar chart.

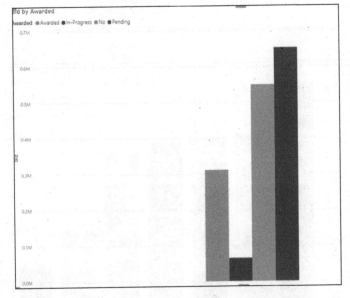

FIGURE 6-13:
A Clustered
Column chart.

100% Stacked Bar charts and 100% Stacked Column charts

When you compare multiple data series in a Stacked Bar chart, you use a 100% Stacked Bar chart or 100% Stacked Column chart. For this type of visualization, the total of each stacked bar or column always equals 100 percent. The goal of this visualization is to show how one part stands in relationship to the whole. In Figures 6-14 and 6-15, two series are being compared: Bid Role (Prime or Sub-Contractor) and Awarded Status. The left is all categories tied to being the Prime, and the right is all Sub-Contractor-related statuses.

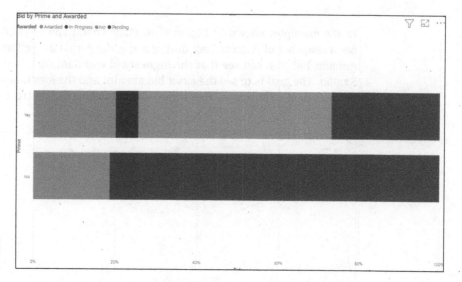

FIGURE 6-14:
A 100% Stacked
Bar chart.

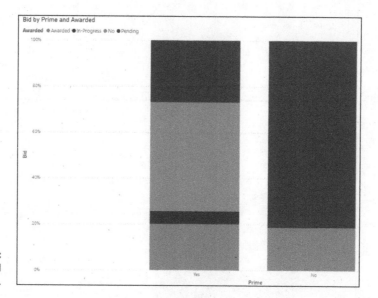

FIGURE 6-15:
A 100% Stacked
Column chart.

Using basic Line charts and Area charts

When trend analysis over a period is your goal, consider using a Line chart or an Area chart. For both chart types, you assign the x-axis a numerical value while the y-axis acts as a key measure. A Line chart connects specific data points by using a straight-line segment. The Area chart is more proper when you're looking for changes among a dataset. Though both adhere to a trend, the Area chart is filled with a particular color or texture to show data variation.

In the examples shown in Figure 6-16 (Line chart) and 6-17 (Area chart), you see a snapshot of Awards Lost during a specific period as well as the figures for Amount Bid. You can see that the highest bid was $261,000, and the lowest bid, $2,000. The goal is to see the exact bid amount and the loss rate across agencies, not necessarily the agency that awarded a bid to specific contractors.

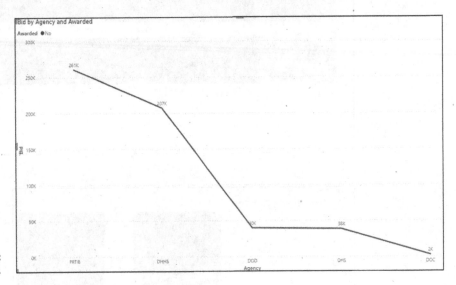

FIGURE 6-16:
A Line chart.

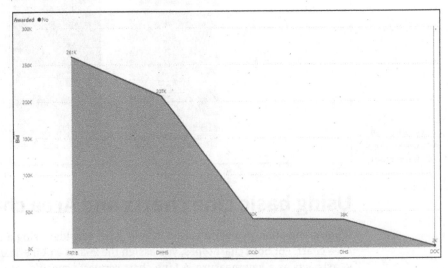

FIGURE 6-17:
An Area chart.

Combining Line charts and Bar charts

There might be times when you're trying to complete an analysis for multiple trends. When the dataset is significant, and you want to put as much information as possible into a single visualization, combining chart types is a possibility. Two choices to consider are the Line and Stacked Column chart and the Line and Clustered Column chart.

Take the example presented in Figure 6-18, which depicts a specific evaluation of the largest number of dollars obligated in three different states. That's one comparison measure. The second comparison measure is how many unique NAICS codes are associated with the dataset. Two states are associated with four NAICS codes, and one state is associated with only three. The volume of award activity, the dollar amount of that activity at the maximum obligation, and the number of distinct NAICS codes tell you that more awards were issued for the state of Maryland than for the state of Georgia.

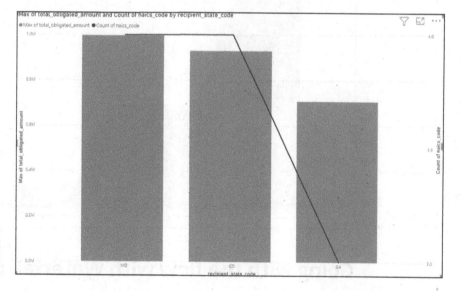

FIGURE 6-18:
A Line chart
and a Stacked
Column chart.

REMEMBER

When you're trying to create comparisons for joint charts, make sure they're relevant to one another. The data comparison shouldn't be too ambiguous because you don't want to dilute the value of your report. Also, be sure not to add too many comparison layers.

Working with Ribbon charts

Should you want to see the values in the order in which they appear as items in a legend, your best choice is to consider the Ribbon chart. A *Ribbon chart* orders items based on which item has most of its measures in a particular axis. When a category has multiple values being evaluated, each category type is represented differently.

In Figure 6-19, notice that Virginia has received the highest number of obligated dollars. In contrast, the District of Columbia has the smallest allocation. In proportion, the number of procurements associated with a given NAICS code is also visible and differentiated by different colors.

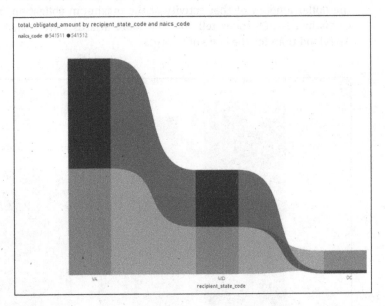

FIGURE 6-19:
A Ribbon chart.

Going with the flow with Waterfall charts

When comparing the strength or weakness of a given value from its start and understanding how the value transforms based on one or more other conditions, consider using a Waterfall chart. A classic use case for a Waterfall chart is a cost analysis or checking account balance. You have intermediate actions displayed in the chart that show positives and negatives.

In the example shown in Figure 6-20, notice that the most significant total financial obligation is attached to the state of Virginia. The difference between the two NAICS codes, 541511 and 541512, creates the gap between financial obligations to the second highest-funded state (beyond Maryland). In this case, the answer is Virginia. The negative represented shows you the difference (or it could be the *added*) funds assigned to a given NAICS code between states.

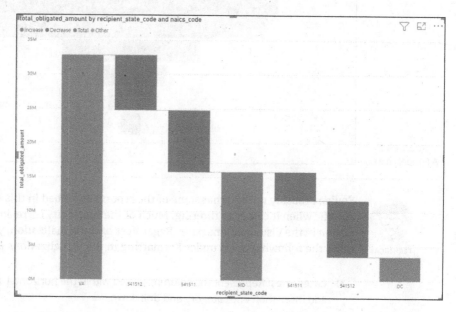

Funneling with Funnel charts

When you're looking for a way to understand linear processes, visualize sequential stages, or rationalize the weight of critical items in a dataset, a Funnel chart is the way to go. Using the Sales Funnel modeling analogy, if the pipeline included bids of various amounts, you could better understand where the bulk of the focus is placed.

In Figure 6-21, the most significant bid opportunity is, hypothetically, the Department of Education with a $340,000 bid. The smallest bid was sent to the Department of Commerce for about $16,800. The smallest amount is 4.9 percent of the overall bid forecast. In contrast, the $340,000 is the most significant bid, as represented by 100% in the funnel.

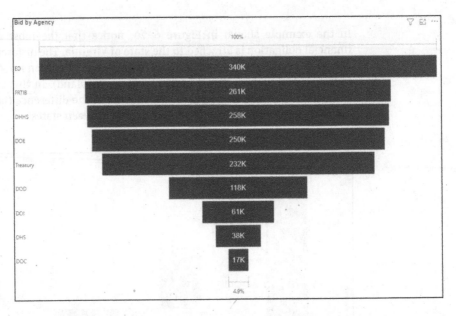

FIGURE 6-21:
A Funnel chart.

**TECHNICAL
STUFF**

You've probably noticed that some of the reports described in this chapter become specific when it comes to filtering. Much of the specificity correlates to field association in the Visualizations pane. Regardless of the visualization, you may need to tailor the following areas under Formatting in the Visualizations pane:

>> **Categories:** Represent the columns placed within the horizontal axis. You can add more than one category and drill down.

>> **Breakdown:** Allows you to show changes between categories.

>> **Values:** Designates the key numerical field that will be plotted.

>> **Tooltip:** Adds field descriptions automatically as a user hovers the mouse cursor over a bar or column in a visualization.

Scattering with Scatter charts

Suppose you have an extensive dataset where you want to find the relationship between one variable found among two axes and then decide the *correlation* — the similarity or lack thereof. In that case, a Scatter chart is a decisive choice to consider. When more cases correlate to a specific behavior, the points are tighter and more aligned, as is the case in Figure 6-22, where you can see the extreme outliers of CA, MD, and VA as well as slight outliers of OH, DC, and CO. Each of these states had a more significant proportion of funds given to IT-related services (NAICS 54151 Series) than the remaining 44 states clustered together in the lower left quadrant of the screen.

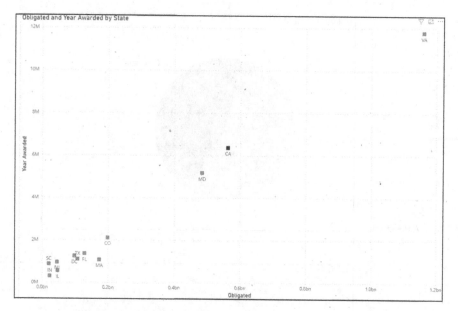

FIGURE 6-22:
Scatter chart.

Sweetening the data using Pie charts and Donut charts

Pie charts are circular graphics that break the values from an individual category into slices (or percentages). The whole piece adds up to 100 percent. The *Donut chart* is an extension of the Pie chart in that it displays categories as arcs with a big hole in the center. The values are precisely the same — it's more about aesthetic design.

In Figure 6-23 (Pie chart) and Figure 6-24 (Donut chart), you see a breakdown of the bid statuses totaling 100 percent distributed to the various award categories based on current awarded standing.

Branching out with treemaps

Weight and proportionality require that a user have a better understanding of data from a hierarchical perspective. The treemap, with its series of nested rectangles of various sizes, offers such a perspective. Corresponding to the summarization of values or frequency, more prominent representations show more activity. In contrast, smaller rectangles represent a smaller subset of data within a branch. The data volume on the left side of a treemap is always proportionally greater than that on the right, as though you're reading a book by its cover from left to right to tell a story.

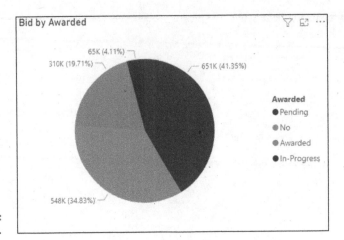

FIGURE 6-23:
A Pie chart.

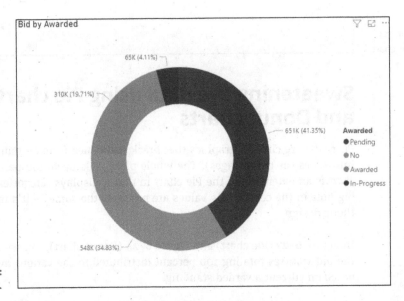

FIGURE 6-24:
A Donut chart.

In the example shown in Figure 6-25, all states where the US government supplied COVID-19-related funding for an IT project are accounted for in this diagram. The more businesses within a given state that benefited from this special allocation, the larger the square in the treemap. Using the treemap, the state of Maryland had the most IT-related COVID-19 acquisitions, followed by the state of Virginia. Four other states (CA, DC, OH, CO) had a disproportionally higher number of added IT purchases. The rest of the US states often had only one or two COVID-19-related emergency procurements.

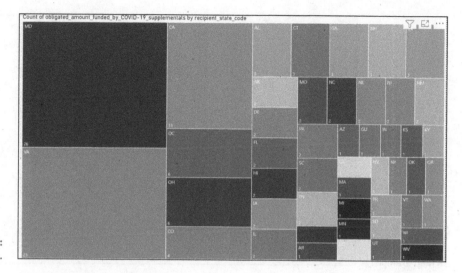
Count of obligated_amount_funded_by_COVID-19_supplementals by recipient_state_code

FIGURE 6-25:
A treemap.

Mapping with maps

If you thought Power BI didn't include geospatial analytics, think again. You're quite able to conduct various analytics evaluations using Power BI based on location, latitude, and longitude as field parameters.

You would use this kind of mapping feature when looking to understand the impact of spatial data compared to geographical distribution. Power BI can automatically zoom in to show the most proper geographical distribution for a visual. To ensure that users have an optimized user experience, they can choose between the Maps and Filled Maps options. Figure 6-26 shows the distribution of funding provided across the United States for obligated COVID-19-related IT emergency expenditures, using geographical distribution as the primary consideration.

Granularity is vital when it comes to mapping. In this particular case of geospatial specificity, the Maps example has an added filter. The parameter set is all obligations that are greater than $500,000 but less than $10 million. The Filled map in Figure 6-27 offers a precise answer to only those states given allocations within that range across the geospatial distribution.

TIP

Mapping requires precision and accuracy. You'll want to geocode as many fields as possible by selecting in the Fields pane the data category that can provide as much laser focus as possible.

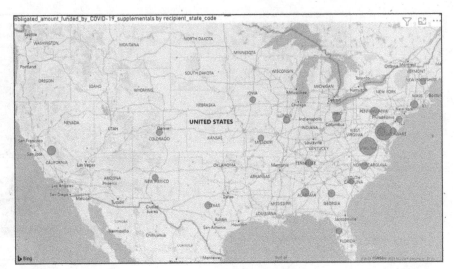

FIGURE 6-26:
A Map example.

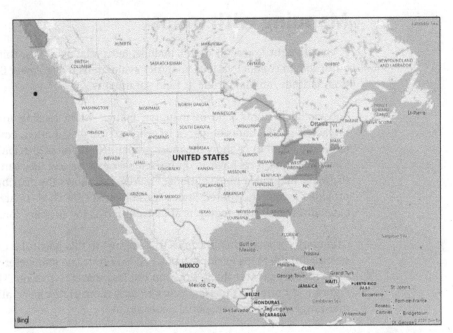

FIGURE 6-27:
A Filled Map
example.

Indicating with indicators

Whenever you're trying to measure the effectiveness of a business goal, you want to compare one or more like-kind measures. Indicators available in Power BI allow a user to be focused on measuring the value their business provides against one or more variables. Several types of critical performance indicator visualizations are available.

Gauges

When you think of key performance indicators (KPI), a gauge is often used as a quick way to display a data point comparing a value to a target range. For example, you're tracking budget financials.

BEST PRACTICE

If you want to be assured that they're in line with your range, you can use a *gauge* — a pictorial representation of how close you are to meeting your target.

In Figure 6-28, the total fiscal year 2021 Budget for Small Businesses with awards under a million dollars distributed was $784.81M. Of that amount, $741.07M was already distributed. The gray area shows that the overall fiscal picture is on track because the gauge doesn't show an overage.

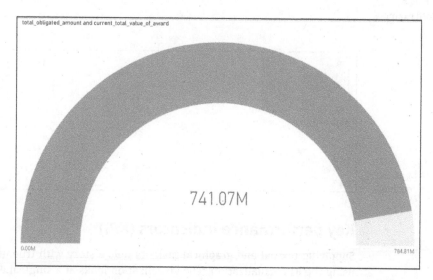

total_obligated_amount and current_total_value_of_award

741.07M

0.00M   784.81M

FIGURE 6-28: Using a gauge.

Cards and multi-cards

Suppose you're looking for a single number to help you address a specific statistic. In that case, the Card indicator can help you track your data. Examples of card uses are total sales, market share, or, as shown in Figure 6-29, the number of contracts awarded.

BEST PRACTICE

When assessing multiple indicators in a single card, you need to add each of those values to the visualization, creating a multi-card indicator. Each field is a new indicator within a card. In Figure 6-30, three indicators are listed as an example of fiscal year spending. The first indicator is the state, the second indicator is the obligated amount, and the third is the total obligated amount.

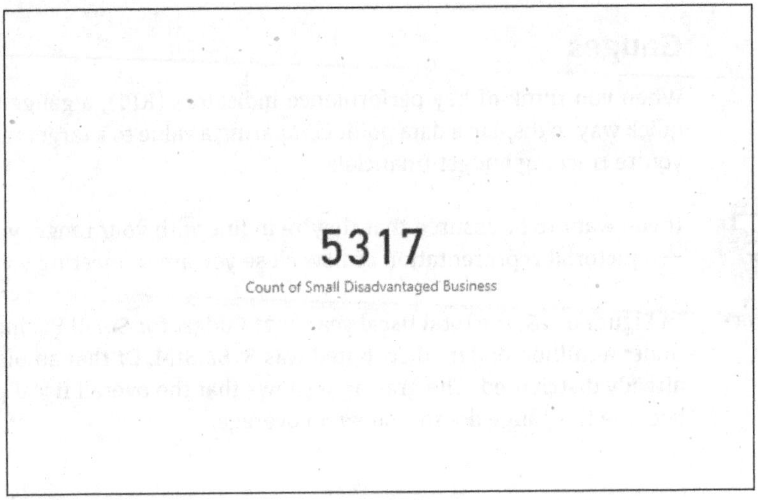

5317

Count of Small Disadvantaged Business

FIGURE 6-29:
A Card example.

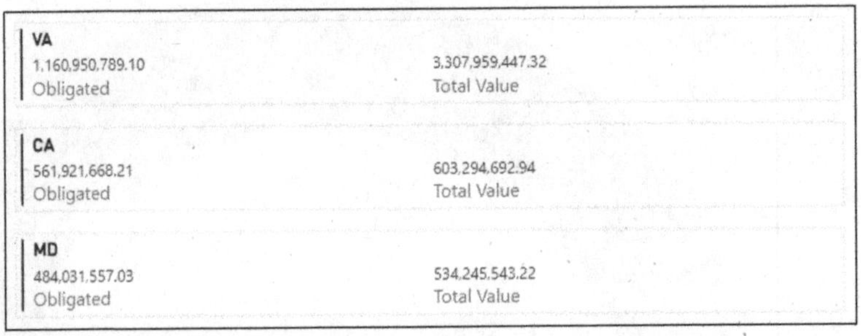

VA	
1,160,950,789.10	3,307,959,447.32
Obligated	Total Value
CA	
561,921,668.21	603,294,692.94
Obligated	Total Value
MD	
484,031,557.03	534,245,543.22
Obligated	Total Value

FIGURE 6-30:
A Multi-card
example.

Key performance indicators (KPI)

Supplying textual and graphical insights tells a story with true impact. Consider using the KPI visualization: The visualization looks at a single measure, evaluating the current value and status against a defined target. You need a base measure that's numerical — a target measure or a value — as well as a threshold goal. The output for a KPI can be both textual and visual, based on the type of trend you're looking to output. With Figure 6-31, using a subset of data in Fiscal Year 2021 that has been filtered, the data in this use case shows that the average highly compensated individuals doing business who have won at least one contract with the US federal government during FY21 earned an average of $1.382 million. The compensation trend is visible in the background with many firms paying their executives around $100,000 with fewer paying $1.5+ million compensation packages on the right side.

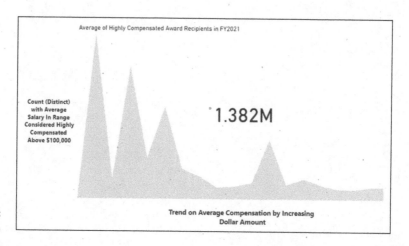

Average of Highly Compensated Award Recipients in FY2021

Count (Distinct) with Average Salary In Range Considered Highly Compensated Above $100,000

1.382M

Trend on Average Compensation by Increasing Dollar Amount

FIGURE 6-31:
A KPI example.

With many indicators, you can only assign a single value. You need to adjust the data category parameters to precisely calculate the output, whether you're looking for average, sum, distinct (single instances), or another measure.

Use the Card visual only if there's a single value to display. If you need to compare a value against more than one target, use the KPI visual — it offers users the ability to add trends in the background. Though it has limited information, the data is nonetheless focused. The multi-card choice can fulfill the business requirement for those looking to put together unrelated metrics on a single page.

Chapter 7

Digging into Complex Visualization and Table Data

Think of each visualization you can create using Power BI as offering a different set of insights for a dataset. Visualizations can also be stand-alone or combined with many other visuals. Either way, the output of a visualization is an end-state deliverable: a report. Though it's not uncommon for a report to include a single visualization, having many visualizations can offer tremendous perspective to an organization. Depending on the user's role, the report can also take on many different lives. Some users may be the report's designer, and others may be the consumer of report data.

This chapter covers how to configure visuals and report settings for end user consumption using Power BI Desktop and Power BI Services. You also see how Microsoft uses AI tools to enhance Power BI's Q&A feature. Finally, you see how to use dashboarding to allow for real-time monitoring of data trends.

Dealing with Table-Based and Complex Visualizations

Sometimes you need a bit more insight than a single graphical representation to tell your story. You may even want to manipulate the dataset or perform sorting activity on a subset of data based on a defined condition. What you want are table-based visualizations, and Power BI is ready to help, with visualization options ranging from slicers to tables to matrices. At other times, you may want to drill down into a many-layered dataset using decomposition trees or key influencers. With each choice, you can manipulate an extensive dataset with the help of Power BI's filtering features.

Zeroing in with slicers

Suppose you want to create a visual drill-down filter on a canvas so the user can sort and filter a report full of data relevant to their needs. In that case, a *slicer* — a dashboard-style tool integrated directly into the report, letting users select values as they analyze the data — may be just what you need. An example of a slicer can be found in Figure 7-1.

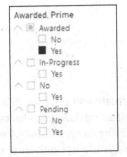

FIGURE 7-1:
A slicer example.

Tabling with table visualizations

You might scratch your head and wonder why you shouldn't just go to the dataset if you want to look at data in a table format. The reason you might want to use a table visualization versus a plain view of the table has to do with sorting and searching. Visualizations can give you a glimpse of the world. Still, a table is handy for displaying precise numerical data and summarized information found in rows and columns. When a table is enabled for sorting and filtering, the end user can better understand what the values behind the graphics mean.

Check out Figure 7-2, which uses sorting and filtering to show which unique company entities (DUNS) were awarded contracts under $1 million for three NAICS codes (541511, 541512, 541519).

State	Count of DUNS Number
VA	223
MD	117
CA	68
FL	37
CO	25
TX	25
NY	23
PA	20
DC	19
GA	18
MA	18
OH	18
NJ	17
IL	15
WA	15
MO	14
NC	14
AZ	12
AL	9
MI	9
OR	9
CT	8
AK	7
NM	7
KS	6
WI	6
HI	5
IN	5
MN	5
OK	5
Total	817

FIGURE 7-2: Table visualization.

Combing through data with matrices

Assume for a moment that you're looking to aggregate data across one or more datasets. Perhaps you need to drill down into the data cross-section to find the needle in the haystack. Your best choice for mixing and matching aggregate data to cross-highlight elements requiring attention is using the Matrix visual. You can select many rows and columns and even drop down to the cellular level to highlight data. In Figure 7-3, you see a cross-section of the contract award status for the fictitious company Data Power, highlighting awarded amounts, pending amounts, in-progress amounts, and lost awards across several federal agencies.

Awarded	DHHS	DHS	DOC	DOD	DOE	DOI	ED	Treasury	Total
Awarded				78,000.00				232,254.00	310,254.00
In-Progress	50,000.00		14,683.20	0.00					64,683.20
No	207,252.45	38,248.10	2,110.24	39,567.00					287,177.79
Pending					250,000.00	60,898.25	340,000.00		650,898.25
Total	257,252.45	38,248.10	16,793.44	117,567.00	250,000.00	60,898.25	340,000.00	232,254.00	1,313,013.24

FIGURE 7-3: A Matrix example.

Decomposing with decomposition trees

When you think of an organization chart, you likely envision a chart that displays leadership to the worker bee. A *decomposition tree* is a type of chart that allows you to visualize data across multiple dimensions. Looking at the top value as an aggregate, you can then drill down into a dataset to a more finite scope. As is the case with Figure 7-4, the decomposition tree shows total obligations for all small businesses awarded contracts under $1 million in a fiscal year (total obligation). The decomposition is the amount distributed per state (aggregate) across all contracts awarded.

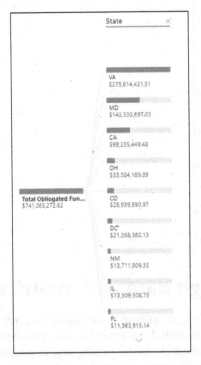

FIGURE 7-4:
A decomposition tree.

Zooming in on key influencers

Ever wonder what the data driver is within a graphic? Or perhaps you're looking to measure performance respective of one or more measures in use based on some form of rank system. Now, it's realistic to understand that not everything ranks as triggering an explicit condition. At other times, you see clear visuals pointing to a scenario where you should pay close attention. Examples of datasets that act as red flags are signs of unusual drops in sales volume or a significant reduction in another specific metric. Another extreme is an outlier that stands out like a sore thumb. Key influencers use the Microsoft AI engine, supported by Azure, to illustrate impacting metrics at speed and scale. If an influencer is designated an identifier, the user can complete various forms of analysis, including segment analysis. As shown in Figure 7-5, a few US states have a huge government contracting presence based on award volume and dollars obligated relative to others.

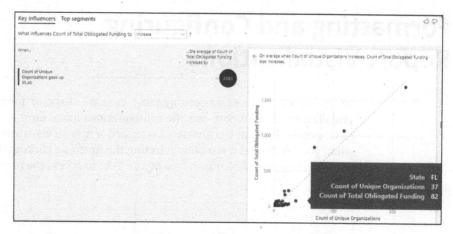

FIGURE 7-5:
Working with key influencers.

Using AI Tools to Create Questions and Answers

It should come as no surprise that Microsoft has integrated its powerful artificial intelligence and machine learning tools inside of Power BI to help users ask questions and provide answers about their data. Microsoft's artificial intelligence engine decides questions for the Q&A feature based on data volume, quality, and attribution. Looking for trends and relationships, Power BI offers users two options: Access prebuilt what-if question scenarios already conceived by the application, or ask the application pointed questions. In Figure 7-6, you can see potential questions crafted based on the finite number of fields associated with a given report. Or, you can come up with your own question, as shown in Figure 7-7.

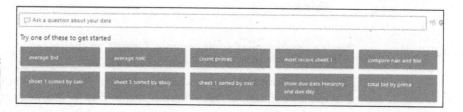

FIGURE 7-6:
Prescribed questions and answers.

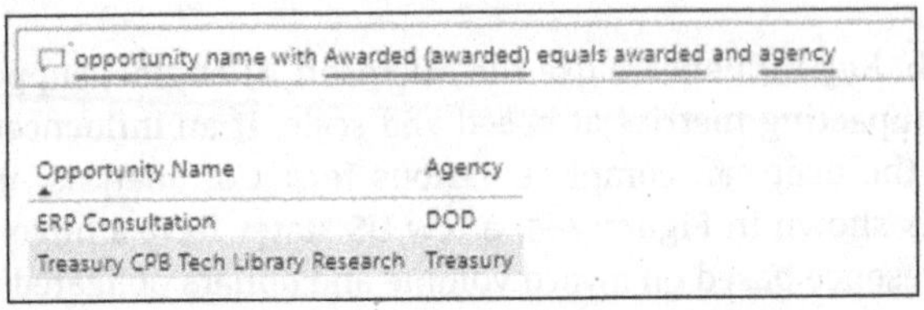

FIGURE 7-7:
Self-created
questions and
answers.

Formatting and Configuring Report Visualizations

All visuals in Power BI are configurable in some shape or form. Though some visualizations have report-specific configurations based on their predefined criteria, many items can be considered standard across all visualizations. No matter what, you can format a visual by selecting the item and clicking the Visualization pane's handy Paint Roller icon (see Figure 7-8) to access the formatting tools.

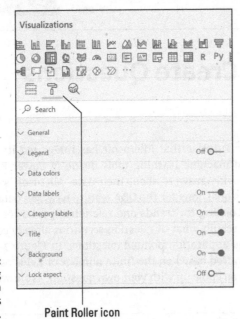

FIGURE 7-8:
Formatting
features found in
the Visualizations
pane.

Paint Roller icon

Here's a description of some common formatting choices:

>> **General formatting:** Here's where you can select the *x*-position, *y*-position, width, height, and *alt text* — the description used for accessibility options.

>> **Title:** Format the title text, text and word wrapping, color (font and background), and text features (alignment, font size, and font face).

>> **Background:** Set the page and visualization background.

>> **Lock aspect:** Lock a visual element based on the proportion of the specific object on the canvas.

>> **Borders:** Format the border colors and radii of your visuals.

>> **Shadow:** Set the shadow color and position.

>> **Tooltips:** Format any default or report-specific tooltips (descriptors).

>> **Headers:** Hide or show headers based on conditions.

REMEMBER

Many other options are available, depending on the visualization. The preceding list covers only the ones you see across all visualizations.

Applying conditional formatting

You may notice an icon on certain formatting areas within the Visualization pane that includes the *fx* symbol. You should be aware that you can customize one or more aspects of the visualization experience whenever you see this. An example of this button can be found under the Data Labels heading, as shown in Figure 7-9.

FIGURE 7-9:
The Conditional
Formatting
button.

A configuration screen appears whenever you press the *fx* symbol, allowing users to configure one or more sides of the user experience under certain conditions. (See Figure 7-10.) For example, for Data Labels, a user can format by color scale, rules, or field value. Upon selecting the preferred choice, you have the option to select the condition based on options including Field, Summarization, Minimum, and Maximum. Of course, there is a Default formatting parameter that is considered the user baseline.

Configuring the report page

Formatting a report page isn't much different from formatting a visual element, except that a report may have multiple visuals. To handle, go straight to the

Visualizations panel. Once there, click the Paint Roller icon. On the screen that appears, you see many options to change the layout and design of your report page, as shown in Figure 7-11. Most of your options focus on positioning, alignment, and color of the overall report experience.

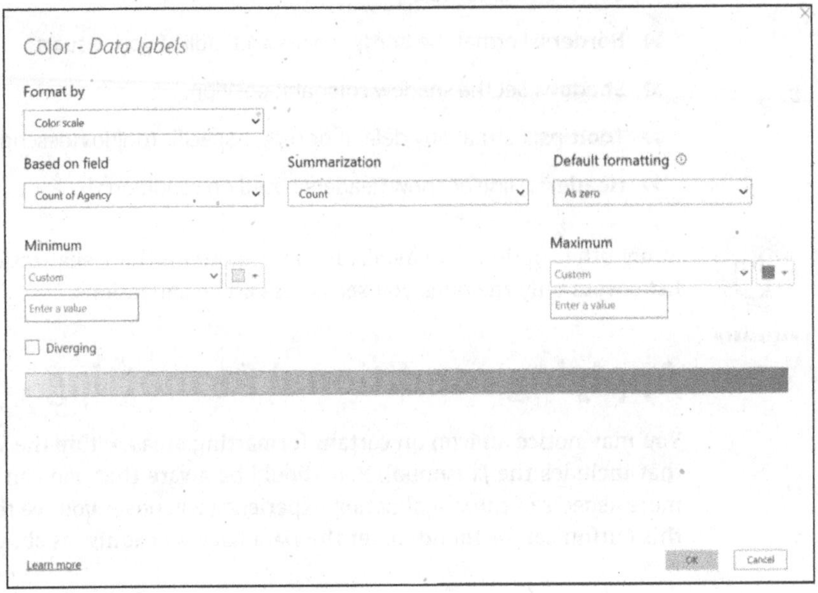

FIGURE 7-10:
The Conditional
Formatting
interface.

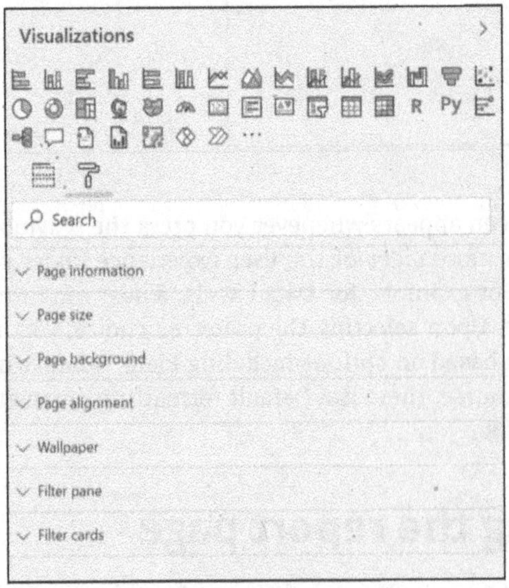

FIGURE 7-11:
Configuring a
report page.

A user can format the following page-related features:

>> **Page information:** Modify the report's name, turn tooltips on and off, and enable Q&A across an entire page, not just a specific visual.

>> **Page size:** Pick the size factor and/or paper type. Depending on how you want to deploy the report, paper sizes and interface options are available.

>> **Page background:** Configure the background color of the report page.

>> **Page alignment:** Decide whether to make the content of their reports flush-left top or flush-left center on a page.

>> **Wallpaper:** Brand a report with specific colors or perhaps a logo to take advantage of the Wallpaper option.

>> **Filter pane:** To change the Filter pane, an integral part of online-based report viewing, a user can configure the user experience to match the paper-style interface with color, transparency, borders, and specific text.

>> **Filter cards:** Like the Filter pane, Filter cards are specific to a given field (a column found in a table, for example). They let a user highlight one or more objects in a report using various aesthetic tools.

REMEMBER

The best way to ensure consistency when it comes to report formatting is to create a page once and duplicate the page configuration multiple times. That saves you the wasted effort of re-creating the wheel several times over.

Exporting reports

Suppose you don't want to save the report you've created to Power BI Services. Your singular aim is to print a snapshot in time, thereby saving the data to a PDF file. That is entirely possible using Power BI Desktop. To export a report without saving to Power BI Services, follow these steps:

1. Choose File ⇨ Export from the main menu.

2. Choose Export from the menu that appears.

3. Save the file either as a Power BI template by providing a description and pressing OK or selecting PDF file, which automatically generates an Adobe Acrobat PDF to your Web browser, as shown in Figure 7-12.

   The export is saved to the desktop.

FIGURE 7-12:
Your export
choices.

A user who selects the Power BI template option gets the equivalent of a Zip file. A Power BI template is based on an existing desktop report template. It has report layout, report pages and visuals, schema, relationships, measures, datasets, and prebuilt data models. Also, part of a definition file may include queries and query parameters. The PDF file, on the other hand, has only static copies of the visualizations accumulated across all tabs.

Perfecting reports for distribution

Yes, you can create a report in Power BI Desktop and export the output as a PDF or print it.

**BEST
PRACTICE**

If your report has many columns, optimize the report for the screen as printing or saving the output into PDF will not yield an optimal output. On the other hand, if there are a contained number of columns, generally 6 – 8 maximum, aim for creating a Paginated Report. The Paginated Report is optimized for print-based output.

But, generally, the real purpose of reporting is to share the data online using either the Power BI service or a mobile app. Microsoft has made it relatively easy for a designer to create rich reports that can fit on either a computer screen or a mobile device. The company has recognized that not everything can fit on one page either — hence, the use of tab management.

Sometimes it makes complete sense to keep any reporting local to the desktop. An example is sales performance forecasting or human resource management distribution. Suppose your goal is to distribute by print or deliver a digital document without an Internet connection. In that case, you should consider creating a paginated report.

BEST PRACTICE

Exporting report visuals to a PDF just doesn't cut it sometimes! That's why you want to use the Power BI Report Builder, an extension found at `www.microsoft.com/en-us/download/details.aspx?id=58158`.

You can use almost any data source you'd expect to find with Power BI Reports on your desktop. In fact, you can even use Power BI Services data if you decide to create one in the application.

Follow these steps to create a Power BI data-based paginated report using Power BI Services:

1. **Go to My Workspace and then find the workspace containing the data you'd like to use for a paginated report.**

2. **Open the workspace.**

3. **Click the workspace's New button and choose Paginated Report from the menu that appears, as shown in Figure 7-13.**

   If this is your first time using Power BI Report Builder, you're asked to download the application. Otherwise, the application launches Power BI Desktop along with the Report Builder.

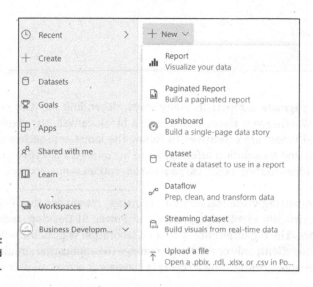

FIGURE 7-13:
The Paginated Report menu.

Digging into Complex
Visualization and Table Data

After the Report Builder launches, you're prompted to create a report using the wizard or a blank report, as shown in Figure 7-14.

4. **Choose Blank Report.**

5. **Using the pane on the left, connect your data sources to the Report Builder so that you can begin to create a paginated report.**

   Notice the blank canvas with some typed-in text, as shown in Figure 7-15.

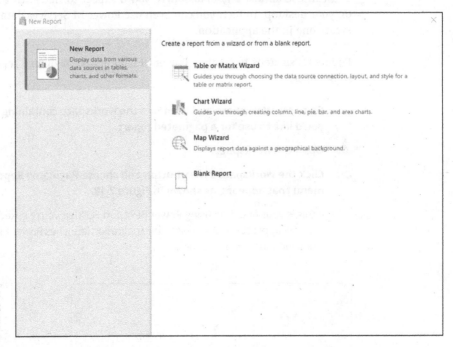

FIGURE 7-14:
The Report
Builder Wizard
screen.

TECHNICAL STUFF

You can paginate a report in many ways, depending on your choice using the wizard. Whether you select a matrix or a blank canvas, the steps to configure a paginated report are extensive. To follow the latest approaches as suggested by Microsoft and its solution offering, go to https://docs.microsoft.com/en-us/power-bi/paginated-reports/paginated-reports-quickstart-aw.

REMEMBER

When formatting visualizations for reporting, remember that Power BI Services offers a virtually identical experience to Power BI Desktop, including the user experience. The big difference is that collaboration is possible online while using the Desktop client; only one user can manage the application simultaneously. What you know about configuring a report is consistent across all user experiences.

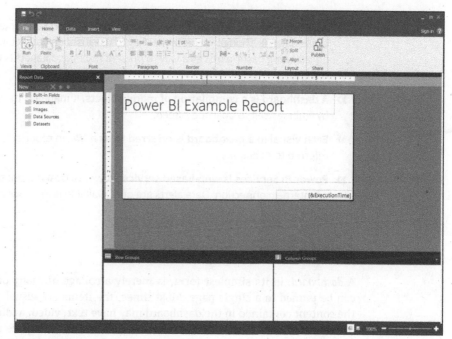

FIGURE 7-15:
The Report
Builder interface.

Diving into Dashboards

Picture this: a mixture of pictures and text neatly organized like a beautiful canvas. It tells you that everything in your organization is running smoothly, but then one of the visuals changes. Alarm bells go off — figurative ones, at least — causing many phones to ring and SMS messages to be sent. And the person responding to the emergency doesn't have to dig too deep, either. Why, might you wonder? Because the organization has collected a series of datasets available in the form of a single user experience, not a collection of ad hoc reports. The datasets on a single canvas all give real-time access to the current state of operations. The dashboard may appear to be a big mush of data, but it's meaningful data presented in a way that those who have mastered the intricacies of the dashboard can immediately see what's wrong. This section introduces you to the mysteries of dashboarding using Power BI Services.

Before your initiation into the mysteries, here are a few critical principles regarding dashboarding with Power BI:

>> **You can only create a dashboard using Power BI Services.** In fact, to truly experience the full breadth of dashboarding, you need to have a Pro or Premium license.

- » **A dashboard is meant to fill a business void.** A report can contain only a single dataset. Though it's perfectly okay to use just one dataset in a dashboard, using dashboards as a way to present multiple datasets is far more common.

- » **A dashboard is a compilation of many objects.** It manages that compilation by limiting itself to only one screen.

- » **Each visual in a dashboard is referred to as a *tile*.** In reports, visuals are referred to as *outputs*.

- » **Power BI Services is web-based service.** Power BI Desktop doesn't require an Internet connection. Data alerts are only available using Power BI Services.

Configuring dashboards

A *dashboard*, in its simplest form, is merely a collage of many data objects that can be pinned to a single page. Most times, the items are visual; at other times, the content contained in the dashboard may have text, video, audio, or navigation to other dashboards and data sources. Dashboards can integrate resources using reports, Excel workbooks, insights, Q&A results, and multimedia across content providers.

Creating a new dashboard

If you're logged into Power BI Services, you should ensure that you have a dataset and some visuals that can be placed on a dashboard. If you've never created a dashboard, follow these steps:

1. In Power BI Services, go to My Workspaces.

2. Click New at the top of My Workspaces.

3. Choose Dashboard from the menu that appears, as shown in Figure 7-16.

4. Enter the name of the new dashboard (see Figure 7-17) and then click Create.

   A blank canvas is set up for you, as shown in Figure 7-18.

FIGURE 7-16:
Creating a
dashboard.

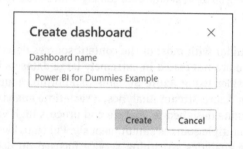

FIGURE 7-17:
Naming a new
dashboard.

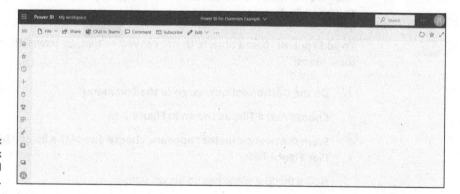

FIGURE 7-18:
A blank
Dashboard
canvas.

Digging into Complex
Visualization and Table Data

Enriching your dashboard with content

You need to keep a couple of points in mind when trying to integrate an object on your Dashboard canvas. The first thing to consider is what type of objects are needed to accentuate a planned report compilation on a dashboard. The second has to do with the layout and number of objects you intend to pin to the canvas.

At this point, you can add a few different items beyond the reports proper:

>> **Web content:** HTML-based web content

>> **Images:** Publicly accessible images exclusively

>> **Text boxes:** Static text that can be formatted

>> **Video:** Videos that can be embedded either on YouTube or Vimeo

>> **Custom streaming data:** Real-time data coming from an API, Azure Stream, or PubNub source

TECHNICAL
STUFF

You are probably familiar with most of the content sources described in the preceding list, but if you are interested in extremely large datasets being presented in a dashboard, consider using Azure Streams or PubNub. Azure Stream is the abbreviated name for Azure Stream Analytics, a real-time analytics and complex event-processing engine designed to analyze and process high volumes of (usually live) data from multiple sources simultaneously. PubNub, like Azure Streams, is another real-time analytics streaming service focused on delivering content using a real-time publish/subscribe messaging process, primarily for Internet of Things (IoT) devices.

To add content-based objects to the canvas — *tiles*, in Power BI-speak — follow these steps:

1. **On the Dashboard canvas, go to the Edit menu.**

2. **Choose Add a Tile, as shown in Figure 7-19.**

3. **From the new menu that appears, choose one of the listed object types. (See Figure 7-20.)**

   Notice that the menu has no Report option.

WARNING

All the content you place on a dashboard must be publicly accessible. Even if authentication or uploading is necessary for a user to view the data, Power BI doesn't presently support such features.

FIGURE 7-19:
Accessing the Add
a Tile menu.

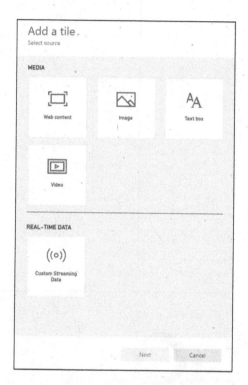

FIGURE 7-20:
Selecting a
tile type.

4. **After choosing an option, use the option's customizing features to place your content the way you want it.**

   For example, if you were to choose the Text Box option, a new screen would appear (see Figure 7-21), where you could add titles, subtitles, and text. You could even tweak whatever you've added by using any of the displayed formatting commands. When you finish, click Apply. Any changes you've made show up on your dashboard, as shown in Figure 7-22.

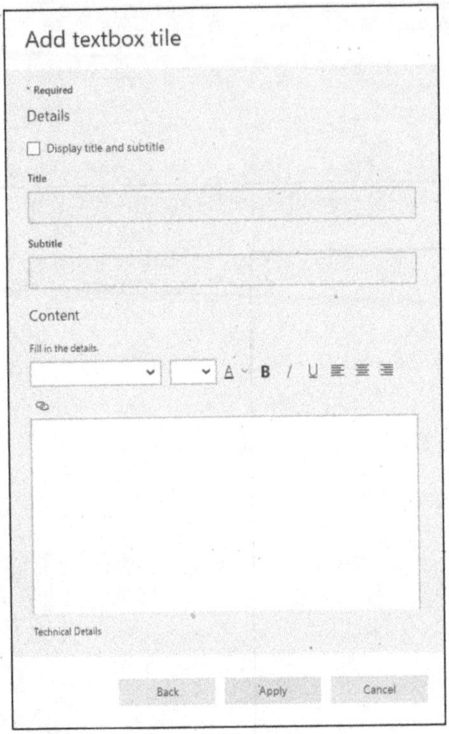

Add textbox tile

* Required

Details

☐ Display title and subtitle

Title

[   ]

Subtitle

[   ]

Content

Fill in the details.

[▼] [▼] A ▼ B *I* U̲ ≡ ≡ ≡

👁

[   ]

Technical Details

[Back]   [Apply]   [Cancel]

FIGURE 7-21:
Configuring a tile.

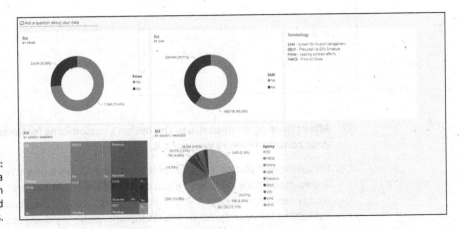

FIGURE 7-22:
Customizing a
content tile on
the Dashboard
canvas.

Once the tile is on the Dashboard canvas, you can move it anywhere you want. By default, it sits flush-left top unless other tiles are in the region. In the earlier example, the tile was moved to the upper right corner so that other tiles can be added later.

Pinning reports

Because you create visualization reports inside Power BI, creating a report Visualization tile is a slightly different process from other content additions. Basically, you pin the existing report visualization to the dashboard rather than create a new tile — the asset is already stored in Power BI, so you don't have to "create" anything. To pin a report visualization, follow these steps:

1. **Go to a workspace that contains a report, including one or more visualizations you'd like to include in a dashboard.**

2. **Locate the Pin icon in the Visual header. (See Figure 7-23.)**

3. **On the new screen that appears, click a radio button to specify whether the visualization will be part of a new dashboard or added to an existing dashboard. (See Figure 7-24.)**

   You'll add the visualization to an existing dashboard, so you should choose that option. You then use the drop-down menu to select the dashboard you want.

4. **After making your selections, click Pin.**

FIGURE 7-23: The Pin icon.

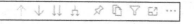

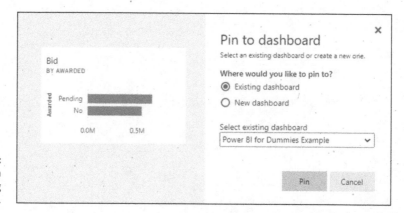

FIGURE 7-24: Opting for a new or existing dashboard.

Repeat Steps 1–4 for as many visualizations as you want to include on your dashboard. The result is a dashboard like the one you see in Figure 7-25.

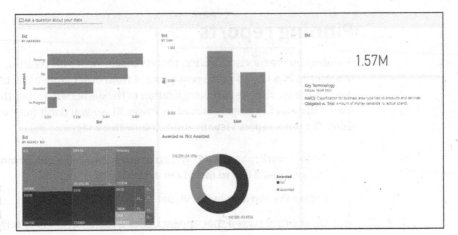

FIGURE 7-25:
A finished
dashboard
with tiles.

REMEMBER

Pinned visualizations aren't interactive. Updates are visible only after you refresh the dataset from which the visualization was derived. If you're looking for real-time data, you use the Custom Streaming Data tile.

Chapter **8**

Sharing and Collaborating with Power BI

After experiencing the entire data lifecycle across data sources, building visualizations, learning the purpose of DAX, and publishing reports, your next step is to share the data from your desktop with everyone who is a stakeholder in your business. To do that, you have to switch gears and move to the web because you're unlikely to want users mangling your Power BI Desktop data. Instead, they should be using Power BI Services to carry out activities using a workspace, which is a crucial feature for collaboration and sharing. In this chapter, you learn about workspaces and how you can collaborate, share, and accelerate your business operations with monitoring tools, all available using Power BI Services.

Working Together in a Workspace

Picture yourself in an art museum. You can explore visuals and read anecdotal tales about each work by yourself or with others by your side. A Power BI workspace, available in Power BI Services, is analogous to curating content for a museum, but of course, it's data! A workspace is created by a Power BI designer to manage a collection of dashboards and reports. Think of a workspace as a filing cabinet. The designer can share the workspace with users based on roles, responsibilities, and permissions. In fact, the designer can even build an app by bundling targeted collections of dashboards and reports and distributing them to their organization, whether that involves just a few users or an entire community. These apps, called *template* apps, are distributable on a variety of devices, including desktop and smartphone.

Defining the types of workspaces

The idea behind a Power BI workspace is that it should contain all content specific to an app. When designers create an app, they bundle all the content assets necessary for use and deployment and make it available in the workspace. The content might include anything from datasets to dashboards to reports.

REMEMBER

A workspace may not necessarily include all content types. It may exclusively contain reports, datasets, or dashboards. It depends on the business purpose and how the designer wants to share and collaborate with other users.

The workspaces shown in Figure 8-1 are intended for sharing and collaboration using a collaboration scheme with others. You access them via your My Workspace (see Figure 8-2), as it is your desktop on the Internet for Power BI. You can publish data from Power BI Desktop to Power BI Services. Then, you can organize, store, and share those assets just published online to one or more workspaces that you might intend to use for collaboration. In Figure 8-3, you find assets that were originally created in Power BI Desktop now available in a workspace. For the purposes of this chapter, the project is referred to as thePipeline Identification project.

Figuring out the nuts and bolts of workspaces

When you go into Power BI Services, you're introduced to the Power BI Services navigation menu. (See Figure 8-4.) To no one's surprise, data ingestion and access are a big part of Services.

At the bottom of the list, you find workspaces-related features. A user has a single My Workspace but can have many workspaces within My Workspace. Just keep in mind that a user can be active in only one workspace at a given time — the one highlighted in the navigation.

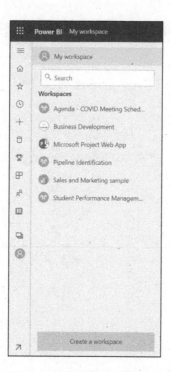

FIGURE 8-1:
A list of
workspace apps.

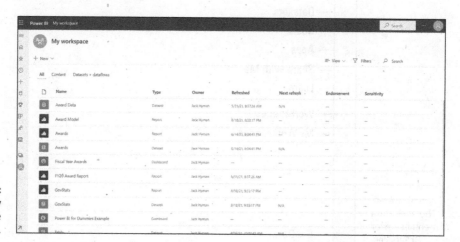

FIGURE 8-2:
The My
Workspace
interface.

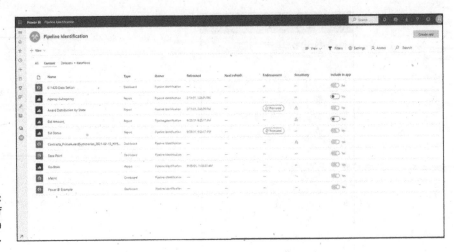

FIGURE 8-3:
The content of a workspace in Power BI.

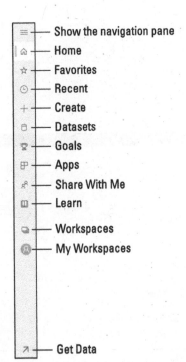

- ≡ — Show the navigation pane
- ⌂ — Home
- ☆ — Favorites
- ⊙ — Recent
- + — Create
- ⊟ — Datasets
- ♔ — Goals
- ⊞ — Apps
- ⋌ — Share With Me
- ▥ — Learn
- ▱ — Workspaces
- ◉ — My Workspaces
- ↗ — Get Data

FIGURE 8-4:
The navigation menu in Power BI Services.

Creating and configuring the workspace

Creating a workspace requires that you configure a few items, including its branding, name, description, access, storage, license mode, app type, and security settings. To complete this configuration, follow these steps:

1. **Click the Workspace icon on the Power BI navigation menu.**

2. **On the menu that appears, click the Create a Workspace button. (See Figure 8-5.)**

3. **In the new window that appears on the right side, use the settings to configure the new workspace.**

   Here are your options, divided between Standard (see Figure 8-6) and Advanced (see Figure 8-7):

   - *Upload:* Save a photo from your desktop to customize the workspace experience.

   - *Workspace Name:* Name the workspace based on its content and datasets. Treat this name as you would for a file collection.

   - *Description:* Describe the purpose of the workspace.

   - *Contact List:* Workspace admins or assigned users receive notifications about updates in each Power BI workspace.

   - *Workspace OneDrive:* This allows a user to configure a Microsoft 365 group whose OneDrive shared library is available to assigned workspace users.

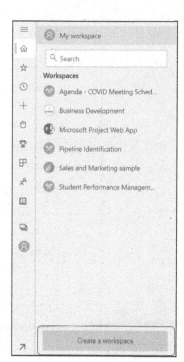

FIGURE 8-5: The Create a Workspace button.

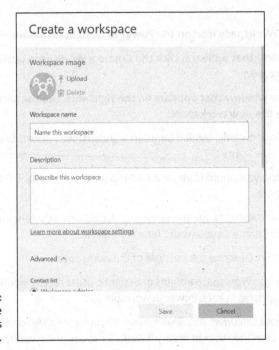

FIGURE 8-6:
Configuring the
standard features
of a workspace.

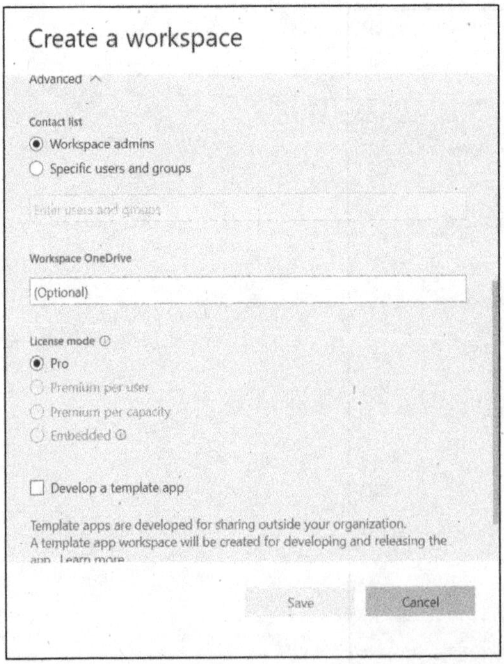

FIGURE 8-7:
Configuring
the advanced
features of a
workspace.

- *License Mode:* Select the license type assigning the right to access content in the workspace. An organization may have access to one type (Pro) or more than one type (Premium-based).

- *Develop a Template App:* Select the check box if you want the workspace to become an app.

- *Security settings:* Selecting this check box allows administrators and contributors to make changes to the workspace.

4. **When you finish, click Save.**

TIP

For a refresher on license types and the difference between Pro and Premium-based licensing, see Book 2, Chapter 1.

Wandering into access management

A big part of sharing and collaborating starts with access management. You must configure who gains access to workspaces and each of the content assets inside the workspaces. You as the designer can assign four distinct role types: admin, member, contributor, or viewer. To change access, follow these steps:

1. **Click the Workspace icon on the Power BI navigation menu.**

2. **Choose the workspace you want to modify from the menu that appears.**

3. **On the right side of the workspace label, select the three vertical dots.**

4. **Click Workspace Access from the menu that appears, as shown in Figure 8-8.**

FIGURE 8-8:
Assigning
workspace
access.

5. **Enter the email addresses or group accounts of those whose access you want to control, along with the workspace roles you want to assign them.**

6. **When you finish, click Close.**

When you create a user group, everyone in that user group gets assigned to the group. Assuming that a user is a part of several user groups, that person is assigned the highest permission level based on their assigned role. However, if you embed the user groups, all contained users get permission.

Your ability to interact with data in workspaces is significantly limited unless you have a Pro or Premium license. You can either view and interact with items or read data stored in workspace dataflows — nothing less, nothing more.

Dealing with settings and storage

Remember all those settings you configured when you first created a workspace? You can modify them at any time, including changing the storage type from Pro to Premium per User, Premium per Capacity, or Embedded. Also, if you're looking to delete a workspace, you can do so under Premium. To make these changes, follow these steps:

1. **Click the Workspace icon on the Power BI navigation menu.**

2. **Choose the workspace you want to modify from the menu that appears.**

3. **On the right side of the workspace label, click the three vertical dots.**

4. **Click Workspace Settings. (Refer to Figure 8-8.)**

   Doing so brings up the Workspace Settings pane on the right side of the screen.

5. **Go to the Premium tab.**

6. **Select the capacity choice that best reflects your need.**

7. **When you finish, click Save.**

Slicing and Dicing Data

As users consume your reports, dashboards, and datasets, you might want to know *how* they consume these content assets. That's why Microsoft has integrated monitoring and alternate data analysis tools within Power BI for those users who have Pro and Premium licensing to evaluate such metrics.

You can slice and dice usage data in several ways. Options include analyzing data in Excel as well as accessing a high-level view of your data with the Quick Insights report. You can also use metrics reports to understand who is accessing and viewing your reports and dashboards. Click the three vertical dots next to any reports or dashboards within a workspace to access these capabilities. You see two options: one for dashboards (see Figure 8-9) and another for reports (see Figure 8-10).

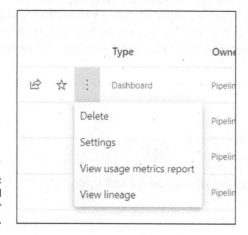

FIGURE 8-9:
The Dashboard menu under Workspaces.

FIGURE 8-10:
The Report menu under Workspaces.

Analyzing in Excel

Sometimes, Power BI may be just a bit too much for a user to evaluate enterprise data comfortably. Users may want to review a subset of data — so we return to Microsoft Excel. With the Analyze in Excel option, you can import Power BI datasets into Excel. Then you can choose to view and interact with the dataset side-by-side or independently. Whether your business goal is to create a PivotTable, chart, table, or Excel output, you need to have the Excel Add-On feature from Power BI downloaded. Don't be alarmed when you see a prompt the first time you try to analyze in Excel, similar to the one you see in Figure 8-11. Once the add-on is downloaded to the computer, you can begin evaluating your datasets.

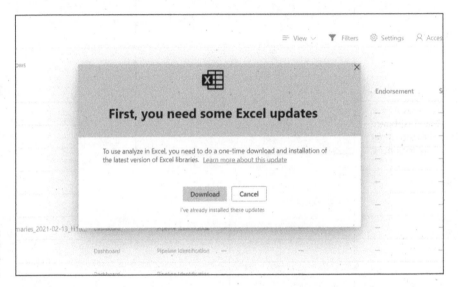

FIGURE 8-11: The Download prompt for the Excel add-on.

Benefiting from Quick Insights

Perhaps you want a quick snapshot of a dataset. Or maybe you're looking for patterns, trends, and ambiguities in your data. The anomalies in the data can be challenging to find if you're first starting out and don't know where to start looking. However, Power BI at least attempts to do the hard work for you. Its artificial intelligence engine finds critical trends, patterns, indicators, and anomalies in your data. With Quick Insights, Power BI automatically produces the top trends it believes are essential in each dataset for a user to consider evaluating. In the example shown in Figure 8-12, you have one federal agency, the State Department, obligating the lowest dollar amount for COVID-19-related projects relative to other federal agencies. Similarly, for counties in Virginia, a greater allocation of dollars was given to Fairfax and Stafford relative to others.

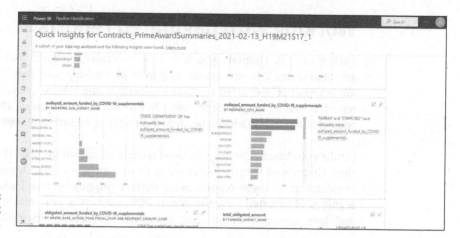

Using Usage Metric reports

Ever want to know how popular a report or dashboard is? Or perhaps who accessed an item in a workspace today, this week, or over time? Microsoft recognized that data access metrics help improve a designer's ability to deliver best-in-class analytics. The Usage Metrics report can help users analyze data points, including distribution types, views, viewers, viewer rank, views per day, and unique views per day, as shown in Figure 8-13.

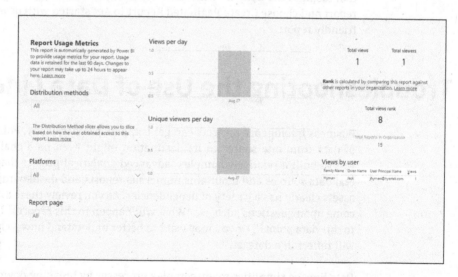

Working with paginated reports

Earlier in this chapter, you see how to create, update, and delete reports as stand-alone content assets in Power BI Desktop and Services. The stand-alone report is optimized for data exploration and interactivity. Another type of report, however, is specific to Power BI Pro and Premium users. That report is the *paginated* report, which can be shared directly or as part of a Power BI app.

Unlike web-based reports, paginated reports are meant for print-based consumption. That means they're formatted to fit well on paper. In fact, you might call the presentation of these reports pixel-perfect. Suppose you're looking to render a highly sophisticated business report PDF, such as a year-end report or profit-and-loss statement. In that case, a paginated report is an excellent choice.

TIP

If you're given access to a paginated report, you can freely share a report with others. Also, you have the option to subscribe yourself and others to a report.

In certain reporting frameworks, you're collating many reports to create a single report. That isn't the case with Power BI — in fact, a report designer is creating a report definition. The definition contains no data; it merely tells you where to acquire the data, which data to obtain from those sources, and how to display the data from those sources. After configuring those three parameters, you run the report, at which time the report processes the definition. The result: a report that displays the data. As with other reports, you click the three dots next to the report and choose Create Paginated Report to get started with developing a user-friendly report.

Troubleshooting the Use of Data Lineage

Business intelligence projects can get complex pretty quickly. Following the flow of data from one source to its destination might even be a challenge. Suppose you've built a relatively complex, advanced analytical project that contains several data sources and maintains numerous reports and dashboards. Each of these assets clearly has a variety of dependencies. As you review these assets, you might come upon questions such as, "What will happen to this report if I make a change to this data point?" Or you may want to better understand how a change you make will reflect in a dataset.

Data lineage simplifies many complex processes by breaking down processes into more manageable steps. Think of it as your little detective! With data lineage, you can see the path your data takes from start to completion, which is crucial when you're scratching your head, having hit many roadblocks. Whether you're managing a workspace with a single report or dashboard or one with many, make sure that the impact of a single change in a dataset is recognized by referring to the data lineage to track those changes. A bonus is that you can resolve many data-refresh concerns with data lineage as well.

To access data lineage information, follow these steps:

1. **Go to the workspace you're targeting.**

2. **Click View.**

3. **Choose Lineage from the menu that appears. (See Figure 8-14.)**

   Lineage view appears, as shown in Figure 8-15.

FIGURE 8-14:
Gaining access to data lineage.

As with other workspace features, only specific roles can access Lineage view. You must be an admin, a contributor, or a member to see Lineage view. Also, you must have a Power BI Pro or Premium license using an app-based workspace to make use of the view.

Once you select Lineage, the view of all items found within the workspace appears on the canvas. Figure 8-15, for example, shows the data lineage for the Pipeline Identification workspace project previously discussed.

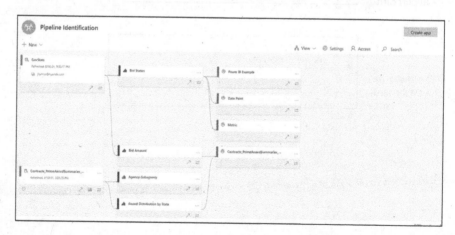

FIGURE 8-15:
An example of data lineage.

Lineage view provides a synopsis of all artifacts found in your workspace — datasets, dataflows, reports, and dashboards, for example. As shown in Figures 8-16 through 8-19, each of the cards on the canvas as represented in Lineage view is a separate asset. The arrows between each of the cards explain the dataflows among assets. Data flows from left to right, letting you observe data as it goes from the source to the destination. Generally, the flow tells a story, such as the one in this list:

>> A source produces one or more datasets. (See Figure 8-16.)

>> Reports are generated from datasets. (See Figure 8-17.)

>> A collection of reports presenting a snapshot in time results in the creation of a dashboard. (See Figure 8-18.)

>> Data flows in particular directions. (See Figure 8-19.)

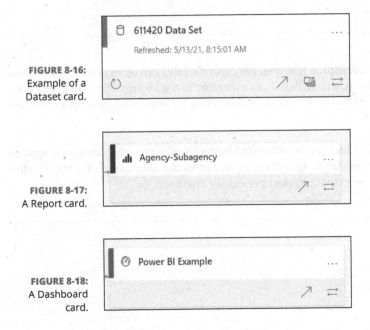

FIGURE 8-16: Example of a Dataset card.

FIGURE 8-17: A Report card.

FIGURE 8-18: A Dashboard card.

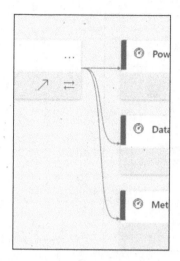

FIGURE 8-19:
Arrows between
each asset in a
workspace.

Datasets, Dataflows, and Lineage

It's not uncommon for datasets and dataflows to be associated with external sources. Some examples may include databases or datasets found in external workspaces. You see that — when reviewing the Dataset card, as shown in Figure 8-20 — a user can drill down to evaluate different factors by choosing one of these three commands. Each command reveals a different aspect of the dataset:

» **View Details and Related Reports:** This command displays all reports tied to the associated datasets or dataflow.

» **Shows Impact Across Workspace:** This command provides you with an impact analysis of how the dataset or dataflow impacts workspace activity. (See Figure 8-21.)

» **Show Lineage:** This command provides you with a micro-level view of the dataset.

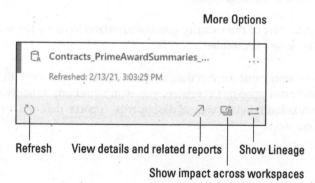

FIGURE 8-20:
Drilling down into
a Dataset card.

FIGURE 8-21:
Showing the impact of an action across a workspace.

Defending Your Data Turf

Can you imagine a sensitive report or dashboard being exposed to an unauthorized user group in your organization? That won't go over too well because that global exposure can potentially harm your data and information security practices. Microsoft integrated a way to codify protection for your data analytics assets. Called *sensitivity labels*, this feature (which is available across the Microsoft 365 product family and integrates with Power BI), which allows users to apply labels to reports, dashboards, datasets, dataflows, and .pbix files. Such labels guard sensitive content against unauthorized access. It is incumbent on you to label your data correctly to ensure that only authorized users access your data.

BEST PRACTICE

For sensitivity labels to work, edit permissions must be enabled for all content you want to label in the workspace. Before edit permissions can even be accessed, a systems administrator must enable sensitivity labels in Settings for users to apply such permissions in the Power BI workspaces. (See Figure 8-22; more on sensitivity labels in a few paragraphs.)

TIP

You must be part of the security group authorized to apply the sensitivity labels; otherwise, access is disabled.

REMEMBER

Data protection must be enabled for your instance of Power BI so that sensitivity labels can appear. Otherwise, you won't find any sensitivity labels in the Sensitivity column in List view of dashboards, reports, datasets, or dataflows with your workspace.

Admin portal

Tenant settings
Usage metrics
Users
Premium Per User
Audit logs
Capacity settings
   Refresh summary
Embed Codes
Organizational visuals
Azure connections
Workspaces
Custom branding
Protection metrics
Featured content

Block classic workspace creation
Enabled for the entire organization

Information protection

▲ Allow users to apply sensitivity labels for Power BI content
Unapplied changes

With this setting enabled, Microsoft Information Protection sensitivity labels published to users by your organization can be applied in Power BI. All prerequisite steps must be completed before enabling this setting.

Note: Sensitivity label settings, such as encryption and content marking for files and emails, are not applied to content within Power BI. Learn more

Visit the M365 Compliance Center to view sensitivity label settings for your organization.

Note: Sensitivity labels and protection are only applied to files exported to Excel, PowerPoint, or PDF files, that are controlled by "Export to Excel" and "Export reports as PowerPoint presentation or PDF documents" settings. All other export and sharing options do not support the application of sensitivity labels and protection.

⬤◯ Enabled

ⓘ The setting below determines which users in the organization can apply and change sensitivity labels. All other users in the organization can only view the labels.

FIGURE 8-22:
Enabling sensitivity labels in Power BI.

WARNING

Your systems administrator must configure sensitivity labels in the Microsoft Information Protect Admin console, separate from Power BI Admin. This step must be completed before sensitivity labels can be enabled and usable by any user.

To make changes to a sensitivity label on a report or a dashboard, follow these steps:

1. **Go to the report or dashboard you want to edit.**

2. **Click the three vertical dots.**

3. **Choose Settings from the menu that appears.**

4. **Locate the Sensitivity Label section in the Settings pane that appears (see Figure 8-23).**

5. **Choose the appropriate sensitivity label.**

6. **When you finish, click Save.**

   In your workspace, the sensitivity label appears in the column under the appropriate report or dashboard, as shown in Figure 8-24.

TIP

To learn how to configure sensitivity labels in Microsoft 365's information protection admin console, go to https://docs.microsoft.com/en-us/microsoft-365/compliance/create-sensitivity-labels.

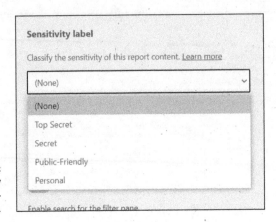

FIGURE 8-23:
The Sensitivity
Label drop-
down menu.

FIGURE 8-24:
Sensitivity labels
in a workspace.

3

Using Tableau for Data Analytics & Visualization

Contents at a Glance

Chapter **1**

Tableau Foundations

Tableau is a business intelligence platform that helps users see and understand their data using highly visual representations. Unlike other enterprise business intelligence platforms, Tableau incorporates business intelligence, data analytics, data science, data mining, and data visualization into a single solution. As a result, its capabilities are considered the broadest and deepest for data evaluation on the market.

In 2019, Salesforce acquired Tableau. At the time, Tableau's focus on data was big but not all-encompassing. It included enterprise data applications, data management and governance, visual analytics, and end-to-end storytelling. As with every other platform on the market, machine learning (ML) and artificial intelligence (AI) have become entrenched in the platform. Salesforce's Einstein AI engine is built into Tableau to help accelerate data analytics predictions, provide a strong recommendation engine, and afford an advanced workflow while touting a low-code development environment.

Tableau is not a single product but a suite of products that includes Tableau Desktop, Tableau Prep, and Tableau Server or Tableau Cloud. Chapter 2 describes the purpose of each in more detail, but in brief, people use Tableau Desktop to create their data models. In contrast, Tableau Prep facilitates data preparation. And when users are ready to collaborate with others, they must publish their outputs from Desktop and Prep to Tableau Server or Tableau Cloud.

Understanding Key Tableau Terms

Tableau has its own product-specific terminology, but there are also terms you can't escape no matter what business intelligence and data analysis tool you use, whether it's Microsoft Excel, Microsoft Power BI, IBM Cognos, or others. This section reviews the most critical Tableau-specific terminology, not the entire business intelligence dictionary.

Data source

A *data source* in Tableau comes from anywhere that Tableau can extract, transport, and load relational and nonrelational data. Sources of data used by Tableau are often divided into four classifications, shown in the following list along with some examples of each classification:

» **Files:** .csv, .txt, Excel

» **Relational databases:** Oracle, SQL Server, DB2

» **Cloud databases and virtualization platforms:** Microsoft Azure SQL, Google Big Query, Amazon Aurora, Denodo

» **ODBC datastores:** Datastores using ODBC-related connections

Figure 1-1 shows an overview of the abundant number of data sources you can connect to in Tableau Desktop.

A Tableau data source may contain multiple data connections to different databases or files, as described previously. The connection information includes where the data is located, such as the filename and path of the network location, or perhaps details on connecting to the data source, such as the database server name and the authentication credentials. Regardless, many data sources can connect in a single instance of Tableau. Still, categorically, they connect to some file or server connection, whether local or cloud-based.

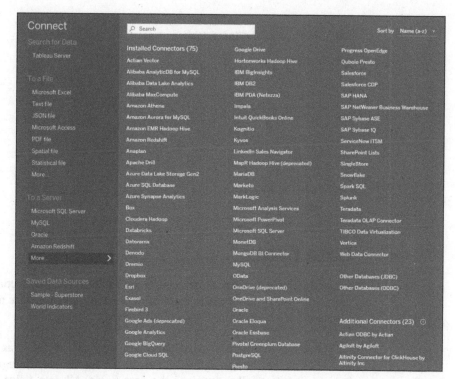

FIGURE 1-1:
A sampling of
Tableau data
sources.

Data type

Going down the data path a bit more, a data field, which is part of a data source (see more details in the next section), must always have a data type. A *data type* reflects whether the field is a number, a type of date, or a string. For example, every area code is an integer (703); a date of birth represents a date (01/01/23); and a state on the U.S. map ("Virginia") is a string. Users can identify the data type they are looking for as part of the data field in the Data pane. Each data type also includes one of several icons, including those represented in Figure 1-2. Although the examples are not exhaustive, you see a few common examples of data type icons mapped against their respective data types. The complete list of Tableau data types includes the following:

- ➤➤ Text (string) value

- ➤➤ Date value

- ➤➤ Date & Time value

- ➤➤ Numerical value

- ➤➤ Boolean value (relational data only)

>> Geographic value (map data)

>> Cluster groups

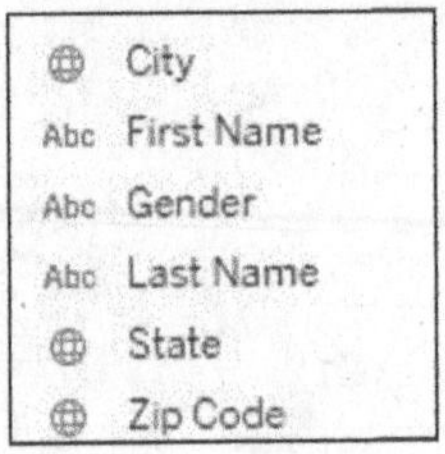

⊕	City
Abc	First Name
Abc	Gender
Abc	Last Name
⊕	State
⊕	Zip Code

FIGURE 1-2:
Examples of data
types icons.

Data fields

Every time you connect a data source to Tableau, the connection presents the users with one or more tables from said source. A table includes many data fields composed of a collection of several data types.

As shown in Figure 1-3, data fields are explicitly defined as dimensions or measures as the Tableau database is created. Based on data integrity and quality, Tableau automatically organized the data fields. All data fields containing text date or Boolean values are dimensions by default. On the other hand, fields containing numerical values are measures. The next section talks about how Tableau deals with dimensions and measures.

Dimensions and measures

In Tableau, dimensions and measures are both data field types. If the field type contains non-numeric data, Tableau references the field as a dimension. Examples include the day of the week, a product category, or geographic data. These variable types don't allow you to complete mathematical equations. Here's an example of an equation with variable types:

State + City / Country = Invalid

All these items are strings because you can't add a state plus a city and divide it by a country to get some magical answer, right?

In Tableau, you can drag each of these fields into a view, which is the part of the Tableau canvas where a visualization is created. Tableau creates headers for each data field. That means you can think of each field as a category or a dimension of data. If the dimension of data is placed in a row, the header label is vertically placed. The label is horizontally placed if the dimension is placed in a column. Figure 1-4 shows an example of data placed in both rows and columns.

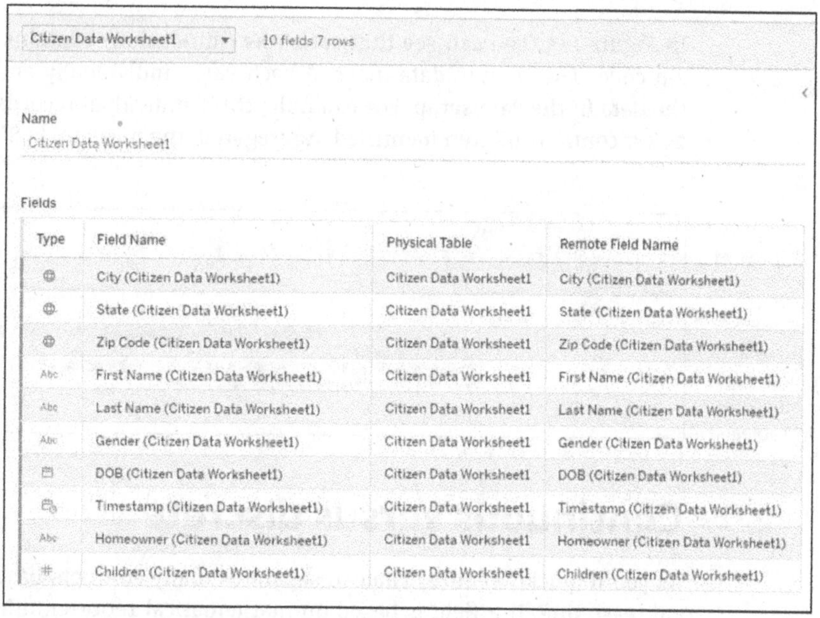

Type	Field Name	Physical Table	Remote Field Name
	City (Citizen Data Worksheet1)	Citizen Data Worksheet1	City (Citizen Data Worksheet1)
	State (Citizen Data Worksheet1)	Citizen Data Worksheet1	State (Citizen Data Worksheet1)
	Zip Code (Citizen Data Worksheet1)	Citizen Data Worksheet1	Zip Code (Citizen Data Worksheet1)
Abc	First Name (Citizen Data Worksheet1)	Citizen Data Worksheet1	First Name (Citizen Data Worksheet1)
Abc	Last Name (Citizen Data Worksheet1)	Citizen Data Worksheet1	Last Name (Citizen Data Worksheet1)
Abc	Gender (Citizen Data Worksheet1)	Citizen Data Worksheet1	Gender (Citizen Data Worksheet1)
	DOB (Citizen Data Worksheet1)	Citizen Data Worksheet1	DOB (Citizen Data Worksheet1)
	Timestamp (Citizen Data Worksheet1)	Citizen Data Worksheet1	Timestamp (Citizen Data Worksheet1)
Abc	Homeowner (Citizen Data Worksheet1)	Citizen Data Worksheet1	Homeowner (Citizen Data Worksheet1)
#	Children (Citizen Data Worksheet1)	Citizen Data Worksheet1	Children (Citizen Data Worksheet1)

FIGURE 1-3: Examples of data fields.

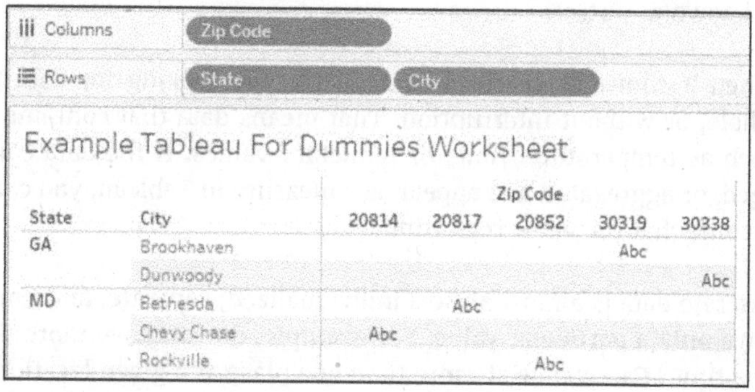

State	City	Zip Code 20814	20817	20852	30319	30338
GA	Brookhaven				Abc	
	Dunwoody					Abc
MD	Bethesda		Abc			
	Chevy Chase	Abc				
	Rockville			Abc		

FIGURE 1-4: Rows and column data for dimensions in Tableau.

Measures are numerical data field types. Tableau assumes that these field types are continuous and tags these values by default. Examples of measures include temperature and financial instruments. Unlike independent dimensions or values that do not rely on other data fields, measures are dependent because they allow you to do the math, as in the following example:

Age (20) + Age (1) / Age (3) = Age (7)

As with dimensions, if you drag a measure into a view, Tableau creates a continuous axis. If a measure is placed in a row, the axis is vertical, whereas a column is horizontal.

In Figure 1-5, you can see that each row (dimension) contains a state, city, and zip code. The column data looks at each value individually and then aggregates the data in the data setup. For example, three individual records in Bethesda, MD 20817 contain children identified. Aggregated, the measure is SUM (3).

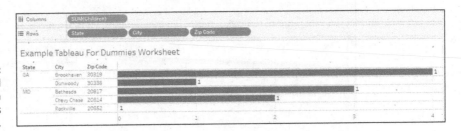

FIGURE 1-5:
Rows and column data for measures in Tableau.

Continuous versus discrete

As you'll quickly realize, Tableau separates many concepts based on mathematical reasoning. If a field is based on mathematical representation, Tableau refers to this data as *continuous*. On the other hand, if the data is non-numeric, the data is known as *discrete*.

When it comes to continuous data, you are looking for data that is unbroken, whole, or without interruption. That means data that contains a range of values such as temperature, time, or monetary values. If the data can be added, averaged, or aggregated and appear as a measure in Tableau, you can almost certainly assume that the value is continuous.

Discrete data is almost always individualized, separate, and unique data. You can have only a particular value. For example, do you have more than one shoe size at a time? Can you be at more than one place at a given location? How many distinct individuals can you claim on a personal tax return? The number 2.39 is not possible; 1, 2, or 3 is more like it.

With discrete data, you have no way to add, average, or aggregate the data points because the values will always be unique by default.

TECHNICAL STUFF

When dragged onto the Tableau View area, discrete data appears as a *blue pill* to form a discrete axis on a chart. Continuous data, on the other hand, appears as a *green pill* to form a continuous axis on a chart.

Filter

The capability for filtering data is one of the essential features of any business intelligence solution associated with big data. Tableau lets a user filter data, whether an individual view contains a few records or an entire data source with millions of records based on dimensions, measures, or values.

As with databases, filtering helps users see only the data they need based on targeted criteria. When using Tableau filters, you can visualize the data in a readable, actionable format. The real benefit of filtering is streamlining data to limit the number of records for improved performance. An example filter would be to filter all the U.S. states with the word *New*. The result set would return a response of New Hampshire, New Jersey, New Mexico, and New York.

Various filter types are available in Tableau, including the extract, data source, context, dimension, measure, and user filters.

Aggregation

Combining data, also known as *aggregation,* is not uncommon in a business intelligence platform. In Tableau, aggregating measures or dimensions is pervasive. However, aggregation is often numerically focused, meaning focused on the use of measures. Suppose you add a measure to a view. In that case, the aggregation is applied to the specific measure by default, which varies based on context.

As an example, pretend for a moment that you're the CEO of a Fortune 100 company (think Walmart, Coca-Cola, or Exxon). One of your data analysts prepares a report for you that presents the minimum, maximum, summary, and average number of sales opportunities for a specific product in each region. The scenario would appear as follows (with the bold signifying each data field that is aggregated).

> **Opportunity Value** = 20,000 **products sold** in five **varieties** across 4 **regions** with a customer population of 1,000,000 **households**.

You've now calculated the opportunity value by utilizing the aggregation functions, a way to calculate a set of values and derive a single value.

WARNING There are limits to what you can aggregate. You can only limit data found in relational data sources. Multidimensional data sources contain data that has already been aggregated, which is impossible to complete. Note that at this time, multidimensional data source aggregation is supported only in the Windows edition of Tableau Desktop.

Workbook and worksheet

Tableau hasn't deviated much from other industry-leading products when it comes to the name of file and formatting conventions. There is a Tableau *workbook*, the main Tableau file, which contains a collection of sheets. The collection of sheets represents the workbook much like that in Microsoft Excel or Microsoft Power BI. In Tableau, a *worksheet* is a single file within a workbook. A worksheet is an element within a dashboard or story.

Although the workbook represents the proverbial catalog of dashboards or stories, the worksheet is a single element or a view. Figure 1-6 represents an example of a single worksheet contained within a Tableau workbook.

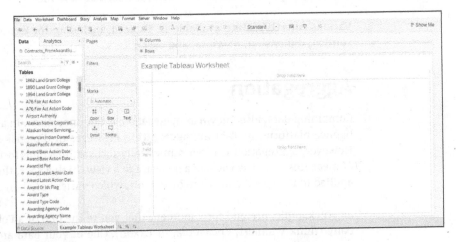

FIGURE 1-6:
A Tableau
worksheet.

REMEMBER

Here are points to consider when thinking about the use of workbooks and worksheets:

>> A Tableau worksheet may contain a single view with many shelves, cards, legends, and analytics panes, which are included as part of a single sidebar on a single page to tell a story.

>> When you add many worksheet pages to a workbook, you can generate a *dashboard*, which is a collection of views from many worksheets.

>> As you create many worksheets within a workbook, you are compiling a *story*, which is a sequence of worksheets that paint a picture to fuse information.

>> Most notably in Tableau Desktop, but also in Tableau Cloud, you can combine views of data by dragging and dropping fields onto the Tableau *shelves*, which are part of a worksheet and which help you create presentations.

In Book 3, Chapter 5, you take a tour of a worksheet and workbook to see how to collect, organize, and extract data.

Getting to Know the Tableau Product Line

Tableau is a business intelligence platform that provides tools for users to engage and interact with data across all phases of the analytics life cycle. Such tools and techniques include data management and governance functionality, visual analytics and storytelling, collaboration and communication, and deep learning that leverages artificial intelligence–powered capabilities.

The Tableau platform brings together all user types at the interaction layer. It offers various analytic and data management options (discussed in upcoming sections), and the connections to all data sources are either cloud based, database ready, or file based. You can deploy all Tableau solutions either in Tableau Cloud, which is a public cloud infrastructure or by hosting them in an on-premises environment. Every layer of the Tableau platform allows for tight integration with industry-standard APIs, and a core tenet of the platform is the application of governance, security, and compliance. Figure 1-7 shows the core platform architecture of Tableau, and the following sections offer an overview of each of the Tableau products. The interaction layer contains each of the end-user connection types. Data connections can be with the cloud, a database, or a file. The deployment options with Tableau include Tableau Cloud, Tableau Server, or Tableau Public. It's the two middle layers, the analytic and data management options, that this book heavily focuses on. Each organization has its own approach, and as you review your data, you figure out what the best choice is for your organization. At any time, as shown on the left side of Figure 1-7, all facets of the model should incorporate security, governance, and compliance. On the right side, APIs, also known as Application Programmable Interfaces, can be integrated to handle one or more of the layers in the Tableau architecture.

WARNING

In this book, coverage is limited to the foundational tools in the Tableau product line. Salesforce has targeted products for data management, artificial intelligence, and CRM integration not covered. Refer to *Tableau For Dummies*, 2nd Edition, for a more in-depth discussion of the other products.

Tableau Desktop

Every dataset doesn't just jump from the data source location to Tableau Cloud or Tableau Server instantly. You follow a process to explore the data and turn it into a meaningful model for consumption. Next, a transformation process must occur to support data visualization, and then you need a mechanism by which to publish the data. Tableau Desktop is where the entire process begins.

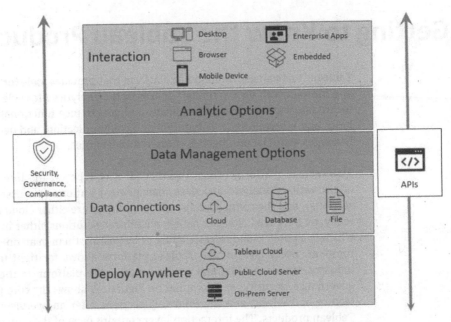

FIGURE 1-7:
The core Tableau platform architecture.

Tableau Desktop is, first and foremost, the platform people use to independently complete data exploration and visualization activities before collaborating with others. Users complete these activities by using an intuitive drag-and-drop interface. Anyone looking to independently evaluate their data and make decisions without cleansing or publishing their data for collaboration can stop at Tableau Desktop. Collaboration requires other tools described in this chapter.

Figure 1-8 depicts the process by which data is consumed and utilized across Tableau, most notably between Tableau Desktop, Tableau Prep, and Tableau Server or Cloud.

As you read the upcoming chapters, you'll recognize that there is a consistent process to handle data ingestion, manipulation, and visualization using Tableau Desktop. Here is a high-level overview of the steps you may take from data ingestion to visualization, starting with Tableau Desktop:

1. **Connect to your data source in Tableau Desktop (raw data source).**

   Remember that there are a few data connection types, some of which allow real-time updates, whereas others require manual updating over time.

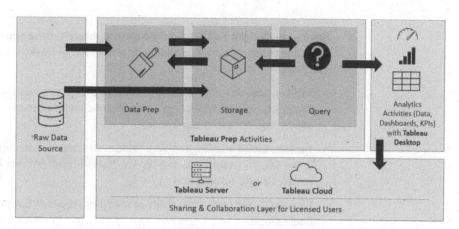

FIGURE 1-8:
How you work
with data across
Tableau Desktop,
Prep, Server,
and Cloud.

2. **After Tableau Desktop recognizes the data source, manipulate the data for data models and visualizations.**

   If you must cleanse and transform data, you need to head to Tableau Prep to complete those activities.

   After the data sources go through the cleansing process (also referred to as Extract, Transform, and Load [ETL]; see Book 3, Chapter 2), Tableau stores that data in its memory.

   You can now create one or more visualizations by querying the dataset in Tableau Desktop, as shown in Figure 1-9.

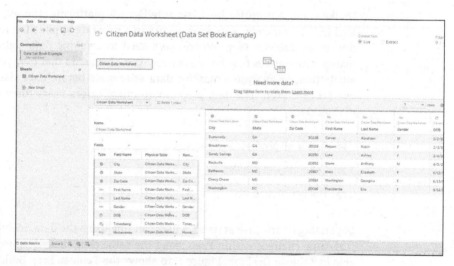

FIGURE 1-9:
The Tableau
Desktop
interface.

3. **Having readied your data for prime time, publish it using one of the following three options, depending on what type of Desktop client you have:**

- **Tableau Server** licensing requires Tableau Desktop to save the workbook to a private, on-premises, or private, cloud-hosted environment. Either option requires a paid subscription.

- **Tableau Cloud** licensing requires Tableau Desktop to save the workbook to the Salesforce software-as-a-service (SaaS)–hosted environment, which requires a paid subscription.

- **Tableau Public** limits your ability to save files anywhere but the Tableau Public Cloud.

REMEMBER

You don't have data-sharing limits if you are licensed for Tableau Desktop Personal or Professional. Suppose you choose not to procure a Tableau license and instead use Tableau Public for free. In that case, you can only share your data with others openly, limiting your ability to protect sensitive data.

TECHNICAL STUFF

Tableau Desktop and Tableau Prep work together. Some users bypass the process of cleansing their data using Tableau Prep and jump straight to Desktop. In fact, you may recognize this being done in some of the examples in this book. Don't panic — no pertinent steps were skipped.

Tableau Prep

Unlike other enterprise business intelligence platforms, the extract, transport, load (ETL), and cleanse process occurs in a separate application within the solution suite, Tableau Prep. When users need to combine data sources, shape and manipulate sources to behave a certain way, clean data that may contain a specific attribution, or analyze a massive dataset at scale before data visualization, they use Tableau Prep. The data prep environment offers users three different views of their data:

>> Row-level profiles

>> Column-level profiles

>> The entire dataset

Depending on the task at hand, a user can fine-tune the data, including by making real-time changes within Prep using the same drag-and-drop experience available in Tableau Desktop. Figure 1-10 shows the Tableau Prep Builder interface.

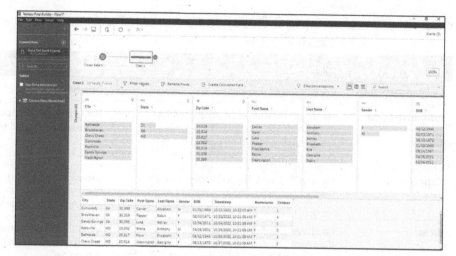

FIGURE 1-10:
The Tableau Prep
Builder interface.

Tableau Prep is often the glue that combines raw data and the final product because raw data often needs some TLC. The more data sources you introduce within Tableau Prep, the more the Tableau artificial intelligence engine works to reconcile the proper business operations given a source's data types and fields. After the data is cleansed, it can go to two possible destinations: Tableau Desktop, to continue with the data visualization and analysis journey, and Tableau Server (on-premises) or Tableau Cloud (online) for storage, with the intent of sharing and collaborating with other end users later.

**TECHNICAL
STUFF**

Data cleansing is a complex process requiring users to evaluate their data for formatting errors, duplicates, incomplete values, inconsistencies, and a host of other potential issues. When you have a bit of data cleansing to do, use Tableau Prep. If you know that your data is sound and the problem is a one-off, updating your work using Tableau Desktop will be just fine.

Tableau Server and Tableau Cloud

There are a few differences between Tableau Server and Tableau Cloud. Still, at the core, their purposes are precisely the same. Tableau Server requires the enterprise user to host the environment. In contrast, Tableau Cloud is a SaaS-hosted infrastructure managed by Salesforce. From a licensing perspective, there are some caveats to using each of these Tableau environments, as noted in Table 1-1.

Server and Cloud are purpose-built to distribute, share, and collaborate user and organizational datasets, visualizations, dashboards, and reports across the Tableau enterprise, most notably between Tableau Desktop and Tableau Prep.

Figure 1-11 shows an example of what the Tableau Cloud user experience provides.

TABLE 1-1   Licensing Differences between Tableau Server and Tableau Cloud

	Tableau Server	Tableau Cloud
License Structure	Core-based or role-based.	Role-based.
Administration	Hardware is required. A server can be virtualized. All updates are the end user's responsibility, including backups and data recovery.	Fully managed by Salesforce in the Tableau Cloud SaaS environment.
Capacity	No specific limits beyond environmental resource constraints.	Site-wide limits exist based on feature type, role-based license type, and utilization of back-end resources.
Sites	Can have an infinite number of sites on the same Tableau Server. A distributed architecture is not allowed.	Multiple sites are charged additional fees, but cross-region support is provided.
Identity Management	Allows identity-management platform support, such as Microsoft Active Directory domain integration for syncing users and groups.	Must use a Tableau Account to log in.
Monitoring	Can only use Server logs and analyze the PostgreSQL repository.	Prebuilt monitoring tools are available through Tableau. No server log access.

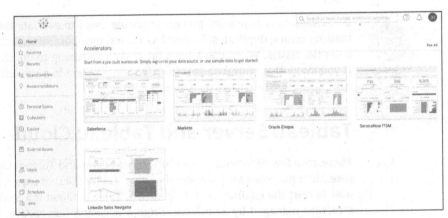

FIGURE 1-11:
The Tableau Cloud user experience.

TECHNICAL STUFF

Organizations requiring tighter security, especially in regulated settings, or perhaps wanting to create custom applications with embedded analytics functionality should consider Tableau Server over Tableau Cloud because SaaS platforms come with obvious shared infrastructure limitations.

Choosing the Right Version

If you've read this entire chapter, you've probably realized by now that purchasing the right Tableau product may require you to purchase more than just one product. That's not to say that Salesforce won't sell users a single license; they will, of course, sell parts of the engine. But getting the whole experience requires buying Tableau as a bundle.

Tableau has come up with product bundles based on user activity type. The bundles are known as Viewer, Explorer, and Creator.

>> **Viewer:** Allows users to access existing dashboards. This option is available only to teams and organizations. The licenses start at $15.00 per user as of this writing.

>> **Explorer:** Allows users to edit existing dashboards. This option is available only to teams and organizations, and the licenses start at $42.00 per user as of this writing.

>> **Creator:** Allows users to connect to data, create vizzes (visualizations), and publish dashboards. Every Tableau subscription requires a minimum of one Tableau Creator license. These licenses start at $70.00 per user as of this writing.

Each Creator license entitlement provides an organization with a single copy of Tableau Desktop and Tableau Prep. The catch is that the Creator license provides an initial single-user license to Tableau Server or Tableau Cloud. Additional Creator licenses are then tied to the original Creator license entitlement of Tableau Server or Tableau Cloud.

TIP

When you purchase the Creator license, it's best to decide early on what server architecture best suits your organization because once you're hooked, it's hard to go back. Your choice is an on-premises server or the cloud.

REMEMBER

If you decide to go with the Explorer or Viewer user type, you must have a minimum of a single Creator license. The license is tied to an organization, hence the team or group requirement noted previously. So, for example, Data Inc. may have one Creator doing all the development work but can have many Explorers and Viewers completing limited activities inside Tableau Desktop. Depending on your license type, features are enabled or disabled upon purchase based on the procured license type.

Knowing What Tools You Need in Each Stage of the Data Life Cycle

The Tableau portfolio isn't a one-and-done solution platform but rather a collection of business intelligence solutions. Undoubtedly, every tool mentioned in this chapter has a place in the Tableau data life cycle. This book focuses on three solutions to bring the life cycle together.

>> **Tableau Desktop:** The solution that helps users create reports, dashboards, stories, and graphs from a workbook containing datasheets. The data can be shared locally or publicly.

>> **Tableau Prep:** The solution within the suite of Tableau products meant to help users prepare data, including combining, shaping, extracting, transforming, and cleansing for analysis in Tableau Desktop.

>> **Tableau Cloud:** The solution that allows users to share, collaborate, and manipulate visualizations and datasets created in Tableau Desktop and Tableau Prep.

Keep in mind that some of the stages in the Tableau Data Life cycle are one hundred percent based on human intervention, meaning that no tool can answer every business intelligence problem. For example, can a tool craft a business hypothesis? Some artificial intelligence agent can probably propose a question or two for you. Still, it doesn't know the dataset's context, hence the need to combine, shape, and transform the data to its destination among the data life cycle stages. Table 1-2 shows which tools you apply to each life cycle stage.

TABLE 1-2 **Tools to Utilize For the Tableau Data Life Cycle**

Life Cycle Stage	Tableau Desktop	Tableau Prep	Tableau Cloud
Identify the question or business need	N/A	N/A	N/A
Get raw data	No	Yes	No
Choose mapping techniques	Yes	No	No
View and prepare datasets	Yes	Yes	No
Develop visual insights	Yes	No	No
Publish and share insights	No	No	Yes

As Table 1-2 reveals, the only stage that requires more than one tool is viewing and preparing data. The cleansed data moves between Tableau Desktop and Tableau Prep when data is extracted, transformed, and loaded during the cleansing and querying process. First, Tableau Prep readies the data. After the data is cleansed, Tableau Prep allows for the data to once again be shared with Tableau Desktop for visualization. To summarize, most of the work in this stage is completed in Tableau Prep because there is cleansing and organization going on, not visualization.

Understanding User Types and Their Capabilities

Previous sections in this chapter provide a brief look at the three user classifications (Viewer, Explorer, and Creator) for the sole purpose of helping you understand what license you need to procure. This section helps you better understand how to get the most out of Tableau as a solution-based platform, and takes a deep dive into what each user type can accomplish.

REMEMBER

There are two licensing models: user-based and core-based. Both Tableau Cloud and Tableau Server require at least one Creator license, which comes as a user-based license. For on-premises users, though, Tableau Server is available on a core (server-based) consumption model. To purchase a Viewer or Explorer license, a Creator license is necessary.

Viewer

The Viewer is by far the most restricted user. Viewers are often the team members who need data gathering and viewing activities, not the data creation tasks. Viewers can interact with the data, dashboards, and visualizations by being informed reviewers of the sources. These users can collaborate within their assigned Tableau environment with other users through commenting, downloading, and creating custom views of existing published data. But that is where their involvement stops. The ability to create new assets is prohibited for the Viewer.

TIP

Viewers who want to learn more about Tableau Cloud's capabilities because most of your interaction occurs when data is published should read Book 3, Chapter 8.

Explorer

As a power user, the Explorer has far more ability to act upon published data, including workbooks. The Explorer can create calculations, change chart types, and craft new filters. Unlike the Viewer, who can only review the data and comment, the Explorer can save the files they modify as separate workbooks or overwrite the original file with the necessary site permissions. The Explorer has a sliver of developer capacity. They can build their workbook from scratch directly on either Tableau Server or Tableau Cloud. However, the entire publishing life cycle is by no means comprehensive like that of the Creator, who has the most access rights.

Creator

The world is your oyster if you are a Creator because you have all the tools to master the entire Tableau data life cycle. Suppose you have a single Creator license. In that case, by default, you are the system administrator for your Tableau Cloud or Tableau Server instance. However, when many parties are involved, including those with Explorer and Viewer licenses, the Creator must assign roles and responsibilities to each licensed Viewer and Explorer. Creators in larger organizations have a varying degree of system administrative privileges, which means that some may be able to provide users with licenses. In contrast, others may have project-level access.

Creators are granted a single license of Tableau Prep to support data acrobatics from cleansing to extracting and loading activities across multiple data sources. In addition, a user is granted access to a full version of Tableau Desktop (not one with reduced functionality), which allows for developing robust data visualization solutions. Finally, at the onset of a user contract, you get to pick between Server or Cloud for publishing and managing your user across all Tableau solutions.

TIP

As a Creator, you'll probably want to read the entire book because all topics are applicable. Still, pay special attention to topics pertaining to Tableau Prep.

WARNING

There are many caveats to be aware of for the Creator user and what activities one might need to engage in, so look carefully before you leap into your licensing selection choice. First, a Server license is often far more expensive in the long run than a Cloud consumption license, especially if you procure based on cores consumed. (*Cores consumed* refers to how many CPUs are on a given server.) Second, after you lock in your adoption of the Server or Cloud model, it's hard to transition from one to another. To learn more about the process of migrating from Server to Cloud or vice versa, head over to https://help.tableau.com/current/blueprint/en-gb/bp_move_to_cloud.htm.

TECHNICAL STUFF

To get into the weeds of each licensing model, go to https://help.tableau.com/current/server/en-us/license_product_keys.htm.

Chapter **2**

Connecting Your Data

Starting up any Tableau product is like turning on a car for the first time. You need a set of keys, some fuel in the car to operate, and a basic understanding of how to operate the vehicle. The data source is the holy grail to running the Tableau engine. If you have no data source, the application won't go very far. More data provides better insights, but if you have a small set, it is still better than nothing.

In this chapter, you explore the various data source options at your fingertips. After showing you how to figure out which option is suitable for your need, the chapter walks you through how to plan the configuration and customization of the data source. Sometimes the process is fluid because only one person needs to access the data, whereas in other situations, thousands, if not millions of users, may access the data, and this chapter looks at these considerations. The last half of the chapter talks about data source construction before you dig deep into the cleansing and prep stage of your data.

Many people want to jump straight to analysis and skip this part, and you may find doing so to be adequate. But if the data impacts a broader audience, the step-by-step process described in this chapter should undoubtedly make you a strong data analyst using Tableau Desktop, Tableau Prep, and Tableau Cloud.

Understanding Data Source Options

Whether you are using Tableau Prep or Desktop, the first activity you must complete is to connect to data. Otherwise, guess what? You'll get nothing out of using Tableau. That's right: zip!

Looking for the Connect button, shown where the arrows point in Figures 2-1 and 2-2, is your golden ticket no matter which Tableau solution you intend to use.

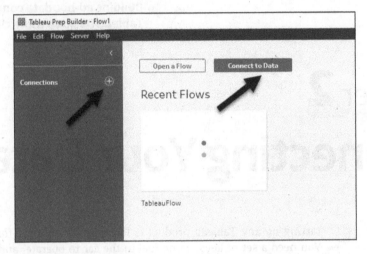

FIGURE 2-1:
The Connect
button in
Tableau Prep.

A few flavors of data sources are available across Tableau Desktop, Tableau Prep, Tableau Server, and Tableau Cloud. Tableau has conveniently broken down your search for options into a few classifications. Users can search for data in the following places:

>> Directly from Tableau Server, in Tableau Server, and Tableau Cloud

>> From files such as text, JSON, Access, PDF, and XLS

>> From a server such as Microsoft SQL, MySQL, Oracle, and Amazon Redshift

Figure 2-3 shows a simple data source login for users with Box accounts, and Figure 2-4 shows a complex data source configuration for users needing to connect to Oracle.

FIGURE 2-2:
The Connect
button in Tableau
Desktop.

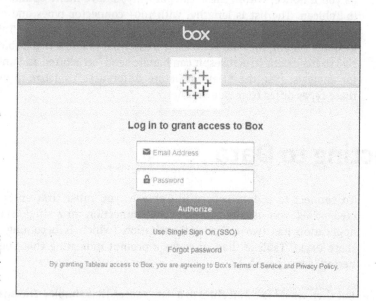

FIGURE 2-3:
A simple data
source login for
users with Box
accounts.

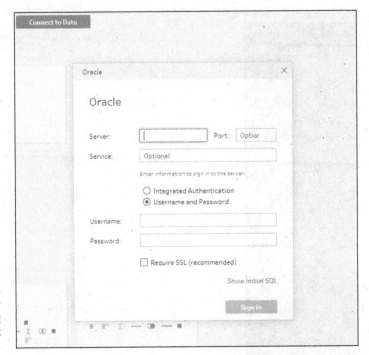

FIGURE 2-4:
A complex
data source
configuration for
users needing
to connect
to Oracle.

As you'll notice, within these categories, you have many options to choose from in Tableau. The list is lengthy, with 100+ connector types and counting across enterprise applications if you have the Professional Edition of Tableau Prep and Desktop. Among the data sources, it's essential to know that Tableau is not married to fixed data structures; it can handle semi-structured and unstructured data for analysis. (See the "Data structure differences" sidebar to understand how these types differ from one another.)

Connecting to Data

To connect to a data source in Tableau, you must first enter the necessary credentials. You usually complete the connection on a single screen unless the application has two-factor authentication (which is becoming more common these days). Tableau then provides a prompt indicating that you are now connected (see Figure 2-5).

But then what? Is connecting to a data source that simple? The answer is yes! You can start playing with your data at this point. In Figure 2-6, you can see the example is connected to a SharePoint list, which is a Microsoft data source. Now you can start importing the data from one or more of the available SharePoint lists.

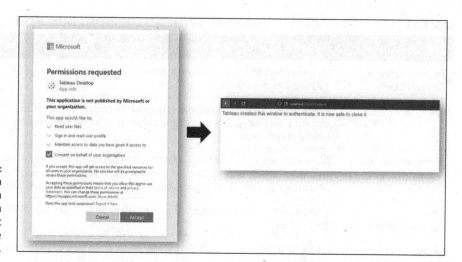

FIGURE 2-5:
Connecting to a
Microsoft data
source, with
the prompt
confirming the
source active.

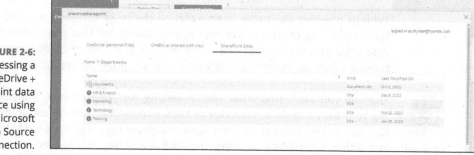

FIGURE 2-6:
Accessing a
OneDrive +
SharePoint data
source using
the Microsoft
Data Source
Connection.

Making the Desktop or Prep connection

Whether you launch Tableau Desktop or Tableau Prep, you make a data connection by using the Connect pane. As described earlier in the chapter, each application has the Connect pane in a slightly different location. Your best bet is always to locate the left panel and find either the Tableau logo (Desktop) or the connection with the plus symbol (Prep) to initiate the connection without fussing around the respective applications. Table 2-1 describes the different data source connection types accessible for Desktop-client users.

REMEMBER

In the Tableau documentation, the term "Connect pane" is specific to Tableau Desktop, whereas "Connections pane" is specific to Tableau Prep. Both terms refer to the same element, however.

Connecting Your Data

TABLE 2-1   Connection Types in Tableau Desktop and Prep

Source Type	Description
Tableau Server or Tableau Cloud	Users connect to the on-premises Tableau Server address or the URL-provided Tableau Cloud address.
File	Users obtain a file by pointing to it on their desktop. There are 25+ file types currently supported. File types can contain structured, semi-structured, and unstructured data.
Server application	Most enterprise applications and enterprise database sources fall into this category. Examples include Oracle, SAP, IBM, Salesforce, and Microsoft applications. You can also integrate with data virtualization platforms such as Denodo and Snowflake.
Other database (JDBC)	Users can create a connection to a Java Database Connectivity (JDBC) API-based data source.
Other database (ODBC)	Users can create a connection to a Microsoft Open Database Connectivity (ODBC) interface data source.

Tableau provides the native connectors to the most common file and database types under the respective Connect menus. Assuming that you cannot find your enterprise data source, you have a few options. If a JDBC or ODBC connection can consume your application, quickly utilize these options to create a data source.

TECHNICAL STUFF

Suppose you can't find what you're looking for? In that case, consider creating your own web data connector or even a connector plug-in using the Tableau Connector SDK. Tableau provides limited support for connection to these options, and details for building such functionality is well beyond the scope of this book.

REMEMBER

Tableau adds new data connector types to its platform all the time. If you have the 2018 edition of Tableau Desktop and Tableau Prep, you are guaranteed to have far fewer data connections available than the version this book is based on (the 2022 edition). To keep up with the latest data connectors, go to `https://help.tableau.com/current/pro/desktop/en-us/exampleconnections_overview.htm`.

Locating the Server and Online connections

Connecting to a data source inside the Tableau ecosystem is easier than connecting to another vendor's product. However, you may expect the process within Tableau to be a bit more descriptive than it is, given that Tableau offers two publishing-oriented products. Still, when you know where to go to get started, connecting within Tableau should go pretty smoothly.

You can find all connections under a single menu, the Server menu. In that menu, you go to the menu option Sign-In, enter the URL of the Tableau Server into the Server field, and then press the Connect button. Or you can connect to Tableau Online using Quick Connect by pressing the link to Tableau Online, as seen in Figure 2-7. Tableau then prompts the user to log in to their Tableau Cloud account, as shown in Figure 2-8.

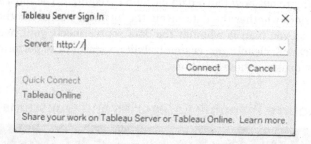

FIGURE 2-7:
The Tableau
Server and
Tableau Cloud
data connection.

FIGURE 2-8:
Log in to Tableau
Online using the
Quick Access link.

TIP

REQUESTING A NEW CONNECTOR

There are thousands of IT products on the market that produce data. It should be no surprise that Tableau does not provide every connector that's available. Someone in the greater Tableau community has likely developed a connector to fill the void. To save yourself some time, head to the Ideas on Community section of the Tableau website to search for your connector first at https://community.tableau.com/s/ideas. If it has been requested, vote for it. Tableau may add it to the commercial product line. Other times, a developer may tinker with the SDK, come up with the one-off connector, and share it with the greater community. Head over to the various open discussions within the Tableau community and see if someone has solved your problem. Most times, you'll find that your problem has already been solved, and you can easily download the solution in a few clicks.

Setting Up and Planning the Data Source

Connecting to a data source doesn't mean you're done with the data source management's planning and design stage. Not even close, in fact. Setting up the data source is step one; bending it to your liking such that it can produce exemplary result sets is a different activity. This and the following sections in this chapter describe how to go about analyzing and preparing the data before data analysis, visualization, and publishing.

Although this is not a self-help book, it's time to ask yourself some critical questions about your wants and needs on data! Is your goal to quickly explore your dataset? If so, you may want to attach your data source to Tableau Desktop or Tableau Prep and take a quick tour of what's under the hood. Perhaps build a few visualizations and see whether you can discern anything of use. You'll get a good sense from your first pass of how good (or bad) the data quality is. And yes, you can figure out how much data cleanup is required. The most significant step is to consider whether the data meets the business needs. Another more pivotal question as you plan is whether the data source meets your needs in terms of source location, cleanliness, customizability, security, and performance maturity. Table 2-2 explores these questions.

TABLE 2-2   Data Source Planning Categories and Questions

Category	Description	Question
Location	Identify where the data source resides.	Is the data source on-premises or cloud-based?
		Is the data source a file or part of an application?
		Is the data source a database?
		Does Tableau offer a data connector? If not, will a data connector need to be created to support the database source, such as an ODBC or JDBC connection?
Access	Identify the specific functionality needed to operate in the location, including authentication and authorization credentials.	Who should have access to the Tableau data source?
		What level of access should the users have based on the data source location?
		What type of user filtering and row-level security may be utilized in accessing the data source?

Category	Description	Question
Cleanliness	Identify how well structured and formatted the data may be, leading to a range of extract, transport, and load (ETL) processes that might be completed using Tableau Prep Builder.	How well structured is the data source? Is Tableau Data Prep required to clean and automate prep flows? Are there any calculations and manipulations that may best be done natively in Tableau? Should data be removed to improve speed and performance or enhance data cleanliness?
Customization	Identify ways that require unique naming conventions or formatting requirements that allow the data to align with Tableau's native capabilities.	Is the data source adequate, or will add-on capabilities be required, such as calculations? Will the tables and fields within the data source require modification to be understood to explore dimensions and measures better?
Scale	Identify the pervasiveness of the data source and how it should be utilized within Tableau. Scaling data includes model maturity and combining of data.	Should data be spread among several systems or centrally contained in a single environment? Does it make sense to combine data from each table into a single source of truth?
Security	Identify where the data source is created and utilized, such as the native workbook or perhaps an embedded data source published to Tableau Server or Tableau Online.	Can the data source remain independent, or does it need to be embedded in another data source? Where will the public data source be published? Who owns the data source, ultimately? What authentication and authorization schema is required for the dataset?
Performance	Identify the type of connection required to support the data source throughout its entire life cycle.	Does the data source require a live connection, or is a data extract adequate? If a data extract is adequate, is a refresh schedule planned using Tableau Server or Tableau Cloud? If Tableau Cloud is being used, will Tableau Bridge also be used?

TECHNICAL STUFF

Regarding data connections, be aware that Tableau Bridge (referenced in the Performance category of Table 2-2) is a unique connection type. Tableau Bridge is a lightweight client software application that sits on the desktop or local server within your computer network (think on-premises). The client software interacts with Tableau Cloud to ensure that the data source on the local machine, which connects to a private network data source that Tableau Cloud can't reach ordinarily, always remains up to date.

Relating and Combining Data Sources

No two data sources come in the same shape and size. The typical scenario with Tableau is to have Tableau from a table in one source, with a second source having another like-kind table. You connect both sources in the same workbook and then drag the two tables onto the canvas to build a single view. But building a single view may be easier said than done, assuming that your data can be combined across multiple databases.

Note: Some of the steps in this chapter use a dataset about Worldwide University rankings found on Kaggle.com, which you can download at https://www.kaggle.com/datasets/aneesayoub/world-universities-ranking-2022. The download contains four CSV files, which you use to extract data into Tableau to complete the following and later steps in this chapter.

To connect to the data sources you've downloaded, follow these steps:

1. **Connect to the data source.**

2. **Drag a table or sheet of data to the canvas, which then releases the table or sheet onto the canvas for manipulation.**

3. **To add another table from the same data source (in this example, that is; see Step 7 to use a different source), drag that second table or sheet to the canvas and release it.**

   One of two things might happen:

   - A "noodle," or a line between two items in the Flow pane, forms indicating that an automatic relationship is created after you map the three like-kind fields. (See Figure 2-9.)

   - The Edit Relationship dialog pops up, prompting you to provide Tableau with the fields that must be mapped, depending on the warning symbol's message. (See Figure 2-10.)

   For Step 3, you want to map the Acceptance Rate for all tables against the Top 300 Universities of the World, resulting in the noodle shown in Figure 2-9. Otherwise, you'll continue to get a result like Figure 2-10.

4. **Continue adding tables to the canvas as needed, assuming that the tables come from the same data source under these conditions.**

   There is a slight modification to the preceding steps if you require multiple data connections.

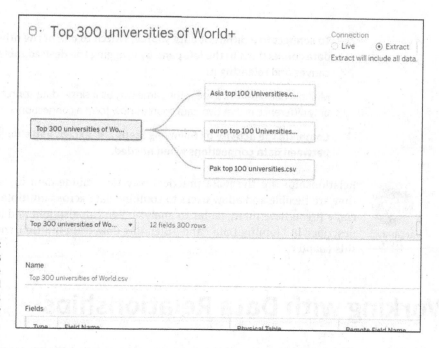

FIGURE 2-9:
Four tables
connect due
to data field
similarities, as
indicated by
the noodle.

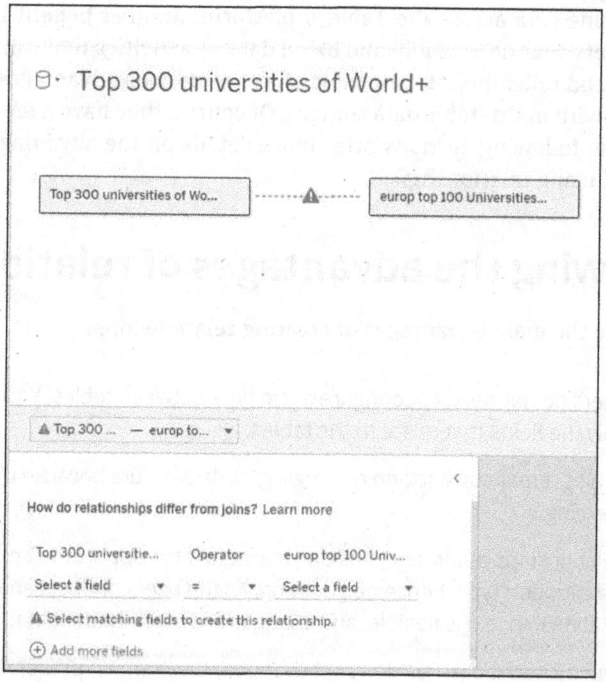

FIGURE 2-10:
An edit
relationship
dialog appears,
prompting the
user to select
the fields.

5. **To connect to a different data source, switch to one of the other available data connections in the left pane by dragging the desired table to the canvas and releasing it.**

   Multiple data sources appear the same way as a single data source does: the only difference is that two data sources now form a connection.

6. **Complete the activity by following Steps 2–4, except you should switch between data connections when needed.**

TECHNICAL STUFF

Relationships are the most practical way to combine data in Tableau because they are flexible and allow users to combine data across multiple sources, especially if you have many tables to analyze. You can also join and blend tables, as described in "Joining Data" and "Blending data from multiple sources," later in this chapter.

Working with Data Relationships

Creating relationships is the cleanest and most simplistic approach a user can use to combine data across the Tableau platform. Another benefit is that a relationship limits your need to join and blend data — activities that can compromise data quality and reliability. Relationships have numerous advantages, especially when dealing with multi-table data sources. Of course, they have a few disadvantages as well. The following sections offer more details on the advantages and disadvantages of using relationships.

Knowing the advantages of relationships

Here are the main advantages of creating relationships:

>> Users do not need to configure a join type between tables. You need to select only the fields that relate to the tables.

>> Tables remain distinct; no comingling of data occurs because there is no data merging.

>> Relationships automate joins on your behalf to support the appropriate visualization type, hence no guessing. As the user conducts analysis, the relationship join is flexible, and changes are made to the data.

>> Unmatched measures don't get dropped; they remain preserved, ensuring that no data loss occurs.

>> Relationships help to avoid data duplication and filtering issues, which often arise with joins.

>> Relationships generate the correct aggregations and join types so that during analysis, you have little concern regarding the data types associated with a field in use within a worksheet.

Seeing the disadvantages of relationships

And now for some of the downsides of relationships:

>> Poorly formatted data, especially multi-table data, can make analysis very complex.

>> Using any data filter can limit Tableau's ability to utilize *join culling*, which involves simplifying queries by eliminating unnecessary join statements.

>> Unmatched values across relationships can be left in limbo.

>> Attempting to mix and match multiple fact tables with multiple-dimension tables, thereby resulting in modeling shared or conformed dimensions, does not yield fruitful results.

WARNING

Using a join can be tricky to manipulate, so use joins cautiously. Furthermore, if you are trying to use a join with published data; doing so is not supported using any version of Tableau.

WARNING

There is one more use case when relationships may not yield the results you want: limited support of relational connections. Tableau has many prebuilt connectors. Some offer exceptional data interoperability, including the use of many logical tables. A few of those connectors limit you to a single logical table, however. You won't be imagining things if you attempt to use sources such as Cubes, SAP HANA, JSON files, or Google Analytics and can pull only a single table, not an infinite number. Other examples of limited support include adding a stored procedure to a connection that commits the connection to a single logical table and publishing data to Tableau Cloud or Tableau Server, where data sources cannot be interrelated.

Creating relationships

To get a grasp of relationship building, it's a good idea to try your data in Tableau Desktop before putting it through Tableau Prep Builder. Doing so lets you see how the fields are labeled and whether any meaningful relationships can be built in the logical layer of the data sources based on the default view of the canvas. Taking the same previous dataset from Kaggle.com (see "Relating and Combining Data Sources," earlier in this chapter), follow these steps to run your data through Tableau Desktop:

1. **Open Tableau Desktop.**

2. **Connect all four csv files into Tableau Desktop as provided in the zip package you've downloaded from Kaggle.com (assuming that you've extracted them all).**

3. **Drag the table derived from the data source Top 300 Universities of World.csv to the canvas (see Figure 2-11).**

4. **Locate the table from the data source Asia Top 100 Universities.csv and drop the table onto the canvas when you see the noodle form between the two tables.**

   A connection forms (see Figure 2-12).

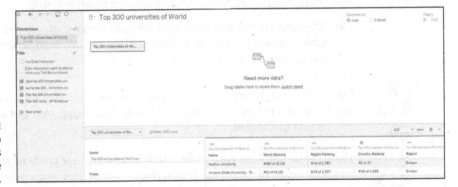

FIGURE 2-11:
Dragging the Top 300 Universities of the World table onto the canvas.

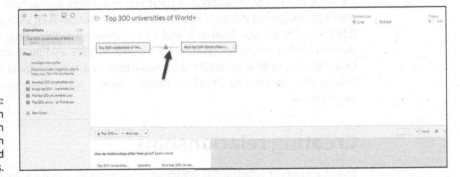

FIGURE 2-12:
A connection forms between two tables when they're dragged onto the canvas.

Editing relationships

Although Tableau attempts to create a relationship between existing data types (for example, string to string or integer to integer) and field names, it may not always find a perfect match. You should anticipate that you'll need to come up with meaningful relationships based on the data types matching appropriately.

To edit the relationships in Tableau Prep Builder, you'll need to identify which columns require editing. After you've identified the specific columns in Tableau Prep Builder, follow these steps:

1. **To change the fields, select the field pairs between the two tables.**

2. **Select the field's name from the two drop-down lists to create a pair of matching fields.**

3. **Repeat Steps 1 and 2 to create multiple field pairs for relationships.**

TECHNICAL STUFF

Sometimes, Tableau doesn't detect constraints, which happens when data has been labeled poorly. Poor labeling is the case with the dataset shown in this chapter, which is why you have had to do a bit of data acrobatics to map fields like *Name* to *name* even though the field names are identical. Tableau isn't perfect. The field names must be identical, including the capitalizations (not kidding here). When these situations occur, you'll have a many-to-many relationship form, leading to referential integrity being set to some record match. Tableau's settings accommodate safe choices, offering flexibility to your data sources. That means your data should accommodate full outer joins (which you find out more about in the next section). Users optimize queries by aggregating table data way before forming joins for the data. The change results in all column and row data becoming available for analysis.

Moving tables to create different relationships

The example using the Top 300 Universities in the World+ dataset in this chapter contains four tables (which you can download from https://www.kaggle.com/datasets/aneesayoub/world-universities-ranking-2022, as mentioned in "Relating and Combining Data Sources," earlier in this chapter.) The primary table, Top 300 Universities in the World.csv, connects with Asia Top 100 Universities.csv, Europe Top 100 Universities.csv, and Pak Top 100 Universities.csv.

Say you wanted to move one of the tables because there may be a better relationship between two tables instead of the primary table, Top 300 Universities. Here are two ways to move a table:

>> Drag the table requiring the change to the new table with which you intend to establish the relationship. In this example, you move the PAK Top 100 Universities next to Asia Top 100 Universities (see Figure 2-13).

>> Alternatively, you can hover over the table and click the arrow. Then select Move To and select your preferred alternative table location (see Figure 2-14).

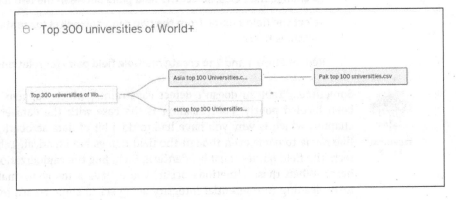

FIGURE 2-13:
Dragging a relationship on the canvas to a new table.

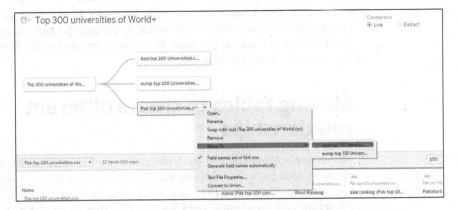

FIGURE 2-14:
Hovering over a table to select an alternative table location.

Changing the root table of a relationship

The root table is considered the primary data table within a Tableau data model. When a model integrates several like-kind tables, but one table offers a superior set of fields, you may want to switch the primary table with one of the connecting tables. For example, if you determine that the connecting table called Asia Top 100 Universities.csv is a superior fit compared to the primary table Top 300 Universities of World+, you can simply swap the corresponding tables, as shown in Figure 2-15. To swap the root table with another, right-click the logical table that should become the primary table in the model. Then select Swap with Root.

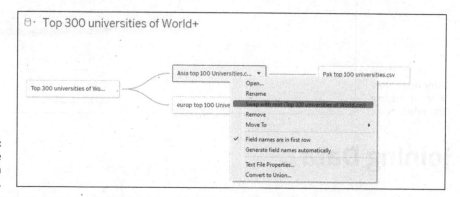

FIGURE 2-15:
Changing the
root table of a
relationship.

Removing tables from a relationship

As you review the data across one or more tables, you may find a table that's not helpful, and removing it from the relationship on the canvas would make sense. To remove a table, follow these steps:

1. **Hover your cursor over the table on the canvas.**

2. **Right-click the table and then select Remove.**

3. **Release the mouse to make the table disappear.**

   Deleting a table on a canvas also automatically deletes all related relationships to the primary descendant table.

In the example shown in Figure 2-16, the table Europe Top 100 Universities.csv is selected for removal.

TIP

Before you remove a table from a relationship, hover your cursor over a noodle to view the relationship status. Check for three things: the relationship between the tables; the cardinality of the relationship; and the fields mapped between the relationship.

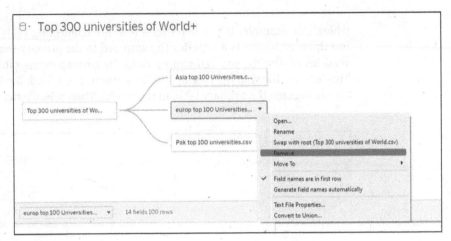

FIGURE 2-16:
Removing a table from an existing data relationship.

Joining Data

Creating relationships is generally the preferred approach to establishing a data source. You may sometimes want to use a join to control data, however. Whether you want to ensure specific types of filtering or reduce filtering deliberately, the join is the technique a data analyst must use to extend the relationship.

A *join* allows the merging of data from two or more tables into a single table. Under ordinary circumstances, if you merge data from many tables into one, you find lots of redundant data, and filtering can be quite cumbersome. Sometimes the values are even returned null or empty. For these reasons, you need to select the correct type of join to determine how Tableau handles your data.

REMEMBER

Joins and the more simplistic relationship act differently in Tableau because they are defined in different data model layers. Relationships are defined at the logical layer of the data source. In contrast, joins are defined at the physical layer of the data source.

TECHNICAL STUFF

Depending on your data-shaping requirements, the Tableau tool you'll use varies. Tableau Desktop is more than adequate when you're looking to complete basic shaping and create standard joins. If you need to create multiple joins or do a bit of data cleanup from modifying field names, changing data types, and establishing filters or sorts, head over to Tableau Prep Builder.

Understanding join types

Most users stick with one of four join types: left, right, inner, and full outer. The other option is union, depicted along with the other types in Figure 2-17. In the following sections, you can see how to create a join, handle various clause types, and deal with null values generated during join creation.

Inner		When using an inner join, the result is a table that contains values that match from both tables only.
Left		When using a left join, the result is a table that contains all values from the left table and only those corresponding matches from the right table. If the table on the left table doesn't contain a corresponding match in the right table, a null value appears.
Right		When using a right join, the result is a table that contains all values from the right table and only those corresponding matches from the left table. If the table on the right table doesn't contain a corresponding match in the left table, a null value appears.
Full outer		When using a full outer join to combine tables, the result is a table that contains all values from both tables. If one or more tables don't contain a match with another table, you see a null value in the data grid.
Union		The union, although not a type of join, is a method to combine two or more tables by appending rows of a table from one table to another. Tables that you attempt to union should have the same types of attribution, such as field names and data types.

FIGURE 2-17: The most commonly used join types.

Setting up join clauses

You perform a join by setting up one or more join clauses. The *join clause* tells Tableau which fields are shared between the tables, including how to match the corresponding rows. For example, rows should be equal when the same identifiers are aligned in the results table using the equal (=) operator. Similarly, you can search for values such as not equal to, less than, less than or equal to, greater than, and greater than or equal to, as shown in the drop-down menu in Figure 2-18.

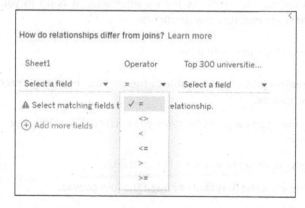

FIGURE 2-18: Operator types supported in forming joins.

Joins are not limited to a single clause, either. They can contain multiple clauses. For example, you may have multiple parameters, such as "Name = Name" and "State = State", as indicated in the .csv files evaluated in this chapter. The conditions must be considered valid for both rows to be joined. Other conditions may include when the Name is shared, but the State is not. The join clause may appear as "Name = Name" and "State <> State".

Unlike other business intelligence platforms, Tableau supports join clauses containing calculations. You can concatenate fields "[City] + [State] = [City]+[State]." That said, only certain data sources support calculations with join clauses. Most file and relational sources are supported, whereas enterprise applications are hit or miss.

Creating a join

To create a join, you need to identify at least one data source, preferably two. You may have a single source, or there may be multiple tables in a database or worksheets in an Excel spreadsheet representing different sources. You may also want to use completely different data sources, which is the case with the example throughout this chapter that uses the four CSV files from Kaggle.com (see "Relating and Combining Data Sources," earlier in this chapter). If you intend to combine tables using a cross-database join, Tableau applies a color scheme to the canvas.

WARNING

Color coding is at the heart of many features within Tableau. Although Tableau offers the user many opportunities to configure dashboards, worksheets, and stories so that they're accessible for public distribution of work, discriminating colors for dimensions and measures inside applications such as Tableau Desktop and Tableau Prep do not support American Disability Act (ADA) Section 508 Compliant standards for its interfaces. As for visualizations, it is up to you to ensure that outputs meet accessibility requirements.

Follow these steps to create a join:

1. **To create a join, drag one table to the canvas; then drag a second table to the canvas.**

   A Join dialog box appears, enabling you to create a data join. Select the join type.

   A relationship forms, as shown in Figure 2-19.

2. **Double-click the first table to open the join canvas.**

   A separate window opens, showing a join canvas on the right with all the tables listed in the left pane (see Figure 2-20).

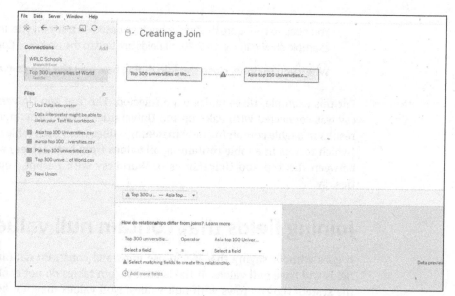

FIGURE 2-19:
A relationship forms when you drag two additional tables to the canvas.

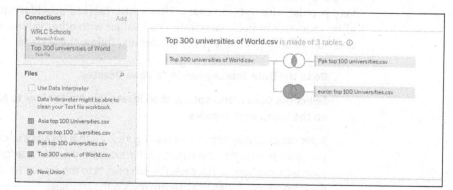

FIGURE 2-20:
Creating a join table.

3. **Select one or more of the tables to create joins.**

   Drag one or more tables onto the first table you've created from the Connections pane, and place it on top of the first table. You'll be asked to create a union or join. Select the join, not a union. At this point, you'll want to select the join type to create after the new relationship has been formed on the canvas.

4. **Repeat this process as many times as you need to by double-clicking another table from the Data Source pane and dragging it to the canvas as needed to build additional join clauses as desired.**

5. **When you have all the desired tables on the canvas, click the join relationship icon to select the join type desired.**

You need to configure the field mappings based on the join type. In the example shown in Figure 2-20, all fields are tied to the Name or Country.

6. **When you're done, close the Join dialog box, and the join canvas is saved.**

For this example, three tables were selected. The Top 300 Universities of World. csv was connected with Pak Top 100 Universities.csv to form an *inner join*, which results in a table containing only matching values from both tables. A *full outer join* (which results in a table containing all values from both tables) was also formed between the Top 300 Universities of World.csv with Europe Top 100 Universities.csv.

Joining fields that contain null values

It goes without saying that if you use joins and constrain data in a table, some fields will have null values. If fields used to join tables do not contain any values, the system returns rows with null values. Null values may not be returned with single-connection data sources, however, and believe it or not, such sources are very popular with Tableau users. That's why Tableau provides various options to allow users to join fields containing null values with other values, which also contain null values. To handle these conditions, follow these steps:

1. **Go to the Data Source page in Tableau Desktop.**

2. **Select the Data menu option, then locate Join Null Values to Null Values on the menu that appears.**

   If this option is grayed out, as it is in Figure 2-21, that means it's not available to your data source. This can happen if, for example, you add a second data source connection. In that case, the join reverts to the default behavior, meaning it has decided to eliminate rows with null values.

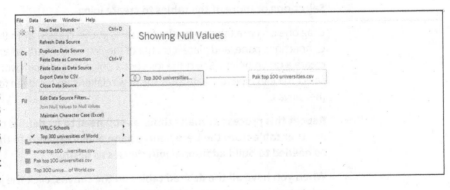

FIGURE 2-21:
Tableau has eliminated rows with null values in this case, as indicated by the greyed-out option.

Blending data from multiple sources

Suppose you want to combine data from multiple sources. In that case, you need to blend your data to bring in additional information across many data sources so it can be displayed with the primary data source within the same view.

Whereas blends and relationships can combine data from multiple data sources, queries don't combine data; they query each source independently. Results are aggregated and presented visually in a single view. Blends, in contrast to queries, can handle different details and work with different published data sources. You should consider using blending, especially when the goal is to link fields across many data sources on a sheet-by-sheet basis when combining data sources.

To blend data, follow these steps:

1. **Connect to your primary data source. Then, in the Data pane, select the sheet that contains the data you want to blend.**

   The first data source becomes the primary.

2. **Click the Data Blending icon in the top-right corner of the screen, which means you can then select the secondary data source you want to blend with the primary data source.**

   This source then becomes the secondary data source.

   Drag a field from the secondary data source to the Filters or Columns/Rows shelf.

   The example uses a workbook that includes Citizen Data and a new data source containing universities in Washington, D.C. The data fields (those in Sheet1) show the potential blending opportunities in Figure 2-22. The blended opportunity, as described in the relationship, is depicted by the noodle in Figure 2-23.

   Watch how Tableau automatically creates a relationship between the two data sources based on the fields you've dragged using the orange noodle, as shown in Figure 2-23.

   If the line is grey, that often means there is a broken link icon. To remedy this situation, click the icon next to the field that links the two data sources. Find a field that is appropriate to match both sides of the match. Then the blended relationships turn orange, representing an active link.

TECHNICAL STUFF

You can't get away with a single data source when blending. There is a mandatory requirement for a primary and secondary data source. The first data source becomes the primary, which defines the view. The secondary source is restricting, helping only to keep values that have corresponding matches to the primary data source. For all purposes, you should consider a blend like a left join.

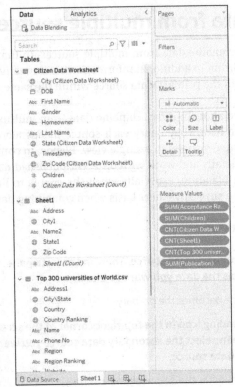

FIGURE 2-22:
Blending data
within the Data
pane using
Tableau Desktop.

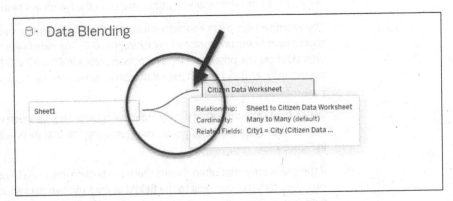

FIGURE 2-23:
How a data
model reflects
blending between
two data sources.

REMEMBER

Joins and blending have subtle differences. Data blending does simulate the traditional left blend. There is one caveat to keep in mind about joins and blending when considering data aggregation. Joins combine data and aggregate after the fact. Blends aggregate first and then combine the data. In other words, it's all about the order in which you combine the data.

Working with clipboard data

Not all your data may be nice and neatly formatted in a data source such as a relational database, enterprise application, or even an organized file format. You may want to pull in data from an outside source for one-off analysis. Rather than spend hours (or days) trying to craft the perfect data source, and then connecting it to Tableau only to be disappointed, you have a quick solution to test your assumptions on the fly. Tableau allows users to copy and paste a sample dataset directly into a workbook, as shown in Figure 2-24.

In a nutshell, to do so Tableau creates a temporary data source on your behalf so that you can begin analyzing the data. As soon as you paste the data onto the data source page, Tableau creates a new connection to the existing data source. Then, if you paste data on a worksheet, Tableau saves the source to your Tableau Repository. Keep reading for more on how to make all this happen.

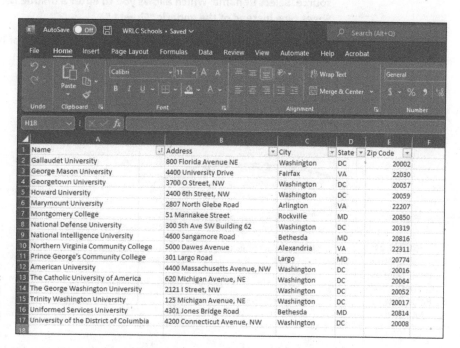

FIGURE 2-24:
An Excel spreadsheet with data being copied to the clipboard.

Next, follow these steps to copy Excel data from your clipboard into Tableau Desktop creating an ad hoc data source:

1. **Open Tableau Desktop and go to the Data Source page.**

2. **Next, go to the Data Menu and either Select Paste Data as Connection or Paste Data as Data Source (Figure 2-25).**

You'll want to select Data as Connection.

A new connection, called Clipboard_221120T195 in this case, is created. A worksheet is also generated consisting of a single table. The worksheet derives field names automatically. In this case, you can rename the field names to more appropriate ones by right-clicking the field name and selecting the Rename option. Note that the field name cannot be the same as the remote field name (the clipboard data field name), as shown in Figure 2-26.

3. **(Optional) To rename the connection, go to the Data Source pane, locate the newly created Data Source, right-click the connection, and select Rename.**

   In this case, the connection is renamed as WRLC Schools, as noted in Figure 2-27.

4. **To rename the worksheet, go to the Flow pane and right-click the data source. Select Rename, which allows you to enter a unique name in the Sheet type instead of the generic "Sheet1."**

   In this example, Sheet1 was renamed to the logical table name of Top 15 WRLC Schools.

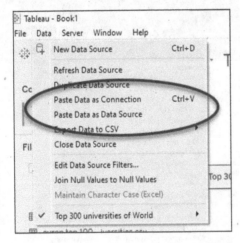

FIGURE 2-25: Choose Paste Data as Connection or Paste Data as Data Source.

After you have saved all your changes, the data source can easily integrate into the existing model, assuming that you've made the necessary relationship tweaks such as streamlining the data in Name, City, State, and Country to be consistent. Figure 2-27 presents the full integration of the Top 15 WRLC Universities into the data model.

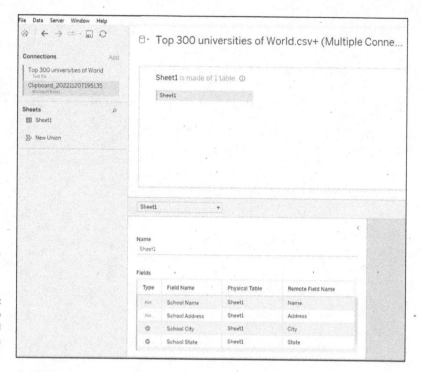

FIGURE 2-26:
Changes made to the newly created data connection and workbook.

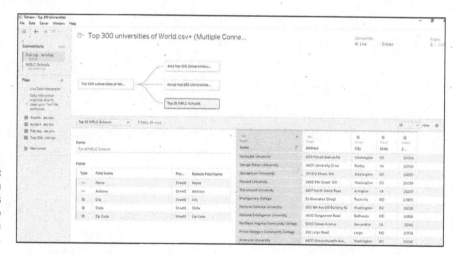

FIGURE 2-27:
Multiple data connections integrated into a single data model.

Chapter **3**

Diving into the Tableau Prep Lifecycle

I f you ask a thousand data analysts what they spend the most time completing, from sourcing data to data visualization and reporting, most folks will say data preparation. Unless you craft the dataset on your own, ensuring that every field maps perfectly to a *T*, you seldom have pure data entry. Tableau recognizes that this issue is one of the complexities in the data life cycle, which is why one of the first products introduced in the solution stack was Tableau Prep Builder. For those needing to twist and bend their data so that it can be shaped and integrated for mass consumption, Tableau Prep Builder is your one-stop shop to handling all these data life cycle activities, from combining, shaping, and cleaning the data before analysis in Tableau Desktop to publishing to Tableau Server or Tableau Cloud.

Tableau Prep Builder is, first and foremost, an Extract, Transport, Load (ETL) tool that connects data from various sources. After connecting to and combining the data sources, users can drag and drop tables into the Flow pane to shape and cleanse the data using a combination of operations such as filtering, pivoting, joining, and unioning data to get it in tip-top shape.

In this chapter, you discover the key capabilities necessary to build flows from inception to execution in Tableau Prep Builder.

Dabbling in Data Flows

Flow is the one term not covered in the Book 3, Chapter 1 discussion of Tableau Fundamentals. That's because the concept is too extensive to compartmentalize into a paragraph. Instead, it requires an entire chapter because Tableau Prep Builder is synonymous with the data flow. So, what is a data flow, exactly?

You have likely heard a smidge about Extract, Transform, Load (ETL). If so, you understand that moving data through one or more cycles or flows is the basic concept of ETL. The flow in Tableau Prep Builder refers to the movement of data between the source and its destination, whether it's the extracted file or a published server, for end-user consumption.

The following pages take you through the steps of the flow life cycle, including connecting data in Tableau Prep Builder, configuring the dataset, adding data, building and organizing flows, and maintaining flows.

Connecting the data dots

You recognize that your data needs a little TLC. A few simple data tweaks inside the database or the file won't cut it. In that case, you must first connect your data to Tableau Prep Builder. To do so, you need to make sure your data source can connect to one of several options available:

>> One of the 100+ built-in connectors provided by Tableau

>> Custom connectors built using the SDK, ODBC, or JDBC offering

>> Prebuilt data sources compatible with Tableau

>> Tableau Data Extracts or Catalogs

Assuming that all the datasets pass muster and you've successfully mastered connecting your data (covered in Book 3, Chapter 2), you're ready to move on to the Tableau Prep Builder panes, and most notably the Flow pane, to create your first flow.

Going down the data flow pathway

After you've connected your data source, the real fun begins. Your first step is to create an input step, and then you can go on your merry way down the Prep Builder pathway of creating flows. The more steps you create, the more actions the data must undergo in the life cycle.

Are you scratching your head yet? The preceding paragraph mentions the word *step*, but you didn't start a flow. Thought that may be confusing! As soon as you associate a data source with Tableau Prep Builder, you've created a data ingestion point so that your data can start flowing down its eventual path. Multiple input steps can exist, as can multiple data files. The chapter covers some of these nuances shortly.

Note: Throughout this chapter's examples, I utilize a specific dataset on salary predictions, found at `https://www.kaggle.com/datasets/thedevastator/jobs-dataset-from-glassdoor`.

If you've added a single file, Tableau Prep Builder automatically adds the input step into the Flow pane (shown in Figure 3-1). All attributes associated with the file are displayed in the Input pane.

Input pane   Flow pane

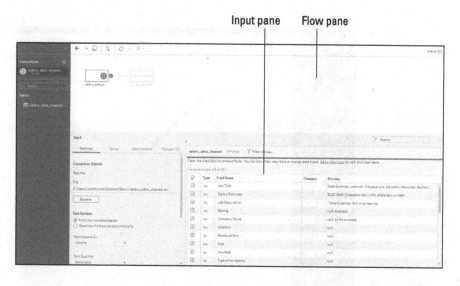

FIGURE 3-1: The Tableau Prep Builder workspace.

The Flow pane is your main workspace to interact with your data visually and build the flows. The Input pane is where you complete all configurations from the time data is ingested. As noted previously, you can see fields, data types, and data-set examples from the Input pane.

Should you want to add multiple files or sources, each data source becomes a new flow, as shown in the Flow pane in Figure 3-2.

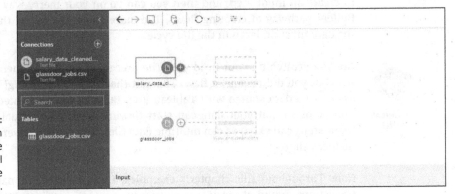

After you create a data flow, you find that Tableau makes it easy to locate the flow right from the Start page of the Tableau Prep Builder application, where you see all recent flows (Figure 3-3). If you're using Tableau Prep Builder on the web, head over to Explore. From there, you can select all web-based flows recently published or created on the internet.

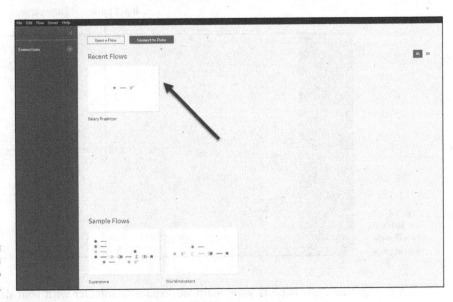

Configuring the data flow

Configuring the dataset after the data connection has been established is the first step in the preparation process. You might not know at this very moment how much work needs to be done to your flow, but you'll get a sense of it as you start to configure. As soon as you add the input to the flow, you'll be able to evaluate what data should be included in the final output.

TECHNICAL STUFF

If you are utilizing an Excel or text file, you can make changes directly from the input step. Other data sources, such as those meaty databases and enterprise applications, require some of the changes discussed to be completed in the data source. It varies by platform.

From the input step, what can you do exactly? If you click the specific item in the Flow pane, your options appear in the Input pane. Such options, indicated by their corresponding letters in Figure 3-4, include the following:

>> **Data Source:** Rename, refresh, and describe the data source.

>> **Settings:** Establish data connection-specific configurations.

>> **Tables:** Select one or more tables to include in Input pane.

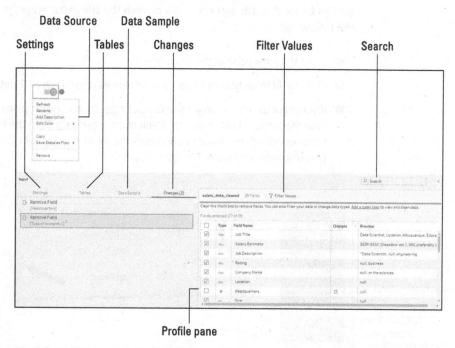

FIGURE 3-4:
Configuring data in the Input pane.

>> **Data Sample:** Produce data samples based on changes made in Input pane.

>> **Changes:** Review all changes made in the Input pane.

>> **Profile pane:** Remove fields from the dataset or modify fields, including changing data types and field names.

>> **Filter Values:** Apply filtering functionality.

>> **Search:** Search for specific fields.

Going with the data flow

Connecting the first data source is easy-breezy. Adding data is where things become a bit more challenging. You have several options: Refresh the native data in the input step, edit the connection to re-recognize the data source and its changes, or create a union among files or database tables in the input step. Read on to find out more about each of these options.

Refreshing data in the input step

When your data source is still active, data changes are inevitable. You'll want to refresh the data, whether it's added to an Excel spreadsheet or becomes more entries to another file structure. To refresh the file input steps, you can do one of the following:

>> Go to the Flow pane at the top menu.

>> Click the Refresh button (Figure 3-5, left image) to refresh all input steps.

>> If you want to refresh only a single input step, locate the drop-down arrow near the Refresh button and then select the input step from the list that requires refreshing. You can also select the input step by right-clicking and pressing Refresh (Figure 3-5, right image).

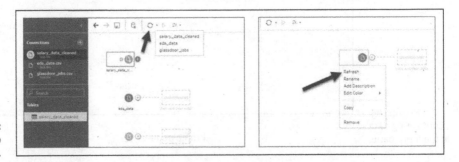

FIGURE 3-5: Input step Refresh options.

Extract input step updates

What I am about to tell you might sound a bit counterintuitive, but it's one of the quirks of Tableau Prep Builder. Suppose you have a Tableau extract or perhaps a database-driven source. In that case, it's best to edit the connection instead of refreshing the data source described in the previous step because data changes can throw off the integrity of the connection if data updates are frequent. You want to be as efficient as possible without having to restart all over again under these conditions.

To ensure the freshest data, follow these steps:

1. **In the Connections pane, right-click your preferred data source.**

2. **In the Flow pane that appears, select Edit on the step for which you'll be editing the connection source.**

   The menu will allow you to edit the source or add additional sources to an existing flow.

3. **Reconnect to the original data source by signing into the database or selecting the Tableau extract.**

TIP

If you believe that your file in the previous step did not refresh properly, reconnect to the data source instead.

What happens when things still don't seem one hundred percent? The folks at Tableau suggest you remove and re-add the step to the flow. Tableau at first indicates that an error exists if you have a complex flow, but this situation is entirely correctable. The steps to ensure that removal and re-addition are successful are as follows:

1. **Go to the Connections pane.**

2. **Right-click the source and select Remove.**

3. **The flow temporarily pauses where the source was formerly.**

4. **Create a connection to the updated file source.**

5. **Drag and drop the table to the Flow pane to initiate the creation of a flow; then, you can add one or more input steps (see Figure 3-6).**

6. **Drag and then drop the new data source onto an Add symbol within a flow to allow it to reconnect with the flow.**

7. **Depending on the source type you've just dropped and added back in to the data flow, you may want to remove the source in the Flow pane, instead of creating a new data source.**

WARNING

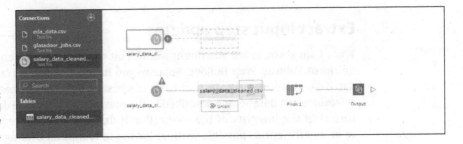

FIGURE 3-6:
Removing and
adding a new
input step.

Creating a union among files or database tables in the input step

Input unions, which are a way to display many tables being queried at a single time, are in their own class because you can create them in Tableau Prep Builder only, unlike the other approaches I've mentioned. Don't worry, however. You can complete some functionality on the web, such as scheduling an input union to run using Tableau Cloud.

A lot of users decide to use Tableau because they want to evaluate many data sources, so they need the ability to cleanse and prep multiple files or database tables. At the same time, with data source complexity comes the desire to search and filter across all the data sources. To create a union with data, if the data sources are files, they must be in the same directory. Before you see how to create a union, here are some other rules that you must consider:

REMEMBER

>> The ability to union data is not available for Tableau extracts.

>> Files can be added only to the same folder that matches specific filter criteria, or the files added to the same folder won't appear automatically within the union.

>> Files don't automatically appear; you need to save your flows and open them again.

>> Packaged flows aren't automatically added as new files, even if they are in the same folder. Instead, you need to open the flow file in Tableau Prep Builder and select the files. Only then can the files be repackaged.

>> If you want to union a database table, the data sources must be in the same database; the database must also support wildcard searches (not all databases offer these features). Those that do support wildcard searches include Amazon Redshift, Microsoft SQL Server, and Oracle. A limited number of open-source databases offer union options.

>> After creating a union, you can refresh the input step if you decide to add or remove tables or files. Otherwise, you can update your flow with available data.

Although there are a few limitations unioning data, the pros still outweigh the cons. Recognize that you are trying to query multiple tables simultaneously with a union, yet you will visualize the data just one time, which can be complicated to achieve. Why, you ask? Except for .csv and Excel files, Tableau Prep Builder does not establish a data union relationship for all files in the same directory. You'll need to manually handle creating file connections to the data source.

For .csv and .xls files, Tableau automatically creates the union on your behalf. Suppose you feel that a better union relationship is available, or that not all the files are necessary. In that case, in the Input pane, you can specify additional filters to find the files and sheets that should be included in the union (see Figure 3-7). You can filter the file being unified in various ways, including by filename, file size, date created, and date modified to tailor files based on specific attributes.

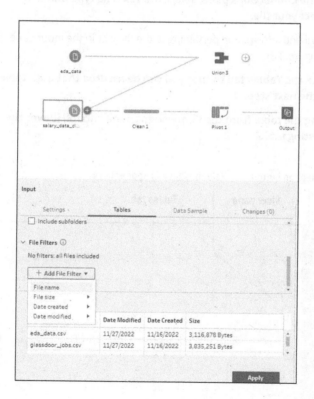

FIGURE 3-7:
The Union filter
for files in the
Input pane.

In Figure 3-8, you'll see that when you add a new step into your flow, all the files are added to the dataset in the file path, which is located in the Profile pane. All fields are added automatically and are visible in both the Profile pane and Data Grid. To add a new step into your flow, follow these steps:

1. **Click the Connect tab on the toolbar.**

   The Connections pane opens so that you can create or access a data connection.

2. **Click the Add Connection button (the plus sign; see Figure 3-8).**

   The Connect pane expands, providing you with various types of connections to create.

3. **In the Connections pane, select the Text File type under To a File; then select your file.**

   You'll find information pertaining to the file within the Input pane (also shown in Figure 3-8).

4. **Click the Tables tab so that you can be assured that both tables connect in the next step.**

5. **Drag the table from the Connections pane and roll it over the existing table.**

Add Connection button   Relationship will appear here

Flow pane   Tables tab

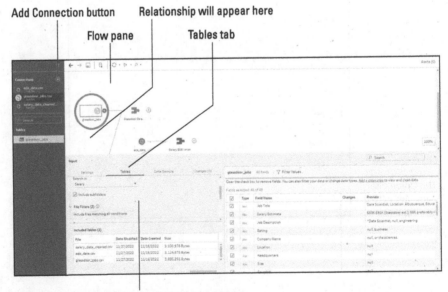

FIGURE 3-8:
The state of the file after an insert step is created.

Find information about the file in the Input pane

6. **Drag the table to the Union (not Join) option below the existing table.**

The relationship between the original table and the new table, which forms a union, can be seen in the Flow pane, also shown in Figure 3-8. Until the union is created, you cannot see the relationship.

7. **Go back to the Input pane and confirm that the data source and relevant data are available under the Settings tab. If you are not satisfied with the data source, click Browse and find the appropriate file located on your desktop or a shared drive and then double-click the file to open it as part of the existing connection.**

After you make the modifications, go back to the Tables tab and click Apply. All panes and data source details update immediately. The most notable change is the Field pane, reflecting the updates from the file union.

TIP

Establishing a union for tables follows the same protocol except that instead of creating a union among files, you are creating a union among multiple tables from one or more data sources. The slight modification occurs in Step 4, whereby the tables aren't files but database tables.

Joining data and input steps

Specific to database-related data, both the desktop version and Tableau Cloud can detect and show users which fields in their tables are unique. Tableau Prep Builder also identifies related fields and shows the names of these fields.

One of three options, as noted in Table 3-1, appears as part of a new column called Linked Keys, which is part of the Input pane.

TABLE 3-1 **Join Relationship Types for Input Step Data Flows**

Relationship Type	Description
Unique identifier	The field is unique for each row in the table. A table can have multiple unique identifiers. Values cannot be blank or null under any circumstance.
Related field	The fields have a relationship to another database table. Multiple related fields in a table can exist.
Both unique identifier and related field	The field is recognized as unique in a table. The field also relates to one or more other tables in a database.

One of the neat things about the linked keys is that you can quickly identify and add related tables to a flow or even create joins as part of the input step. So long as the database connector is supported where tables are defined, linked key relationships are widely available. To successfully leverage linked keys, use the steps that follow. If all you need to do is create a join relationship, click the + (plus sign) icon in the Flow pane and select Add Join; then, you can skip most of these steps. However, if you do need to bring multiple data source types together, follow these steps:

1. **Connect to the database that contains the relationships for fields, which may include unique identifiers (primary keys) and related fields (foreign keys).**

2. **Click the field marked as a related field or as a unique identifier and related field in the Input pane.**

   A list of related tables appears in the Profile pane.

3. **Review the tables and hover your cursor over the table you want to add or join to the input step.**

4. **Click the plus sign to add a table to your flow, or if you already have multiple tables available, click the Join button to join two or more tables together.**

Nurturing a flow

To get to the stage of cleansing and preparing your data, you must face a deluge of data, as you now understand if you've read the previous sections. Cleansing requires you to remove all the errors that might be found in your dataset, causing a potential result set to be skewed. The problem could be words that are inappropriately capitalized, items with too few or too many spaces, misspellings, or even extraneous numbers after a decimal. Those are just a few specific reasons you may need to clean your data. When you reach the point of cleansing and preparation, you should be ready to add new steps to the flow, insert new steps, and organize steps. Also, at this point, you can add *context*, meaning a way to individualize items to the flows. Context can be integrated into a flow through the use of the colors, descriptions, and naming conventions needed to support a flow layout. See Figure 3-9. Each of these attributes can be included as part of the specific flow, which incorporates two data sources, a single cleaning step, a pivot step, and a singular output.

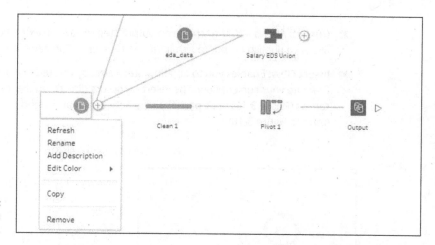

FIGURE 3-9:
Formatting a
flow step.

Whether you intend to add a step at the beginning or insert a step anywhere throughout a flow, these options are accessible by right-clicking or pressing the + (plus sign) next to a step (highlighted) in the Input pane, as shown in Figure 3-10. Even removing a flow requires only one step of right-clicking the input step and selecting Remove. Here are the available options:

>> **Clean Step:** Allows you to add a step that supports cleaning actions.

>> **New Rows:** Generates new rows to a sequential dataset that fill in dataset gaps.

>> **Aggregate:** Helps to bring steps together between existing fields and change the level of detail provided.

>> **Pivot:** Creates a pivot step between two existing steps to perform actions such as converting column data to rows or rows data to columns. Users can also create wildcard pivots to add additional data to an existing pivot automatically.

>> **Join:** Creates a join step between existing steps. There are two ways to create joins, either manually from the menu or by dragging and dropping steps on top of an existing step to create a join.

>> **Union:** Creates a union between tables. Like a join, there are two ways to create a union step, either by using the Add option or by dragging and dropping to an existing step.

>> **Script:** If you need to utilize a scripting language such as R or Python in a flow, you use this option; however, as of this writing, Tableau Cloud does not support using script steps.

>> **Prediction:** If you have access to the Einstein Discovery–powered models, you can incorporate predictive modeling capabilities into your flows.

» **Output:** Allows a user to create an output step to save an extract or a .csv file, or to publish output to either Tableau Server or Tableau Cloud.

» **Insert Flow:** Enables you to add flow steps already created in a previous flow into your current flow. The insertion occurs directly on the Input pane canvas (Figure 3-11) or as part of a step between or at the end of a flow (refer to Figure 3-10).

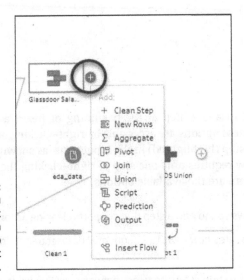

FIGURE 3-10:
The menu options that appear when right-clicking to add or insert a step.

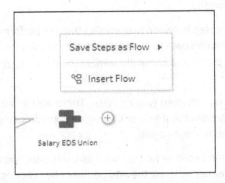

FIGURE 3-11:
Inserting a step into a flow.

To remove a flow step, right-click to bring up the option to remove a step (the link) between two inserts (see Figure 3-12).

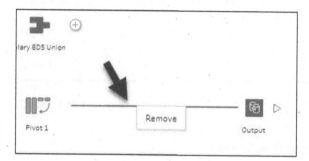

FIGURE 3-12:
Removing a step
from a flow.

Grouping flows

Suppose you have a set of steps in your flow that are connected and repetitive. The flow might have steps occurring across many lanes, as shown in Figure 3-13. In that case, you can consolidate the connected steps into a single group.

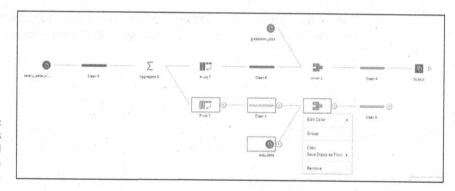

FIGURE 3-13:
Selecting items
to be included
within a
group flow.

To begin a group, you click the two or more steps in the single flow that you want to group. Then right-click the steps you've selected and select Group from the menu that appears. The result is a folder consolidating all the steps into a nice, neat package, as shown in Figure 3-14. Notice how each group flow is represented with a different color, offering you context indicating that two separate flows are occurring.

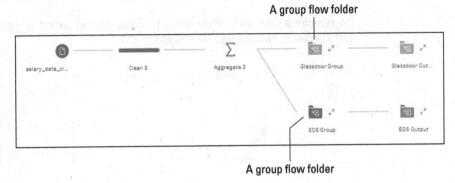

A group flow folder

A group flow folder

FIGURE 3-14:
Presenting
when all steps
are compressed
into a group
flow folder.

With a group flow, you can

>> Click the double arrows next to the folder, which is the same as a group, to expand or collapse a group.

>> Expand a group anytime and add more steps to the existing group before collapsing the folder to create a compact group.

>> Expand a group anytime and remove unwanted steps in an existing group before collapsing the folder.

>> To format the group, manage the group settings such as expand or ungroup, copy group steps, or remove a group, right-click the group folder, as shown in Figure 3-15.

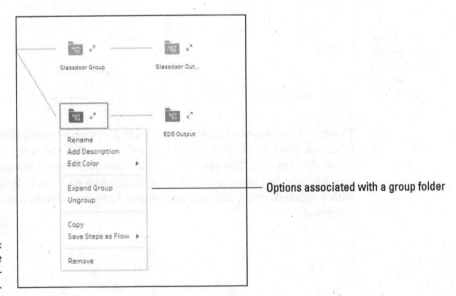

Options associated with a group folder

FIGURE 3-15:
Options available
when you right-
click a group flow.

Filtering flows

One of the features touted by Tableau is its ability to filter data with a single click. You can hide data using the Keep Only or Exclude options on a specific field in a profile card, Data Grid, or result card. Alternatively, you can select from numerous filtering options at the field level when you require more complex filtering.

Users can filter data at any step within a flow. For example, suppose you want to change a specific value. In that case, you can edit the value within the field or isolate the value with a null by directly clicking the field, assuming that you have a cleaning step available to present the field, as seen in Figure 3-16. You'd use the cleaning step in Tableau when your data requires refinement. Each time a flow cycles, the step will look to complete activities such as filter, rename, split, group, or remove fields.

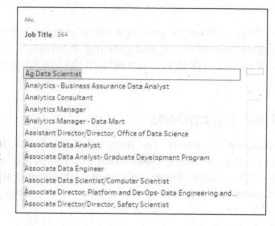

FIGURE 3-16: You can edit a field value by directly updating within a cleaning step.

Many filtering functions are available at the field level. You find these options by clicking the ellipsis referred to as "More Options" in Tableau Prep Builder. Some of the options you can choose from are shown in Figure 3-17 and include the following:

» **Rename Field:** Enables a user to rename a specific field.

» **Duplicate Field:** Enables a user to duplicate a field and all the values within that field.

» **Keep Only Field:** Hides all fields except for the ones selected.

» **Hide Field:** Temporarily hides the specific field selected from the dataset.

» **Remove:** Removes the field entirely from the dataset.

FIGURE 3-17:
Filtering options
that appear
after clicking
the ellipsis next
to a field.

The menu also offers options to complete more complex filtering, cleaning, grouping, creating calculated fields, and splitting of values. You can also create calculated fields or publish a field as a data role. In the following sections, we will address these items.

Advanced filtering options

There are four filtering categories. The first, Calculated Value, lets you narrow down string data or create calculated values based on numerical fields, depending on the field type. The example shown in Figure 3-18 incorporates a CONTAINS filter, and all jobs must have a Location field containing CA and a Headquarters field containing CA.

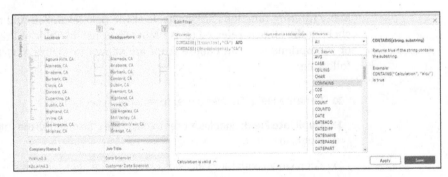

FIGURE 3-18:
A calculated
value filter.

After you create a string that contains the calculated values for the filter, click Apply. You can see the changes appear in the dataset after you've created a targeted filter.

The Selected Values Filter allows you to search a specific field value and then narrow down the values using the Keep Only or Exclude parameters to tighten the results further. In the example shown in Figure 3-19, the parameter searched on the left is MD (for Maryland). On the right, the Exclude field indicates the removal of all Baltimore, MD instances from the dataset. If you wanted to keep only specific values, you would go to the Keep Only option and select from the remaining cities in the state of MD.

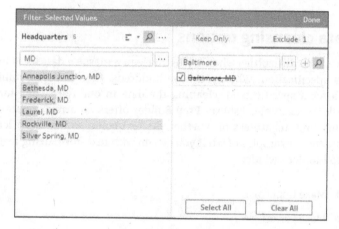

FIGURE 3-19:
Using the
Selected
Values filter.

Wildcard Search works similarly to Selected Values; however, you could filter on specific values. Then, on the right side using Boolean parameters, you can further narrow down the options by Contains, Starts With, Ends With, or Exact Match. Again, the parameters can be set for you to Exclude or Keep Only. In the example shown in Figure 3-20, the initial search looks for all Headquarters locations containing the value GA. On the right side, the qualifying parameter is set to keep only those entries that end with the letters GA. As a result, only three locations match these criteria.

The remaining filter is Null Values. It offers only two options: to narrow the dataset to null and non-null values. You may wonder why someone would heavily restrict values to null values, but it's the quickest way to evaluate what data does not exist in a field because quickly creating restrictions helps reduce anomalies.

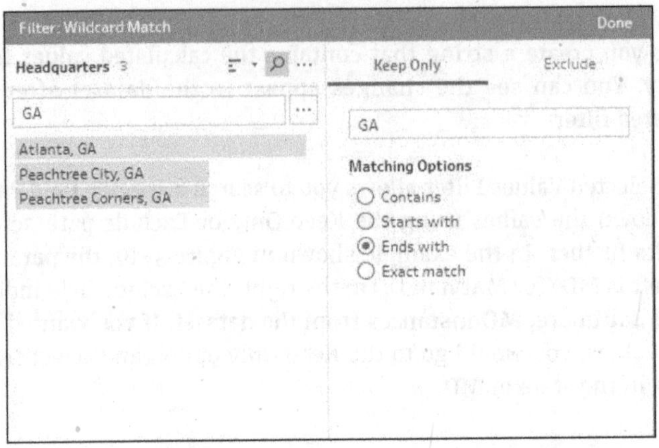

FIGURE 3-20:
The Wildcard
Search filter.

Data cleansing options

One of the difficulties when trying to clean a massive dataset is formatting items to a specification. When you have hundreds, thousands, or millions of rows of data for a specific field, cleaning the data in one fell swoop for consistency is ideal. For example, Tableau Prep Builder offers an array of options to clean text formatting, regardless of whether the text contains numbers, letters, or special characters. Examples of what you can do with text-formatting features in Tableau Prep Builder include:

>> Make Uppercase

>> Make Lowercase

>> Remove Letters

>> Remove Numbers

>> Remove Punctuation

>> Trim Spaces

>> Remove Extra Spaces

>> Remove All Spaces

Suppose you had one entry that was Vancouver BC. Another entry was Vancouver, BC. A third was Vancouver Bc. The formatting here presents three different scenarios. To ensure consistency, you'll want to consider streamlining all entries to one format. In this case, the entry should be Vancouver BC. You would follow these steps to make all entries conform to that format:

1. **To thoroughly clean the operations, select Remove Punctuation on the drop-down menu.**

2. **Type** BC **in the search box, which acts as a filter, and make sure the** *BC* **is all uppercase.**

3. **Select Remove All Extra Spaces.**

   In this case, where the comma is located, you should truncate from two spaces to one.

Using Split Value

Some users find that when they filter, they wind up with too many rows of data in a field. In those cases, you may have a way to classify specific data better. With the Split Value Filter, Tableau Prep Builder can use its recommendation engine to split values based on patterns and known behaviors. Alternatively, you can select which rows should be made into a new column, leading users to go from one column to two or more columns.

An example of using the Split Value Filter for one of the location fields is to split headquarters locations from A–Z to A–L and M–Z.

Saving Prep Data

Saving your work often is paramount to successfully using any software application and Tableau Prep Builder is no exception. A nice feature with Tableau Prep Builder is the ability to automatically save your data when creating or editing flows on the web. For the desktop, though, you need to save items manually.

A significant consideration that links data freshness and saving items in Tableau Prep Builder is how often a flow is executed. Of course, you can run flows manually and, if you want, save items periodically by utilizing a schedule with Tableau Server or Tableau Cloud. This section presents a variety of approaches to automate saving data across Tableau Prep Builder, but it's important to note that server or cloud-based configuration is often required as part of the scheduling cycle.

Automating flows

Changes are automatically saved when you create or edit a flow using Tableau Server or Tableau Cloud. Saved changes include the data source connection as well as inserted, added, and customized steps. So, take a deep breath; you won't lose your work. But there are a few catches, of course:

REMEMBER

>> You must log in to the server to which you are saving your flows.

>> You need to head to the Push menu (click File ⇨ Push) to set up the Publishing parameters if you want to publish a flow to a different server's project.

>> Draft flows are visible to only one person: you! You must publish them before they are available to others to collaborate and share. That's only the half of it. You also need to set permissions to access the project; permissions are not configured when you click Publish.

>> Until a flow is published, you see the badge Never Been Published next to a badge showing Draft.

The most important consideration to keep in mind about automated flows is that when a flow is published, and you then decide to edit and republish the draft, each new version of the flow is kept in the Revision History dialog box, accessible on the Explore Page of either Tableau Server or Tableau Cloud from the actions menu.

Crafting published data sources

If you are reading this section, it probably means you are ready to create a published data source. You have reached the last step in the cleansing and preparation cycle (unless you are looking to make some advanced data enhancements, as described in Book 3, Chapter 4).

The published data source requires a bit of configuration. Here is how to get there:

1. **Locate the +(plus sign) icon on a step where you want to produce an output.**

2. **Select the Output option (see Figure 3-21).**

   An Output Pane opens, showing you a data snapshot (see Figure 3-22). To the left, you have some options to choose from: Save Output to a File, Published Data Source, or Database.

   Depending on the output type, you will be required to configure one or more parameters using one of these approaches:

- If you select File, you're prompted to select the location where the file is saved and the output type. Also, you need to determine the Write type, either Create Table or Append to Table.

TECHNICAL STUFF

- To create a Tableau Extract, set the Save Output to Save As File and the Output Type to Tableau Data Extract (.hyper).

  Selecting Published Data Source requires you to log in to Tableau Server or Tableau Cloud.

If you decide to save the output to a database table, you need to select the connection type, allowing you to utilize 10+ connectors. Alternatively, you can point to a Custom SQL Query.

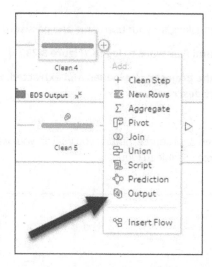

FIGURE 3-21:
Selecting the output to run.

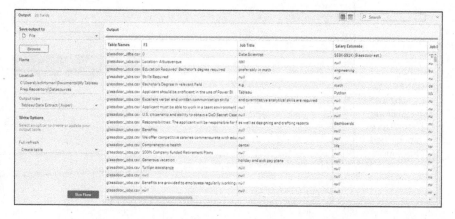

FIGURE 3-22:
Snapshot in the Output pane, along with ways to save published data sources.

TIP

The most efficient way to save and publish work is to use Tableau Cloud. To publish the data source, follow these steps:

1. **Go to the Save Output drop-down menu and select Published Data Source.**

2. **Pick one option from the drop-down menu, either Select a Server or Sign-In.**

3. **Upon selecting Sign into Tableau Online with your user credentials, you're prompted to log in to Tableau Cloud.**

4. **You can either enter the Tableau Server address or select Tableau Online, but because you want Tableau Cloud, in this case, select Tableau Online.**

5. **Click Connecting.**

   A pop-up screen appears asking for your username and password.

6. **Enter your Username and Password to log in. (Figure 3-23.)**

7. **At the prompt, select the project to be loaded and extracted, the project's name, and the project's description.**

8. **Press Run Flow.**

   You now have a published data source, putting you well on your way to using the Published Data Source in Tableau Cloud.

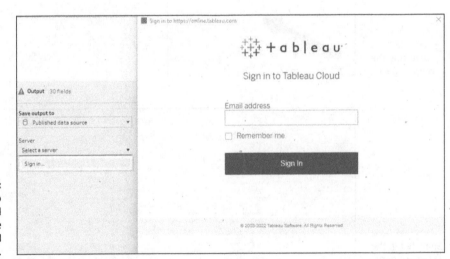

FIGURE 3-23:
Log into
Tableau Cloud
to configure
a published
data source.

Chapter 4

Advanced Data Prep Approaches in Tableau

After you've completed the preparation and cleansing phase covered in Book 3, Chapters 2 and 3, your data is on its way to being in tip-top shape, and you're just about ready to make the transition from Tableau Prep Builder back to Tableau Desktop. But first, you need to know about a few remaining items in the bag of magic tricks — fundamental concepts that, whether you are in Tableau Prep Builder or Tableau Desktop, can get you from data glut to harmony.

In this chapter, you take a final quick tour around Tableau Prep Builder to explore features that help streamline your data before heading to Tableau Desktop and Tableau Cloud for the remainder of Book 3.

Peering into Data Structures

When data is in its raw form, you have control over the data structure because you manipulate and move things all over the place. As soon as you transition to a Tableau product, though, you lose a bit of that control. Tableau assumes that you have access to the raw data as well as sufficient access within the toolset to shape the dataset using Tableau Prep. Some situations won't allow pivoting (explained in more detail in "Pivoting with data: Tall versus wide," later in this chapter), aggregating, or blending data because of how Tableau ingests and presents the data. You can conduct the analysis, but to be successful, you'll need to change how you approach your data, from how you generate calculations to formatting your rows and columns. The following sections address some of these data structure complexities.

Rows and records

It might seem odd to talk about rows and records in this chapter, but aspects of data structure and placement of data are relevant, as your goal should be to focus on data granularity.

As you prepare your data, you should adhere to the following best practices concerning rows and records:

>> Each row should contain a unique identifier (UID).

>> Each row should have a unique purpose.

>> Each time you have a value such as ExTableName(Count) as a field, you should know precisely what that value adds to a row.

Your data structure is likely poor if you fail the litmus test for each condition. The top image in Figure 4-1 shows an example of the data structure, which almost but not quite meets the litmus test on the left side. To establish a patient's medical conditions, Four data requirements are captured in the medical record: weight, height, temperature, and blood pressure, and the date is recorded. Although each row of data indicates health care data that is independent and unique, certain fields, such as the Patient ID (PID), must be included to ensure 100 percent uniqueness.

In this case, condition one is not met. Each row may appear unique, but what happens if two patients have the same patient profile, including weight, height, temperature, and blood pressure captured on the same day? In that case, a user would be unable to differentiate the record from one patient to another, so condition two is not met because each row does not have a unique purpose. In the case of condition three regarding calculated fields, the name of a field should be clearly labeled. The example has no calculated fields, so that condition does not apply to this use case. By simply adding the PID row, shown in the bottom image of Figure 4-1, your data structure passes the litmus test because each patient's records can be grouped in conjunction with a unique record ID (not seen).

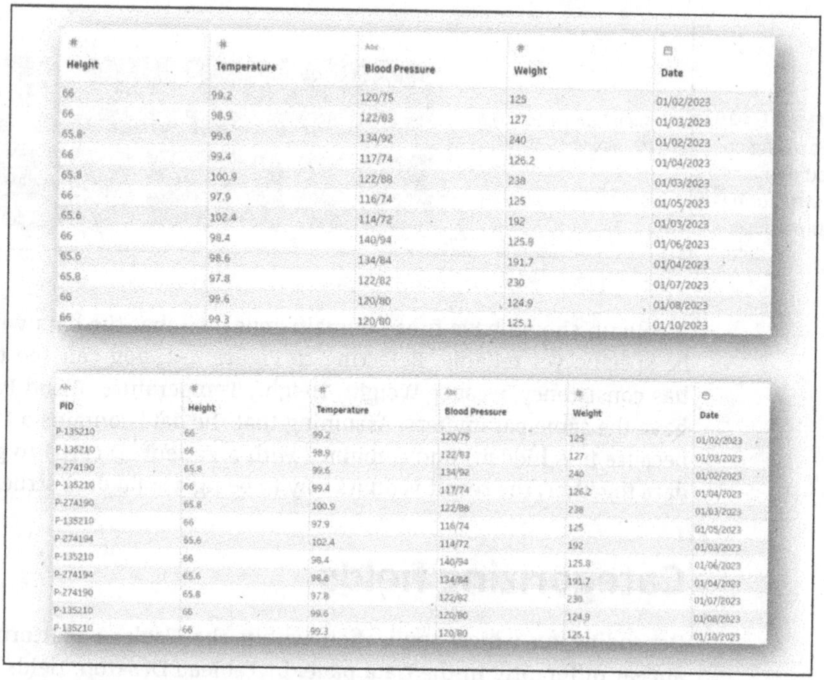

Height	Temperature	Blood Pressure	Weight	Date
66	99.2	120/75	125	01/02/2023
66	98.9	122/83	127	01/03/2023
65.8	99.6	134/92	240	01/02/2023
66	99.4	117/74	126.2	01/04/2023
65.8	100.9	122/88	238	01/03/2023
66	97.9	116/74	125	01/05/2023
65.6	102.4	114/72	192	01/03/2023
66	98.4	140/94	125.8	01/06/2023
65.6	98.6	134/84	191.7	01/04/2023
65.8	97.8	122/82	230	01/07/2023
66	99.6	120/80	124.9	01/08/2023
66	99.3	120/80	125.1	01/10/2023

PID	Height	Temperature	Blood Pressure	Weight	Date
P-135210	66	99.2	120/75	125	01/02/2023
P-135210	66	98.9	122/83	127	01/03/2023
P-274190	65.8	99.6	134/92	240	01/02/2023
P-135210	66	99.4	117/74	126.2	01/04/2023
P-274190	65.8	100.9	122/88	238	01/03/2023
P-135210	66	97.9	116/74	125	01/05/2023
P-274194	65.6	102.4	114/72	192	01/03/2023
P-135210	66	98.4	140/94	125.8	01/06/2023
P-274194	65.6	98.6	134/84	191.7	01/04/2023
P-274190	65.8	97.8	122/82	230	01/07/2023
P-135210	66	99.6	120/80	124.9	01/08/2023
P-135210	66	99.3	120/80	125.1	01/10/2023

FIGURE 4-1: A rows and records example that doesn't meet all three best practices for data structure.

Columns and fields

In the preceding section's example, a column is introduced when you need to make a record set unique to a specific individual or subject, such as a product type. In that example, the creation of the PID allowed the patient's records to be aggregated. Hence, a unique identity capturing an entire medical history is now available. Combined with a record ID, which is not seen in Tableau Prep Builder, each row is then deemed unique. Fields and columns are considered interchangeable terms, especially in Tableau Desktop. But for Tableau Prep Builder, you should address a data field relative to how data is grouped with data and their relationships. An analyst must articulate the field's association in terms of domain groups. For example, the domain of shoes may have four different groups: men's, children's, women's, and unisex (see Figure 4-2).

On the other hand, the more granular items that fall under each domain, such as sneakers, boots, and slippers, are all item types, not shoe classifications. In other words, the shoe domain is limited to a focused classification, not an expansive list of options. Here's another example: Education, College, and Grades. College is a type of schooling (education). The Grades category is too broad and could fit in various ways, so the concept needs to be narrower.

FIGURE 4-2:
Focusing on
targeted domains
in structuring
column-based
data.

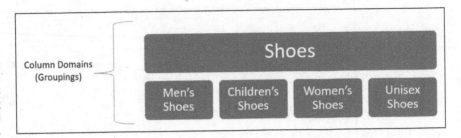

Column Domains
(Groupings)

A column should have broad domain appeal so that the data within the field can be specific yet reliable. Referring to Figure 4-1, you can see that each column has consistency because Weight, Height, Temperature, Blood Pressure, and Date have the same parameters. Assuming that the data contains a UID (which it does because it is hidden) and combined with a Patient ID (PID) to group like patient data together, the result is on its way to being a solid data structure.

Categorizing fields

Depending on which application within the Tableau platform you use, fields appear differently in the Data pane. In Tableau Desktop, fields are either treated as a dimension or measures, indicated by lines in a table in the Data pane. Furthermore, dimensions or measures are considered discrete or continuous, using a color-coding scheme of blue fields for discrete and green fields for continuous. Blue and green indicators are referred to as pills, as mentioned in Book 3, Chapter 1.

WARNING

If you have difficulty seeing colors or want an alternative way to discriminate blue from green, you can't. The blue/green pills are a set-in-stone feature within Tableau.

To better understand how to categorize field-level data, take a look at Table 4-1.

REMEMBER

An axis in Tableau is created when you drag a measure that can be aggregated onto the View. You'll see an axis because there will be a label with a measure's name, and it will include a range of values. Tableau creates an axis to scale based on your dataset.

In Figure 4-3, the Year field is set to continuous, creating a horizontal axis along the bottom. The green pill for both fields shows that both the row and column are representative of continuous fields. The line across the time horizon also indicates a continuous measure.

TABLE 4-1   **Field Types Categories**

Type	Definition
Dimension	Refers to a qualitative field type, meaning it is described as not measurable. Examples of dimensions include City, State, Hair Color, or Brand. Notice that none of these is a numerical term. Dimensions are associated with being discrete because qualitative data describe items.
Measure	Refers to a quantitative field type, meaning it's described as having data points that can be measured using numbers. Examples of measures include income earned, number of clicks, or quantity. In Tableau Desktop, measures are aggregated by default using SUM. You can change the way data is aggregated. Measures are generally continuous, but not always.
Discrete	When you are looking for distinct values, you are describing discrete data. Restaurants such as McDonald's and Starbucks are two specific (discrete) brands.
Continuous	Continuous data is associated with constant numeric values and order. Examples of numeric order include distance, time, and weight. In Tableau Desktop, continuous values are presented on the axis.

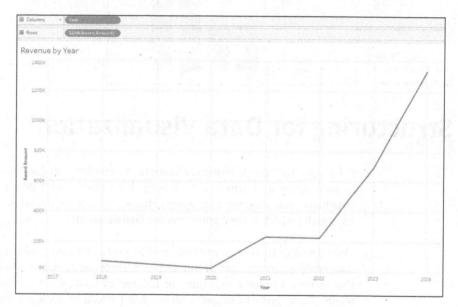

FIGURE 4-3:
Example of a
continuous
measure.

Figure 4-4 shows that the Year field has been set to Discrete. The field creates a horizontal header of an axis. The blue background (using the blue pill) and horizontal headers illustrate that the data is discrete.

**TECHNICAL
STUFF**

Tableau Prep Builder does not distinguish dimensions and measures because it's a data-cleansing and preparation tool. In cleansing and preparation, you must know (generally speaking) the difference between discrete or continuous values to help shape the data as required.

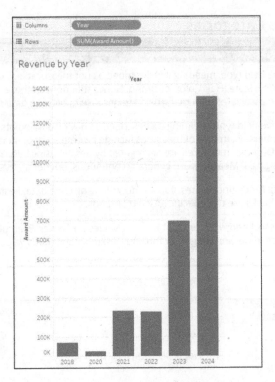

FIGURE 4-4:
Example of a
discrete measure.

Structuring for Data Visualization

For proper and compelling visualizations, the underlying data must be structured in such a way as to make it logical for both users and Tableau itself. Properly structured data ensures that aggregations and other calculations are computed accurately, which is the foundation for visualizations.

The following sections show you how to group data for optimal readability and data analysis. In the case of binning and histograms, you see how to group data that follows a pattern into bins, or focused groupings using a histogram-based model. Data tends to follow a structured pattern or data distribution for large datasets. When the data falls outside the normal range of values, interpreting the validity of outliers — the odd values in the dataset — is important to improve data visualization quality. The last section covers how you present your data to avoid data redundancy and quality concerns. When creating a wide formatted dataset, data does not repeat in at least one column, usually the first. An example is a unique record ID. If you utilize tall datasets, minimizing the use of columns, you will have data repetition, likely resulting in a need to cleanse your data with a tool such as Tableau Prep Builder.

Binning and histograms

Fixed values are continuous. Your age is an example. It doesn't change for 365 days, so there is a distance between one year and the next. Think about the time. Can you change the fact that there are 60 minutes in an hour, 24 hours in a day, or seven days a week? Not a chance.

When someone asks a 42-year-old person how old they are, do they exclaim from the rooftops, "42 years old, 7 months, 23 days, and 13 hours old." Okay, that is a bit extreme, but generally people say their age in terms of their latest birthday (or they say 39 going on whatever). A cute little seven-year-old may get into the nitty-gritty of years, months, and days, but they won't when they get older.

Speaking of one's age this way is an example of *binning* — in this case, by using a time-bound reference, age. *Binning* is a way to group related values together rather than have an exorbitant number of distinct, redundant values. When you create a fixed value despite having a more precise answer available, you lump all the facts into a grouping of sorts. How many surveys have you taken in which you were asked to select your age: 18–24, 25–34, 35–44, and so on? That type of grouping is another example of binning.

Tableau Prep Builder uses histograms to visualize the distribution of numerical data using binning. The histogram is similar to the bar chart, but it spans a grouping across a continuous axis, such as the range of ages in a survey or time horizons. The height of the bar, as represented by the bar's rectangle shape, is determined by the frequency of values using the count function.

In the example presented in Figure 4-5, you see two variables, Mobile Devices and Age.

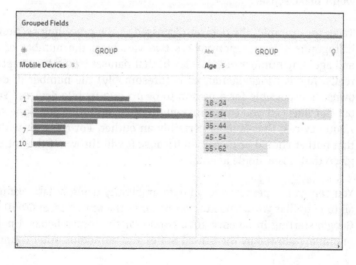

FIGURE 4-5: An example of binning and histogram structures.

In the figure, both variables have been binned so that you can see two perspectives. The summary view illustrates that owners of mobile devices aged 18–62 own anywhere from one to ten devices. Each bar represents the aggregation of values, demonstrating how often a user may have a specific number of devices. Of the range of ten possible answers, there are eight unique binned values that Tableau has determined should be grouped together for the count of mobile devices. Each bar represents the number of people within the sample with a given number of mobile devices. For example, there might be five respondents with four mobile devices, whereas one respondent in this example has ten or more.

For the detailed view of the age of those owning mobile devices, each group was aggregated, illustrating the binning of range-bound data. In the survey response, the detailed view shows how many respondents participated in the mobile device survey. For example, 6 of the 30 respondents were aged 25–34, representing the largest bar in the model. The binning was derived by evaluating the ages reported by the participants and then aggregating the results into the appropriate groups.

Distributions and outliers

After your data is consistent enough to be evaluated, having been cleaned in Tableau Prep Builder, you'll want to complete an activity that allows you to understand its range of possible values, known as *distribution*. This is also the time to determine whether you have any one-off data points, known as *outliers*.

Distributions give you an idea of how your data is shaped within the histogram. Depending on the size of the dataset and the range of the bins within the histogram view, ensuring that your data is complete can be tricky. You can be sure that the shape is rock-solid only if you know your data; otherwise, the distribution won't make sense.

Take, for example, the dataset discussed in the preceding section, "Binning and histograms." The section covers two variables: the number of mobile devices and age. Any number of variables in that dataset would be acceptable, right? Not really. Age is range-bound, as is (presumably) the number of devices a person owns. Is it possible for a person to own 1,000 mobile devices? Yes, it's possible but not likely. If you saw a maximum of 10, and then someone said they owned 1,000 devices, that is most certainly an outlier. For the user with 1,000 devices, that outlier should be discarded because it will throw off the entire visualization, given that it is a single anomaly.

You can gain a perspective on data ambiguity using a data example everyone is all too familiar with. The number of times the search term *COVID-19* appeared on Google starting in January 2020 is one for the record books. Upon the lockdown in China, followed by the United States and numerous other countries, the search term *COVID-19* peaked on March 12, 2020. It was the number one search trend before the news, weather, music, and sports (really) until April 26, 2020. Since then, *COVID-19* has been considered a common search term on Google. So, what do we learn from this trend? There was a date-based trend that had *COVID-19* as the predominant search term, not at a single point in time. In this case, the data should not be discarded because a unique trending distribution over a given period exists.

To zoom in a bit more: March 2, 2020, to April 26, 2020, should for all purposes be considered an outlier because the value is extreme relative to other search values in Google's search engine history. Although some may say that Google exaggerates their numbers from time to time (they don't; robots do the counting), errors within a range are possible. For this example, it's not likely, though, given the nature of the global lockdown. The outliers are correct, given that the outliers were part of a trend over a particular period, not a single blip on the radar, which indicates that natural data anomalies can be introduced into binning and histogram data.

TIP

To review the COVID-19 Google Search dataset, go to `https://trends.google.com/trends/explore?date=today%205-y&geo=US&q=COVID-19&hl=en`.

Pivoting with data: Tall versus wide

Most data analysts are accustomed to exploring wide spreadsheets with many columns of data and few rows. The wide-versus-tall debate often leads folks like you and me to manipulate our data sources because complex data makes us feel unsettled. In a typical business productivity application, pivoting functionality helps you shape your data from tall to wide and vice versa. For those using Tableau's pivot functionality, the word *pivot* suggests going from people-facing (wide) to machine-readable (tall or long) by transforming columns into rows.

TECHNICAL
STUFF

Pivoting data is a complex exercise in both Tableau Desktop and Tableau Prep Builder. Depending on the quality of the data source and needed searchability, the requirements vary greatly. To learn more about data pivot-based preparation requirements in Tableau Prep Builder, go to `https://help.tableau.com/current/prep/en-us/prep_pivot.htm`.

Have you ever seen publicly accessible government data before? It's dizzying for any expert analyst to interpret, never mind anyone not in that field. There are numerous top-level agencies in the United States and hundreds, if not thousands, of government departments and branches that roll up under the 15 or so big agencies. So it goes without saying that the interpretation of data would yield a separate column representing each agency's data. Then you'd have a minimum number of rows of data depending on how many years of data is available. Manageable, but quite the eye sore.

The table in Figure 4-6 shows a dataset provided by the White House, reformatted to be readable in Tableau using Microsoft Excel. You can access the raw data files at `https://www.whitehouse.gov/omb/budget/historical-tables/`. The dataset contains the Executive Branch Civilian Full-Time Equivalent Employees count as a percentage from 1981–2023. Given there are 11 agencies where data is reported over a 42-year period, the dataset is a good example of a wide dataset because there are 43 columns and just 11 rows of data.

	DoD	Agriculture	HHS, Education, Social Security Admin.	Homeland Security	Interior	Justice	Transportation	Treasury	Veterans	Other
1981	44.9	5.6	7.3	1.8	3.8	2.3	2.5	4.8	10.2	16.8
1982	47.2	5.4	7.1	1.8	3.5	2.2	2.6	4.6	10.4	15.3
1983	47.4	5.3	7.1	1.9	3.5	2.3	2.7	4.7	10.5	14.7
1984	48.0	5.2	6.8	1.8	3.5	2.4	2.7	4.9	10.5	14.2
1985	48.7	5.0	6.5	1.8	3.4	2.4	2.6	5.0	10.5	13.9
1986	49.3	4.9	6.3	1.8	3.3	2.6	2.6	5.2	10.4	13.6
1987	49.0	4.9	6.0	2.0	3.3	2.6	2.6	5.4	10.5	13.6
1988	47.7	5.1	5.8	2.2	3.3	2.7	2.7	6.0	10.5	13.9
1989	48.0	5.1	5.7	2.2	3.4	3.0	2.7	6.0	10.0	13.8
1990	46.3	5.1	5.6	2.2	3.3	3.0	2.7	6.0	9.8	15.9
1991	45.9	5.2	6.0	2.3	3.4	3.4	2.8	6.3	10.3	14.4
1992	44.9	5.2	6.2	2.5	3.5	3.6	2.9	6.2	10.6	14.6
1993	43.6	5.3	6.4	2.5	3.7	3.8	2.9	6.2	10.9	14.7
1994	42.3	5.4	6.4	2.6	3.7	3.9	2.9	6.3	11.4	15.1
1995	41.7	5.3	6.5	2.7	3.7	4.2	2.9	6.6	11.6	14.8
1996	41.2	5.3	6.7	3.1	3.5	4.4	3.0	6.5	11.7	14.5
1997	40.7	5.4	6.9	3.4	3.6	4.8	3.1	6.4	11.5	14.3
1998	39.5	5.4	7.1	3.7	3.7	5.1	3.2	6.3	11.6	14.5
1999	38.3	5.4	7.1	3.7	3.8	5.3	3.3	6.4	11.6	15.1
2000	36.4	5.2	7.0	3.7	3.7	5.3	3.1	6.3	11.2	18.1
2001	37.4	5.6	7.4	4.0	4.0	5.5	3.3	6.6	11.9	14.3
2002	37.0	5.5	7.2	4.6	4.0	5.5	3.5	6.6	11.9	14.1
2003	35.5	5.6	7.0	7.9	3.9	5.4	3.2	6.3	11.6	13.5

FIGURE 4-6:
A wide dataset from whitehouse.gov.

If you read the document as is, you can understand which agencies support the most personnel relative to the U.S. Executive Branch budget. However, to successfully cleanse the data and bring it into either Tableau Desktop or Tableau Prep Builder, you must do the following:

>> Ensure that the dataset has a single field per column.

>> Ensure that each agency has only a single data point per year based on a percentage of total employees.

Although presenting this dataset may look easy in Excel, porting the data into either Tableau Desktop or Tableau Prep Builder complicates the data's appearance because your data is transformed. Each field will be represented in a separate column. In other words, each agency will have a distinct row (single field), and each year will have a distinct column (many fields). The dataset here is wide, as shown in Figure 4-7.

Wide Date Example

	2004	2005	2006	2007	2008	2009	2010	2011	2012	2013	2014	2015	2016	2017	2018	2019
Agriculture	6.50	5.40	5.30	5.20	5.00	4.80	4.50	4.60	4.40	4.30	4.20	4.20	4.20	4.20	4.10	3.90
DoD	36.70	35.70	36.10	36.00	35.80	35.50	34.80	36.70	36.60	35.90	35.60	35.50	35.30	35.20	35.40	35.60
HHS, Educa..	7.00	7.00	6.90	6.80	6.70	6.60	6.50	6.70	6.60	6.60	6.60	6.80	6.80	6.80	6.70	6.60
Homeland S..	7.50	7.80	7.90	8.10	8.40	8.60	8.10	8.50	8.80	8.90	9.00	8.80	8.90	8.90	9.00	9.20
Interior	3.90	3.80	3.70	3.70	3.60	3.50	3.30	3.40	3.30	3.30	3.20	3.10	3.10	3.10	3.10	3.00
Justice	5.60	5.60	5.70	5.70	5.70	5.50	5.30	5.50	5.50	5.60	5.50	5.60	5.60	5.70	5.50	5.40
Other	13.40	13.40	18.40	13.20	12.90	13.40	16.10	12.60	12.50	12.50	12.40	12.30	12.10	11.90	11.70	11.60
Transpor-t..	3.10	3.00	2.90	2.90	2.90	2.90	2.70	2.70	2.70	2.70	2.70	2.70	2.60	2.70	2.60	2.60
Treasury	6.20	6.00	5.90	5.90	5.70	5.50	5.30	5.30	5.10	5.00	4.90	4.70	4.50	4.50	4.30	4.20
Veterans	12.00	12.10	12.10	12.60	13.30	13.80	13.40	14.10	14.40	15.20	15.90	16.40	16.80	17.00	17.60	18.00

FIGURE 4-7:
A wide dataset in
Tableau Desktop.

If you were to swap rows for columns in the Excel worksheet, you'd then create tall data. Now, technically, you could have pivoted this data in Tableau Desktop. Because the dataset is a tad overwhelming, however, you might want to instead have a column for each agency and then list each agency's percentage per year.

Tableau Desktop consolidates your dataset from the Excel document, which is in the tall format, to a compressed set of five rows of data (years) and four distinct columns representing the sum result of each agency. In Figure 4-8, only a subset of the agencies in this dataset have been posted.

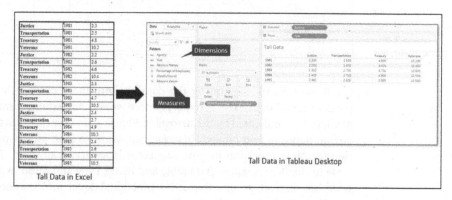

FIGURE 4-8:
Tableau
transforms
an Excel
spreadsheet
into a Tableau-
readable tall
dataset.

Compared to the Excel spreadsheet shown on the left in Figure 4-8 containing 20 rows and 3 columns of discrete data, Tableau Desktop has transformed the dataset by listing dates in a single column and having each agency represented as its unique column versus row, as shown in the wide data example in the previous section. Because each row has some form of unique attribution: date, agency, and percentage of the employee population, the dataset is optimized to be readable as a machine-ready format, hence the definition of tall data.

Normalizing Data

Generally, you don't think about normalizing data when addressing a single table. Relational databases often contain several tables sharing a common bond. Each table contains one or more unique identifiers, known as primary and secondary keys, on a per-record (row) basis. By joining keys, records become related so that information can be contained in a single table. If you can link the tables to find commonality, you can reduce data duplication.

Think about when you go to a doctor. Every doctor has an electronic health record system containing medical data on you, their patient. Some common data elements include name, date of birth, phone number, and perhaps your unique patient ID. There are two possibilities for how your data can be presented. The first aggregates all data into a single table, as shown in Figure 4-9. Although this approach may be ideal if all clinicians operate in the same medical practice, it is not likely because most patients go to many doctors across many medical practices.

FIGURE 4-9:
A single table before normalization.

PID	Patient Last Name	Patient First Name	Patient Phone	Age	Blind	Blood Donor	City	State	Zip Code
1Z4Q4J	Smith	James	617-555-1234	32	No	Yes	Phoenix	AZ	72901
2Z4Q4J	Jones	Barbara	617-555-1412	49	No	Yes	Scotsdale	AZ	72922
3Z4Q4J	Brown	Randall	202-555-1922	52	No	No	Washington	DC	20005
4Z4Q4J	Irving	Rebecca	202-555-9151	19	Yes	No	Bethesda	MD	20814
5Z4Q4J	Washington	Simon	757-555-2412	48	No	Yes	Virginia Beach	VA	23455
6Z4Q4J	Clayton	Maura	703-555-3933	22	Yes	No	Arlington	VA	22201
7Z4Q4J	Gibson	Brooklyn	404-555-0667	17	No	Yes	Atlanta	GA	30318

For these reasons, separating the datasets into more discrete blocks that compartmentalize data into groups is more suited to patient-centered data. The primary key (indicated by the arrows in Figure 4-10) synthesizes the record association between two tables. However, you want to look at group-level information for more precision in grouping records for trend analysis. The examples of State in the Demographic Data table and Blood Type and Blind in the Medical Data table are distinct groups that offer individual-level information with grouping opportunities.

When you break down tables into more discrete datasets, there is often the possibility of common fields within one or more columns. This process is called *normalization*. When you normalize data, you are helping to reduce redundant data found in the database.

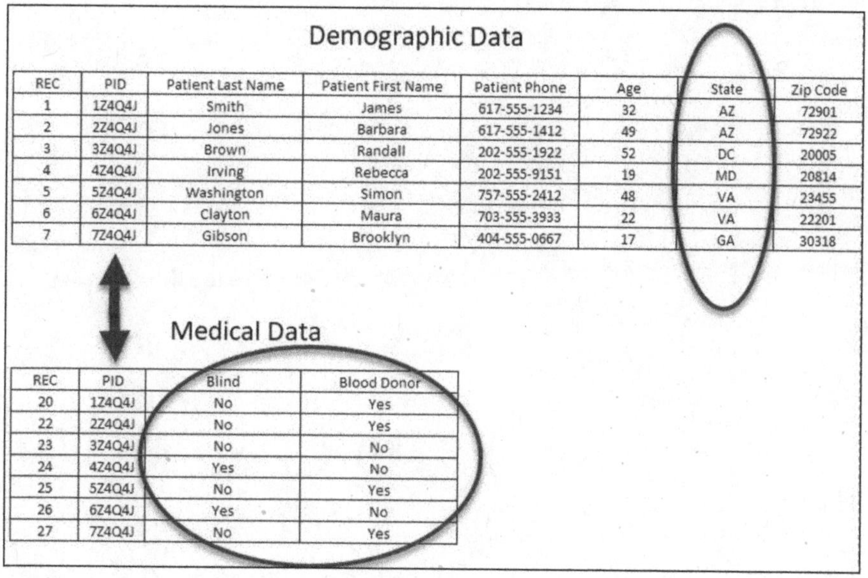

Demographic Data

REC	PID	Patient Last Name	Patient First Name	Patient Phone	Age	State	Zip Code
1	1Z4Q4J	Smith	James	617-555-1234	32	AZ	72901
2	2Z4Q4J	Jones	Barbara	617-555-1412	49	AZ	72922
3	3Z4Q4J	Brown	Randall	202-555-1922	52	DC	20005
4	4Z4Q4J	Irving	Rebecca	202-555-9151	19	MD	20814
5	5Z4Q4J	Washington	Simon	757-555-2412	48	VA	23455
6	6Z4Q4J	Clayton	Maura	703-555-3933	22	VA	22201
7	7Z4Q4J	Gibson	Brooklyn	404-555-0667	17	GA	30318

Medical Data

REC	PID	Blind	Blood Donor
20	1Z4Q4J	No	Yes
22	2Z4Q4J	No	Yes
23	3Z4Q4J	No	No
24	4Z4Q4J	Yes	No
25	5Z4Q4J	No	Yes
26	6Z4Q4J	Yes	No
27	7Z4Q4J	No	Yes

FIGURE 4-10:
Tables are broken to address the group and individual-level information for normalization.

Chapter **5**

Touring Tableau Desktop

O f all the applications in the Tableau product suite, Tableau Desktop is by far the one you'll use most as a data analyst. Tableau Desktop was the first application developed back when its founding company started in the late 1990s. It remained the industry leader because of its rich feature set. To create reports, dashboards, KPIs, and stories, you must use Tableau Desktop.

This chapter walks you through the key features of Tableau Desktop so that you can transform data into visualization masterpieces, allowing you to tell a story with your data.

Getting Hands-On in the Tableau Desktop Workspace

Tableau Desktop touts itself as an all-inclusive data analytics and business intelligence solution. *All-inclusive* is the key phrase because all activity is completed in the Tableau workspace, which consists of menus, toolbars, data panes, cards, shelves, and sheets. A *sheet* can represent one or more worksheets, dashboards, and stories.

In Figure 5-1, notice the conglomeration of capabilities built into the Tableau Desktop, including

>> **Workbook name:** The name of your workbook, which may consist of worksheets, dashboards, and stories. The workbook name in Figure 5-1 is PSC Code for Tableau.

>> **Cards and shelves:** A drag-and-drop interface in the workspace used to add data among one or more views. In the figure, the card Product Or Service Codes has been dragged from the Rows shelf to the Filters shelf. Doing so allows a user to create a filter for Product Or Service Codes.

>> **Views:** The primary canvas where visualizations (referred to as a *vizzes*) are created. The figure shows a listing of Federal Agencies that purchased products or services under PSC Code 7030 or DA10. Each bar represents the SUM dollar amount obligated for the specific agency.

>> **Toolbar:** The central location of commands and navigation aids to complete your analysis.

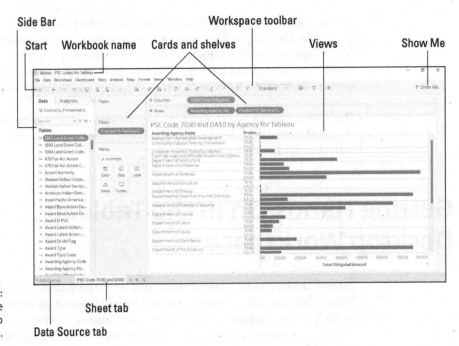

FIGURE 5-1:
Overview of the
Tableau Desktop
interface.

>> **Start:** Your ability to connect to new data sources begins with the Start icon.

>> **Side Bar:** Provides direct access to the Data and Analytics panes.

>> **Data Source tab:** This tab serves as the central location to access the Data Source pages so that you can view your data.

>> **Sheet tab:** Tabs in Tableau Desktop provide access to various workbook pages, whether a worksheet, dashboard, or story.

>> **Show Me:** Enables you to select the appropriate viz, based on the number of dimensions and measures included on the cards and shelves. Assuming that a viz is active, you'd click once, and the viz updates in the View area.

The remainder of this chapter describes these specific areas of the Tableau Desktop. These are the critical launch points to managing data, creating visualizations, and conducting analysis.

Making Use of the Tableau Desktop Menus

Menus in Tableau are one way to access all the features available to your workspace. Whereas the toolbar visualizes vital features, the menu categorizes each feature based on business functionality. For example, all worksheet, dashboard, and story capabilities fall under their respective menus. In contrast, you can access a complete set of analysis capabilities on the Analysis menu. The following sections dig a bit deeper into each of the menus and the critical capabilities within Tableau Desktop.

File menu

The File menu (Figure 5-2) is the central point where you save Tableau Desktop products and export Desktop files to alternative file formats. You can also import data into Tableau, set your data locale, and configure outputs to be print-ready. If you want to start a new workspace (choose New), open an existing workspace (choose Open), or close the current workspace (choose Close), you can complete each of these essential functions directly from this menu.

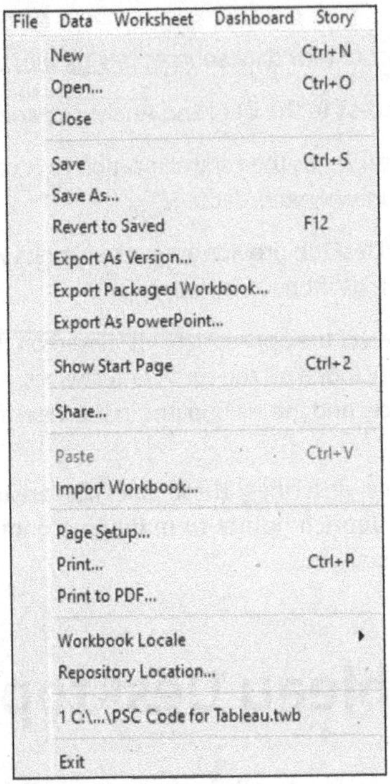

File	Data	Worksheet	Dashboard	Story
New				Ctrl+N
Open...				Ctrl+O
Close				
Save				Ctrl+S
Save As...				
Revert to Saved				F12
Export As Version...				
Export Packaged Workbook...				
Export As PowerPoint...				
Show Start Page				Ctrl+2
Share...				
Paste				Ctrl+V
Import Workbook...				
Page Setup...				
Print...				Ctrl+P
Print to PDF...				
Workbook Locale				▶
Repository Location...				
1 C:\...\PSC Code for Tableau.twb				
Exit				

FIGURE 5-2:
The File menu.

Data menu

Data is at the heart of Tableau Desktop. The features that are available as part of the workspace vary somewhat from those you can access on the Data Source page. When you want to fully exploit all the features within a data source that's already connected to Tableau Desktop, you go to the worksheet and click the Data menu. Most features are greyed out unless you are copying and pasting across multiple data sources. You can connect to a new data source from the Data menu, as you can by clicking the Tableau icon.

Most configurable features on the Data menu can be accessed under the active Data Source page. Active options include adding, removing, or extracting data from the data source. In addition, you can publish a data source and append existing data sources. You also find functionality such as configuring data source names and ensuring that referential integrity exists on the Data menu within a workspace, as shown in Figure 5-3. After you create a new data source for the Tableau workspace, you see a Data menu that varies slightly (see Figure 5-4). Each option in this menu allows you to complete a more detailed data-related task that you can see within one click.

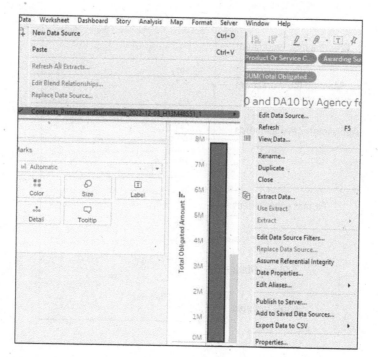

FIGURE 5-3:
The Data Source
menu under the
Worksheet menu.

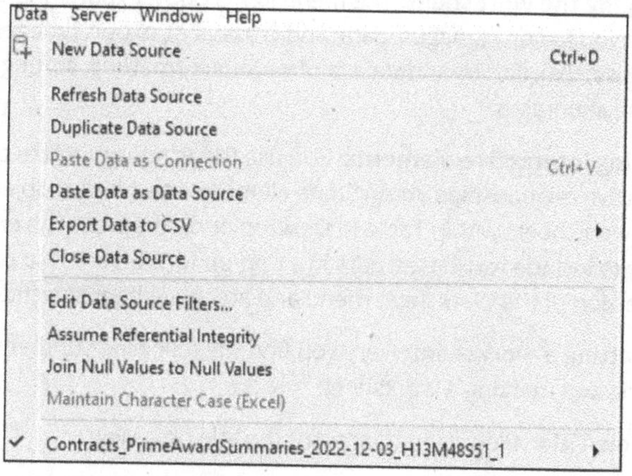

FIGURE 5-4:
The Data
Source menu
on the Data
Source page.

Worksheet menu

The Worksheet menu combines all the features needed to create, format, and build interactive experiences for a given worksheet. The Worksheet menu breaks out into subsections (see Figure 5-5), which include these capabilities:

>> **Creating a new worksheet:** Allows a user to create a new worksheet.

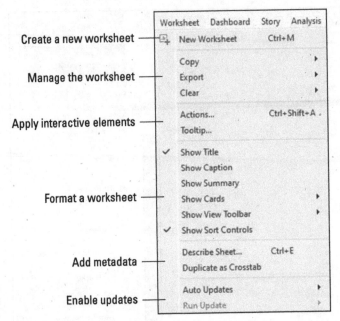

Create a new worksheet — New Worksheet   Ctrl+M

Manage the worksheet — Copy / Export / Clear

Apply interactive elements — Actions...   Ctrl+Shift+A / Tooltip...

Format a worksheet — Show Title / Show Caption / Show Summary / Show Cards / Show View Toolbar / Show Sort Controls

Add metadata — Describe Sheet...   Ctrl+E / Duplicate as Crosstab

Enable updates — Auto Updates / Run Update

FIGURE 5-5:
The Worksheet menu.

>> **Managing the worksheet:** The menu items Copy, Export, and Clear enable you to copy (images, data, and crosstabs), export (images, data, and crosstabs), and clear datasets of various formatting, sorting, and filtering anomalies.

>> **Applying interactive elements:** You use the Actions menu to create interactive relationships among data elements, dashboard objects, and other worksheets within Tableau Desktop or on the web. The *tooltips* (a way to include text-based data in a pop-up format) are also part of this section of the Worksheet menu and are worksheet specific.

>> **Formatting a worksheet:** Here you find the following submenus related to labeling and marking a worksheet:

- **Show Title:** Allows you to present the title on a view.

- **Show Caption:** Allows you to better understand the visualization through a textual description authored entirely by Tableau.

- **Show Summary:** A type of card that helps you understand the breadth of the Tableau dataset included within a view.

- **Show Cards:** Enables you to select which areas of the interface should be visible (or not). For example, a Filters card can be shown or hidden.

- **Show View Toolbar:** To maximize the screen real estate, you may want to hide the toolbars on the top. In this case, you can show or hide the toolbars.

- **Show Sort Controls:** Data can be presented as either ascending or descending. To ensure that the sort order is present, you want to make sure that the Show Sort Controls is enabled.

» **Adding metadata to the worksheet:** If you need to add context or duplicate the crosstabs, this menu segment includes all the firepower under two options:

- **Describe Sheet:** Allows you to see details about elements used in a visualization.

- **Duplicate as Crosstab:** Allows you to insert one or more worksheets into a workbook, and then populate the sheet with a cross-tab view of the data from the original worksheet.

» **Enabling updates:** There are two options to choose from: Auto Updates and Run Update. You can have the system auto update the data source in real time, or you can select Run Update to update when you prefer.

TIP

Many of the features listed also have like-kind buttons on the toolbar. With the menu, you get all the features. On the toolbar, you're limited to the critical capabilities for a worksheet.

Dashboard menu

Similarly to the Worksheet menu, the Dashboard menu is divided into sections, using a horizontal line to break up features. Given that a dashboard's purpose combines worksheets, you don't see many formatting-related options on the Dashboard menu. Instead, the Dashboard menu focuses on how to present the data on various devices such as desktops or tablets. Because dashboards also present a variety of datasets, Tableau Desktop allows you to add grids to each worksheet so that you can complete a more detailed analysis. The Dashboard menu (Figure 5-6) is broken out into key sections as follows:

» **New Dashboard:** Allows you to create a new dashboard.

» **Device Layouts:** Allows you to choose desktop, phone, or tablet.

» **Grids:** Provides a matrix design to organize and present specific visual elements on a canvas, enabling you to understand how they relate to one another.

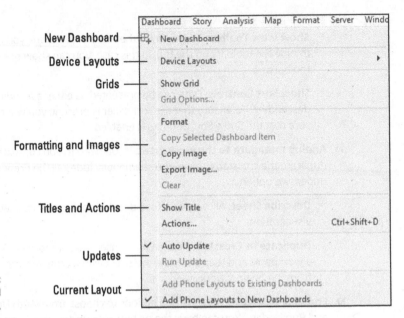

New Dashboard

Device Layouts

Grids

Formatting and Images

Titles and Actions

Updates

FIGURE 5-6:
The Dashboard
menu.

Current Layout

>> **Formatting and Images:** Allows you to format the dashboard with text-based elements or to add external images.

>> **Titles and Actions:** Allows you to add a meaningful title or *actions,* a means of adding context or interactivity to a dashboard.

>> **Updates:** Allows a user to configure Auto Updates or run a manual update on a dashboard dataset.

>> **Current Layout:** Presents the current layouts available.

To save and export a dashboard as a graphic, which is a static picture showing data, you can either copy a worksheet as a viz or export a worksheet to create a single snapshot of the data in the form of a .png graphic file.

TIP

Sometimes users hide the dashboard title because data may not be entirely related to all the visualizations. Select the Show Title option if you want to show the dashboard title.

Story menu

The Story menu, shown in Figure 5-7, appears to have few options. You can format, copy images, export images, clear the story, and enable or disable the title and backward and forward buttons, and that's seemingly all you can do — unless you look at the expandable cards. In contrast to some other features with full menus, the story features take advantage of cards instead. For example, when you select Format, a card appears on the left side of the Tableau Desktop interface. That card enables you to format the story experience using options such as the following:

>> **New Story:** Allows you to create a new story.

>> **Format:** Offers various formatting options including background enhancements, navigation enhancements, and font/image options.

>> **Title and Navigator:** Allows you to add a title and create the story's navigation using story points.

>> **Updates:** Allows you to refresh the data.

FIGURE 5-7:
The Story menu.

WARNING

You find out more about creating a story in Book 3, Chapter 6. Note that the design terminology that is standard for most analytics platforms does not apply to a story. You need to know more lingo for this area of Tableau.

Analysis menu

The Analysis menu is full of bells and whistles. As with other menus, it has distinct sections, as shown in Figure 5-8. Here's an overview of the Analysis menu sections:

>> **Labels/Measures/Marks/Data:** This menu section enables you to label, view, and explain your data by applying different approaches. You can either aggregate measures or keep them distinct.

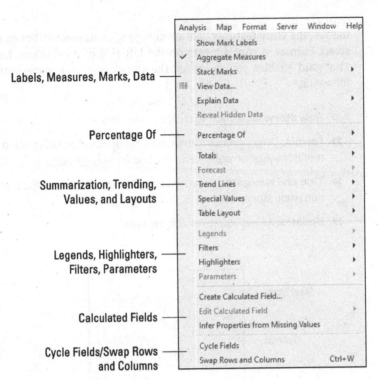

Labels, Measures, Marks, Data

Percentage Of

Summarization, Trending, Values, and Layouts

Legends, Highlighters, Filters, Parameters

Calculated Fields

Cycle Fields/Swap Rows and Columns

FIGURE 5-8:
The Analysis menu.

» **Percentage Of:** Depending on the measurement type selected, each measure on a worksheet is expressed as a percentage of a given measure within one or more panes in a view.

» **Summarization, Trending, Values, and Layouts:** This segment offers a real hodge-podge of analysis options, enabling you to establish grand totals, look at trend-line analysis, show/hide particular values created, and show/hide empty values if applicable in a dataset.

» **Legends, Highlighters, Filters, Parameters:** This is another section with a boatload of tools that enable data filters, support data parameterization using calculations, and offer more aesthetic approaches to your presentation by highlighting data or adding legends for data awareness.

» **Calculated Fields:** If the data doesn't exist, you can create targeted fields to enhance the dataset with calculated fields. This section is also where you go to create a calculated field (or edit the field if one has already been created).

» **Cycle Fields/and Swap Rows and Columns:** These two options are grouped but have polar-opposite impacts on the data. Whereas you use Cycle Fields to flip-flop the order of the rows and columns in the dataset, often changing the accuracy of data, you use Swap Rows and Columns to change the visualization from left/right to top/bottom. The data is merely presented from a different visual perspective.

Map menu

Unless you are using one of the map-based visualizations, the Map menu is of little value to you. Likewise, if your dataset has no map data such as city, state, or county, you can skip this menu. But if you do have some demographic-oriented data, you'll find that Tableau's mapping functionality is second to none. You have various ways to display your map output, whether in light, dark, or normal mode, using the following options shown in Figure 5-9:

>> **Background Maps:** Offers map-rendering types such as street, outdoor, satellite, light, dark, offline.

>> **Background Images:** Allows you to add a custom background to your map. For example, you can add a state seal if you're creating a map for a specific state in the United States.

>> **Geocoding:** Lets you integrate geocoding targets into a Tableau map visualization.

>> **Edit Locations:** Enables you to edit the map targets to be more specific, based on a geographic region such as a state or country, depending on geographic parameters in the map type.

>> **Map Legend:** Lets you add color variations to a map.

>> **Background Layers:** Allows you to add textures to your map such as land cover, terrain, coastlines, or streets or highways based on map granularity.

>> **Map Options:** Lets you select which controls should be enabled or disabled in the Tableau Map Viewer, such as search, layer control, pan and zoom, scale, and units of measure.

FIGURE 5-9:
The Map menu.

When you need to look for more granular details, you can get down to street level, outdoor, or satellite views so that your data appears in 2-D or 3-D. If you prefer to add third-party mapping data sources, you find such options within the Background Maps menu (WMS/Mapbox Options).

You can also add multiple layers to your maps, depending on how many data-sets are integrated into a single workspace. Suppose, for example, you have three worksheets. Each worksheet can be a layer of a map brought together as a single visualization.

Format menu

You can modify the look and feel of any object from using the Format menu in Tableau. No questions asked.

The single menu is your single source to locate formatting options, which is helpful if you don't know which card controls which formatting function. Most features in Tableau use the point-and-click method, so you can simply high-light an item in a specific card, go to the Format menu, select the formatting feature you want, and then follow the prompt. Options such as Font, Alignment, Shading, Borders, and Lines align to the more traditional formatting activity on a document. Visualization-rich formatting options also appear on this menu, including these:

>> **Panes:** Enables the Worksheet, Dashboard, or Story Format panes.

>> **Format:** Enables the specific panes for fonts, alignment, shading, borders, and lines.

>> **Animation:** Enables the Animation pane for you to integrate interactivity into your Tableau workspace.

>> **Lines, labels, and captions:** Allows you to enhance your visualization using reference lines, drop lines, annotations, titles, captions, or field labels. Each menu option enables a new pane.

>> **Visualization enhancements:** You can enhance visualizations with the use of legends, filters, highlighters, or parameters.

>> **Themes:** Enables you to create a targeted look and feel to workbooks and cells.

>> **Copy/Paste Formatting:** Lets you capture formatting once and reuse it.

>> **Clear:** You can clear the formatting of the worksheet, dashboard, or story.

Figure 5-10 shows the Format menu.

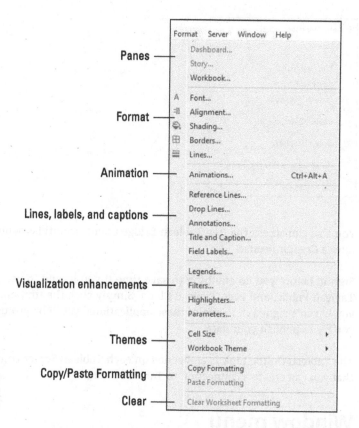

Panes

Format

Animation

Lines, labels, and captions

Visualization enhancements

Themes

Copy/Paste Formatting

Clear

FIGURE 5-10:
The Format
menu.

WARNING

You may notice some repetition of option names on certain menus. For example, the Format menu contains many Analysis options such as Highlight, Filter, Legends, and Parameters because they are also deemed to be formatting options. Although they appear to replicate options of the same name elsewhere, they actually vary in feature functionality. On the Format menu, options are specific to data formatting, whereas on the Analysis menu, they relate to creating or evolving the data elements.

Server menu

You can think of the Server menu, shown in Figure 5-11, as your candy store for all things relating to public and server data. This menu enables you to access the most popular Tableau Public datasets, publish your own datasets for the world to explore via Tableau Public, or take the traditional approach by using Tableau Server (or Cloud) for publishing workbooks, data sources, and filters. The menu specifically points out what features are unique to Tableau Public versus Tableau Server and Tableau Cloud.

FIGURE 5-11:
The Server menu.

You also can access the free Tableau Bridge Client from this menu so long as you have a Creator license.

TIP

Sign in before you do anything to save time if you intend to use Tableau Server, Tableau Public, and even Tableau Cloud. Simply click the first option, Sign-In. If you haven't signed in to one of these applications, you'll be prompted every time you try to publish your data.

REMEMBER

The Tableau Online Link is embedded on each Tableau Server connection page so that you can create a connection to Tableau Cloud.

Window menu

You can use the Window menu (Figure 5-12) as your cheat sheet for accessing all your worksheets, dashboards, and story tabs. Instead of going to the bottom of the screen to find all your worksheets, dashboards, or stories, click the Window tab to the Window menu on the Tableau toolbar to see how many items you've generated. If you want to focus on a specific item, select that item with a single click.

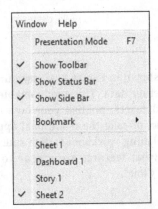

FIGURE 5-12:
The Window
menu.

The other feature offered by the Window menu is the capability to show and hide standard features, such as toolbars, status bars, and sidebars. Again, it takes only a single click on the menu option to make one of these bars appear or disappear — nothing less, nothing more.

Help menu

Tableau heavily emphasizes using self-help resources. As you can see in Figure 5-13, the Help menu offers Open Help (Forums), Get Support (Ask the Community or Pay for Support), Watch Training Videos, and Check for Product Updates.

FIGURE 5-13:
The Help menu.

REMEMBER

You find a few features in Help that most users would expect to find on a different menu, such as File, which is typically where application preferences and licensing details are located. Not with Tableau. You modify all your application-wide settings, preferences, licenses, and language selection choices using the Help menu.

Tooling Around in the Toolbar

The toolbar appears across the top of Tableau Desktop (see Figure 5-14). Although it's not as robust as the menus, the toolbar clusters key features that are necessary to manipulate and analyze data and fully exploit the visualization options available. As you work through the toolbar, you notice that it is divided into sections. The first section is specific to creating data sources and handling standard application functions such as undoing and redoing previous actions. The following list describes the tools found on this first section of the toolbar, also shown in Figure 5-15:

» **Show Start Page:** Enables a user to go back to the Start page.

» **Undo:** Reverses the most recent actions in a workbook. A user can reverse an unlimited number of times, back to when Tableau was most recently opened.

» **Redo:** Repeats the last actions reversed, assuming that you've selected the Undo button at least one or more times.

» **Replay Animation:** When you have one or more states within a visualization, you can see the various states by pressing this quasi-Play button. Various speeds are available with the Replay Animation button.

» **Save:** Saves changes made in a workbook.

» **New Data Source:** Opens the Connect pane to create a new connection or to enable a user to access an existing saved connection.

» **Pause Auto Update:** Allows you to control where Tableau updates the view when you make changes.

» **Run Auto Update:** If running a query, you can manually update your data to make changes, assuming that Auto Update is turned off.

FIGURE 5-14:
The full Tableau Desktop toolbar.

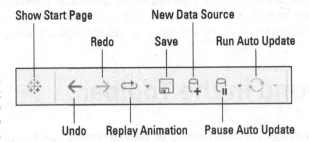

FIGURE 5-15:
Tools on the first section of the Tableau Desktop toolbar.

The next section of the toolbar functionality, shown in Figure 5-16, centers around creation and filtering tasks. You must put your magnifying glasses on to see the itsy-bitsy menus. Each toolbar option has a drop-down menu with sub-functions. For example, the first button allows you to create a new worksheet. When you click the button, options appear for creating a new dashboard or new story. Depending on what feature you're using (worksheet, dashboard, or story), the other two toolbar buttons vary in drop-down capability. The second button always creates a duplicate feature, and the third is intended for clearing a sheet, residual formatting, and filters.

Duplicate

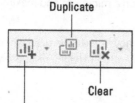

FIGURE 5-16:
Core worksheet, dashboard, and story functionality.

Clear

Drop down to create new worksheet, dashboard, or story

The next segment of buttons, shown in Figure 5-17, is nifty because these buttons enable you to manipulate visualizations and data sort order. The Swap button allows you to swap rows and columns order visually without touching a single data cell. The Ascend and Descend buttons enable visualization sort order differentiation; one is for data to ascend, and the other is to descend. Depending on the visualization type you're applying in the canvas, the data presentation may be entirely text-based or a mix of visual and text, with the items displayed as descending or ascending.

Swap Rows and Columns

Sort Descending

FIGURE 5-17:
The swap and sort order functionality on the Tableau Desktop toolbar.

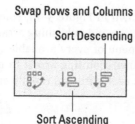

Sort Ascending

After you've nailed down the visualization (viz) type you prefer, formatting to perfection is an essential ingredient for the data analyst. You use the next series of buttons (see Figure 5-18) to format your visualizations. These buttons, which are loaded with various options, appear from left to right in the figure:

>> **Highlight:** Enables you to highlight selected sheet features. You can define how values appear in a menu.

>> **Group Members:** Allows for creating groups of selected values by combining selected values. When you select multiple dimensions, you can choose whether to apply them to one grouping or all groupings.

>> **Show/Hide Mark Labels:** Click to show or hide all markings on a current worksheet. An example of a marking is to provide a text-label equivalent on a viz.

>> **Fix Axes:** You can lock the axis or show specific ranges. You can also establish a dynamic axis that can adjust based on a minimum and maximum value established within a view.

>> **Fit:** Select from the drop-down menu how the view is sized within a window. Several options include Standard, Fit Width, Fit Height, or Entire View.

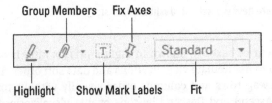

FIGURE 5-18:
Visualization formatting buttons.

WARNING

Tableau has many hidden menus. Within the visualization formatting toolbar options, you have three complete sets of options — one for worksheets, one for dashboards, and one for stories. Although the icons are virtually the same, the capabilities are vastly different.

The rightmost section of the toolbar, shown in Figure 5-19, consists of a series of shortcuts for users to execute presentation and publishing actions quickly. The first button, Show/Hide Cards, offers a menu of every available card that can be shown or hidden. When you click the down-pointing arrow to make the drop-down menu appear, you can single-click each card and rapidly enable or disable an option.

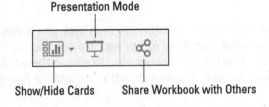

FIGURE 5-19:
The rightmost section of the Tableau Desktop toolbar.

You use the next button, Presentation Mode, to put your worksheet, dashboard, or story into presentation mode. Think of this button as creating the ultimate executive presentation view with one click.

The final button on the Tableau Desktop toolbar is Share Workbook with Others. Ring a bell? This is a code phrase for publishing to one of several Tableau server-based platforms such as Tableau Public, Tableau Server, or Tableau Cloud. After clicking the button, you need to enter the Tableau Server URL or select the Tableau Online link. You are then on your way to publishing your workbook, dashboard, or story to the masses.

Understanding Sheets versus Workbooks

Much like other business productivity suites, Tableau uses the same naming nomenclature and file structure of the workbook and sheet file structure. A workbook (package) can contain many sheets. A sheet can be in the form of a worksheet, dashboard, or story:

>> **A worksheet** contains a single view of data along with shelves, cards, legends, data, and analytics panes along the Side Bar.

>> **A dashboard** is a compilation of views across many worksheets. The Dashboard and Layout panes are available on the Side Bar.

>> **A story page** takes a sequence of worksheets or dashboards and integrates navigations to piece together a cohesive message that cannot be told on a single screen or page. The Story and Layout panes are also available on the Side Bar.

You have several ways to create new sheets in a workbook, but the easiest is to head straight to the tabs at the bottom of the Tableau Desktop interface. To create a worksheet, dashboard, or story, go to the bottom of a given workbook, near the status bar. You'll see three icons with + (plus signs): one to create a new worksheet, one to create a new dashboard, and one to create a new story (see Figure 5-20).

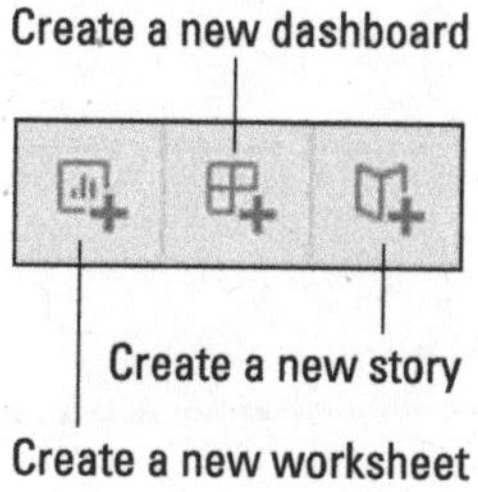

Create a new dashboard

FIGURE 5-20:
Click a + (plus sign) button to create a worksheet, dashboard, or story.

Create a new story

Create a new worksheet

Renaming sheets

To rename a worksheet, dashboard, or story within a workbook, you double-click the tab at the bottom of the workbook and then type in the alternative title in the highlighted space. If you're renaming a sheet, you type the new name in when the tab turns to a different color. When you're done entering the new name, press the Enter key to commit the change.

Deleting sheets

Just because you may *want* to delete a sheet doesn't mean you'll be able to. A few conditions must be met before you can remove a worksheet from a workbook:

>> At least one worksheet must exist within a workbook.

>> If you've used a worksheet as part of a dashboard or a story, you've committed the data to the workbook until you remove the dashboard or story. Your only option is to hide rather than delete the worksheet.

>> If you have used a worksheet as a viz within a tooltip, you can hide it or delete it, but any associated data with a viz is lost upon deleting the worksheet.

If you consider all these conditions and are still okay with proceeding, select the active sheet you want to delete from a workbook. Right-click the active sheet, select the Delete option, and click OK when prompted. If worksheets are dependent on what you attempt to delete, the software prompts you to hide, unhide, delete, or cancel the worksheet.

Chapter **6**

Storytelling Foundations in Tableau

Tableau is an excellent tool for analyzing data and crafting visualizations, even utilizing a single worksheet and data source. But the real power of Tableau reveals itself when you're looking to share and collaborate on data with others, which provides multidimensional perspectives. Dashboards enable you to bring together several perspectives so that the audience can interact with the data holistically.

In this chapter, you find out how to engage in two forms of data collaboration beyond a worksheet: the dashboard and the story.

Working with Dashboards

The workbook and its worksheets are obviously important, but there is only so much a worksheet can accomplish. You may, for example, need to compare a variety of data views simultaneously, such as the revenue produced by various departments of an entire company in one view. Or perhaps you want to break out a geographic region using a map view in a second view. In a third view, you may even want to pinpoint the product or service accelerating revenue growth in a specific region. Instead of having separate worksheets present the data, you can create a single view of the data. That single view is your *dashboard*.

You create dashboards similarly to how you create a worksheet, using the tabs at the bottom of the workbook. Data in sheets and dashboards are connected at the hip. If you modify a sheet, your dashboard reflects the change and vice versa.

In Figure 6-1, several worksheets from Book 3, Chapter 5 have been combined into a single dashboard, and a filter was added.

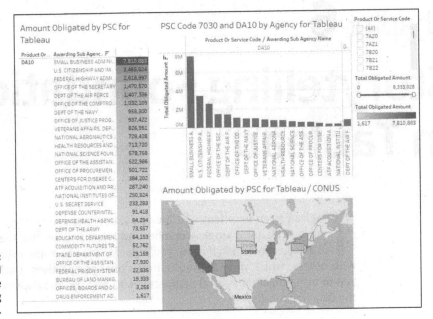

FIGURE 6-1:
A dashboard made up of three worksheets along with a filter.

Configuring the dashboard

Consistency is critical with Tableau. You have several ways to create a dashboard. One is to click Dashboard on the top of the page to open the Dashboard menu and choose the New Dashboard option (see Figure 6-2). Or you can click the New Workbook icon in the toolbar to open the drop-down list and then click the Dashboard button on the Tableau toolbar (see Figure 6-3). The third way to create a dashboard is to head to the bottom of the workspace near the status bar and select the New Dashboard icon, shown in Figure 6-4.

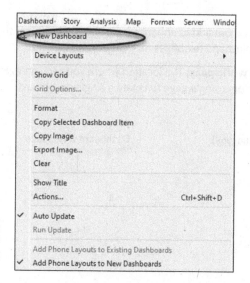

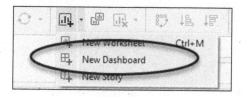

Whichever way you create a new dashboard, the outcome is always the same: You've added a new dashboard workspace. The interface for your new dashboard workspace (shown in Figure 6-5) consists of many features that enable you to create a multifaceted visualization, including the Dashboard pane and Layout pane.

The Dashboard pane contains a few dashboard-specific functions, including

>> **The interface type and its size:** You can choose whether the dashboard is meant for the Desktop or a mobile device based on how many views you expect to integrate into a single dashboard.

>> **Sheets:** A compilation of all worksheets that you can include as part of a single dashboard.

>> **Objects:** Items you can add to enhance a dashboard, including shapes to highlight data points and textboxes for headers and footers.

>> **The dashboard workspace:** The location where you can aggregate various worksheet views on a single page to create a single dashboard.

Interface card (size and type)　　　　Dashboard workspace

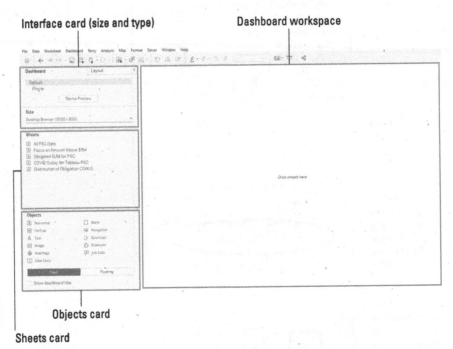

FIGURE 6-5:
A blank
dashboard
workspace.　　Objects card

　　Sheets card

To create a dashboard, drag one or more sheets from the Sheets card on the Dashboard pane to the Dashboard's workspace (as shown in Figure 6-6). In the Dashboard pane, select the appropriate size for presenting the visualization, rendered for either a desktop or mobile device. A grey workspace indicates that a new object is being added. You repeat this activity numerous times, adding all the sheets from the Sheets card and Objects card that you want until you feel that your dashboard is complete.

Customizing the dashboard

To create the ultimate dashboard, you may also want to utilize layout objects, found on the Objects section of the Dashboard pane (under Sheets). For example, you may want to include the horizontal and vertical layout so that when you drag a sheet to the workspace, the page is more aesthetically pleasing and balanced. To use a layout object, drag one or more objects to the dashboard workspace.

Then place one or more sheets from the Sheets card on the workspace to create the desired dashboard result. Figure 6-7 shows an example of a layout using the Horizontal object (Figure 6-7), and Figure 6-8 shows the layout using the Vertical object (Figure 6-8).

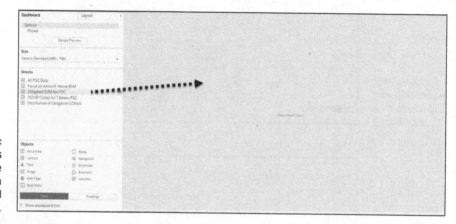

FIGURE 6-6: Dragging sheets and sizing the visualization in the dashboard workspace.

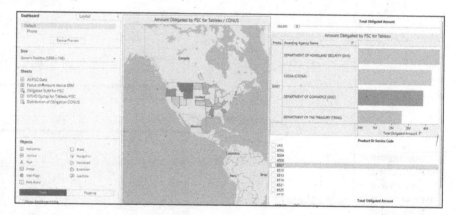

FIGURE 6-7: A horizontal layout of sheets for a dashboard.

The Blank object, shown in Figure 6-9, is a glorified spacer that helps to separate the sheets and keep them from being on top of one another. You use the Blank object for other reasons as well. First, it helps you focus on individual visualizations when you're including multiple sheets in your dashboard. More important, though, is that the spacer can also be used for nonlayout-specific objects, discussed in depth in the next section.

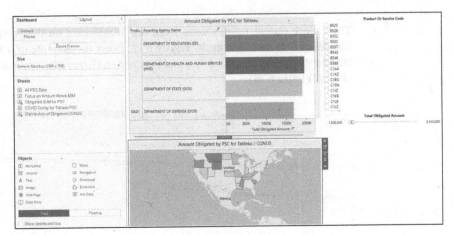

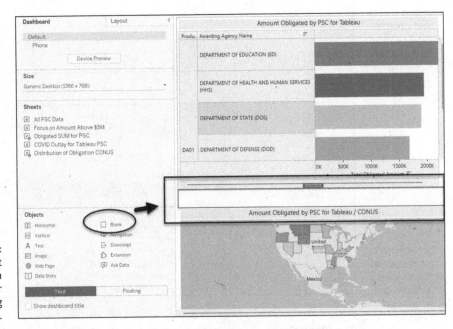

Adding objects to dashboards

In contrast to a worksheet and a story, you can add objects to enhance your dashboard. Because the dashboard represents a collection of various visualizations, you may need to incorporate logos, images, shapes, or even embedded content, such as a web page. The icons in Figure 6-10 represent the various object types that you can incorporate into a dashboard, including text, images, and embedded web pages.

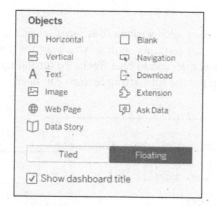

FIGURE 6-10:
Choose an option for the dashboard.

Figure 6-11 shows how to drag the object to the workspace. In the following sections, you discover how to integrate text, images, web pages, button types, and extensions into your dashboard.

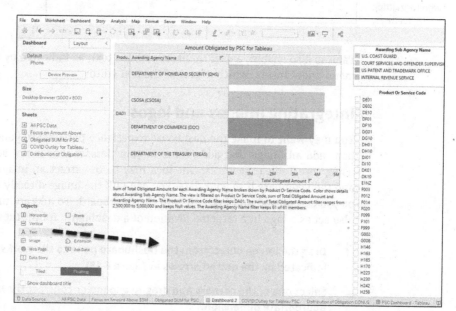

FIGURE 6-11:
Drag an object to the workspace.

Tackling text, fonts, and color

The Text object has many of the same features as your run-of-the-mill text editor, such as selecting fonts, changing font size, and applying bold, underlining, italics, and positioning options. The Text object, however, lets you add an object to the dashboard to augment a caption or data story with self-written text. You are not married to sticking with a specific font or size or making the text black;

Storytelling Foundations in Tableau

in fact, you can craft a textbox with various font faces, sizes, and shapes if you want, as exemplified by Figure 6-12. As soon as you drag the Text object to the dashboard, a pop-up window asks you to type freely. To format the text, highlight it and then click the button for the formatting feature you need.

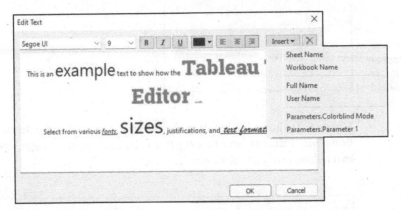

FIGURE 6-12:
Example text-box with formatting features.

Tableau also enables a user to insert prebuilt text, as indicated by the drop-down menu under Insert, which is part of the text editor.

Integrating images and logos

You may want to make the dashboard experience personal to your brand or perhaps add an image that adds value to your dataset that is not self-explanatory using core Tableau features. One idea may be to extract an image from a report and then compare it to your data. You can pull the image directly from a website, or you can upload and insert it into the dashboard. To add an image, which can also act as a logo in a targeted location of a dashboard, follow these steps:

1. **Drag the Image object from the Dashboard pane to the workspace (as indicated by the dotted arrows in Figure 6-13).**

2. **Select one of the corners and drag to expand or contract the image to the appropriate dimension.**

3. **Double-click the image box to open the Edit Image screen.**

4. **Upload the image to the workspace, or point to the URL by selecting Link to Image; then enter the URL.**

   The image uploads from the internet to the dashboard.

5. **At the bottom of the Edit Image Object screen, add appropriate alt text for usability purposes.**

Alt text helps a user with visual challenges to better understand what an image object describes. Additionally, if you're looking to position an image within the given space provided, you can select the boxes under the options to center or fit the image (or both).

6. **When you're finished adding your image, click OK.**

7. **Drag the completed image to its destination.**

The ideal logo placement is on the left side of the title of your dashboard.

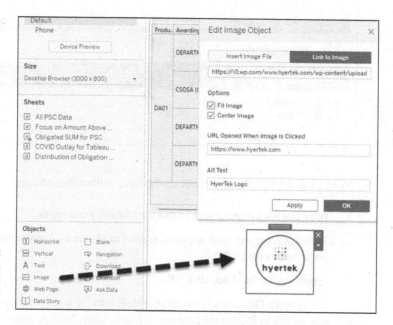

FIGURE 6-13:
Placing a corporate logo on the bottom of the dashboard.

Weaving in web pages

Including a web page within a dashboard may sound unusual, but it can be useful when you're pulling data from a targeted source or want to provide additional insights into a data point. In that case, you can create a Web Page card on the dashboard. By including procurement data on the dashboard from another source and then allowing a user to compare the Tableau-generated visualizations, you can map the source to aggregate data in a single view. The single view incorporates the various sheets from one or more workbooks and the data source itself (which is usaspending.gov in the example in Figure 6-14).

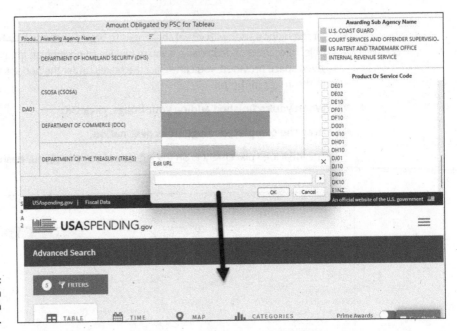

FIGURE 6-14:
Embedding a
web page into a
dashboard.

To add a web page object to your dashboard, follow these steps:

1. **Drag the Web Page object to the dashboard workspace.**

2. **In the pop-up box that appears, shown in Figure 6-14, enter the website parameters (the URL).**

3. **When you're finished, click OK.**

   The Website Object loads the targeted URL into the layout container, which you can modify to fit onto the dashboard comfortably. The *layout container* allows you to group related dashboard items so that they can be positioned to meet your specific needs quickly.

Buttoning up the dashboard

Buttons can enhance the interactivity of Tableau dashboard by enabling users to trigger specific actions or events. The two main types of buttons are the Navigation and Download buttons. Navigation buttons enable users to navigate between worksheets, dashboards, and stories within Tableau. Download buttons let users download items from a specified URL by clicking the button. These buttons can add an extra dimension to dashboards by allowing users to interact with the data and navigate through the content in a more targeted and customized way.

You can see both button types near the bottom of Figure 6-15. To configure these buttons, you must fill in all fields on the Edit Button page. Key items to configure include navigation location, button style, and tooltips to describe the button's purpose. The figure also shows an example interface for configuring the Navigation buttons.

FIGURE 6-15: Configuring Navigation and Download buttons to place on the dashboard workspace.

Extending the dashboard

Tableau extensions are add-ons that allow you to extend the functionality of Tableau dashboards and worksheets. Extensions can be created by folks like you and me or by other enterprise software organizations to enhance Tableau dashboards or worksheets.

Many extensions are available, including ones that allow you to integrate with external applications, add custom visualizations, or add new features to your dashboards. To use an extension, you need to install it in Tableau and then add it to your dashboard layout just as you do any other dashboard object.

In Figure 6-16, you'll find an example of what the Extensions interface looks like after you drag and drop the Extension object onto the workspace.

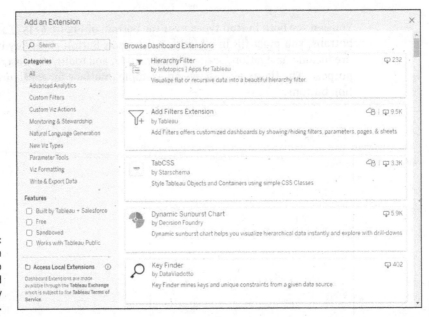

FIGURE 6-16:
Adding an
extension to
the dashboard
using third-party
sources.

**TECHNICAL
STUFF**

Each extension has its own configuration requirements, but the process to select, drag, and drop is the same for all. Follow the developer's instructions to incorporate an extension into your dashboard.

Adhering to best practices for dashboard design

**BEST
PRACTICE**

When creating a dashboard, it's essential to keep in mind the guidelines for making an effective dashboard. You can't just consider the data, although that is important. You should also strive to balance aesthetic clarity, conciseness, and appropriateness. Also, it would be best to remember that users often face unique circumstances when reviewing visualizations, especially ones full of color that may be complex to understand. Follow these principles, at a minimum, for design best practices. A bit later in the chapter, you find out about applying accessible features to Tableau.

>> **Keep it simple:** A dashboard should include only the most crucial information and be clear of unnecessary details.

>> **Use clear and concise labels:** Use clear and concise labels to help users understand the purpose and context of each view or visualization.

>> **Use appropriate visualizations:** Choose the correct type of visualization to convey the information effectively. For example, use a bar chart to show quantitative comparisons and a pie chart to show proportions.

>> **Use color effectively:** Color should be used only to highlight important information and create a visual hierarchy; also, using too many colors can be overwhelming.

>> **Test and refine:** Test your dashboard with users to gather feedback, and refine it based on their needs and insights.

Following these guidelines, you can create a compelling and informative dashboard in Tableau that helps users quickly understand and analyze data.

Creating a Compelling Story

A story is a sequence of visualizations; it could be a worksheet or dashboard coming together to convey information. The story is intended to tell a narrative, provide context, and demonstrate how outcomes are derived. You can also use a story to present a streaming use case, from the conception of data to the conclusion.

Like the worksheet and dashboard, a story is nothing more than a sheet in Tableau. Therefore, the mechanics used to create, name, and manage the story don't deviate from the worksheet or dashboard. The big difference is in the sequencing of the worksheets. You'll need to correctly name and label every worksheet because each one becomes a story point — a navigation point in the story sequence.

Figure 6-17 shows which of the continental 48 United States had recognized federal sales of Tableau between 2018 and 2022. The second story point (not shown) shows a breakdown in how much was spent by each federal agency.

Synthesizing data through a Tableau story

The Tableau *story* is a powerful tool for creating an interactive data visualization based on a sequence of information. The story feature lets you easily connect to various data sources, not just one, to build dashboards and charts. You can also share your insights with others by aggregating visualizations using workbook sheets.

REMEMBER

The story is a sheet, not a workbook. The method you use to create, name, and manage the worksheets and dashboards should be consistent with a story. There is a catch, however: A story is a collection of sheets, so you'll need to figure out the sequence of those sheets and create story points. A *story point* is a single sheet representing a single concept throughout the story.

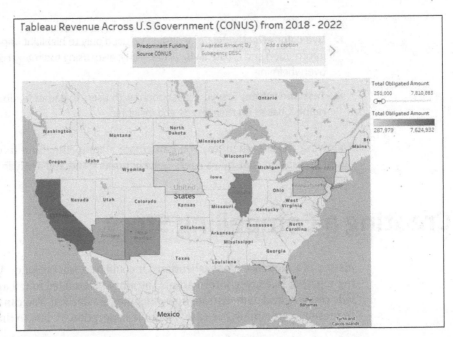

FIGURE 6-17:
An example of a story consisting of multiple worksheets.

Formatting updates may include the appearance of your charts and dashboards. You can also add interactive elements to the charts and dashboards for each story point, including filters, parameters, and actions.

After you've assembled your story, the final step is to share it with others by publishing it to Tableau Cloud. You can also embed a story on a website or blog.

Planning your story to perfection

Have you ever experienced a dataset as a hodge-podge because no theme connects the data and facts to the scenario? It's happened to me, and I'm sure it has happened to all of us at some point.

Before creating your story, it's essential to consider its purpose and the experience you want your viewers to have. Are you trying to persuade them to take action, or do you just want to offer a straightforward narrative or present an extended use case? Different purposes require different strategies to achieve your goal:

>> **Spurring your audience to action:** The most powerful stories in this category get to the punchline immediately by showing the outcome. A story can present a doom-and-gloom scenario, the a-ha revelatory moment, or the visionary goal. In each of these cases, you want to start with the result, followed by walking the user through how you got there. Ultimately, you want

to remind the user why taking action is essential. Using analytics to give a sales pitch is an example of how to take action.

>> **Offering a narrative:** The good ol' line about a picture being worth a thousand words applies here. Simple, straightforward graphics are best for a straightforward narrative, with less interaction and more interpretation. A good narrative focuses on showing the impact before, during, or after a targeted event.

>> **Presenting a use case:** For this type of story, you need to consider whether you want to present data points that build toward a conclusion, or that start with a conclusion and then show the supporting data points. The latter approach can be practical for engaged audiences. Health care use cases are ripe for storytelling using the use case method.

TIP

This tip may sound like it defeats the purpose of Tableau, but you may find it helpful to sketch out your story on paper or a whiteboard before building it in Tableau. You are laying out the targeted data points to help identify any potential issues with the sequence and ensure that your story flows smoothly. Another reason an advance sketch is helpful is that it helps you focus on delivery speed and ensure that the dataset fits in the worksheet comfortably, which leads to better readability.

TIP

Tableau explores numerous ways to tell a compelling story based on the business need. When deciding whether you want to take action, create a narrative, or author the use case, the various approaches can help you laser-focus even more. To discover more about how to craft each story type, start at `https://help.tableau.com/current/pro/desktop/en-us/story_best_practices.htm`.

Surveying the story workspace

The story workspace is pretty simplistic. It has only six major areas to be aware of, as shown in Figure 6-18:

>> **Buttons for adding story points:** Click the Blank button in the Story pane to add a story point. Alternatively, if you want to duplicate the behaviors of a worksheet, click the Duplicate button to use a current story point as your starting point.

>> **Story pane:** From here is where you drag relevant dashboards, sheets, and text descriptions within your workbook to the story sheet. You can set the size of your story and its display by going to the Size drop-down menu on the bottom of the Story pane (which is also where you can hide the title, if you want). To hide a feature, just deselect the check box next to its name.

>> **Layout pane:** In this pane, which is next to the Story pane, you can select the navigator style and hide the forward and back arrows.

>> **Story menu:** When trying to format, copy, or export content, including images for a story, you use the Story menu, which you access via the toolbar. Clearing a story in this menu may include hiding the navigator and story title.

>> **Story toolbar:** Mousing over the navigator (described in the next bullet) enables the Story toolbar. You can reverse changes or handle story point updates using the Story toolbar.

>> **Navigator:** Right above the Story view is the navigator, a central hub for editing and organizing the story points. You'll come to the navigator when you want to show your audience how to step through a story. The navigator has a variety of styles, which you can change in the Layout pane.

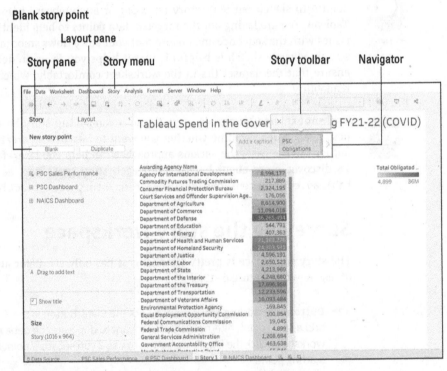

FIGURE 6-18:
The story workspace.

Crafting the story

Crafting a story in Tableau is a similar process to creating worksheets and dashboards. The difference is that all activities start with the Story tab or menu, as shown in Figure 6-19.

FIGURE 6-19:
The Story tab.

REMEMBER

When you click the Story tab, Tableau opens a screen for a new story (see Figure 6-20). Remember, though, that each worksheet and dashboard previously created are listed in the Story pane. These assets are required first if you haven't created other worksheets or dashboards.

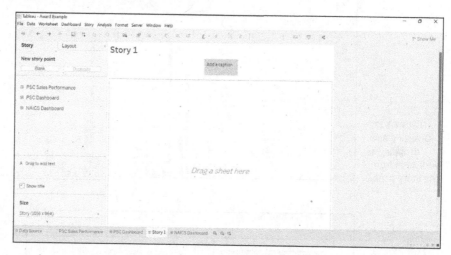

FIGURE 6-20:
A blank story
workspace.

When you have your assets ready in the Story pane, your next step is to set the story size (Figure 6-21) and apply story points. You can incorporate one story point, or a hundred; each point presents a targeted message.

FIGURE 6-21:
Select the story
interface size.

In the lower-left corner of the screen, select the size interface based on pixels, as seen in Figure 6-21.

TIP

Your story's title is based on the original worksheet name. Titles can be modified by renaming your worksheet.

After setting up the basic story configuration, it's time to start building the story. Double-click a worksheet from the Story pane to add it as a story point. You can also drag and drop the worksheet into the workspace. As shown in Figure 6-22,

Storytelling
Foundations in Tableau

there is one blank space, indicated by Add a Caption. You can double-click a worksheet or drag it to the circled location. The other two story points integrate existing worksheets. Either you can modify the title of the story (Figure 6-23) or save changes by clicking Update, as shown in Figure 6-24.

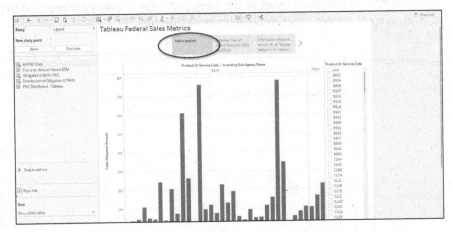

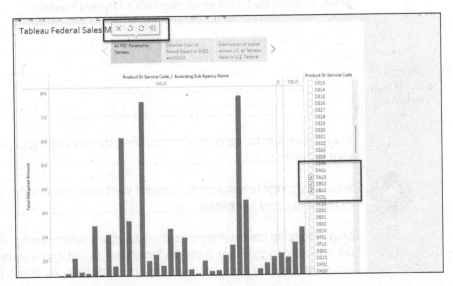

WARNING

Each sheet you add to a story becomes a story point. The story point is directly tied to the worksheet. If you remove the worksheet, your story immediately changes.

After you've landed the story point where you want it, it's time to add captions to the story for descriptive purposes (shown in Figure 6-23). To modify functionality such as filters and story-point order, make changes using the features in the areas outlined in Figure 6-24. The impact of any changes you make is immediate. In this case, the name of the caption was changed, as were the filters in the filters pane.

After creating your first story point, drag one of your sheets next to the recently created caption, as indicated by the arrow in Figure 6-25. This adds a new story point to the workspace. The only significant activity you need to complete is modifying the caption to reflect the sheet moving forward. Repeat this action as many times as needed to provide more descriptive explanations of each story point.

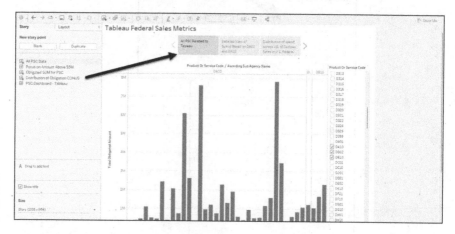

FIGURE 6-25:
Dragging a sheet to create a story point.

Formatting the story

Formatting is the most prevalent feature within the story user experience. The changes you make for formatting are more like nuanced modifications to a worksheet and the aesthetics of a story point. Changes you make across the Story and Layout panes are more global to the story. Here are some key formatting concepts to consider:

TECHNICAL STUFF

>> **Navigator options:** Modifying the navigator style can be completed in the Layout pane.

>> **Resizing captions:** Expand and contract the size of your caption from the left and right corners, as you would a typical image. Resizing can only be done in Tableau Desktop.

>> **Sizing dashboards within a story:** It's one thing to size a worksheet, but sizing a dashboard means retrofitting numerous visualizations to a screen. Tableau can do that for you automatically under the Size section of the Layout pane.

>> **Format the story:** The look and feel created in a worksheet may not be desired. Instead, highlight a specific item and choose Format ⇨ Story to open the Formatting pane to modify the format (see Figure 6-26).

>> **Deleting a story:** Select the caption and then click the X. You'll be able to delete the story point quickly. Don't worry, however. Your data won't go missing.

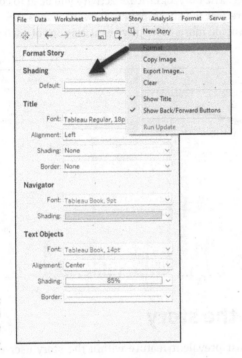

FIGURE 6-26:
Formatting a
story using the
Format menu.

Chapter **7**

Visualizing Data in Tableau

ableau makes it easy to figure out whether a visualization requires a measure or dimension and whether the data should use discrete or continuous behavior using the Show Me recommendations, which include more than 20 choices. But one of the challenges people often face is having skipped the data cleansing or realizing that "whoops," our data has some flubs. That realization is perfectly okay, however, because Tableau allows you to filter and hide data anomalies. Before you take a deep dive into the visualization realm, consider that your dataset size and quality drive the visualization. At the same time, Tableau is fantastic at interpreting the data; only *you* know whether the visualization and explanations are on the money.

This chapter shows how to create each visualization type in the Show Me pane, with the focus on the importance of data types using measures and dimensions. Then it shows how you can spruce up visualizations by using some of the customizations provided in Tableau. And finally, you find out how to publish your visualization to Tableau Online.

Introducing the Visualizations

A visualization, referred to as a *viz* for short in Tableau, is the graphical representation of data in tables, pivots, charts, graphs, plots, or maps. Tableau provides a wide range of visualization types and customization options, allowing users to choose the best way to display their data and convey their message. Often, Tableau provides best-fit recommendations based on your data when you drag and drop fields from a data source onto the source. Based on the fields dragged and dropped onto the canvas (the visualization-specific workspace area) from the highlighted area in Figure 7-1, a desired visualization type can form in the Show Me pane, shown in Figure 7-2.

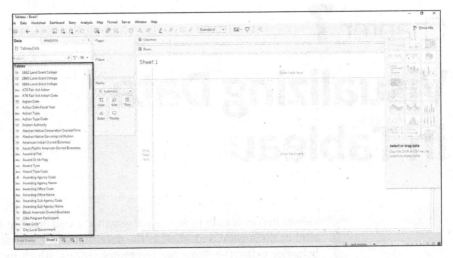

FIGURE 7-1:
The Tableau Desktop canvas, including data fields on the left.

The appearance and formatting of the visualization can be customized using the options in the Marks card and the Formatting pane.

The text table

The text table places one dimension on a Rows shelf and another on a Columns shelf. You then complete the view creation by adding more measures to the text as you see fit. A text table leverages the *text mark type,* which is a way to display numerical data in a text-based manner when dimensional data exists. Tableau uses the *mark type,* which is a way to add color, size, shape, and typeface, assuming that the view is constructed using dimensions exclusively (remember that it's automatic).

FIGURE 7-2:
The Show Me
pane's best-fit
examples.

Two dimensions in the dataset are Awarding Agency Name and Recipient State Code. To create a text table visualization, drag both dimensions to the Rows shelf, and drag one dimension into the area of the mark, which is Total Obligation. The result is a visualization, as shown in Figure 7-3.

Funding Agency Name	Recipient State Code	
Null	NH	60,309
AGENCY FOR INTERNATIONAL DEVELOPMENT (USAID)	DC	204,148
	MO	67,604,206
	VA	15,149,879
	WA	100,121
COMMODITY FUTURES TRADING COMMISSION (CFTC)	CA	23,319
	MD	54,175
	VA	32,472
CONSUMER FINANCIAL PROTECTION BUREAU (CFPB)	DC	845,911
	MD	415,288
	VA	18,098,897
CORPS OF ENGINEERS - CIVIL WORKS (USACE)	MD	3,958
COURT SERVICES AND OFFENDER SUPERVISION AGENCY (CSOSA)	VA	369,246
DEPARTMENT OF AGRICULTURE (USDA)	AZ	17,869
	CO	208,012
	DC	4,869
	GA	2,231,562
	MD	7,190,404
	ME	22,000
	MI	4,881
	NH	21,584
	OR	1,156,892
	VA	651,025,529
	WA	48,178
DEPARTMENT OF COMMERCE (DOC)	CO	37,680
	DC	58,035
	MD	526,202
	VA	16,046,708

Tableau Sales by State in the U.S. Federal Government

FIGURE 7-3:
A text table
visualization.

You may be wondering why you move items into the marks area versus to a Rows or Columns shelf. If you add fields on shelves, you are creating visualization structure. To increase the level of detail and control the number of marks in the view, which may include increasing or decreasing data granularity, you'll want to add data to the Marks cards. By adding specific fields to Marks cards, you are encoding the visualization with context using color, size, text, or numerical translation.

The heat map and highlight table

A heat map in Tableau is a visualization that uses color to encode values in a table or matrix. This type of map helps to compare the relative values of data points within a dataset and identify patterns and trends. The highlight table in Tableau is a visualization type that displays the values of a single measure or a series of measures in a table format, with the ability to highlight the highest or lowest values.

Creating a heat map

To create a heat map in Tableau, you need one or more dimensions and measures. The example in Figure 7-4 uses one measure and two dimensions. To create the heat map in this example, follow these steps:

1. **Drag one dimension to the Columns shelf (Recipient State Code), and drag the other dimension to the Rows shelf (Funding Agency Name).**

   The measure is to the left of the chart, as shown in Figure 7-4 under Marks: SUM(Total Obligations Amount).

2. **Right-click each of the dimensions and select Filter; next, select the desired parameters; and finally, click OK.**

   Two filters for this visualization now appear under the Filters card:

   - One wildcard on Awarding Agency Name, where anything containing the word *Department* should appear

   - A filter on the Recipient State Code

   In this example, any state containing the letter *A* appears. As you can see, the viz is significantly filtered. The marks that are proportionally larger than others indicate greater spending.

Using a heat map to assist in understanding who is getting more money may be helpful for a scientific presentation or to wow someone. However, with business reports, it's all about the data. That's why you'll want to use a highlight table instead.

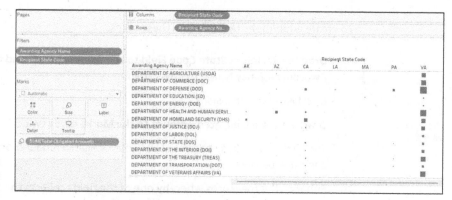

FIGURE 7-4:
A heat map
visualization.

Creating a highlight table

You can have the values in the table sorted in ascending or descending order. You can format the table to display the values differently, using colors, font sizes, or symbols to highlight specific values. A highlight table can quickly identify trends or patterns in the data and compare values across different categories or dimensions. It's a valuable tool for presenting data clearly and concisely and can be easily included in dashboards or reports. Figure 7-5 presents the same dataset created in the heat map in the highlight table. You can see many of the most significant awards in the State of Virginia. Volume-wise, large orders were also placed in California and Washington State (headquarters to Salesforce and Tableau, respectively).

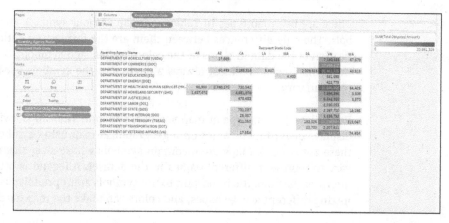

FIGURE 7-5:
A highlight table.

To create a highlight table, follow these steps:

1. **Drag the Recipient State Code Field to the Columns shelf and the Awarding Agency Name to Rows shelf.**

   Both fields are dimensions.

2. **Drag the Total Obligated Amount to the Marks cards twice.**

   The field automatically becomes SUM(Total Obligated Amount). Both of these items are measures.

3. **Enhance the measures whereby one of the fields reflects the text marking, and another reflects the color marking.**

4. **Right-click both dimensions and create a filter for each:**

   a. **For the Recipient State Code, go to the wildcard and pick only states where the letter _A_ is in the State Code name.**

   b. **For the awarding agency name, select only those where the word _Department_ exists in the name.**

   The dataset dramatically shrinks, and the result is a highlight table, as shown in Figure 7-5, with the State of Virginia seeming to have the most dollars obligated across key departments in the U.S. federal government.

Maps with and without symbols

There are two map types in Tableau, a map without symbols and one with symbols. The only differences between them are the formatting options and sophistication of the data in terms of the colors, styles, and symbols. On a normal map, the symbol used is almost always a circle, but the symbols used with a symbol map can vary.

Regardless of what type of map you use, a map in Tableau is a visualization that displays quantitative values on a geographical map using symbols (again, often these are circles). Maps often contain symbols whose size, shape, and color can vary to represent different values in the dataset. A legend is often used to help interpret the map. It's important to use symbols appropriately; using too many or mixing different sizes, shapes, and colors can make the map hard to understand.

TIP

Proportional symbol maps, which use symbols scaled in size according to the data values, can help compare limited datasets across a geographical area. However, you should take care to ensure that the symbols are distinct from the actual size of the location. It's also essential to ensure that the variables on the map are related.

Figure 7-6 shows a symbol map. To create a symbol map that shows the depth of symbols, colors, and size based on the data points or map, like the one in Figure 7-7, as well as illustrates more traditional map details such as terrain and streets if you zoom in close enough, follow these steps:

1. **From the dataset on the left pane, drag Recipient State Code and Recipient City Name to the Rows shelf.**

2. **Drag Total Current Value of Award to the Rows shelf.**

   The difference between Step 2 and Step 1 is a measure versus a row. The measure automatically SUMs the Total Obligation per City and State Symbol.

3. **Right-click the measure and select Edit Filter.**

4. **Enter a range of values from 50,000 to 1,000,000.**

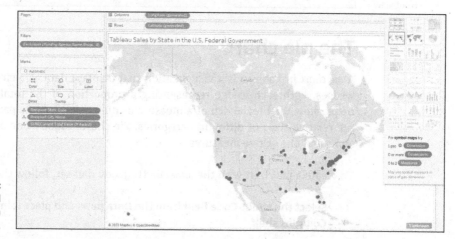

Visualizing Data in Tableau

FIGURE 7-6:
A symbol map with limited detail.

If you select the symbol map from Show Me, you can see very distinct circle sizes depending on dollar amounts. Selecting Maps initially differentiates the map by shades, which is normal behavior. As you can see in Figure 7-7, though, by going to the Maps menu, you can change and adjust the background, in effect also removing the color scheme. You then see more density relative to the area. For the example in Figure 7-7, bigger circles appear for the activity occurring in the Washington, D.C., metro area, where more significant procurements occurred.

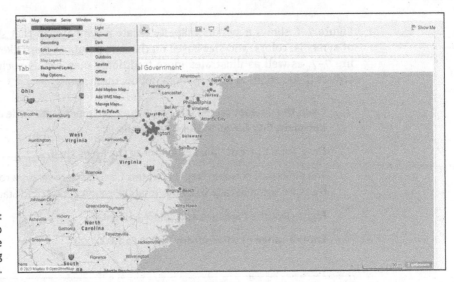

FIGURE 7-7:
A symbol map
with more
details, including
street view.

The pie chart

A *pie chart* in Tableau is a visualization that displays data as a circle divided into wedges, with each wedge representing a proportion of the total. The pie chart helps show the breakdown of a measure or dimension into its parts. It compares the relative sizes of different categories. Pie charts require one or more dimensions and one or two measures.

To create a pie chart with the usaspending.gov dataset, follow these steps.

1. **Select the NAICS Code field from the Data pane and place it in the Columns shelf.**

2. **Drag the Total Obligations from the Data pane to the Rows shelf.**

3. **Go to the NAICS Code and right-click Filter.**

   A Filter window appears, allowing a user to create a General, Wildcard, Condition, or Top filter.

4. **Select the NAICS Codes 541511, 541512, 541513, 541519 under the General Filter tab, then click OK.**

5. **Click the Label button under Marks and select Show Mark Labels. Click anywhere on the screen to hide the Show Mark Labels screen.**

   A pie chart is created.

This example pie chart, shown in Figure 7-8, enables you to understand the proportionality for all Tableau sales under NAICS Codes 541511, 541512, 541513, and 541519 in the U.S government.

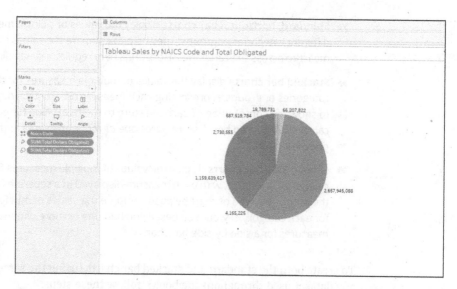

WARNING

Pie charts are not among the friendliest graphics in Tableau. You need to use tooltips to interpret data where you have several measures and dimensions. You can have only one label, which is numerical and, therefore, a measure. Figure 7-9 shows an example of including a tooltip.

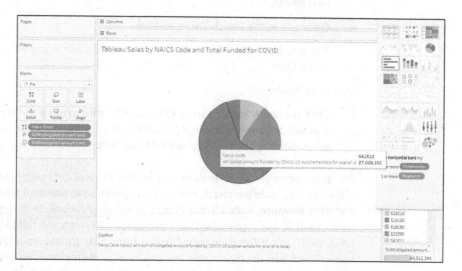

Visualizing Data in
Tableau

The bar chart

Tableau offers three types of bar charts in Tableau: horizontal (which is standard), stacked, and side by side. Here are some differences among the three:

>> **Standard, horizontal bar charts** display the values of a single measure for different categories or groups. They help to compare the values of the measure across the categories. Horizontal bars require a single dimension.

>> **Stacked bar charts** display the values of multiple measures for different categories or groups, representing each measure differently. They help to show the contribution of each measure to the total value for each category. A stacked bar chart requires one or more measures and at least one dimension.

>> **Side-by-side bar charts** display the values of multiple measures for different categories or groups, with each measure displayed in a separate bar next to the other. This type of chart helps to compare the values of multiple measures for each category. It would be best if you had one or more dimensions and measures for a side-by-side bar chart.

To create both the standard and stacked bar charts (using the same usaspending.gov dataset used throughout the book), follow these steps:

1. **Select the NAICS Code field and place it within the Marks card.**

2. **Drag the Total Obligated Amount field to the Rows shelf.**

3. **Click the Wildcard tab and select the Contains option in the menu that opens.**

4. **Enter 541 in the Match Value textbox.**

   This step filters the NAICS Code field for all values containing 541 as part of the NAICS Code.

5. **Click Apply.**

6. **Click the Show Me button on the top-right side to open the Show Me pane and select either Horizontal (Standard) Bars or Stacked Bars to see examples like those in Figures 7-10 and 7-11.**

The only option for those looking to compare several data points using a bar chart is the side-by-side bar chart. Figure 7-12 shows an example of what you see when a second measure, called Total Potential Value of Award, is dragged to the Rows shelf. Tableau automatically SUMs the value. Although the field is dragged to the Rows shelf, it's ultimately transformed into measure values relative to measure names. Notice in the figure that two columns are being evaluated, which results in the automatic generation of a legend, also shown in Figure 7-12.

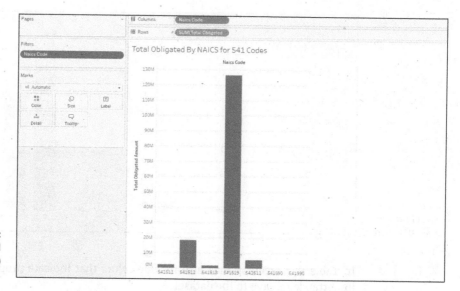

FIGURE 7-10:
A horizontal (standard) bar chart.

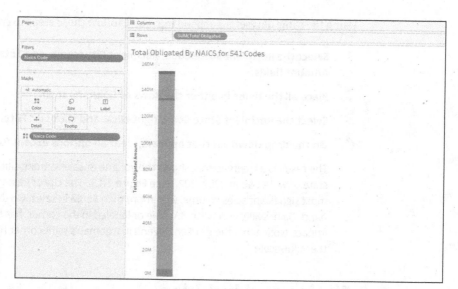

FIGURE 7-11:
A stacked bar chart.

The treemap

A treemap offers you a way to visualize and display hierarchical data using nested rectangles. The area of each rectangle is proportional to the quantity it represents. The rectangles are arranged in a way that avoids overlap, so it's easy to see the structure of the data. Treemaps can help to compare proportions within a hierarchy and to identify data patterns. People often use them to display data about categories, such as sales by product, geographical regions, or customer segments.

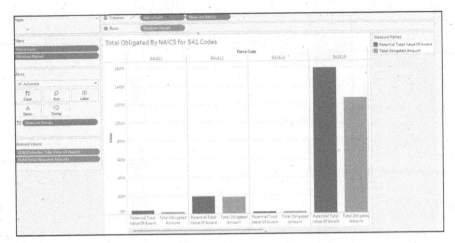

FIGURE 7-12:
A side-by-side
bar chart.

In Tableau, a treemap may also include colors that indicate proportionality and importance relative to the dataset.

Using the same dataset (usaspending.gov), follow these steps to create a treemap:

1. **Select the Recipient State Code, Recipient City Name, and Total Obligated Amount fields.**

2. **Place all the fields in either the Rows or Columns shelf.**

3. **Select the Recipient State Code, right-click, and click Edit Filter.**

4. **On the drop-down list that appears, clear all options except for V.**

   The result is a treemap that shows the volume of sales among cities in the state of VA between 2007–2022 (see Figure 7-13). The city of Reston had the most significant sales volume, with more than $50M in sales. On the other hand, Gainesville, which is not visible or labeled in the corner, has the slightest impact. Notice that the gradient legend in treemap's right corner helps to show the value scale.

Circles and bubbles

People often confuse circles with bubbles in Tableau, but they shouldn't. Also, the names of these diagrams are a bit misleading because the Circle view visualization in Tableau is a traditional scatter plot. The scatter plot displays data points as circles (or other shapes) on a two-dimensional grid. A single circle represents each data point, and the circle's position on the grid represents the values of the data point along the x and y axes. You often use scatter plots to visualize the relationships between different datasets or to identify patterns and trends in the data. For example, you may want to use a scatter plot to visualize the relationship between a company's revenue and its profits, or to identify stock market trends. Scatter plots are a valuable tool for exploring and understanding data. You can customize them in various ways to highlight different aspects of the data.

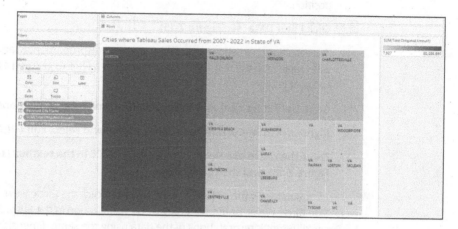

FIGURE 7-13:
A treemap.

A second type of circle visualization is the side-by-side Circle view. This type of visualization displays two datasets as circles. One set of circles is positioned next to another to compare the values of two datasets or to show how two datasets are related. You often use side-by-side Circle views to compare data about categories, such as sales by product, geographical regions, or customer segments. You can also use them to compare data about individual observations, such as the size of a company and its revenue or profit.

The last of the circle-type charts is a bubble, even though bubbles and circles are the same. The bubble chart in Tableau is a visualization that displays data as circles shown on a two-dimensional chart. Each bubble represents a single data point, with its position on the chart determined by its values on two numeric axes. You can also use the bubble size to encode additional data, such as the volume of a particular product sold or the population of a particular city. People often use bubble charts to compare multiple datasets, identify trends and patterns, and find outliers in the data. Bubble charts can help to visualize data with three or more dimensions, such as data that includes a third numeric or categorical variable.

Using the following steps with the usaspending.gov dataset, you can create each circle chart using the same variables: Recipient State Code, Current Total Value of Award, and Total Obligated Amount.

1. **For the Circle view, place the two measures on the Rows shelf and the dimension on the Columns shelf.**

2. **On the bottom of the page, you see that nulls exist. Click the nulls link to indicate that you want to filter all values (see Figure 7-14).**

   A pop-up menu appears, asking you to filter or show data at the default position.

3. **Click Filter Data (see Figure 7-15).**

   The resulting chart shows that one state has a disproportionate amount of sales relative to the rest. The next step creates a filter to give you a better sense of reality.

4. **Go to the Filters card and select SUM(Current Total Obligations).**

5. **Right-click SUM(Current Total Obligations) and select Edit Filters.**

6. **Enter the range of values** $50,000 – $2,500,000 **in the textbox (see Figure 7-16), and then click OK.**

   After you follow the preceding steps, you can click the Circle views, Side-By-Side Circle views, or Bubble Chart views visualization in the Show Me pane to see different interpretations of the data using the same dimensions and measures utilized. Regardless of the view, you'll see three consistent circle and bubble charts appear, presenting the same message in terms of sales value by state, given the range $50,000–$2,500,000 NET from 2007–2022 using the Circle view, Side-by-Side Circle view, and a bubble chart, as shown in Figures 7-17 through 7-19.

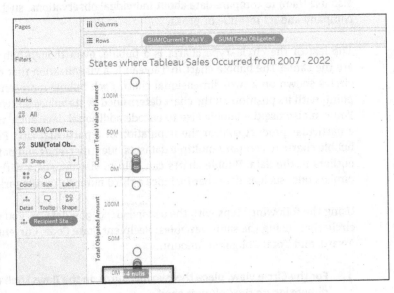

FIGURE 7-14:
Filtering nulls from a visualization.

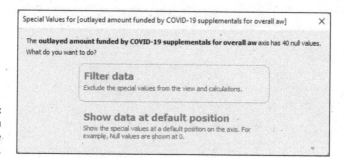

FIGURE 7-15:
A pop-up menu
lets you choose
to filter data.

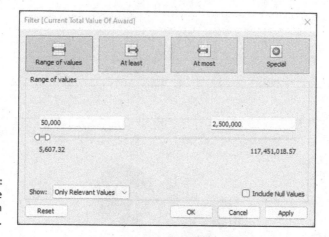

FIGURE 7-16:
Set a range
of values in
the filter.

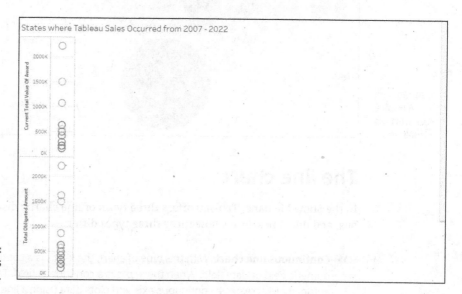

FIGURE 7-17:
A Circle views
visualization.

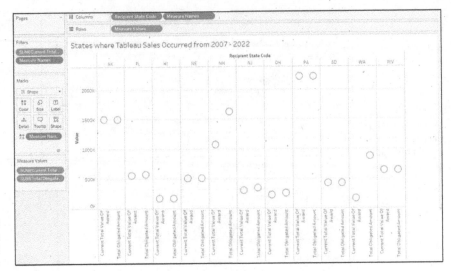

FIGURE 7-18:
A Side-By-Side
Circle views
visualization.

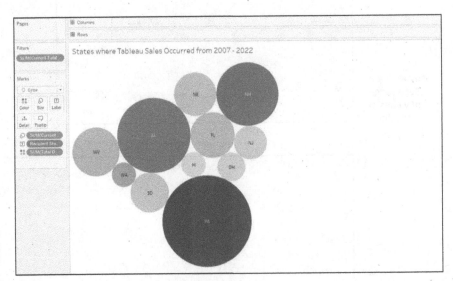

FIGURE 7-19:
A Bubble
Chart views
visualization.

The line chart

In the Show Me pane, Tableau offers three types of line charts: discrete, continuous, and dual line. Here's how these three types differ:

>> **Continuous line chart:** With this type of chart, the x-axis is a continuous numeric field or date field. When the x-axis is a continuous field, Tableau automatically creates a continuous axis and plots data using a line.

>> **Discrete line chart:** With this type of chart, the x-axis is a discrete field containing a finite number of distinct values. Tableau creates a discrete axis and plots data using discrete data points rather than a continuous line.

>> **Dual-line chart:** Also referred to as a dual axis, this type of chart displays two measures on a y-axis. Using this chart type is proper when comparing two measures that have different scales. You may have one measure with a range of 0–100 and another that ranges from 200–500. If you try to measure these on the same axis, it would not be easy to see the difference between them. Using dual-scale axes allows you to compare the two values more effectively than using a single-line discrete or continuous-line evaluation.

To create a continuous line chart from the sample dataset (usaspending.gov), follow these steps:

1. **Locate these two data fields: Current Period of Performance and Total Obligated Amount.**

2. **Drag the Current Period of Performance field to the Columns shelf.**

3. **Drag the Total Obligated Amount field to the Rows shelf.**

   A continuous line chart like the one shown in Figure 7-20 appears.

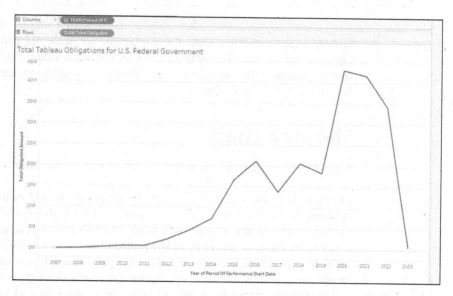

FIGURE 7-20:
A continuous line chart.

Each time you add another field to the Rows shelf — for example, the Potential Value of Award — another line will be added to the visualization. If you want to create a discrete line chart instead, you'll need to apply the changes to the y-axis (Columns shelf), as shown in Figure 7-21.

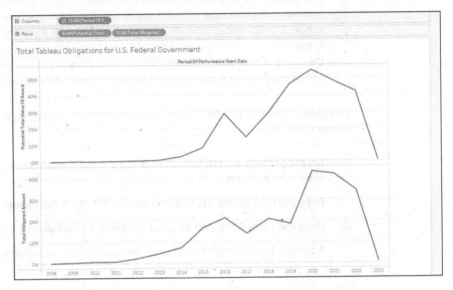

FIGURE 7-21:
A discrete
line chart.

You can make use of the dual-line option on the Show Me pane without adding more data points. The notable difference between Obligated versus Potential emerges clearly with this type of chart, shown in Figure 7-22, especially with the different colors for each line.

The area chart

As with the line chart, the area chart offers a continuous and discrete view.

The area chart displays data as a series of points connected by lines, except that between the lines and the x-axis, the space is filled with color or a gradient. You use area charts to demonstrate trends over time or to compare several measures. If you used the data points from the previous section's example, you would see little differentiation between discrete and continuous lines versus area charts except for the areas being filled. Figure 7-23 uses the data points Year of the Period of Performance Start Date and the sum of the Potential Value of the Total Award to show a like-kind line in the area chart.

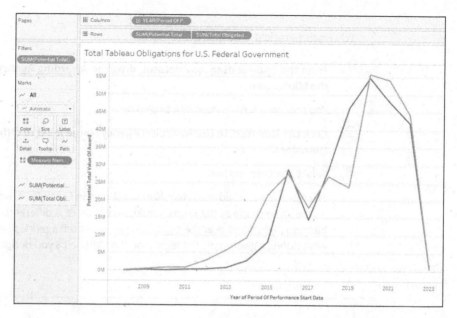

FIGURE 7-22:
A dual-line chart.

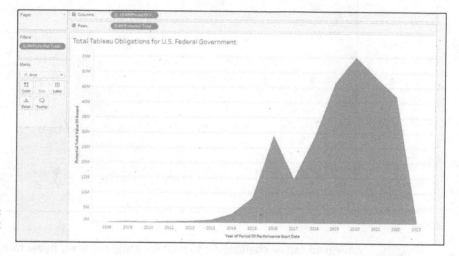

FIGURE 7-23:
An area chart (continuous).

What happens, though, if you add an extra layer? You may want to understand who is spending the money. You can add an extra layer and create a stacked area chart, which is not an option available on the Show Me pane.

To create a stacked area chart:

1. **From the usaspending.gov dataset, drag the Awarding Agency field to the Marks card.**

   You see many lines instead of a single line.

2. **Click the icon next to the Awarding Agency Name label to differentiate the colors.**

3. **Select the Color option.**

   The result is a stacked area chart like that shown in Figure 7-24. Notice that it's the same shape as the original chart, except there is differentiation because if you scroll over the chart, you can see which agencies have spent what during a given year. The legend on the right helps you decipher the color coding.

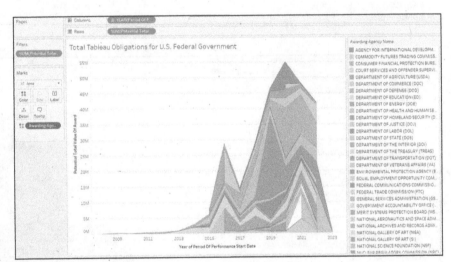

FIGURE 7-24: A stacked area chart.

TIP

A legend can be challenging to read for a sighted user, never mind a person with color challenges. Tableau does offer an accessible, compliant palette for those needing to meet Section 508 and WCAG standards. Also, the usaspending.gov dataset has many data points. Filtering should help reduce the number of tones and shades for better readability in a stacked area chart.

The dual combination chart

In Tableau, a dual combination is a visualization that combines two separate views of the same data onto a single sheet. Dual combinations help to compare two targeted values given a specific period or value in the exact visualization, or the same measure or dimension across different periods.

To create a dual combination chart in Tableau, you need two measures and one date. Dimensions are optional. To create a dual combination chart using the usaspending.gov dataset as an example, follow these steps:

1. **Drag the Period of Performance Start Date data field to the Columns shelf.**

2. **Drag the Potential Total Value of Award and Total Obligated Amount data fields to the Rows shelf.**

   The initial result is shown in Figure 7-25. Notice the bars and line.

3. **(Optional) You can swap the line for an alternative combination, such as areas, circles, and symbols (Figure 7-26). To accomplish this, go to each value under the Marks card and select one of the following from the drop-down list (by default, the list is set to automatic):**

   • Area Chart for Total Obligations

   • Line Chart for the Potential Total Value of the Award

   In Figure 7-27, you can see the changes made when both fields were changed from a line or bar given the options found under the drop-down menu.

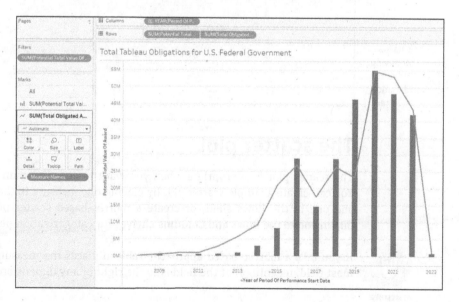

Visualizing Data in Tableau

FIGURE 7-25: A dual combination chart with bars and a single line.

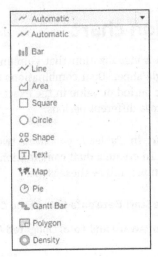

FIGURE 7-26:
Alternative
charting design
combinations.

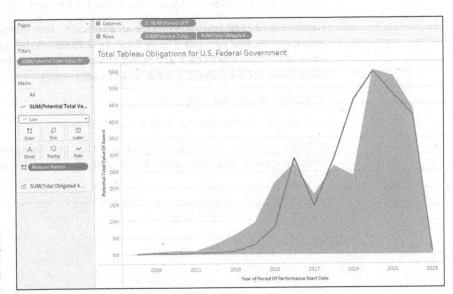

FIGURE 7-27:
Modifying
the dual
combination
chart.

The scatter plot

The scatter plot is appropriate when you want to visualize numerical variables. You can create a simple scatter plot by placing one measure in the Columns shelf and one in the Rows shelf, or create a matrix-based scatter plot by adding a dimension to the Rows and Columns shelves for categorization purposes.

REMEMBER

If you take a matrix-based approach, Tableau places the measure as the inner-most field, meaning that the field is to the right of any dimension on a shelf.

In the following example using the usaspending.gov dataset, you follow these steps to evaluate the number of awards per the NAICS Code and Product and Service Code (which are both dimensions), by including the Current Total Value of Awards and Number of Offers Received fields:

1. **Drag the Current Total Value of Awards field to the Rows shelf.**

2. **Drag the Number of Offers Received field to the Columns shelf.**

3. **Drag the NAICS Code and Product and Service Code fields to the Marks card.**

   At this point, you see a scatter plot with a highly dense region in the lower-left corner (see Figure 7-28). However, to better understand data, consider applying filters on the dimensions and measures. Creating a specific filter for each measure and dimension helps you to view all scenarios and achieve greater clarity.

WARNING

4. **To apply filters, right-click each of the dimensions or measures and select Show Filter.**

   Each filter appears on the right side of the screen.

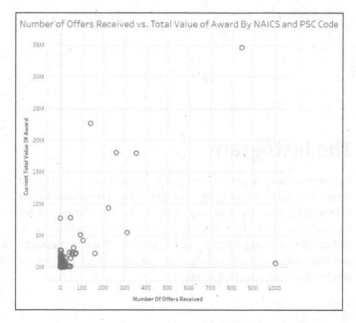

FIGURE 7-28:
A scatter plot with no filters on dimensions or measures.

5. **Adjust the filters as follows:**

- **For Product and Service Code: Enter** D.

- **For SUM(Numbers of Offers Received): Set the range to 0–100.**

- **For SUM(Current Total Values of Award): Set the range to 250,000–1,000,000.**

- **Keep the NAICS Codes as they are.**

The new scatter plot shows the finite number of Tableau-related acquisitions where the SUM was between $250,000 and $1,000,000 for specific NAICS and PSCs combined. An example is shown in Figure 7-29.

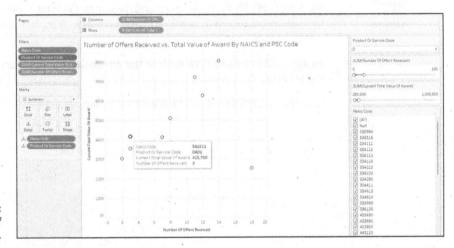

The histogram

Histograms help users understand data distributions. Using a bar chart to group values for data comparison, you can better understand data based on grouped values of continuous measures or bins. In other words, you may have many small transactions. Still, the transactions are lumped together under a single umbrella and classified using a range. For example, all store transactions with a value of less than $99.99 would fall into one range, and transactions above that threshold would comprise a second range.

That's the case in Figure 7-30, where *bins*, a grouping of like-kind values, are grouped for the Current Total Value of the Award, which is the only data field you need to drag to the Rows and Columns shelves. Each of the smaller transactions matched to like-kind properties are paired in bins and then classified, which is the same in the sampling you've just created in the previous section, "The scatter plot."

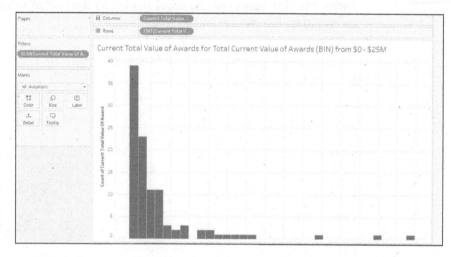

WARNING

You have little control over histogram bins; therefore, you should filter the dataset to target a realistic view of a histogram. Such filtering has been applied to the histogram in Figure 7-30 to keep the range of values from exceeding 25,000,000. All anomalous data ranges have been removed.

The box and whisker plot

The *box and whisker plot*, also called a *box plot*, is a chart type that allows users to display minimum values, 25 percent quartile, median, 75 percent quartile, and maximum range values. Values that exceed the thresholds are called *outliers*. Using a box and whisker plot helps you understand the distribution and spread of your dataset.

Visualizing Data in
Tableau

To create a box and whisker plot, you need two dimensions on the Columns shelf and one measure on the Rows shelf. Ensure that the Marks card is set to a circle and the reference line is set to a box plot.

After you place your data fields on the shelves, the resulting chart (using the usaspending.gov dataset) looks like the one in Figure 7-31, which illustrates the total value of awards based on a given contract type. As you can tell from the figure, the Firm Fixed Fee and Labor Hours had the bulk of federal dollars allocated during the award period.

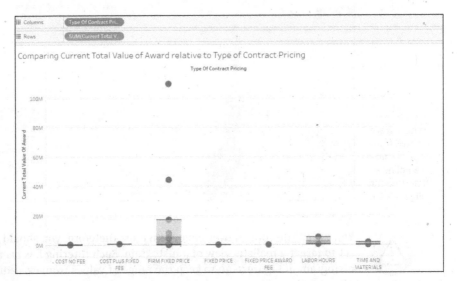

FIGURE 7-31:
A box and
whisker plot.

The Gantt chart

You use a Gantt chart to illustrate the duration of a data point. A Gantt chart requires one date measure in the Columns shelf and one dimension in the Rows shelf. The Tableau Gantt chart is different from the traditional project management tool such as Microsoft Project because you can't create a discrete line item and assign a start date and end date to a specific item. Quite the opposite, in fact. With Tableau, you're looking at the date at a given moment in time. For example, say that a transaction occurred in January 2023. On a Gantt chart, a tick mark would appear, representing the period of January 2023. Depending on the granularity, it could be one mark representing the month (January 2023) or a series of marks representing part of a quarter (Q1 2023). The marks are not spelled out for the duration of the contract; they just show a moment in time. That's the case with the Gantt chart you see in Figure 7-32, with each mark representing a unit of one month.

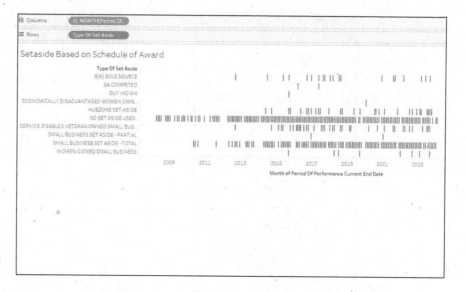

FIGURE 7-32:
A Gantt chart.

To create a Gantt chart using the usaspending.gov dataset as an example, follow these steps:

1. **Drag the Month of Period of Performance Current End Date field to the Columns shelf.**

2. **Drag the Type of Set Aside field to the Rows shelf.**

3. **Right-click the Period of Performance Current End Date field, and change the time frame from Years to Months (it's the second option, which includes the month and year notation).**

Your Gantt chart ticks are now a bit more granular.

4. **Click Gantt Chart on the Show Me pane.**

A Gantt chart like the one in Figure 7-32 appears.

TECHNICAL STUFF

Out of the box, Tableau defaults to the Year setting for every tick mark on the Gantt Chart. To change this setting, right-click the date-based measure and then click an alternative parameter such as Year, Quarter, Month, or Day to modify the bounds. The example in Figure 7-33 shows Month as the setting.

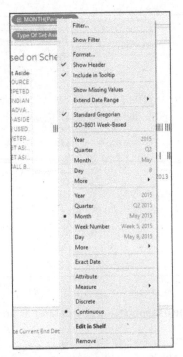

FIGURE 7-33:
Setting date-
based measures
for a Gantt chart.

The bullet chart

The *bullet chart* displays data in much the same way as a horizontal bar chart, except that it's condensed, given that it contains two data points. A bullet chart compares a single measure to a targeted value. This type of chart is ideal when you're trying to gauge performance over time. The bar represents the tracked measure, and the horizontal line indicates the target value. Knowing the bar's position relative to the line helps you quickly ascertain whether you're on target to meet the measured objective. A bullet chart does allow for the comparison of multiple measures in the same target value.

To create an example bullet chart using the usaspending.gov dataset, follow these steps:

1. **Drag the Award Type data field to the Rows shelf.**

2. **Drag the Total Potential Value of Award and Total Obligated Amount data fields to the Columns shelf.**

3. **Select the Bullet Chart option on the Show Me pane.**

   The bullet chart shown in Figure 7-34 appears.

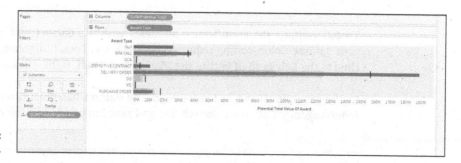

FIGURE 7-34:
A bullet chart.

Converting a Visualization to a Crosstab

You can take any visualization in Tableau and convert it to a cross tabulation table, or crosstab. A *crosstab* converts a visualization into a text-based table, showing the data in a textual form. Like the text table discussed in the section "The text table," earlier in the chapter, the crosstab table comprises one or more dimensions and measures. A crosstab can also integrate various calculations for the measure fields, including running totals and percentage totals. To convert a visualization to a crosstab using the usaspending.gov dataset, follow these steps:

1. **Drag the Period of Performance Start Date field to the Columns shelf.**

2. **Drag the Funding Agency Name and Awarding Office Name fields to the Rows shelf.**

3. **Drag the measure Total Obligated Amount to the Labels shelf under the Marks card.**

   A simple crosstab is created (see Figure 7-35).

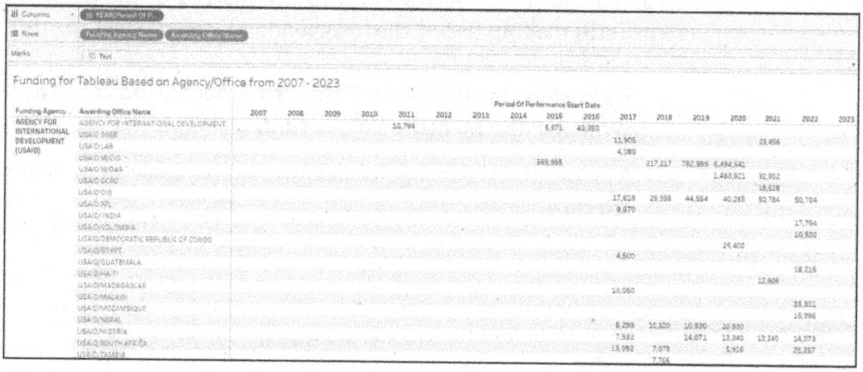

FIGURE 7-35:
A simple crosstab table.

To differentiate the significance of values within a dataset, you can color-code your dataset. Color-coding requires you to add the Total Obligation field one more time to the Labels shelf within the Marks card. Then, right-click and select Color.

In the example shown in Figure 7-36, the dataset has been filtered to only one federal agency. Still, the color scheme and range in values and colors are apparent.

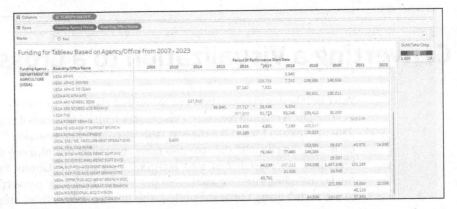

FIGURE 7-36:
A crosstab
with colors.

TIP

If your range of values is quite broad — say, 0 to a billion — be sure to pick a gradient range that's easy to differentiate. Having too many similar shades can confuse people and defeat the purpose of using color.

Finally, you may want to review data using a standard calculation. Out of the box, Tableau incorporates various calculations that can be autogenerated in a crosstab table. The options, which appear in Figure 7-37, are frequently updated.

To add a calculation to the chart to use instead of the dollar values, follow these steps (still making use of the usaspending.gov dataset for this example):

1. **Right-click the SUM(Total Obligated Amount) indicated by the text symbol in the Measure Values card.**

   A list of options appears, including Add Table Calculation, which you'll be selecting.

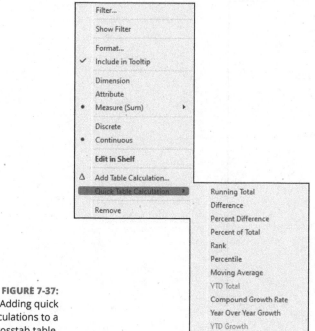

FIGURE 7-37:
Adding quick
calculations to a
crosstab table.

2. **Select the Add Table Calculations option.**

   A pop-up window appears, enabling you to create a Table Calculation
   (see Figure 7-38).

3. **On the first drop-down menu, select Table Calculation Type: Percent
   Difference From.**

4. **On the second drop-down menu, select Compute Using Table (across).**

   When you close the window, the crosstab immediately changes to show yearly
   percentages (see Figure 7-39.) The percentages indicate the increase and
   decrease in total obligated spending relative to the previous year for a given
   agency and its corresponding office.

Visualizing Data in
Tableau

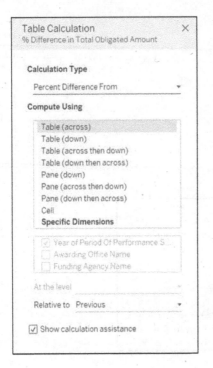

FIGURE 7-38:
Table calculation types.

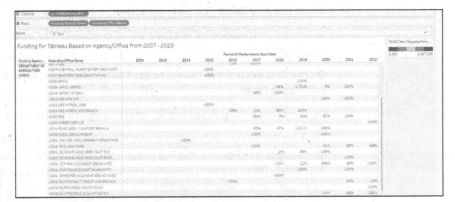

FIGURE 7-39:
A crosstab using table calculations.

Publishing Visualizations

Tableau Desktop has several paths for users to take to get their work product from Tableau Desktop to Tableau Server or Cloud. You can complete and publish a worksheet containing your visualization by doing one of the following:

>> On the Server menu, select Publish Workbook.

>> On the toolbar, click the last button, Share Workbook with Others.

>> On the File menu, choose Export your Visualization as a Package.

>> Create a PDF, PowerPoint, or alternative file format for mass use.

If your goal is to share and collaborate with other users in the organization who have Creator, Explorer, or Viewer licenses, publishing the workbook to a Tableau project is your optimal choice. If a system administrator has configured a project on your behalf, follow these steps to save your worksheet using either the Server or toolbar approach; the prompts are the same.

1. **Click the Share Workbook with Others button on the toolbar.**

   A pop-up menu appears (see Figure 7-40).

2. **Select the project.**

3. **Under Name, enter a worksheet name.**

4. **Under Description, provide a document description.**

5. **Under Tags, click Add to add tags.**

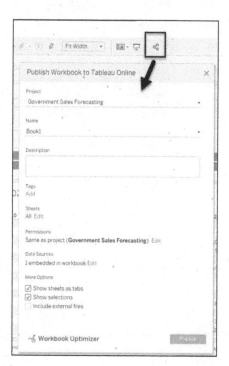

FIGURE 7-40:
A common publishing dialog box for Tableau Cloud and Server.

Visualizing Data in Tableau

6. **Under Permissions, click Edit to list who may or may not have access to the file in the future.**

7. **Under Data Sources, click Edit to validate the data source parameters using the Workbook Optimizer.**

   By default, it is usually embedded.

8. **If you are satisfied with what Workbook Optimizer indicates, you can execute publishing directly, or close the window and click the Back button to return to the previous window and then click Publish.**

WARNING

At this point, the file should be ready for publishing. One last step could be to optimize the file. In this case, the dataset used so far contains more than 280 fields, but only a handful have been used for the exercises. That's okay, because you'll use some other fields in subsequent chapters. However, if you want to optimize the dataset, follow the guidance provided using Workbook Optimizer (shown in Figure 7-41), which offers you a way to ensure that the dataset you're publishing is healthy.

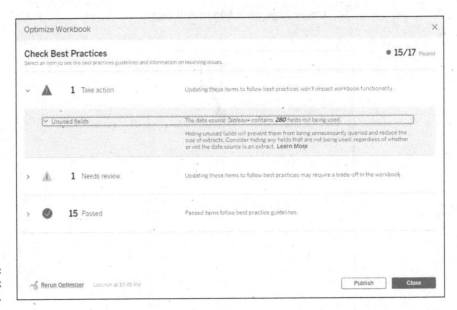

FIGURE 7-41:
Workbook
Optimizer.

Chapter **8**

Collaborating and Publishing with Tableau Cloud

L ike other heavyweight enterprise business intelligence platforms, Tableau offers an online and desktop version of its servers. Many folks try to figure out why to opt for online versus Tableau Desktop and Tableau Server, beyond the fact that you can access all the tools on the internet. After all, doesn't the online version lack certain features that Tableau Desktop and Tableau Server offer? My answer is yes, yes, and yes! But the online version also has capabilities that you can't get anywhere else affordably.

The significant difference boils down to nuances with worksheet, dashboard, and story features available only on Tableau Desktop and Tableau Server. With Tableau Cloud, the user experience is more fluid in that it integrates many of the applications you need to utilize on your local computer desktop in a single platform. However, Tableau Cloud requires you to take more steps to complete a straightforward activity than you have to take in both Tableau Desktop and Tableau Server, which are not browser-based. That's the big negative. The positive of being on the internet is the ability to share and collaborate with users at a highly granular level, assuming that you are licensed to do so. You get a cadre of collaboration options in the cloud that you don't get in any other environment.

This chapter covers the end-user aspect of Tableau Cloud, emphasizing how to collaborate and publish worksheets, dashboards, and stories with others. Although add-on features such as Data Management, Advanced Management, and Analytics can be enabled in Tableau Cloud, those features are specifically for targeted enterprise use cases, which are well beyond the scope of this book.

Strolling through the Tableau Cloud Experience

The Tableau Cloud experience combines three tools: a Sharing and Collaboration platform, a Systems Administrator console for those using Tableau in the enterprise, and an online companion to Tableau Desktop and Tableau Prep Builder that enables a user to create full workbooks and flows online. However, the interface doesn't divide the platform components as cut-and-dried as this book does. Figure 8-1 shows the key interface elements.

>> **Personal features:** All the features to control the Tableau Cloud experience personally and for those looking to collaborate with others

>> **System administrative features:** All the features relevant to administering Tableau Cloud using automation, feeds, templates, and configurable options

>> **Features of Tableau applications in the cloud features:** All the key features available in Tableau Desktop for New Workbook, Tableau Prep Builder for New Flow, and New Data Source

REMEMBER

Tableau workbooks, and by default, worksheets are the equivalent of a spreadsheet created using Google Sheets or Microsoft Excel. Both products produce a workbook (a single file) that may or may not contain many sheets (worksheets) in which visualizations are produced.

If you want to complete a universal search of all views, metrics, workbooks, collections, and data sources, or even search by Content Owner, go to the Tableau Cloud search bar (shown in Figure 8-2) and type in a relevant term. For the figure, two terms were input for search: external assets and Tableau, which could appear in any of the objects saved within the instance of Tableau Cloud across all the object types.

Personal features

Tableau applications in the cloud

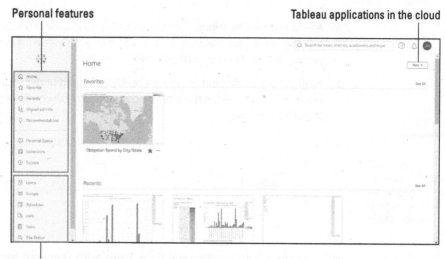

FIGURE 8-1:
The Tableau
Cloud interface.

System administrative features

FIGURE 8-2:
Performing a
Tableau Cloud
search.

Next to the search bar, you'll find three icons: a question mark in a circle, a bell, and two letters (my initials, in Figure 8-3). Each item represents a specific function:

>> **Help:** All help functionality is available when you click the question mark icon for Tableau Cloud. Help options include Tableau Help, Support, System Status, What's New, and About Tableau.

>> **Alerts and Notifications:** Alerts and Notifications appear under the bell. For example, when you create an item to share or you receive a share notification, you see the notification under the bell.

>> **Profile:** Your profile and activity are centrally housed under your initials. Features include Personal Space, My Content, My Account Settings, Set as Start Page, and Logout.

FIGURE 8-3:
Help, notification, and profile functionality in Tableau Cloud.

Next, you see a button below the three icons with the word New. If you expand the arrows, you find the New menu, which contains all the features you can use as part of Tableau Cloud, just as if you were using Tableau Desktop, except for the additional capability to upload files. This option, Upload Workbook (shown in Figure 8-4), enables files to be edited in the cloud.

FIGURE 8-4:
The New menu in Tableau Cloud.

Although creating a project and collection is specific to Tableau Cloud, as you find out in the upcoming pages, you can select New Workbook to create a new workbook, which includes a combination of worksheets, dashboards, or stories using Tableau Cloud. The Tableau Cloud interface that allows users to manage their workbooks and data online is called the Tableau Cloud Workbook Editor. Using the Tableau Cloud Workbook Editor is similar to the native user experience in Tableau Desktop to create new worksheets. Figure 8-5 shows an example of a new workbook being created in the Tableau Cloud Workbook Editor.

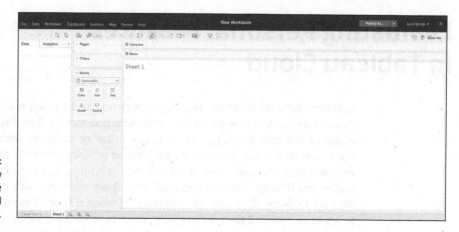

FIGURE 8-5:
Creating a new workbook in the Tableau Cloud Workbook Editor.

You can also create a new flow that's like the entire user experience available in Tableau Prep Builder. However, before you get to the full editor, you must connect to a data source so that the online Flow Editor can fully operate. (See Book 3, Chapters 2 through 4 on Tableau Prep Builder for more details.)

TECHNICAL STUFF

Users often assume that data sources previously defined in Tableau Cloud are brought into a Tableau Cloud flow, but that assumption is inaccurate. Each time you want to create a new flow, you need to define your sources, just as in Tableau Prep Builder, and then build the flow from scratch. This process was followed in Figure 8-6 using the Tableau Cloud Flow Builder web Authoring tool. Remember, Tableau Cloud tries to replicate the experience with the Desktop companion, Tableau Prep Builder, but subtle differences should be evident across features and functionality.

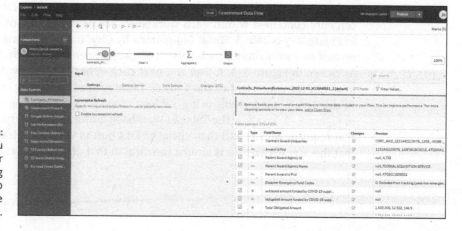

FIGURE 8-6:
Using the Tableau Cloud Flow Editor is similar to using Tableau Prep Builder to create a flow.

Evaluating Personal Features in Tableau Cloud

Transferring a simile of the Desktop experience to the cloud is often a tall order. Tableau has done a fine job of accomplishing just that by focusing on integrating many of the best concepts across many industry products within its product. For example, the concept of the cloud-based personal folder is mimicked by the Personal Space feature. Like other industry solutions that leverage bookmarking and recent history, Tableau has replicated those concepts with its Favorites and Recents. Collectively, users can make use of Personal Space, Favorites, and Recents to organize and find their data rapidly, often in one click if well enough organized. The following sections tell you more about each of these features.

Personal Space

If you've used Google Drive, Microsoft One Drive, SharePoint Document Libraries, Dropbox, Box, or other document collaboration solutions, you should be at ease using the Personal Space feature. The Personal Space is just that: personal. It's a private location for the Creators and Explorers (see Book 3, Chapter 1 for more about these user types) to create, edit, and save their work using Tableau Cloud. Any time you save content to a Personal Space, it can't be shared with other users until you move it to a project, which is when it's ready for others to see and explore.

You can save workbooks to a Personal Space. Workbooks may consist of worksheets, dashboards, or stories. In the example shown in Figure 8-7, two workbooks are saved. If you click the name of each workbook, you can then view the contents contained within each workbook. For example, one of the workbooks in Figure 8-7 is called "Total Obligations by City/State." Clicking that workbook reveals two worksheets, each with "Obligation Spend by City/State" in the title, as shown in Figure 8-8. A user can next click either of these worksheets to open it within the equivalent of the Tableau Desktop read-only view but on the cloud. At this level, you can edit using Tableau Cloud's web authoring tools, as shown in Figure 8-9. To show the Tableau Workbook Editor, go to the specific workbook that requires editing and then click the Edit button within Tableau Cloud. Notice that the user experience is almost identical to that of Tableau Desktop.

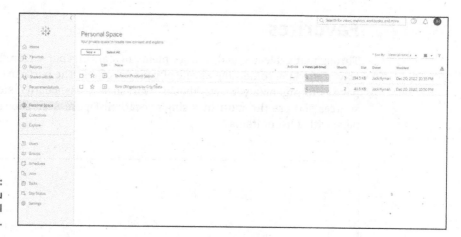

FIGURE 8-7:
The Tableau
Cloud Personal
Space feature.

FIGURE 8-8:
Click the
workbook
title to see its
worksheets.

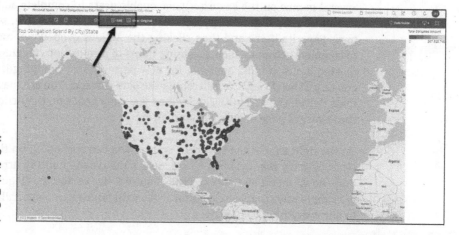

FIGURE 8-9:
Click the Edit tab
to fully edit the
worksheet
using Tableau
Cloud's web
authoring tools.

Favorites

Throughout Tableau Cloud, you see plenty of stars on your screen. The star is your way of marking something as one of your Favorites. The purpose of the Favorites page is to organize your workbooks, worksheets, dashboards, stories, and data sources you use the most in a single location. Figure 8-10 shows the Favorites page with a list of items.

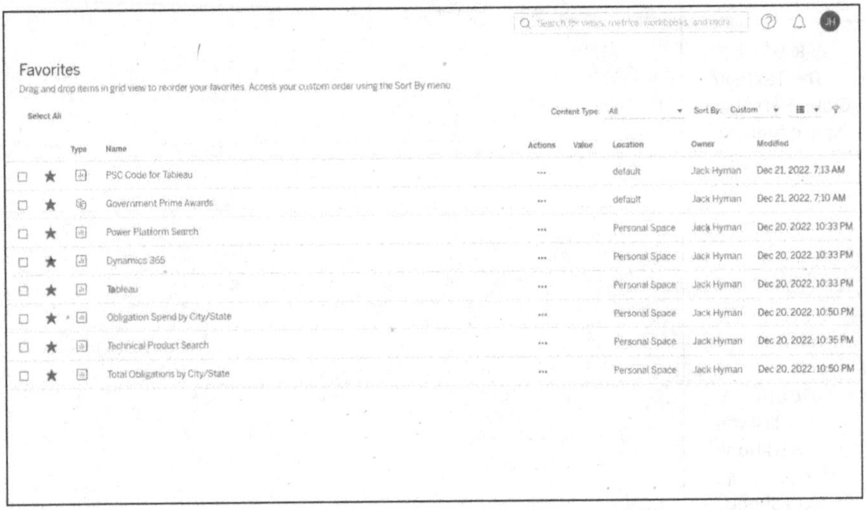

FIGURE 8-10: The Favorites page.

Several menus on the Favorites page enable users to complete additional actions as long as they have the appropriate permissions. For example, selecting one or more Favorite items and then clicking the Actions drop-down menu allows you to complete activities such as adding items to a collection, tagging items in bulk, moving items in bulk, applying for new permissions, changing item ownership, creating Tabbed views, or refreshing the data extracts. You also have the option to mass delete. (Be careful!) The options you can choose on the Actions menu from the Favorites page appear in Figure 8-11.

On the right side of the Favorites screen, you can sort based on the type of content you have marked with a star. Select the down-pointing arrow to open the drop-down menu by Content Type (Figure 8-12) or Sort By (Figure 8-13). These are simple ways to review your favorites with laser focus, especially if you happen to like everything you create.

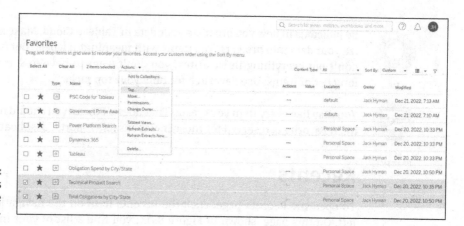

FIGURE 8-11:
The Actions menu on the Favorites page.

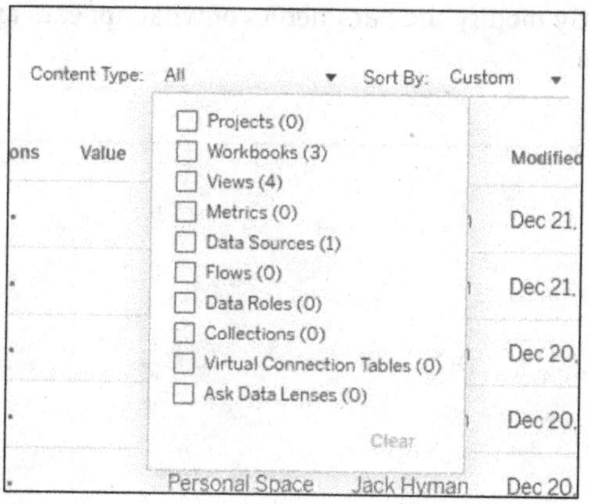

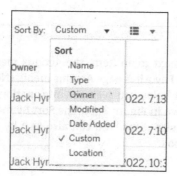

FIGURE 8-12:
The Content Type menu on the Favorites page.

FIGURE 8-13:
The Sort By menu on the Favorites page.

Be judicious in how you organize your data in Tableau Cloud. Make sure you organize your data into projects. Tag items with meaningful labels. But most important, don't put everything in Favorites; you don't want to have to sort through a very long list of items. Use Favorites for only your top picks.

You may like every item you create. That doesn't mean you should make it a Favorite. A Favorite is reserved for those indispensable reports, dashboards, and stories.

Recents

To open the Recents page, click the Recents item on the navigation pane on the left. On this page, shown in Figure 8-14, you find a list of your most accessed or recent activity. Tableau uses the combination of the two metrics to populate the page. You can slightly modify the parameters of what appears and for how long it appears on the page.

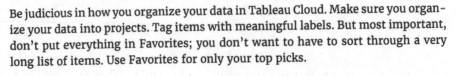

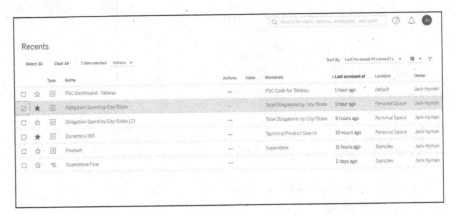

FIGURE 8-14:
Recents page.

When you select the check box next to an item, the Actions menu appears with the same options as those on the Favorites page Actions menu. (Notice a repetitive theme yet?) The only menu that helps you seek out information based on chronology is the Sort By menu, shown in Figure 8-15. The Sort By menu can help you sort from oldest to newest and vice versa. You can also sort by owner, location, last accessed, name, and workbook.

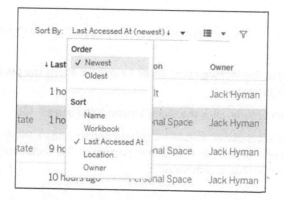

FIGURE 8-15:
The Sort By menu on the Recents page.

Sharing Experiences and Collaborating with Others

Tableau Cloud's shared experience is limited to users who are actively licensed in your organization as Creators, Explorers, and Viewers. Any user without an active license won't be able to view, edit, or create content unless they use the Tableau Public release. As noted elsewhere in the book, if you use Tableau Public, you are required to publish your findings to the world; you can't target your group of users, who may have varying levels of permissiveness.

For licensed users, especially Creators or Explorers, your ability to control object-level visibility can be pretty granular, down to the data source, view, workbook, or flow level.

Sharing content

When you're ready to let your content be shared with others, follow these steps:

1. **Go to the item you want to share and then select the drop-down menu under Actions.**

   The Actions menu opens.

2. **Choose Share.**

   A pop-up asking whom you want to share the data with appears, along with a link to the document to be shared.

3. **Under Share with People, enter at least one other username (they must be licensed) to access the content.**

As you type, the names of licensed users within your Tableau Cloud domain appear.

4. **(Optional) In the Message box, enter a message about the purpose of the shared documents.**

5. **When you're ready, click the Share button (see Figure 8-16).**

   The document is shared, and each user you decide to share the document with receives a notification about the shared document. The document also appears on the Shared with Me page.

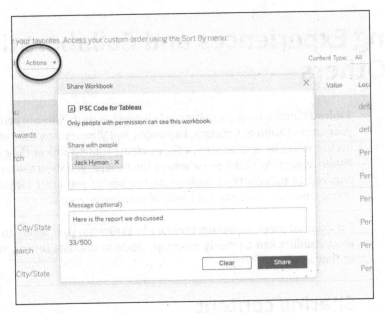

FIGURE 8-16:
Sharing content with other users.

Shared with Me

In the previous section, you click the Share button to share the document with others. You should then receive an email notification with a link to the content. If, on the other hand, someone shares a document with you, open the Shared with Me page navigation and click the page to see a list of documents that have been shared.

Your ability to manipulate the file with Tableau Desktop, Tableau Prep Builder, or Tableau Cloud depends entirely on the permissions the party sharing the file has assigned to that file. In the example shown in Figure 8-17, a single item has been shared, which also triggered a received email, viewable in Figure 8-18.

FIGURE 8-17:
The Shared with
Me page.

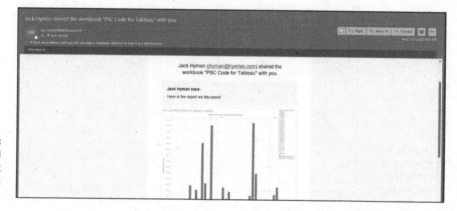

FIGURE 8-18:
An email
notification that
an item has been
shared with you.

Click the check box within the filters pane next to the visualization to choose various options from the Actions menu that opens (see Figure 8-19). If you happen to have permission to edit the file, you can do so by downloading the file or opening the file directly in Tableau Desktop. You can then edit the workbook and publish it back to your workspace and that of the owners.

BEST PRACTICE

Make sure you know what level of access you have to the relevant content. You might be a Creator in one instance versus a Viewer in another case. It is up to you (or the content creator) to assign relevant permissions.

Collections

Organization is the key to success with Tableau Cloud. You may have a well-organized system if you've put some thought into how to organize your computer files. Most people, though, always have files that fall through the cracks. A *collection* is a virtual folder that lets you place related items in an easy-to-access list to organize items based on your specific topic or theme. Collections also enable you to break down items based on visibility and ownership. You can keep a project private or make it public, assigning it to a user or a group of users within your Tableau site.

FIGURE 8-19:
The Actions menu on the Shared with Me page.

TECHNICAL STUFF

Although you can give access to others for a collection, you should not worry about exposing data because collections are permission neutral. Users can see only the items to which they are given access. Furthermore, when selecting an item and heading to the Actions menu, you have limited options depending on your permissions. Those given the most permission can modify and delete a file from a collection.

Previous sections mention that users can select the check box and move an item to a collection. Assuming that a collection has already been created, the user selects the collection to which the item should be saved. Then, it appears as part of the virtual list.

For the examples in the following figures, items are assigned to specific collections based on the files uploaded to Personal Space. Tableau Desktop automatically loads files published to Tableau Cloud into the default folder. It is up to you to move the file to another collection. Figure 8-20 provides a representative example of two collections, and Figure 8-21 offers a glimpse of how you can organize items in a collection (in this case, the collection is named "Government Procurement Data").

FIGURE 8-20:
The Collections
page listing two
collections.

FIGURE 8-21:
Items stored
within a named
collection.

REMEMBER

You may have noticed a tab called My Collections on the Collections page. The My Collections tab houses only collections you've created, not ones that have been shared with you by others.

Explore

The Explore feature in Tableau Cloud is the equivalent of the Windows File Explorer or the Apple Finder, with a twist concerning the capability to create folders and files. Because you are in the cloud, Explore presents all your file systems on the Explore home page. Each project, represented by a new folder, can contain a combination of objects, including workbooks, flows, and published data sources.

To create a new workbook, flow, or published data source or to upload a workbook, click the New drop-down menu in the upper-left corner of the Explore page (see Figure 8-22).

What happens, though, when you've been using Tableau for months if not years, and you've collected thousands of documents in your Explore repository, much like in your My Documents folder? You'll want a quick and easy way to search for the documents. That's where filters come in handy. Right next to the word *Explore* in the upper-left corner of the Explore page, the name of the default filter, Top-Level Projects, appears. When you click the down-pointing arrow next to that filter, you open a drop-down menu (see Figure 8-23) that lists all the ways you can filter and thereby organize your documents and folders.

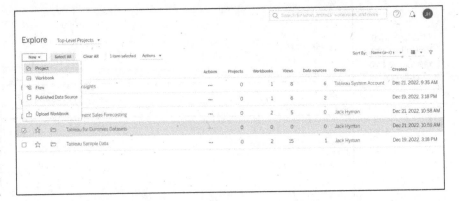

FIGURE 8-22:
Click New on the Explore page to create new workbooks, flows, or published data sources.

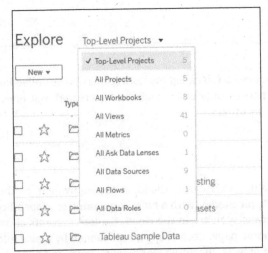

FIGURE 8-23:
Filtering options in Explore.

Recommendations

Tableau Cloud has a "big brother" element to it as well. But don't worry: No trackers are looking at your activities online other than in Tableau Cloud. Instead, Tableau Cloud offers recommendations that it thinks may be useful to you. Its "recommendation engine" notices what content you view the most and looks for trends of popular content on your site. It also picks out the popular content of others who share content with you. Recommendations then appear on your site that best match what you've looked at most and what has been trending for a given period, generally one week.

TIP

You may not like the recommendation. That's okay; Tableau won't take offense if you want to hide its recommendations. To do so, select the Actions menu ellipsis and then choose Hide on the menu that appears.

TECHNICAL STUFF

In the Recommendation for You section of the Recommendations page, you'll likely find the names of others, not just yours, who have looked at the content. Don't worry; no one has inappropriately accessed your Tableau instance. These users have access to view the same content as you do.

4

Extracting Information with SQL

Contents at a Glance

IN THIS CHAPTER

» **Relating SQL to the relational model**

» **Figuring out functional dependencies**

» **Discovering keys, views, users, privileges, schemas, and catalogs**

» **Checking out connections, sessions, and transactions**

» **Understanding routines and paths**

Chapter **1**

SQL Foundations

Thisthis chapter offers a brief introduction to the (somewhat complicated) relationship between SQL and the relational database model. The chapter highlights how certain important terms and concepts may have slightly different meanings in the (practical) SQL world as opposed to the (theoretical) relational database world. The chapter also provides some general, all-inclusive definitions for good measure.

SQL and the Relational Model

SQL is a software tool designed to deal with relational database data. It does far more than just execute queries. Yes, of course, you can use it to retrieve the data you want from a database using a query. However, you can also use SQL to create and destroy databases, as well as modify their structure. In addition, you can add, modify, and delete data with SQL. Even with all that capability, SQL is still considered only a *data sublanguage*, which means that it does not have all the features of general-purpose programming languages such as C, C++, C#, or Java.

SQL is specifically designed for dealing with relational databases and thus does not include a number of features needed for creating useful application programs. As a result, to create a complete application — one that handles queries as well as provides access to a database — you must write the code in one of the general-purpose languages and embed SQL statements within the program whenever it communicates with the database.

The *relational database*, a type of data model, stores and provides access to data points that are related to one another, existed as a theoretical model for almost a decade before the first relational database product appeared on the market. Now, it turns out that the first commercial implementation of the relational model — a software program from the company that later became Oracle — did not even use SQL, which IBM had not yet released. In those early days, there were a number of competing data sublanguages. Gradually, SQL became a de facto standard, thanks in no small part to IBM's dominant position in the market, and the fact that Oracle started offering it as an alternative to its own language early on.

Although SQL was developed to work with a relational database management system, it's not entirely consistent with the relational model. However, it is close enough, and in many cases, it even offers capabilities not present in the relational model. Some of the most important aspects of SQL are direct analogs of some aspects of the relational model. Others are not.

Sets, Relations, Multisets, and Tables

The relational model is based on the mathematical discipline known as *set theory*. In set theory, a *set* is defined as a collection of unique objects — duplicates are not allowed. This carries over to the relational model. A *relation* is defined as a collection of unique objects called *tuples* — no duplicates are allowed among tuples.

In SQL, the equivalent of a relation is a table. However, tables are not exactly like relations in that a table can have duplicate rows. For that reason, tables in a relational database are not modeled on the sets of set theory but rather on *multisets*, which are similar to sets, except they allow duplicate objects.

Although a relation is not exactly the same thing as a table, the terms are often used interchangeably. Because relations were defined by theoreticians, they have a very precise definition. The word *table*, on the other hand, is in general use and is often much more loosely defined. This book uses the word *table*, in a more restricted sense, as being an alternate term for *relation*. The attributes and tuples of a relation are strictly equivalent to the columns and rows of a table.

So, what's an SQL relation? Formally, a relation is a two-dimensional table that has the following characteristics:

>> Every cell in the table must contain a single value if it contains any value at all. Repeating groups and arrays are not allowed as values. (In this context, *groups* and *arrays* are examples of collections of values.)

>> All the entries in any column must be the same. For example, if a column contains an employee name in one row, it must contain employee names in all rows that contain values.

>> Each column has a unique name.

>> The order of the columns doesn't matter.

>> The order of the rows doesn't matter.

>> No two rows may be identical.

If and only if a table meets all these criteria, it is a relation. You might have tables that fail to meet one or more of these criteria. For example, a table might have two identical rows. It is still a table in the loose sense, but it is not a relation.

Functional Dependencies

Functional dependencies are relationships between or among attributes. Consider the example of two attributes of the CUSTOMER relation, Zipcode and State. If you know the customer's zip code, the state can be obtained by a simple lookup because each zip code resides in one and only one state. This means that State is *functionally dependent* on Zipcode or that Zipcode *determines* state. Zipcode is called a *determinant* because it determines the value of another attribute. The reverse is not true. State does not determine Zipcode because states can contain multiple Zipcodes. You denote functional dependencies as follows:

```
Zipcode ⇨ State
```

A group of attributes may act as a determinant. If one attribute depends on the values of multiple other attributes, that group of attributes, collectively, is a determinant of the first attribute.

Consider the relation INVOICE, made up as it is of the following attributes:

>> **InvNo:** Invoice number.

>> **CustID:** Customer ID.

>> **WorR:** Wholesale or retail. I'm assuming that products have both a wholesale and a retail price, which is why I've added the WorR attribute to tell me whether this is a wholesale or a retail transaction.

» **ProdID:** Product ID.

» **Quantity:** Quantity.

» **Price:** You guessed it.

» **Extprice:** Extended price (which I get by multiplying Quantity and Price.)

With our definitions out of the way, check out what depends on what by following the handy determinant arrow:

```
(WorR, ProdID) ⇨ Price
(Quantity, Price) ⇨ Extprice,
```

W/R tells you whether you are charging the wholesale or the retail price. ProdID shows which product you are considering. Thus, the combination of WorR and ProdID determines Price. Similarly, the combination of Quantity and Price determines Extprice. Neither WorR nor ProdID by itself determines Price; they are both needed to determine Price. Both Quantity and Price are needed to determine Extprice.

Keys

A *key* is an attribute (or group of attributes) that uniquely identifies a tuple (a unique collection of attributes) in a relation. One of the characteristics of a relation is that no two rows (tuples) are identical. You can guarantee that no two rows are identical if at least one field (attribute) is guaranteed to have a unique value in every row, or if some combination of fields is guaranteed to be unique for each row.

Table 1-1 shows an example of the PROJECT relation. It lists researchers affiliated with the Gentoo Institute's Penguin Physiology Lab, the project that each participant is working on, and the location at which each participant is conducting his or her research.

In this table, each researcher is assigned to only one project. Is this a rule? Must a researcher be assigned to only one project, can a researcher be assigned to more than one? If a researcher can be assigned to only one project, ResearcherID is a key. It guarantees that every row in the PROJECT table is unique. What if there is no such rule? What if a researcher may work on multiple projects at the same time? Table 1-2 shows this situation.

TABLE 1-1   **PROJECT Relation**

ResearcherID	Project	Location
Pizarro	Why penguin feet don't freeze	Bahia Paraiso
Whitehead	Why penguins don't get the bends	Port Lockroy
Shelton	How penguin eggs stay warm in pebble nests	Peterman Island
Nansen	How penguin diet varies by season	Peterman Island

TABLE 1-2   **PROJECTS Relation**

ResearcherID	Project	Location
Pizarro	Why penguin feet don't freeze	Bahia Paraiso
Pizarro	How penguin eggs stay warm in pebble nests	Peterman Island
Whitehead	Why penguins don't get the bends	Port Lockroy
Shelton	How penguin eggs stay warm in pebble nests	Peterman Island
Shelton	How penguin diet varies by season	Peterman Island
Nansen	How penguin diet varies by season	Peterman Island

In this scenario, Dr. Pizarro works on the cold feet and the warm eggs projects, whereas Professor Shelton works on the warm eggs and the varied diet projects. Clearly, ResearcherID cannot be used as a key. However, the combination of ResearcherID and Project is unique and is thus a key.

You're probably wondering how you can reliably tell what is a key and what isn't. Looking at the relation in Table 1-1, it looks like ResearcherID is a key because every entry in that column is unique. However, this could be due to the fact that you are looking at a limited sample, and any minute now, someone could add a new row that duplicates the value of ResearcherID in one of the existing rows. How can you be sure that won't happen? Easy. Ask the users.

The relations you build are models of the mental images that the users have of the system they are dealing with. You want your relational model to correspond as closely as possible to the model the users have in their minds. If they tell you, for example, that in their organization, researchers never work on more than one project at a time, you can use ResearcherID as a key. On the other hand, if it is even remotely possible that a researcher might be assigned to two projects simultaneously, you have to revert to a composite key made up of both ResearcherID and Project.

REMEMBER

A question that might arise in your mind is, "Is it possible for a relation to exist that has no key?" By the definition of a relation, the answer is no. Every relation *must* have a key. One of the characteristics of a relation is that no two rows may be exactly the same. That means that you are always able to distinguish rows from each other, although you may have to include all the relation's attributes in the key to do it.

Views

Although the most fundamental constituent of a relational database is undoubtedly the table, another important concept is the virtual table or *view*. Unlike an ordinary table, a view has no physical existence until it is called upon in a query. There is no place on the disk where the rows in the view are stored. The view exists only in the metadata as a definition. The definition describes how to pull data from tables and present it to the user in the form of a view.

From the user's perspective, a view looks just like a table. You can do almost everything to a view that you can do to a table. The major exception is that you cannot always update a view the same way that you can update a table. The view may contain columns that are the result of some arithmetic operation on the data in columns from the tables upon which the view is based. You can't update a column that doesn't exist in your permanent storage device. Despite this limitation, views, after they're formulated, can save you considerable work: You don't need to code the same complex query every time you want to pull data from multiple tables. Create the view once, and then use it every time you need it.

Users

Although it may seem a little odd to include them, the users are an important part of any database system. After all, without the users, no data would be written into the system, no data would be manipulated, and no results would be displayed. When you think about it, the users are mighty important. Just as you want your hardware and software to be of the highest quality you can afford in order to produce the best results, and for the same reason, you want the highest-quality people. To ensure that only the people who meet your standards have access to the database system, you should have a robust security system that enables authorized users to do their job, and at the same time, prevents access to everyone else.

Privileges

A good security system not only keeps out unauthorized users but also provides authorized users with access privileges tailored to their needs. The night watchman has different database needs from those of the company CEO. One way of handling privileges is to assign every authorized user an authorization ID. When the person logs on with his authorization ID, the privileges associated with that authorization ID become available to him. This could include the ability to read the contents of certain columns of certain tables, the ability to add new rows to certain tables, delete rows, update rows, and so on.

A second way to assign privileges is with roles, which were introduced in SQL:1999. *Roles* are simply a way for you to assign the same privileges to multiple people, and they are particularly valuable in large organizations where a number of people have essentially the same job and, thus, the same needs for data.

For example, a security guard working the nightshift might have the same data needs as other security guards. You can grant a suite of privileges to the SECURITY_GUARD role. From then on, you can assign the SECURITY_GUARD role to any new guards, and all the privileges appropriate for that role are automatically assigned to them. When a person leaves, or changes jobs, revoking their role can be just as easy.

Schemas

Relational database applications typically use multiple tables. As a database grows to support multiple applications, it becomes more and more likely that an application developer will try to give one of her tables the same name as a table already in the database. This can cause problems and frustration. To get around this problem, SQL has a hierarchical namespace structure. A developer can define her tables as being members of a *schema*.

With this structure, one developer can have a table named CUSTOMER in her schema, whereas a second developer can also have an entirely different table, also named CUSTOMER, but in a different schema.

Catalogs

These days, organizations can be so big that if every developer had a schema for each of her applications, the number of schemas itself could be a problem. Someone might inadvertently give a new schema the same name as an existing schema. An additional level was added at the top of the namespace hierarchy to head off this possibility. A *catalog* can contain multiple schemas, which in turn can contain multiple tables. The smallest organizations don't have to worry about either catalogs or schemas, but those levels of the namespace hierarchy are there if they're needed. If your organization is big enough to worry about duplicate catalog names, it is big enough to figure out a way to deal with the problem.

Connections, Sessions, and Transactions

A database management system is typically divided into two main parts: a *client* side, which interfaces with the user, and a *server* side, which holds the data and operates on it. To operate on a database, a user must establish a *connection* between their client and the server that holds the data they want to access. Generally, the first thing you must do — if you want to work on a database at all — is to establish a connection to it. You can do this with a CONNECT statement that specifies your authorization ID and names the server you want to connect to. The exact implementation of this varies from one DBMS to another. (Most people today would use the DBMS's graphical user interface to connect to a server instead of using the SQL CONNECT statement.)

REMEMBER

A *session* is the context in which a single user executes a sequence of SQL statements, using a single connection. A *user* can either be a person entering SQL statements at the client console, or a program running on the client machine.

A *transaction* is a sequence of SQL statements that is atomic with respect to recovery. This means that if a failure occurs while a transaction is in progress, the effects of the transaction are erased so that the database is left in the state it was in before the transaction started. *Atomic* in this context means indivisible. Either the transaction runs to completion, or it aborts in such a way that any changes it made before the abort are undone.

Routines

Routines are procedures, functions, or methods that can be invoked either by an SQL CALL statement or by the host language program that the SQL code is operating with. *Methods* are a kind of function used in object-oriented programming.

Routines enable SQL code to take advantage of calculations performed by host language code and enable host language code to take advantage of data operations performed by SQL code.

Because either a host language program or SQL code can invoke a routine, and because the routine being invoked can be written either in SQL or in host language code, routines can cause confusion. A few definitions help to clarify the situation:

» **Externally invoked routine:** A procedure, written in SQL and residing in a module located on the client, which is invoked by the host language program

» **SQL-invoked routine:** Either a procedure or a function residing in a module located on the server, which could be written in either SQL or the host language that is invoked by SQL code

» **External routine:** Either a procedure or a function residing in a module located on the server, which is written in the host language, but is invoked by SQL

» **SQL routine:** Either a procedure or a function residing in a module located on either the server or the client, which is written in SQL and invoked by SQL

Paths

A *path* in SQL, similar to a path in operating systems, tells the system in what order to search locations to find a routine that has been invoked. For a system with several schemas (perhaps one for testing, one for QA, and one for production), the path tells the executing program where to look first, where to look next, and so on, to find an invoked routine.

IN THIS CHAPTER

» **Executing SQL statements**

» **Using (and misusing) reserved words**

» **Working with SQL's data types**

» **Handling null values**

» **Applying constraints**

Chapter **2**

Drilling Down to the SQL Nitty-Gritty

This chapter gets into the nitty-gritty of SQL. This is knowledge you need to master before you embark on actually writing SQL statements. SQL has some similarities to computer languages you may already be familiar with and some important differences. The chapter touches on some of these similarities and differences, but others are discussed later in this book (Book 4) at the appropriate points in a complete discussion of SQL.

Executing SQL Statements

SQL is not a complete language, but a data sublanguage. As such, you cannot write a program in the SQL language like you can with C or Java. That doesn't mean SQL is useless, though. There are several ways that you *can* use SQL. Say you have a query editor up on your screen, and all you want is the answer to a simple question. Just type an SQL query, and the answer, in the form of one or more lines of data, appears on your screen. This mode of operation is called *interactive SQL*.

If your needs are more complex, you have two additional ways of making SQL queries:

>> You can write a program in a host language, such as C or Java, and embed single SQL statements here and there in the program as needed. This mode of operation is called *embedded SQL*.

>> You can write a module containing SQL statements in the form of procedures, and then call these procedures from a program written in a language such as C or Java. This mode of operation is called *module language*.

Interactive SQL

Interactive SQL consists of entering SQL statements into a database management system such as SQL Server, Oracle, or DB2. The DBMS then performs the commands specified by the statements. You could build a database from scratch this way, starting with a CREATE DATABASE statement and building everything from there. You could fill it with data, and then type queries to selectively pull information out of it.

Although it's possible to do everything you need to do to a database with interactive SQL, this approach has a couple of disadvantages:

>> It can get awfully tedious to enter everything in the form of SQL statements from the keyboard.

>> Only people fluent in the SQL language can operate on the database, and most people have never even heard of SQL, let alone are able to use it effectively.

SQL *is* the only language that most relational databases understand, so there is no getting around using it. However, the people who interact with databases the most — those folks that ask questions of the data — do not need to be exposed to naked SQL. They can be protected from that intimidating prospect by wrapping the SQL in a blanket of code written in another language. With that other language, a programmer can generate screens, forms, menus, and other familiar objects for the user to interact with. Ultimately, those things translate the user's actions to SQL code that the DBMS understands. The desired information is retrieved, and the user sees the result.

Challenges to combining SQL with a host language

SQL has these fundamental differences from host languages that you might want to combine it with:

>> **SQL is nonprocedural.** One basic feature of all common host languages is that they are *procedural*, meaning that programs written in those languages execute procedures in a step-by-step fashion. They deal with data the same way, one row at a time. Because SQL is nonprocedural, it does whatever it is going to do all at once and deals with data a set of rows at a time. Procedural programmers coming to SQL for the first time need to adjust their thinking in order to use SQL effectively as a data manipulation and retrieval tool.

>> **SQL recognizes different data types than whatever host language you are using with it.** Because there are a large number of languages out there that could serve as host languages for SQL, and the data types of any one of them do not necessarily agree with the data types of any other, the committee that created the ANSI/ISO standard defined the data types for SQL that they thought would be most useful, without referring to the data types recognized by any of the potential host languages. This data type incompatibility presents a problem if you want to perform calculations with your host language on data that was retrieved from a database with SQL. The problem is not serious; you just need to be aware of it. (It helps that SQL provides the CAST statement for translating one data type into another.)

Embedded SQL

Until recently, the most common form of SQL has been embedded SQL. This method uses a general-purpose computer language such as C, C++, or COBOL to write the bulk of an application. Such languages are great for creating an application's user interface. They can create forms with buttons and menus, format reports, perform calculations, and basically do all the things that SQL cannot do. In a database application, however, sooner or later, the database must be accessed. That's a job for SQL.

It makes sense to write the application in a host language and, when needed, drop in SQL statements to interact with the data. It is the best of both worlds. The host language does what it's best at, and the embedded SQL does what *it's* best at. The only downside to the cooperative arrangement is that the host language compiler will not recognize the SQL code when it encounters it and will issue an error message. To avoid this problem, a precompiler processes the SQL before the host language compiler takes over. When everything works, this is a great arrangement. Before everything works, however, debugging can be tough because a host language debugger doesn't know how to handle any SQL that it encounters. Nevertheless, embedded SQL remains the most popular way to create database applications.

For example, look at a fragment of C code that contains embedded SQL statements. This particular fragment is written in Oracle's Pro*C dialect of the C language and is code that might be found in an organization's human resources department. This particular code block is designed to authenticate and log on a user, and then enable the user to change the salary and commission information for an employee.

```
EXEC SQL BEGIN DECLARE SECTION;
    VARCHAR uid[20];
    VARCHAR pwd[20];
    VARCHAR ename[10];
    FLOAT salary, comm;
    SHORT salary_ind, comm_ind;
EXEC SQL END DECLARE SECTION;
main()
{
    int sret;           /* scanf return code */
    /* Log in */
    strcpy(uid.arr,"Mary");     /* copy the user name */
    uid.len=strlen(uid.arr);
    strcpy(pwd.arr,"Bennett");   /* copy the password */
    pwd.len=strlen(pwd.arr);
    EXEC SQL WHENEVER SQLERROR STOP;
    EXEC SQL WHENEVER NOT FOUND STOP;
    EXEC SQL CONNECT :uid;
    printf("Connected to user: percents \n",uid.arr);
    printf("Enter employee name to update:  ");
    scanf("percents",ename.arr);
    ename.len=strlen(ename.arr);
    EXEC SQL SELECT SALARY,COMM INTO :salary,:comm
                FROM EMPLOY
                WHERE ENAME=:ename;
    printf("Employee: percents salary: percent6.2f
            comm: percent6.2f \n", ename.arr, salary, comm);
    printf("Enter new salary:  ");
    sret=scanf("percentf",&salary);
    salary_ind = 0;
    if (sret == EOF !! sret == 0)   /* set indicator */
        salary_ind =-1;   /* Set indicator for NULL */
```

```
        printf("Enter new commission:  ");
        sret=scanf("percentf",&comm);
        comm_ind = 0;    /* set indicator */
        if (sret == EOF !! sret == 0)
            comm_ind=-1;        /* Set indicator for NULL */
    EXEC SQL UPDATE EMPLOY
                SET SALARY=:salary:salary_ind
                SET COMM=:comm:comm_ind
                WHERE ENAME=:ename;
    printf("Employee percents updated. \n",ename.arr);
    EXEC SQL COMMIT WORK;
    exit(0);
}
```

Here's a closer look at what the code does:

>> First comes an SQL declaration section, where variables are declared.

>> Next, C code accepts a username and password.

>> A couple of SQL error traps follow, and then a connection to the database is established. (If an SQL error code or Not Found code is returned from the database, the run is aborted before it begins.)

>> C code prints out some messages and accepts the name of the employee whose record will be changed.

>> SQL retrieves that employee's salary and commission data.

>> C displays the salary and commission data and solicits new salary and commission data.

>> SQL updates the database with the new data.

>> C displays a successful completion message.

>> SQL commits the transaction.

>> C terminates the program.

In this implementation, every SQL statement is introduced with an EXEC SQL directive. This is a clue to the compiler not to try to compile what follows but instead to pass it directly to the DBMS's database engine.

REMEMBER

Some implementations have deprecated embedded SQL or discontinued it entirely. For example, embedded SQL was deprecated in SQL Server 2008, meaning it was still present but may not be in a subsequent version. Software vendors recommend that deprecated features not be included in new development efforts.

Embedded SQL is now absent from MySQL and SAP SQL Anywhere, although an independently developed preprocessor is available for MySQL.

Module language

Module language is similar to embedded SQL in that it combines the strengths of SQL with those of a host language. However, it does it in a slightly different way. All the SQL code is stored — as procedures — in a module separate from the host language program. Whenever the host language program needs to perform a database operation, it calls a procedure from the SQL module to do the job. With this arrangement, all your SQL is kept out of the main program, so the host language compiler has no problem, and neither does the debugger. All they see is host language code, including the procedure calls. The procedures themselves cause no difficulty because they are in a separate module, and the compiler and debugger just skip over them.

Another advantage of module language over embedded SQL is that the SQL code is separated from the host language code. Because high skill in *both* SQL and any given host language is rare, it is difficult to find good people to program embedded SQL applications. Because a module language implementation separates the languages, you can hire the best SQL programmer to write the SQL and the best host language programmer to write the host language code. Neither one has to be an expert in the other language.

To see how this would work, check out the following module definition, which shows you the syntax you'd use to create a module that contains SQL procedures:

```
MODULE [module-name]
    [NAMES ARE character-set-name]
    LANGUAGE {ADA|C|COBOL|FORTRAN|MUMPS|PASCAL|PLI|SQL}
    [SCHEMA schema-name]
    [AUTHORIZATION authorization-id]
    [temporary-table-declarations...]
    [cursor-declarations...]
    [dynamic-cursor-declarations...]
    procedures...
```

The MODULE declaration is mandatory, but the module name is not. (It's a good idea to name your modules anyway, just to reduce the confusion.) With the optional NAMES ARE clause, you can specify a character set — Hebrew, for example, or Cyrillic. The default character set will be used if you don't include a NAMES ARE clause.

The next line lets you specify a host language — something you definitely have to do. Each language has different expectations about what the procedure will look like, so the LANGUAGE clause determines the format of the procedures in the module.

Although the SCHEMA clause and the AUTHORIZATION clause are both optional, you must specify at least one of them. The AUTHORIZATION clause is a security feature. If your authorization ID does not carry sufficient privileges, you won't be allowed to use the procedures in the module.

REMEMBER

If any of the procedures use temporary tables, cursors, or dynamic cursors, they must be declared before they are used.

Using Reserved Words Correctly

Given the fact that SQL makes constant use of command words such as CREATE and ALTER, it stands to reason that it would probably be unwise to use these same words as the names of tables or variables. To do so is a guaranteed way to confuse your DBMS. In addition to such command words, a number of other words also have a special meaning in SQL. These *reserved words* should also not be used for any purpose other than the one for which they are designed. Consider the following SQL statement:

```
SELECT CustomerID, FirstName, LastName
    FROM Customer
    WHERE CustomerID < 1000;
```

SELECT is a command word, and FROM and WHERE are reserved words. SQL has hundreds of reserved words, and you must be careful not to inadvertently use any of them as the names of objects or variables. Allen G. Taylor's *SQL All-in-One For Dummies*, 3rd Edition (Wiley) provides a list of reserved words in ISO/IEC SQL:2016.

SQL's Data Types

SQL is capable of dealing with many different data types — as this aptly named section will soon make clear. From the beginning, SQL has been able to handle the common types of numeric and character data, but more recently, new types have been added that enable SQL to deal with nontraditional data types, such as

BLOB, CLOB, and BINARY. At present, there are eleven major categories of data types: exact numerics, approximate numerics, character strings, binary strings, Booleans, datetimes, intervals, XML type, collection types, REF types, and user-defined types. Within each category, one or more specific types may exist.

REMEMBER

Your SQL implementation may not support all the data types described in this section. Furthermore, your implementation may support nonstandard data types that I don't describe here.

With that proviso out of the way, read on to find brief descriptions of each of the categories as well as enumerations of the standard types they include.

Exact numerics

Because computers store numbers in registers of finite size, there is a limit to how large or small a number can be and still be represented exactly. There is a range of numbers centered on zero that can be represented exactly. The size of that range depends on the size of the registers that the numbers are stored in. Thus, a machine with 64-bit registers can exactly represent a range of numbers wider than the range that can be exactly represented on a machine with 32-bit registers.

After doing all the complex math, you're left with six standard exact numeric data types. They are

- » INTEGER
- » SMALLINT
- » BIGINT
- » NUMERIC
- » DECIMAL
- » DECFLOAT

The next few sections drill down deeper into each type.

INTEGER

Data of the INTEGER type is numeric data that has no fractional part. Any given implementation of SQL will have a limit to the number of digits that an integer can have. If, for some reason, you want to specify a maximum size for an integer that is less than the default maximum, you can restrict the maximum number of digits by specifying a *precision* argument. By declaring a variable as having type INTEGER (10), you are saying numbers of this type can have no more than ten digits, even if the system you are running on is capable of handling more digits. Of course, if you specify a precision that exceeds the maximum capacity of the system, you're not gonna get it no matter how much you whine. You cannot magically expand the sizes of the hardware registers in a machine with an SQL declaration.

TIP

If there is a possibility that sometime in the near or distant future, your application may be ported to a system that has a different default precision for exact numeric numbers, you should specify a precision. That way, the precision you have planned on will carry over to the new system. If you rely on the default precision, and the default precision of the system you port to is different, your operations may produce different results from those produced by your original system. On the other hand, you may be fine. For example, both Microsoft SQL Server and MySQL reserve the same amount of space for a number of the INTEGER type; thus, the precision is the same for both.

SMALLINT

The SMALLINT data type is similar to the INTEGER type, but how it differs from the INTEGER type is implementation-dependent. It may not differ from the INTEGER type at all. The only constraint on the SMALLINT type is that its precision may be no larger than the precision of the INTEGER type.

For systems where the precision of the SMALLINT type actually is less than the precision of the INTEGER type, it may be advantageous to specify variables as being of the SMALLINT type if you can be sure that the values of those variables will never exceed the precision of the SMALLINT type. This saves you some storage space. If storage space is not an issue, or if you cannot be absolutely sure that the value of a variable will never exceed the precision of the SMALLINT type, you may be better off specifying it as being of the INTEGER type.

BIGINT

The BIGINT type is similar to the SMALLINT type. The only difference is that the precision of the BIGINT type can be no *smaller* than the precision of the INTEGER type. As is the case with SMALLINT, the precision of the BIGINT type could be the same as the precision of the INTEGER type.

If the precision of the BIGINT type for any given implementation is actually larger than the precision of the INTEGER type, a variable of the BIGINT type will take up more storage space than a variable of the INTEGER type. Only use the BIGINT type if there is a possibility that the size of a variable may exceed the precision of the INTEGER type.

NUMERIC

Data of the NUMERIC type *does* have a fractional part. This means the number contains a decimal point and zero or more digits to the right of the decimal point. For NUMERIC data, you can specify both precision and scale. The *scale* of a number is the number of digits to the right of the decimal point. For example, a variable declared as type NUMERIC (10, 2) would have a maximum of ten digits, with two of those digits to the right of the decimal point. The largest number you can represent with this type is 99,999,999.99. If the system you are running on happens to be able to handle numbers with precision greater than ten, only the precision you specify will be used.

DECIMAL

Data of the DECIMAL type is similar to data of the NUMERIC type with one difference. For data of the DECIMAL type, if the system you are running on happens to be able to handle numbers with larger precision than what you have specified, the extra precision will be used.

TIP

The NUMERIC data type is better if portability is a possibility. When you use the NUMERIC type, you can be sure the precision you specify will be the precision that is used, regardless of the system's capabilities. This ensures consistent results across diverse platforms.

DECFLOAT

DECFLOAT is a new exact numeric data type in SQL:2016. It was added to ISO/IEC standard SQL specifically for business applications that deal with exact decimal values. Floating point data types, such as REAL and DOUBLE, can handle larger numbers than exact numerics such as NUMERIC and DECIMAL. However, they cannot be counted on to produce exact decimal values. DECFLOAT can handle larger numbers than other exact numeric data types and retain the exactness of an exact numeric type.

Approximate numerics

The approximate numeric types (all three of them) exist so that you can represent numbers either too large or too small to be represented by an exact numeric type. If, for example, a system has 32-bit registers, then the largest number that can be represented with an *exact* numeric type is the largest number that can be represented with 32 binary digits — which happens to be 4,294,967,295 in decimal.

If you have to deal with numbers larger than that, you must move to *approximate* numerics or buy a computer with 64-bit registers. Using approximate numerics may not be much of a hardship: For most applications, after you get above four billion, approximations are good enough.

Similarly, values very close to zero cannot be represented with exact numerics either. The smallest number that can be represented exactly on a 32-bit machine has a one in the least significant bit position and zeros everywhere else. This is a very small number, but there are a lot of numbers of interest, particularly in science, that are smaller. For such numbers, you must also rely on approximate numerics.

With that intro out of the way, it's time to meet the three approximate numeric types: REAL, DOUBLE PRECISION, and FLOAT.

REAL

The REAL data type is what you would normally use for single-precision floating-point numbers. The exact meaning of the term *single precision* depends on the implementation. This is hardware-dependent, and a machine with 64-bit registers will generally have a larger precision than a machine with 32-bit registers. How much larger may vary from one implementation to another.

REMEMBER

A *floating-point number* is a number that contains a radix point. In the case of decimal numbers, that means a decimal point. The decimal point could appear anywhere in the number, which is why it is called floating. 2.7, 2.73, 27.3, and 2735.53894 are all examples of floating-point numbers. Although we humans are accustomed to seeing numbers expressed in this form, approximate numerics are expressed as a combination of a mantissa and an exponent. This form is a little less user friendly but enables the approximate representation of very large and very small numbers in a compact form. 6.626×10^{-34}, for example, is a very small number, being as it is an approximation of Planck's constant, also a very small number. 6.626 is the mantissa, and -34 is the exponent. It would not be possible to represent a number that small exactly with any currently existing hardware.

DOUBLE PRECISION

A double-precision number, which is the basis for the double precision (DOUBLE) data type, on any given system has greater precision than a real number on the same system. However, despite the name, a double-precision number does not necessarily have twice the precision of a real number. The most that can be said in general is that a double-precision number on any given system has greater precision than does a real number on the same system. On some systems, a double-precision number may have a larger mantissa than a real number. On other systems, a double-precision number may support a larger exponent (absolute value). On yet other systems, both mantissa and exponent of a double-precision number may be larger than for a real number. You will have to look at the specifications for whatever system you are using to find out what is true for you.

FLOAT

The FLOAT data type is very similar to the REAL data type. The difference is that with the FLOAT data type, you can specify a precision. With the REAL and DOUBLE PRECISION data types, the default precision is your only option. Because the default precision of these data types can vary from one system to another, porting your application from one system to another could be a problem. With the FLOAT data type, specifying the precision of an attribute on one machine guarantees that the precision will be maintained after porting the application to another machine. If a system's hardware supports double-precision operations and the application requires double-precision operations, the FLOAT data type automatically uses the double-precision circuitry. If single-precision is sufficient, it uses that.

Character strings

After numbers, the next most common thing to be stored is strings of alphanumeric characters. SQL provides several character string types, each with somewhat different characteristics. The three main types are CHARACTER, CHARACTER VARYING, and CHARACTER LARGE OBJECT. These three types are mirrored by NATIONAL CHARACTER, NATIONAL CHARACTER VARYING, and NATIONAL CHARACTER LARGE OBJECT deals with character sets other than the default character set, which is usually the character set of the English language.

CHARACTER

A column defined as being of type CHARACTER or CHAR can contain any of the normal alphanumeric characters of the language being used. A column definition also includes the maximum length allowed for an item of the CHAR type. Consider this example:

```
Name CHAR (15)
```

This field can hold a name up to 15 characters long. If the name is less than 15 characters long, the remaining spaces are filled with blank characters to bring the total length up to 15. Thus, a CHARACTER field always takes up the same amount of space in memory, regardless of how long the actual data item in the field is.

CHARACTER VARYING

The CHARACTER VARYING or VARCHAR data type is like the CHARACTER type in all respects, except that short entries are not padded out with blanks to fill the field to the stated maximum.

```
Name VARCHAR (15)
```

The VARCHAR data type doesn't add blanks on the end of a name. Thus, if the Name field contains Joe, the length of the field that is stored will be only three characters rather than fifteen.

CHARACTER LARGE OBJECT (CLOB)

Any implementation of SQL has a limit to the number of characters that are allowed in a CHARACTER or CHARACTER VARYING field. For example, the maximum length of a character string in Oracle 11g is 1,024 characters. If you want to store text that goes beyond that limit, you can use the CHARACTER LARGE OBJECT data type. The CLOB type, as it is affectionately known, is much less flexible than either the CHAR or VARCHAR types in that it does not allow you to do many of the fine-grained manipulations that you can do in those other types. You can compare two CLOB items for equality, but that's about all you can do. With CHARACTER type data you can, for example, scan a string for the first occurrence of the letter W, and display where in the string it occurs. This type of operation is not possible with CHARACTER LARGE OBJECT data.

Here's an example of the declaration of a CHARACTER LARGE OBJECT:

```
Dream CLOB (8721)
```

Another restriction on CLOB data is that a CLOB data item may not be used as a primary key or a foreign key. Furthermore, you cannot apply the UNIQUE constraint to an item of the CLOB type. The bottom line is that the CLOB data type enables you to store and retrieve large blocks of text, but it turns out you can't do much with them beyond that.

NATIONAL CHARACTER, NATIONAL CHARACTER VARYING, and NATIONAL CHARACTER LARGE OBJECT

Different languages use different character sets. For example, Spanish and German have letters with diacritical marks that change the way the letter is pronounced. Other languages, such as Russian, have an entirely different character set. To store character strings that contain these different character sets, the various national character types have been added to SQL. If the English character type is the default on your system, as it is for most people, you can designate a different character set as your national character set. From that point on, when you specify a data type as NATIONAL CHARACTER, NATIONAL CHARACTER VARYING, or NATIONAL CHARACTER LARGE OBJECT, items in columns so specified use the chosen national character set rather than the default character set.

In addition to whatever national character set you specify, you can use multiple other character sets in a table definition by specifying them explicitly. Here's an example where the national character set is Russian, but you explicitly add Greek and Kanji (Japanese) to the mix:

```
CREATE TABLE BOOK_TITLE_TRANSLATIONS (
    English      CHARACTER (40),
    Greek        VARCHAR (40)          CHARACTER SET GREEK,
    Russian      NATIONAL CHARACTER (40),
    Japanese     CHARACTER (40)        CHARACTER SET KANJI
) ;
```

WARNING

Some implementations may not support all the character sets. For example, MySQL does not currently support Kanji.

Binary strings

The various binary string data types were added to SQL:2008. Binary strings are like character strings, except the only characters allowed are 1 and 0. There are three different types of binary strings: BINARY, BINARY VARYING, and BINARY LARGE OBJECT.

BINARY

A string of binary characters of the BINARY type must be some multiple of eight bits long. You can specify such a string with BINARY (x), where x is the number of bytes of binary data contained in the string. For example, if you specify a binary string with BINARY (2), then the string will be two bytes, or 16 bits long. Byte one is defined as the first byte of the string.

BINARY VARYING

The BINARY VARYING or VARBINARY type is like the BINARY type except the string length need not be x bytes long. A string specified as VARBINARY (x) can be a minimum of zero bytes long and a maximum of x bytes long.

BINARY LARGE OBJECT (BLOB)

The BINARY LARGE OBJECT (BLOB) type is used for a really large binary number. That large binary number may represent the pixels in a graphical image, or something else that doesn't seem to be a number. However, at the most fundamental level, it is a number.

The BLOB type, like the CLOB type, was added to the SQL standard to reflect the reality that more and more of the things people want to store in databases do not fall into the classical categories of being either numbers or text. You cannot perform arithmetic operations on BLOB data, but at least you can store it in a relational database and perform some elementary operations.

Booleans

A column of the BOOLEAN data type, named after 19th-century English mathematician George Boole, will accept any of three values: TRUE, FALSE, and UNKNOWN. The fact that SQL entertains the possibility of NULL values expands the traditional restriction of Boolean values from just TRUE and FALSE to TRUE, FALSE, and UNKNOWN. If a Boolean TRUE or FALSE value is compared to a NULL value, the result is UNKNOWN. Of course, comparing a Boolean UNKNOWN value to any value also gives an UNKNOWN result.

Datetimes

You often need to store either dates, times, or both, in addition to numeric and character data. ISO/IEC standard SQL defines five datetime types. Because considerable overlap exists among the five types, not all implementations of SQL include all five types. This could cause problems if you try to migrate a database from a platform that uses one subset of the five types to a platform using a different subset. There is not much you can do about this except deal with it when the issue arises.

DATE

The DATE data type is the one to use if you care about the date of something but could not care less about the time of day within a date. The DATE data type stores a year, month, and day in that order, using ten character positions in the form yyyy-mm-dd. If you were recording the dates that humans first landed on the Moon, the entry for Apollo 11 would be 1969-07-20.

TIME WITHOUT TIME ZONE

Suppose you want to store the time of day but don't care which day, and furthermore, don't even care which time zone the time refers to. In that case, the TIME WITHOUT TIME ZONE data type is just the ticket. It stores hours, minutes, and seconds. The hours and minutes data occupy two digits apiece. The seconds data also occupies two digits but may include a fractional part for fractions of a second. If you specify a column as being of TIME WITHOUT TIME ZONE type, with no parameter, it will hold a time with no fractional seconds. An example is 02:56:31, which is fifty-six minutes and thirty-one seconds after two in the morning.

For greater precision in storing a time value, you can use a parameter to specify the number of digits beyond the decimal point that will be stored for seconds. Here's an example of such a definition:

```
Smallstep TIME WITHOUT TIME ZONE (2),
```

In this example, there are two digits past the decimal point, so time is measured down to a hundredth of a second. It would take the form of 02:56:31.17.

TIME WITH TIME ZONE

The TIME WITH TIME ZONE data type gives you all the information that you get in the TIME WITHOUT TIME ZONE data type and adds the additional fact of the time zone the time refers to. All time zones around the Earth are referenced to Coordinated Universal Time (UTC), formerly known as Greenwich Mean Time (GMT). Coordinated Universal Time is the time in Greenwich, U.K., which was the place where people first started being concerned with highly accurate timekeeping. Of course, the United Kingdom is a fairly small country, so UTC is in effect throughout the entire U.K. In fact, a huge "watermelon slice" of the Earth, running from the North Pole to the South Pole, is also in the same time zone as Greenwich. There are 24 such slices that girdle the Earth. Times around the Earth range from eleven hours and fifty-nine minutes behind UTC to twelve hours ahead of UTC (not counting Daylight Saving Time). If Daylight Saving Time is in effect, the offset from UTC could be as much as −12:59 or +13:00. The International Date Line is theoretically exactly opposite Greenwich on the other side of the world but is offset in spots so as to keep some countries in one time zone.

TIMESTAMP WITHOUT TIME ZONE

Just as sometimes you will need to record dates and other times you will need to record times, it's certain that there will also be times when you need to store both times and dates. That is what the TIMESTAMP WITHOUT TIME ZONE data type is for. It is a combination of the DATE type and the TIME WITHOUT TIMEZONE type.

The one difference between this data type and the `TIME WITHOUT TIMEZONE` type is that the default value for fractions of a second is six digits rather than zero. You can, of course, specify zero fractional digits, if that is what you want. Suppose you specified a database table column as follows:

```
Smallstep TIMESTAMP WITHOUT TIME ZONE (0),
```

A valid value for Smallstep would be 1969-07-21 02:56:31. That was the date and time in Greenwich when Neil Armstrong's foot first touched the lunar soil. It consists of ten date characters, a blank space separator, and eight time characters.

TIMESTAMP WITH TIME ZONE

If you have to record the time zone that a date and time refers to, use the `TIMESTAMP WITH TIME ZONE` data type. It's the same as the `TIMSESTAMP WITHOUT TIME ZONE` data type, with the addition of an offset that shows the time's relationship to Coordinated Universal Time. Here's an example:

```
Smallstep TIMESTAMP WITH TIME ZONE (0),
```

In this case, Smallstep might be recorded as 1969-07-20 21:56:31-05:00. That is the date and time in Houston when Neil Armstrong's foot first touched the lunar soil. Houston time is normally six hours ahead of Greenwich time, but in July, it is only five hours ahead due to Daylight Saving Time.

Intervals

An *interval* is the difference between two dates, two times, or two datetimes. There are two different kinds of intervals, the year-month interval and the day-hour-minute-second interval. A day always has 24 hours. An hour always has 60 minutes. A minute always has 60 seconds. However, a month may have 28, 29, 30, or 31 days. Because of that variability, you cannot mix the two kinds of intervals. A field of the `INTERVAL` type can store the difference in time between two instants in the same month but cannot store an interval such as 2 years, 7 months, 13 days, 5 hours, 6 minutes, and 45 seconds.

XML type

The SQL/XML:2003 update to the ISO/IEC SQL standard introduced the XML data type. Values in the XML type are XML values, meaning you can now manage and query XML data in an SQL database.

With SQL/XML:2006, folks moved to the XQuery Data Model, which means that any XML value is also an XQuery sequence. The details of the XQuery Data Model are beyond the scope of this book. Refer to *Querying XML*, by Jim Melton and Stephen Buxton (published by Morgan Kaufmann) for detailed coverage of this topic.

With the introduction of SQL/XML:2006, three specific subtypes of the XML type were defined. They are XML(SEQUENCE), XML(CONTENT), and XML(DOCUMENT). The three subtypes are related to each other hierarchically. An XML(SEQUENCE) is any sequence of XML nodes, XML values, or both. An XML(CONTENT) is an XML(SEQUENCE) that is an XML fragment wrapped in a document node. An XML(DOCUMENT) is an XML(CONTENT) that is a well-formed XML document.

Every XML value is at least an XML(SEQUENCE). An XML(SEQUENCE) that is a document node is an XML(CONTENT). An XML(CONTENT) that has legal document children is an XML(DOCUMENT).

XML types may be associated with an XML schema. There are three possibilities:

>> UNTYPED: There is no associated XML schema.

>> XMLSCHEMA: There is an associated XML schema.

>> ANY: There may or may not be an associated XML schema.

So, a document of type XML(DOCUMENT(ANY)) may or may not have an associated XML schema. If you specify a column as being of type XML with no modifiers, it must be either XML(SEQUENCE), XML(CONTENT(ANY)), or XML(CONTENT(UNTYPED)). Which of those it is depends on the implementation.

ROW type

The ROW type, introduced in the 1999 version of the ISO/IEC SQL standard (SQL:1999), represents the first break of SQL away from the relational model, as defined by its creator, Dr. E.F. Codd. With the introduction of this type, SQL databases can no longer be considered pure relational databases. One of the defining characteristics of Codd's First Normal Form (1NF) is the fact that no field in a table row may be multivalued. Multivalued fields are exactly what the ROW type introduces. The ROW type enables you to place a whole row's worth of data into a single field, effectively nesting a row within a row. To see how this works, create a ROW type.

Note: The normal forms constrain the structure of database tables as a defense against anomalies, which are inconsistencies in table data or even outright wrong values. 1NF is the least restrictive of the normal forms and, thus, the easiest to satisfy. Notwithstanding that, a table that includes a ROW type fails the test of First Normal Form. According to Dr. Codd, such a table is not a relation and, thus, cannot be present in a relational database.

```
CREATE ROW TYPE address_type (
    Street      VARCHAR (25),
    City        VARCHAR (20),
    State       CHAR (2),
    PostalCode  VARCHAR (9)
    ) ;
```

This code effectively compresses four attributes into a single type. After you have created a ROW type — such as address_type in the preceding example — you can then use it in a table definition.

```
CREATE TABLE VENDOR (
    VendorID    INTEGER PRIMARY KEY,
    VendorName  VARCHAR (25),
    Address     address_type,
    Phone       VARCHAR (15)
) ;
```

If you have tables for multiple groups, such as vendors, employees, customers, stockholders, or prospects, you have to declare only one attribute rather than four. That may not seem like much of a savings, but you're not limited to putting just four attributes into a ROW type. What if you had to type the same 40 attributes into 100 tables?

REMEMBER

Like many other relatively recent aspects of SQL, the ROW type has not yet been included in many of the most popular SQL implementations. Even Oracle, which is one of the closest implementations to the SQL:2016 standard, does not currently support the ROW type. Instead, it supports object types that perform a similar function.

Collection types

The introduction of ROW types in SQL:1999 was not the only break from the iron-clad rules of relational database theory. In that same version of the standard, the ARRAY type was introduced, and in SQL:2003, the MULTISET type was added. Both of these collection types violate the ol' First Normal Form (1NF) and, thus, take SQL databases a couple of steps further away from relational purity.

ARRAY

The ARRAY type violates 1NF, but not in the same way that the ROW type does. The ARRAY type enables you to enhance a field of an existing type by putting more than one entry into it. This creates a repeating group, which was demonized in Codd's original formulation of the relational model but now reappears as a desirable feature. Arrays are ordered in the sense that each element in the array corresponds to exactly one ordinal position.

You might ask how a repeating group of the ARRAY type differs from the ROW type's ability to put "a whole row's worth of data into a single field." The distinction is subtle. The ROW type enables you to compress multiple *different* attributes into a single field, such as a street, city, state, and postal code. The repeating group of the ARRAY type enables you to put multiple instances of the *same* attribute into a single field, such as a phone number and three alternate phone numbers.

For example, suppose you want to have alternate ways of contacting your vendors if main telephone number does not work for you. Perhaps you would like the option of storing as many as four telephone numbers, just to be safe. A slight modification to the code shown previously will do the trick.

```
CREATE TABLE VENDOR (
    VendorID    INTEGER PRIMARY KEY,
    VendorName  VARCHAR (25),
    Address     address_type,
    Phone       VARCHAR (15)  ARRAY [4]
) ;
```

When he created the relational model, Dr. Codd made a conscious decision to sacrifice some functional flexibility in exchange for enhanced data integrity. The addition of the ARRAY type, along with the ROW type and later the MULTISET type, takes back some of that flexibility in exchange for added complexity. That added complexity could lead to data integrity problems if it is not handled correctly. The more complex a system is, the more things that can go wrong and the more opportunities there are for people to make mistakes.

Multiset

Whereas an *array* is an ordered collection of elements, a *multiset* is an unordered collection. You cannot reference individual elements in a multiset because you don't know where they are located in the collection. If you want to have multiples of an attribute, such as phone numbers but don't care what order they are listed in, you can use a multiset rather than an array.

REF types

REF types are different from distinct data types such as INTEGER or CHAR. They are used in obscure circumstances by highly skilled SQL wizards and just about nobody else. Instead of holding values, an REF type references a user-defined structured type associated with a typed table. Typed tables are beyond the scope of this book, but I mention REF type here for the sake of completeness.

REF types are not a part of core SQL. This means that database vendors can claim compliance with the SQL standard without implementing REF types.

The REF type is an aspect of the object-oriented nature of SQL since the SQL:1999 standard. If object-oriented programming seems obscure to you, as it does to many programmers of a more traditional bent, you can probably survive quite well without ever needing the REF type.

User-defined types

User-defined types (UDTs) are another addition to SQL imported from the world of object-oriented programming. If the data types enumerated here are not enough for you, you can define your own data types. To do so, use the principles of abstract data types (ADTs) that are major features of such object-oriented languages as C++.

REMEMBER

SQL is not a complete programming language, and as such must be used with a host language that is complete, such as C. One of the problems with this arrangement is that the data types of the host language often do not match the data types of SQL. User-defined types come to the rescue here. You can define a type that matches the corresponding type in the host language.

The object-oriented nature of UDTs becomes evident when you see that a UDT has attributes and methods encapsulated within it. The attribute definitions and the results of the methods are visible to the outside world, but the ways the methods are actually implemented are hidden from view. In this object-oriented world, you can declare attributes and methods to be public, private, or protected. A *public* attribute or method is available to anyone who uses the UDT. A *private* attribute or method may be used only by the UDT itself. A *protected* attribute or method may be used only by the UDT itself and its subtypes. (If this sounds familiar to you, don't be surprised — an SQL UDT is much like a class in object-oriented programming.)

There are two kinds of UDTs: distinct types and structured types. The next sections take a look at each one in turn.

Distinct types

A *distinct* type is very similar to a regular predefined SQL type. In fact, a distinct type is derived directly from a predefined type, called the *source* type. You can create multiple distinct types from a single source type, each one distinct from all the others and from the source type. Here's how to create a distinct type from a predefined type:

```
CREATE DISTINCT TYPE USdollar AS DECIMAL (10,2) ;
```

This definition (USdollar) creates a new data type for (wait for it) U.S. dollars, based on the predefined DECIMAL type. You can create additional distinct types in the same way:

```
CREATE DISTINCT TYPE Euro AS DECIMAL (10,2) ;
```

Now you can create tables that use the new types:

```
CREATE TABLE USinvoice (
    InvoiceNo    INTEGER PRIMARY KEY,
    CustomerID   INTEGER,
    SalesID      INTEGER,
    SaleTotal    USdollar,
    Tax          USdollar,
    Shipping     USdollar,
    GrandTotal   USdollar
    ) ;
```

```
CREATE TABLE Europeaninvoice (
    InvoiceNo    INTEGER PRIMARY KEY,
    CustomerID   INTEGER,
    SalesID      INTEGER,
    SaleTotal    Euro,
    Tax          Euro,
    Shipping     Euro,
    GrandTotal   Euro
    ) ;
```

The USdollar type and the Euro type are both based on the DECIMAL type, but you cannot directly compare a USdollar value to a Euro value, nor can you directly compare either of those to a DECIMAL value. This is consistent with reality because one U.S. dollar is not equal to one euro. However, it is possible to exchange dollars for euros and vice versa when traveling. You can make that exchange with SQL too, but not directly. You must use a CAST operation, as described in Book 4, Chapter 3.

Structured types

Structured types are not based on a single source type as are the distinct types. Instead, they are expressed as a list of attributes and methods. When you create a structured UDT, the DBMS automatically creates a constructor function, a mutator function, and an observer function. The *constructor* for a UDT is given the same name as the UDT. Its job is to initialize the UDT's attributes to their default values. When you invoke a *mutator* function, it changes the value of an attribute of a structured type. You can then use an *observer* function to retrieve the value of an attribute of a structured type. If you include an observer function in a SELECT statement, it will retrieve values from the database.

SUBTYPES AND SUPERTYPES

A hierarchical relationship can exist between two structured types. One structured type can be a "child" or subtype of a "parent" or supertype. Consider an example involving books. Suppose you have a UDT named BookUDT, which has a subtype named NovelUDT and another subtype named TechBookUDT. BookUDT is a supertype of both subtypes. Suppose further that TechBookUDT has a subtype named DatabaseBookUDT. DatabaseBookUDT is not only a subtype of TechBookUDT but also a subtype of BookUDT. Because DatabaseBookUDT is a direct child of TechBookUDT, it is considered a *proper subtype* of TechBookUDT. Since DatabaseBookUDT is not a direct child of BookUDT but rather a grandchild, it is not considered a proper subtype of BookUDT.

A structured type that has no supertype is considered a *maximal supertype*, and a structured type that has no subtypes is considered a *leaf subtype*.

STRUCTURED TYPE EXAMPLE

Here's how you can create structured UDTs:

```
/* Create a UDT named BookUDT */
CREATE TYPE BookUDT AS
/* Specify attributes */
    Title       CHAR (40),
    Author      CHAR (40),
    MyCost      DECIMAL (9,2),
    ListPrice   DECIMAL (9.2)
/* Allow for subtypes */
    NOT FINAL ;


/* Create a subtype named TechBookUDT */
CREATE TYPE TechBookUDT UNDER BookUDT NOT FINAL ;
```

```
/* Create a subtype named DatabaseBookUDT */
CREATE TYPE DatabaseBookUDT UNDER TechBookUDT FINAL ;
```

Note: In this code, comments are enclosed within /* comment */ pairs. The NOT
FINAL keywords indicate that even though a semicolon is closing out the statement, there is more to come. Subtypes are about to be defined under the supertype. The lowest level subtype closes out with the keyword FINAL.

Now that the types are defined, you can create tables that use them.

```
CREATE TABLE DATABASEBOOKS (
    StockItem    DatabaseBookUDT,
    StockNumber INTEGER
    ) ;
```

Now that the table exists, you can add data to it.

```
BEGIN
    /* Declare a temporary variable x */
    DECLARE x = DatabaseBookUDT;
    /* Execute the constructor function */
    Set x = DatabaseBookUDT() ;
    /* Execute the first mutator function */
    SET x = x.Title('SQL for Dummies') ;
    /* Execute the second mutator function */
    SET x = x.Author('Allen G. Taylor') ;
    /* Execute the third mutator function */
    SET x = x.MyCost(23.56) ;
    /* Execute the fourth mutator function */
    SET x = x.ListPrice(29.99) ;
    INSERT INTO DATABASEBOOKS VALUES (x, 271828) ;
END
```

Handling Null Values

SQL is different from practically any computer language that you may have
encountered up to this point in that it allows null values. Other languages don't.
Allowing null values gives SQL a flexibility that other languages lack, but also
contributes to the impedance mismatch between SQL and host languages that it
must work with in an application. If an SQL database contains null values the host

language does not recognize, you have to come up with a plan that handles that difference in a consistent way.

The term *impedance mismatch* comes from the world of electrical engineering. If, for example, you've set up your stereo system using speaker cable with a characteristic impedance of 50 ohms feeding speakers with an impedance of 8 ohms, you've got yourself a case of impedance mismatch, and you'll surely get fuzzy, noisy sound — definitely low fidelity. If a data type of a host language does not exactly match the corresponding data type of SQL, you have a similar situation: bad communication across the interface between the two.

A *null value* is a nonvalue. If you are talking about numeric data, a null value is not the same as zero, which is a definite value. It is one less than one. If you are talking about character data, a null value is not the same as a blank space. A blank space is also a definite value. If you are talking about Boolean data, a null value is not the same as FALSE. A false Boolean value is a definite value, too.

A null value is the absence of a value.

A field may contain a null value for several reasons:

>> A field may have a definite value, but the value is currently unknown.

>> A field may not yet have a definite value, but it may gain one in the future.

>> For some rows in a table, a particular field in that row may not be applicable.

>> The old value of a field has been deleted, but it has not yet been replaced with a new value.

In any situation where knowledge is incomplete, null values are possible. Because in most application areas, knowledge is never complete, null values are very likely to appear in most databases.

Applying Constraints

Constraints are one of the primary mechanisms for keeping the contents of a database from turning into a misleading or confusing mess. By applying constraints to tables, columns, or entire databases, you prevent the addition of invalid data or the deletion of data required to maintain overall consistency. A constraint can also identify invalid data that already exists in a database. If an operation that you perform in a transaction causes a constraint to be violated, the DBMS will prevent the transaction from taking effect (being *committed*). This protects the database from being put into an inconsistent state.

Column constraints

You can constrain the contents of a table column. In some cases, that means constraining what the column *must* contain, and in other cases, what it *may not* contain. There are three kinds of column constraints: the NOT NULL, UNIQUE, and CHECK constraints.

NOT NULL

Although SQL allows a column to contain null values, there are times when you want to be sure that a column always has a distinct value. In order for one row in a table to be distinguished from another, there must be some way of telling them apart. This is usually done with a primary key, which must have a unique value in every row. Because a null value in a column could be anything, it might match the value for that column in any of the other rows. Thus, it makes sense to disallow a null value in the column used to distinguish one row from the rest. You can do this with a NOT NULL constraint, as shown in the following example:

```
CREATE TABLE CLIENT (

    ClientName      CHAR (30)      NOT NULL,
    Address1        CHAR (30),
    Address2        CHAR (30),
    City            CHAR (25),
    State           CHAR (2),
    PostalCode      CHAR (10),
    Phone           CHAR (13),
    Fax             CHAR (13),
    ContactPerson   CHAR (30)
    ) ;
```

When entering a new client into the CLIENT table, you must make an entry in the ClientName column.

UNIQUE

The NOT NULL constraint is a fairly weak constraint. You can satisfy the constraint as long as you put anything at all into the field, even if what you put into it would allow inconsistencies into your table. For example, suppose you already had a client named David Taylor in your database and someone tried to enter another record with the same client name. If the table was protected only by a NOT NULL constraint, the entry of the second David Taylor would be allowed. Now, when you go to retrieve David Taylor's information, which one will you get? How will you tell whether you have the one you want? A way around this problem is to use the stronger UNIQUE constraint. The UNIQUE constraint will not only disallow the entry of a null value in a column but also disallow the entry of a value that matches a value already in the column.

CHECK

Use the CHECK constraint for preventing the entry of invalid data that goes beyond maintaining uniqueness. For example, you can check to make sure that a numeric value falls within an allowed range. You can also check to see that a particular character string is not entered into a column.

Here's an example that ensures that the charge for a service falls within the acceptable range. It insures that a customer is not mistakenly given a credit rather than a debit, and that they are not charged a ridiculously high amount.

```
CREATE TABLE TESTS (
    TestName          CHARACTER (30)      NOT NULL,
    StandardCharge    NUMERIC (6,2)
        CHECK (StandardCharge >= 0.00
          AND StandardCharge <= 200.00)
    ) ;
```

The constraint is satisfied only if the charge is positive and less than or equal to $200.

Table constraints

Sometimes, a constraint applies not just to a column but to an entire table. The PRIMARY KEY constraint is the principal example of a table constraint; it applies to an entire table.

Although a primary key *may* consist of a single column, it could also be made up of a combination of two or more columns. Because a primary key must be guaranteed to be unique, multiple columns may be needed if one column is not enough to guarantee uniqueness.

To better understand what this means, check out the following, which shows a table with a single-column primary key:

```
CREATE TABLE PROSPECT (
    ProspectName    CHAR (30)     PRIMARY KEY,
    Address1        CHAR (30),
    Address2        CHAR (30),
```

```
City              CHAR (25),
State             CHAR (2),
PostalCode        CHAR (10),
Phone             CHAR (13),
Fax               CHAR (13)
) ;
```

The primary key constraint, in this case, is listed with the ProspectName column, but it is nonetheless a table constraint because it guarantees that the table contains no duplicate rows. By applying the primary key constraint to ProspectName, you are guaranteeing that ProspectName cannot have a null value, and no entry in the ProspectName column may duplicate another entry in the ProspectName column. Because ProspectName is guaranteed to be unique, every row in the table must be distinguishable from every other row.

ProspectName may not be a particularly good choice for a proposed primary key. Some people have rather common names— Joe Wilson or Jane Adams. It is quite possible that two people with the same name might both be prospects for your business. You could overcome that problem by using more than one column for the primary key. Here's one way to do that:

```
CREATE TABLE PROSPECT (
    ProspectName      CHAR (30)      NOT NULL,
    Address1          CHAR (30)      NOT NULL,
    Address2          CHAR (30),
    City              CHAR (25),
    State             CHAR (2),
    PostalCode        CHAR (10),
    Phone             CHAR (13),

    CONSTRAINT prospect_pk PRIMARY KEY
          (ProspectName, Address1)
    ) ;
```

A composite primary key is made up of both ProspectName and Address1.

You might ask, "What if a father and son have the same name and live at the same address?" The more such scenarios you think up, the more complex things tend to get. In many cases, it's best to make up a unique ID number for every row in a table and let that be the primary key. If you use an autoincrementer to generate the keys, you can be sure they are unique. This keeps things relatively simple. You can also program your own unique ID numbers by storing a value in memory and incrementing it by one after each time you add a new record that uses the stored value as its primary key.

```
CREATE TABLE PROSPECT (
   ProspectID          INTEGER              PRIMARY KEY,
   ProspectName        CHAR (30),
   Address1            CHAR (30),
   Address2            CHAR (30),
   City                CHAR (25),
   State               CHAR (2),
   PostalCode          CHAR (10),
   Phone               CHAR (13)
   ) ;
```

Many database management systems automatically create autoincrementing primary keys for you as you enter new rows into a table.

Foreign key constraints

Relational databases are categorized as they are because the data is stored in tables that are *related* to each other in some way. The relationship occurs because a row in one table may be directly related to one or more rows in another table.

For example, in a retail database, the record in the CUSTOMER table for customer Lisa Mazzone is directly related to the records in the INVOICE table for purchases that Ms. Mazzone has made. To establish this relationship, one or more columns in the CUSTOMER table must have corresponding columns in the INVOICE table.

The primary key of the CUSTOMER table uniquely identifies each customer. The primary key of the INVOICE table uniquely identifies each invoice. In addition, the primary key of the CUSTOMER table acts as a foreign key in INVOICE to link the two tables. In this setup, the foreign key in each row of the INVOICE table identifies the customer who made this particular purchase. Here's an example:

```
CREATE TABLE CUSTOMER (
   CustomerID          INTEGER              PRIMARY KEY,
   CustomerName        CHAR (30),
   Address1            CHAR (30),
   Address2            CHAR (30),
   City                CHAR (25),
   State               CHAR (2),
   PostalCode          CHAR (10),
   Phone               CHAR (13)
   ) ;
```

```
CREATE TABLE SALESPERSON (
    SalespersonID     INTEGER              PRIMARY KEY,
    SalespersonName   CHAR (30),
    Address1          CHAR (30),
    Address2          CHAR (30),
    City              CHAR (25),
    State             CHAR (2),
    PostalCode        CHAR (10),
    Phone             CHAR (13)
    ) ;

CREATE TABLE INVOICE (
    InvoiceNo         INTEGER PRIMARY KEY,
    CustomerID        INTEGER,
    SalespersonID     INTEGER,

    CONSTRAINT customer_fk FOREIGN KEY (CustomerID)
        REFERENCES CUSTOMER (CustomerID),
    CONSTRAINT salesperson_fk FOREIGN KEY (SalespersonID)
        REFERENCES SALESPERSON (SalespersonID)
    ) ;
```

Each invoice is related to the customer who made the purchase and the salesperson who made the sale.

Using constraints in this way is what makes relational databases relational. This is the core of the whole thing right here! How do the tables in a relational databases relate to each other? They relate by the keys they hold in common. The relationship is established but also constrained by the fact that a column in one table has to match a corresponding column in another table. The only relationships present in a relational database are those where there is a key-to-key link mediated by a foreign key constraint.

Assertions

Sometimes, a constraint may apply not just to a column or a table, but to multiple tables or even an entire database. A constraint with such broad applicability is called an *assertion*.

Suppose a small bookstore wants to control its exposure to dead inventory by not allowing total inventory to grow beyond 20,000 items. Suppose further that stocks of books and DVDs are maintained in different tables — the BOOKS and DVD tables. An assertion can guarantee that the maximum is not exceeded.

```
CREATE TABLE BOOKS (
    ISBN          INTEGER,
    Title         CHAR (50),
    Quantity      INTEGER ) ;

CREATE TABLE DVD (
    BarCode       INTEGER,
    Title         CHAR (50),
    Quantity      INTEGER ) ;

CREATE ASSERTION
    CHECK ((SELECT SUM (Quantity)
            FROM BOOKS)
        + (SELECT SUM (Quantity)
            FROM DVD)
          < 20000) ;
```

This assertion adds up all the books in stock, then all the DVDs in stock, and finally adds those two sums together. It then checks to see that the sum of them all is less than 20,000. Whenever an attempt is made to add a book or DVD to inventory, and that addition would push total inventory to 20,000 or more, the assertion is violated and the addition is not allowed.

Most popular implementations do not support assertions. For example, SQL Server 2016, DB2, Oracle Database 18c, SAP SQL Anywhere, MySQL, and PostgreSQL do not. Assertions may become available in the future since they are a part of SQL:2003, but it would not be wise to hold your breath until this functionality appears. Although a feature that would be nice to have, assertions are far down on the list of features to add for most DBMS vendors.

Chapter **3**

Values, Variables, Functions, and Expressions

This chapter describes the tools that ISO/IEC standard SQL provides to operate on data. In addition to specifying the value of a data item, you can slice and dice an item in a variety of ways. Instead of just retrieving raw data as it exists in the database, you can preprocess it to deliver just the information you want, in the form that you want it.

Entering Data Values

After you've created a database table, the next step is to enter data into it. SQL supports a number of different data types. Within any specific data type, the data can take any of several forms. The five different forms that can appear in table rows are

» Row values

» Column references

» Literal values

» Variables

» Special variables

Each form is discussed in turn throughout this section.

Row values have multiple parts

A *row value* includes the values of all the data in all the columns in a row in a table. It is actually multiple values rather than just one. The intersection of a row and a column, called a *field*, contains a single, so-called "atomic" value. All the values of all the fields in a row, taken together, are that single row's row value.

Identifying values in a column

Just as you can specify a row value consisting of multiple values, you can specify the value contained in a single column.

```
SELECT * FROM CUSTOMER
    WHERE LastName = 'Smith' ;
```

This query returns all the rows in the CUSTOMER table, where the value in the LastName column is `Smith`.

Literal values don't change

In SQL, a value can either be a constant or it can be represented by a variable. Constant values are called *literals*. Table 3-1 shows sample literals for each of the SQL data types.

REMEMBER

Numeric literals are just the values that they represent. Nonnumeric literals are enclosed in single quotes.

TABLE 3-1   Sample Literals of Various Data Types

Data Type	Sample Literal
BIGINT	8589934592
INTEGER	186282
SMALLINT	186
NUMERIC	186282.42
DECIMAL	186282.42
DECFLOAT (16)	1234567890123456
REAL	6.02257E23
DOUBLE PRECISION	3.1415926535897E00
FLOAT	6.02257E23
BINARY (2)	'0110011111101010'
VARBINARY (1)	'10011'
CHARACTER(15)	'GREECE '

Note: Fifteen total characters and spaces are between the quote marks above.

Data Type	Sample Literal
VARCHAR (CHARACTER VARYING)	'lepton'
NATIONAL CHARACTER(15)	'ΕΛΛΑΣ ' [1]

Note: Fifteen total characters and spaces are between the quote marks above.

Data Type	Sample Literal
NATIONAL CHARACTER VARYING	'λεπτον' [2]
CHARACTER LARGE OBJECT (CLOB)	(A really long character string)
BINARY LARGE OBJECT (BLOB)	(A really long string of ones and zeros)
DATE	DATE '1969-07-20'
TIME(2)	TIME '13.41.32.50'
TIMESTAMP(0)	TIMESTAMP '2007-07-25-13.03.16.000000'
TIME WITH TIMEZONE(4)	TIME '13.41.32.5000-08.00'
TIMESTAMP WITH TIMEZONE(0)	TIMESTAMP '2007-07-25-13.03.16.0000+02.00'
INTERVAL DAY	INTERVAL '7' DAY

[1] This term is the word that Greeks use to name their own country in their own language. (The English equivalent is Hellas.)
[2] This term is the word lepton in Greek national characters.

Variables vary

Literals that explicitly hold a single value are fine if that value appears only once or twice in an application. However, if a value appears multiple times, and there is any chance that value might change in the future, you should represent it with a variable. That way, if changes are necessary, you have to change the code in one place only, where the value is assigned to the variable, rather than in all the places in the application where that value appears.

For example, suppose an application dealing with a table containing the archives of a magazine retrieves information from various sections of the current issue. One such retrieval might look like this:

```
SELECT Editorial FROM PENGUINLIFE
    WHERE Issue = 47 ;
```

Another could be

```
SELECT LeadStory FROM PENGUINLIFE
    WHERE Issue = 47 ;
```

There could be many more like these two in the application. When next week rolls around, and you want to run the application again for the latest issue, you must go through the program by hand and change all the instances of 47 to 48. Computers are supposed to rescue us from such boring, repetitive tasks, and they do. Instead of using literals in such cases, use variables instead, like this:

```
SELECT Editorial FROM PENGUINLIFE
    WHERE Issue = :IssueNumber ;
```

You have to change the IssueNumber variable in one place only, and the change affects all the places in the application where the variable appears.

Special variables hold specific values

SQL has a few special variables that hold information about system usage. In multiuser systems, you often need to know who is using the system at any given time. This information can be captured in a log file using the special variables. The special variables are

>> SESSION_USER, which holds a value that's equal to the user authorization identifier of the current SQL session. If you write a program that performs a monitoring function, you can interrogate SESSION_USER to find out who is executing SQL statements.

» CURRENT_USER, which stores a user-specified authorization identifier. If a module has no such identifier, CURRENT_USER has the same value as SESSION_USER.

» SYSTEM_USER, which contains the operating system's user identifier. This identifier may differ from that user's identifier in an SQL module. A user may log onto the system as ANDREW, for example, but identify himself to a module as DIRECTOR. The value in SESSION_USER is DIRECTOR. If he makes no explicit specification of the module identifier, and CURRENT_USER also contains DIRECTOR, SYSTEM_USER holds the value ANDREW.

One use of the SYSTEM_USER, SESSION_USER, and CURRENT_USER special variables is to track who is using the system. You can maintain a log table and periodically insert the values into that table that SYSTEM_USER, SESSION_USER, and CURRENT_USER contain. The following example shows how:

```
INSERT INTO USAGELOG (SNAPSHOT)
    VALUES ('User ' || SYSTEM_USER ||
        ' with ID ' || SESSION_USER ||
        ' active at ' || CURRENT_TIMESTAMP) ;
```

This statement produces log entries similar to the following example:

```
User ANDREW with ID DIRECTOR active at 2019-03-03-23.50.00
```

Working with Functions

Functions perform computations or operations that are more elaborate than what you would expect a simple command statement to do. SQL has two kinds of functions: set functions and value functions. *Set functions* are so named because they operate on a set of rows in a table rather than on a single row. *Value functions* operate on the values of fields in a table row.

Summarizing data with set functions

When dealing with a set of table rows, often what you want to know is some aggregate property that applies to the whole set. SQL has five such aggregate or set functions: COUNT, AVG, MAX, MIN, and SUM. To see how these work, consider the example data in Table 3-2. It is a price table for photographic papers of various sizes and characteristics.

TABLE 3-2   ## Photographic Paper Price List per 20 Sheets

Paper Type	Size8	Size11
Dual-sided matte	8.49	13.99
Card stock dual-sided matte	9.49	16.95
Professional photo gloss	10.99	19.99
Glossy HW 9M	8.99	13.99
Smooth silk	10.99	19.95
Royal satin	10.99	19.95
Dual-sided semigloss	9.99	17.95
Dual-sided HW semigloss	--	--
Universal two-sided matte	--	--
Transparency	29.95	--

The fields that contain dashes do not have a value. The dash in the table represents a null value.

COUNT

The COUNT function returns the number of rows in a table or the number of rows that meet a specified condition. In the simplest case, you have

```
SELECT COUNT (*)
   FROM PAPERS ;
```

This returns a value of 10 because there are ten rows in the PAPERS table. You can add a condition to see how many types of paper are available in Size 8:

```
SELECT COUNT (Size8)
   FROM PAPERS ;
```

This returns a value of 8 because, of the ten types of paper in the PAPERS table, only eight are available in size 8. You might also want to know how many different prices there are for papers of size 8. That is also easy to determine:

```
SELECT COUNT (DISTINCT Size8)
   FROM PAPERS ;
```

This returns a value of 6 because there are six distinct values of Size 8 paper. Null values are ignored.

AVG

The AVG function calculates and returns the average of the values in the specified column. It works only on columns that contain numeric data.

```
SELECT AVG (Size8)
   FROM PAPERS ;
```

This returns a value of 12.485. If you wonder what the average price is for the Size 11 papers, you can find out this way:

```
SELECT AVG (Size11)
   FROM PAPERS ;
```

This returns a value of 17.539.

MAX

As you might expect, the MAX function returns the maximum value found in the specified column. Find the maximum value in the Size 8 column:

```
SELECT MAX (Size8)
   FROM PAPERS ;
```

This returns 29.95, the price for 20 sheets of Size 8 transparencies.

MIN

The MIN function gives you the minimum value found in the specified column.

```
SELECT MIN (Size8)
   FROM PAPERS ;
```

Here the value returned is 8.49.

SUM

Calculating the sum of all the prices for the papers being offered for sale doesn't make much sense in the photographic paper example, but this type of calculation can be valuable in other applications. Just in case you want to know what it would cost to buy 20 sheets of every Size 11 paper being offered, you could make the following query:

```
SELECT SUM (Size11)
   FROM PAPERS ;
```

It would cost 122.77 to buy 20 sheets of each of the 7 kinds of Size 11 paper that are available.

LISTAGG

LISTAGG is a set function, defined in the SQL:2016 ISO/IEC specification. Its purpose is to transform the values from a group of rows into a list of values delimited by a character that does not occur within the data. An example would be to transform a group of table rows into a string of comma-separated values (CSV).

```
SELECT LISTAGG(LastName, ', ')
          WITHIN GROUP (ORDER BY LastName) "Customer"
   FROM CUSTOMER
   WHERE Zipcode = 97201;
```

This statement will return a list of all customers residing in the 97201 zip code, in ascending order of their last names. This will work as long as there are no commas in the LastName field of any customer.

Dissecting data with value functions

A number of data manipulation operations occur fairly frequently. SQL provides value functions to perform these tasks. There are four types of value functions:

>> String value functions

>> Numeric value functions

>> Datetime value functions

>> Interval value functions

The following subsections examine the functions available in each of these categories.

String value functions

String value functions take one character string as input and produce another character string as output. There are eight string value functions.

- >> SUBSTRING (FROM)
- >> SUBSTRING (SIMILAR)
- >> UPPER
- >> LOWER
- >> TRIM
- >> TRANSLATE
- >> CONVERT
- >> OVERLAY

SUBSTRING (FROM)

The operation of SUBSTRING (FROM) is similar to substring operations in many other computer languages. Here's an example:

```
SUBSTRING ('manual transmission' FROM 8 FOR 4)
```

This returns tran, the substring that starts in the eighth character position and continues for four characters. You want to make sure that the starting point and substring length you specify locate the substring entirely within the source string. If part or all of the substring falls outside the source string, you could receive an unexpected result.

SUBSTRING (SIMILAR)

SUBSTRING (SIMILAR) is a regular expression substring function. It divides a string into three parts and returns the middle part. Formally, a regular expression is a string of legal characters. A substring is a particular designated part of that string. Consider this example:

```
SUBSTRING ('antidisestablishmentarianism'
          SIMILAR 'antidis\"[:ALPHA:]+\"arianism'
          ESCAPE '\' )
```

The original string is the first operand. The operand following the SIMILAR keyword is a character string literal that includes a regular expression in the form of another character string literal, a separator (\"), a second regular expression that means "one or more alphabetic characters," a second separator (\"), and a third regular expression in the form of a different character string literal. The value returned is

```
establishment
```

UPPER

The UPPER function converts its target string to all uppercase.

```
UPPER ('ChAoTic')                returns 'CHAOTIC'
```

The UPPER function has no effect on character sets, such as Hebrew, that do not distinguish between upper- and lowercase.

LOWER

The LOWER function converts its target string to all lowercase.

```
LOWER ('INTRUDER ALERT!')        returns 'intruder alert!'
```

As is the case for UPPER, LOWER has no effect on character sets that do not include the concept of case.

TRIM

The TRIM function enables you to crop a string, shaving off characters at the front or the back of the string — or both. Here are a few examples:

```
TRIM (LEADING ' ' FROM ' ALERT ')     returns 'ALERT '
TRIM (TRAILING ' ' FROM ' ALERT ')    returns ' ALERT'
TRIM (BOTH ' ' FROM ' ALERT ')        returns 'ALERT'
TRIM (LEADING 'A' FROM 'ALERT')       returns 'LERT'
```

If you don't specify what to trim, the blank space (' ') is the default.

TRANSLATE AND CONVERT

The TRANSLATE and CONVERT functions take a source string in one character set and transform the original string into a string in another character set. Examples might be Greek to English or Katakana to Norwegian. The conversion functions that specify these transformations are implementation-specific, so those details aren't relevant here.

These functions do not really translate character strings from one language to another. All they do is translate a character from the first character set to the corresponding character in the second character set. In going from Greek to English, it would convert Ελλασ to Ellas instead of translating it as Greece. ("Ελλασ" is what the Greeks call their country, which English speakers call Greece).

OVERLAY

The OVERLAY function is a SUBSTRING function with a little extra functionality. As with SUBSTRING, it finds a specified substring within a target string. However, instead of returning the string that it finds, it replaces it with a different string. For example:

```
OVERLAY ('I Love Paris' PLACING 'Tokyo' FROM 8 FOR 5)
```

This changes the string to

```
I Love Tokyo
```

This won't work if you want to change I Love Paris to I Love London. The number of letters in London does not match the number in Paris.

Numeric value functions

Numeric value functions can take a variety of data types as input but the output is always a numeric value. SQL has 14 types of numeric value functions. The defining characteristic of a function is that it returns a value of some sort. Numeric value functions always return a numeric value. Thus, the square root function will return a value that is the square root of the input, the natural logarithm function will return a value that is the natural logarithm of the input, and so on.

>> Position expression (POSITION)

>> Extract expression (EXTRACT)

>> Length expression (CHAR_LENGTH, CHARACTER_LENGTH, OCTET_LENGTH)

>> Cardinality expression (CARDINALITY)

>> Absolute value expression (ABS)

>> Modulus expression (MOD)

>> Trigonometric functions (SIN, COS, TAN, ASIN, ACOS, ATAN, SINH, COSH, TANH)

>> Logarithmic functions (LOG, LOG10, LN)

>> Exponential function (EXP)

>> Power function (POWER)

>> Square root (SQRT)

>> Floor function (FLOOR)

>> Ceiling function (CEIL, CEILING)

>> Width bucket function (WIDTH_BUCKET)

POSITION

POSITION searches for a specified target string within a specified source string and returns the character position where the target string begins. The syntax is as follows:

```
POSITION (target IN source)
```

If the function doesn't find the target string, the POSITION function returns a zero value. If the target string has zero length (as in the last example), the POSITION function always returns a value of 1. If any operand in the function has a null value, the result is a null value.

EXTRACT

The EXTRACT function extracts a single field from a datetime or an interval. The following statement, for example, returns 12:

```
EXTRACT (MONTH FROM DATE '2018-12-04')
```

CHARACTER_LENGTH

The CHARACTER_LENGTH function returns the number of characters in a character string. The following statement, for example, returns 20:

```
CHARACTER_LENGTH ('Transmission, manual')
```

REMEMBER

As you can see, commas and even blank spaces count as characters. Note that this function is not particularly useful if its argument is a literal like 'Transmission, manual'. You can write 20 just as easily as you can write CHARACTER_LENGTH ('Transmission, manual'). In fact, writing 20 is easier. This function is more useful if its argument is an expression rather than a literal value.

OCTET_LENGTH

In music, a vocal ensemble made up of eight singers is called an *octet*. Typically, the parts that the ensemble represents are first and second soprano, first and second alto, first and second tenor, and first and second bass. In computer terminology, an ensemble of eight data bits is called a *byte*. The word *byte* is clever in that the term clearly relates to *bit* but implies something larger than a bit. A nice wordplay — but unfortunately, nothing in the word *byte* conveys the concept of "eightness." By borrowing the musical term, a more apt description of a collection of eight bits becomes possible.

Practically all modern computers use eight bits to represent a single alphanumeric character. More complex character sets (such as Chinese) require 16 bits to represent a single character. The OCTET_LENGTH function counts and returns the number of octets (bytes) in a string. If the string is a bit string, OCTET_LENGTH returns the number of octets you need to hold that number of bits. If the string is an English-language character string (with one octet per character), the function returns the number of characters in the string. If the string is a Chinese character string, the function returns a number that is twice the number of Chinese characters. The following string is an example:

```
OCTET_LENGTH ('Brakes, disc')
```

This function returns 12 because each character takes up one octet.

Some character sets use a variable number of octets for different characters. In particular, some character sets that support mixtures of Kanji and Latin characters use *escape* characters to switch between the two character sets. A string that contains both Latin and Kanji may have, for example, 30 characters and require 30 octets if all the characters are Latin; 62 characters if all the characters are Kanji (60 characters plus a leading and trailing shift character); and 150 characters if the characters alternate between Latin and Kanji (because each Kanji character needs two octets for the character and one octet each for the leading and trailing shift characters). The OCTET_LENGTH function returns the number of octets you need for the current value of the string.

CARDINALITY

Cardinality deals with collections of elements such as arrays or multisets, where each element is a value of some data type. The cardinality of the collection is the number of elements that it contains. One use of the CARDINALITY function is something like this:

```
CARDINALITY (TeamRoster)
```

This function would return 12, for example, if there were 12 team members on the roster. TeamRoster, a column in the TEAM table, can be either an array or a multiset. An *array* is an ordered collection of elements, and a *multiset* is an unordered collection of elements. For a team roster, which changes frequently, a multiset makes more sense.

ABS

The ABS function returns the absolute value of a numeric value expression.

```
ABS (-273)
```

This returns 273.

TRIGONOMETRIC FUNCTIONS SIN, COS, TAN, ASIN, ACOS, ATAN, SINH, COSH, TANH

The trig functions give you the values you would expect, such as the sine of an angle or the hyperbolic tangent of one.

LOGARITHMIC FUNCTIONS LOG10, LN, LOG (<BASE>, <VALUE>)

The logarithmic functions enable you to generate the logarithm of a number, either a base-10 logarithm, a natural logarithm, or a logarithm to a base that you specify.

MOD

The MOD function returns the *modulus* — the remainder of division of one number by another — of two numeric value expressions.

```
MOD (6,4)
```

This function returns 2, the modulus of six divided by four.

EXP

This function raises the base of the natural logarithms *e* to the power specified by a numeric value expression:

```
EXP (2)
```

This function returns something like 7.389056. The number of digits beyond the decimal point is implementation-dependent.

POWER

This function raises the value of the first numeric value expression to the power of the second numeric value expression:

```
POWER (3,7)
```

This function returns 2187, which is three raised to the seventh power.

SQRT

This function returns the square root of the value of the numeric value expression:

```
SQRT (9)
```

This function returns 3, the square root of nine.

FLOOR

This function rounds the numeric value expression to the largest integer not greater than the expression:

```
FLOOR (2.73)
```

This function returns 2.0.

CEIL OR CEILING

This function rounds the numeric value expression to the smallest integer not less than the expression.

```
CEIL (2.73)
```

This function returns 3.0.

WIDTH_BUCKET

The WIDTH_BUCKET function, used in online application processing (OLAP), is a function of four arguments returning an integer between the value of the second (minimum) argument and the value of the third (maximum) argument. It assigns the first argument to an equiwidth partitioning of the range of numbers between the second and third arguments. Values outside this range are assigned to either the value of zero or one more than the fourth argument (the number of buckets).

For example:

```
WIDTH_BUCKET (PI, 0, 10, 5)
```

Suppose PI is a numeric value expression with a value of 3.141592. The example partitions the interval from zero to ten into five equal *buckets*, each with a width of two. The function returns a value of 2 because 3.141592 falls into the second bucket, which covers the range from two to four.

Datetime value functions

SQL includes three functions that return information about the current date, current time, or both. CURRENT_DATE returns the current date; CURRENT_TIME returns the current time; and CURRENT_TIMESTAMP returns the current date and the current time. CURRENT_DATE doesn't take an argument, but CURRENT_TIME and CURRENT_TIMESTAMP take a single argument. The argument specifies the precision for the seconds part of the time value that the function returns. Datetime data types and the precision concept are described in Book 4, Chapter 2.

The following table offers some examples of these datetime value functions.

This Statement	Returns
CURRENT_DATE	2019-01-23
CURRENT_TIME (1)	08:36:57.3
CURRENT_IMESTAMP (2)	2019-01-23 08:36:57.38

The date that CURRENT_DATE returns is DATE type data. The time that CURRENT_TIME (p) returns is TIME type data, and the timestamp that CURRENT_TIMESTAMP (p) returns is TIMESTAMP type data. The precision (p) specified is the number of digits beyond the decimal point showing fractions of a second. Because SQL retrieves date and time information from your computer's system clock, the information is correct for the time zone in which the computer resides.

In some applications, you may want to deal with dates, times, or timestamps as character strings to take advantage of the functions that operate on character data. You can perform a type conversion by using the CAST expression, which is described later in this chapter.

Polymorphic table functions

A table function is a user-defined function that returns a table as a result. A polymorphic table function, first described in SQL:2016, is a table function whose row type is not declared when the function is created. Instead, the row type may depend on the function arguments used when the function is invoked.

Using Expressions

An *expression* is any combination of elements that reduces to a single value. The elements can be numbers, strings, dates, times, intervals, Booleans, or more complex things. What they are doesn't matter as long as the result is a single value after all operations have taken place.

Numeric value expressions

The operands in a numeric value expression can be numbers of an exact numeric type or of an approximate numeric type. (Exact and approximate numeric types are discussed in Book 4, Chapter 2.) Operands of different types can be used within a single expression. If at least one operand is of an approximate type, the result is of an approximate type. If all operands are of exact types, the result is of an exact type. The SQL specification does not specify exactly what type the result of any given expression will be due to the wide variety of platforms that SQL runs on.

Here are some examples of valid numeric value expressions:

>> −24

>> 13+78

>> 4*(5+8)

>> Weight/(Length*Width*Height)

>> Miles/5280

String value expressions

String value expressions can consist of a single string or a concatenation of strings. The concatenation operator (||) joins two strings together and is the only one you can use in a string value expression. Table 3-3 shows some examples of string value expressions and the strings that they produce.

From the first two rows in Table 3-3, you see that concatenating two strings produces a result string that has seamlessly joined the two original strings. The third row shows that concatenating a null value with two source strings produces the same result as if the null were not there. The fourth row shows concatenation of two strings while retaining a blank space in between. The fifth row shows the concatenation of two variables with a blank space in between, which produces a string consisting of the values of those variables separated by a blank space. Finally, the

Values, Variables, Functions, and Expressions

last line of Table 3-3 shows the concatenation of two binary strings. The result is a single binary string that is a seamless combination of the two source strings.

TABLE 3-3 ## Examples of String Value Expressions

String Value Expression	Resulting String
`'nanotechnology'`	`'nanotechnology'`
`'nano' || 'technology'`	`'nanotechnology'`
`'nano' || '' || 'technology'`	`'nanotechnology'`
`'Isaac' || '' || 'Newton'`	`'Isaac Newton'`
`FirstName || ' ' || LastName`	`'Isaac Newton'`
`B'10101010' || B'01010101'`	`B'1010101001010101'`

Datetime value expressions

Datetime value expressions perform operations on dates and times. Such data is of the DATE, TIME, TIMESTAMP, or INTERVAL type. The result of a datetime value expression is always of the DATE, TIME, or TIMESTAMP type. Intervals are not one of the datetime types, but an interval can be added to or subtracted from a datetime to produce another datetime. Here's an example datetime value expression that makes use of an added interval:

```
CURRENT_DATE + INTERVAL '2' DAY
```

This expression evaluates to the day after tomorrow.

Datetimes can also include time zone information. The system maintains times in Coordinated Universal Time (UTC), which until recently was known as Greenwich Mean Time (GMT). (I guess the feeling was that Greenwich was too provincial, and a more general name for world time was called for.) You can specify a time as being either at your local time, or as an offset from UTC. An example is

```
TIME '13:15:00' AT LOCAL
```

for 1:15 p.m. local time. Another example is

```
TIME '13:15:00' AT TIME ZONE INTERVAL '-8:00' HOUR TO MINUTE
```

for 1:15 p.m. Pacific Standard Time. (Pacific Standard Time is eight hours earlier than UTC.)

Interval value expressions

An *interval* is the difference between two datetimes. If you subtract one datetime from another, the result is an interval. It makes no sense to add two datetimes, so SQL does not allow you to do it.

There are two kinds of intervals: year-month and day-time. This situation is a little messy but necessary because not all months contain the same number of days. Because a month can be 28, 29, 30, or 31 days long, there is no direct translation from days to months. As a result, when using an interval, you must specify which kind of interval it is. Suppose you expect to take an around-the-world cruise after you retire, starting on June 1, 2045. How many years and months is that from now? An interval value expression gives you the answer.

```
(DATE '2045-06-01' - CURRENT_DATE) YEAR TO MONTH
```

You can add two intervals to obtain an interval result.

```
INTERVAL '30' DAY + INTERVAL '14' DAY
```

However, you cannot do the following:

```
INTERVAL '30' DAY + INTERVAL '14' MONTH
```

The two kinds of intervals do not mix. Besides addition and subtraction, multiplication and division of intervals are also allowed. The expression

```
INTERVAL '7' DAY * 3
```

is valid and gives an interval of 21 days. The expression

```
INTERVAL '12' MONTH / 2
```

is also valid and gives an interval of 6 months. Intervals can also be negative.

```
INTERVAL '-3' DAY
```

gives an interval of -3 days. Aside from the literals used in the previous examples, any value expression or combination of value expressions that evaluates to an interval can be used in an interval value expression.

Boolean value expressions

Only three legal Boolean values exist: TRUE, FALSE, and UNKNOWN. The UNKNOWN value becomes operative when a NULL is involved. Suppose the Boolean variable Signal1 is TRUE and the Boolean variable Signal2 is FALSE. The following Boolean value expression evaluates to TRUE:

```
Signal1 IS TRUE
```

So does this one:

```
Signal1 IS TRUE OR Signal2 IS TRUE
```

However, the following Boolean value expression evaluates to FALSE.

```
Signal1 IS TRUE AND Signal2 IS TRUE
```

The AND operator means that both predicates must be true for the result to be true. (A *predicate* is an expression that asserts a fact about values.) Because Signal2 is false, the entire expression evaluates to a FALSE value.

Array value expressions

You can use a couple of types of expressions with arrays. The first has to do with cardinality. The maximum number of elements an array can have is called the array's *maximum cardinality*. The actual number of elements in the array at a given time is called its *actual cardinality*. You can combine two arrays by concatenating them, summing their maximum cardinalities in the process. Suppose you want to know the actual cardinality of the concatenation of two array-type columns in a table, where the first element of the first column has a given value. You can execute the following statement:

```
SELECT CARDINALITY (FirstColumn || SecondColumn)
    FROM TARGETTABLE
WHERE FirstColumn[1] = 42 ;
```

The CARDINALITY function gives the combined cardinality of the two arrays, where the first element in the first array has a value of 42.

Note: The first element of an SQL array is considered to be element 1, rather than element 0 as is true for some other languages.

Conditional value expressions

The value of a conditional value expression depends on a condition. SQL offers three variants of conditional value expressions: CASE, NULLIF, and COALESCE. The following sections cover each of these separately.

Handling different cases

The CASE conditional expression was added to SQL to give it some of the functionality that all full-featured computer languages have, the ability to do one thing if a condition holds and another thing if the condition does not hold. Originally conceived as a data sublanguage that was concerned only with managing data, SQL has gradually gained features that enable it to take on more of the functions needed by application programs.

SQL actually has two different CASE structures: the CASE expression described here and a CASE statement. The CASE expression, like all expressions, evaluates to a single value. You can use a CASE expression anywhere where a value is legal. The CASE statement, on the other hand, doesn't evaluate to a value. Instead, it executes a block of statements.

The CASE expression searches a table, one row at a time, taking on the value of a specified result whenever one of a list of conditions is TRUE. If the first condition is not satisfied for a row, the second condition is tested, and if it is TRUE, the result specified for it is given to the expression, and so on, until all conditions are processed. If no match is found, the expression takes on a NULL value. Processing then moves to the next row.

SEARCHING FOR TABLE ROWS THAT SATISFY VARIOUS CONDITIONS

You can specify the value to be given to a CASE expression based on which of several conditions is satisfied. Here's the syntax:

```
CASE
    WHEN condition1 THEN result1
    WHEN condition2 THEN result2
    ...
    WHEN conditionN THEN resultN
    ELSE resultx
END
```

If, in searching a table, the CASE expression finds a row where condition1 is true, it takes on the value of result1. If condition1 is not true but condition2 is true, it takes on the value of result2. This continues for all conditions. If none of the conditions are met and there is no ELSE clause, the expression is given the NULL value. Here's an example of usage:

```
UPDATE MECHANIC
    Set JobTitle = CASE
                        WHEN Specialty = 'Brakes'
                            THEN 'Brake Fixer'
                        WHEN Specialty = 'Engines'
                            THEN 'Motor Master'
                        WHEN Specialty = 'Electrical'
                            THEN 'Wizard'
                        ELSE 'Apprentice'
                    END ;
```

THE EQUALITY CONDITION ALLOWS A COMPACT CASE VALUE EXPRESSION

A shorthand version of the CASE statement can be used when the condition, as in the previous example, is based on one thing being equal (=) to one other thing. The syntax is as follows:

```
CASE valuet
    WHEN value1 THEN result1
    WHEN value2 THEN result2
    ...
    WHEN valueN THEN resultN
    ELSE resultx
END
```

For the preceding example, this translates to

```
UPDATE MECHANIC
    Set JobTitle = CASE Specialty
                        WHEN 'Brakes' THEN 'Brake Fixer'
                        WHEN 'Engines' THEN 'Motor Master'
                        WHEN 'Electrical' THEN 'Wizard'
                        ELSE 'Apprentice'
                    END ;
```

If the condition involves anything other than equality, the first, nonabbreviated form must be used.

The NULLIF special CASE

SQL databases are unusual in that NULL values are allowed. A NULL value can represent an unknown value, a known value that has just not been entered into the database yet, or a value that does not exist. Most other languages that deal with data do not support nulls, so whenever a situation arises in such databases where a value is not known, not yet entered, or nonexistent, the space is filled with a value that would not otherwise occur, such as –1 in a field that never holds a negative value, or ∗∗∗ in a character field in which asterisks are not valid characters.

To migrate data from a database that does not support nulls to a SQL database that does, you can use a CASE statement such as

```
UPDATE MECHANIC
    SET Specialty = CASE Specialty
                        WHEN '***' THEN NULL
                        ELSE Specialty
                END ;
```

You can do the same thing in a shorthand manner, using a NULLIF expression, as follows:

```
UPDATE MECHANIC
    SET Specialty = NULLIF(Specialty, '***') ;
```

Admittedly, this looks more cryptic than the CASE version, but it does save some tedious typing. You could interpret it as, "Update the MECHANIC table by setting the value of Specialty to NULL if its current value is '∗∗∗'".

Bypassing null values with COALESCE

The COALESCE expression is another shorthand version of CASE that deals with NULL values. It examines a series of values in a table row and assumes the value of the first one that is not NULL. If all the listed values are NULL, the COALESCE expression takes on the NULL value. Here's the syntax for a CASE expression that does this:

```
CASE
    WHEN value1 IS NOT NULL
        THEN value1
    WHEN value2 IS NOT NULL
        THEN value2
    ...
    WHEN valueN is NOT NULL
        THEN valueN
```

```
        ELSE NULL
   END
```

Here's the syntax for the equivalent COALESCE expression:

```
COALESCE(value1, value2, ..., valueN)
```

If you are dealing with a large number of cases, the COALESCE version can save you quite a bit of typing.

Converting data types with a CAST expression

Book 4, Chapter 2 describes the data types that SQL recognizes. The host languages that SQL statements are often embedded in also recognize data types, and those host language data types are never an exact match for the SQL data types. This could present a problem, except that, with a CAST expression, you can convert data of one type into data of another type. Whereas the first type might not be compatible with the place you want to send the data, the second type is. Of course, not all conversions are possible. If you have a character string such as '2019-02-14', you can convert it to the DATE type with a CAST expression. However, SQL doesn't let you convert a character string such as 'rhinoceros' to the DATE type. The data to be converted must be compatible with the destination type.

Casting one SQL data type to another

The simplest kind of cast is from one SQL data type to another. Even for this operation, however, you cannot indiscriminately make any conversion you want. The data you are converting must be compatible with the target data type. For example, suppose you have a table named ENGINEERS with a column named SSN, which is of the NUMERIC type. Perhaps you have another table, named MANAGERS that has a column named SocSecNo, which is of the CHAR (9) type. A typical entry in SSN might be 987654321. To find all the engineers who are also managers, you can use the following query. The CAST expression converts the CHAR (9) type to the NUMERIC type so that the operation can proceed.

```
SELECT * FROM ENGINEER
    WHERE ENGINEER.SSN = CAST(MANAGER.SocSecNo AS INTEGER) ;
```

This returns all the rows from the ENGINEER table that have Social Security Numbers that match Social Security Numbers in the MANAGERS table. To do so, it changes the Social Security Number from the MANAGER table from the CHAR (9) type to the INTEGER type, for the purposes of the comparison.

Using CAST to overcome data type incompatibilities between SQL and its host language

Problems arise when you want to send data between SQL and its host language. For example, SQL has the DECIMAL and NUMERIC types, but some host languages, such as FORTRAN and Pascal, do not. One way around this problem is to use CAST to put a numeric value into a character string, and then put the character string into a host variable that the host language can take in and deal with.

Suppose you maintain salary information as REAL type data in the EMPLOYEE table. You want to make some manipulations on that data that SQL is not well-equipped to perform but your host language is. You can cast the data into a form the host language can accept, operate on it at the host level, and then cast the result back to a form acceptable to the SQL database.

```
SELECT CAST(Salary AS CHAR (10)) INTO :salary_var
    FROM EMPLOYEE
    WHERE EmpID = :emp_id_var ;
```

That puts the salary value where the host language can grab it and in a form that the host language understands. After the host language is finished operating on the data item, it can return to the SQL database via a similar path:

```
UPDATE EMPLOYEE
    SET Salary = CAST(:salary_var AS DECIMAL(10,2))
        WHERE EmpID = :emp_id_var ;
```

Row value expressions

Row value expressions (as distinct from mere row values, which are covered at the beginning of this chapter) enable you to deal with the data in an entire table row or a subset of a row. The other expressions I've shown deal with only a single field in a row at a time. Row value expressions are useful for adding new data to a table a row at a time or to specify the retrieval of multiple fields from a table row. Here's an example of a row value expression used to enter a new row of data into a table:

```
INSERT INTO CERTIFICATIONS
    (CertificationNo, CertName, MechanicID, Expires)
```

```
VALUES
    (1, 'V8 Engines', 34, 2023-07-31) ;
```

One advantage of using row value expressions is that many SQL implementations can process them faster than the equivalent one-field-at-a-time operations. This could make a significant difference in performance at runtime.

Chapter 4

SELECT Statements and Modifying Clauses

The main purpose of storing data on a computer is to be able to retrieve specific elements of the data when you need them. As databases grow in size, the proportion that you are likely to want on any given occasion becomes smaller. As a result, SQL provides tools that enable you to make retrievals in a variety of ways. With these tools — SELECT statements and modifying clauses — you can zero in on the precise pieces of information that you want, even though they may be buried among megabytes of data that you're not interested in at the moment.

Finding Needles in Haystacks with the SELECT Statement

SQL's primary tool for retrieving information from a database is the SELECT statement. In its simplest form, with one modifying clause (a FROM clause), it retrieves everything from a table. By adding more modifying clauses, you can whittle down what it retrieves until you are getting exactly what you want, no more and no less.

Suppose you want to display a complete list of all the customers in your CUSTOMER table, including every piece of data that the table stores about each one. That is the simplest retrieval you can do. Here's the syntax:

```
SELECT * FROM CUSTOMER ;
```

The asterisk (*) is a wildcard character that means *all columns*. This statement returns all the data held in all the rows of the CUSTOMER table. Sometimes that is exactly what you want. At other times, you may only want *some* of the data on *some* of the customers: those that satisfy one or more conditions. For such refined retrievals, you must use one or more modifying clauses.

Modifying Clauses

In any SELECT statement, the FROM clause is mandatory. You *must* specify the source of the data you want to retrieve. Other modifying clauses are optional. They serve several different functions:

>> The WHERE clause specifies a condition. Only those table rows that satisfy the condition are returned.

>> The GROUP BY clause rearranges the order of the rows returned by placing rows together that have the same value in a grouping column.

>> The HAVING clause filters out groups that do not meet a specified condition.

>> The ORDER BY clause sorts whatever is left after all the other modifying clauses have had a chance to operate.

The next few sections look at these clauses in greater detail.

FROM clauses

The FROM clause is easy to understand if you specify only one table, as in the previous example.

```
SELECT * FROM CUSTOMER ;
```

This statement returns all the data in all the rows of every column in the CUSTOMER table. You can, however, specify more than one table in a FROM clause. Consider the following example:

```
SELECT *
    FROM CUSTOMER, INVOICE ;
```

This statement forms a virtual table that combines the data from the CUSTOMER table with the data from the INVOICE table. Each row in the CUSTOMER table combines with every row in the INVOICE table to form the new table. The new virtual table that this combination forms contains the number of rows in the CUSTOMER table multiplied by the number of rows in the INVOICE table. If the CUSTOMER table has 10 rows and the INVOICE table has 100, the new virtual table has 1,000 rows.

This operation is called the *Cartesian product* of the two source tables. The Cartesian product is a type of JOIN. Book 4, Chapter 7 covers JOIN operations in detail.

In most applications, the majority of the rows that form as a result of taking the Cartesian product of two tables are meaningless. In the case of the virtual table that forms from the CUSTOMER and INVOICE tables, only the rows where the CustomerID from the CUSTOMER table matches the CustomerID from the INVOICE table would be of any real interest. You can filter out the rest of the rows by using a WHERE clause.

Row pattern recognition is a new capability that was added to the FROM clause in SQL:2016. It enables you to find patterns in a data set. The capability is particularly useful in finding patterns in time series data, such as stock market quotes or any other data set where it would be helpful to know when a trend reverses direction. The row pattern recognition operation is accomplished with a MATCH_RECOGNIZE clause within an SQL statement's FROM clause. The syntax of the row pattern recognition operation is more complex than required for this overview of modifying clauses. It is described in detail in ISO/IEC TR 19075-5:2016(E), Section 3, which is available for free from ISO. As of this writing, of the major RDBMS products, only Oracle implements row pattern recognition.

WHERE clauses

This book often uses the WHERE clause without really explaining it because its meaning and use are obvious: A statement performs an operation (such as a SELECT, DELETE, or UPDATE) only on table rows where a stated condition is TRUE. The syntax of the WHERE clause is as follows:

```
SELECT column_list
    FROM table_name
    WHERE condition ;
```

```
DELETE FROM table_name
    WHERE condition ;

UPDATE table_name
    SET column₁=value₁, column₂=value₂, ..., columnₙ=valueₙ
    WHERE condition ;
```

The condition in the WHERE clause may be simple or arbitrarily complex. You may join multiple conditions together by using the logical connectives AND, OR, and NOT (discussed later in this chapter) to create a single condition.

The following statements show you some typical examples of WHERE clauses:

```
WHERE CUSTOMER.CustomerID = INVOICE.CustomerID
WHERE MECHANIC.EmployeeID = CERTIFICATION.MechanicID
WHERE PART.QuantityInStock < 10
WHERE PART.QuantityInStock > 100 AND PART.CostBasis > 100.00
```

The conditions that these WHERE clauses express are known as predicates. A *predicate* is an expression that asserts a fact about values.

The predicate PART.QuantityInStock < 10, for example, is True if the value for the current row of the column PART.QuantityInStock is less than 10. If the assertion is True, it satisfies the condition. An assertion may be True, False, or UNKNOWN. The UNKNOWN case arises if one or more elements in the assertion are null. The *comparison predicates* (=, <, >, <>, <=, and >=) are the most common, but SQL offers several others that greatly increase your capability to distinguish or filter out a desired data item from others in the same column. The following list notes the predicates that give you that filtering capability:

>> Comparison predicates

>> BETWEEN

>> IN [NOT IN]

>> LIKE [NOT LIKE]

>> NULL

>> ALL, SOME, and ANY

>> EXISTS

>> UNIQUE

>> DISTINCT

>> OVERLAPS

>> MATCH

The mechanics of filtering can get a bit complicated, so the following sections explain the mechanics of each predicate in the preceding list.

Comparison predicates

The examples in the preceding section show typical uses of comparison predicates in which you compare one value to another. For every row in which the comparison evaluates to a True value, that value satisfies the WHERE clause, and the operation (SELECT, UPDATE, DELETE, or whatever) executes upon that row. Rows that the comparison evaluates to FALSE are skipped. Consider the following SQL statement:

```
SELECT * FROM PART
    WHERE QuantityInStock < 10 ;
```

This statement displays all rows from the PART table that have a value of less than 10 in the QuantityInStock column.

Six comparison predicates are listed in Table 4-1.

TABLE 4-1

SQL's Comparison Predicates

Comparison	Symbol
Equal	=
Not equal	<>
Less than	<
Less than or equal	<=
Greater than	>
Greater than or equal	>=

BETWEEN

Sometimes, you want to select a row if the value in a column falls within a specified range. One way to make this selection is by using comparison predicates. For example, you can formulate a WHERE clause to select all the rows in the PART table that have a value in the QuantityInStock column greater than 10 and less than 100, as follows:

```
WHERE PART.QuantityInStock > 10 AND PART.QuantityInStock < 100
```

This comparison doesn't include parts with a quantity in stock of exactly 10 or 100 — only those values that fall in between these two numbers. To include the end points, you can write the statement as follows:

```
WHERE PART.QuantityInStock >= 10 AND PART.QuantityInStock <= 100
```

Another (potentially simpler) way of specifying a range that includes the end points is to use a BETWEEN predicate, like this:

```
WHERE PART.QuantityInStock BETWEEN 10 AND 100
```

This clause is functionally identical to the preceding example, which uses comparison predicates. This formulation saves some typing and is a little more intuitive than the one that uses two comparison predicates joined by the logical connective AND.

WARNING

The BETWEEN keyword may be confusing because it doesn't tell you explicitly whether the clause includes the end points. In fact, the clause *does* include these end points. BETWEEN also fails to tell you explicitly that the first term in the comparison must be equal to or less than the second. If, for example, PART.Quantity InStock contains a value of 50, the following clause returns a TRUE value:

```
WHERE PART.QuantityInStock BETWEEN 10 AND 100
```

However, a clause that you may think is equivalent to the preceding example returns the opposite result, False:

```
WHERE PART.QuantityInStock BETWEEN 100 AND 10
```

REMEMBER

If you use BETWEEN, you must be able to guarantee that the first term in your comparison is always equal to or less than the second term.

You can use the BETWEEN predicate with character, bit, and datetime data types as well as with the numeric types. You may see something like the following example:

```
SELECT FirstName, LastName
    FROM CUSTOMER
    WHERE CUSTOMER.LastName BETWEEN 'A' AND 'Mzzz' ;
```

This example returns all customers whose last names are in the first half of the alphabet.

IN and NOT IN

The IN and NOT IN predicates deal with whether specified values (such as GA, AL, and MS) are contained within a particular set of values (such as the states of the United States). You may, for example, have a table that lists suppliers of a commodity that your company purchases regularly. You want to know the phone numbers of those suppliers in the southern United States. You can find these numbers by using comparison predicates, such as those shown in the following example:

```
SELECT Company, Phone
   FROM SUPPLIER
   WHERE State = 'GA' OR State = 'AL' OR State = 'MS' ;
```

You can also use the IN predicate to perform the same task, as follows:

```
SELECT Company, Phone
   FROM SUPPLIER
   WHERE State IN ('GA', 'AL', 'MS') ;
```

This formulation is more compact than the one using comparison predicates and logical OR.

The NOT IN version of this predicate works the same way. Say that you have locations in New York, New Jersey, and Connecticut, and to avoid paying sales tax, you want to consider using suppliers located anywhere except in those states. Use the following construction:

```
SELECT Company, Phone
   FROM SUPPLIER
   WHERE State NOT IN ('NY', 'NJ', 'CT') ;
```

Using the IN keyword this way saves you a little typing. Saving a little typing, however, isn't that great an advantage. You can do the same job using comparison predicates, as shown in this section's first example.

TIP

You may have another good reason to use the IN predicate rather than comparison predicates, even if using IN doesn't save much typing. Your DBMS probably implements the two methods differently, and one of the methods may be significantly faster than the other on your system. You may want to run a performance comparison on the two ways of expressing inclusion in (or exclusion from) a group and then use the technique that produces the quicker result. A DBMS with a good optimizer will probably choose the more efficient method regardless of which kind of predicate you use. A performance comparison gives you some idea of how good your DBMS's optimizer is. If a significant difference between the run times of the two statements exists, the quality of your DBMS's optimizer is called into question.

The IN keyword is valuable in another area, too. If IN is part of a subquery, the keyword enables you to pull information from two tables to obtain results that you can't derive from a single table. Book 4, Chapter 6 covers subqueries in detail, but following is an example that shows how a subquery uses the IN keyword.

Suppose that you want to display the names of all customers who've bought the flux capacitor product in the last 30 days. Customer names are in the CUSTOMER table, and sales transaction data is in the PART table. You can use the following query:

```
SELECT FirstName, LastName
  FROM CUSTOMER
  WHERE CustomerID IN
    (SELECT CustomerID
      FROM INVOICE
      WHERE SalesDate >= (CurrentDate - 30) AND InvoiceNo IN
        (SELECT InvoiceNo
          FROM INVOICE_LINE
          WHERE PartNo IN
            (SELECT PartNo
              FROM PART
              WHERE NAME = 'flux capacitor' ) ;
```

The inner SELECT of the INVOICE table nests within the outer SELECT of the CUSTOMER table. The inner SELECT of the INVOICE_LINE table nests within the outer SELECT of the INVOICE table. The inner select of the PART table nests within the outer SELECT of the INVOICE_LINE table. The SELECT on the INVOICE table finds the CustomerID numbers of all customers who bought the flux capacitor product in the last 30 days. The outermost SELECT (on the CUSTOMER table) displays the first and last names of all customers whose CustomerID is retrieved by the inner SELECT statements.

LIKE and NOT LIKE

You can use the LIKE predicate to compare two character strings for a partial match. Partial matches are valuable if you don't know the exact form of the string for which you're searching. You can also use partial matches to retrieve multiple rows that contain similar strings in one of the table's columns.

To identify partial matches, SQL uses two wildcard characters. The percent sign (%) can stand for any string of characters that have zero or more characters. The underscore (_) stands for any single character. Table 4-2 provides some examples that show how to use LIKE.

TABLE 4-2

SQL's LIKE Predicate

Statement	Values Returned
WHERE String LIKE 'auto%'	auto
	automotive
	automobile
	automatic
	autocracy
WHERE String LIKE '%ode%'	code of conduct
	model citizen
WHERE String LIKE '_o_e'	mope
	tote
	rope
	love
	cone
	node

The NOT LIKE predicate retrieves all rows that don't satisfy a partial match, including one or more wildcard characters, as in the following example:

```
WHERE Email NOT LIKE '%@databasecentral.info'
```

This example returns all the rows in the table where the email address is not hosted at www.DatabaseCentral.Info.

NULL

The NULL predicate finds all rows where the value in the selected column is null. In the photographic paper price list table described in Book 4, Chapter 3, several rows have null values in the Size11 column. You can retrieve their names by using a statement such as the following:

```
SELECT (PaperType)
    FROM PAPERS
    WHERE Size11Price IS NULL ;
```

This query returns the following values:

```
Dual-sided HW semigloss
Universal two-sided matte
Transparency
```

As you may expect, including the NOT keyword reverses the result, as in the following example:

```
SELECT (PaperType)
    FROM PAPERS
    WHERE Size11Price IS NOT NULL ;
```

This query returns all the rows in the table except the three that the preceding query returns.

WARNING

The statement Size11Price IS NULL is not the same as Size11Price = NULL. To illustrate this point, assume that, in the current row of the PAPERS table, both Size11Price and Size8Price are null. From this fact, you can draw the following conclusions:

>> Size11Price IS NULL is True.

>> Size8Price IS NULL is True.

>> (Size11Price IS NULL AND Size8Price IS NULL) is True.

>> Size11Price = Size8Price is unknown.

Size11Price = NULL is an illegal expression. Using the keyword NULL in a comparison is meaningless because the answer always returns as *unknown*.

Why is Size11Price = Size8Price defined as unknown, even though Size11Price and Size8Price have the same (null) value? Because NULL simply means, "I don't know." You don't know what Size11Price is, and you don't know what Size8Price is; therefore, you don't know whether those (unknown) values are the same. Maybe Size11Price is 9.95, and Size8Price is 8.95; or maybe Size11Price is 10.95, and Size8Price is 10.95. If you don't know both the Size11 value and the Size8 value, you can't say whether the two are the same.

ALL, SOME, and ANY

Thousands of years ago, the Greek philosopher Aristotle formulated a system of logic that became the basis for much of Western thought. The essence of this logic is to start with a set of premises that you know to be true, apply valid operations to these premises, and thereby arrive at new truths. The classic example of this procedure is as follows:

> *Premise 1:* All Greeks are human.
>
> *Premise 2:* All humans are mortal.
>
> *Conclusion:* All Greeks are mortal.

Another example:

> *Premise 1:* Some Greeks are women.
>
> *Premise 2:* All women are human.
>
> *Conclusion:* Some Greeks are human.

Another way of stating the same logical idea of this second example is as follows:

> If any Greeks are women and all women are human, then some Greeks are human.

ANY CAN BE AMBIGUOUS

The original SQL used the word ANY for existential quantification. This usage turned out to be confusing and error-prone because the English language connotations of *any* are sometimes universal and sometimes existential:

- "Do any of you know where Wilbur Street is?"
- "I can eat more pizza than any of you."

The first sentence is probably asking whether at least one person knows where Wilbur Street is. *Any* is used as an existential quantifier. The second sentence, however, is a boast that states I can eat more pizza than the biggest eater among all you people can eat. In this case, *any* is used as a universal quantifier.

Thus, for the SQL-92 standard, the developers retained the word ANY for compatibility with early products but added the word SOME as a less confusing synonym. SQL continues to support both existential quantifiers.

The first example uses the universal quantifier ALL in both premises, enabling you to make a sound deduction about all Greeks in the conclusion. The second example uses the existential quantifier SOME in one premise, enabling you to make a deduction about some, but not all, Greeks in the conclusion. The third example uses the existential quantifier ANY, which is a synonym for SOME, to reach the same conclusion you reach in the second example.

Look at how SOME, ANY, and ALL apply in SQL.

Consider an example in baseball statistics. Baseball is a physically demanding sport, especially for pitchers. A pitcher must throw the baseball from the pitcher's mound, at speeds up to 100 miles per hour, to home plate between 90 and 150 times during a game. This effort can be very tiring, and many times, the starting pitcher becomes ineffective, and a relief pitcher must replace him before the game ends. Pitching an entire game is an outstanding achievement, regardless of whether the effort results in a victory.

Suppose that you're keeping track of the number of complete games that all Major League pitchers pitch. In one table, you list all the American League pitchers, and in another table, you list all the National League pitchers. Both tables contain the players' first names, last names, and number of complete games pitched.

The American League permits a designated hitter (DH) (who isn't required to play a defensive position) to bat in place of any of the nine players who play defense. Usually, the DH bats for the pitcher because pitchers are notoriously poor hitters. (Pitchers must spend so much time and effort on perfecting their pitching that they do not have as much time to practice batting as the other players.)

Say that you speculate that, on average, American League starting pitchers throw more complete games than National League starting pitchers. This is based on your observation that designated hitters enable hard-throwing but weak-hitting, American League pitchers to stay in close games. Because the DH is already batting for them, the fact that they are poor hitters is not a liability. In the National League, however, a pinch hitter would replace a comparable National League pitcher in a close game because he would have a better chance of getting a hit. To test your idea, you formulate the following query:

```
SELECT FirstName, LastName
    FROM AMERICAN_LEAGUER
    WHERE CompleteGames > ALL
        (SELECT CompleteGames
            FROM NATIONAL_LEAGUER) ;
```

The subquery (the inner SELECT) returns a list showing every National League pitcher and the number of complete games he pitched. The outer query returns the first and last names of all American Leaguers who pitched more complete games than ALL of the National Leaguers. In other words, the query returns the names of those American League pitchers who pitched more complete games than the pitcher who has thrown the most complete games in the National League.

Consider the following similar statement:

```
SELECT FirstName, LastName
   FROM AMERICAN_LEAGUER
   WHERE CompleteGames > ANY
      (SELECT CompleteGames
         FROM NATIONAL_LEAGUER) ;
```

In this case, you use the existential quantifier ANY rather than the universal quantifier ALL. The subquery (the inner, nested query) is identical to the subquery in the previous example. This subquery retrieves a complete list of the game statistics for all the National League pitchers. The outer query returns the first and last names of all American League pitchers who pitched more complete games than ANY National League pitcher. Because you can be virtually certain that at least one National League pitcher hasn't pitched a complete game, the result probably includes all American League pitchers who've pitched at least one complete game.

If you replace the keyword ANY with the equivalent keyword SOME, the result is the same. If the statement that at least one National League pitcher hasn't pitched a complete game is true, you can then say that SOME National League pitcher hasn't pitched a complete game.

EXISTS

You can use the EXISTS predicate in conjunction with a subquery to determine whether the subquery returns any rows. If the subquery returns at least one row, that result satisfies the EXISTS condition, and the outer query executes. Consider the following example:

```
SELECT FirstName, LastName
   FROM CUSTOMER
   WHERE EXISTS
      (SELECT DISTINCT CustomerID
         FROM INVOICE
         WHERE INVOICE.CustomerID = CUSTOMER.CustomerID);
```

The INVOICE table contains all your company's sales transactions. The table includes the CustomerID of the customer who makes each purchase, as well as other pertinent information. The CUSTOMER table contains each customer's first and last names but no information about specific transactions.

The subquery in the preceding example returns a row for every customer who has made at least one purchase. The DISTINCT keyword assures you that you retrieve only one copy of each CustomerID, even if a customer has made more than one purchase. The outer query returns the first and last names of the customers who made the purchases that the INVOICE table records.

UNIQUE

As you do with the EXISTS predicate, you use the UNIQUE predicate with a subquery. Although the EXISTS predicate evaluates to TRUE only if the subquery returns at least one row, the UNIQUE predicate evaluates to TRUE only if no two rows that the subquery returns are identical. In other words, the UNIQUE predicate evaluates to TRUE *only* if all rows that its subquery returns are unique. Consider the following example:

```
SELECT FirstName, LastName
   FROM CUSTOMER
   WHERE UNIQUE
     (SELECT CustomerID FROM INVOICE
        WHERE INVOICE.CustomerID = CUSTOMER.CustomerID);
```

This statement retrieves the names of all first-time customers for whom the INVOICE table records only one sale. Two null values are considered not equal to each other and thus unique. When the UNIQUE keyword is applied to a result table containing only two null rows, the UNIQUE predicate evaluates to True.

DISTINCT

The DISTINCT predicate is similar to the UNIQUE predicate, except in the way it treats nulls. If all the values in a result table are UNIQUE, they're also DISTINCT from each other. However, unlike the result for the UNIQUE predicate, if the DISTINCT keyword is applied to a result table that contains only two null rows, the DISTINCT predicate evaluates to False. Two null values are *not* considered distinct from each other, while at the same time, they are considered to be unique. This strange situation seems contradictory, but there's a reason for it. In some situations, you may want to treat two null values as different from each other, whereas, in other situations, you want to treat them as if they're the same. In the first case, use the UNIQUE predicate. In the second case, use the DISTINCT predicate.

OVERLAPS

You use the OVERLAPS predicate to determine whether two time intervals overlap each other. This predicate is useful for avoiding scheduling conflicts. If the two intervals overlap, the predicate returns a True value. If they don't overlap, the predicate returns a False value.

You can specify an interval in two ways: either as a start time and an end time or as a start time and a duration. Following are a few examples:

```
(TIME '2:55:00', INTERVAL '1' HOUR)
OVERLAPS
(TIME '3:30:00', INTERVAL '2' HOUR)
```

The preceding example returns a True because 3:30 is less than one hour after 2:55.

```
(TIME '9:00:00', TIME '9:30:00')
OVERLAPS
(TIME '9:29:00', TIME '9:31:00')
```

The preceding example returns a True because you have a one-minute overlap between the two intervals.

```
(TIME '9:00:00', TIME '10:00:00')
OVERLAPS
(TIME '10:15:00', INTERVAL '3' HOUR)
```

The preceding example returns a False because the two intervals don't overlap.

```
(TIME '9:00:00', TIME '9:30:00')
OVERLAPS
(TIME '9:30:00', TIME '9:35:00')
```

This example returns a False because even though the two intervals are contiguous, they don't overlap.

MATCH

Referential integrity involves maintaining consistency in a multitable database. You can lose integrity by adding a row to a child table that doesn't have a corresponding row in the child's parent table. You can cause similar problems by deleting a row from a parent table if rows corresponding to that row exist in a child table.

Say that your business has a CUSTOMER table that keeps track of all your customers and a TRANSACT table that records all sales transactions. You don't want to add a row to TRANSACT until after you enter the customer making the purchase into the CUSTOMER table. You also don't want to delete a customer from the CUSTOMER table if that customer made purchases that exist in the TRANSACT table. Before you perform an insertion or deletion, you may want to check the candidate row to make sure that inserting or deleting that row doesn't cause integrity problems. The MATCH predicate can perform such a check.

To examine the MATCH predicate, consider an example that employs the CUSTOMER and TRANSACT tables. CustomerID is the primary key of the CUSTOMER table and acts as a foreign key in the TRANSACT table. Every row in the CUSTOMER table must have a unique, nonnull CustomerID. CustomerID isn't unique in the TRANSACT table because repeat customers buy more than once. This situation is fine and does not threaten integrity because CustomerID is a foreign key rather than a primary key in that table.

TIP

Seemingly, CustomerID can be null in the TRANSACT table because someone can walk in off the street, buy something, and walk out before you get a chance to enter their name and address into the CUSTOMER table. This situation can create a row in the child table with no corresponding row in the parent table. To overcome this problem, you can create a generic customer in the CUSTOMER table and assign all such anonymous sales to that customer.

Say that a customer steps up to the cash register and claims that they bought a flux capacitor on January 15, 2019. They now want to return the device because they have discovered that their DeLorean lacks time circuits, and so the flux capacitor is of no use. You can verify their claim by searching your TRANSACT database for a match. First, you must retrieve their CustomerID into the variable vcustid; then you can use the following syntax:

```
... WHERE (:vcustid, 'flux capacitor', '2019-01-15')
        MATCH
        (SELECT CustomerID, ProductName, Date
            FROM TRANSACT)
```

If a sale exists for that customer ID for that product on that date, the MATCH predicate returns a True value. Take back the product and refund the customer's money. (Note: If any values in the first argument of the MATCH predicate are null, a True value always returns.)

TECHNICAL STUFF

SQL's developers added the MATCH predicate and the UNIQUE predicate for the same reason — to provide a way to explicitly perform the tests defined for the implicit referential integrity (RI) and UNIQUE constraints. (See the next section for more on referential integrity.)

The general form of the MATCH predicate is as follows:

```
Row_value MATCH [UNIQUE] [SIMPLE| PARTIAL | FULL ] Subquery
```

The UNIQUE, SIMPLE, PARTIAL, and FULL options relate to rules that come into play if the row value expression R has one or more columns that are null. The rules for the MATCH predicate are a copy of corresponding referential integrity rules.

The MATCH predicate and referential integrity

Referential integrity rules require that the values of a column or columns in one table match the values of a column or columns in another table. You refer to the columns in the first table as the *foreign key* and the columns in the second table as the *primary key* or *unique key*. For example, you may declare the column EmpDeptNo in an EMPLOYEE table as a foreign key that references the DeptNo column of a DEPT table. This matchup ensures that if you record an employee in the EMPLOYEE table as working in department 123, a row appears in the DEPT table, where DeptNo is 123.

This situation is fairly straightforward if the foreign key and primary key both consist of a single column. The two keys can, however, consist of multiple columns. The DeptNo value, for example, may be unique only within a Location; therefore, to uniquely identify a DEPT row, you must specify both a Location and a DeptNo. If both the Boston and Tampa offices have a department 123, you need to identify the departments as ('Boston', '123') and ('Tampa', '123'). In this case, the EMPLOYEE table needs two columns to identify a DEPT. Call those columns EmpLoc and EmpDeptNo. If an employee works in department 123 in Boston, the EmpLoc and EmpDeptNo values are 'Boston' and '123'. And the foreign key declaration in EMPLOYEE is as follows:

```
FOREIGN KEY (EmpLoc, EmpDeptNo)
    REFERENCES DEPT (Location, DeptNo)
```

Drawing valid conclusions from your data is complicated immensely if the data contains nulls. Sometimes, you want to treat null-containing data one way, and sometimes, you want to treat it another way. The UNIQUE, SIMPLE, PARTIAL, and FULL keywords specify different ways of treating data that contains nulls. If your data does not contain any null values, you can save yourself a lot of head-scratching by merely skipping to the section called "Logical connectives" later in this chapter. If your data *does* contain null values, drop out of Evelyn Wood speed-reading mode now and read the following paragraphs slowly and carefully. Each paragraph presents a different situation with respect to null values and tells how the MATCH predicate handles it.

If the values of EmpLoc and EmpDeptNo are both nonnull or both null, the referential integrity rules are the same as for single-column keys with values that are null or nonnull. But if EmpLoc is null and EmpDeptNo is nonnull — or EmpLoc is nonnull and EmpDeptNo is null — you need new rules. What should the rules be if you insert or update the EMPLOYEE table with EmpLoc and EmpDeptNo values of (NULL, '123') or ('Boston', NULL)? You have six main alternatives: SIMPLE, PARTIAL, and FULL, each either with or without the UNIQUE keyword. The UNIQUE keyword, if present, means that a matching row in the subquery result table must be unique in order for the predicate to evaluate to a True value. If both components of the row value expression R are null, the MATCH predicate returns a True value regardless of the contents of the subquery result table being compared.

If neither component of the row value expression R is null, SIMPLE is specified, UNIQUE is not specified, and at least one row in the subquery result table matches R, the MATCH predicate returns a True value. Otherwise, it returns a False value.

If neither component of the row value expression R is null, SIMPLE is specified, UNIQUE is specified, and at least one row in the subquery result table is both unique and matches R, the MATCH predicate returns a True value. Otherwise, it returns a False value.

If any component of the row value expression R is null and SIMPLE is specified, the MATCH predicate returns a True value.

If any component of the row value expression R is nonnull, PARTIAL is specified, UNIQUE is not specified, and the nonnull parts of at least one row in the subquery result table matches R, the MATCH predicate returns a True value. Otherwise, it returns a False value.

If any component of the row value expression R is nonnull, PARTIAL is specified, UNIQUE is specified, and the nonnull parts of R match the nonnull parts of at least one unique row in the subquery result table, the MATCH predicate returns a True value. Otherwise, it returns a False value.

If neither component of the row value expression R is null, FULL is specified, UNIQUE is not specified, and at least one row in the subquery result table matches R, the MATCH predicate returns a True value. Otherwise, it returns a False value.

If neither component of the row value expression R is null, FULL is specified, UNIQUE is specified, and at least one row in the subquery result table is both unique and matches R, the MATCH predicate returns a True value. Otherwise, it returns a False value.

If any component of the row value expression R is null and FULL is specified, the MATCH predicate returns a False value.

Logical connectives

Often, as a number of previous examples show, applying one condition in a query isn't enough to return the rows that you want from a table. In some cases, the rows must satisfy two or more conditions. In other cases, if a row satisfies any of two or more conditions, it qualifies for retrieval. On other occasions, you want to retrieve only rows that don't satisfy a specified condition. To meet these needs, SQL offers the logical connectives AND, OR, and NOT.

AND

If multiple conditions must all be True before you can retrieve a row, use the AND logical connective. Consider the following example:

```
SELECT InvoiceNo, SaleDate, SalesPerson, TotalSale
    FROM SALES
    WHERE SaleDate >= '2019-01-16'
        AND SaleDate <= '2019-01-22' ;
```

The WHERE clause must meet the following two conditions:

» SaleDate must be greater than or equal to January 16, 2019.

» SaleDate must be less than or equal to January 22, 2019.

Only rows that record sales occurring during the week of January 16 meet both conditions. The query returns only these rows.

WARNING

Notice that the AND connective is strictly logical. This restriction can sometimes be confusing because people commonly use the word *and* with a looser meaning. For example, suppose that your boss says to you, "I'd like to see the sales for Acheson and Bryant." They said, "Acheson and Bryant," so you may write the following SQL query:

```
SELECT *
    FROM SALES
    WHERE Salesperson = 'Acheson'
        AND Salesperson = 'Bryant';
```

Well, don't take that answer back to your boss. The following query is more like what they had in mind:

```
SELECT *
    FROM SALES
    WHERE Salesperson IN ('Acheson', 'Bryant') ;
```

The first query won't return anything, because none of the sales in the SALES table were made by *both* Acheson and Bryant. The second query returns the information on all sales made by either Acheson or Bryant, which is probably what the boss wanted.

OR

If any one of two or more conditions must be True to qualify a row for retrieval, use the OR logical connective, as in the following example:

```
SELECT InvoiceNo, SaleDate, Salesperson, TotalSale
    FROM SALES
        WHERE Salesperson = 'Bryant'
            OR TotalSale > 200 ;
```

This query retrieves all of Bryant's sales, regardless of how large, as well as all sales of more than $200, regardless of who made the sales.

NOT

The NOT connective negates a condition. If the condition normally returns a True value, adding NOT causes the same condition to return a False value. If a condition normally returns a False value, adding NOT causes the condition to return a True value. Consider the following example:

```
SELECT InvoiceNo, SaleDate, Salesperson, TotalSale
    FROM SALES
        WHERE NOT (Salesperson = 'Bryant') ;
```

This query returns rows for all sales transactions completed by salespeople other than Bryant.

WARNING

When you use AND, OR, or NOT, sometimes the scope of the connective isn't clear. To be safe, use parentheses to make sure that SQL applies the connective to the predicate you want. In the preceding example, the NOT connective applies to the entire predicate (Salesperson = 'Bryant').

GROUP BY clauses

Sometimes, instead of retrieving individual records, you want to know something about a group of records. The GROUP BY clause is the tool you need. The following examples use the AdventureWorks2017 sample database designed to work with Microsoft SQL Server 2017.

REMEMBER

SQL Server Express is a version of Microsoft SQL Server that you can download for free from www.microsoft.com.

Suppose you're the sales manager and you want to look at the performance of your sales force. You could do a simple SELECT such as the following:

```
SELECT SalesOrderId, OrderDate, LastName, TotalDue
    FROM Sales.SalesOrderHeader, Person.Person
    WHERE BusinessEntityID = SalesPersonID
        AND OrderDate >= '2011-05-01'
        AND OrderDate < '2011-05-31'
```

You would receive a result similar to that shown in Figure 4-1. In this database, SalesOrderHeader is a table in the Sales schema and Person is a table in the Person schema. BusinessEntityID is the primary key of the SalesOrderHeader table, and SalesPersonID is the primary key of the Person table. SalesOrderID, OrderDate, and TotalDue are rows in the SalesOrderHeader table, and LastName is a row in the Person table.

This result gives you some idea of how well your salespeople are doing because relatively few sales are involved. Thirty-eight rows were returned. However, in real life, a company would have many more sales, and it wouldn't be as easy to tell whether sales objectives were being met. To do that, you can combine the GROUP BY clause with one of the *aggregate* functions (also called *set* functions) to get a quantitative picture of sales performance. For example, you can see which salesperson is selling more of the profitable high-ticket items by using the average (AVG) function as follows:

```
SELECT LastName, AVG(TotalDue)
    FROM Sales.SalesOrderHeader, Person.Person
    WHERE BusinessEntityID = SalesPersonID
        AND OrderDate >= '2011-05-01'
        AND OrderDate < '2011-05-31'
    GROUP BY LastName;
```

You would receive a result similar to that shown in Figure 4-2. The GROUP BY clause causes records to be grouped by LastName and the groups to be sorted in ascending alphabetical order.

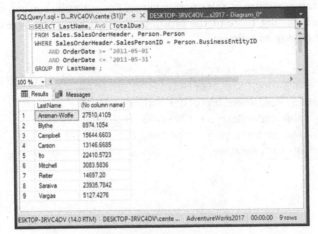

FIGURE 4-1:
The result set for
retrieval of sales
for May 2011.

As shown in Figure 4-2, Ansman-Wolfe has the highest average sales. You can compare total sales with a similar query — this time using SUM:

```
SELECT LastName, SUM(TotalDue)
    FROM Sales.SalesOrderHeader, Person.Person
    WHERE BusinessEntityID = SalesPersonID
        AND OrderDate >= '2011-05-01'
        AND OrderDate < '2011-05-31'
    GROUP BY LastName;
```

FIGURE 4-2:
Average sales for
each salesperson.

This gives the result shown in Figure 4-3. As in the previous example, the GROUP BY clause causes records to be grouped by LastName and the groups to be sorted in ascending alphabetical order.

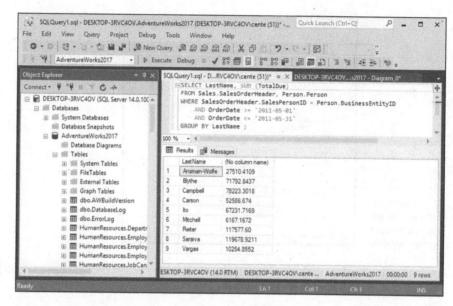

FIGURE 4-3:
Total sales for
each salesperson.

Saraiva has the highest total sales for the month. Ansman-Wolfe has apparently sold only high-ticket items, but Saraiva has sold more across the entire product line.

HAVING clauses

You can analyze the grouped data further by using the HAVING clause. The HAVING clause is a filter that acts similar to a WHERE clause, but the filter acts on groups of rows rather than individual rows. To illustrate the function of the HAVING clause, suppose Saraiva has just resigned, and the sales manager wants to display the overall data for the other salespeople. You can exclude Saraiva's sales from the grouped data by using a HAVING clause as follows:

```
SELECT LastName, SUM(TotalDue)
    FROM Sales.SalesOrderHeader, Person.Person
    WHERE BusinessEntityID = SalesPersonID
        AND OrderDate >= '2011-05-01'
        AND OrderDate <  '2011-05-31'
    GROUP BY LastName
    HAVING LastName <> 'Saraiva';
```

This gives the result shown in Figure 4-4. Only rows where the salesperson is *not* Saraiva are returned. As before, the GROUP BY clause causes records to be grouped by LastName and the groups to be sorted in ascending alphabetical order.

FIGURE 4-4: Total sales for all salespeople except Saraiva.

ORDER BY clauses

You can use the ORDER BY clause to display the output table of a query in either ascending or descending alphabetical order. Whereas the GROUP BY clause gathers rows into groups and sorts the groups into alphabetical order, ORDER BY sorts individual rows. The ORDER BY clause must be the last clause that you specify in a query. If the query also contains a GROUP BY clause, the clause first arranges the output rows into groups. The ORDER BY clause then sorts the rows within each group. If you have no GROUP BY clause, the statement considers the entire table as a group, and the ORDER BY clause sorts all its rows according to the column (or columns) that the ORDER BY clause specifies.

To illustrate this point, consider the data in the SalesOrderHeader table. The SalesOrderHeader table contains columns for SalesOrderID, OrderDate, DueDate, ShipDate, and SalesPersonID, among other things. If you use the following example, you see all the SALES data, but in an arbitrary order:

```
SELECT * FROM Sales.SalesOrderHeader ;
```

In one implementation, this order may be the one in which you inserted the rows in the table, and in another, the order may be that of the most recent updates. The order can also change unexpectedly if anyone physically reorganizes the database.

Usually, you want to specify the order in which you want to display the rows. You may, for example, want to see the rows in order by the OrderDate, as follows:

```
SELECT * FROM Sales.SalesOrderHeader ORDER BY OrderDate ;
```

This example returns all the rows in the SalesOrderHeader table in ascending order by OrderDate.

For rows with the same OrderDate, the default order depends on the implementation. You can, however, specify how to sort the rows that share the same OrderDate. You may want to see the orders for each OrderDate in order by SalesOrderID, as follows:

```
SELECT * FROM Sales.SalesOrderHeader ORDER BY OrderDate,
    SalesOrderID ;
```

This example first orders the sales by OrderDate then for each OrderDate, it orders the sales by SalesOrderID. But don't confuse that example with the following query:

```
SELECT * FROM Sales.SalesOrderHeader ORDER BY SalesOrderID,
    OrderDate ;
```

This query first orders the sales by SalesOrderID. Then for each different SalesOrderID, the query orders the sales by OrderDate. This probably won't yield the result you want because it is unlikely that multiple order dates exist for a single sales order number.

The following query is another example of how SQL can return data:

```
SELECT * FROM Sales.SalesOrderHeader ORDER BY SalesPersonID,
    OrderDate ;
```

This example first orders by salesperson and then by order date. After you look at the data in that order, you may want to invert it, as follows:

```
SELECT * FROM Sales.SalesPersonID ORDER BY OrderDate,
    SalesPersonID ;
```

This example orders the rows first by order date and then by salesperson.

All these ordering examples are ascending (ASC), which is the default sort order. In the AdventureWorks2017 sample database, this last SELECT would show earlier sales first and, within a given date, show sales for 'Ansman-Wolfe' before

'Blythe'. If you prefer descending (DESC) order, you can specify this order for one or more of the order columns, as follows:

```
SELECT * FROM Sales.SalesPersonID ORDER BY OrderDate DESC,
    SalesPersonID ASC;
```

This example specifies a descending order for order date, showing the more recent orders first, and an ascending order for salespeople.

IN THIS CHAPTER

» **Avoiding retrieving duplicate records**

» **Managing multiple selection conditions**

» **Saving resources with temporary tables**

» **Filtering out groups that don't meet a search condition**

» **Working with indexes**

Chapter **5**

Tuning Queries

Performance is almost always a top priority for any organizational database system. As the usage of the system goes up, if resources such as processor speed, cache memory, and hard disk storage do not go up proportionally, performance starts to suffer, and users start to complain. Clearly, one thing that a system administrator can do is increase the resources — install a faster processor, add more cache, buy more hard disks. These solutions may give the needed improvement and may even be necessary, but you should try a cheaper solution first: improving the efficiency of the queries that are loading down the system.

Generally, there are several different ways that you can obtain the information you want from a database; in other words, there are several different ways that you can code a query. Some of those ways are more efficient than others. If one or more queries that are run on a regular basis are bogging down the system, you may be able to bring your system back up to speed without spending a penny on additional hardware. You may just have to recode the queries that are causing the bottleneck.

Popular database management systems have query optimizers that try to eliminate bottlenecks for you, but they don't always do as well as you could if you tested various alternatives and picked the one with the best performance.

Unfortunately, no general rules apply across the board. The way a database is structured and the columns that are indexed have definite effects. In addition, a coding practice that would be optimal if you use Microsoft SQL Server might result in the worst possible performance if you use Oracle. Because the different DBMSs do things in different ways, what is good for one is not necessarily good for another. There are some things you can do, however, that enable you to find good query plans. This chapter shows you some common situations.

SELECT DISTINCT

You use SELECT DISTINCT when you want to make sure there are no duplicates in records you retrieve. However, the DISTINCT keyword potentially adds overhead to a query that could impact system performance. The impact it may or may not have depends on how it is implemented by the DBMS. Furthermore, including the DISTINCT keyword in a SELECT operation may not even be needed to ensure there are no duplicates. If you are doing a select on a primary key, the result set is guaranteed to contain no duplicates anyway, so adding the DISTINCT keyword provides no advantage.

Instead of relying on general rules such as, "Avoid using the DISTINCT keyword if you can," if you suspect that a query that includes a DISTINCT keyword is inefficient, test it to see. First, make a typical query into Microsoft's Adventure-Works2017 sample database. The AdventureWorks2017 database contains records typical of a commercial enterprise. There is a Customer table and a SalesOrder-Header table, among others. One thing you might want to do is see what companies in the Customer table have actually placed orders, as recorded in the Orders table. Because a customer may place multiple orders, it makes sense to use the DISTINCT keyword so that only one row is returned for each customer. Here's the code for the query:

```
SELECT DISTINCT SalesOrderHeader.CustomerID, Customer.StoreID, SalesOrderHeader.
    TotalDue
  FROM Sales.Customer, Sales.SalesOrderHeader
  WHERE Customer.CustomerID = SalesOrderHeader.CustomerID ;
```

Before executing this query, click on the Include Client Statistics icon to select it. Then click the Execute button.

You can see the result in Figure 5-1, which shows the first few customer ID numbers of the 31,349 companies that have placed at least one order.

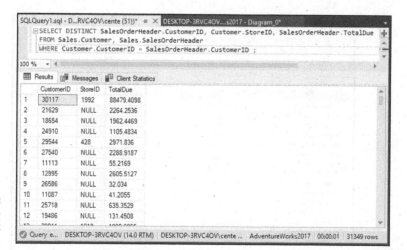

FIGURE 5-1:
Customers who have placed at least one order.

This query uses CustomerID to link the Customer table to the SalesOrderHeader table so that information can be pulled from both.

It would be interesting to see how efficient this query is. Use Microsoft SQL Server 2017's tools to find out. First, look at the execution plan that was followed to run this query in Figure 5-2. To see the execution plan, click the Estimated Execution Plan icon in the toolbar.

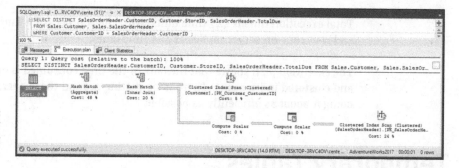

FIGURE 5-2:
The SELECT DISTINCT query execution plan.

The execution plan shows that a hash match on an aggregation operation takes 48% of the execution time, and a hash match on an inner join takes another 20%. A clustered index scan on the primary key of the customer table takes 5% of the time, and a clustered index scan on the primary key of the SalesOrderHeader table takes 26%. To see how well or how poorly things are going, view the client statistics (Figure 5-3) by clicking the Include Client Statistics icon in the toolbar.

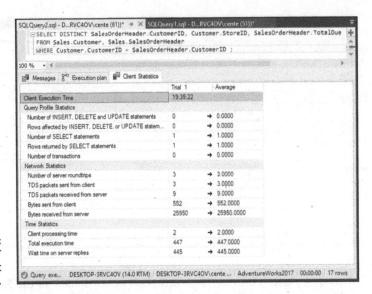

Book 4, Chapter 7 covers *inner joins*. A *clustered index scan* is a row-by-row examination of the index on a table column. In this case, the index of SalesOrderHeader.CustomerID is scanned. The hash match on the aggregation operation and the hash match on the inner join are the operations used to match up the CustomerID from the Customer table with the CustomerID from the SalesOrderHeader table.

Total execution time is 447 time units, with client processing time at 2 time units and wait time on server replies at 445 time units.

The execution plan shows that the bulk of the time consumed is due to hash joins and clustered index scans. There is no getting around these operations, and it is doing it about as efficiently as possible.

Temporary Tables

SQL is so feature-rich that there are multiple ways to perform many operations. Not all those ways are equally efficient. Often, the DBMS's optimizer dynamically changes an operation that was coded in a suboptimal way into a more efficient operation. Sometimes, however, this doesn't happen. To be sure your query is running as fast as possible, code it using a few different approaches, and then test each approach. Settle on the one that does the best job. Sometimes, the best method on one type of query performs poorly on another, so take nothing for granted.

One method of coding a query that has multiple selection conditions is to use temporary tables. Think of a temporary table as a scratchpad. You put some data in it as an intermediate step in an operation. When you are done with it, it disappears. Consider an example. Suppose you want to retrieve the last names of all the AdventureWorks employees whose first name is Janice. First, you can create a temporary table that holds the information you want from the Person table in the Person schema:

```
SELECT PersonType, FirstName, LastName INTO #Temp
    FROM Person.Person
    WHERE PersonType = 'EM' ;
```

As you can see from the code, the result of the select operation is placed into a temporary table named #Temp rather than being displayed in a window. In SQL Server, local temporary tables are identified with a # sign as the first character.

Now you can find the Janices in the #Temp table:

```
SELECT FirstName, LastName
    FROM #Temp
    WHERE FirstName = 'Janice' ;
```

Running these two queries consecutively gives the result shown in Figure 5-4.

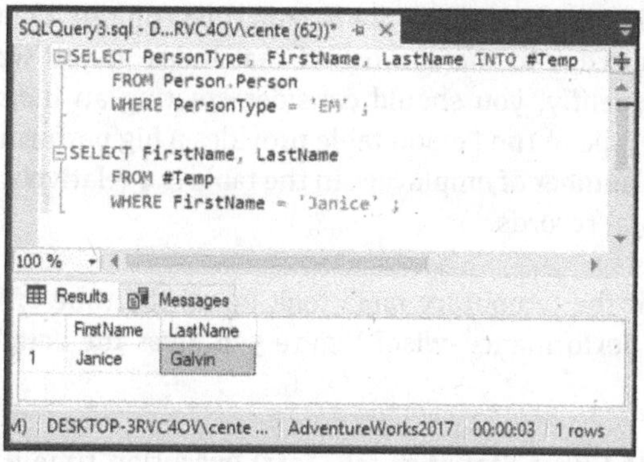

FIGURE 5-4: Retrieve all employees named Janice from the Person table.

The summary at the bottom of the screen shows that AdventureWorks has only one employee named Janice. Look at the execution plan (see Figure 5-5) to see how this retrieval was done.

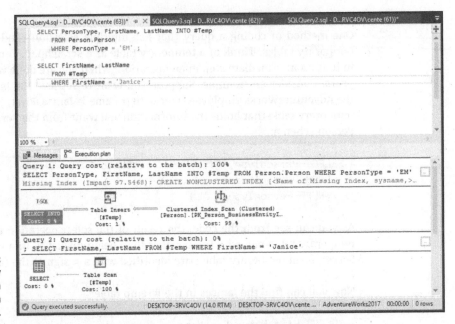

```
SELECT PersonType, FirstName, LastName INTO #Temp
  FROM Person.Person
  WHERE PersonType = 'EM' ;

SELECT FirstName, LastName
  FROM #Temp
  WHERE FirstName = 'Janice' ;
```

100 %

Messages   Execution plan

```
Query 1: Query cost (relative to the batch): 100%
SELECT PersonType, FirstName, LastName INTO #Temp FROM Person.Person WHERE PersonType = 'EM'
Missing Index (Impact 97.5468): CREATE NONCLUSTERED INDEX [<Name of Missing Index, sysname,>...
```

```
T-SQL              Table Insert <=========  Clustered Index Scan (Clustered)
SELECT INTO          [#Temp]               [Person].[PK_Person_BusinessEntityI...
Cost: 0 %          Cost: 1 %                      Cost: 99 %
```

```
Query 2: Query cost (relative to the batch): 0%
; SELECT FirstName, LastName FROM #Temp WHERE FirstName = 'Janice'
```

```
SELECT           Table Scan
Cost: 0 %          [#Temp]
                 Cost: 100 %
```

Query executed successfully.   DESKTOP-3RVC4OV (14.0 RTM)   DESKTOP-3RVC4OV\cente ...   AdventureWorks2017   00:00:00   0 rows

FIGURE 5-5:
SELECT query execution plan using a temporary table.

Creation of the temporary table to separate the employees is one operation, and finding all the Janices is another. In the Table Creation query, creating the temporary table took up only 1% of the time used. A clustered index scan on the primary key of the Person table took up the other 99%. Also, notice that a missing index was flagged with an impact of over 97, followed by a recommendation to create a nonclustered index on the PersonType column. Considering the huge impact on runtime due to the absence of that index, if you were to run queries such as this frequently, you should consider creating an index on PersonType. Indexing PersonType in the Person table provides a big performance boost in this case because the number of employees in the table is a relatively small number out of over 31,000 total records.

The table scan of the temporary table took up all the time of the second query. How did you do performance-wise? Figure 5-6 gives the details from the Client Statistics tab.

As you see in the Client Statistics tab, total execution time was 65 time units, with two units going to client processing time and 63 units waiting for server replies. 374 bytes were sent from the client, and 148 bytes were returned by the server. These figures will vary from one run to the next due to caching and other factors.

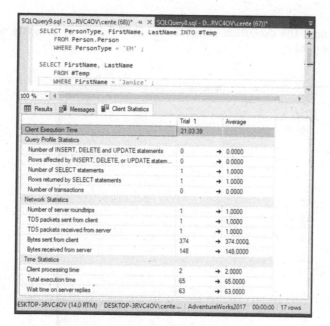

FIGURE 5-6:
SELECT query execution client statistics using a temporary table.

Now, suppose you performed the same operation without using a temporary table. You could do so with the following code:

```
SELECT FirstName, LastName
  FROM Person.Person
  WHERE PersonType = 'EM'
  AND FirstName = 'Janice';
```

EM is AdventureWorks' code for a PersonType of employee. You get the same result (shown in Figure 5-7) as in Figure 5-4. Janice Galvin is the only employee with a first name of Janice.

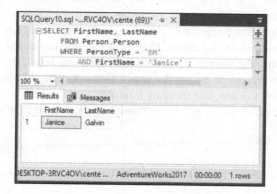

FIGURE 5-7:
SELECT query result with a compound condition.

How does the execution plan (shown in Figure 5-8) compare with the one in Figure 5-5?

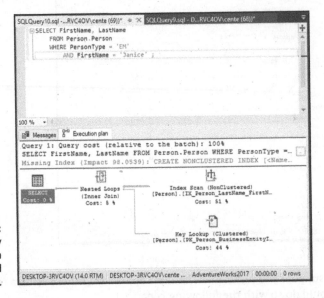

FIGURE 5-8:
SELECT query
execution plan
with a compound
condition.

As you can see, the same result was obtained by a completely different execution plan. A nonclustered index scan took up 77% of the total execution time, a key lookup took 15%, and the remaining 7% was consumed by an inner join. Once again, a recommendation for a nonclustered index has been made, this time on the combined PersonType and FirstName columns. The real story, however, is revealed in the client statistics (shown in Figure 5-9). How does performance compare with the temporary table version?

Hmmm. Total execution time is 307 time units, most of which is due to wait time for server replies. That's more than the 65 time units consumed by the temporary table formulation. The client sent 236 bytes, which is significantly less than the upstream traffic in the temporary table case. In addition, only 119 bytes were sent from the server down to the client. That's comparable to the 148 bytes that were downloaded using the temporary table. All things considered, the performance of both methods turns out to be about a wash. There may be situations where using one or the other is better, but creating a nonclustered index on [PersonType] in the first case or on [PersonType, FirstName] in the second case will have a much bigger impact.

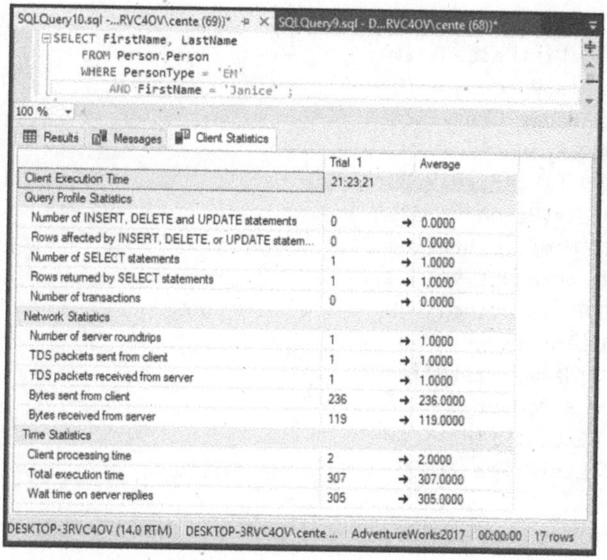

FIGURE 5-9:
SELECT query client statistics, with a compound condition.

The ORDER BY Clause

The ORDER BY clause can be expensive in terms of both bandwidth between the server and the client and execution time simply because ORDER BY initiates a sort operation, and sorts consume large amounts of both time and memory. If you can minimize the number of ORDER BY clauses in a series of queries, you may save resources. This is one place where using a temporary table might perform better. Consider an example. Suppose you want to do a series of retrievals on your Products table in which you see which products are available in several price ranges. For example, you want one list of products priced between 10 dollars and 20 dollars, ordered by unit price. Then, you want a list of products priced between 20 dollars and 30 dollars, similarly ordered, and so on. To cover four such price ranges, you could make four queries, all four with an ORDER BY clause. Alternatively, you could create a temporary table with a query that uses an ORDER BY clause, and then draw the data for the ranges in separate queries that do not have ORDER BY clauses. Compare the two approaches. Here's the code for the temporary table approach:

```
SELECT Name, ListPrice INTO #Product
  FROM Production.Product
  WHERE ListPrice > 10
  AND ListPrice <= 50
  ORDER BY ListPrice;
SELECT Name, ListPrice
  FROM #Product
```

```
    WHERE ListPrice > 10
    AND ListPrice <= 20;
SELECT Name, ListPrice
  FROM #Product
    WHERE ListPrice > 20
    AND ListPrice <= 30;
SELECT Name, ListPrice
  FROM #Product
    WHERE ListPrice > 30
    AND ListPrice <= 40;
SELECT Name, ListPrice
  FROM #Product
    WHERE ListPrice > 40
    AND ListPrice <= 50;
```

The execution plan for this series of queries is shown in Figure 5-10.

FIGURE 5-10: Execution plan, minimizing occurrence of ORDER BY clauses.

The first query, the one that creates the temporary table, has the most complex execution plan. By itself, it takes up 64% of the allotted time, and the other four queries take up the remaining 36%. Figure 5-11 shows the client statistics measuring resource usage.

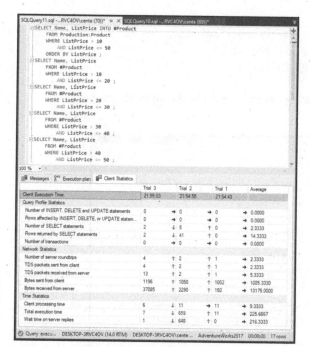

FIGURE 5-11:
Client statistics,
minimizing
occurrence
of ORDER BY
clauses.

Total execution time varies from run to run because of variances in the time spent waiting to hear back from the server, and an average of 13,175 bytes were received from the server. Now compare that with no temporary table, but four separate queries, each with its own ORDER BY clause. Here's the code:

```
SELECT Name, ListPrice
  FROM #Product
  WHERE ListPrice > 10
  AND ListPrice <= 20
  ORDER BY ListPrice ;
SELECT Name, ListPrice
  FROM #Product
  WHERE ListPrice > 20
  AND ListPrice <= 30
  ORDER BY ListPrice ;
SELECT Name, ListPrice
  FROM #Product
  WHERE ListPrice > 30
  AND ListPrice <= 40
  ORDER BY ListPrice ;
SELECT Name, ListPrice
  FROM #Product
```

```
    WHERE ListPrice > 40
    AND ListPrice <= 50
ORDER BY ListPrice ;
```

The resulting execution plan is shown in Figure 5-12.

FIGURE 5-12:
Execution plan,
queries with
separate ORDER
BY clauses.

Each of the four queries involves a sort, which consumes 48% of the total time of the query. This could be costly. Figure 5-13 shows what the client statistics look like.

Total execution time varies from one run to the next, primarily due to waiting for a response from the server. The number of bytes returned by the server also varies. A cursory look at the statistics does not determine whether this latter method is slower than the temporary table method; averages over multiple independent runs will be required. At any rate, as table sizes increase, the time it takes to sort them goes up exponentially. For larger tables, the performance advantage tips strongly to the temporary table method.

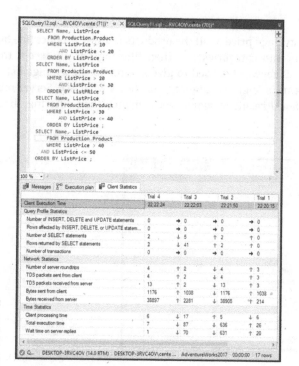

FIGURE 5-13:
Client statistics,
queries with
separate ORDER
BY clauses.

The HAVING Clause

Think about the order in which you do things. Performing operations in the correct order can make a big difference in how long it takes to complete those operations. Whereas the WHERE clause filters out rows that don't meet a search condition, the HAVING clause filters out entire groups that don't meet a search condition. It makes sense to filter first (with a WHERE clause) and group later (with a GROUP BY clause) rather than group first and filter later (with a HAVING clause). If you group first, you perform the grouping operation on everything. If you filter first, you perform the grouping operation only on what is left after the rows you don't want have been filtered out.

This line of reasoning sounds good. To see if it is borne out in practice, consider this code:

```
SELECT AVG(ListPrice) AS AvgPrice, ProductLine
   FROM Production.Product
   GROUP BY ProductLine
   HAVING ProductLine = 'T' ;
```

It finds the average price of all the products in the T product line by first grouping the products into categories and then filtering out all except those in product line T. The AS keyword is used to give a name to the average list price — in this case, the name is AvgPrice. Figure 5-14 shows what SQL Server returns. This formulation *should* result in worse performance than filtering first and grouping second.

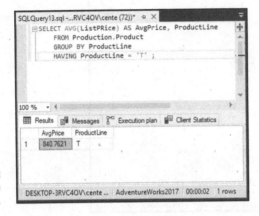

FIGURE 5-14: Retrieval with a HAVING clause.

The average price for the products in product line T is $840.7621. Figure 5-15 shows what the execution plan tells us.

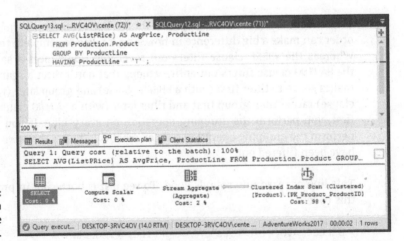

FIGURE 5-15: Retrieval with a HAVING clause execution plan.

A clustered index scan takes up most of the time. This is a fairly efficient operation. The client statistics are shown in Figure 5-16.

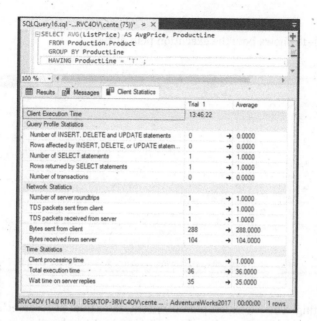

FIGURE 5-16:
Retrieval with a
HAVING clause
client statistics.

Client execution time is about 13 time units. Now, try filtering first and grouping second.

```
SELECT AVG(ListPrice) AS AvgPrice
  FROM Production.Product
  WHERE ProductLine = 'T' ;
```

There is no need to group because all product lines except product line T are filtered out by the WHERE clause. Figure 5-17 shows that the result is the same as in the previous case, $840.7621.

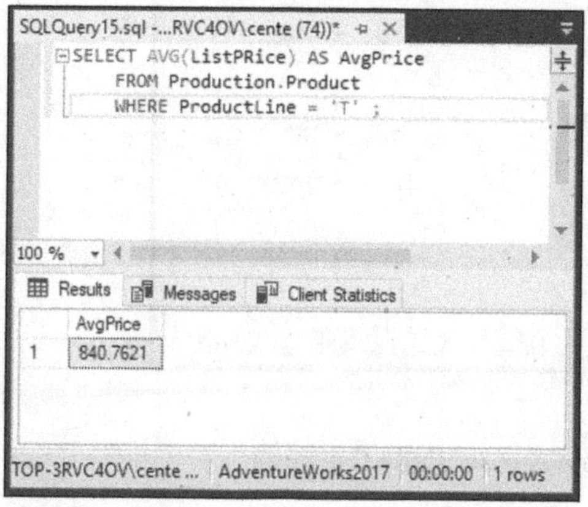

FIGURE 5-17:
Retrieval without
a HAVING clause.

Figure 5-18 shows how the execution plan differs.

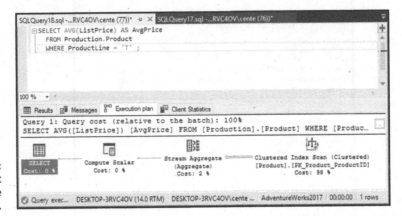

FIGURE 5-18: Retrieval without a HAVING clause execution plan.

Interesting! The execution plan is exactly the same. SQL Server's optimizer has done its job and optimized the less efficient case. Are the client statistics the same too? Check Figure 5-19 to find out.

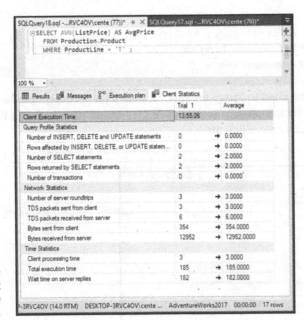

FIGURE 5-19: Retrieval without a HAVING clause client statistics.

Client execution time is essentially the same.

The OR Logical Connective

Some systems never use indexes when expressions in a WHERE clause are connected by the OR logical connective. Check your system to see if it does. See how SQL Server handles it.

```
SELECT ProductID, Name
  FROM Production.Product
  WHERE ListPrice < 20
  OR SafetyStockLevel < 30 ;
```

Check the execution plan to see if SQL Server uses an index (like the one shown in Figure 5-20). SQL Server *does* use an index in this situation, so there is no point in looking for alternative ways to code this type of query.

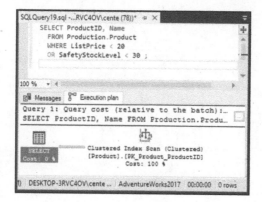

FIGURE 5-20: Query with an OR logical connective.

IN THIS CHAPTER

» Defining subqueries

» Discovering how subqueries work

» Nesting subqueries

» Tuning nested subqueries

» Tuning correlation subqueries

» Using relational operators

Chapter **6**

Complex Query Design

Relational databases have multiple tables. That's where the word *relational* comes from — multiple tables that relate to each other in some way. One consequence of the distribution of data across multiple tables is that most queries need to pull data from more than one of them. There are a couple of ways to do this. One is to use relational operators, and the other method is to use subqueries. This chapter covers both methods.

In some cases, you may find that using the JOIN operator makes more sense. This operator is considerably more flexible than the relational operators covered in this chapter. Book 4, Chapter 7 covers the various joins and their operations.

What Is a Subquery?

A *subquery* is an SQL statement embedded within another SQL statement. It's possible for a subquery to be embedded within another subquery, which is in turn embedded within an outermost SQL statement. Theoretically, there is no limit to the number of levels of subquery that an SQL statement may include, although any given implementation has a practical limit. A key feature of a subquery is that the table or tables it references need not be the same as the table or tables referenced by its enclosing query. This has the effect of returning results based on the information in multiple tables.

What Subqueries Do

Subqueries are located within the WHERE clause of their enclosing statement. Their function is to set the search conditions for the WHERE clause. The combination of a subquery and its enclosing query is called a *nested query*. Different kinds of nested queries produce different results. Some subqueries produce a list of values that is then used as input by the enclosing statement. Other subqueries produce a single value that the enclosing statement then evaluates with a comparison operator. A third kind of subquery, called a *correlated subquery*, operates differently (see the upcoming "Correlated subqueries" section).

Subqueries that return multiple values

A key concern of many businesses is inventory control. When you are building products that are made up of various parts, you want to make sure that you have an adequate supply of all the parts. If just one part is in short supply, it could bring the entire manufacturing operation to a screeching halt. To see how many products are impacted by the lack of a part they need, you can use a subquery.

Subqueries that retrieve rows satisfying a condition

Suppose your company (Penguin Electronics, Inc.) manufactures a variety of electronic products, such as audio amplifiers, FM radio tuners, and handheld metal detectors. You keep track of inventory of all your products — as well as all the parts that go into their manufacture — in a relational database. The database has a PRODUCTS table that holds the inventory levels of finished products and a PARTS table that holds the inventory levels of the parts that go into the products.

A part could be included in multiple products, and each product is made up of multiple parts. This means that there is a many-to-many relationship between the PRODUCTS table and the PARTS table. Because this could present problems, you decide to insert an intersection table between PRODUCTS and PARTS, transforming the problematical many-to-many relationship into two easier-to-deal-with one-to-many relationships. The intersection table, named PROD_PARTS, takes the primary keys of PRODUCTS and PARTS as its only attributes. You can create these three tables with the following code:

```
CREATE TABLE PRODUCTS (
    ProductID            INTEGER       PRIMARY KEY,
    ProductName          CHAR (30),
    ProductDescription   CHAR (50),
    ListPrice            NUMERIC (9,2),
    QuantityInStock      INTEGER ) ;
```

```
CREATE TABLE PARTS (
   PartID                INTEGER       PRIMARY KEY,
   PartName              CHAR (30),
   PartDescription       CHAR (50),
   QuantityInStock       INTEGER ) ;


CREATE TABLE PROD_PARTS (
   ProductID             INTEGER       NOT NULL,
   PartID                INTEGER       NOT NULL ) ;
```

Suppose some of your products include an APM-17 DC analog panel meter. To your horror, you now find that you are completely out of the APM-17 part. You can't complete the manufacture of any product that includes it. It is time for management to take some emergency actions. One is to check on the status of any outstanding orders to the supplier of the APM-17 panel meters. Another is to notify the sales department to stop selling all products that include the APM-17, and switch to promoting products that do not include it.

To discover which products include the APM-17, you can use a nested query such as the following:

```
SELECT ProductID
   FROM PROD_PARTS
   WHERE PartID IN
    (SELECT PartID
       FROM PARTS
      WHERE PartDescription = 'APM-17') ;
```

SQL processes the innermost query first, so it queries the PARTS table, returning the PartID of every row in the PARTS table where the PartDescription is APM-17. There should be only one such row. Only one part should have a description of APM-17. The outer query uses the IN keyword to find all the rows in the PROD_PARTS table that include the PartID that appears in the result set from the inner query. The outer query then extracts from the PROD_PARTS table the ProductIDs of all the products that include the APM-17 part. These are the products that the Sales department should stop selling.

Subqueries that retrieve rows that don't satisfy a condition

Because sales are the lifeblood of any business, it is even more important to determine which products the Sales team can continue to sell than it is to tell them what not to sell. You can do this with another nested query. Use the query just executed in the preceding section as a base, add one more layer of query to it, and return the ProductIDs of all the products not affected by the APM-17 shortage.

```
SELECT ProductID
  FROM PROD_PARTS
  WHERE ProductID NOT IN
    (SELECT ProductID
      FROM PROD_PARTS
      WHERE PartID IN
        (SELECT PartID
          FROM PARTS
          WHERE PartDescription = 'APM-17') ;
```

The two inner queries return the ProductIDs of all the products that include the APM-17 part. The outer query returns all the ProductIDs of all the products that are not included in the result set from the inner queries. This final result set is the list of ProductIDs of products that do not include the APM-17 analog panel meter.

Subqueries that return a single value

Introducing a subquery with one of the six comparison operators (=, <>, <, <=, >, >=) is often useful. In such a case, the expression preceding the operator evaluates to a single value, and the subquery following the operator must also evaluate to a single value. An exception is the case of the *quantified comparison operator*, which is a comparison operator followed by a quantifier (ANY, SOME, or ALL).

To illustrate a case in which a subquery returns a single value, look at another piece of Penguin Electronics' database. It contains a CUSTOMER table that holds information about the companies that buy Penguin products. It also contains a CONTACT table that holds personal data about individuals at each of Penguin's customer organizations. The following code creates Penguin's CUSTOMER and CONTACT tables.

```
CREATE TABLE CUSTOMER (
    CustomerID          INTEGER         PRIMARY KEY,
    Company             CHAR (40),
    Address1            CHAR (50),
    Address2            CHAR (50),
    City                CHAR (25),
    State               CHAR (2),
    PostalCode          CHAR (10),
    Phone               CHAR (13) ) ;
```

```
CREATE TABLE CONTACT (
   CustomerID              INTEGER      PRIMARY KEY,
   FirstName               CHAR (15),
   LastName                CHAR (20),
   Phone                   CHAR (13),
   Email                   CHAR (30),
   Fax                     CHAR (13),
   Notes                   CHAR (100),
   CONSTRAINT ContactFK FOREIGN KEY (CustomerID)
      REFERENCES CUSTOMER (CustomerID) ) ;
```

Say that you want to look at the contact information for the customer named Baker Electronic Sales, but you don't remember that company's CustomerID. Use a nested query like this one to recover the information you want:

```
SELECT *
   FROM CONTACT
      WHERE CustomerID =
         (SELECT CustomerID
            FROM CUSTOMER
               WHERE Company = 'Baker Electronic Sales') ;
```

The result looks something like this:

```
CustomerID FirstName LastName Phone        Notes
---------- --------- -------- ------------ --------------
       787 David     Lee      555-876-3456 Likes to visit
                                           El Pollo Loco
                                           when in Cali.
```

You can now call Dave at Baker and tell him about this month's special sale on metal detectors.

When you use a subquery in an "=" comparison, the subquery's SELECT list must specify a single column (CustomerID in the example). When the subquery is executed, it must return a single row in order to have a single value for the comparison.

For this example, assume that the CUSTOMER table has only one row with a Company value of Baker Electronic Sales. If the CREATE TABLE statement for CUSTOMER specified a UNIQUE constraint for Company, such a statement guarantees that the subquery in the preceding example returns a single value (or no value). Subqueries like the one in the example, however, are commonly used on columns not specified to be UNIQUE. In such cases, you are relying on some other reasons for believing that the column has no duplicates.

If more than one CUSTOMER has a value of Baker Electronic Sales in the Company column (perhaps in different states), the subquery raises an error.

If no Customer with such a company name exists, the subquery is treated as if it were null, and the comparison becomes unknown. In this case, the WHERE clause returns no row (because it returns only rows with the condition True and filters rows with the condition False or Unknown). This would probably happen, for example, if someone misspelled the COMPANY as Baker Electronics Sales.

Although the equals operator (=) is the most common, you can use any of the other five comparison operators in a similar structure. For every row in the table specified in the enclosing statement's FROM clause, the single value returned by the subquery is compared to the expression in the enclosing statement's WHERE clause. If the comparison gives a True value, a row is added to the result table.

You can guarantee that a subquery returns a single value if you include a set function in it. Set functions, also known as *aggregate* functions, always return a single value. Of course, this way of returning a single value is helpful only if you want the result of a set function.

Say that you are a Penguin Electronics salesperson, and you need to earn a big commission check to pay for some unexpected bills. You decide to concentrate on selling Penguin's most expensive product. You can find out what that product is with a nested query:

```
SELECT ProductID, ProductName, ListPrice
    FROM PRODUCT
        WHERE ListPrice =
            (SELECT MAX(ListPrice)
                FROM PRODUCT) ;
```

This is an example of a nested query where both the subquery and the enclosing statement operate on the same table. The subquery returns a single value: the maximum list price in the PRODUCTS table. The outer query retrieves all rows from the PRODUCTS table that have that list price.

The next example shows a comparison subquery that uses a comparison operator other than =:

```
SELECT ProductID, ProductName, ListPrice
    FROM PRODUCTS
```

```
WHERE ListPrice <
    (SELECT AVG(ListPrice)
    FROM PRODUCTS) ;
```

The subquery returns a single value: the average list price in the PRODUCTS table. The outer query retrieves all rows from the PRODUCTS table that have a list price less than the average list price.

In the original SQL standard, a comparison could have only one subquery, and it had to be on the right side of the comparison. SQL:1999 allowed either or both operands of the comparison to be subqueries, and later versions of SQL retain that expanded capability.

Quantified subqueries return a single value

One way to make sure a subquery returns a single value is to introduce it with a quantified comparison operator. The universal quantifier ALL and the existential quantifiers SOME and ANY, when combined with a comparison operator, process the result set returned by the inner subquery, reducing it to a single value.

Look at an example. From the 1960s through the 1980s, there was fierce competition between Ford and Chevrolet to produce the most powerful cars. Both companies had small-block V-8 engines that went into Mustangs, Camaros, and other performance-oriented vehicles.

Power is measured in units of horsepower. In general, a larger engine delivers more horsepower, all other things being equal. Because the displacements (sizes) of the engines varied from one model to another, it's unfair to look only at horsepower. A better measure of the efficiency of an engine is horsepower per displacement. Displacement is measured in cubic inches (CID). Table 6-1 shows the year, displacement, and horsepower ratings for Ford small-block V-8s between 1960 and 1980.

The Shelby GT350 was a classic muscle car — not a typical car for the weekday commute. Emission regulations taking effect in the early 1970s halved power output and brought an end to the muscle car era. Table 6-2 shows what Chevy put out during the same timeframe.

Here again, you see the effect of the emission regulations that kicked in circa 1971 — a drastic drop in horsepower per displacement.

TABLE 6-1 ## Ford Small-Block V-8s, 1960–1980

Year	Displacement (CID)	Maximum Horsepower	Notes
1962	221	145	
1963	289	225	4bbl carburetor
1965	289	271	289HP model
1965	289	306	Shelby GT350
1969	351	290	4bbl carburetor
1975	302	140	Emission regulations

TABLE 6-2 ## Chevy Small-Block V-8s, 1960–1980

Year	Displacement (CID)	Maximum Horsepower	Notes
1960	283	315	
1962	327	375	
1967	350	295	
1968	302	290	
1968	307	200	
1969	350	370	Corvette
1970	400	265	
1975	262	110	Emission regulations

Use the following code to create tables to hold these data items:

```
CREATE TABLE Ford (
   EngineID          INTEGER        PRIMARY KEY,
   ModelYear         CHAR (4),
   Displacement      NUMERIC (5,2),
   MaxHP             NUMERIC (5,2),
   Notes             CHAR (30) ) ;

CREATE TABLE Chevy (
   EngineID          INTEGER        PRIMARY KEY,
   ModelYear         CHAR (4),
   Displacement      NUMERIC (5,2),
   MaxHP             NUMERIC (5,2),
   Notes             CHAR (30) ) ;
```

After filling these tables with the data in Tables 6-1 and 6-2, you can run some queries. Suppose you are a dyed-in-the-wool Chevy fan and are quite certain that the most powerful Chevrolet has a higher horsepower-to-displacement ratio than any of the Fords. To verify that assumption, enter the following query:

```
SELECT *
  FROM Chevy
  WHERE (MaxHP/Displacement) > ALL
    (SELECT (MaxHP/Displacement) FROM Ford) ;
```

This returns the result shown in Figure 6-1:

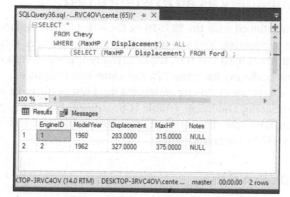

FIGURE 6-1:
Chevy muscle cars with horsepower to displacement ratios higher than any of the Fords listed.

The subquery (SELECT (MaxHP/Displacement) FROM Ford) returns the horsepower-to-displacement ratios of all the Ford engines in the Ford table. The ALL quantifier says to return only those records from the Chevy table that have horsepower-to-displacement ratios higher than all the ratios returned for the Ford engines. Two different Chevy engines had higher ratios than any Ford engine of that era, including the highly regarded Shelby GT350. Ford fans should not be bothered by this result, however. There's more to what makes a car awesome than just the horsepower-to-displacement ratio.

What if you had made the opposite assumption? What if you had entered the following query?

```
SELECT *
  FROM Ford
  WHERE (MaxHP/Displacement) > ALL
    (SELECT (MaxHP/Displacement) FROM Chevy) ;
```

Because none of the Ford engines has a higher horsepower-to-displacement ratio than *all* of the Chevy engines, the query doesn't return any rows.

Correlated subqueries

In all the nested queries shown in the previous sections, the inner subquery is executed first, and then its result is applied to the outer enclosing statement. A *correlated subquery* first finds the table and row specified by the enclosing statement, and then executes the subquery on the row in the subquery's table that correlates with the current row of the enclosing statement's table.

Using a subquery as an existence test

Subqueries introduced with the EXISTS or the NOT EXISTS keyword are examples of correlated subqueries. The subquery returns one or more rows, or it returns none. If it returns at least one row, the EXISTS predicate succeeds, and the enclosing statement performs its action. In the same circumstances, the NOT EXISTS predicate fails, and the enclosing statement does not perform its action. After one row of the enclosing statement's table is processed, the same operation is performed on the next row. This action is repeated until every row in the enclosing statement's table has been processed.

TESTING FOR EXISTENCE

Say that you are a salesperson for Penguin Electronics and you want to call your primary contact people at all of Penguin's customer organizations in New Hampshire. Try the following query:

```
SELECT *
   FROM CONTACT
   WHERE EXISTS
      (SELECT *
          FROM CUSTOMER
          WHERE State = 'NH'
             AND CONTACT.CustomerID = CUSTOMER.CustomerID) ;
```

Notice the reference to CONTACT.CustomerID, which is referencing a column from the outer query and comparing it with another column, CUSTOMER.CustomerID, from the inner query. For each candidate row of the outer query, you evaluate the inner query using the CustomerID value from the current CONTACT row of the outer query in the WHERE clause of the inner query.

The CustomerID column links the CONTACT table to the CUSTOMER table. SQL looks at the first record in the CONTACT table, finds the row in the CUSTOMER table that has the same CustomerID, and checks that row's State field. If CUSTOMER.State = 'NH', the current CONTACT row is added to the result table. The next CONTACT record is then processed in the same way, and so on, until the entire CONTACT table has been processed. Because the query specifies SELECT * FROM CONTACT, all the CONTACT table's fields are returned, including the contact's name and phone number.

TESTING FOR NONEXISTENCE

In the previous example, the Penguin salesperson wants to know the names and numbers of the contact people of all the customers in New Hampshire. Imagine that a second salesperson is responsible for all of the United States except New Hampshire. They can retrieve their contacts by using NOT EXISTS in a query similar to the preceding one:

```
SELECT *
    FROM CONTACT
    WHERE NOT EXISTS
        (SELECT *
            FROM CUSTOMER
            WHERE State = 'NH'
                AND CONTACT.CustomerID = CUSTOMER.CustomerID) ;
```

Every row in CONTACT for which the subquery does not return a row is added to the result table.

Introducing a correlated subquery with the IN keyword

As noted in a previous section of this chapter, subqueries introduced by IN or by a comparison operator need not be correlated queries, but they can be. The "Subqueries that retrieve rows satisfying a condition" section gives examples of how a noncorrelated subquery can be used with the IN predicate. To show how a correlated subquery may use the IN predicate, ask the same question that came up with the EXISTS predicate: What are the names and phone numbers of the contacts at all of Penguin's customers in New Hampshire? You can answer this question with a correlated IN subquery:

```
SELECT *
    FROM CONTACT
    WHERE 'NH' IN
        (SELECT State
```

```
            FROM CUSTOMER
            WHERE CONTACT.CustomerID = CUSTOMER.CustomerID) ;
```

The statement is evaluated for each record in the CONTACT table. If, for that record, the CustomerID numbers in CONTACT and CUSTOMER match, the value of CUSTOMER.State is compared to 'NH'. The result of the subquery is a list that contains, at most, one element. If that one element is 'NH', the WHERE clause of the enclosing statement is satisfied, and a row is added to the query's result table.

Introducing a correlated subquery with a comparison operator

A correlated subquery can also be introduced by one of the six comparison operators, as shown in the next example.

Penguin pays bonuses to its salespeople based on their total monthly sales volume. The higher the volume, the higher the bonus percentage. The bonus percentage list is kept in the BONUSRATE table:

MinAmount	MaxAmount	BonusPct
0.00	24999.99	0.
25000.00	49999.99	0.01
50000.00	99999.99	0.02
100000.00	249999.99	0.03
250000.00	499999.99	0.04
500000.00	749999.99	0.05
750000.00	999999.99	0.06

If a person's monthly sales total is between $100,000.00 and $249,999.99, the bonus is 3 percent of sales.

Sales are recorded in a transaction master table named TRANSMASTER, which is created as follows:

```
CREATE TABLE TRANSMASTER (
    TransID       INTEGER        PRIMARY KEY,
    CustID        INTEGER        FOREIGN KEY,
    EmpID         INTEGER        FOREIGN KEY,
    TransDate     DATE,
    NetAmount     NUMERIC,
    Freight       NUMERIC,
    Tax           NUMERIC,
    InvoiceTotal  NUMERIC) ;
```

Sales bonuses are based on the sum of the NetAmount field for all of a person's transactions in the month. You can find any person's bonus rate with a correlated subquery that uses comparison operators:

```
SELECT BonusPct
    FROM BONUSRATE
        WHERE MinAmount <=
            (SELECT SUM(NetAmount)
                FROM TRANSMASTER
                    WHERE EmpID = 133)
        AND MaxAmount >=
            (SELECT SUM(NetAmount)
                FROM TRANSMASTER
                    WHERE EmpID = 133) ;
```

This query is interesting in that it contains two subqueries, making use of the logical connective AND. The subqueries use the SUM aggregate operator, which returns a single value: the total monthly sales of employee 133. That value is then compared against the MinAmount and the MaxAmount columns in the BONUSRATE table, producing the bonus rate for that employee.

If you had not known the EmpID but had known the person's name, you could arrive at the same answer with a more complex query:

```
SELECT BonusPct
    FROM BONUSRATE
        WHERE MinAmount <=
            (SELECT SUM(NetAmount)
                FROM TRANSMASTER
                    WHERE EmpID =
                        (SELECT EmployeeID
                            FROM EMPLOYEE
                                WHERE EmplName = 'Thornton'))
        AND MaxAmount >=
            (SELECT SUM(NetAmount)
                FROM TRANSMASTER
                    WHERE EmpID =
                        (SELECT EmployeeID
                            FROM EMPLOYEE
                                WHERE EmplName = 'Thornton'));
```

This example uses subqueries nested within subqueries, which, in turn, are nested within an enclosing query to arrive at the bonus rate for the employee named Thornton. This structure works only if you know for sure that the company has one, and only one, employee whose name is Thornton. If you know that more than one employee is named Thornton, you can add terms to the WHERE clause of the innermost subquery until you're sure that only one row of the EMPLOYEE table is selected.

Correlated subqueries in a HAVING clause

You can have a correlated subquery in a HAVING clause just as you can in a WHERE clause. As covered in Book 4, Chapter 5, a HAVING clause is normally preceded by a GROUP BY clause. The HAVING clause acts as a filter to restrict the groups created by the GROUP BY clause. Groups that don't satisfy the condition of the HAVING clause are not included in the result. When used this way, the HAVING clause is evaluated for each group created by the GROUP BY clause. In the absence of a GROUP BY clause, the HAVING clause is evaluated for the set of rows passed by the WHERE clause, which is considered a single group. If neither a WHERE clause nor a GROUP BY clause is present, the HAVING clause is evaluated for the entire table:

```
SELECT TM1.EmpID
    FROM TRANSMASTER TM1
        GROUP BY TM1.EmpID
        HAVING MAX(TM1.NetAmount) >= ALL
            (SELECT 2 * AVG (TM2.NetAmount)
                FROM TRANSMASTER TM2
                WHERE TM1.EmpID <> TM2.EmpID) ;
```

This query uses two aliases for the same table, enabling you to retrieve the EmpID number of all salespeople who had a sale of at least twice the average value of all the other salespeople. Short aliases such as TM1 are often used to eliminate excessive typing when long table names such as TRANSMASTER are involved. But in this case, aliases do more than just save some typing. The TRANSMASTER table is used for two different purposes, so two different aliases are used to distinguish between them. The query works as follows:

1. The outer query groups TRANSMASTER rows by the EmpID. This is done with the SELECT, FROM, and GROUP BY clauses.

2. The HAVING clause filters these groups. For each group, it calculates the MAX of the NetAmount column for the rows in that group.

3. The inner query evaluates twice the average NetAmount from all rows of TRANSMASTER whose EmpID is different from the EmpID of the current group of the outer query. Each group contains the transaction records for an employee whose biggest sale had at least twice the value of the average of the sales of all the other employees. Note that in the last line, you need to

reference two different EmpID values, so in the FROM clauses of the outer and inner queries, you use different aliases for TRANSMASTER.

4. You then use those aliases in the comparison of the query's last line to indicate that you're referencing both the EmpID from the current row of the inner subquery (TM2.EmpID) and the EmpID from the current group of the outer subquery (TM1.EmpID).

Using Subqueries in INSERT, DELETE, and UPDATE Statements

In addition to SELECT statements, UPDATE, DELETE, and INSERT statements can also include WHERE clauses. Those WHERE clauses can contain subqueries in the same way that SELECT statement WHERE clauses do.

For example, Penguin has just made a volume purchase deal with Baker Electronic Sales and wants to retroactively provide Baker with a 10 percent credit for all its purchases in the last month. You can give this credit with an UPDATE statement:

```
UPDATE TRANSMASTER
    SET NetAmount = NetAmount * 0.9
    WHERE CustID =
        (SELECT CustID
            FROM CUSTOMER
            WHERE Company = 'Baker Electronic Sales') ;
```

You can also have a correlated subquery in an UPDATE statement. Suppose the CUSTOMER table has a column LastMonthsMax, and Penguin wants to give the same 10 percent credit for purchases that exceed LastMonthsMax for the customer:

```
UPDATE TRANSMASTER TM
    SET NetAmount = NetAmount * 0.9
    WHERE NetAmount >
        (SELECT LastMonthsMax
            FROM CUSTOMER C
            WHERE C.CustID = TM.CustID) ;
```

Note that this subquery is correlated: The WHERE clause in the last line references both the CustID of the CUSTOMER row from the subquery and the CustID of the current TRANSMASTER row that is a candidate for updating.

A subquery in an UPDATE statement can also reference the table being updated. Suppose that Penguin wants to give a 10 percent credit to customers whose purchases have exceeded $10,000:

```
UPDATE TRANSMASTER TM1
    SET NetAmount = NetAmount * 0.9
    WHERE 10000 < (SELECT SUM(NetAmount)
                    FROM TRANSMASTER TM2
                          WHERE TM1.CustID = TM2.CustID);
```

The inner subquery calculates the SUM of the NetAmount column for all TRANSMASTER rows for the same customer. What does this mean? Suppose that the customer with CustID = 37 has four rows in TRANSMASTER with values for NetAmount: 3000, 5000, 2000, and 1000. The SUM of NetAmount for this CustID is 11000.

REMEMBER

The order in which the UPDATE statement processes the rows is defined by your implementation and is generally not predictable. The order may differ depending on how the rows are arranged on the disk. Assume that the implementation processes the rows for this CustID in this order: first the TRANSMASTER row with a NetAmount of 3000, and then the one with NetAmount = 5000, and so on. After the first three rows for CustID 37 have been updated, their NetAmount values are 2700 (90 percent of 3000), 4500 (90 percent of 5000), and 1800 (90 percent of 2000). Then when you process the last TRANSMASTER row for CustID 37, whose NetAmount is 1000, the SUM returned by the subquery would seem to be 10000 — that is, the SUM of the *new* NetAmount values of the first three rows for CustID 37 and the *old* NetAmount value of the last row for CustID 37. Thus, it would seem that the last row for CustID 37 isn't updated because the comparison with that SUM is not True, since 10000 is not less than SELECT SUM (NetAmount). But that is not how the UPDATE statement is defined when a subquery references the table being updated. All evaluations of subqueries in an UPDATE statement reference the *old* values of the table being updated. In the preceding UPDATE for CustID 37, the subquery returns 11000 — the original SUM.

The subquery in an UPDATE statement WHERE clause operates the same as it does in a SELECT statement WHERE clause. The same is true for DELETE and INSERT. To delete all of Baker's transactions, use this statement:

```
DELETE FROM TRANSMASTER
    WHERE CustID =
        (SELECT CustomerID
            FROM CUSTOMER
            WHERE Company = 'Baker Electronic Sales') ;
```

As with UPDATE, DELETE subqueries can also be correlated and can also reference the table whose rows are being deleted. The rules are similar to the rules for UPDATE subqueries. Suppose you want to delete all rows from TRANSMASTER for customers whose total NetAmount is larger than $10,000:

```
DELETE FROM TRANSMASTER TM1
    WHERE 10000 < (SELECT SUM(NetAmount)
        FROM TRANSMASTER TM2
            WHERE TM1.CustID = TM2.CustID) ;
```

This query deletes all rows from TRANSMASTER referencing customers with purchases exceeding $10,000 — including the aforementioned customer with CustID 37. All references to TRANSMASTER in the subquery denote the contents of TRANSMASTER before any deletes by the current statement. So even when you are deleting the last TRANSMASTER row, the subquery is evaluated on the original TRANSMASTER table, identified by TM1.

BEST PRACTICE

When you update, delete, or insert database records, you risk making a table's data inconsistent with other tables in the database. If you delete TRANSMASTER records and a TRANSDETAIL table depends on TRANSMASTER, you must delete the corresponding records from TRANSDETAIL too. This operation is called a *cascading delete* because the deletion of a parent record cascades to its associated child records. Otherwise, the undeleted child records become orphans. In this case, they would be invoice detail lines that are in limbo because they are no longer connected to an invoice record. Your database management system will give you the option to either specify a cascading delete or not.

INSERT can include a SELECT clause. One use for this statement is filling *snapshot tables* — tables that take a snapshot of another table at a particular moment in time. For example, to create a table with the contents of TRANSMASTER for October 27, do this:

```
CREATE TABLE TRANSMASTER_1027
    (TransID INTEGER, TransDate DATE,
    ...) ;

INSERT INTO TRANSMASTER_1027
    (SELECT * FROM TRANSMASTER
        WHERE TransDate = 2018-10-27) ;
```

The CREATE TABLE statement creates an empty table; the INSERT INTO statement fills it with the data that was added on October 27. Or you may want to save rows only for large NetAmounts:

```
INSERT INTO TRANSMASTER_1027
    (SELECT * FROM TRANSMASTER
        WHERE TRANSMASTER.NetAmount > 10000
            AND TransDate = 2018-10-27) ;
```

Tuning Considerations for Statements Containing Nested Queries

How do you tune a nested query? In some cases, there is no need because the nested query is about as efficient as it can be. In other cases, nested queries are not particularly efficient. Depending on the characteristics of the database management system you're using, you may want to recode a nested query for higher performance. As mentioned at the beginning of this chapter, many tasks performed by nested queries could also be performed using relational operators. In some cases, using a relational operator yields better performance than a nested query that produces the same result. If performance is an issue in a given application and a nested query seems to be the bottleneck, you might want to try a statement containing a relational operator instead and compare execution times.

As mentioned earlier in this chapter, there are two kinds of subqueries, noncorrelated and correlated. Let's look at a noncorrelated subquery without a set function.

```
SELECT SalesOrderID
    FROM Sales.SalesOrderDetail
    WHERE ProductID IN
        (SELECT ProductID
            FROM Production.ProductInventory
            WHERE Quantity = 0) ;
```

This query takes data from both the ProductInventory table and the SalesOrder-Detail table. It returns the SalesOrderIDs of all orders that include out-of-stock products. Figure 6-2 shows the result of the query. Figure 6-3 shows the execution plan, and Figure 6-4 shows the client statistics.

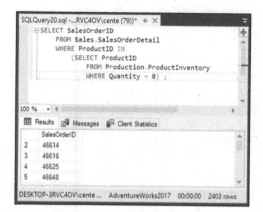

FIGURE 6-2:
Orders that contain products that are out of stock.

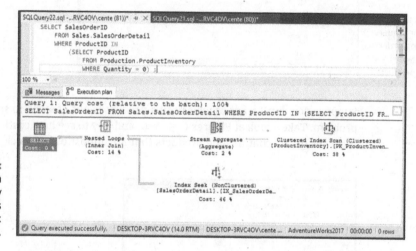

FIGURE 6-3:
An execution plan for a query showing orders for out-of-stock products.

This was a pretty efficient query; 12,089 bytes were transferred from the server, but total execution time was only 2 time units. The execution plan shows that a nested loop join was used, taking up 14% of the total time consumed by the query.

How would performance change if the WHERE clause condition was inequality rather than equality?

```
SELECT SalesOrderID
  FROM Sales.SalesOrderDetail
  WHERE ProductID IN
    (SELECT ProductID
       FROM Production.ProductInventory
       WHERE Quantity < 10) ;
```

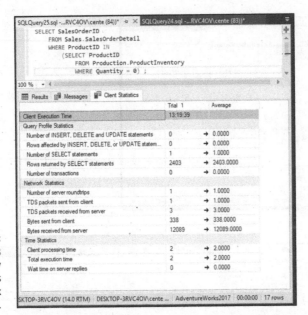

FIGURE 6-4:
Client statistics
for a query
showing orders
for out-of-stock
products.

Suppose you don't want to wait until a product is out of stock to see if you have a problem. Take a look at Figures 6-5, 6-6, and 6-7 to see how costly a query is that retrieves orders that include products that are almost out of stock.

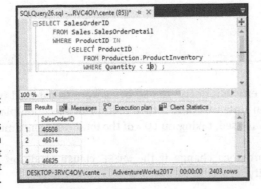

FIGURE 6-5:
A nested query
showing orders
that contain
products that
are almost out
of stock.

Figure 6-4 shows that 2403 rows were returned, and Figure 6-7 shows that 2404 rows were returned. This must mean that there is one item where between 1 and 9 units are still in stock.

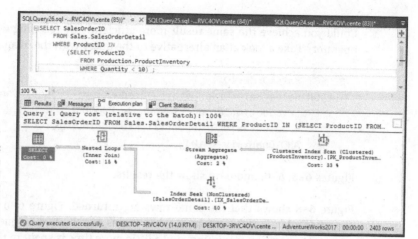

FIGURE 6-6:
An execution plan for a nested query showing orders for almost out-of-stock products.

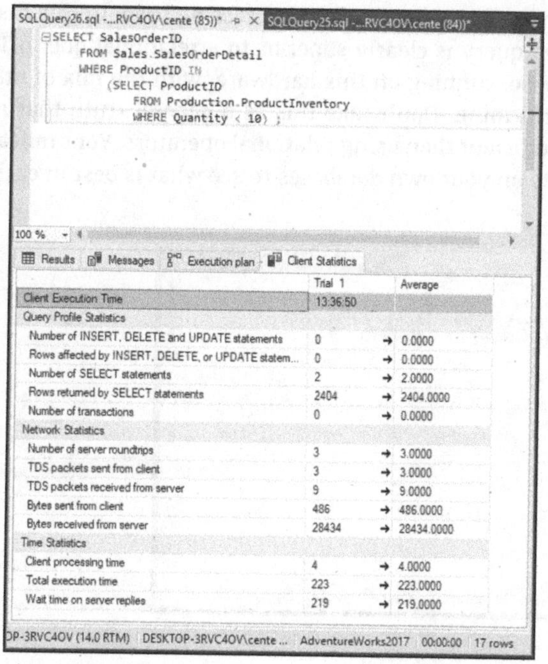

FIGURE 6-7:
Client statistics for a nested query showing orders for almost out-of-stock products.

The execution plan is the same in both cases. This indicates that the query optimizer figured out which of the two formulations was more efficient and performed the operation the best way rather than the way it was coded. The client statistics vary. The difference could have been due to other things the system was doing at the same time. To determine whether there is any real difference between the two formulations, they would each have to be run a number of times and an average taken.

Could you achieve the same result more efficiently by recoding with a relational operator? Take a look at an alternative to the query with the inequality condition:

```
SELECT SalesOrderID
   FROM Sales.SalesOrderDetail, Production.ProductInventory
   WHERE Production.ProductInventory.ProductID
        = Sales.SalesOrderDetail.ProductInventory
        AND Quantity < 10) ;
```

Figures 6-8, 6-9, and 6-10 show the results.

Figure 6-8 shows that the same rows are returned. Figure 6-9 shows that the execution plan is different from what it was for the nested query. The stream aggregate operation is missing, and a little more time is spent in the nested loops. Figure 6-10 shows that total execution time has increased substantially, a good chunk of the increase being in client processing time. In this case, it appears that using a nested query is clearly superior to a relational query. This result is true for this database, running on this hardware, with the mix of other work that the system is performing. Don't take this as a general truth that nested selects are always more efficient than using relational operators. Your mileage may vary. Run your own tests on your own databases to see what is best in each particular case.

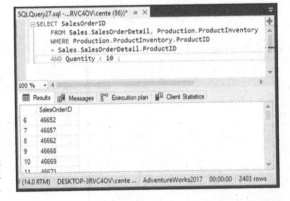

FIGURE 6-8:
A relational query showing orders that contain products that are almost out of stock.

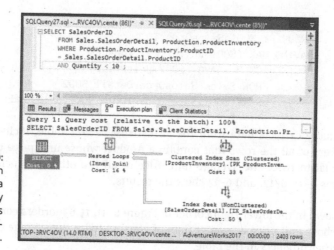

```
SELECT SalesOrderID
    FROM Sales.SalesOrderDetail, Production.ProductInventory
    WHERE Production.ProductInventory.ProductID
    = Sales.SalesOrderDetail.ProductID
    AND Quantity < 10 ;
```

FIGURE 6-9: The execution plan for a relational query showing orders for almost out-of-stock products.

```
SELECT SalesOrderID
    FROM Sales.SalesOrderDetail, Production.ProductInventory
    WHERE Production.ProductInventory.ProductID
    = Sales.SalesOrderDetail.ProductID
    AND Quantity < 10 ;
```

	Trial 1	Average
Client Execution Time	15:54:13	
Query Profile Statistics		
Number of INSERT, DELETE and UPDATE statements	0	→ 0.0000
Rows affected by INSERT, DELETE, or UPDATE statem...	0	→ 0.0000
Number of SELECT statements	2	→ 2.0000
Rows returned by SELECT statements	2404	→ 2404.0000
Number of transactions	0	→ 0.0000
Network Statistics		
Number of server roundtrips	3	→ 3.0000
TDS packets sent from client	3	→ 3.0000
TDS packets received from server	9	→ 9.0000
Bytes sent from client	542	→ 542.0000
Bytes received from server	26602	→ 26602.0000
Time Statistics		
Client processing time	18	→ 18.0000
Total execution time	421	→ 421.0000
Wait time on server replies	403	→ 403.0000

FIGURE 6-10: Client statistics for a relational query showing orders for almost out-of-stock products.

Tuning Correlated Subqueries

Compare a correlated subquery to an equivalent relational query and see if a performance difference shows up:

```
SELECT SOD1.SalesOrderID
    FROM Sales.SalesOrderDetail SOD1
```

```
      GROUP BY SOD1.SalesOrderID
      HAVING MAX (SOD1.UnitPrice) >= ALL
          (SELECT 2 * AVG (SOD2.UnitPrice)
          FROM Sales.SalesOrderDetail SOD2
          WHERE SOD1.SalesOrderID <> SOD2.SalesOrderID) ;
```

The query extracts data from the SalesOrderDetail table, including the order numbers of all the rows that contain a product whose unit price is greater than or equal to twice the average unit price of all the other products in the table. Figures 6-11, 6-12, and 6-13 show the results.

As shown in the lower right corner of Figure 6-11, 13,831 orders contained a product whose unit price is greater than or equal to twice the average unit price of all the other products in the table.

FIGURE 6-11:
A correlated
subquery
showing orders
that contain
products at least
twice as costly
as the average
product.

Figure 6-12 shows the most complex execution plan in this book. Correlated subqueries are intrinsically more complex than the noncorrelated variety. Many parts of the plan have minimal cost, but the clustered index seek takes up 71% of the total, and the stream aggregate due to the MAX set function takes up 29%. The query took much longer to run than any of the queries discussed so far in this chapter.

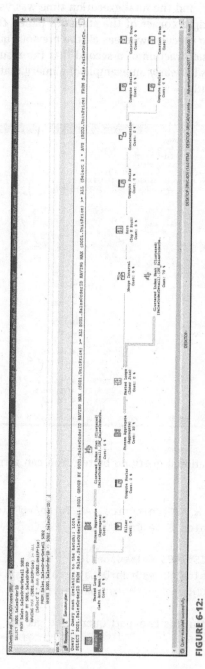

FIGURE 6-12:

An execution plan for a correlated subquery showing orders at least twice as costly as the average product.

The client statistics table in Figure 6-13 shows that 69,341 bytes were returned by the server, and the total execution time was 759,145 time units. As shown in the bottom right corner of the statistics panel, the query took 12 minutes and 39 seconds to execute, whereas all the previous queries in this chapter executed in such a small fraction of a second that the result seemed to appear instantaneously. This is clearly an example of a query that anyone would like to perform more efficiently.

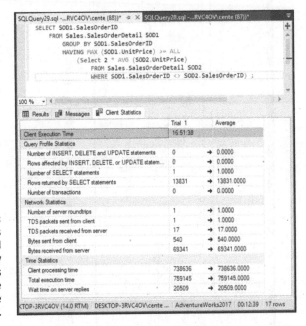

FIGURE 6-13: Client statistics for a correlated subquery showing orders at least twice as costly as the average product.

Would a relational query do better? You can formulate one, using a temporary table:

```
SELECT 2 * AVG(UnitPrice) AS TwiceAvgPrice INTO #TempPrice
  FROM Sales.SalesOrderDetail ;

SELECT DISTINCT SalesOrderID
  FROM Sales.SalesOrderDetail, #TempPrice
  WHERE UnitPrice >= twiceavgprice ;
```

When you run this two-part query, you get the results shown in Figures 6-14, 6-15, and 6-16.

FIGURE 6-14:
Relational query
showing orders
that contain
products at least
twice as costly
as the average
product.

This query returns the same result as the previous one, but the difference in execution time is astounding. This query ran in 8 seconds rather than over 12 minutes.

Figure 6-15 shows the execution plans for the two parts of the relational query. In the first part, a clustered index scan takes up most of the time (93%). In the second part, a clustered index scan and an inner join consume the time.

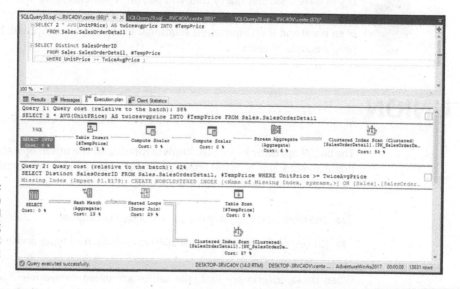

FIGURE 6-15:
An execution plan
for a relational
query showing
orders for almost
out-of-stock
products.

Figure 6-16 shows a tremendous difference in performance with the correlated subquery in Figure 6-13, which produced exactly the same result. Execution time is reduced to 8 seconds compared to 12 minutes and 39 seconds.

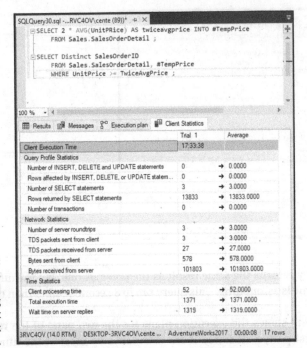

```
SQLQuery30.sql -...RVC4OV\cente (89))*  -₄  ×
 ⊟SELECT 2 * AVG(UnitPRice) AS twiceavgprice INTO #TempPrice
     FROM Sales.SalesOrderDetail ;

 ⊟SELECT Distinct SalesOrderID
     FROM Sales.SalesOrderDetail, #TempPrice
     WHERE UnitPrice >= TwiceAvgPrice ;
```

	Trial 1	Average
Client Execution Time	17:33:38	
Query Profile Statistics		
Number of INSERT, DELETE and UPDATE statements	0	→ 0.0000
Rows affected by INSERT, DELETE, or UPDATE statem...	0	→ 0.0000
Number of SELECT statements	3	→ 3.0000
Rows returned by SELECT statements	13833	→ 13833.0000
Number of transactions	0	→ 0.0000
Network Statistics		
Number of server roundtrips	3	→ 3.0000
TDS packets sent from client	3	→ 3.0000
TDS packets received from server	27	→ 27.0000
Bytes sent from client	578	→ 578.0000
Bytes received from server	101803	→ 101803.0000
Time Statistics		
Client processing time	52	→ 52.0000
Total execution time	1371	→ 1371.0000
Wait time on server replies	1319	→ 1319.0000

3RVC4OV (14.0 RTM)   DESKTOP-3RVC4OV\cente ...   AdventureWorks2017   00:00:08   17 rows

FIGURE 6-16:
Client statistics
for a relational
query showing
orders for almost
out-of-stock
products.

TIP

If you have a similar query that will be run repeatedly, give serious consideration to performing a relational query rather than a correlated subquery if performance is an issue and if an equivalent relational query can be composed. It is worth running a couple of tests.

UNION

The UNION operator is the SQL implementation of the union operator used in relational algebra. SQL's UNION operator enables you to draw information from two or more tables that have the same structure. *Same structure* means

>> The tables must all have the same number of columns.

>> Corresponding columns must all have identical data types and lengths.

When these criteria are met, the tables are *union-compatible*. The union of two tables returns all the rows that appear in either table and eliminates duplicates.

Suppose you have created a database for a business named Acme Systems that sells and installs computer products. Acme has two warehouses that stock the products, one in Fort Deposit, Alabama, and the other in East Kingston, New Hampshire. It contains two union-compatible tables named DEPOSIT and KINGSTON. Both tables have two columns, and the corresponding columns are the same type. In fact, corresponding columns have identical column names (although this condition isn't required for union compatibility).

DEPOSIT lists the names and quantities in stock of products in the Fort Deposit warehouse. KINGSTON lists the same information about the East Kingston warehouse. The UNION of the two tables gives you a virtual result table containing all the rows in the first table plus all the rows in the second table. This example shows just a few rows in each table to illustrate the operation:

```
SELECT * FROM DEPOSIT ;

ProductName      QuantityInStock
-----------      ---------------
185_Express            12
505_Express            5
510_Express            6
520_Express            2
550_Express            3

SELECT * FROM KINGSTON ;

ProductName      QuantityInStock
-----------      ---------------
185_Express            15
505_Express            7
510_Express            6
520_Express            2
550_Express            1

SELECT * FROM DEPOSIT
UNION
SELECT * FROM KINGSTON ;

ProductName      QuantityInStock
-----------      ---------------
185_Express            12
185_Express            15
505_Express            5
505_Express            7
```

510_Express	6
520_Express	2
550_Express	3
550_Express	1

The UNION DISTINCT operator functions identically to the UNION operator without the DISTINCT keyword. In both cases, duplicate rows are eliminated from the result set. In this example, because both warehouses had the same number of 510_Express and 520_Express products, those rows in both tables were exact duplicates, only one of which was returned.

This example shows how UNION works, but it isn't very practical. In most cases, you might imagine Acme's manager would not care which products were stocked in exactly the same numbers at both warehouses and thus partially removed from the result set. All the information is present, but the user must be savvy enough to realize that the total number of units of 510_Express is actually 12 rather than 6, and the total number of units of 520_Express is 4 rather than 2.

WARNING

I use the asterisk (*) as shorthand for all the columns in a table. This shortcut is fine most of the time, but it can get you into trouble when you use relational operators in embedded or module-language SQL. What if you add one or more new columns to one table and not to another, or you add different columns to the two tables? The two tables are then no longer union-compatible, and your program is invalid the next time it's recompiled. Even if the same new columns are added to both tables so that they remain union-compatible, your program is probably not prepared to deal with this additional data. So, explicitly listing the columns that you want rather than relying on the * shorthand is generally a good idea. When you're entering ad hoc SQL from the console, the asterisk will probably work fine because you can quickly display the table structure to verify union compatibility if your query isn't successful.

UNION ALL

As mentioned previously, the UNION operation normally eliminates any duplicate rows that result from its operation, which is the desired result most of the time. Sometimes, however, you may want to preserve duplicate rows. On those occasions, use UNION ALL.

The following code shows you what UNION ALL produces when it's used with the DEPOSIT and KINGSTON tables:

```
SELECT * FROM DEPOSIT
UNION ALL
```

```
SELECT * FROM KINGSTON ;

ProductName      QuantityInStock
-----------      ---------------
185_Express           12
505_Express            5
510_Express            6
520_Express            2
550_Express            3
185_Express           15
505_Express            7
510_Express            6
520_Express            2
550_Express            1
```

UNION CORRESPONDING

You can sometimes form the union of two tables even if they are not union-compatible. If the columns you want in your result set are present and compatible in both source tables, you can perform a UNION CORRESPONDING operation. Only the specified columns are considered, and they are the only columns displayed in the result set.

Suppose ACME Systems opens a third warehouse in Jefferson, Maine. A new table named JEFFERSON is added to the database, which includes Product and QuantityInStock columns (as the DEPOSIT and KINGSTON tables do), but also has an additional column named QuantityOnHold. A UNION or UNION ALL of JEFFERSON with either DEPOSIT or KINGSTON would not return any rows because there is not a complete match between all the columns of JEFFERSON and all the columns of the other two tables. However, you can still add the JEFFERSON data to either DEPOSIT or KINGSTON by specifying only the columns in JEFFERSON that correspond with the columns in the other table. Here's a sample query:

```
SELECT *
   FROM JEFFERSON
UNION CORRESPONDING BY
   (ProductName, QuantityInStock)
SELECT *
   FROM KINGSTON ;
```

The result table holds the products and the quantities in stock at both warehouses. As with the simple UNION, duplicates are eliminated. Thus, if the Jefferson warehouse happens to have the same quantity of a particular product that the Kingston warehouse has, the UNION CORRESPONDING operation loses one of those rows. To avoid this problem, use UNION ALL CORRESPONDING.

INTERSECT

The UNION operation produces a result table containing all rows that appear in at least one of the source tables. If you want only rows that appear in all the source tables, you can use the INTERSECT operation, which is the SQL implementation of relational algebra's intersect operation. To illustrate INTERSECT, the following example returns the Acme Systems warehouse table:

```
SELECT * FROM DEPOSIT ;

ProductName        QuantityInStock
-----------        ---------------
185_Express              12
505_Express               5
510_Express               6
520_Express               2
550_Express               3


SELECT * FROM KINGSTON ;

ProductName        QuantityInStock
-----------        ---------------
185_Express              15
505_Express               7
510_Express               6
520_Express               2
550_Express               1
```

Only rows that appear in all source tables show up in the INTERSECT operation's result table:

```
SELECT *
   FROM DEPOSIT
INTERSECT
SELECT *
   FROM KINGSTON;
```

```
ProductName        QuantityInStock
-----------        ----------------
510_Express               6
520_Express               2
```

The result table shows that the Fort Deposit and East Kingston warehouses both have exactly the same number of 510_Express and 520_Express products in stock, a fact of dubious value. Note that, as was the case with UNION, INTERSECT DISTINCT produces the same result as the INTERSECT operator used alone. In this example, only one of the identical rows displaying each of two products is returned.

The ALL and CORRESPONDING keywords function in an INTERSECT operation the same way they do in a UNION operation. If you use ALL, duplicates are retained in the result table. If you use CORRESPONDING, the intersected tables need not be union-compatible, although the corresponding columns need to have matching types and lengths.

Consider another example: A municipality keeps track of the phones carried by police officers, firefighters, parking enforcement officers, and other city employees. A database table called PHONES contains data on all phones in active use. Another table named OUT, with an identical structure, contains data on all phones that have been taken out of service. No cellphone should ever exist in both tables. With an INTERSECT operation, you can test to see whether such an unwanted duplication has occurred:

```
SELECT *
   FROM PHONES
INTERSECT CORRESPONDING BY (PhoneID)
SELECT *
   FROM OUT ;
```

If the result table contains any rows, you know you have a problem. You should investigate any PhoneID entries that appear in the result table. The corresponding phone is either active or out of service; it can't be both. After you detect the problem, you can perform a DELETE operation on one of the two tables to restore database integrity.

EXCEPT

The UNION operation acts on two source tables and returns all rows that appear in *either* table. The INTERSECT operation returns all rows that appear in *both* the first and the second table. In contrast, the EXCEPT (or EXCEPT DISTINCT) operation returns all rows that appear in the first table but that *do not* also appear in the second table.

Returning to the municipal phone database example, say that a group of phones that had been declared out of service and returned to the vendor for repairs have now been fixed and placed back into service. The PHONES table was updated to reflect the returned phones, but the returned phones were not removed from the OUT table as they should have been. You can display the PhoneID numbers of the phones in the OUT table, with the reactivated ones eliminated, using an EXCEPT operation:

```
SELECT *
   FROM OUT
EXCEPT CORRESPONDING BY (PhoneID)
SELECT *
   FROM PHONES;
```

This query returns all the rows in the OUT table whose PhoneID is not also present in the PHONES table. These are the phones still out of service.

Chapter 7

Joining Data Together in SQL

The preceding chapter describes how to use subqueries and relational operators to pull data from multiple tables in relational databases. This chapter shows how to collect information from multiple tables by using JOIN operators. A number of different joins exist, and each performs a somewhat different operation. Depending on what you want in terms of information retrieved from multiple tables, one or another of the joins or the other relational operators is likely to give it to you.

JOINS

The UNION, INTERSECT, and EXCEPT operators are valuable in multitable databases in which the tables are union-compatible. In many cases, however, you want to draw data from multiple tables that have very little in common. JOINs are powerful relational operators that combine data from multiple tables into a single result table. The source tables may have little (or even nothing) in common with each other.

SQL supports a number of types of JOINs. The best one to choose in a given situation depends on the result you're trying to achieve.

Cartesian product or cross join

Any multitable query is a type of JOIN. The source tables are joined in the sense that the result table includes information taken from all the source tables. The simplest JOIN is a two-table SELECT that has no WHERE clause qualifiers. Every row of the first table is joined to every row of the second table. The result table is referred to as the *Cartesian product* of the two source tables — the direct product of the two sets. (The less fancy name for the same thing is *cross join*.) The number of rows in the result table is equal to the number of rows in the first source table multiplied by the number of rows in the second source table.

For example, imagine that you're the personnel manager for a company and that part of your job is to maintain employee records. Most employee data, such as home address and telephone number, is not particularly sensitive. However, some data, such as current salary, should be available only to authorized personnel. To maintain security of the sensitive information, you'd probably keep it in a separate table that is password protected. Consider the following pair of tables:

```
EMPLOYEE                              COMPENSATION
--------                              ------------

EmpID                                 Employ
FName                                 Salary
LName                                 Bonus
City
Phone
```

Fill the tables with some sample data:

```
EmpID    FName    LName    City      Phone
-----    -----    -----    ----      -----
    1    Jenny    Smith    Orange    555-1001
    2    Bill     Jones    Newark    555-3221
    3    Val      Brown    Nutley    555-6905
    4    Justin   Time     Passaic   555-8908


Employ   Salary   Bonus
------   ------   -----
    1    63000    10000
    2    48000     2000
    3    54000     5000
    4    52000     7000
```

Create a virtual result table with the following query:

```
SELECT *
  FROM EMPLOYEE, COMPENSATION ;
```

which can also be written

```
SELECT *
  FROM EMPLOYEE CROSS JOIN COMPENSATION ;
```

Both of the previous formulations do the same thing. This query produces:

EmpID	FName	LName	City	Phone	Employ	Salary	Bonus
1	Jenny	Smith	Orange	555-1001	1	63000	10000
1	Jenny	Smith	Orange	555-1001	2	48000	2000
1	Jenny	Smith	Orange	555-1001	3	54000	5000
1	Jenny	Smith	Orange	555-1001	4	52000	7000
2	Bill	Jones	Newark	555-3221	1	63000	10000
2	Bill	Jones	Newark	555-3221	2	48000	2000
2	Bill	Jones	Newark	555-3221	3	54000	5000
2	Bill	Jones	Newark	555-3221	4	52000	7000
3	Val	Brown	Nutley	555-6905	1	63000	10000
3	Val	Brown	Nutley	555-6905	2	48000	2000
3	Val	Brown	Nutley	555-6905	3	54000	5000
3	Val	Brown	Nutley	555-6905	4	52000	7000
4	Justin	Time	Passaic	555-8908	1	63000	10000
4	Justin	Time	Passaic	555-8908	2	48000	2000
4	Justin	Time	Passaic	555-8908	3	54000	5000
4	Justin	Time	Passaic	555-8908	4	52000	7000

The result table, which is the Cartesian product of the EMPLOYEE and COMPENSATION tables, contains considerable redundancy. Furthermore, it doesn't make much sense. It combines every row of EMPLOYEE with every row of COMPENSATION. The only rows that convey meaningful information are those in which the EmpID number that came from EMPLOYEE matches the Employ number that came from COMPENSATION. In those rows, an employee's name and address are associated with that same employee's compensation.

When you're trying to get useful information out of a multitable database, the Cartesian product produced by a cross join is almost never what you want, but it's almost always the first step toward what you want. By applying constraints to the JOIN with a WHERE clause, you can filter out the unwanted rows. The most common JOIN that uses the WHERE clause filter is the equi-join.

Equi-join

An *equi-join* is a cross join with the addition of a WHERE clause containing a condition specifying that the value in one column in the first table must be equal to the value of a corresponding column in the second table. Applying an equi-join to the example tables from the previous section brings a more meaningful result:

```
SELECT *
    FROM EMPLOYEE, COMPENSATION
    WHERE EMPLOYEE.EmpID = COMPENSATION.Employ ;
```

This produces the following:

EmpID	FName	LName	City	Phone	Employ	Salary	Bonus
1	Jenny	Smith	Orange	555-1001	1	63000	10000
2	Bill	Jones	Newark	555-3221	2	48000	2000
3	Val	Brown	Nutley	555-6905	3	54000	5000
4	Justin	Time	Passaic	555-8908	4	52000	7000

In this result table, the salaries and bonuses on the right apply to the employees named on the left. The table still has some redundancy because the EmpID column duplicates the Employ column. You can fix this problem by specifying in your query which columns you want selected from the COMPENSATION table:

```
SELECT EMPLOYEE.*,COMPENSATION.Salary,COMPENSATION.Bonus
    FROM EMPLOYEE, COMPENSATION
    WHERE EMPLOYEE.EmpID = COMPENSATION.Employ ;
```

This produces the following result:

EmpID	FName	LName	City	Phone	Salary	Bonus
1	Jenny	Smith	Orange	555-1001	63000	10000
2	Bill	Jones	Newark	555-3221	48000	2000
3	Val	Brown	Nutley	555-6905	54000	5000
4	Justin	Time	Passaic	555-8908	52000	7000

This table tells you what you want to know but doesn't burden you with any extraneous data. The query is somewhat tedious to write, however. To avoid ambiguity, it makes sense to qualify the column names with the names of the tables they came from. However, writing those table names repeatedly can be tiresome.

You can cut down on the amount of typing by using aliases (or *correlation names*). An *alias* is a short name that stands for a table name. If you use aliases in recasting the preceding query, it comes out like this:

```
SELECT E.*, C.Salary, C.Bonus
    FROM EMPLOYEE E, COMPENSATION C
    WHERE E.EmpID = C.Employ ;
```

In this example, E is the alias for EMPLOYEE, and C is the alias for COMPENSATION. The alias is local to the statement it's in. After you declare an alias (in the FROM clause), you must use it throughout the statement. You can't use both the alias and the long form of the table name.

Mixing the long form of table names with aliases creates confusion. Consider the following example, which is confusing:

```
SELECT T1.C, T2.C
    FROM T1 T2, T2 T1
    WHERE T1.C > T2.C ;
```

In this example, the alias for T1 is T2, and the alias for T2 is T1. Admittedly, this isn't a smart selection of aliases, but the rules don't forbid it. If you mix aliases with long-form table names, you can't tell which table is which.

The preceding example with aliases is equivalent to the following SELECT with no aliases:

```
SELECT T2.C, T1.C
    FROM T1, T2
    WHERE T2.C > T1.C ;
```

SQL enables you to join more than two tables. The maximum number varies from one implementation to another. The syntax is analogous to the two-table case:

```
SELECT E.*, C.Salary, C.Bonus, Y.TotalSales
    FROM EMPLOYEE E, COMPENSATION C, YTD_SALES Y
    WHERE E.EmpID = C.Employ
        AND C.Employ = Y.EmpNo ;
```

This statement performs an equi-join on three tables, pulling data from corresponding rows of each one to produce a result table that shows the salespeople's names, the amount of sales they are responsible for, and their compensation. The sales manager can quickly see whether compensation is in line with production.

TIP

Storing a salesperson's year-to-date sales in a separate YTD_SALES table ensures better performance and reliability than keeping that data in the EMPLOYEE table. The data in the EMPLOYEE table is relatively static. A person's name, address, and telephone number don't change very often. In contrast, the year-to-date sales change frequently. (You hope.) Because the YTD_SALES table has fewer columns than EMPLOYEE, you may be able to update it more quickly. If, in the course of updating sales totals, you don't touch the EMPLOYEE table, you decrease the risk of accidentally modifying EMPLOYEE information that should stay the same.

Natural join

The *natural join* is a special case of an equi-join. In the WHERE clause of an equi-join, a column from one source table is compared with a column of a second source table for equality. The two columns must be the same type and length and must have the same name. In fact, in a natural join, *all* columns in one table that have the same names, types, and lengths as corresponding columns in the second table are compared for equality.

Imagine that the COMPENSATION table from the preceding example has columns EmpID, Salary, and Bonus rather than Employ, Salary, and Bonus. In that case, you can perform a natural join of the COMPENSATION table with the EMPLOYEE table. The traditional JOIN syntax looks like this:

```
SELECT E.*, C.Salary, C.Bonus
    FROM EMPLOYEE E, COMPENSATION C
    WHERE E.EmpID = C.EmpID ;
```

This query is a natural join. An alternate syntax for the same operation is the following:

```
SELECT E.*, C.Salary, C.Bonus
    FROM EMPLOYEE E NATURAL JOIN COMPENSATION C ;
```

Condition join

A *condition join* is like an equi-join, except the condition being tested doesn't have to be equality (although it can be). It can be any well-formed predicate. If the condition is satisfied, the corresponding row becomes part of the result table. The syntax is a little different from what you have seen so far, in that the condition is contained in an ON clause rather than a WHERE clause.

Suppose Acme Systems wants to know which products the Fort Deposit warehouse has in larger numbers than does the East Kingston warehouse. This question is a job for a condition join:

```
SELECT *
    FROM DEPOSIT JOIN KINGSTON
    ON DEPOSIT.QuantityInStock > KINGSTON.QuantityInStock ;
```

Within the predicate of a condition join, ON syntax is used in place of WHERE syntax.

Column-name join

The *column-name join* is like a natural join, but it's more flexible. In a natural join, all the source table columns that have the same name are compared with each other for equality. With the column-name join, you select which same-name columns to compare. You can choose them all if you want, making the column-name join effectively a natural join. Or you may choose fewer than all same-name columns. In this way, you have a great degree of control over which cross product rows qualify to be placed into your result table.

Suppose you are Acme Systems, and you have shipped the exact same number of products to the East Kingston warehouse that you have shipped to the Fort Deposit warehouse. So far, nothing has been sold, so the number of products in inventory in East Kingston should match the number in Fort Deposit. If there are mismatches, it means that something is wrong. Either some products were never delivered to the warehouse, or they were misplaced or stolen after they arrived. With a simple query, you can retrieve the inventory levels at the two warehouses.

```
SELECT * FROM DEPOSIT ;

ProductName       QuantityInStock
-----------       ---------------
185_Express             12
505_Express              5
510_Express              6
520_Express              2
550_Express              3

SELECT * FROM KINGSTON ;
```

```
ProductName      QuantityInStock
-----------      ---------------
185_Express             15
505_Express              7
510_Express              6
520_Express              2
550_Express              1
```

For such small tables, it is fairly easy to see which rows don't match. However, it's not so easy for a table with thousands of rows. You can use a column-name join to see whether any discrepancies exist. I show only two columns of the DEPOSIT and KINGSTON tables to make it easy to see how the various relational operators work on them. In any real application, such tables would have additional columns, and the contents of those additional columns would not necessarily match. With a column-name join, the join operation considers only the columns specified.

```
SELECT *
    FROM DEPOSIT JOIN KINGSTON
    USING (ProductName, QuantityInStock) ;
```

Note the USING keyword, which tells the DBMS which columns to use.

The result table shows only the rows for which the number of products in stock at Fort Deposit equals the number of products in stock at East Kingston:

```
ProductName QuantityInStock ProductName QuantityInStock
----------- --------------- ----------- ---------------
510_Express        6        510_Express        6
520_Express        2        520_Express        2
```

Wow! Only two products match. There is a definite "shrinkage" problem at one or both warehouses. Acme needs to get a handle on security.

Inner join

By now, you're probably getting the idea that joins are pretty esoteric and that it takes an uncommon level of spiritual discernment to deal with them adequately. You may have even heard of the mysterious *inner join* and speculated that it probably represents the core or essence of relational operations. Well, ha! The joke is on you: There's nothing mysterious about inner joins. In fact, all the joins covered so far in this chapter are inner joins. The column-name join in the last example could be formulated as an inner join by using the following syntax:

```
SELECT *
  FROM DEPOSIT INNER JOIN KINGSTON
  USING (ProductName, QuantityInStock) ;
```

The result is the same.

The inner join is so named to distinguish it from the outer join. An *inner join* discards all rows from the result table that don't have corresponding rows in both source tables. An *outer join* preserves unmatched rows. That's the difference. Nothing metaphysical about it.

Outer join

When you're joining two tables, the first one (call it the one on the left) may have rows that don't have matching counterparts in the second table (the one on the right). Conversely, the table on the right may have rows that don't have matching counterparts in the table on the left. If you perform an inner join on those tables, all the unmatched rows are excluded from the output. *Outer joins*, however, don't exclude the unmatched rows. Outer joins come in three types: the left outer join, the right outer join, and the full outer join.

Left outer join

In a query that includes a join, the left table is the one that precedes the keyword JOIN, and the right table is the one that follows it. The *left outer join* preserves unmatched rows from the left table but discards unmatched rows from the right table.

To understand outer joins, consider a corporate database that maintains records of the company's employees, departments, and locations. Tables 7-1, 7-2, and 7-3 contain the database's sample data.

TABLE 7-1

LOCATION

LocationID	CITY
1	Boston
3	Tampa
5	Chicago

	TABLE 7-2	**DEPT**		
		DeptID	LocationID	NAME
		21	1	Sales
		24	1	Admin
		27	5	Repair
		29	5	Stock

	TABLE 7-3	**EMPLOYEE**		
		EmpID	DeptID	NAME
		61	24	Kirk
		63	27	McCoy

Now suppose that you want to see all the data for all employees, including department and location. You get this with an equi-join:

```
SELECT *
    FROM LOCATION L, DEPT D, EMPLOYEE E
    WHERE L.LocationID = D.LocationID
        AND D.DeptID = E.DeptID ;
```

This statement produces the following result:

```
1    Boston    24    1    Admin    61    24    Kirk
5    Chicago   27    5    Repair   63    27    McCoy
```

This results table gives all the data for all the employees, including their location and department. The equi-join works because every employee has a location and a department.

Suppose now that you want the data on the locations with the related department and employee data. This is a different problem because a location without any associated departments may exist. To get what you want, you have to use an outer join, as in the following example:

```
SELECT *
    FROM LOCATION L LEFT OUTER JOIN DEPT D
        ON (L.LocationID = D.LocationID)
    LEFT OUTER JOIN EMPLOYEE E
        ON (D.DeptID = E.DeptID);
```

This join pulls data from three tables. First, the LOCATION table is joined to the DEPT table. The resulting table is then joined to the EMPLOYEE table. Rows from the table on the left of the LEFT OUTER JOIN operator that have no corresponding row in the table on the right are included in the result. Thus, in the first join, all locations are included, even if no department associated with them exists. In the second join, all departments are included, even if no employee associated with them exists. The result is as follows:

1	Boston	24	1	Admin	61	24	Kirk
5	Chicago	27	5	Repair	63	27	McCoy
3	Tampa	NULL	NULL	NULL	NULL	NULL	NULL
5	Chicago	29	5	Stock	NULL	NULL	NULL
1	Boston	21	1	Sales	NULL	NULL	NULL

The first two rows are the same as the two result rows in the previous example. The third row (3 Tampa) has nulls in the department and employee columns because no departments are defined for Tampa and no employees are stationed there. (Perhaps Tampa is a brand new location and has not yet been staffed.) The fourth and fifth rows (5 Chicago and 1 Boston) contain data about the Stock and the Sales departments, but the employee columns for these rows contain nulls because these two departments have no employees. This outer join tells you everything that the equi-join told you, plus the following:

>> All the company's locations, whether or not they have any departments

>> All the company's departments, whether or not they have any employees

The rows returned in the preceding example aren't guaranteed to be in the order you want. The order may vary from one implementation to the next. To make sure that the rows returned are in the order you want, add an ORDER BY clause to your SELECT statement, like this:

```
SELECT *
    FROM LOCATION L LEFT OUTER JOIN DEPT D
        ON (L.LocationID = D.LocationID)
    LEFT OUTER JOIN EMPLOYEE E
        ON (D.DeptID = E.DeptID)
    ORDER BY L.LocationID, D.DeptID, E.EmpID;
```

TIP

You can abbreviate the left outer join language as LEFT JOIN because there's no such thing as a left inner join.

Right outer join

I'm sure you have figured out by now how the right outer join behaves. It preserves unmatched rows from the right table but discards unmatched rows from the left table. You can use it on the same tables and get the same result by reversing the order in which you present tables to the join:

```
SELECT *
    FROM EMPLOYEE E RIGHT OUTER JOIN DEPT D
        ON (D.DeptID = E.DeptID)
    RIGHT OUTER JOIN LOCATION L
        ON (L.LocationID = D.LocationID) ;
```

In this formulation, the first join produces a table that contains all departments, whether they have an associated employee or not. The second join produces a table that contains all locations, whether they have an associated department or not.

You can abbreviate the right outer join language as RIGHT JOIN because there's no such thing as a right inner join.

Full outer join

The *full outer join* combines the functions of the left outer join and the right outer join. It retains the unmatched rows from both the left and the right tables. Consider the most general case of the company database used in the preceding examples. It could have

» Locations with no departments

» Locations with no employees

» Departments with no locations

» Departments with no employees

» Employees with no locations

» Employees with no departments

REMEMBER

Whereas the preceding named conditions are unusual, they can happen, particularly in a startup situation, and when they do, you'll be glad you have outer joins to deal with them. As soon as you say that a certain situation is not possible, reality will conk you on the head with an example of that very situation.

To show all locations, departments, and employees, regardless of whether they have corresponding rows in the other tables, use a full outer join in the following form:

```
SELECT *
    FROM LOCATION L FULL OUTER JOIN DEPT D
        ON (L.LocationID = D.LocationID)
    FULL OUTER JOIN EMPLOYEE E
        ON (D.DeptID = E.DeptID) ;
```

TIP

You can abbreviate the full outer join language as FULL JOIN because there's no such thing as a full inner join.

ON versus WHERE

The function of the ON and WHERE clauses in the various types of joins is potentially confusing. These facts may help you keep things straight:

>> The ON clause is part of the inner, left, right, and full joins. The cross join and UNION join don't have an ON clause because neither of them does any filtering of the data.

>> The ON clause in an inner join is logically equivalent to a WHERE clause; the same condition could be specified either in the ON clause or a WHERE clause.

>> The ON clauses in outer joins (left, right, and full joins) are different from WHERE clauses. The WHERE clause simply filters the rows returned by the FROM clause. Rows rejected by the filter are not included in the result. The ON clause in an outer join first filters the rows of a cross product and then includes the rejected rows, extended with nulls.

Join Conditions and Clustering Indexes

The performance of queries that include joins depends, to a large extent, on which columns are indexed and whether or not the index is clustering. A table can have only one clustering index, where data items that are near each other logically, such as 'Smith' and 'Smithson', are also near each other physically on disk. Using a clustering index to step through a table sequentially speeds up hard disk retrievals and thus maximizes performance.

REMEMBER

An index is a separate table that corresponds to a data table but is sorted in some order. A clustering index is an index sorted in the same order that items are stored in memory and thus provides the fastest retrievals.

A clustering index works well with multipoint queries, which look for equality in nonunique columns. This is similar to looking up names in a telephone book. All the Smiths are listed together on consecutive pages. Most or all of them are located on the same hard disk cylinder. You can access multiple Smiths with a single disk seek operation. A nonclustering index, on the other hand, would not have this advantage. Each record typically requires a new disk seek, greatly slowing down operation. Furthermore, you probably have to touch every index to be sure you have not missed one. This is analogous to searching the greater Los Angeles telephone book for every instance of Area Code 626. Most of the numbers are in Area 213, but there will be instances of 626 sprinkled throughout the book.

Consider the following sample query:

```
SELECT Employee.FirstName, Employee.LastName, Student.Major
   FROM Employee, Students
   WHERE Employee.IDNum = Student.IDNum ;
```

This query returns the first and last names and the majors of university employees who are also students. How long it takes to run the query depends on how the tables are indexed. If Employee has a clustering index on IDNum, records searched are on consecutive pages. If Employee and Student both have clustering indexes on IDNum, the DBMS will likely use a merge join, which reads both tables in sorted order, minimizing the number of disk accesses needed. Such clustering often eliminates the need for a costly ORDER BY clause because the records are already sorted in the desired order.

The one disadvantage of clustered indexes is that they can become "tired" (meaning less helpful) after a number of updates have been performed, causing the generation of overflow pages, which require additional disk seeks. Rebuilding the index corrects this problem. Every time you add or delete a record, the index loses some of its advantage. A deleted record must be skipped over and added records must be put on an overflow page, which will usually require a couple of extra disk seeks.

BEST PRACTICE

When performance slows, or data slows down, it's generally a good idea to reindex as it's a sign the data is fragmented due to being "tired."

Some modern DBMS products perform automatic clustered index maintenance, meaning they rebuild clustered indexes without having to be told to do so. If you have such a product, then the disadvantage noted previously goes away.

5

Performing Statistical Data Analysis & Visualization with R Programming

Contents at a Glance

Chapter **1**

Using Open Source R for Data Science

D ata science involves the skillful application of math, coding, and subject matter expertise in ways that allow data scientists to generate reliable and accurate predictions from data. While the last element — subject matter expertise — is unique to each practitioner, if you apply data science within a business context, then you'd want to make sure you've got a good handle on the needed business acumen and the math-and-statistics requirements of data science (Book 1, Chapter 3). Another important data science constituent to consider is coding, which can be done using the open source programming language R, as covered in this chapter, or Python (covered in Book 6).

This chapter describes the fundamental concepts of programming with R (such as data types, functions, and classes). The machine learning models you build with R or Python can serve as the *decision engines* within AI SaaS products you build for your company. The chapter also introduces some of the best R packages for manipulating data, performing statistical computations, creating data visualizations, and completing other data science tasks.

Downloading Open Source R

R is an open-source, free statistical software system that, like Python (covered in Book 6), has been widely adopted across the data science sector over the past decade. In fact, a somewhat never-ending squabble takes place among data science types about which programming language is best suited for data science. Practitioners who favor R generally do so because of its advanced statistical programming and data visualization capabilities — capabilities that simply can't be replicated in Python. When it comes to data science practitioners, specifically, R's user base is broader than Python's.

You can download the R programming language and the packages that support it from http://cran.r-project.org.

R isn't as easy to learn as Python, but R can be more powerful for certain types of advanced statistical analyses. Although R's learning curve is somewhat steeper than Python's, the programming language is nonetheless relatively straightforward. All you really need to do is master the basic vocabulary used to describe the language, and then it shouldn't be too hard to grasp how the software works.

Comprehending R's Basic Vocabulary

Although the vocabulary associated with R may sound exotic at first, with practice you can quickly become comfortable with it. For starters, you can run R in one of two modes:

» **Non-interactive:** You run your R code by executing it as an .r file directly from the command line. (The .r file extension is the one that's assigned to script files created for execution by the R program.)

» **Interactive:** You generally work in a separate software application that interacts with you by prompting you to enter your data and R code. In an R session using interactive mode, you can import datasets or enter the raw data directly; assign names to variables and data objects; and use functions, operators, and built-in iterators to help you gain some insight into your source data.

REMEMBER

R is an *object-oriented* language, which simply means that the different parts that comprise the language belong to classes — each class has its own specific definition and role. A specific example of a class is known as an *instance* of that class; as an instance, it inherits the class's characteristics. Classes are also referred to as *polymorphic*, meaning the subclasses of a class can have their own set of unique behaviors yet share some of the same functionality as the parent class. To illustrate this concept, consider R's print function: print( ). Because this function is polymorphic, it works slightly differently depending on the class of the object it's told to print. Thus, this function and many others perform the same general job in many classes but differ slightly according to class. The section "Observing How Objects Work," later in this chapter, elaborates on object-oriented programming and its advantages, but for now, this section simply introduces objects by giving you their names and definitions.

Here goes!

R works with the following main object types:

>> **Vector:** A *vector* is an ordered list of the same mode — character (alphanumeric), numeric, or Boolean. Vectors can have any number of dimensions. For instance, the vector A = ["a", "cat", "def"] is a 3-dimensional Character vector. B = [2, 3.1, –5, 33] is a 4-dimensional Numerical vector. To identify specific elements of these vectors, you can enter the following codes at the prompt in Interactive mode to get R to generate the following returns: A[[1]] = "a" or A[[2]] = "cat" or A[[3]] = "def" or B[[1]] = 2 or B[[2]] = 3.1 or B[[3]] = –5 or B[[4]] = 33. R views a single number as a vector of dimension one. Because vectors can't be broken down further in R, they're also known as *atomic vectors*. An atomic vector can be logical , integer , numeric , complex , character, or raw; it can have any attributes except a dimension attribute. An atomic vector though can have only one type, not many. R's treatment of atomic vectors gives the language tremendous advantages with respect to speed and efficiency (see the section "Iterating in R," later in this chapter).

>> **Matrix:** Think of a *matrix* as a collection of vectors. A matrix can be of any mode (numerical, character, or Boolean), but all elements in the matrix must be of the same mode. A matrix is also characterized by its number of dimensions. Unlike a vector, a matrix has only two dimensions: number of rows and number of columns.

>> **List:** A *list* is a list of items of arbitrary modes, including other lists or vectors.

TECHNICAL STUFF

Lists are sometimes also called *generic vectors* because some of the same operations performed on vectors can be performed on lists as well.

>> **Data frame:** A data frame is a type of list that's analogous to a table in a database. Technically speaking, a data frame is a list of vectors, each of which is the same length. A row in a table contains the information for an individual record, but elements in the row most likely won't be of the same mode. All elements in a specific column, however, are of the same mode. Data frames are structured in this same way — each vector in a data frame corresponds to a column in a data table, and each possible index for these vectors is a row.

There are two ways to access members of vectors, matrices, and lists in R:

>> **Single brackets** [ ] give a vector, matrix, or list (respectively) of the element(s) that are indexed.

>> **Double brackets** [[ ]] give a single element.

R users sometimes disagree about the proper use of the brackets for indexing. Generally speaking, the double bracket has several advantages over the single bracket. For example, the double bracket returns an error message if you enter an index that's out of bounds — or, in other words, an index value that does not exist within the given object. If, however, you want to indicate more than one element of a vector, matrix, or list, you should use a single bracket.

Now that you have a grasp of R's basic vocabulary, you're probably eager to see how it works with some actual programming. Imagine that you're using a simple EmployeeRoll dataset and entering the dataset into R by hand. You'd come up with something that looks like Listing 1-1.

LISTING 1-1: **Assigning an Object and Concatenating in R**

```
> EmployeeRoll <- data.frame(list(EmployeeName=c("Smith, John","O'Bannon,
  Tom","Simmons, Sarah"),Grade=c(10,8,12),Salary=c(100000,75000,125000),
  Union=c(TRUE, FALSE, TRUE)))
> EmployeeRoll
EmployeeName Grade Salary Union
1 Smith,John 10 100000 TRUE
2 O'Bannon, Tom 8 75000 FALSE
3 Simmons, Sarah 12 125000 TRUE
```

The combined symbol <- in the first line of Listing 1-1 is pronounced "gets." It assigns the contents on its right to the name on its left. You can think of this relationship in even simpler terms by considering the following statement, which assigns the number 3 to the variable c:

```
> c <- 3
```

Line 1 of Listing 1-1 also exhibits the use of R's concatenate function — c( ) — which is used to create a vector. The concatenate function is being used to form the atomic vectors that comprise the vector list that makes up the EmployeeRoll data frame. Line 2 of Listing 1-1, EmployeeRoll, instructs R to display the object's contents on the screen. (Figure 1-1 breaks out the data in more diagrammatic form.)

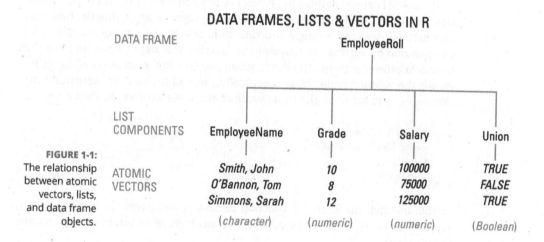

DATA FRAMES, LISTS & VECTORS IN R

FIGURE 1-1:
The relationship between atomic vectors, lists, and data frame objects.

One other object within R is vitally important: the function. *Functions* use atomic vectors, matrices, lists, and data frames to accomplish whatever analysis or computation you want done. (The following section covers functions more thoroughly. For now, you should simply understand their general role.) Each analysis you perform in R may be done in one or more sessions, which consists of entering a set of instructions that tells R what you want it to do with the data you've entered or imported. In each session, you specify the functions of your script. Then the blocks of code process any input that's received and return an output. A function's input (also known as a function's *arguments*) can be any R object or combination of objects — vectors, matrices, arrays, data frames, tables, or even other functions.

Invoking a function in R is known as *calling* a function.

Delving into Functions and Operators

You can choose one of two methods when writing your functions: a quick, simple method and a more complex, but ultimately more useful, method. Of course, you achieve the same result from choosing either approach, but each method is advantageous in its own way. If you want to call a function and generate a result as simply and quickly as possible and don't think you'll want to reuse the function later, use Method 1. If you want to write a function that you can call for different purposes and use with different datasets in the future, use Method 2 instead.

To illustrate the difference between these two methods, consider again the EmployeeRoll dataset defined in Listing 1-1. Say you want to come up with a function you can use to derive a mean value for employee salary. Using the first, simpler method, you call a single function to handle that task: You simply define an operation by writing the name of the function you want to use, and you then include whatever argument(s) the function requires in the set of parentheses following the function name. More specifically, you call the built-in statistical function mean( ) to calculate the mean value of employee salaries, as shown here:

```
> #Method 1 of Calculating the Mean Salary
> MeanSalary1 <- mean(EmployeeRoll$Salary)
> MeanSalary1
[1] 1e+05
```

In this method, the mean( ) function calculates and saves the average salary, 100,000 (or 1e+05, in scientific notation) as an object (a vector, of course!) named MeanSalary1.

TECHNICAL
STUFF

The $ symbol points R to a particular field in the dataset. In this example, it points R to the Salary field of the EmployeeRoll dataset.

Method 2 illustrates a more complicated but possibly more useful approach. Rather than define only a single operation, as in Method 1, Method 2's function can define a series of separate operations if they're needed; therefore, the method can oftentimes grow quite complex. In the following chunk of code, the statement MeanSalary2 <- function(x) creates a function named MeanSalary2, which takes one argument, x. The statements between the curly braces ({ }) make up this function. The job of {return(mean(x))} is to calculate the mean of some entity x and then return that value as a result to the computer screen:

```
> #Method 2 of Calculating the Mean Salary
> #This method allows the user to create a custom set of instructions for R that
    can be used again and again.
```

```
> MeanSalary2 <- function(x) {return(mean(x))}
>
> MeanSalary2(EmployeeRoll$Salary)
[1] 1e+05
```

The argument of the function definition isn't the `Salary` field from the `EmployeeRoll` dataset because this type of function can be called and used for different purposes on different datasets and different fields of said datasets. Also, nothing happens when you finish typing the function and press Return after entering the ending curly brace; in the next line, you just get another prompt (>). That's because you set up the function correctly. (You know it's correct because you didn't get an error message.) You can now call this function when you actually need it — that's what the last instruction entered at the prompt in the preceding code does. Typing `MeanSalary2(EmployeeRoll$Salary)` is a *function call,* and it replaces the function's placeholder argument x with `EmployeeRoll$Salary` — a real object that allows the function to generate a solution.

Of course, the function that's written in Method 2 yields the same mean salary as did the function in Method 1, but the Method 2 function can now be reused for different applications. To illustrate how you'd use this same function on a different dataset, imagine that you have another business with its own payroll. It has five employees with the following salaries: $500,000; $1,000,000; $75,000; $112,000; and $400,000. If you want to call and use the `MeanSalary2` function to find the mean salary of these employees, you can simply write

```
> MeanSalary2(c(500000,1000000,75000,112000,400000))
[1] 417400
```

As instructed in Method 2, the `MeanSalary2` function quickly generates a mean value for this new dataset — in this case, $417,400.

The primary benefit of using functions in R is that they make it easier to write cleaner, more concise code that's easy to read and more readily reusable. But at the most fundamental level, R is simply using functions to apply operators. Although applying operators and calling functions both serve the same purpose, you can distinguish the two techniques by their differing syntaxes.

Speaking of operators, R uses many of the same ones used in other programming languages. Table 1-1 lists the more commonly used operators.

REMEMBER

Operators act as functions in R. (I *warned* you that learning the vocabulary of R can be tricky!)

TABLE 1-1

Popular Operators

Operation	Operator
Plus	+
Minus	–
Times	*
Divide	/
Modulo	%%
Power	^
Greater than	>
Greater than or equal to	>=
Less than	<
Less than or equal to	<=
Equals	==
Not equals	!=
Not (logical)	!
And (logical)	&
Or (logical)		
Is assigned; gets	<-
Is assigned to	->

The code snippet shows several examples of where operators are used as functions:

```
> "<"(2,3)
[1] TRUE
> "<"(100,10)
[1] FALSE
> "+"(100,1)
[1] 101
> "/"(4,2)
[1] 2
> "+"(2,5,6,3,10)
Error in `+`(2, 5, 6, 3, 10) : operator needs one or two arguments
```

In the preceding snippet, the Boolean operators less-than (<) and greater-than (>) return a value of either TRUE or FALSE. Also, do you see the error message that's generated by the last line of code? That error happened because the operator + can take only one or two arguments, and in that example, I provided three arguments more than it could handle.

TIP

You can use the + operator to add two numbers or two vectors. In fact, all arithmetic operators in R can accept both numbers and vectors as arguments. For more on arithmetic operators, check out the following section.

Iterating in R

Because of the way R handles vectors, programming in R offers an efficient way to handle loops and iterations. Essentially, R has built-in iterators that automatically loop over elements without the added hassle of having to write out the loops yourself.

To better conceptualize this process, called *vectorization*, imagine that you want to add a constant c = 3 to a series of three numbers that you've stored as a vector, m = [10, 6, 9]. You can use the following code:

```
> c <- 3
> m <- c(10, 6, 9)
> x <- m + c
> x
[1] 13 9 12
```

The preceding method works because of an R property known as *recyclability*: If you perform operations on two vectors of different lengths, R repeats and reuses the smaller vector to make the operation work. In this example, c was a 1-dimensional vector, but R reused it to convert it to a 3-dimensional vector so that the operation could be performed on m.

Here's the logic behind this process:

```
10 + 3 = 13
6 + 3 = 9
9 + 3 = 12
```

This method works also because of the vectorization of the + operator, which performs the + operation on the vectors m and c — in effect, looping through each of the vectors to add their corresponding elements.

Here's another way of writing this process that makes the vectorization of the + operator obvious:

```
> x <- "+"(m,c)
```

R vectorizes all arithmetic operators, including +, -, /, *, and ^.

When you're using conditional statements within iterative loops, R uses vectorization to make this process more efficient. If you've used other programming languages, you've probably seen a structure that looks something like this:

```
for (y = 1 through 5) { if (3*y <= 4) then z = 1 else z = 0}
```

This loop iterates the code within the brackets ({ }) sequentially for each y equal to 1, 2, 3, 4, and 5. Within this loop, for each y-value, the conditional statement $3*y <= 4$ generates either a TRUE or a FALSE statement. For y-values that yield TRUE values, z is set to 1; otherwise, it's set to 0. This loop thus generates the following:

```
| y | 3*y | 3*y <= 4 | z |
| 1 | 3   | TRUE     | 1 |
| 2 | 6   | FALSE    | 0 |
| 3 | 9   | FALSE    | 0 |
| 4 | 12  | FALSE    | 0 |
| 5 | 15  | FALSE    | 0 |
```

Now check out how you can do this same thing using R:

```
> y <- 1:5
> z <- ifelse(3*y <= 4, 1, 0)
> z
[1] 1 0 0 0 0
```

It's much more compact, right? In the preceding R code, the y term represents the numerical vector [1, 2, 3, 4, 5]. As was the case earlier, in the R code the operator <= is vectorized, and recyclability is again applied so that the scalar 4 is treated as a 5-dimensional vector [4, 4, 4, 4, 4] to make the vector operation work. As before, only where y = 1 is the condition met and, consequently, z[[1]] = 1 and z[2:5] = 0.

In R, you often see something that looks like 1:10. This *colon operator* notates a sequence of numbers — the first number, the last number, and the sequence that lies between them. Thus, the vector 1:10 is equivalent to 1, 2, 3, 4, 5, 6, 7, 8, 9, 10 and 2:5 is equal to 2, 3, 4, 5.

Observing How Objects Work

R's object-oriented approach makes deploying and maintaining code relatively quick and easy. As part of this object-oriented functionality, objects in R are distinguished by characteristics known as *attributes*. Each object is defined by its attributes; more specifically, it is defined by its class attribute.

For example, the USDA provides data on the percentages of insect-resistant and herbicide-tolerant corn planted yearly for years ranging from 2000 through 2014. You could use a linear regression function on this information to predict the percentage of herbicide-tolerant corn planted in Illinois from 2000 to 2014, from the percentage of insect-resistant corn planted in Illinois during these same years. The dataset and function are shown in Listing 1-2.

LISTING 1-2: **Exploring Objects in R**

```
> GeneticallyEngineeredCorn <- data.frame(list(year=c(2000, 2001, 2002,
    2003, 2004, 2005, 2006, 2007, 2008, 2009, 2010, 2011, 2012, 2013,
    2014),Insect =c(13, 12,18,23,26,25,24,19,13, 10, 15, 14, 14, 4, 3),
    herbicide=c(3,3,3,4,5,6,12,15,15,15,15,17,18,7,5)))
> GeneticallyEngineeredCorn
   year Insect herbicide
1  2000    13       3
2  2001    12       3
3  2002    18       3
4  2003    23       4
5  2004    26       5
6  2005    25       6
7  2006    24      12
8  2007    19      15
9  2008    13      15
10 2009    10      15
11 2010    15      15
12 2011    14      17
13 2012    14      18
14 2013     4       7
15 2014     3       5
> PredictHerbicide <- lm(GeneticallyEngineeredCorn$herbicide
    GeneticallyEngineeredCorn$Insect)
> attributes(PredictHerbicide)$names
 [1] "coefficients"  "residuals"     "effects"       "rank"
 [5] "fitted.values" "assign"        "qr"            "df.residual"
 [9] "xlevels"       "call"          "terms"         "model"
> attributes(PredictHerbicide)$class
 [1] "lm"
```

```
> PredictHerbicide$coef
                (Intercept) GeneticallyEngineeredCorn$Insect
    10.52165581                          -0.06362591
```

In Listing 1-2, the expression `PredictHerbicide <- lm(GeneticallyEngineered`
`Corn$herbicide ~ GeneticallyEngineeredCorn$Insect)` instructs R to perform a linear regression and assign the results to the `PredictHerbicide` object.
In the linear regression, `GeneticallyEngineeredCorn` is defined as the source
dataset, the `Insect` column acts as the independent variable, and the `herbicide`
column acts as the dependent variable.

R's `attribute` function returns information about an object's attributes. In this
example, typing in the function `attribute(PredictHerbicide)$names` instructs
R to name all attributes of the `PredictHerbicide` object, and the function
`attribute(PredictHerbicide)$class` instructs R to identify the object's classes.
You can see from Listing 1-2 that the `PredictHerbicide` object has 12 attributes
and has class `lm` (which stands for linear model).

R allows you to request specifics on each of these attributes, but to keep this
example brief, simply ask R to specify the coefficients of the linear regression
equation. Looking back, you can see that this is the first attribute provided for the
`PredictHerbicide` object. To ask R to show the coefficients obtained by fitting the
linear model to the data, enter `PredictHerbicide$coef`, as shown in Listing 1-2,
and R returns the following information:

```
    (Intercept) GeneticallyEngineeredCorn$Insect
    10.52165581                          -0.06362591
```

In plain math, the preceding result translates into the equation shown in
Figure 1-2.

FIGURE 1-2:
Linear regression
coefficients from
R, translated
into a plain math
equation.

$$\left(\% _{\text{herbicide-resistant corn}}\right)_{\text{Illinois, 2000-2014}} = 10.52165581 - 0.06362591 \left(\% _{\text{insect-resistance corn}}\right)_{\text{Illinois, 2000-2014}}$$

Translated into mathematical terms, this is equivalent to the following:

Percentage of Genetically Engineered Herbicide-Tolerant Corn = 10.5 – 0.06 *
Percentage of Genetically Engineered Insect-Resistant Corn

Thus, l the relationship between the two variables appears rather weak so the percentage of genetically engineered, insect-resistant corn planted wouldn't provide a good predictor of the percentage of herbicide-resistant corn planted.

This example also illustrates the polymorphic nature of generic functions in R — that is, where the same function can be adapted to the class it's used with, thus making that function applicable to many different classes. The polymorphic function of this example is R's attributes( ) function. This function is applicable to the lm (linear model) class, the mean class, the histogram class, and many others.

REMEMBER

If you want to get a quick orientation when working with instances of an unfamiliar class, R's polymorphic generic functions can come in handy. These functions generally tend to make R a more efficiently mastered programming language.

Sorting Out R's Popular Statistical Analysis Packages

R has a plethora of easy-to-install packages and functions, many of which are quite useful in data science. In an R context, *packages* are bundles composed of specific functions, data, and code suited for performing specific types of analyses or sets of analyses, including forecasting, multivariate analysis, and factor analysis The CRAN site lists the current packages available for download at http://cran.r-project.org/web/packages, along with directions on how to download and install them. This section discusses some popular packages and then delves deeper into the capabilities of a few of the more advanced packages available.

Let me start with R's forecast package, which contains various forecasting functions that you can adapt to use for AutoRegressive Integrated Moving Average (ARIMA) time series forecasting, or for other types of univariate time series forecasts. Or perhaps you want to use R for quality management? You can use R's Quality Control Charts package (qcc) for quality and statistical process control.

In the practice of data science, you're likely to benefit from almost any package that specializes in multivariate analysis. If you want to carry out logistic regression, you can use R's *multinomial logit model* (mlogit), in which observations of a known class are used to "train" the software so that it can identify classes of other observations whose classes are unknown.

If you want to use R to take undifferentiated data and identify which of its factors is significant for some specific purpose, you can use factor analysis. To better illustrate the fundamental concept of factor analysis, imagine that you own a restaurant. You want to do everything you can to make sure its customer satisfaction rating is as high as possible, right? Well, factor analysis can help you determine which exact factors have the largest impact on customer satisfaction ratings — those could coalesce into the general factors of ambience, restaurant layout, and employee appearance, attitude, and knowledge. With this knowledge, you can work on improving these factors to increase customer satisfaction and, with it, brand loyalty.

TIP

For information on additional R packages, check out the R Project website at www.r-project.org. You can find a lot of existing online documentation to help you identify which packages best suit your needs. Also, coders in R's active community are making new packages and functions available all the time.

Examining Packages for Visualizing, Mapping, and Graphing in R

The following sections introduce some powerful R packages for data visualization, network graph analysis, and spatial point pattern analysis.

Visualizing R statistics with ggplot2

If you're looking for a fast and efficient way to produce good-looking data visualizations that you can use to derive and communicate insights from your datasets, look no further than R's ggplot2 package. It was designed to help you create all different types of data graphics in R, including histograms, scatterplots, bar charts, boxplots, and density plots. It offers a wide variety of design options as well, including choices in colors, layout, transparency, and line density. Admittedly, ggplot2 probably isn't the best option if you're looking to do data storytelling or data art, but it's definitely useful for data showcasing.

To better understand how the ggplot2 package works, consider the following example. Figure 1-3 shows a simple scatterplot that was generated using ggplot2. This scatterplot depicts the concentrations (in parts per million, or ppm) of four types of pesticides detected in a stream between the years 2000 and 2013. The scatterplot could have been designed to show only the pesticide concentrations for each year, but ggplot2 provides an option for fitting a regression line to each pesticide type. (The regression lines are the solid lines shown on the plot.) You can also have ggplot2 present these pesticide types in different colors. The colored areas enclosing the regression lines represent 95 percent confidence intervals for the regression models.

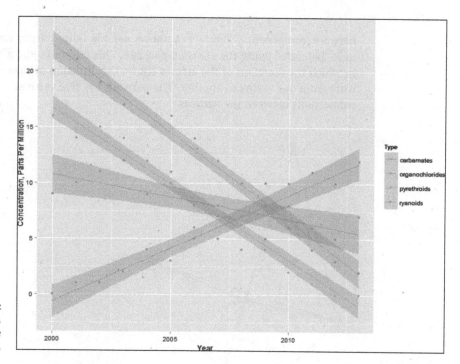

FIGURE 1-3:
A scatterplot,
generated in the
ggplot2 package.

The scatterplot chart makes it clear that all pesticides except for ryanoids are showing decreasing stream concentrations. Organochlorides had the highest concentration in 2000, but then exhibited the greatest decrease in concentration over the 13-year period.

Analyzing networks with statnet and igraph

Social networks and social network data volumes have absolutely exploded over the past decade. Therefore, knowing how to make sense of network data has become increasingly important for analysts. Social network analysis skills enable you to analyze social networks to uncover how accounts are connected and the ways in which information is shared across those connections. You can use network analysis methods to determine how fast information spreads across the Internet. You can even use network analysis methods in genetic mapping to better understand how one gene affects and influences the activity of other genes or use them in hydraulic modeling to figure out how to best design a water-distribution or sewer-collection system.

Two R packages were explicitly written for network analysis purposes: statnet and igraph. You can use either one to collect network statistics or statistics about network components. Figure 1-4 shows sample output from network analysis in R, generated using the statnet package. This output is just a simple network in which the direction of the arrows shows the direction of flow within the network from one vertex to another. The network has five vertices and nine *faces* — connections between the vertices.

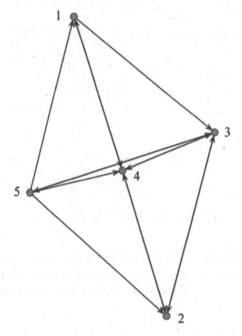

Mapping and analyzing spatial point patterns with spatstat

If you want to analyze spatial data in R, you can use the spatstat package. This package is most commonly used in analyzing the patterns of spatial data points — also called *point pattern data* — but you can also use it to analyze line patterns, pixels, and linear network data. By default, the package installs with geographical, ecological, and environmental datasets that you can use to support your analyses, if appropriate. With its space-time point pattern analysis capabilities, spatstat can help you visualize a spatiotemporal change in one or several variables over time. The package even comes with 3-dimensional graphing capabilities. Because spatstat is a geographic data analysis package, it's commonly used in ecology, geosciences, and botany, or for environmental studies, although the package could easily be used for location-based studies that relate to business, logistics, sales, marketing, and more.

IN THIS CHAPTER

» **Introducing statistics**

» **Getting R and RStudio on your computer**

» **Starting a session with R**

» **Working with R functions**

» **Working with R structures**

Chapter **2**

R: What It Does and How It Does It

Before we go any further, it probably makes sense to learn a little about R and its history. R is a versatile programming language created in the 1990s for statistical computing and graphics by Ross Ihaka and Robert Gentleman, professors at the University of Auckland. R shines in data analysis, offering a vast range of statistical techniques and extensive graphical capabilities for insightful data visualization. The secret sauce of R is in its open-source packages, a collection of functions, data, and compiled code in a structured format that is contributed by users worldwide. What sets R apart is its active community and extensibility. Users not only use R for analysis but also contribute by creating new packages, enhancing the language's capabilities.

Before getting into the details of how R operates, this chapter introduces the foundational concepts of data and statistics pertaining to R.

The Statistical (and Related) Ideas You Just Have to Know

The analytical tools that R provides are based on the statistical concepts explored in this section. As you'll see, these concepts are based on common sense.

Samples and populations

If you watch TV on election night, you know that one of the main events is the prediction of the outcome immediately after the polls close (and before all the votes are counted). How is it that pundits almost always get it right?

The idea is to talk to a *sample* of voters right after they vote. If they're truthful about how they marked their ballots, and if the sample is representative of the *population* of voters, analysts can use the sample data to draw conclusions about the population.

That, in a nutshell, is what statistics is all about — using the data from samples to draw conclusions about populations.

Here's another example. Imagine that your job is to find the average height of 10-year-old children in the United States. Because you probably wouldn't have the time or the resources to measure every child, you'd measure the heights of a representative sample. Then you'd average those heights and use that average as the estimate of the population average.

Estimating the population average is one kind of *inference* that statisticians make from sample data. This chapter discusses inference in more detail in the later section "Inferential statistics: Testing hypotheses."

REMEMBER

Here's some important terminology: Properties of a population (like the population average) are called *parameters*, and properties of a sample (like the sample average) are called *statistics*. If your only concern is the sample properties (like the heights of the children in your sample), the statistics you calculate are *descriptive*. If you're concerned about estimating the population properties, your statistics are *inferential*.

BEST PRACTICE

Now for an important convention about notation: Statisticians use Greek letters (μ, σ, ρ) to stand for parameters, and English letters ($\bar{X}$, s, r) to stand for statistics. Figure 2-1 summarizes the relationship between populations and samples, and between parameters and statistics.

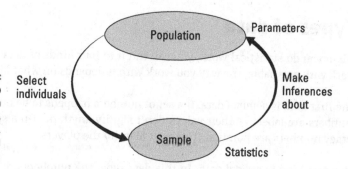

FIGURE 2-1:
The relationship
between
populations,
samples,
parameters, and
statistics.

Variables: Dependent and independent

A *variable* is something that can take on more than one value — like your age, the value of the dollar against other currencies, or the number of games your favorite sports team wins. Something that can have only one value is a *constant*. Scientists tell us that the speed of light is a constant, and we use the constant π to calculate the area of a circle.

Statisticians work with *independent* variables and *dependent* variables. In any study or experiment, you'll find both kinds. Statisticians assess the relationship between them.

For example, imagine a computerized training method designed to increase a person's IQ. How would a researcher find out whether this method does what it's supposed to do? First, the researcher would randomly assign a sample of people to one of two groups. One group would receive the training method, and the other would complete another kind of computer-based activity — like reading text on a website. Before and after each group completes its activities, the researcher measures each person's IQ. What happens next? This chapter discusses that topic in the later section "Inferential statistics: Testing hypotheses."

For now, understand that the independent variable here is Type of Activity. The two possible values of this variable are IQ Training and Reading Text. The dependent variable is the change in IQ from Before to After.

REMEMBER

A dependent variable is what a researcher *measures*. In an experiment, an independent variable is what a researcher *manipulates*. In other contexts, a researcher can't manipulate an independent variable. Instead, they note naturally occurring values of the independent variable and how they affect a dependent variable.

Types of data

When you do statistical work, you can run into four kinds of data. And when you work with a variable, the way you work with it depends on what kind of data it is:

The first kind is *nominal* data. If a set of numbers happens to be nominal data, the numbers are labels — their values don't signify anything. On a sports team, the jersey numbers are nominal. They just identify the players.

The next kind is *ordinal* data. In this data type, the numbers are more than just labels. As the name *ordinal* might tell you, the order of the numbers is important. If you were to ask a person to rank ten foods from the one they like best (1) to the one they like least (10), you'd have a set of ordinal data.

But the difference between a person's third-favorite food and their fourth-favorite food might not be the same as the difference between their ninth-favorite and their tenth-favorite. So this type of data lacks equal intervals and equal differences.

Interval data gives equal differences. The Fahrenheit scale of temperature is a good example. The difference between 30° and 40° is the same as the difference between 90° and 100°. So each degree is an interval.

People are sometimes surprised to find out that on the Fahrenheit scale, a temperature of 80° is not twice as hot as 40°. For ratio statements ("twice as much as," "half as much as") to make sense, *zero* has to mean the complete absence of the thing you're measuring. A temperature of 0° F doesn't mean the complete absence of heat — it's just an arbitrary point on the Fahrenheit scale. (The same holds true for Celsius.)

The fourth kind of data, *ratio*, provides a meaningful zero point. On the Kelvin scale of temperature, *zero* means absolute zero, where all molecular motion (the basis of heat) stops. So 200° Kelvin is twice as hot as 100° Kelvin. Another example is length. Eight inches is twice as long as 4 inches. *Zero inches* means a complete absence of length.

REMEMBER

An independent variable or a dependent variable can be either nominal, ordinal, interval, or ratio. The analytical tools you use depend on the type of data you work with.

A little probability

When statisticians make decisions, they use probability to express their confidence about those decisions. They can never be absolutely certain about what they decide. They can tell you only how probable their conclusions are.

What do statisticians mean by *probability*? Mathematicians and philosophers might give you complex definitions. The best way to understand probability is usually in terms of examples.

Here's a simple example: If you toss a coin, what's the probability that it turns up heads? If the coin is fair, you might figure that you have a 50-50 chance of heads and a 50-50 chance of tails. And you'd be right. In terms of the kinds of numbers associated with probability, that's ½.

Think about rolling a fair die (one member of a pair of dice). What's the probability that you roll a 4? Well, a die has six faces and one of them is 4, so that's ⅙.

Still another example: Select one card at random from a standard deck of 52 cards. What's the probability that it's a diamond? A deck of cards has four suits, so that's ¼.

These examples tell you that if you want to know the probability that an event occurs, count how many ways that event can happen and divide by the total number of events that can happen. In the first two examples (heads, 4), the event you're interested in happens only one way. For the coin, we divide 1 by 2. For the die, we divide 1 by 6. In the third example (diamond), the event can happen 13 ways (Ace through King), so we divide 13 by 52 (to get ¼).

Now for a slightly more complicated example. Toss a coin and roll a die at the same time. What's the probability of tails and a 4? Think about all the possible events that can happen when you toss a coin and roll a die at the same time. You could have tails and 1 through 6, or heads and 1 through 6. That adds up to 12 possibilities. The tails-and-4 combination can happen only one way. So the probability ¹⁄₁₂.

In general, the formula for the probability that a particular event occurs is

$$\text{Pr(event)} = \frac{\text{Number of ways the event can occur}}{\text{Total number of possible events}}$$

As stated in the beginning of this section, statisticians express their confidence about their conclusions in terms of probability, which is why the chapter brings all this up in the first place. This line of thinking leads to *conditional probability* — the probability that an event occurs given that some other event occurs. Suppose that a person rolls a die, looks at it (so that you don't see it), and tells you that they rolled an odd number. What's the probability that they've rolled a 5? Ordinarily, the probability of a 5 is 1/6, but "I rolled an odd number" narrows it down. That piece of information eliminates the three even numbers (2, 4, 6) as possibilities. Only the three odd numbers (1,3, 5) are possible, so the probability is 1/3.

Inferential statistics: Testing hypotheses

Before a statistician does a study, they draw up a tentative explanation — a *hypothesis* that tells why the data might come out a certain way. After gathering all the data, the statistician has to decide whether to reject the hypothesis.

That decision is the answer to a conditional probability question — what's the probability of obtaining the data, given that this hypothesis is correct? Statisticians have tools that calculate the probability. If the probability turns out to be low, the statistician rejects the hypothesis.

Back to coin-tossing for an example: Imagine that you're interested in whether a particular coin is fair — whether it has an equal chance of heads or tails on any toss. Let's start with "The coin is fair" as the hypothesis.

To test the hypothesis, you'd toss the coin a number of times — let's say 100. These 100 tosses are the sample data. If the coin is fair (as per the hypothesis), you'd expect 50 heads and 50 tails.

If it's 99 heads and 1 tail, you'd surely reject the fair-coin hypothesis: The conditional probability of 99 heads and 1 tail given a fair coin is very low. Of course, the coin could still be fair, and you could, quite by chance, get a 99–1 split, right? Sure. You never really know. You have to gather the sample data (the 100 toss results) and then decide. Your decision might be right, or it might not.

Juries make these types of decisions. In the United States, the starting hypothesis is that the defendant is not guilty ("innocent until proven guilty"). Think of the evidence as data. Jury members consider the evidence and answer a conditional probability question: What's the probability of the evidence, given that the defendant is not guilty? Their answer determines the verdict.

Null and alternative hypotheses

Think again about that coin-tossing study mentioned in the preceding section. The sample data are the results from the 100 tosses. As stated in that section, you can start with the hypothesis that the coin is fair. This starting point is called the *null hypothesis*. The statistical notation for the null hypothesis is H_o. According to this hypothesis, any heads–tails split in the data is consistent with a fair coin. Think of it as the idea that nothing in the sample data is out of the ordinary.

An alternative hypothesis is possible — that the coin isn't a fair one, and it's biased to produce an unequal number of heads and tails. This hypothesis says that any heads–tails split is consistent with an unfair coin. This alternative hypothesis is called, believe it or not, the *alternative hypothesis*. The statistical notation for the alternative hypothesis is H_1.

Now toss the coin 100 times and note the number of heads and tails. If the results are something like 90 heads and 10 tails, it's a good idea to reject H_0. If the results are around 50 heads and 50 tails, don't reject H_0.

Similar ideas apply to the IQ example given earlier (see the section, "Variables: Dependent and independent"). One sample receives the computer-based IQ training method, and the other participates in a different computer-based activity — like reading text on a website. Before and after each group completes its activities, the researcher measures each person's IQ. The null hypothesis, H_0, is that one group's improvement isn't different from the other. If the improvements are greater with the IQ training than with the other activity — so much greater that it's unlikely that the two aren't different from one another — reject H_0. If they're not, don't reject H_0.

BEST PRACTICE

Note that statisticians never say "accept H_0." The way the logic works, you *never* accept a hypothesis. You either reject H_0 or don't reject H_0. In a jury trial, the verdict is either "guilty" (reject the null hypothesis of "not guilty") or "not guilty" (don't reject H_0). "Innocent" (acceptance of the null hypothesis) is not a possible verdict.

In the coin-tossing example, the language used is "around 50 heads and 50 tails." What does *around* mean? Also, the example indicates that if it's 90-10, reject H_0. What about 85-15? 80-20? 70-30? Exactly how much different from 50-50 does the split have to be for you to reject H_0? In the IQ training example, how much greater does the IQ improvement have to be to reject H_0?

TECHNICAL STUFF

To find out more about the decision rules statisticians have formulated for situations like this, see *R All-in-One For Dummies*.

Two types of error

Whenever you evaluate data and decide to reject or not reject H_0, you can never be absolutely sure. You never really know the "true" state of the world. In the coin-tossing example, that means you can't be certain whether the coin is fair. All you can do is make a decision based on the sample data. If you want to know for sure about the coin, you have to have the data for the entire population of tosses — which means you have to keep tossing the coin until the end of time.

Because you're never certain about your decisions, you can make an error either way you decide. As mentioned earlier, the coin could be fair, and you just happen to get 99 heads in 100 tosses. That's not likely, and that's why you reject H_0 if that happens. It's also possible that the coin is biased, yet you just happen to toss 50 heads in 100 tosses. Again, that's not likely, and you don't reject H_o in that case.

Although those errors are not likely, they are possible. They lurk in every study that involves inferential statistics. Statisticians have named them Type I errors and Type II errors.

If you reject H_o and you shouldn't, that's a *Type I* error. In the coin example, that's rejecting the hypothesis that the coin is fair, when in reality it is a fair coin.

If you don't reject H_o and you should have, that's a *Type II* error. It happens if you don't reject the hypothesis that the coin is fair, and in reality it's biased.

How do you know if you've made either type of error? You don't — at least not right after you make the decision to reject or not reject H_o. (If it's possible to know, you wouldn't make the error in the first place!) All you can do is gather more data and see whether the additional data is consistent with your decision.

If you think of H_o as a tendency to maintain the status quo and not interpret anything as being out of the ordinary (no matter how it looks), a Type II error means you've missed out on something big. In fact, some iconic mistakes are Type II errors.

Here's a classic example that illustrates a Type II error. On New Year's Day in 1962, a rock group consisting of three guitarists and a drummer auditioned in the London studio of a major recording company. Legend has it that the recording executives didn't like what they heard, didn't like what they saw, and believed that guitar groups were on the way out. Although the musicians played their hearts out, the group failed the audition.

Who was that group? The Beatles!

And *that's* a Type II error.

Getting R

If you don't already have R on your computer, the first thing to do is to download R and install it.

You'll find the appropriate software on the website of the Comprehensive R Archive Network (CRAN). In your browser, type this web address:

```
https://cran.rstudio.com
```

Click the appropriate link to download R for your computer.

Getting RStudio

Working with R is a lot easier if you do it through an application called RStudio. Computer honchos refer to RStudio as an IDE (Integrated Development Environment). Think of it as a tool that helps you write, edit, run, and keep track of your R code, and as an environment that connects you to a world of helpful hints about R.

Here's the web address for this terrific tool:

```
www.rstudio.com/products/rstudio/download
```

Click the link for the installer for your flavor of computer and again follow the usual installation procedures. (You'll want RStudio Desktop.) Figure 2-2 shows an example of RStudio installed.

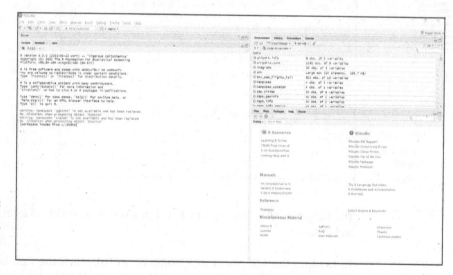

FIGURE 2-2:
RStudio,
immediately after
you install it and
click its icon.

The large Console pane on the left runs R code. One way to run R code is to type it directly into the Console pane. You see another way a little later in the chapter.

The other two panes provide helpful information as you work with R. The Environment and History pane is in the upper right. The Environment tab keeps track of the things you create (which R calls *objects*) as you work with R. The History tab tracks R code that you enter.

Get used to the word *object*. Everything in R is an object.

The Files, Plots, Packages, and Help pane is in the lower right. The Files tab shows files you create. The Plots tab holds graphs you create from your data. The Packages tab shows add-ons (called *packages*) that have downloaded with R. Bear in mind that *downloaded* doesn't mean "ready to use." To use a package's capabilities, one more step is necessary.

Figure 2-3 shows the Packages tab.

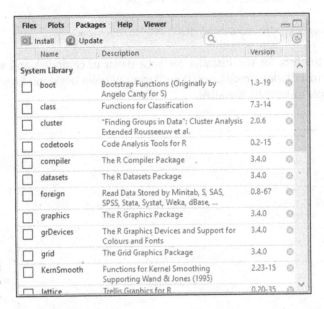

FIGURE 2-3: The RStudio Packages tab.

The Help tab, shown in Figure 2-4, links you to a wealth of information about R and RStudio.

To tap into the full power of RStudio as an IDE, click the icon in the rightmost upper corner of the Console pane. (It looks like a tall folder with a gray band across the top.) That changes the appearance of RStudio so that it looks like Figure 2-5.

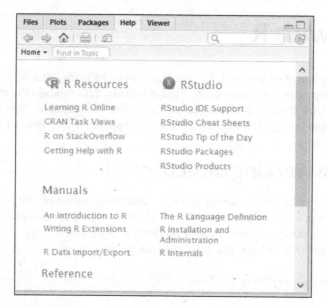

FIGURE 2-4:
The RStudio
Help tab.

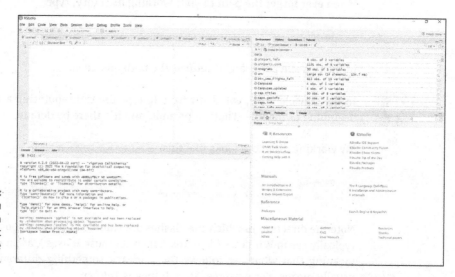

FIGURE 2-5:
RStudio, after you
click the icon in
the upper right
corner of the
Console pane.

The Console pane relocates to the lower left. The new pane in the upper left is the Scripts pane. You type and edit code in the Scripts pane, press Ctrl+Enter (Command+Enter on the Mac), and then the code executes in the Console pane.

TIP

You can also highlight lines of code in the Scripts pane and choose Code ⇨ Run Selected Line(s) from RStudio's main menu.

A Session with R

Before you start working, choose File ⇨ Save As from RStudio's main menu and then save the blank pane as My First R Session. This relabels the tab in the Scripts pane with the name of the file and adds the .R extension. This also causes the filename (along with the .R extension) to appear on the Files tab.

The working directory

When you follow my advice and save something called My First R Session, what exactly is R saving and where does R save it? What R saves is called the *workspace*, which is the environment you're working in. R saves the workspace in the *working directory*. In Windows, the default working directory is

```
C:\Users\<User Name>\Documents
```

If you ever forget the path to your working directory, type

```
> getwd()
```

in the Console pane, and R returns the path onscreen.

TIP

In the Console pane, you don't have to type the right-pointing arrowhead at the beginning of the line. That's a prompt, and it's there by default.

My working directory looks like this:

```
> getwd()
[1] "C:/Users/Joseph Schmuller/Documents"
```

Note the direction in which the slashes are slanted. They're opposite to what you typically see in Windows file paths. This is because R uses \ as an *escape character*, meaning that whatever follows the \ means something different from what it usually means. For example, \t in R means *Tab key*.

TIP

You can also write a Windows file path in R as

```
C:\\Users\\<User Name>\\Documents
```

If you like, you can change the working directory:

```
> setwd(<file path>)
```

Another way to change the working directory is to choose Session ⇨ Set Working Directory ⇨ Choose Directory from R Studio's main menu.

Getting started

Let's get down to business and start writing R code. In the Scripts pane, type

```
x <- c(5,10,15,20,25,30,35,40)
```

and then press Ctrl+Enter.

That puts this line into the Console pane:

```
> x <- c(5,10,15,20,25,30,35,40)
```

REMEMBER

The right-pointing arrowhead (the greater-than sign) is a prompt that R puts in the Console pane. You don't see it in the Scripts pane.

Here's what R just did: The arrow sign says that x gets assigned whatever is to the right of the arrow sign. Think of the arrow sign as R's *assignment operator*.

So the set of numbers 5, 10, 15, 20 . . . 40 is now assigned to x.

REMEMBER

In R-speak, a set of numbers like this is a *vector*. I tell you more about this topic in the later section "R Structures." That c in front of the parentheses is what does the actual vector-creating.

You can read that line of code as "x gets the vector 5, 10, 15, 20."

Type **x** into the Scripts pane and press Ctrl+Enter, and here's what you see in the Console pane:

```
> x
[1] 5 10 15 20 25 30 35 40
```

The 1 in square brackets is the label for the first line of output. So this signifies that 5 is the first value.

Here you have only one line, of course. What happens when R outputs many values over many lines? Each line gets a bracketed numeric label, and the number corresponds to the first value in the line. For example, if the output consists of 23 values and the 18th value is the first one on the second line, the second line begins with [18].

Creating the vector x adds the line in Figure 2-6 to the Environment tab.

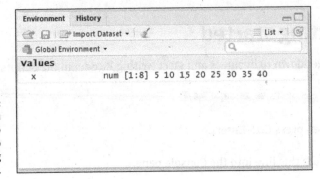

FIGURE 2-6:
A line in
the RStudio
Environment tab
after creating
the vector x.

TIP

Another way to see the objects in the environment is to type

```
ls()
```

into the Scripts pane and then press Ctrl+Enter. Or you can type

```
> ls()
```

directly into the Console pane and press Enter. Either way, the result in the Console pane is

```
[1] "x"
```

Now you can work with x. First, add all the numbers in the vector. Typing

```
sum(x)
```

in the Scripts pane (be sure to follow with pressing Ctrl+Enter) executes the following line in the Console pane:

```
> sum(x)
[1] 180
```

How about the average of the numbers in vector x?

That would be

```
mean(x)
```

in the Scripts pane, which (when followed by pressing Ctrl+Enter) executes

```
> mean(x)
[1] 22.5
```

in the Console pane.

As you type in the Scripts pane or in the Console pane, you see that helpful information pops up. As you become experienced with RStudio, you learn how to use that information.

Variance is a measure of how much a set of numbers differ from their mean. Here's how to use R to calculate variance:

```
> var(x)
[1] 150
```

After R executes all these commands, the History tab looks like the one in Figure 2-7.

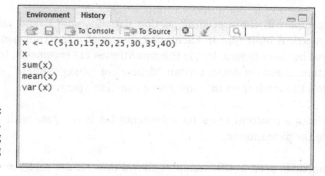

FIGURE 2-7:
The History tab, after creating and working with a vector.

To end a session, choose File ⇨ Quit Session from R Studio's main menu or press Ctrl+Q. As Figure 2-8 shows, a dialog box opens and asks what you want to save from the session. Saving the selections enables you the next time you open RStudio to reopen the session where you left off (although the Console pane doesn't save your work).

The instructions for the examples provided in this book don't always specify "Type this code into the Scripts pane and press Ctrl+Enter." The examples just show the code and its output, as in the var() example.

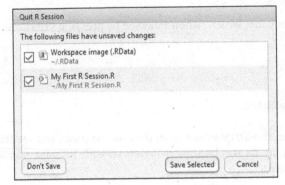

FIGURE 2-8:
The Quit
R Session
dialog box.

REMEMBER

Also, sometimes code appears in this book with the › prompt, and sometimes without. Generally, the prompt appears when the book shows R code and its results. The prompt doesn't appear when the book shows R code created in the Scripts pane.

R Functions

The examples in the preceding section use c(), sum(), and var(). These are three *functions* built into R. Each one consists of a function name immediately followed by parentheses. Inside the parentheses are *arguments*. In the context of a function, *argument* doesn't mean "debate" or "disagreement" or anything like that. It's the math term for whatever a function operates on.

REMEMBER

Sometimes a function takes no arguments (as is the case with ls()). You still include the parentheses.

The functions used in the examples shown thus far are pretty simple: Supply an argument, and each one gives you a result. Some R functions, however, take more than one argument.

R has a couple of ways for you to deal with multiargument functions. One way is to list the arguments in the order that they appear in the function's definition. R calls this *positional mapping*.

Here's an example. As shown previously, you can create the vector x as follows:

```
x <- c(5,10,15,20,25,30,35,40)
```

Another way to create a vector of those numbers is with the function seq( ):

```
> y <- seq(5,40,5)
> y
[1] 5 10 15 20 25 30 35 40
```

Think of seq( ) as creating a "sequence." The first argument to seq( ) is the number to start the sequence *from* (5). The second argument is the number that ends the sequence — the number the sequence goes *to* (40). The third argument is the increment of the sequence — the amount the sequence increases *by* (5, in this case).

If you *name* the arguments, it doesn't matter how you order them:

```
> z <- seq(to=40,by=5,from=5)
> z
[1] 5 10 15 20 25 30 35 40
```

So if you name a function when using it, you can place the function's arguments out of order. R calls this *keyword matching*. This comes in handy when you use an R function that has many arguments. If you can't remember their order, use their names, and the function works.

TIP

For help with a particular function — seq( ), for example — type **?seq** and press Ctrl+Enter to open helpful information on the Help tab.

User-Defined Functions

R enables you to create your own functions, and here are the fundamentals on how to do it.

The form of an R function is

```
myfunction <- function(argument1, argument2, ...){
  statements
  return(object)
}
```

Here's a function for dealing with right triangles. Remember them? A right triangle has two sides that form a right angle and a third side called a *hypotenuse*. You might also remember that a guy named Pythagoras showed that if one side has length a, and the other side has length b, the length of the hypotenuse, c, is $c = \sqrt{a^2 + b^2}$

So here's a simple function called hypotenuse() that takes two numbers a and b, (the lengths of the two sides of a right triangle) and returns c, the length of the hypotenuse.

```
hypotenuse <- function(a,b){
  hyp <- sqrt(a^2+b^2)
  return(hyp)
}
```

Type that code snippet into the Scripts pane and highlight it. Then press Ctrl+Enter. Here's what appears in the Console pane:

```
> hypoteneuse <- function(a,b){
+ hyp <- sqrt(a^2+b^2)
+ return(hyp)
+ }
```

Each plus sign is a *continuation prompt*. It just indicates that a line continues from the preceding line.

And here's how to use the function:

```
> hypoteneuse(3,4)
[1] 5
```

Comments

A *comment* is a way of annotating code. Begin a comment with the # symbol, which, as everyone knows, is called an *octothorpe*. (Wait. What? "Hashtag?" Getattahere!) This symbol tells R to ignore everything to the right of it.

Comments help someone who has to read the code you've written. For example:

```
hypoteneuse <- function(a,b){ # list the arguments
  hyp <- sqrt(a^2+b^2) # perform the computation
  return(hyp) # return the value
}
```

Note: To make concepts easier to grasp, this book often provides detailed descriptions rather than the comments you might usually see added to lines of code.

R Structures

As mentioned in the "R Functions" section earlier in this chapter, an R function can have many arguments. An R function can also have many outputs. To understand the possible inputs and outputs, you must understand the structures that R works with.

Vectors

The *vector* is the fundamental structure in R. A vector is an array of elements of the same type. The data elements in a vector are called *components*.

To create a vector, use the function c( ), as done in the earlier example:

```
x <- c(5,10,15,20,25,30,35,40)
```

In the vector x, of course, the components are numbers.

In a *character vector*, the components are quoted text strings:

```
> beatles <- c("john","paul","george","ringo")
```

It's also possible to have a *logical vector*, whose components are TRUE and FALSE, or the abbreviations T and F:

```
> w <- c(T,F,F,T,T,F)
```

To refer to a specific component of a vector, follow the vector name with a bracketed number:

```
> beatles[2]
[1] "paul"
```

Within the brackets, you can use a colon (:) to refer to two consecutive components:

```
> beatles[2:3]
[1] "paul" "george"
```

Want to refer to non-consecutive components? That's a bit more complicated, but doable via c( ):

```
> beatles[c(2,4)]
[1] "paul" "ringo"
```

Numerical vectors

In addition to c(), R provides two shortcut functions for creating numerical vectors. One, seq(), was shown earlier:

```
> y <- seq(5,40,5)
> y
[1] 5 10 15 20 25 30 35 40
```

Without the third argument, the sequence increases by 1:

```
> y <- seq(5,40)
> y
 [1] 5 6 7 8 9 10 11 12 13 14 15 16 17 18 19 20 21 22 23 [20] 24 25 26 27 28 29
    30 31 32 33 34 35 36 37 38 39 40
```

On computer screens, all the elements in y appear on one line. The printed page, however, is not as wide as the Console pane. This book separates the output into two lines and adds the R-style bracketed number [20].

R has a special syntax for creating a numerical vector whose elements increase by 1:

```
> y <- 5:40
> y
 [1] 5 6 7 8 9 10 11 12 13 14 15 16 17 18 19 20 21 22 23 [20] 24 25 26 27 28 29
    30 31 32 33 34 35 36 37 38 39 40
```

Another function, rep(), creates a vector of repeating values:

```
> quadrifecta <- c(7,8,4,3)
> repeated_quadrifecta <- rep(quadrifecta,3)
> repeated_quadrifecta
 [1] 7 8 4 3 7 8 4 3 7 8 4 3
```

You can also supply a vector as the second argument:

```
> rep_vector <-c(1,2,3,4)
> repeated_quadrifecta <- rep(quadrifecta,rep_vector)
```

The vector specifies the number of repetitions for each element. So here's what happens:

```
> repeated_quadrifecta
 [1] 7 8 8 4 4 4 3 3 3 3
```

The first element repeats once, the second, twice, the third, three times; and the fourth, four times.

You can use append() to add an item at the end of a vector:

```
> xx <- c(3,4,5)
> xx
[1] 3 4 5
> xx <- append(xx,6)
> xx
[1] 3 4 5 6
```

How many items are in a vector? That's

```
> length(xx)
[1] 4
```

Matrices

A *matrix* is a two-dimensional array of data elements of the same type. You can have a matrix of numbers:

| 5 | 30 | 55 | 80 |

| 10 | 35 | 60 | 85 |

| 15 | 40 | 65 | 90 |

| 20 | 45 | 70 | 95 |

| 25 | 50 | 75 | 100 |

or a matrix of character strings:

| "john" | "paul" | "george" | "ringo" |

| "groucho" | "harpo" | "chico" | "zeppo" |

| "levi" | "duke" | "larry" | "obie" |

The numbers are a 5 (rows) X 4 (columns) matrix. The character strings matrix is 3 X 4.

To create this particular 5 X 4 numerical matrix, first create the vector of numbers from 5 to 100 in steps of 5:

```
> num_matrix <- seq(5,100,5)
```

Then you use R's dim() function to turn the vector into a two-dimensional matrix:

```
> dim(num_matrix) <- c(5,4)
> num_matrix
     [,1] [,2] [,3] [,4]
[1,] 5 30 55 80
[2,] 10 35 60 85
[3,] 15 40 65 90
[4,] 20 45 70 95
[5,] 25 50 75 100
```

Note how R displays the bracketed row numbers along the side and the bracketed column numbers along the top.

Transposing a matrix interchanges the rows with the columns. The t() function takes care of that:

```
> t(num_matrix)
     [,1] [,2] [,3] [,4] [,5]
[1,] 5 10 15 20 25
[2,] 30 35 40 45 50
[3,] 55 60 65 70 75
[4,] 80 85 90 95 100
```

The function matrix() gives you another way to create matrices:

```
> num_matrix <- matrix(seq(5,100,5),nrow=5)
> num_matrix
     [,1] [,2] [,3] [,4]
[1,] 5 30 55 80
[2,] 10 35 60 85
[3,] 15 40 65 90
[4,] 20 45 70 95
[5,] 25 50 75 100
```

If you add the argument byrow=T, R fills the matrix by rows, like this:

```
> num_matrix <- matrix(seq(5,100,5),nrow=5,byrow=T)
> num_matrix
     [,1] [,2] [,3] [,4]
[1,] 5 10 15 20
```

```
[2,]  25 30 35 40
[3,]  45 50 55 60
[4,]  65 70 75 80
[5,]  85 90 95 100
```

How do you refer to a specific matrix component? You type the matrix name and then, in brackets, the row number, a comma, and the column number:

```
> num_matrix[5,4]
[1] 100
```

To refer to a whole row (like the third one):

```
> num_matrix[3,]
[1] 45 50 55 60
```

and to a whole column (like the second one):

```
> num_matrix[,2]
[1] 10 30 50 70 90
```

Although it's a column, R displays it as a row in the Console pane.

Lists

In R, a *list* is a collection of objects that aren't necessarily the same type. Suppose you're putting together some information on the Beatles:

```
> beatles <- c("john","paul","george","ringo")
```

One piece of important information might be each Beatle's age when he joined the group. John and Paul started singing together when they were 17 and 15, respectively, and 14-year-old George joined them soon after. Ringo, a late arriver, became a Beatle when he was 22. So

```
> ages <- c(17,15,14,22)
```

To combine the information into a list, you use the list() function:

```
> beatles_info <-list(names=beatles,age_joined=ages)
```

Naming each argument (names, age_joined) causes R to use those names as the names of the list components.

And here's what the list looks like:

```
> beatles_info
$names
[1] "john" "paul" "george" "ringo"

$age_joined
[1] 17 15 14 22
```

R uses the dollar sign ($) to indicate each component of the list. If you want to refer to a list component, you type the name of the list, the dollar sign, and the component name:

```
> beatles_info$names
[1] "john" "paul" "george" "ringo"
```

And to zero in on a particular Beatle, like the fourth one? You can probably figure out that it's

```
> beatles_info$names[4]
[1] "ringo"
```

R also allows you to use criteria inside the brackets. For example, to refer to members of the Fab Four who were older than 16 when they joined:

```
> beatles_info$names[beatles_info$age_joined > 16]
[1] "john" "ringo"
```

Data frames

A list is a good way to collect data. A *data frame* is even better. Why? When you think about data for a group of individuals, you typically think in terms of rows that represent the individuals and columns that represent the data variables. And that's a data frame. If the terms *data set* or *data matrix* come to mind, you have the right idea.

Suppose you have a set of six people:

```
> name <- c("al","barbara","charles","donna","ellen","fred")
```

and you have each person's height (in inches) and weight (in pounds):

```
> height <- c(72,64,73,65,66,71)
> weight <- c(195,117,205,122,125,199)
```

You also tabulate each person's gender:

```
> gender <- c("M","F","M","F","F","M")
```

Before you can combine all these vectors into a data frame, you need to know one more thing. The components of the gender vector are character strings. For purposes of data summary and analysis, it's a good idea to turn them into categories — the Male category and the Female category. To do this, you use the factor() function:

```
> factor_gender <-factor(gender)
> factor_gender
[1] M F M F F M
Levels: F M
```

In the last line of output, *Levels* is the term that R uses for categories.

The function data.frame() works with the vectors to create a data frame:

```
> d <- data.frame(name,factor_gender,height,weight)
> d
     name factor_gender height weight
1 al M 72 195
2 barbara F 64 117
3 charles M 73 205
4 donna F 65 122
5 ellen F 66 125
6 fred M 71 199
```

Want to know the height of the third person?

```
> d[3,3]
[1] 73
```

How about all the information for the fifth person:

```
> d[5,]
     name factor_gender height weight
5 ellen F 66 125
```

Like lists, data frames use the dollar sign. In this context, the dollar sign identifies a column:

```
> d$height
[1] 72 64 73 65 66 71
```

You can calculate statistics, like the average height:

```
> mean(d$height)
[1] 68.5
```

As is the case with lists, you can put criteria inside the brackets. This is often done with data frames in order to summarize and analyze data within categories. To find the average height of the females:

```
> mean(d$height[d$factor_gender == "F"])
[1] 65
```

The double equal sign (==) in the brackets is a *logical operator*. Think of it as "if d$factor_gender is equal to 'F'".

REMEMBER

The double equal sign (a == b) distinguishes the logical operator ("if a equals b") from the assignment operator (a = b; "set a equal to b").

If you'd like to eliminate $ signs from your R code, you can use the function with( ). You put your code inside the parentheses after the first argument, which is the data you're using.

TIP

For example,

```
> with(d,mean(height[factor_gender == "F"]))
```

is equivalent to

```
> mean(d$height[d$factor_gender == "F"])
```

How many rows are in a data frame?

```
> nrow(d)
[1] 6
```

And how many columns?

```
> ncol(d)
[1] 4
```

To add a column to a data frame, I use cbind( ). Begin with a vector of scores

```
> aptitude <- c(35,20,32,22,18,15)
```

Then add that vector as a column:

```
> d.apt <- cbind(d,aptitude)
> d.apt
     name factor_gender height weight aptitude
1 al M 72 195 35
2 barbara F 64 117 20
3 charles M 73 205 32
4 donna F 65 122 22
5 ellen F 66 125 18
6 fred M 71 199 15
```

for Loops and if Statements

Like many programming languages, R provides a way of iterating through its structures to get things done. R's way is called the *for* loop. And, like many languages, R gives you a way to test against a criterion — the *if* statement.

The general format of a for loop is

```
for counter in start:end{
        statement 1



        statement n
}
```

As you might imagine, counter tracks the iterations.

The simplest general format of an if statement is

```
if(test){statement to execute if test is TRUE}
else{statement to execute if test is FALSE}
```

Here is an example that incorporates both. If you have one vector xx:

```
> xx
[1] 2 3 4 5 6
```

And another vector yy with nothing in it at the moment:

```
> yy <-NULL
```

You want the components of yy to reflect the components of xx: If a number in xx is an odd number, you want the corresponding component of yy to be "ODD" and if the xx number is even, you want the yy component to be "EVEN".

How do you test a number to see whether it's odd or even? Mathematicians have developed *modular arithmetic*, which is concerned with the remainder of a division operation. If you divide *a* by *b* and the result has a remainder of *r*, mathematicians say that "a *modulo* b is r." So 10 divided by 3 leaves a remainder of 1, and 10 modulo 3 is 1. Typically, *modulo* gets shortened to *mod*, so that would be "10 mod 3 = 1."

Most computer languages write 10 mod 3 as mod(10,3). (Excel does that, in fact.) R does it differently: R uses the double percent sign (%%) as its *mod operator*:

```
> 10 %% 3
[1] 1
> 5 %% 2
[1] 1
> 4 %% 2
[1] 0
```

You're probably getting the picture: if xx[i] %% 2 == 0, then xx[i] is even. Otherwise, it's odd.

Here, then, is the for loop and the if statement:

```
for(i in 1:length(xx)){
if(xx[i] %% 2 == 0){yy[i]<- "EVEN"}
else{yy[i] <- "ODD"}
}

> yy
[1] "EVEN" "ODD" "EVEN" "ODD" "EVEN"
```

Chapter **3**

Getting Graphical

D ata visualization is an important part of statistics. A good graph enables you to spot trends and relationships you might otherwise miss if you look only at numbers. Graphics are valuable for another reason: They help you present your ideas to groups.

This concept is especially important in the data science field. Organizations rely on data scientists to make sense of huge amounts of data so that decision-makers can formulate strategy. Graphics enable data scientists to explain patterns in the data to managers and to nontechnical personnel.

Finding Patterns

Data often resides in long, complex tables. Often, you have to visualize only a portion of the table to find a pattern or a trend. A number of good examples reside in the MASS package, so download this package into your R library by selecting the check box next to MASS on the Packages tab.

This chapter uses the Cars93 data frame, which holds data on 27 variables for 93 car models that were available in 1993.

Figure 3-1 shows part of the data frame in the Data Editor window that opens after you type

```
> edit(Cars93)
```

Close the Data Editor window, and you can move on to visualizing the data.

	Manufacturer	Model	Type	Min.Price	Price	Max.Price	MPG.city
1	Acura	Integra	Small	12.9	15.9	18.8	25
2	Acura	Legend	Midsize	29.2	33.9	38.7	18
3	Audi	90	Compact	25.9	29.1	32.3	20
4	Audi	100	Midsize	30.8	37.7	44.6	19
5	BMW	535i	Midsize	23.7	30	36.2	22
6	Buick	Century	Midsize	14.2	15.7	17.3	22
7	Buick	LeSabre	Large	19.9	20.8	21.7	19
8	Buick	Roadmaster	Large	22.6	23.7	24.9	16
9	Buick	Riviera	Midsize	26.3	26.3	26.3	19
10	Cadillac	DeVille	Large	33	34.7	36.3	16
11	Cadillac	Seville	Midsize	37.5	40.1	42.7	16
12	Chevrolet	Cavalier	Compact	8.5	13.4	18.3	25
13	Chevrolet	Corsica	Compact	11.4	11.4	11.4	25
14	Chevrolet	Camaro	Sporty	13.4	15.1	16.8	19
15	Chevrolet	Lumina	Midsize	13.4	15.9	18.4	21
16	Chevrolet	Lumina_APV	Van	14.7	16.3	18	18
17	Chevrolet	Astro	Van	14.7	16.6	18.6	15
18	Chevrolet	Caprice	Large	18	18.8	19.6	17
19	Chevrolet	Corvette	Sporty	34.6	38	41.5	17

FIGURE 3-1:
Part of the
Cars93 data
frame.

Graphing a distribution

One pattern that might be of interest is the distribution of all the car prices listed in the Cars93 data frame. If you had to examine the entire data frame to determine this, it would be a tedious task. A graph, however, provides the information immediately. Figure 3-2, a *histogram*, shows what this means.

The histogram is appropriate when the variable on the x-axis is an interval variable or a ratio variable. (See Book 5, Chapter 2 for more on these variables.) With interval and ratio variables, the numbers have meaning (as opposed to nominal variables, where numbers are just labels).

You can distinguish between independent variables and dependent variables. Here, Price is the independent variable, and Frequency is the dependent variable. In most (but not all) graphs, the independent variable is on the x-axis, and the dependent variable is on the y-axis.

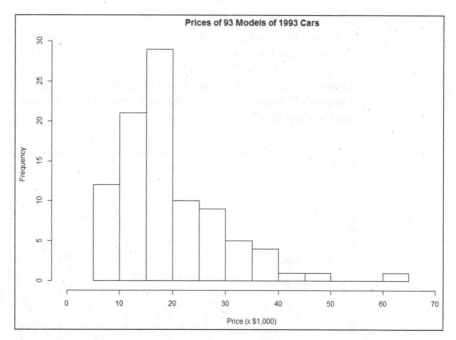

FIGURE 3-2:
Histogram of
prices of cars
in the Cars93
data frame.

Bar-hopping

For nominal variables (again, see Book 5, Chapter 2), numbers are just labels. In fact, the levels of a nominal variable (also called a *factor*) can be names. Case in point: Another possible point of interest is the frequencies of the different types of cars (sporty, midsize, van, and so on) in the data frame. So "Type" is a nominal variable. If you looked at every entry in the data frame and created a table of these frequencies, it would look like Table 3-1.

TABLE 3-1

Types and Frequencies of Cars in the Cars93 Data Frame

Type	Frequency
Compact	16
Large	11
Midsize	22
Small	21
Sporty	14
Van	9

The table shows some trends — more midsize and small car models than large cars and vans. Compact cars and sporty cars are in the middle.

Figure 3-3 shows this information in graphical form. This type of graph is a *bar graph*. The spaces between the bars emphasize that Type, on the x-axis, is a nominal variable.

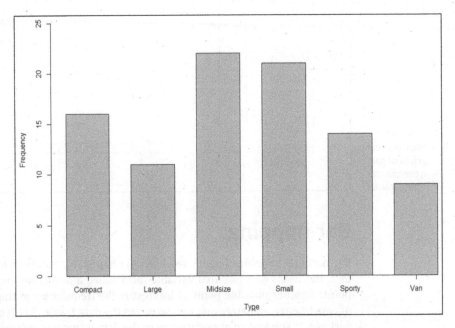

FIGURE 3-3:
Table 3-1 as a
bar graph.

Although the table is pretty straightforward, an audience would prefer to see the picture. Eyes that glaze over when looking at numbers often shine brighter when looking at pictures.

Slicing the pie

The *pie graph* is another type of picture that shows the same data in a slightly different way. Each frequency appears as a slice of a pie, as shown in Figure 3-4. In a pie graph, the area of the slice represents the frequency.

The plot of scatter

Another potential pattern of interest is the relationship between miles per gallon for city driving and horsepower. One type of graph well-suited to demonstrating the nature of this relationship is a *scatter plot*. Figure 3-5 shows the scatter plot for these two variables.

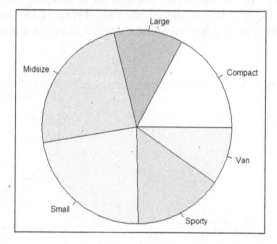

FIGURE 3-4:
Table 3-1 as a
pie graph.

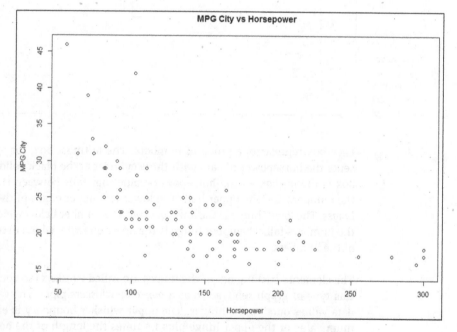

FIGURE 3-5:
MPG in city
driving and
horsepower
for the data
in Cars93.

Each small circle represents one of the 93 cars. A circle's position along the *x*-axis (its *x-coordinate*) is its horsepower, and its position along the *y*-axis (its *y-coordinate*) is its MPG for city driving.

Getting Graphical

Of boxes and whiskers

What about the relationship between horsepower and the number of cylinders in a car's engine? You would expect horsepower to increase with cylinders, and Figure 3-6 shows that this is indeed the case. Invented by famed statistician John Tukey, this type of graph is called a *box plot*, and it's a nice, quick way to visualize data.

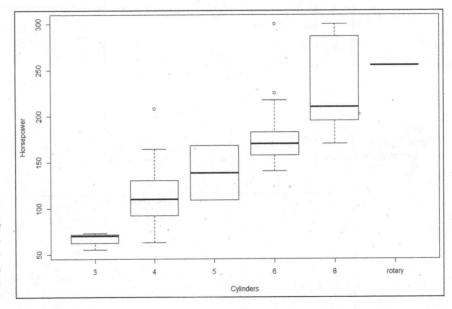

Each box represents a group of numbers. The leftmost box, for example, represents the horsepower of cars with three cylinders. The black solid line inside the box is the *median* — the horsepower-value that falls between the lower half of the numbers and the upper half. The lower and upper edges of the box are called *hinges*. The lower hinge is the *lower quartile*, the number below which 25 percent of the numbers fall. The upper hinge is the *upper* quartile, which exceeds 75 percent of the numbers.

The elements sticking out of the hinges are called *whiskers* (so you sometimes see this type of graph referred to as a *box-and-whiskers* plot). The whiskers include data values outside the hinges. The upper whisker boundary is either the maximum value or the upper hinge plus 1.5 times the length of the box, whichever is *smaller*. The lower whisker boundary is either the minimum value or the lower hinge minus 1.5 times the length of the box, whichever is *larger*. Data points outside the whiskers are *outliers*. The box plot shows that the data for four and six cylinders has outliers.

Note that the graph shows only a solid line for "rotary," an engine type that occurs just once in the data.

Doing the Basics: Base R Graphics, That Is

The capability to create the graphs like the ones shown in earlier sections of this chapter comes with your R installation, which makes these graphs part of the *base R graphics* covered in this section. Book 5, Chapter 4 shows you the very useful ggplot2 package.

In base R, the general format for creating graphics is

```
graphics_function(data, arg1, arg2, ...)
```

Histograms

Time to take another look at that Cars93 data frame introduced in the "Finding Patterns" section at the beginning of this chapter. To create a histogram of the distribution of prices in that data frame, you enter

```
> hist(Cars93$Price)
```

which produces Figure 3-7, the histogram in the Plots pane.

You'll note that this isn't quite as spiffy-looking as Figure 3-2. You can spruce it up by adding arguments.

One often-used argument in base R graphics changes the label of the *x*-axis from R's default into something more meaningful. It's called xlab. For the *x*-axis in Figure 3-2, the following was added to the arguments:

```
xlab= "Price (x $1,000)"
```

You can use ylab to change the *y*-axis label, but this isn't necessary for the example.

For the *x*-axis to extend from a lower limit of 0 to an upper limit of 70, you use the argument xlim. Because this argument works with a vector, the following was added for the example:

```
xlim = c(0,70)
```

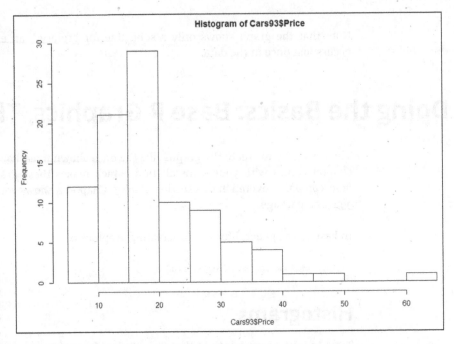

FIGURE 3-7:
Initial histogram
of the distribution
of prices
in Cars93.

To change the title, you use main:

```
main = "Prices of 93 Models of 1993 Cars"
```

To produce the histogram in Figure 3-2, the whole megillah is

```
> hist(Cars93$Price, xlab="Price (x $1,000)", xlim = c(0,70), main = "Prices of
          93 Models of 1993 Cars")
```

TIP

When creating a histogram, R figures out the best number of columns for a nice-looking appearance. Here, R decided that 12 is a pretty good number. You can vary the number of columns by adding an argument called breaks and setting its value. R doesn't always give you the value you set. Instead, it provides something close to that value and tries to maintain a nice-looking appearance. To see this effect in action, add the breaks argument and set its value (breaks =4, for example).

Graph features

An important aspect of base R graphics is the ability to add features to a graph after you create it. To illustrate graph features, the example used in this section starts with a slightly different type of graph.

Another way of showing histogram information is to think of the data as *probabilities* rather than frequencies. So, instead of the frequency of a particular price range, you graph the probability that a car selected from the data is in that price range. To do this, you add

```
probability = TRUE
```

to the arguments. Now the R code looks like this:

```
> hist(Cars93$Price, xlab="Price (x $1,000)", xlim = c(0,70), main = "Prices of
          93 Models of 1993 Cars",probability = TRUE)
```

The result appears in Figure 3-8. The *y*-axis measures *density*, which is a concept related to probability. The graph is called a *density plot*.

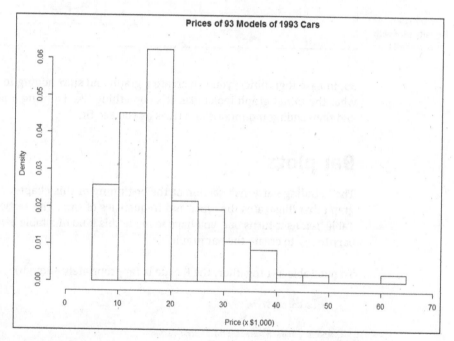

FIGURE 3-8:
Density plot of
the distribution of
prices in Cars93.

The point of all this is what you do next. After you create the graph, you can use an additional function called lines() to add a line to the density plot:

```
> lines(density(Cars93$Price))
```

The graph now looks like Figure 3-9.

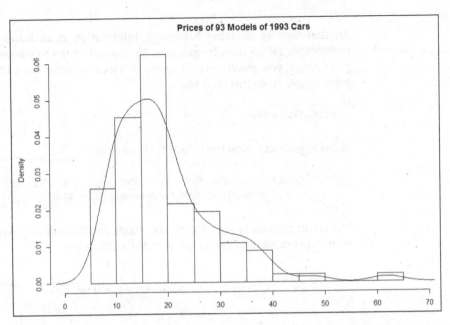

FIGURE 3-9:
Density plot with
an added line.

So, in base R graphics, you can create a graph and start adding to it after you see what the initial graph looks like. It's something like painting a picture of a lake and then adding mountains and trees as you see fit.

Bar plots

The "Finding Patterns" section at the beginning of this chapter shows you a bar graph that illustrates the types and frequencies of cars. The section also contains Table 3-1. As it turns out, you have to make this kind of a table before you can use `barplot()` to create the bar graph.

To put Table 3-1 together, the R code is (appropriately enough)

```
> table(Cars93$Type)

Compact Large Midsize Small Sporty Van
    16   11     22    21     14   9
```

For the bar graph, then, it's

```
> barplot(table(Cars93$Type))
```

which creates the graph in Figure 3-10.

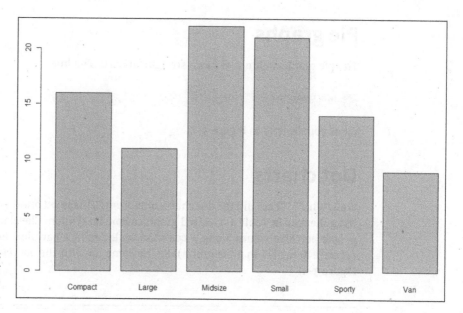

FIGURE 3-10:
The initial bar
plot of `table`
(`Cars93$Type`).

Again, it's not as jazzy as the final product shown in Figure 3-3. Additional arguments do the trick. To put 0 through 25 on the *y*-axis, you use `ylim`, which, like `xlim`, works with a vector:

```
ylim = c(0,25)
```

For the *x*-axis label and *y*-axis label, you use

```
xlab = "Type"
ylab = "Frequency"
```

To draw a solid axis, you work with `axis.lty`. Think of this as "axis linetype," which you set to `solid` by typing

```
axis.lty = "solid"
```

The values `dashed` and `dotted` for `axis.lty` result in different looks for the *x*-axis.

Finally, you use `space` to increase the spacing between bars:

```
space = .05
```

Here's the entire function for producing the graph shown earlier, in Figure 3-3:

```
> barplot(table(Cars93$Type),ylim=c(0,25), xlab="Type", ylab="Frequency",
          axis.lty = "solid", space = .05)
```

Pie graphs

The pie graph couldn't be more straightforward. The line

```
> pie(table(Cars93$Type))
```

takes you directly to Figure 3-4.

Dot charts

Wait. What? Where did the dot chart come from? This is yet another way of visualizing the data in Table 3-1. Noted graphics honcho William Cleveland believes that people perceive values along a common scale (as in a bar plot) better than they perceive areas (as in a pie graph). So, he came up with the *dot chart*, as shown in Figure 3-11.

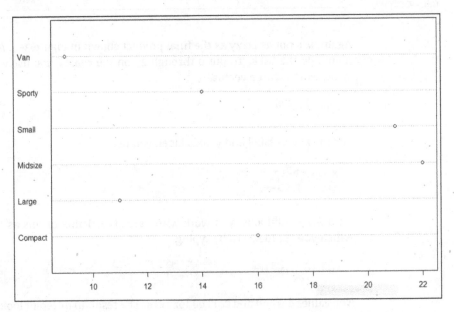

FIGURE 3-11:
Dot chart for the data in Table 3-1.

Looks a little like an abacus laid on its side, doesn't it? This is one of those infrequent cases where the independent variable is on the *y*-axis and the dependent variable is on the *x*-axis.

The format for the function that creates a dot chart is

```
> dotchart(x, labels, arg1, arg2 ...)
```

The first two arguments are vectors, and the others are optional arguments for modifying the appearance of the dot chart. The first vector is the vector of values (the frequencies). The second is pretty self-explanatory — in this case, it's labels for the types of vehicles.

To create the two necessary vectors (one for the type of car, the other for the frequency), you have to turn the table (which is a single vector) into a data frame:

```
> type.frame <- data.frame(table(Cars93$Type))
> type.frame
     Var1 Freq
1 Compact 16
2 Large 11
3 Midsize 22
4 Small 21
5 Sporty 14
6 Van 9
```

After you have the data frame, this line produces the dot chart:

```
> dotchart(type.frame$Freq,type.frame$Var1)
```

The type.frame$Freq specifies that the Frequency column in the data frame is the x-axis, and type.frame$Var1 specifies that the Var1 column (which holds the car types) is the y-axis.

This line works, too:

```
> dotchart(type.frame[,2],type.frame[,1])
```

Note that [,2] means "column 2" and [,1] means "column 1."

Bar plots revisited

In all the preceding graphs in this chapter, the dependent variable has been frequency. Many times, however, the dependent variable is a data point rather than a frequency.

Table 3-2 shows the data for commercial space revenues for the early 1990s. (The data is from the US Department of Commerce, via the Statistical Abstract of the US.)

The data are the numbers in the cells, which represent revenue in thousands of dollars. A base R bar plot of the data in this table appears in Figure 3-12.

TABLE 3-2 US Commercial Space Revenues 1990–1994 (in Millions of Dollars)

Industry	1990	1991	1992	1993	1994
Commercial satellites delivered	1,000	1,300	1,300	1,100	1,400
Satellite services	800	1,200	1,500	1,850	2,330
Satellite ground equipment	860	1,300	1,400	1,600	1,970
Commercial launches	570	380	450	465	580
Remote sensing data	155	190	210	250	300

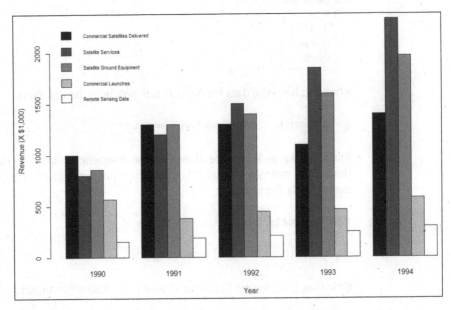

FIGURE 3-12:
Bar plot of the data in Table 3-2.

This graph is called a *grouped bar plot*. How do you create a plot like this one in base R?

The first thing to do is create a vector of the values in the cells:

```
rev.values <- c(1000,1300,1300,1100,1400,800,1200,1500,1850,2330,860,1300,1400,
                1600,1970,570,380,450,465,580,155,190,210,250,300)
```

WARNING

Although commas appear in the values in the table (for values greater than a thousand), you can't have commas in the values in the vector! (For the obvious reason: Commas separate consecutive values in the vector.)

Next, you turn this vector into a matrix. You have to let R know how many rows (or columns) will be in the matrix, and that the values load into the matrix row-by-row:

```
space.rev <- matrix(rev.values,nrow=5,byrow = T)
```

Finally, you supply column names and row names to the matrix:

```
colnames(space.rev) <- c("1990","1991","1992","1993","1994")
rownames(space.rev) <- c("Commercial Satellites Delivered","Satellite
            Services","Satellite Ground Equipment","Commercial
            Launches","Remote Sensing Data")
```

Let's have a look at the matrix:

```
> space.rev
                            1990 1991 1992 1993 1994
Commercial Satellites Delivered 1000 1300 1300 1100 1400
Satellite Services 800 1200 1500 1850 2330
Satellite Ground Equipment 860 1300 1400 1600 1970
Commercial Launches 570 380 450 465 580
Remote Sensing Data 155 190 210 250 300
```

Perfect. It looks just like Table 3-2.

With the data in hand, you move on to the bar plot. You create a vector of colors for the bars:

```
color.names = c("black","grey25","grey50","grey75","white")
```

TIP

A word about those color names: You can join any number from 0 to 100 with "grey" and get a color: "grey0" is equivalent to "black" and "grey100" is equivalent to "white".

And now for the plot:

```
> barplot(space.rev, beside = T, xlab= "Year",ylab= "Revenue (X $1,000)",
            col=color.names)
```

beside = T means the bars will be, well, beside each other. (You ought to try this without that argument and see what happens.) The col=color.names argument supplies the colors you specified in the vector.

The resulting plot is shown in Figure 3-13.

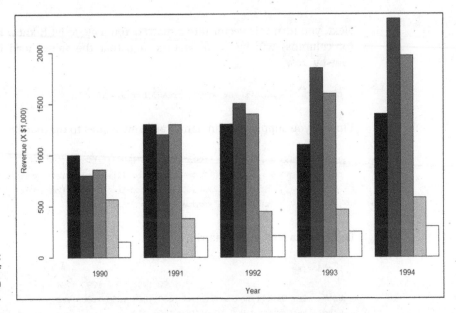

FIGURE 3-13:
Initial bar plot of
the data shown
in Table 3-2.

What's missing, of course, is the legend. You add that with the legend() function to produce Figure 3-12:

```
> legend(1,2300,rownames(space.rev), cex=0.7, fill = color.names, bty = "n")
```

The first two values are the *x*- and *y*-coordinates for locating the legend. (That took a *lot* of tinkering!) The next argument shows what goes into the legend (the names of the industries). The cex argument specifies the size of the characters in the legend. The value, 0.7, indicates that you want the characters to be 70 percent of the size they would normally be. That's the only way to fit the legend on the graph. (Think of cex as "character expansion," although in this case it's "character contraction.") fill = color.names puts the color swatches in the legend, next to the row names. Setting bty (the "border type") to "n" ("none") is another little trick to fit the legend into the graph.

Scatter plots

To visualize the relationship between horsepower and MPG for city driving (as shown earlier, in Figure 3-5), you use the plot() function:

```
> plot(Cars93$Horsepower, Cars93$MPG.city, xlab="Horsepower",ylab="MPG City",
        main ="MPG City vs Horsepower")
```

As you can see, this example adds the arguments for labeling the axes and for the title.

Another way to do this is to use the tilde operator (~). So, if you want the R code to show that MPG-city depends on horsepower, you type

```
> plot(Cars93$MPG.city ~ Cars93$Horsepower, xlab="Horsepower",ylab="MPG City",
        main ="MPG City vs Horsepower")
```

to produce the same scatter plot.

The tilde operator (~) means "depends on."

A plot twist

R enables you to change the symbol that depicts the points in the graph. Figure 3-5 shows that the default symbol is an empty circle. To change the symbol, which is called the *plotting character*, set the argument pch. R has a set of built-in numerical values (0–25) for pch that correspond to a set of symbols. The values 0–15 correspond to unfilled shapes, and 16–25 are filled.

The default value is 1. To change the plotting character to squares, set pch to 0. For triangles, it's 2, and for filled circles, it's 16:

```
> plot(Cars93$Horsepower,Cars93$MPG.city, xlab="Horsepower", ylab="MPG City",
        main = "MPG City vs Horsepower",pch=16)
```

Figure 3-14 shows the plot with the filled circles.

You can also set the argument col to change the color from "black" to "blue" or to a variety of other colors (which wouldn't show up well on the black-and-white page you're looking at).

Scatter plot matrix

Base R provides a nice way of visualizing relationships among more than two variables. If you add price into the mix and want to show all the pairwise relationships among MPG-city, price, and horsepower, you'd need multiple scatter plots. R can plot them all together in a matrix, as Figure 3-15 shows.

The names of the variables are in the cells of the main diagonal. Each off-diagonal cell shows the scatter plot for its row variable (on the *y*-axis) and its column variable (on the *x*-axis). For example, the scatter plot in the first row, second column, shows MPG-city on the *y*-axis and price on the *x*-axis. In the second row, first column, the axes are reversed: MPG city is on the *x*-axis, and price is on the *y*-axis.

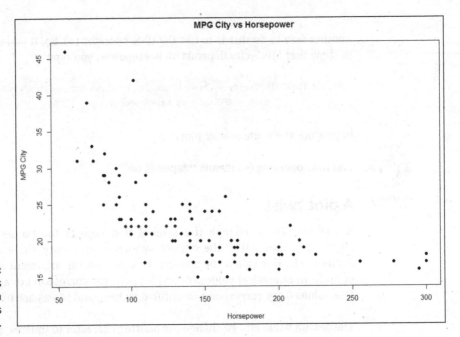

FIGURE 3-14:
MPG City versus
Horsepower with
filled-in circles
(pch = 16).

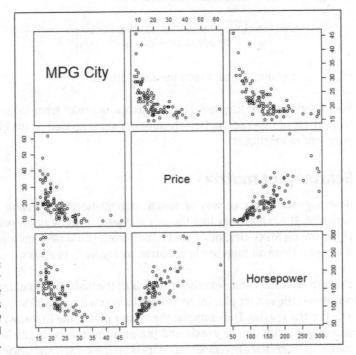

FIGURE 3-15:
Multiple scatter
plots for the
relationships
among city
MPG, price, and
horsepower.

The R function for plotting this matrix is `pairs()`. To calculate the coordinates for all scatter plots, this function works with numerical columns from a matrix or a data frame.

For convenience, you create a data frame that's a subset of the `Cars93` data frame. This new data frame consists of just the three variables to plot. The function `subset()` handles that nicely:

```
> cars.subset <- subset(Cars93, select = c(MPG.city,Price,Horsepower))
```

The second argument to `subset` creates a vector of exactly what to select out of `Cars93`. Just to make sure the new data frame is the way you want it, use the `head()` function to take a look at the first six rows:

```
> head(cars.subset)
  MPG.city Price Horsepower
1 25 15.9 140
2 18 33.9 200
3 20 29.1 172
4 19 37.7 172
5 22 30.0 208
6 22 15.7 110
```

And now,

```
> pairs(cars.subset)
```

creates the plot in Figure 3-15.

This capability isn't limited to three variables, nor to continuous ones. To see what happens with a different type of variable, add `Cylinders` to the vector for `select` and then use the `pairs()` function on `cars.subset`.

Box plots

To draw a box plot like the one shown earlier in Figure 3-6, you use a formula to show that `Horsepower` is the dependent variable and `Cylinders` is the independent variable:

```
> boxplot(Cars93$Horsepower ~ Cars93$Cylinders,
          xlab="Cylinders",ylab="Horsepower")
```

If you get tired of typing the $ signs, here's another way:

```
> boxplot(Horsepower ~ Cylinders, data = Cars93, xlab="Cylinders",
          ylab="Horsepower")
```

TIP

With the arguments laid out as in either of the two preceding code examples, `plot()` works exactly like `boxplot()`.

Chapter **4**

Kicking It Up a Notch to ggplot2

The base R graphics toolset will get you started, but if you want to shine at visualization, it's a good idea to learn ggplot2. Created by R megastar Hadley Wickham, the *gg* in the package name stands for "grammar of graphics," and that's a good indicator of what's ahead. That's also the title of the book (by Leland Wilkinson) that is the source of the concepts for this package.

In general, a *grammar* is a set of rules for combining things. In the grammar that people are most familiar with, the things happen to be words, phrases, and clauses. The grammar of our language tells you how to combine these components to produce valid sentences.

So, a "grammar of graphics" is a set of rules for combining graphics components to produce graphs. Wilkinson proposed that all graphs have underlying common components — like data, a coordinate system (the *x*- and *y*-axes you know so well, for example), statistical transformations (like frequency counts), and objects within the graph (dots, bars, lines, or pie slices, for example — to name just a few).

Just as combining words and phrases produces grammatical sentences, combining graphics components produces graphs. And just as some sentences are grammatical but make no sense ("Colorless green ideas sleep furiously"), some ggplot2 creations are beautiful graphs that aren't always useful. It's up to the speaker/writer to make sense for their audiences, and it's up to the graphics developer to create useful graphs for people who use them.

Histograms

In ggplot2, Wickham's implementation of Wilkinson's grammar is an easy-to-learn structure for R graphics code. To learn that structure, make sure you have ggplot2 in the library so that you can follow what comes next. (Find ggplot2 on the Packages tab and select its check box.)

A graph starts with ggplot(), which takes two arguments. The first argument is the source of the data. The second argument maps the data components of interest into components of the graph. The function that does the job is aes().

To begin a histogram for Price in Cars93, the function is

```
> ggplot(Cars93, aes(x=Price))
```

The aes() function associates Price with the *x*-axis. In ggplot-world, this is called an *aesthetic mapping*. In fact, each argument to aes() is called an *aesthetic*.

This line of code draws Figure 4-1, which is just a grid with a gray background and Price on the *x*-axis.

Well, what about the *y*-axis? Does anything in the data map into it? No. That's because this is a histogram and nothing explicitly in the data provides a *y*-value for each x. So, you can't say "y=" in aes(). Instead, you let R do the work to calculate the heights of the bars in the histogram.

And what about that histogram? How do you put it into this blank grid? You have to add something indicating that you want to plot a histogram and let R take care of the rest. What you add is a geom function. (*Geom* is short for "geometric object.")

These geom functions come in a variety of types. ggplot2 supplies one for almost every graphing need and provides the flexibility to work with special cases. To draw a histogram, the geom function to use is called geom_histogram().

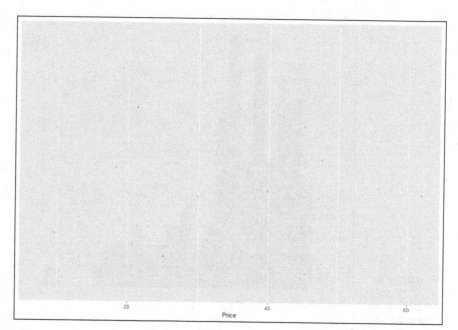

FIGURE 4-1:
Applying
ggplot() and
nothing else.

You add `geom_histogram()` to `ggplot()` by using a plus sign:

```
ggplot(Cars93, aes(x=Price)) +
   geom_histogram()
```

This snippet produces Figure 4-2. The grammar rules tell `ggplot2` that when the geometric object is a histogram, R does the necessary calculations on the data and produces the appropriate plot.

At the bare minimum, `ggplot2` graphics code has to have data, aesthetic mappings, and a geometric object. It's like answering a logical sequence of questions: What's the source of the data? What parts of the data are you interested in? Which parts of the data correspond to which parts of the graph? How do you want the graph to look?

Beyond those minimum requirements, you can modify the graph. Each bar is called a *bin*, and by default, `ggplot()` uses 30 of them. After plotting the histogram, `ggplot()` displays an onscreen message that advises experimenting with `binwidth` (which, unsurprisingly, specifies the width of each bin) to change the graph's appearance. Accordingly, you use `binwidth = 5` as an argument in `geom_histogram()`.

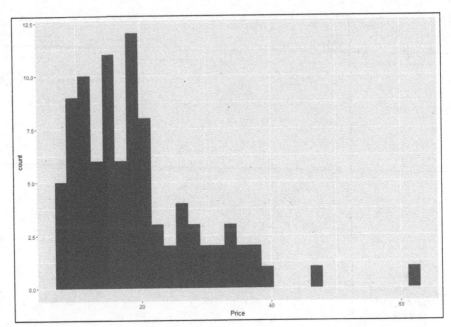

FIGURE 4-2:
The initial
histogram for
Price in Cars93.

Additional arguments modify the way the bars look:

```
geom_histogram(binwidth=5, color = "black", fill = "white")
```

With another function, labs(), you modify the labels for the axes and supply a title for the graph:

```
labs(x = "Price (x $1000)", y="Frequency",title="Prices of 93 Models of 1993
    Cars")
```

Altogether now:

```
ggplot(Cars93, aes(x=Price)) +
  geom_histogram(binwidth=5,color="black",fill="white") +
  labs(x = "Price (x $1000)", y="Frequency", title="Prices of 93 Models of 1993
             Cars")
```

The result is shown in Figure 4-3.

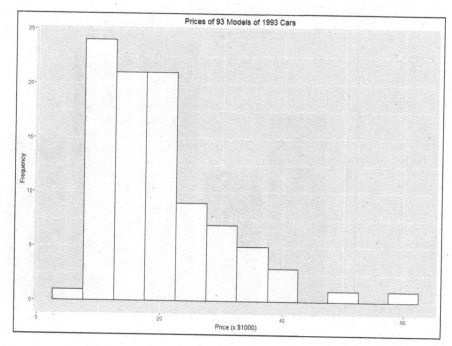

Prices of 93 Models of 1993 Cars

FIGURE 4-3:
The finished Price
histogram.

Bar Plots

Drawing a bar plot in ggplot2 is a little easier than drawing one in base R: It's not necessary to first create a table in order to draw the graph. As in the example in the preceding section, you don't specify an aesthetic mapping for y. This time, the geom function is geom_bar(), and the rules of the grammar tell ggplot2 to do the necessary work with the data and then draw the plot:

```
ggplot(Cars93, aes(x=Type))+
  geom_bar() +
  labs(y="Frequency", title="Car Type and Frequency in Cars93")
```

Figure 4-4 shows the resulting bar plot.

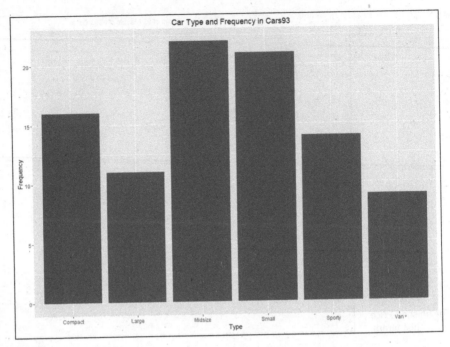

FIGURE 4-4:
Bar plot
for Car Type.

Dot Charts

In the preceding chapter (Book 5, Chapter 3), you see how to use the dot chart as an alternative to the pie graph. In this section, you find out how to use ggplot() to draw one.

Making a dot chart begins much the same as in base R: You create a table for ype, and you turn the table into a data frame:

```
type.frame <- data.frame(table(Cars$93.Type))
```

To ensure that you have meaningful variable names for the aesthetic mapping, you apply the colnames() function to name the columns in this data frame

```
colnames(type.frame)<- c("Type","Frequency")
```

Now, type.frame looks just like Table 3-1 in the preceding chapter:

```
> type.frame
    Type Frequency
1 Compact 16
```

```
2 Large 11
3 Midsize 22
4 Small 21
5 Sporty 14
6 Van 9
```

On to the graph. To orient the dot chart as shown in the preceding chapter, you map Frequency to the *x*-axis and Type to the *y*-axis:

```
ggplot(type.frame, aes(x=Frequency,y= Type))
```

Again, usually the independent variable is on the *x*-axis and the dependent variable is on the *y*-axis, but that's not the case in this graph.

Next, you add a geom function.

WARNING

A geom function called geom_dotplot() is available, but surprisingly, it's not appropriate here. That one draws something else. In ggplot-world, a dot *plot* is different from a dot *chart*.

The geom function for the dot chart is geom_point(). So, this code:

```
ggplot(type.frame, aes(x=Frequency,y=Type)) +
  geom_point()
```

results in Figure 4-5.

A couple of modifications are in order. First, with a graph like this, it's a nice touch to rearrange the categories on the *y*-axis concerning how they order on what you're measuring on the *x*-axis. That necessitates a slight change in the aesthetic mapping to the *y*-axis:

```
ggplot(type.frame,
  aes(x=Frequency,y=reorder(Type,Frequency)))
```

Larger dots would make the chart look a little nicer:

```
geom_point(size =4)
```

Additional functions modify the graph's overall appearance. One family of these functions is called *themes*. One member of this family, theme_bw(), removes the gray background. Adding theme() with appropriate arguments a) removes the

Kicking It Up a Notch to ggplot2

vertical lines in the grid and b) blackens the horizontal lines and makes them dotted:

```
theme_bw() +
theme(panel.grid.major.x=element_blank(),
      panel.grid.major.y=element_line(color = "black", linetype = "dotted"))
```

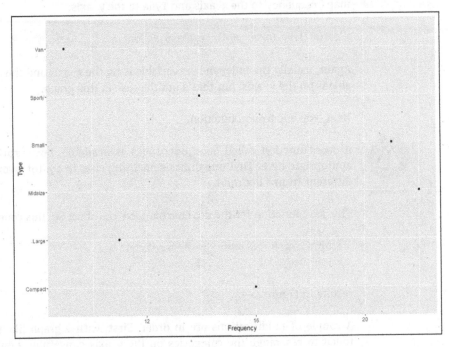

FIGURE 4-5:
The initial dot
chart for Type.

Finally, labs() changes the y-axis label:

```
labs(y= "Type")
```

Without that change, the y-axis label would be reorder(Type,Frequency). Though picturesque, that label makes little sense to the average viewer.

Here's the code from beginning to end:

```
ggplot(type.frame, aes(x=Frequency,y=reorder(Type,Frequency))) +
    geom_point(size = 4) +
    theme_bw() +
    theme(panel.grid.major.x=element_blank(),
          panel.grid.major.y=element_line(color = "black",linetype = "dotted"))+
    labs(y="Type")
```

Figure 4-6 shows the dot chart.

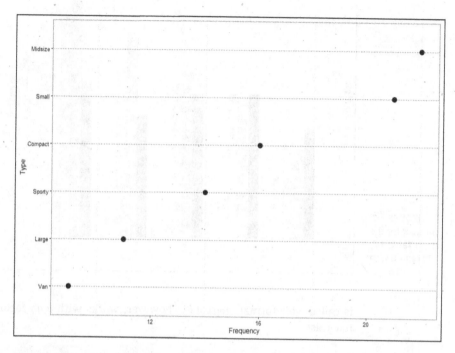

Bar Plots Re-revisited

As was the case with the first few graphs in base R (Book 5, Chapter 3), the graphs shown so far in this chapter have frequencies (or "counts") as the dependent variable. And, of course, as shown in the preceding chapter, that's not always the case. Here, you see how to use ggplot() to create one from space.rev, the data set created from the data in Table 3-2 (Book 5, Chapter 3). The finished product will look like Figure 4-7.

The first order of business is to get the data ready. It's not in the format that ggplot() uses. This format

```
> space.rev
                              1990 1991 1992 1993 1994
Commercial Satellites Delivered 1000 1300 1300 1100 1400
Satellite Services 800 1200 1500 1850 2330
Satellite Ground Equipment 860 1300 1400 1600 1970
Commercial Launches 570 380 450 465 580
Remote Sensing Data 155 190 210 250 300
```

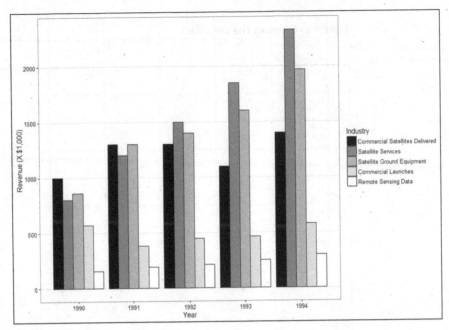

FIGURE 4-7:
Bar plot for the
data in Table 3-2,
created with
ggplot().

is called *wide* format. ggplot(), however, works with *long* format, which looks like this:

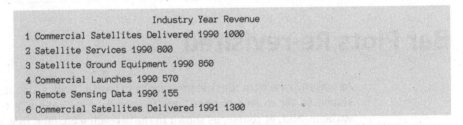

```
              Industry Year Revenue
1 Commercial Satellites Delivered 1990 1000
2 Satellite Services 1990 800
3 Satellite Ground Equipment 1990 860
4 Commercial Launches 1990 570
5 Remote Sensing Data 1990 155
6 Commercial Satellites Delivered 1991 1300
```

Those are just the first six rows for this data set. The total number of rows is 25 (because 5 rows and 5 columns are in the wide format).

Hadley Wickham (there's that name again!) created a package called reshape2 that provides everything for a seamless transformation. The function melt() turns wide format into long. Another function, cast(), does the reverse. These functions are a huge help because they eliminate the need to go schlepping around in spreadsheets to reshape a data set.

So, with `reshape2` in the library (select its check box on the Packages tab), the code is

```
> space.melt <- melt(space.rev)
```

Yes, that's really all there is to it:

```
> head(space.melt)
                                Var1 Var2 value
1 Commercial Satellites Delivered 1990 1000
2 Satellite Services 1990 800
3 Satellite Ground Equipment 1990 860
4 Commercial Launches 1990 570
5 Remote Sensing Data 1990 155
6 Commercial Satellites Delivered 1991 1300
```

Next, you give meaningful names to the columns:

```
> colnames(space.melt) <- c("Industry","Year","Revenue")
> head(space.melt)
                          Industry Year Revenue
1 Commercial Satellites Delivered 1990 1000
2 Satellite Services 1990 800
3 Satellite Ground Equipment 1990 860
4 Commercial Launches 1990 570
5 Remote Sensing Data 1990 155
6 Commercial Satellites Delivered 1991 1300
```

And now you're ready to roll. You start with `ggplot()`. The aesthetic mappings are straightforward:

```
ggplot(space.melt, aes(x=Year,y=Revenue,fill=Industry))
```

You add the `geom` function for the bar, and you specify three arguments:

```
geom_bar(stat = "identity", position = "dodge", color ="black")
```

The first argument is necessary for a graph of this type. If left on its own, `geom_bar` defaults to the bar plot shown earlier — a graph based on frequencies. Because you defined an aesthetic mapping for `y`, and that type of graph is incompatible with an aesthetic for `y`, not setting this argument results in an error message.

Accordingly, you let `ggplot()` know that this is a graph based on explicit data values. So `stat="identity"` means "use the given numbers as the data."

The value for the next argument, `position`, is a cute name that means the bars "dodge" each other and line up side-by-side. (Omit this argument and see what happens.) It's analogous to "`beside =T`" in base R.

The third argument sets the color of the borders for each bar. The fill-color scheme for the bars is the province of the next function:

```
scale_fill_grey(start = 0,end = 1)
```

As its name suggests, this function fills the bars with shades of gray (or "grey"). The `start` value, 0, is black, and the `end` value, 1, is white. (Reminiscent of "grey0" = "black" and "grey100" = "white.") The effect is to fill the five bars with five shades from black to white.

You'd like to relabel the y-axis, so that's

```
labs(y="Revenue (X $1,000)")
```

and then remove the gray background

```
theme_bw()
```

and, finally, remove the vertical lines from the grid

```
theme(panel.grid.major.x = element_blank())
```

The whole chunk for producing Figure 4-8 is

```
ggplot(space.melt, aes(x=Year,y=Revenue,fill=Industry)) +
  geom_bar(stat = "identity", position = "dodge", color="black") +
  scale_fill_grey(start = 0,end = 1)+
  labs(y="Revenue (X $1,000)")+
  theme_bw()+
  theme(panel.grid.major.x = element_blank())
```

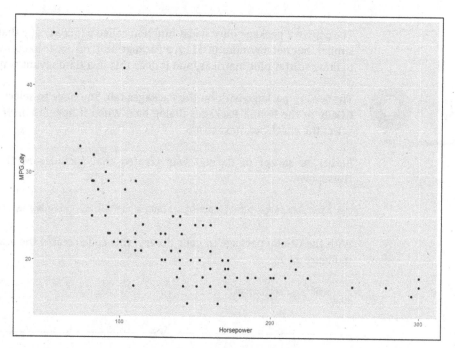

FIGURE 4-8:
MPG.city versus
Horsepower
in Cars93.

Scatter Plots

A scatter plot is a great way to show the relationship between two variables, like horsepower and miles per gallon for city driving. And ggplot() is a great way to draw the scatter plot. If you've been following along, the grammar of this will be easy for you:

```
ggplot(Cars93,aes(x=Horsepower,y=MPG.city))+
  geom_point()
```

Figure 4-8 shows the scatter plot. You may want to change the y-axis label to "Miles per Gallon (City)" and add a descriptive title.

Scatter Plot Matrix

A *matrix* of scatter plots shows the pairwise relationships among more than two variables. In the preceding chapter (Book 5, Chapter 3), you see how the base R pairs() function draws this kind of matrix.

The ggplot2 package once had a function called plotpairs() that did something similar, but not anymore. GGally, a package built on ggplot2, provides ggpairs() to draw scatter plot matrices, and it does this in a flamboyant way.

TIP

The GGally package isn't on the Packages tab. You have to select Install and type **GGally** in the Install Packages dialog box. When it appears on the Packages tab, select the check box next to it.

Earlier, a subset of Cars93 was created that includes MPG.city, Price, and Horsepower:

```
> cars.subset <- subset(Cars93, select = c(MPG.city,Price,Horsepower))
```

With the GGally package in your library, this code creates the scatter plot matrix in Figure 4-9:

```
> ggpairs(cars.subset)
```

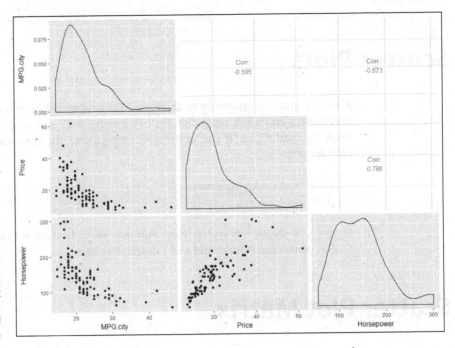

FIGURE 4-9:
Scatter plot matrix for MPG.city, Price, and Horsepower.

As Figure 4-9 shows, this one's a beauty. The cells along the main diagonal present density plots of the variables. (See the discussion of graph features in Book 5, Chapter 3.) One drawback is that the *y*-axis is visible for the variable MPG.city only in the first row and first column.

The three scatter plots are in the cells below the main diagonal. Rather than show the same scatter plots with the axes reversed in the cells above the main diagonal (like pairs() does), each above-the-diagonal cell shows a *correlation coefficient* that summarizes the relationship between the cell's row variable and its column variable.

For a real visual treat, add Cylinders to cars.subset and then apply ggpairs():

```
> cars.subset <- subset(Cars93, select = c(MPG.city,Price,Horsepower,Cylinders))
> ggpairs(cars.subset)
```

Figure 4-10 shows the new scatter plot matrix in all its finery.

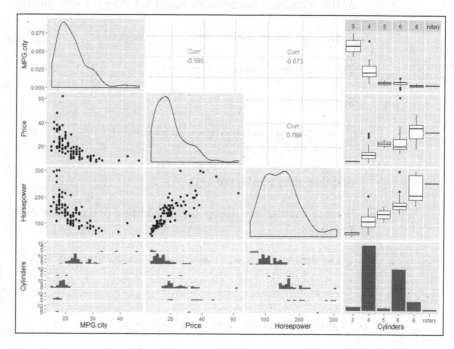

FIGURE 4-10: Adding Cylinders produces this scatter plot matrix.

Cylinders is not a variable that lends itself to scatter plots, density plots, or correlation coefficients. (Thought question: Why not?) Thus, the cell in the fourth column, fourth row, has a bar plot rather than a density plot. Bar plots relating Cylinders (on each y-axis) to the other three variables (on the x-axes) are in the remaining three cells in row 4. Box plots relating Cylinders (on each x-axis) to the other three variables (on the y-axes) are in the remaining three cells in column 4.

Box Plots

Statisticians use box plots to quickly show how groups differ from one another. As in the base R example in Book 5, Chapter 3, this section shows the box plot for Cylinders and Horsepower. This is a replication of the graph in row 3, column 4 of Figure 4-10.

At this point, you can probably figure out the ggplot() function:

```
ggplot(Cars93, aes(x=Cylinders, y= Horsepower))
```

The geom function is geom_boxplot().

So the code is

```
ggplot(Cars93, aes(x=Cylinders,y=Horsepower)) +
  geom_boxplot()
```

And that gives you Figure 4-11.

Want to show all the data points in addition to the boxes? Add the geom function for points:

```
ggplot(Cars93, aes(x=Cylinders,y=Horsepower)) +
  geom_boxplot()+
  geom_point()
```

to produce the graph shown in Figure 4-12.

Remember, this is data for 93 cars. You don't see 93 data points, of course, because many points overlap. Graphics gurus refer to this as *overplotting*.

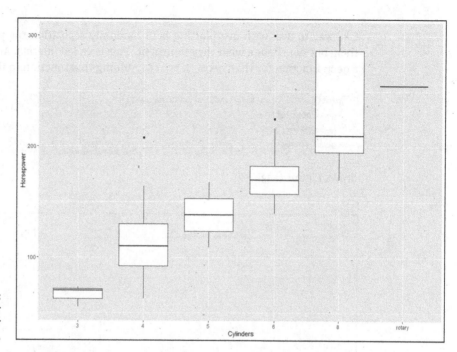

FIGURE 4-11:
Box plot for
Horsepower
versus Cylinders.

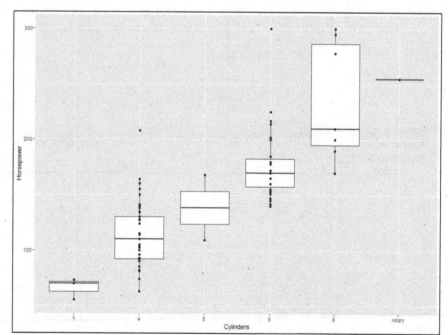

FIGURE 4-12:
Box plot with
data points.

One way to deal with overplotting is to randomly reposition the points to reveal them but not change what they represent. This is called *jittering*. And ggplot2 has a geom function for that: geom_jitter(). Adding this function to the code

```
gplot(Cars93, aes(x=Cylinders,y=Horsepower)) +
  geom_boxplot()+
  geom_point()+
  geom_jitter()
```

draws Figure 4-13.

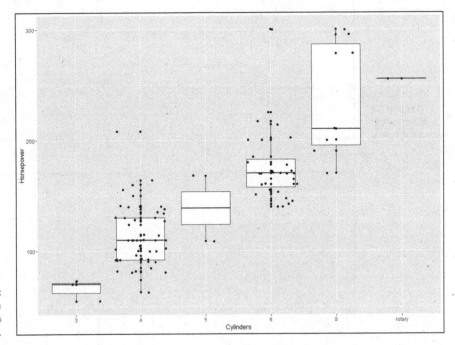

FIGURE 4-13:
Boxplot with
jittered data
points.

6

Applying Python Programming to Data Science

Contents at a Glance

Chapter **1**

Discovering the Match between Data Science and Python

D ata science is the person behind the partition in the experience of the wonderment of technology. Without data science, much of what you accept as typical and expected today wouldn't even be possible. This is the reason that being a data scientist is one of the most interesting jobs of the 21st century. You can read more about data science in Book 1, Chapter 3.

Python is uniquely suited to making it easier to work with data science. For one thing, Python provides an incredible number of math-related libraries that help you perform tasks with a less-than-perfect understanding of precisely what is going on. However, Python goes further by supporting multiple coding styles (programming paradigms) and doing other things to make your job easier. Therefore, yes, you could use other languages to write data science applications, but Python reduces your workload, so it's a natural choice for those who really don't want to work hard but rather to work smart.

This chapter gets you started with Python. Even though this book isn't designed to provide you with a complete Python tutorial, exploring some basic Python issues will reduce the time needed to get you up to speed. (If you do need a good starting tutorial, please get *Beginning Programming with Python For Dummies*, 3rd Edition, by John Mueller [Wiley]). You'll find that the book provides pointers to tutorials and other aids as needed to fill in any gaps that you may have in your Python education.

Creating the Data Science Pipeline

Data science is partly art and partly engineering. Recognizing patterns in data, considering what questions to ask, and determining which algorithms work best are all part of the art side of data science. However, to make the art part of data science realizable, the engineering part relies on a specific process to achieve specific goals. This process is the data science pipeline, which requires the data scientist to follow particular steps in the preparation, analysis, and presentation of the data. The following list helps you understand the data science pipeline better so that you can understand how the book employs it during the presentation of examples:

» **Preparing the data:** The data that you access from various sources doesn't come in an easily packaged form, ready for analysis. The raw data may vary substantially in format and require that you transform it to make all the data sources cohesive and amenable to analysis.

» **Performing exploratory data analysis:** The math behind data analysis relies on engineering principles in that the results are provable and consistent. However, data science provides access to a wealth of statistical methods and algorithms that help you discover patterns in the data. A single approach doesn't ordinarily do the trick. You typically use an iterative process to rework the data from a number of perspectives. The use of trial and error is part of the art of data science.

» **Learning from data:** As you iterate through various statistical analysis methods and apply algorithms to detect patterns, you begin learning from the data. The data may not tell the story that you originally thought it would, or it may have many stories to tell. Discovery is part of being a data scientist. If you have preconceived ideas of what the data contains, you won't find the information it actually does contain.

» **Visualizing:** Visualization means seeing the patterns in the data and then being able to react to those patterns. It also means seeing when data is not part of the pattern. Think of yourself as a data sculptor, removing the data that lies outside the patterns (the outliers) so that others can see the masterpiece of information beneath.

>> **Obtaining insights and data products:** The data scientist may seem to simply be looking for unique methods of viewing data. However, the process doesn't end until you have a clear understanding of what the data means. The insights you obtain from manipulating and analyzing the data help you to perform real-world tasks. For example, you can use the results of an analysis to make a business decision.

Understanding Python's Role in Data Science

Given the right data sources, analysis requirements, and presentation needs, you can use Python for every part of the data science pipeline. In fact, that's precisely what you do in this book. Every example uses Python to help you understand another part of the data science equation. Of all the languages you could choose for performing data science tasks, Python is the most flexible and capable because it supports so many third-party libraries devoted to the task. The following sections help you better understand why Python is such a good choice for many (if not most) data science needs.

Considering the shifting profile of data scientists

Some people view the data scientist as an unapproachable nerd who performs miracles on data with math. The data scientist is the person behind the curtain in an Oz-like experience. However, this perspective is changing. In many respects, the world now views the data scientist as either an adjunct to a developer or as a new type of developer. The ascendance of applications of all sorts that can learn is the essence of this change. For an application to learn, it has to be able to manipulate large databases and discover new patterns in them. In addition, the application must be able to create new data based on the old data — making an informed prediction of sorts. The new kinds of applications affect people in ways that would have seemed like science fiction just a few years ago. Of course, the most noticeable of these applications define the behaviors of robots that will interact far more closely with people tomorrow than today.

From a business perspective, the necessity of fusing data science and application development is obvious: Businesses must perform various sorts of analysis on the huge databases it has collected — to make sense of the information and use it to predict the future. In truth, however, the far greater impact of the melding of these two branches of science — data science and application development — will be felt in terms of creating altogether new kinds of applications, some of which aren't even possible to imagine with clarity today. For example, new applications could help students learn with greater precision by analyzing their learning trends and creating new instructional methods that work for that particular student. This combination of sciences may also solve a host of medical problems that seem impossible to solve today — not only in keeping disease at bay but also by solving problems, such as how to create truly usable prosthetic devices that look and act like the real thing.

Working with a multipurpose, simple, and efficient language

Many different ways are available for accomplishing data science tasks. This book covers only one of the myriad methods at your disposal. However, Python represents one of the few single-stop solutions that you can use to solve complex data science problems. Instead of having to use a number of tools to perform a task, you can simply use a single language, Python, to get the job done. The Python difference is the large number of scientific and math libraries created for it by third parties. Plugging in these libraries greatly extends Python and allows it to easily perform tasks that other languages could perform only with great difficulty.

TIP

Python's libraries are its main selling point; however, Python offers more than reusable code. The most important thing to consider with Python is that it supports four different coding styles:

>> **Functional:** Treats every statement as a mathematical equation and avoids any form of state or mutable data. The main advantage of this approach is that it has no side effects to consider. In addition, this coding style lends itself better than the others to parallel processing because there is no state to consider. Many developers prefer this coding style for recursion and lambda calculus.

>> **Imperative:** Performs computations as a direct change to program state. This style is especially useful when manipulating data structures and produces elegant but simple code.

>> **Object-oriented:** Relies on data fields that are treated as objects and manipulated only through prescribed methods. Python doesn't fully support this coding form because it can't implement features such as data hiding. However, this is a useful coding style for complex applications because it supports encapsulation and polymorphism. This coding style also favors code reuse.

>> **Procedural:** Treats tasks as step-by-step iterations where common tasks are placed in functions called as needed. This coding style favors iteration, sequencing, selection, and modularization.

Learning to Use Python Fast

It's time to try using Python to see the data science pipeline in action. Don't worry about understanding every aspect of the process at this point. The purpose of these sections is to help you understand the flow of using Python to perform data science tasks. Many of the details may seem difficult to understand at this point, but the rest of the book will help you understand them.

The examples in this book rely on a web-based application named Jupyter Notebook. The screenshots you see in this and other chapters reflect how Jupyter Notebook looks in Chrome on a Windows 10/11 system. The view you see will contain the same data, but the actual interface may differ a little depending on the platform (such as using a notebook instead of a desktop system), operating system, and browser. Don't worry if you see some slight differences between your display and the screenshots in the book.

Loading data

Before you can do anything, you need to load some data. Figure 1-1 shows how to load a dataset called California Housing that contains housing prices and other facts about houses in California. It was obtained from StatLib repository (see `https://www.dcc.fc.up.pt/~ltorgo/Regression/cal_housing.html` for details). The code places the entire dataset in the `housing` variable and then places parts of that data in variables named X and y. Think of variables as you would storage boxes. The variables are important because they make it possible to work with the data. The output shows that the dataset contains 20,640 entries with eight features each. The second output shows the name of each of the features.

Training a model

Now that you have some data to work with, you can do something with it. All sorts of algorithms are built into Python. Figure 1-2 shows a linear regression model. As shown in the figure, Python lets you perform the linear regression using just two statements. You place the result in a variable named `hypothesis`.

Learning to Use Python Fast

Loading data

```
In [1]: from sklearn.datasets import fetch_california_housing
        housing = fetch_california_housing()
        X, y = housing.data,housing.target
        print("The size of the data set is {}".format(X.shape))
        print("The names of the data columns are {}", housing.feature_names)

        The size of the data set is (20640, 8)
        The names of the data columns are {} ['MedInc', 'HouseAge', 'AveRooms', 'AveBed
        rms', 'Population', 'AveOccup', 'Latitude', 'Longitude']
```

FIGURE 1-1:
Loading data
into variables
so that you can
manipulate it.

Training a model

```
In [2]: from sklearn.linear_model import LinearRegression
        hypothesis = LinearRegression()
        hypothesis.fit(X,y)

Out[2]: LinearRegression()
```

FIGURE 1-2:
Using the
variable content
to train a linear
regression model.

Viewing a result

Performing any sort of analysis doesn't pay unless you obtain some benefit from
it in the form of a result. This book shows all sorts of ways to view output, but
Figure 1-3 starts with something simple. In this case, you see the coefficient output from the linear regression analysis. Notice that there is one coefficient for
each of the dataset features.

Viewing a result

```
In [3]: print(hypothesis.coef_)

        [ 4.36693293e-01  9.43577803e-03 -1.07322041e-01  6.45065694e-01
         -3.97638942e-06 -3.78654265e-03 -4.21314378e-01 -4.34513755e-01]
```

FIGURE 1-3:
Outputting
a result as a
response to
the model.

TIP

One of the reasons this book uses Jupyter Notebook is that the product helps you
to create nicely formatted output as part of creating the application. Look again
at Figure 1-3, and you see a report that you could simply print and offer to a colleague. The output isn't suitable for many people, but those experienced with
Python and data science will find it quite usable and informative.

Working with Python

This book doesn't provide you with a full Python tutorial. (However, you can get a great start with *Beginning Programming with Python For Dummies*, 3rd Edition, by John Paul Mueller [Wiley]). The following sections provide a brief but helpful overview of what Python looks like and how you interact with it.

Contributing to data science

Because this is a book about data science, you're probably wondering how Python contributes to better data science and what the word *better* actually means in this case. Knowing that a lot of organizations use Python doesn't help you because it doesn't say much about how they use Python, and if you want to match your choice of language to your particular need, understanding how other organizations use Python becomes important.

One such example appears at `https://www.datasciencegraduateprograms.com/python`. In this case, the article talks about `Forecastwatch.com` (`https://forecastwatch.com`), which actually does watch the weather and try to make predictions better. Every day, `Forecastwatch.com` compares 36,000 forecasts with the weather that people actually experience and then uses the results to create better forecasts. Trying to aggregate and make sense of the weather data for 800 U.S. cities is daunting, so `Forecastwatch.com` needed a language that could do these tasks with the least amount of fuss. Here are the reasons `Forecast.com` chose Python:

>> **Library support:** Python provides support for a large number of libraries, more than any one organization will ever need. According to `https://www.python.org/about/success/forecastwatch`, `Forecastwatch.com` found the regular expression, thread, object serialization, and gzip data compression libraries especially useful.

>> **Parallel processing:** Each forecast is processed as a separate thread so that the system can work through them quickly. The thread data includes the web page URL with the required forecast and category information, such as city name.

>> **Data access:** This huge amount of data can't all exist in memory, so `Forecast.com` relies on a MySQL database accessed through the MySQLdb (`https://sourceforge.net/projects/mysql-python`) library, which is one of the few libraries that hasn't moved on to Python 3.*x* yet. However, the associated website promises the required support soon. In the meantime, if you need to use MySQL with Python 3.*x*, then using mysqlclient

(https://pypi.org/project/mysqlclient/) will be a good replacement because it adds Python 3.x support to MySQLdb.

>> **Data display:** Originally, the PHP scripting language produced the Forecastwatch.com output. However, by using Quixote (https://www.mems-exchange.org/software/quixote), which is a display framework, Forecastwatch.com was able to move everything to Python. (An update of this framework is DurusWorks, at https://www.mems-exchange.org/software/DurusWorks.)

Getting a taste of the language

Python is designed to provide clear language statements but does so in an incredibly small space. A single line of Python code may perform tasks that another language usually takes several lines to perform. For example, if you want to display something on-screen, you simply tell Python to print it, like this:

```
print("Hello There!")
```

The point is that you can simply tell Python to output text, an object, or anything else using a simple statement. You don't really need too much in the way of advanced programming skills. When you want to end your session using a command line environment such as IDLE, you simply type quit() and press Enter. This book relies on a much better environment, Jupyter Notebook (or Google Colab as an alternative), which really does make your code look as though it came from someone's notebook.

Understanding the need for indentation

Python relies on indentation to create various language features, such as conditional statements. One of the most common errors that developers encounter is not providing the proper code indentation. You see this principle in action later in the book, but for now, always be sure to pay attention to indentation as you work through the book examples. For example, here is an if statement (a conditional that says that if something meets the condition, perform the following code) with proper indentation.

```
if 1 < 2:
    print("1 is less than 2")
```

WARNING

The print statement must appear indented below the conditional statement. Otherwise, the condition won't work as expected, and you may see an error message, too.

TECHNICAL STUFF

Throughout this book, you'll be leveraging a combination of both Jupyter Notebook and Google Colab. Google Colab is used as a way to test code as part of the Anaconda installation you create later on in this book. Google Colab and Jupyter Notebook are Integrated Desktop Environments (IDE). They help create correct code and perform targeted tasks to manage the code base's appearance.

This book mostly relies on Jupyter Notebook (with code also tested using Google Colab), which is part of the Anaconda installation you create in Chapter 3. Jupyter Notebook is used in Chapter 1 and again later in the book. The presentation for Google Colab is similar to, but not precisely the same as, Jupyter Notebook, and you see Google Colab in detail in Chapter 4. The purpose behind using an Integrated Development Environment (IDE) such as Jupyter Notebook and Google Colab is that they help you create correct code and perform some tasks, such as indentation, automatically. An IDE can also give your code a nicer appearance and give you a means for making report-like output with graphics and other noncode features.

Using the Python Ecosystem for Data Science

To perform data science tasks in Python, you first must load *libraries*, a collection of code to make using Python more efficient. The following sections provide an overview of the Python libraries most often used to perform data science tasks.

Accessing scientific tools using SciPy

The SciPy stack (`http://www.scipy.org`) contains a host of other libraries that you can also download separately. These libraries provide support for mathematics, science, and engineering. When you obtain SciPy, you get a set of libraries designed to work together to create various types of applications. These libraries are

- » NumPy
- » SciPy
- » Matplotlib
- » Jupyter

» Sympy

» pandas

The SciPy library focuses on numerical routines, such as routines for numerical integration and optimization. SciPy is a general-purpose library that provides functionality for multiple problem domains. It also supports domain-specific libraries, such as Scikit-learn, Scikit-image, and statsmodels.

Performing fundamental scientific computing using NumPy

The NumPy library (http://www.numpy.org) provides the means for performing n-dimensional array manipulation, which is critical for data science work. The California Housing dataset used in the examples in this chapter is an example of an n-dimensional array, and you couldn't easily access it without NumPy functions that include support for linear algebra, Fourier transform, and random-number generation (see the listing of functions at http://docs.scipy.org/doc/numpy/reference/routines.html).

Performing data analysis using pandas

The pandas library (http://pandas.pydata.org) supports data structures and data analysis tools. The library is optimized to perform data science tasks especially fast and efficiently. The basic principle behind pandas is to provide data analysis and modeling support for Python is similar to other languages, such as R (covered in Book 5).

Implementing machine learning using Scikit-learn

The Scikit-learn library (http://scikit-learn.org/stable) is one of a number of Scikit libraries that build on the capabilities provided by NumPy and SciPy to allow Python developers to perform domain-specific tasks. In this case, the library focuses on data mining and data analysis. It provides access to the following sorts of functionality:

» Classification

» Regression

» Clustering

>> Dimensionality reduction

>> Model selection

>> Preprocessing

A number of these functions appear as chapter headings in the book. As a result, you can assume that Scikit-learn is the most important library for the book (even though it relies on other libraries to perform its work).

Going for deep learning with Keras and TensorFlow

Keras (https://keras.io) is an application programming interface (API) used to train deep learning models. An *API* often specifies a model for doing something but doesn't provide an implementation. Consequently, you need an implementation of Keras to perform useful work, which is where the machine learning platform TensorFlow (https://www.tensorflow.org) comes into play because Keras runs on top of it.

When working with an API, you're looking for ways to simplify things. Keras makes things easy by offering the following features:

>> **A consistent interface:** The Keras interface is optimized for common use cases with an emphasis on actionable feedback for fixing user errors.

>> **A building-block approach:** Using a black-box approach makes it easy to create models by connecting configurable building blocks together with only a few restrictions on how you can connect them.

>> **Extendability:** You can easily add custom building blocks to express new ideas for research that include new layers, loss functions, and models.

>> **Parallel processing:** To run applications fast today, you need good parallel processing support. Keras runs on both CPUs and GPUs. It will also make use of multiple CPUs, when available.

>> **Direct Python support:** You don't have to do anything special to make the TensorFlow implementation of Keras work with Python, which can be a major stumbling block when working with other sorts of APIs.

Plotting the data using Matplotlib

The Matplotlib library (http://matplotlib.org/) gives you a MATLAB-like interface for creating data presentations of the analysis you perform. The library is currently limited to 2-D output, but it still provides you with the means to express graphically the data patterns you see in the data you analyze. Without this library, you couldn't create output that people outside the data science community could easily understand.

Creating graphs with NetworkX

To properly study the relationships between complex data in a networked system (such as that used by your GPS setup to discover routes through city streets), you need a library to create, manipulate, and study the structure of network data in various ways. In addition, the library must provide the means to output the resulting analysis in a form that humans understand, such as graphical data. NetworkX (https://networkx.github.io) enables you to perform this sort of analysis. The advantage of NetworkX is that nodes can be anything (including images) and edges can hold arbitrary data. These features allow you to perform a much broader range of analysis with NetworkX than using custom code would (and such code would be time-consuming to create).

Chapter **2**

Using Python for Data Science and Visualization

This chapter introduces the fundamental concepts of programming with Python (such as data types, loops, functions, and classes). As with R (covered in Book 5), the machine learning models you build with Python can serve as the *decision engines* within AI SaaS products you build for your company. This chapter also covers some of the best Python libraries for manipulating data, performing statistical computations, creating data visualizations, and completing other data science tasks.

Using Python for Data Science

Although popular programming languages like Java and C++ are good for developing stand-alone desktop applications, Python's versatility makes it an ideal programming language for processing, analyzing, and visualizing data. For this reason, Python has earned a reputation of excellence in the data science field, where it has been widely adopted over the past decade. In fact, Python has become so popular that it's actually stolen a lot of ground from R — the other free, widely adopted programming language for data science applications. (Book 5 covers programming with R for data analytics and visualization.) Python's status as one of the more popular programming languages out there can be linked to the fact that it's relatively easy to learn, and it allows users to accomplish several tasks using just a few lines of code.

TIP

Though this book wasn't designed to teach readers either the mechanics of programming or the implementation of machine learning algorithms, you can find plenty of helpful coding demonstrations and course recommendations on the companion website, www.businessgrowth.ai. If you want to get started using Python to implement data science, you may want to check it out.

You can use Python to do anything, from simple mathematical operations to data visualizations and even machine learning and predictive analytics. Here's an example of a basic math operation in Python:

```
>>> 2.5+3
5.5
```

Figure 2-1 shows an example — taken from Python's MatPlotLib library — of a more advanced output based on topographical data sets created by the National Oceanic and Atmospheric Administration (NOAA).

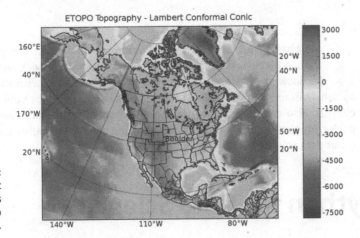

FIGURE 2-1:
Sample output from Python's MatPlotLib library.

Regardless of the task at hand, you should always study the most basic concepts of a language before attempting to delve into its more specialized libraries. So, to start, keep in mind that because Python is an object-oriented programming language, everything in Python is considered an object. In Python, an *object* is anything that can be assigned to a variable or passed as an argument to a function. The following items are all considered objects in the Python programming language:

- » Numbers
- » Strings
- » Lists
- » Tuples
- » Sets
- » Dictionaries
- » Functions
- » Classes

Additionally, all these items (except the last two in the list) function as basic data types in plain ol' Python, which is Python with no external extensions added. (You can find out more about the external Python libraries NumPy, SciPy, Pandas, MatPlotLib, and Scikit-learn later in this chapter, in the section "Checking out some useful Python libraries." When you add these libraries, additional data types become available.)

In Python, functions do basically the same thing they do in plain math — they accept data inputs, process them, and output the result. Output results depend wholly on the task the function was programmed to do. Classes, on the other hand, are prototypes of objects that are designed to output additional objects.

REMEMBER

If your goal is to write fast, reusable, easy-to-modify code in Python, you must use functions and classes. Doing so helps keep your code efficient and organized.

Sorting Out the Various Python Data Types

If you do much work with Python, you need to know how to work with different data types. The main data types in Python and the general forms they take are described in this list:

- » **Numbers:** Plain old numbers, obviously
- » **Strings:** '...' or "..."
- » **Lists:** [...] or [..., ..., ...]

» **Tuples:** (. . .) or (. . ., . . ., . . .)

» **Sets:** Rarely used

» **Dictionaries:** {'Key': 'Value', . . .}.

Numbers and strings are the most basic data types. You can incorporate them inside other, more complicated data types. All Python data types can be assigned to variables.

In Python, numbers, strings, lists, tuples, sets, and dictionaries are classified as both object types and data types.

Numbers in Python

The Numbers data type represents numeric values that you can use to handle all types of mathematical operations. Numbers come in the following types:

» **Integer:** A whole-number format

» **Long:** A whole-number format with an unlimited digit size

» **Float:** A real-number format, written with a decimal point

» **Complex:** An imaginary-number format, represented by the square root of –1

Strings in Python

Strings are the most often used data type in Python — and in every other programming language, for that matter. Simply put, a *string* consists of one or more characters written inside single or double quotes. The following code represents a string:

```
>>> variable1='This is a sample string'
>>> print(variable1)
This is a sample string
```

In this code snippet, the string is assigned to a variable and the variable subsequently acts like a storage container for the string value.

To print the characters contained inside the variable, simply use the predefined function, print.

TIP

Python coders often refer to lists, tuples, sets, and dictionaries as data *structures* rather than data *types*. *Data structures* are basic functional units that organize data so that it can be used efficiently by the program or application you're working with.

REMEMBER

Lists, tuples, sets, and dictionaries are data structures but keep in mind that they're still composed of one or more basic data types (numbers and/or strings, for example).

Lists in Python

A *list* is a sequence of numbers and/or strings. To create a list, you simply enclose the elements of the list (separated by commas) within square brackets. Here's an example of a basic list:

```
>>> variable2=["ID","Name","Depth","Latitude","Longitude"]
>>> depth=[0,120,140,0,150,80,0,10]
>>> variable2[3]
'Latitude'
```

Every element of the list is automatically assigned an index number, starting from 0. You can access each element using this index, and the corresponding value of the list is returned. If you need to store and analyze long arrays of data, use lists — storing your data inside a list makes it fairly easy to extract statistical information. The following code snippet is an example of a simple computation to pull the mean value from the elements of the depth list created in the preceding code example:

```
>>> sum(depth)/len(depth)
62.5
```

In this example, the average of the list elements is computed by first summing up the elements via the sum function and then dividing them by the number of the elements contained in the list — a number you determine with the help of the len function, which returns the *length* (the number of elements, in other words) in a string, an array, or a list. The len function in the denominator returns the average value of items in the object. See? It's as simple as 1-2-3!

Tuples in Python

Tuples are just like lists, except that you can't modify their content after you create them. Also, to create tuples, you need to use normal brackets instead of squared ones.

REMEMBER

"Normal brackets" refers to refers to parentheses in the form of (. . .) or (. . ., . . ., . . .)

Here's an example of a tuple:

```
>>> depth=(0,120,140,0,150,80,0,10)
```

In this case, you can't modify any of the elements as you would with a list. To ensure that your data stays in a read-only format, use tuples.

Sets in Python

A *set* is another data structure that's similar to a list. In contrast to lists, however, elements of a *set* are unordered. This disordered characteristic of a set makes it impossible to index, so it's not a commonly used data type.

Dictionaries in Python

Dictionaries are data structures that consist of pairs of keys and values. In a dictionary, every value corresponds to a certain key, and consequently, each value can be accessed using that key. The following code snippet shows a typical key/value pairing:

```
>>> variable4={"ID":1,"Name":"Valley City","Depth":0,"Latitude":49.6,
               "Longitude":-98.01}
>>> variable4["Longitude"]
-98.01
```

Putting Loops to Good Use in Python

When working with lists in Python, you typically access a list element by using the element index number. In a similar manner, you can access other elements of the list by using their corresponding index numbers. The following code snippet illustrates this concept:

```
>>>variable2=["ID","Name","Depth","Latitude","Longitude"]
>>> print(variable2[3])
Latitude
>>> print(variable2[4])
Longitude
```

WARNING

Don't let the index numbering system confuse you. Every element of the list is automatically assigned an index number starting from 0 — *not* starting from 1. That means the fourth element in an index actually bears the index number 3.

When you're analyzing considerable amounts of data, and you need to access each element of a list, this technique becomes quite inefficient. In these cases, you should use a looping technique instead.

You can use *looping* to execute the same block of code multiple times for a sequence of items. Consequently, rather than manually accessing all elements one by one, you simply create a loop to automatically *iterate* (or pass through in successive cycles) each element of the list.

You can use two types of loops in Python: the `for` loop and the `while` loop. The most often used looping technique is the `for` loop — designed especially to iterate through sequences, strings, tuples, sets, and dictionaries. The following code snippet illustrates a `for` loop iterating through the `variable2` list created in the preceding code snippet:

```
>>> for element in variable2:print(element)
ID
Name
Depth
Latitude
Longitude
```

The other available looping technique in Python is the `while` loop. Use a `while` loop to perform actions while a given condition is true.

REMEMBER

Looping is crucial when you work with long arrays of data, such as when you're working with raster images. Looping lets you apply certain actions to all data or to apply those actions to only predefined groups of data.

Having Fun with Functions

Functions (and classes, which I describe in the following section) are the crucial building blocks of almost every programming language. They provide a way to build organized, reusable code. Functions are blocks of code that take an input, process it, and return an output. Function inputs can be numbers, strings, lists, objects, or other functions. Python has two types of functions: built-in and custom. *Built-in* functions are predefined inside Python. You can use them by just typing their names.

The following code snippet is an example of the built-in function `print`:

```
>>> print("Hello")
Hello
```

This oft-used, built-in function `print` prints a given input. The code behind `print` has already been written by the people who created Python. Now that this code stands in the background, you don't need to know how to code it yourself — you simply call the `print` function. The people who created the Python library couldn't guess every possible function to satisfy everyone's needs, but they managed to provide users with a way to create and reuse their own functions when necessary.

In the section "Sorting out the various Python data types," earlier in this chapter, the following code snippet from that section (listed again here) was used to sum up the elements in a list and calculate the average:

```
>>> depth=[0,120,140,0,150,80,0,10]
>>> sum(depth)/len(depth)
62.5
```

The preceding data represents snowfall and snow depth records from multiple point locations. As you can see, the points where snow depth measurements were collected have an average depth of 62.5 units. These are depth measurements taken at only one time, though. In other words, all the data bears the same time-stamp. When modeling data using Python, you often see scenarios in which sets of measurements were taken at different times — known as *time-series* data.

Here's an example of time-series data:

```
>>> december_depth=[0,120,140,0,150,80,0,10]
>>> january_depth=[20,180,140,0,170,170,30,30]
>>> february_depth=[0,100,100,40,100,160,40,40]
```

You could calculate December, January, and February average snow depth in the same way you averaged values in the previous list, but that would be cumbersome. This is where custom functions come in handy:

```
>>> def average(any_list):return(sum(any_list)/len(any_list))
```

This code snippet defines a function named `average`, which takes any list as input and calculates the average of its elements. The function isn't executed yet, but the code defines what the function does when it later receives some input values. In this snippet, `any_list` is just a variable that's later assigned the given value when the function is executed. To execute the function, all you need to do is pass it a value. In this case, the value is a real list with numerical elements:

```
>>> average(february_depth)
72
```

Executing a function is straightforward. You can use functions to do the same thing repeatedly, as many times as you need for different input values. The beauty here is that once the functions are constructed, you can reuse them without having to rewrite the calculating algorithm.

Keeping Cool with Classes

Classes are blocks of code that put together functions and variables to produce other objects. As such, they're slightly different from functions, which take an input and produce an output. The set of functions and classes tied together inside a class describes the blueprint of a certain object. In other words, classes spell out what has to happen in order for an object to be created. After you come up with a class, you can generate the actual object instance by calling a class instance. In Python, this is referred to as *instantiating* an object — creating an instance of that class, in other words.

REMEMBER

Functions that are created inside a class are called *methods,* and variables within a class are called *attributes.* Methods describe the actions that generate the object, and attributes describe the actual object properties.

To better understand how to use classes for more efficient data analysis, consider the following scenario: Imagine that you have snow depth data from different locations and times, and you're storing it online on an FTP server. The dataset contains different ranges of snow depth data, depending on the month of the year. Now imagine that every monthly range is stored in a different location on the FTP server.

Your task is to use Python to fetch all monthly data and then analyze the entire dataset, so you need to use different operations on the data ranges. First, you need to download the data from within Python by using an FTP handling library, such as ftplib. Then, to be able to analyze the data in Python, you need to store it in proper Python data types (in lists, tuples, or dictionaries, for example). After you fetch the data and store it as recognizable data types in a Python script, you can then apply more advanced operations that are available from specialized libraries such as NumPy, SciPy, Pandas, MatPlotLib, and Scikit-learn.

In this scenario, you want to create a class that creates a list containing the snow depth data for each month. Every monthly list would be an object instance generated by the class. The class would tie together the FTP downloading functions and the functions that store the downloaded records inside the lists. You can then instantiate the class for as many months as you need in order to carry out a thorough analysis. The code to do something like this is shown in Listing 2-1.

Defining a Class in Python

```
class Download:
    def __init__(self,ftp=None,site,dir,fileList=[]):
        self.ftp =ftp
        self.site=site
        self.dir=dir
        self.fileList=fileList
        self.Login_ftp()
            self.store_in_list()
    def Login_ftp(self):
        self.ftp=ftplib.FTP(self.site)
        self.ftp.login()
    def store_in_list(self):
        fileList=[]
        self.ftp.cwd("/")
        self.ftp.cwd(self.dir)
        self.ftp.retrlines('NLST',fileList.append)
        return fileList
```

Defining a class probably looks intimidating right now; use this section just to get a feeling for the basic structure and observe the class methods involved.

Delving into Listing 2-1, the keyword class defines the class, and the keyword def defines the class methods. The init function is a default function that you should always define when creating classes because you use it to declare class variables. The Login_ftp method is a custom function that you define to log in to the FTP server. After you log in using the Login_ftp method and set the required directory where the data tables are located, you then store the data in a Python list using the custom function store_in_list.

After you finish defining the class, you can use it to produce objects. You just need to instantiate the class:

```
>>> Download("ftpexample.com","ftpdirectory")
```

And that's it! With this brief snippet, you've just declared the particular FTP domain and the internal FTP directory where the data is located. After you execute this last line, a list appears, giving you data that you can manipulate and analyze as needed.

Checking Out Some Useful Python Libraries

In Python, a *library* is a specialized collection of scripts that were written by someone else to perform specialized sets of tasks. To use specialized libraries in Python, you must first complete the installation process. After you install your libraries on your local hard drive, you can import any library's function into a project by simply using the `import` statement. For example, if you want to import the `ftplib` library, you write

```
>>> import ftplib
```

REMEMBER

Be sure to import the library into your Python project before attempting to call its functions in your code.

After you import the library, you can use its functionality inside any of your scripts. Simply use *dot notation* (a shorthand way of accessing modules, functions, and classes in one line of code) to access the library. Here's an example of dot notation:

```
>>> ftplib.any_ftp_lib_function
```

The dot notation you see above tells the computer to open the "any_ftp_lib_function" that is found in the ftplib library.

REMEMBER

Though you can choose from countless libraries to accomplish different tasks in Python, the Python libraries most commonly used in data science are MatPlotLib, NumPy, Pandas, Scikit-learn, and SciPy. The NumPy and SciPy libraries were specially designed for scientific uses, Pandas was designed for optimal data analysis performance, and MatPlotLib library was designed for data visualization. Scikit-learn is Python's premiere machine learning library.

Saying hello to the NumPy library

NumPy is the Python package that primarily focuses on working with n-dimensional array objects, and SciPy, described next, extends the capabilities of the NumPy library. When working with plain Python (Python with no external extensions, such as libraries, added to it), you're confined to storing your data in 1-dimensional lists. If you extend Python by using the NumPy library, however, you're provided a basis from which you can work with n-dimensional arrays. (Just in case you were wondering, n-dimensional arrays are arrays of one dimension or of multiple dimensions.)

To enable NumPy in Python, you must first install and import the NumPy library. After that, you can generate multidimensional arrays.

To see how generating n-dimensional arrays works in practice, start by checking out the following code snippet, which shows how you'd create a 1-dimensional NumPy array:

```
import numpy
>>> array_1d=numpy.arange(8)
>>> print(array_1d)
[0 1 2 3 4 5 6 7]
```

The numpy.arange method returns evenly spaced values from within a user specified interval. If you don't specify a number for numpy.arange to start with, then it starts with 0. In this case, we specified that we want 8 values, so numpy.arange returns [0 1 2 3 4 5 6 7]

After importing numpy, you can use it to generate n-dimensional arrays, such as the 1-dimensional array just shown. One-dimensional arrays are referred to as *vectors*. You can also create multidimensional arrays using the reshape method, like this:

```
>>> array_2d=numpy.arange(8).reshape(2,4)
>>> print(array_2d)
[[0 1 2 3]
 [4 5 6 7]]
```

The preceding example is a 2-dimensional array, otherwise known as a 2 × 4 *matrix*. The only difference between this and the preceding example is that we called the .reshape method, and passed in a 2 and a 4 value — telling numpy to take the array and transform it into a 2*4 matrix.

Standard matrix notation is m*n, where m is the number of rows and n specifies the number of columns in the matrix.

Using the .arange and reshape method is just one way to create NumPy arrays. You can also generate arrays from lists and tuples.

In the snow dataset contained in the earlier section "Having fun with functions," the snow depth data for different locations is stored inside three separate Python lists — one list per month:

```
>>> december_depth=[0,120,140,0,150,80,0,10]
>>> january_depth=[20,180,140,0,170,170,30,30]
>>> february_depth=[0,100,100,40,100,160,40,40]
```

It would be more efficient to have the measurements stored in a better-consolidated structure. For example, you can easily put all those lists in a single NumPy array by using the following code snippet:

```
>>>depth=numpy.array([december_depth,january_depth,february_depth])
>>> print(depth)
[[  0 120 140   0 150  80   0  10]
 [ 20 180 140   0 170 170  30  30]
 [  0 100 100  40 100 160  40  40]]
```

Using this structure allows you to pull out certain measurements more efficiently. For example, if you want to calculate the average of the snow depth for the first location in each of the three months, you'd extract the first elements of each horizontal row (values 0, 20, and 0, to be more precise). You can complete the extraction in a single line of code by taking a slice of the dataset and then calculating the mean by way of the NumPy mean function. The term slicing refers to taking a slice out of dataset. Here's an example:

```
>>> numpy.mean(depth[:,1])
133.33333333333334
```

The preceding code snippet instructs the computer to go to column index position 1 and calculate the mean of the value in that column. The values in the column at column index 1 are 120, 180, and 100. When you calculate the mean value of the numbers, you get 133.3.

Beyond using NumPy to extract information from single matrices, you can use it to interact with different matrices as well — applying standard mathematical operations between matrices, for example, or even applying nonstandard operators, such as matrix inversion, summarize, and minimum/maximum operators.

REMEMBER

Array objects have the same rights as any other objects in Python. You can pass them as parameters to functions, set them as class attributes, or iterate through array elements to generate random numbers.

Getting up close and personal with the SciPy library

SciPy is a collection of mathematical algorithms and sophisticated functions that extends the capabilities of the NumPy library. The SciPy library adds some specialized scientific functions to Python for more specific tasks in data science. To use SciPy's functions within Python, you must first install and import the SciPy library.

Some sticklers out there consider SciPy to be an extension of the NumPy library. That's because SciPy was *built on top of* NumPy — it uses NumPy functions but adds to them.

SciPy offers functionalities and algorithms for a variety of tasks, including vector quantization, statistical functions, discrete Fourier transform-algorithms, orthogonal distance regression, airy functions, sparse eigenvalue solvers, maximum entropy fitting routines, *n*-dimensional image operations, integration routines, interpolation tools, sparse linear algebra, linear solvers, optimization tools, signal-processing tools, sparse matrices, and other utilities that aren't served by other Python libraries. Impressive, right? Yet that's not even a complete listing of the available SciPy utilities. If you're dying to get hold of a complete list, running the following code snippet in Python opens an extensive help module that explains the SciPy library:

```
>>> import scipy
>>> help(scipy)
```

You need to first download and install the SciPy library before you can use this code.

The help function used in the preceding code snippet returns a script that lists all utilities that comprise SciPy and documents all SciPy's functions and classes. This information helps you understand what's behind the prewritten functions and algorithms that make up the SciPy library.

Because SciPy is still under development and therefore, changing and growing, regularly check the help function to see what's changed.

Bonding with MatPlotLib for data visualization

Generally speaking, data science projects usually culminate in visual representations of objects or phenomena. In Python, things are no different. After taking baby steps (or some not-so-baby steps) with NumPy and SciPy, you can use Python's MatPlotLib library to create complex visual representations of your dataset or data analysis findings. MatPlotLib, when combined with NumPy and SciPy, creates an excellent environment in which to work when solving problems using data science.

Looking more closely at MatPlotLib, you may notice that it is a 2-dimensional plotting library you can use in Python to produce figures from data. You can use MatPlotLib to produce plots, histograms, scatterplots, and a variety of other data graphics. What's more, because the library gives you full control of your visualization's symbology, line styles, fonts, and colors, you can even use MatPlotLib to produce publication-quality data graphics.

REMEMBER

As is the case with all other libraries in Python, in order to work with MatPlotLib, you first need to install and import the library into your script. After you complete those tasks, it's easy to get started producing graphs and charts.

To illustrate how to use MatPlotLib, consider the following NumPy array (which was created in the "Saying hello to the NumPy library" section, earlier in this chapter):

```
>>> print(depth)
[[ 0 120 140  0 150 80  0 10]
 [ 20 180 140  0 170 170 30 30]
 [ 0 100 100 40 100 160 40 40]]
```

With the following few lines of code, using just a `for` loop and a MatPlotLib function — `pyplot` — you can easily plot all measurements in a single graph within Python:

```
>>> import matplotlib.pyplot as plt
>>> for month in depth:
    plt.plot(month)
>>> plt.show()
```

TECHNICAL STUFF

Heads up for MacOS users who may have recently upgraded to Big Sur and already used MatPlotLib before (but didn't update), the first line of code generates a "Segmentation Error 11." The best way to fix this is to uninstall & re-install MatPlotLib. Learn more here: https://stackoverflow.com/questions/64841082/segmentation-fault-11-python-after-upgrading-to-os-big-sur

The preceding code snippet instantly generates the line chart you see in Figure 2-2.

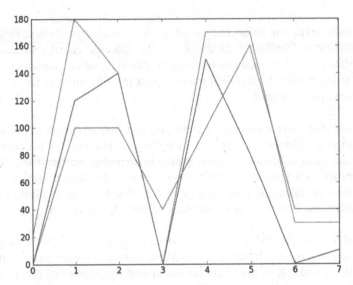

FIGURE 2-2:
Time-series plot
of monthly snow
depth data.

Each line in the graph represents the depth of snow at different locations in the same month. The preceding code you use to build this graph is simple; if you want to make a better representation, you can add color or text font attributes to the plot function. Of course, you can also use other types of data graphics, depending on which types best show the data trends you want to display. What's important here is that you know when to use each of these important libraries and that you understand how you can use the Python programming language to make data analysis both easy and efficient.

Peeking into the Pandas offering

The pandas library makes data analysis much faster and easier with its accessible and robust data structures. Its precise purpose is to improve Python's performance with respect to data analysis and modeling. It even offers some data visualization functionality by integrating small portions of the MatPlotLib library. The two main Pandas data structures are described in this list:

>> **Series:** A Series object is an array-like structure that can assume either a horizontal or vertical dimension. You can think of a Pandas Series object as being similar to one row or one column from an Excel spreadsheet.

>> **DataFrame:** A DataFrame object acts like a tabular data table in Python. Each row or column in a DataFrame can be accessed and treated as its own Pandas Series object.

Indexing is integrated into both data structure types, making it easy to access and manipulate your data. Pandas offers functionality for reading in and writing out your data, which makes it easy to use for loading, transferring, and saving datasets in whatever formats you want. Lastly, Pandas offers excellent functionality for reshaping data, treating missing values, and removing outliers, among other tasks. This makes Pandas an excellent choice for data preparation and basic data analysis tasks. If you want to carry out more advanced statistical and machine learning methods, you'll need to use the Scikit-learn library. The good news is that Scikit-learn and Pandas play well together.

Learning from data with Scikit-learn

Scikit-learn is far and away Python's best machine learning library. With it, you can execute all sorts of machine learning methods, including classification, regression, clustering, dimensionality reduction, and more. The library also offers a preprocessing module that is wonderfully supportive whenever you need to prepare your data for predictive modeling. Scikit-learn offers a model selection module that's readily available with all sorts of metrics to help you build your models and choose the best-performing model among a selection.

BEST PRACTICE

You'll want to write clear, concise documentation within your Python code to detail how and why the code works. You can also write comments within your Python code by simply starting the comment line with a *hash symbol* — the # symbol. The Python interpreter will ignore anything written after the #.

Chapter **3**

Getting a Crash Course in Matplotlib

P ython makes the task of converting your textual data into graphics relatively easy using Matplotlib, which is actually a simulation of the MATLAB application. MATLAB and Matplotlib are both prominent data visualization tools, essentially with the same technical backbone. However, the tools cater to different preferences and environments. MATLAB is a comprehensive, commercial platform known for its numerical analysis and wide-ranging application-specific toolboxes, offering a cohesive environment. There is a financial cost associated with using MATLAB as it is distributed by a software vendor. In contrast, Matplotlib is a free, open-source plotting library within the Python ecosystem, specifically designed for data science-targeted activities. While MATLAB offers an all-in-one proprietary environment with robust support, Matplotlib appeals to those who prefer the open nature of the Python community and seek a flexible tool for creating a wide variety of 2D and 3D visualizations. The choice between them often hinges on specific project needs, budget constraints, and programmatic integration requirements. This chapter is solely focused on the matplotlib library, the open-source platform.

TECHNICAL STUFF

You can see a comparison of Matplotlib and MATLAB at `https://pyzo.org/python_vs_matlab.html`. (If you don't know how to use MATLAB, see *MATLAB For Dummies*, by John Paul Mueller [Wiley]), if you'd like to learn.)

Starting with a Graph

A graph or chart is simply a visual representation of numeric data. Matplotlib makes a large number of graph and chart types available to you. Of course, you can choose any of the common graph and graph types such as bar charts, line graphs, or pie charts. You can also access a huge number of statistical plot types, such as boxplots, error bar charts, and histograms. You can see a gallery of the various graph types that Matplotlib supports at https://matplotlib.org/gallery.html. Remember, though, that you can combine graphic elements in almost infinite ways to create your own presentation of data, no matter how complex that data may be. The following sections describe how to create a basic graph, but you have access to a lot more functionality than these sections tell you about.

Defining the plot

Plots show graphically what you've defined numerically. To define a plot, you need some values, the matplotlib.pyplot module, and an idea of what you want to display, as shown in the following code:

```
import matplotlib.pyplot as plt
%matplotlib inline

values = [1, 5, 8, 9, 2, 0, 3, 10, 4, 7]
plt.plot(range(1,11), values)
plt.show()
```

In this case, the code tells the plt.plot() function to create a plot using x-axis values between 1 and 11 and y-axis values as they appear in the values variable. Calling plot.show() displays the plot in a separate dialog box, as shown in Figure 3-1. Notice that the output is a line graph. Book 6, Chapter 4 shows you how to create other chart and graph types.

TECHNICAL STUFF

The %matplotlib inline magic function (used for embedding plots and other images) has become optional in newer versions of Python. However, including it is still a good idea, especially if you share your code with other people.

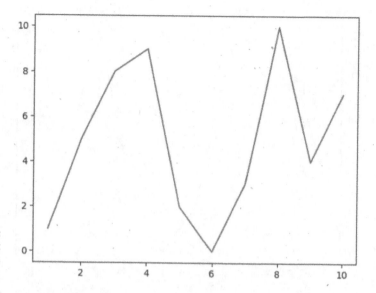

FIGURE 3-1:
Creating a basic
plot that shows
just one line.

Drawing multiple lines and plots

You encounter many situations in which you must use multiple plot lines, such as when comparing two sets of values. To create such plots using Matplotlib, you simply call plt.plot() multiple times — once for each plot line, as shown in the following example:

```
import matplotlib.pyplot as plt
%matplotlib inline

values = [1, 5, 8, 9, 2, 0, 3, 10, 4, 7]
values2 = [3, 8, 9, 2, 1, 2, 4, 7, 6, 6]
plt.plot(range(1,11), values)
plt.plot(range(1,11), values2)
plt.show()
```

When you run this example, you see two plot lines, as shown in Figure 3-2. Even though you can't see it in the printed book, the line graphs are different colors (chosen by the library) so you can tell them apart.

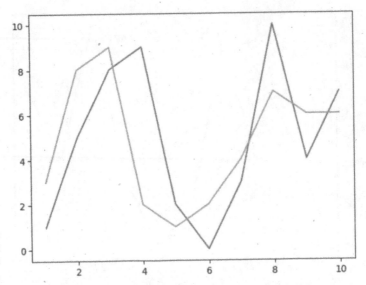

FIGURE 3-2:
Defining a plot
that contains
multiple lines.

Saving your work to disk

Jupyter Notebook makes it easy to include your graphs within the notebooks you create, enabling you to define reports that everyone can easily understand. When you need to save a copy of your work to disk for later reference or to use it as part of a larger report, you save the graphic programmatically using the `plt.savefig()` function, as shown in the following code:

```
import matplotlib.pyplot as plt
%matplotlib auto

values = [1, 5, 8, 9, 2, 0, 3, 10, 4, 7]
plt.plot(range(1,11), values)
plt.ioff()
plt.savefig('MySamplePlot.png', format='png')
```

In this case, you must provide a minimum of two inputs. The first input is the filename. You may optionally include a path for saving the file. The second input is the file format. In this case, the example saves the file in Portable Network Graphic (PNG) format, but you have other options: Portable Document Format (PDF), Postscript (PS), Encapsulated Postscript (EPS), and Scalable Vector Graphics (SVG).

REMEMBER

Note the presence of the `%matplotlib auto` magic in this case. Using this call removes the inline display of the graph. You do have options for other Matplotlib backends, depending on which version of Python and Matplotlib you use. For example, some developers prefer the `notebook` backend to the `inline` backend because it provides additional functionality. However, to use the `notebook` backend, you must also restart the kernel, and you may not always see what you expect. To see the backend list, use the `%matplotlib -l` magic. In addition, calling `plt.ioff()` turns plot interaction off.

Setting the Axis, Ticks, and Grids

It's hard to know what the data actually means unless you provide a unit of measure or at least some means of performing comparisons. The use of axes, ticks, and grids makes it possible to illustrate graphically the relative size of data elements so that the viewer gains an appreciation of comparative measure. You won't use these features with every graphic, and you may employ the features differently based on viewer needs, but it's important to know that these features exist and how you can use them to help document your data within the graphic environment.

TECHNICAL STUFF

The following examples use the `%matplotlib notebook` magic so that you can see the difference between it and the `%matplotlib inline` magic. The two inline displays rely on a different graphic engine. Consequently, you must choose Kernel ⇨ Restart to restart the kernel before you run any of the examples in the sections that follow.

Getting the axes

The axes define the x and y plane of the graphic. The x axis runs horizontally, and the y axis runs vertically. In many cases, you can allow Matplotlib to perform any required formatting for you. However, sometimes you need to obtain access to the axes and format them manually. The following code shows how to obtain access to the axes for a plot:

```
import matplotlib.pyplot as plt
%matplotlib notebook

values = [0, 5, 8, 9, 2, 0, 3, 10, 4, 7]
ax = plt.axes()
plt.plot(range(1,11), values)
plt.show()
```

The reason you place the axes in a variable, `ax`, instead of manipulating them directly is to make writing the code simpler and more efficient. In this case, you simply turn on the default axes by calling `plt.axes()`; then you place a handle to the axes in ax. A *handle* is a sort of pointer to the axes. Think of it as you would a frying pan. You wouldn't lift the frying pan directly but would instead use its handle when picking it up.

Formatting the axes

Simply displaying the axes won't be enough in many cases. Instead, you may want to change the way Matplotlib displays them. For example, you may not want the highest value to reach to the top of the graph. The following example shows just a small number of tasks you can perform after you have access to the axes:

```
import matplotlib.pyplot as plt
%matplotlib notebook
plt.figure()

values = [0, 5, 8, 9, 2, 0, 3, 10, 4, 7]
ax = plt.axes()
ax.set_xlim([0, 11])
ax.set_ylim([-1, 11])
ax.set_xticks([1, 2, 3, 4, 5, 6, 7, 8, 9, 10])
ax.set_yticks([0, 1, 2, 3, 4, 5, 6, 7, 8, 9, 10])
plt.plot(range(1,11), values)
plt.show()
```

In this case, the set_xlim() and set_ylim() calls change the axes limits — the minimum and maximum coordinate values of each axis. The set_xticks() and set_yticks() calls change the ticks used to display data. The ways in which you can change a graph using these calls can become quite detailed. For example, you can choose to change individual tick labels if you want.

REMEMBER

Notice also the call to plt.figure(). If you don't make this call, the code will modify the first plot (figure) from the previous section (Figure 3-2) rather than create a new figure. In fact, it will actually add to that previous figure, so what you end up with is a mess that no one can figure out! Figure 3-3 shows the output from this example. Notice how the changes affect how the line graph displays.

TECHNICAL
STUFF

As you can see by viewing the differences between Figures 3-1, 3-2, and 3-3, the %matlplotlib notebook magic produces a significantly different display. The controls at the bottom of the display let you pan and zoom the display, move between views you've created, and download the figure to disk when working with Jupyter Notebook (they may not work at all in Google Colab). The button to the right of the Figure 2 heading in Figure 3-3 lets you stop interacting with the graph after you've finished working with it. Any changes you've made to the presentation of the graph remain afterward so that anyone looking at your notebook will see the graph in the manner you intended. The ability to interact with the graph ends when you display another graph.

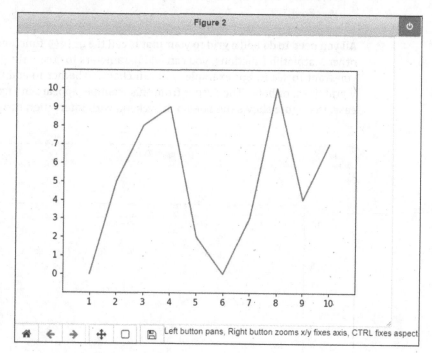

FIGURE 3-3:
Specifying how the axes should appear to the viewer.

Adding grids

Grid lines enable you to see the precise value of each element of a graph. You can more quickly determine both the x and y coordinates, which allow you to perform comparisons of individual points with greater ease. Of course, grids also add noise (added information) and make seeing the actual flow of data harder. The point is that you can use grids to good effect to create particular effects. The following code shows how to add a grid to the graph in the previous section:

```
import matplotlib.pyplot as plt
%matplotlib notebook
plt.figure()

values = [0, 5, 8, 9, 2, 0, 3, 10, 4, 7]
ax = plt.axes()
ax.set_xlim([0, 11])
```

```
ax.set_ylim([-1, 11])
ax.set_xticks([1, 2, 3, 4, 5, 6, 7, 8, 9, 10])
ax.set_yticks([0, 1, 2, 3, 4, 5, 6, 7, 8, 9, 10])
ax.grid()
plt.plot(range(1,11), values)
plt.show()
```

All you need to do add a grid to your plot is call the grid() function. As with many other Matplotlib functions, you can add parameters to create the grid precisely as you want to see it. For example, you can choose whether to add the x grid lines, y grid lines, or both. The output from this example appears in Figure 3-4. In this case, the figure shows the notebook backend with interaction turned off.

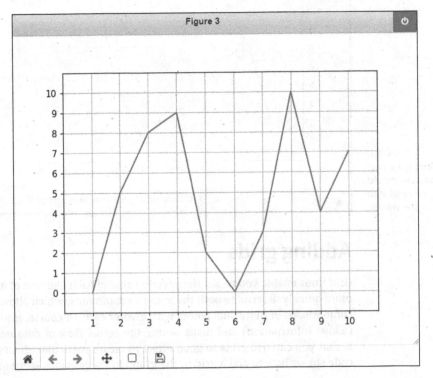

FIGURE 3-4:
Adding grids makes the values easier to read.

Defining the Line Appearance

Just drawing lines on a page won't do much for you if you need to help the viewer understand the importance of your data. In most cases, you need to use different line styles to ensure that the viewer can tell one data grouping from another. However, to emphasize the importance or value of a particular data grouping, you need to employ color. The use of color communicates all sorts of ideas to the viewer. For example, green often denotes that something is safe, and red communicates danger. The following sections help you understand how to work with line style and color to communicate ideas and concepts to the viewer without using any text.

Working with line styles

Line styles help differentiate graphs by drawing the lines in various ways. Using a unique presentation for each line helps you distinguish each line so that you can call it out (even when the printout is in shades of gray). You could also call out a particular line graph by using a different line style for it (and using the same style for the other lines). Table 3-1 shows the various Matplotlib line styles.

The line style appears as a third argument to the plot() function call. You simply provide the desired string for the line type, as shown in the following example.

```
import matplotlib.pyplot as plt
%matplotlib inline

values = [1, 5, 8, 9, 2, 0, 3, 10, 4, 7]
values2 = [3, 8, 9, 2, 1, 2, 4, 7, 6, 6]
plt.plot(range(1,11), values, '--')
plt.plot(range(1,11), values2, ':')
plt.show()
```

BEST PRACTICE

MAKING GRAPHICS ACCESSIBLE

Avoiding assumptions about someone's ability to see your graphic presentation is essential. For example, someone who is color blind may not be able to tell that one line is green and the other red. Likewise, someone with low vision may not be able to distinguish between a dashed line and one that combines dashes and dots. Using multiple methods to distinguish each line helps ensure that everyone can see your data in a manner that is comfortable for each person.

TABLE 3-1

Matplotlib Line Styles

Character	Line Style
'-'	Solid line
'--'	Dashed line
'-.'	Dash-dot line
':'	Dotted line

In this case, the first line graph uses a dashed line style, while the second line graph uses a dotted line style. (Note that you must restart the kernel again to switch from the %matplotlib notebook to the %matplotlib inline style.) You can see the results of the changes in Figure 3-5.

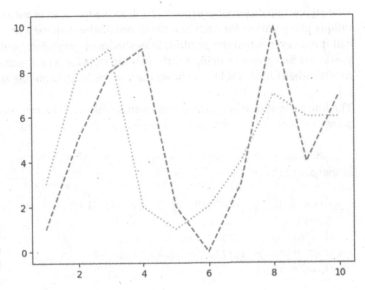

FIGURE 3-5:
Line styles help differentiate between plots.

Using colors

Color is another way in which to differentiate line graphs. Of course, this method has certain problems. The most significant problem occurs when someone makes a black-and-white copy of your colored graph — hiding the color differences as shades of gray. Another problem is that someone with color blindness may not be able to tell one line from the other. All this said, color does make for a brighter, eye-grabbing presentation. Table 3-2 shows the colors that Matplotlib supports.

TABLE 3-2

Matplotlib Colors

Character	Color
'b'	Blue
'g'	Green
'r'	Red
'c'	Cyan
'm'	Magenta
'y'	Yellow
'k'	Black
'w'	White

As with line styles, the color appears in a string as the third argument to the `plot()` function call. In this case, the viewer sees two lines — one in red and the other in magenta. The data points are the same as those used for Figure 3-2, just with different colors. If you're reading the printed version of the book, Figure 3-2 appears in shades of gray instead of color, as does this new presentation.

```
import matplotlib.pyplot as plt
%matplotlib inline

values = [1, 5, 8, 9, 2, 0, 3, 10, 4, 7]
values2 = [3, 8, 9, 2, 1, 2, 4, 7, 6, 6]
plt.plot(range(1,11), values, 'r')
plt.plot(range(1,11), values2, 'm')
plt.show()
```

Adding markers

Markers add a special symbol to each data point in a line graph. Unlike line style and color, markers tend to be a little less susceptible to accessibility and printing issues. Even when the specific marker isn't clear, people can usually differentiate one marker from the other. Table 3-3 shows the list of markers that Matplotlib provides.

TABLE 3-3

Matplotlib Markers

Character	Marker Type
'.'	Point
','	Pixel
'o'	Circle
'v'	Triangle 1 down
'^'	Triangle 1 up
'<'	Triangle 1 left
'>'	Triangle 1 right
'1'	Triangle 2 down
'2'	Triangle 2 up
'3'	Triangle 2 left
'4'	Triangle 2 right
's'	Square
'p'	Pentagon
'*'	Star
'h'	Hexagon style 1
'H'	Hexagon style 2
'+'	Plus
'x'	X
'D'	Diamond
'd'	Thin diamond
'|'	Vertical line
'_'	Horizontal line

As with line style and color, you add markers as the third argument to a plot()
call. In the following example, you see the effects of combining line style with a
marker to provide a unique line-graph presentation.

```
import matplotlib.pyplot as plt
%matplotlib inline
```

```
values = [1, 5, 8, 9, 2, 0, 3, 10, 4, 7]
values2 = [3, 8, 9, 2, 1, 2, 4, 7, 6, 6]
plt.plot(range(1,11), values, 'o--')
plt.plot(range(1,11), values2, 'v:')
plt.show()
```

Notice how the combination of line style and marker makes each line stand out in Figure 3-6. Even when printed in black and white, you can easily differentiate one line from the other, which is why you usually want to combine presentation techniques.

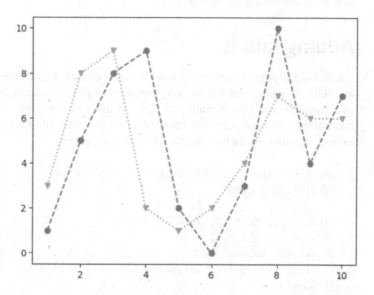

FIGURE 3-6:
Markers help
to emphasize
individual values.

Using Labels, Annotations, and Legends

To fully document your graph, you usually have to resort to labels, annotations, and legends. Each of these elements has a different purpose, as follows:

>> **Label:** Provides positive identification of a particular data element or grouping. The purpose is to make it easy for the viewer to know the name or kind of data illustrated.

>> **Annotation:** Augments the information the viewer can immediately see about the data with notes, sources, or other useful information. In contrast to a label, the purpose of annotation is to help extend the viewer's knowledge of the data rather than simply identify it.

>> **Legend:** Presents a listing of the data groups within the graph and often provides cues (such as line type or color) to make identification of the data group easier. For example, all the red points may belong to group A, and all the blue points may belong to group B.

The following sections help you understand the purpose and usage of various documentation aids provided with Matplotlib. These documentation aids help you create an environment in which the viewer is certain of the source, purpose, and usage of data elements. Some graphs work just fine without any documentation aids, but in other cases, you may find that you need to use all three in order to communicate with your viewer fully.

Adding labels

Labels help people understand the significance of each axis of any graph you create. Without labels, the values portrayed don't have any significance. In addition to a moniker, such as rainfall, you can add units of measure, such as inches or centimeters, so your audience knows how to interpret the data shown. The following example shows how to add labels to your graph:

```python
import matplotlib.pyplot as plt
%matplotlib inline

values = [1, 5, 8, 9, 2, 0, 3, 10, 4, 7]
plt.xlabel('Entries')
plt.ylabel('Values')
plt.plot(range(1,11), values)
plt.show()
```

The call to xlabel() documents the x axis of your graph, while the call the ylabel() documents the y axis of your graph. Figure 3-7 shows the output of this example.

Annotating the chart

You use annotation to draw special attention to points of interest on a graph. For example, you may want to point out that a specific data point is outside the usual range expected for a particular dataset. The following example shows how to add annotation to a graph:

```python
import matplotlib.pyplot as plt
%matplotlib inline
```

```
values = [1, 5, 8, 9, 2, 0, 3, 10, 4, 7]
plt.annotate(xy=[1,1], text='First Entry')
plt.plot(range(1,11), values)
plt.show()
```

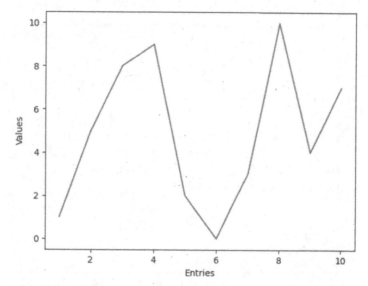

FIGURE 3-7:
Use labels to
identify the axes.

The call to annotate() provides the labeling you need. You must provide a location for the annotation by using the xy parameter, as well as provide text to place at the location by using the text parameter. The annotate() function also provides other parameters that you can use to create special formatting or placement onscreen. Figure 3-8 shows the output from this example.

Creating a legend

A legend documents the individual elements of a plot. Each line is presented in a table that contains a label for it so that people can differentiate between each line. For example, one line may represent sales for one year and another line may represent sales during the next year, so you include an entry in the legend for each line that is labeled with the years. The following example shows how to add a legend to your plot.

```
import matplotlib.pyplot as plt
%matplotlib inline

values = [1, 5, 8, 9, 2, 0, 3, 10, 4, 7]
```

```
values2 = [3, 8, 9, 2, 1, 2, 4, 7, 6, 6]
line1 = plt.plot(range(1,11), values)
line2 = plt.plot(range(1,11), values2)
plt.legend(['First', 'Second'], loc=4)
plt.show()
```

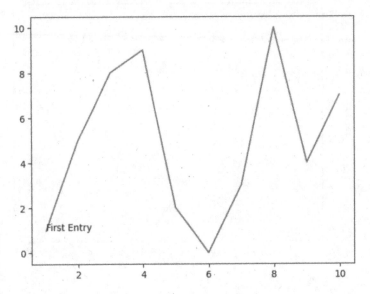

FIGURE 3-8:
Annotation can
identify points
of interest.

The call to legend() occurs after you create the plots, not before, as with some of
the other functions described in this chapter. The call contains a list of the labels
you want to use in the order of the plots you generate. So, 'First' is associated
with line1, and 'Second' is associated with line2.

TIP

The default location for the legend is the upper-right corner of the plot, which
proved inconvenient for this particular example. Adding the loc parameter lets
you place the legend in a different location. See the legend() function documentation at https://matplotlib.org/2.0.2/api/pyplot_api.html#matplotlib.
pyplot.figlegend for additional legend locations. Figure 3-9 shows the output
from this example.

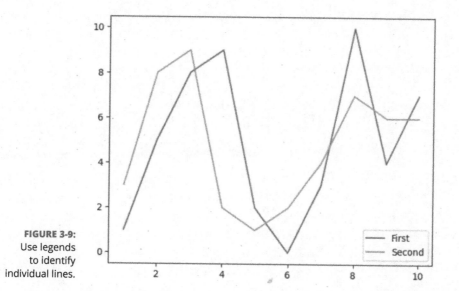

Chapter **4**

Visualizing the Data

ook 6, Chapter 3 helps you understand the mechanics of working with
Matplotlib, which is an important first step toward using it. This chapter
takes the next step in helping you use Matplotlib to perform useful work.
The main goal of this chapter is to help you visualize your data in various ways.
Creating a graphic presentation of your data is essential if you want to help other
people understand what you're trying to say. Even though you can see what the
numbers mean in your mind, other people will likely need graphics to see what
point you're trying to make by manipulating data in various ways.

The chapter starts by looking at some basic graph types that Matplotlib supports.
You don't find the full list of graphs and plots listed in this chapter — it could
take an entire book to explore them all in detail. However, you do find the most
common types.

In the remainder of the chapter, you begin exploring specific sorts of plotting
as it relates to data science. Of course, no book on data science would be complete without exploring scatterplots, which are used to help people see patterns
in seemingly unrelated data points. Because much of the data that you work with
today is time related or geographic in nature, the chapter devotes two special
sections to these topics. You also get to work with both directed and undirected
graphs, which is fine for social media analysis.

Choosing the Right Graph

The kind of graph you choose determines how people view the associated data, so choosing the right graph from the outset is important. For example, when you want people to form opinions on how data elements compare through the use of precise counts, you use a bar chart. The idea is to choose a graph that naturally leads people to draw the conclusion that you need them to draw about the data that you've carefully massaged from various data sources. (You also have the option of using line graphs — a technique demonstrated in Book 6, Chapter 3.) The following sections describe the various graph types and provide you with basic examples of how to use them.

Creating comparisons with bar charts

Bar charts make comparing values easy. The wide bars and segregated measurements emphasize the differences between values rather than the flow of one value to another as a line graph does. Fortunately, you have all sorts of methods at your disposal for emphasizing specific values and performing other tricks. The following example shows just some of the things you can do with a vertical bar chart:

```
import matplotlib.pyplot as plt
%matplotlib inline

values = [5, 8, 9, 10, 4, 7]
widths = [0.7, 0.8, 0.7, 0.7, 0.7, 0.7]
colors = ['b', 'r', 'b', 'b', 'b', 'b']
plt.bar(range(0, 6), values, width=widths,
        color=colors, align='center')

plt.show()
```

To create even a basic bar chart, you must provide a series of x coordinates and the heights of the bars. The example uses the range() function to create the x coordinates, and values contains the heights.

Of course, you may want more than a basic bar chart, and Matplotlib provides a number of ways to get the job done. In this case, the example uses the width parameter to control the width of each bar, emphasizing the second bar by making it slightly larger. The larger width shows up even in a black-and-white printout. It also uses the color parameter to change the color of the target bar to red (the rest are blue).

As with other chart types, the bar chart provides some special features that you can use to make your presentation stand out. The example uses the `align` parameter to center the data on the x coordinate (the standard position is to the left). You can also use other parameters, such as `hatch`, to enhance the visual appearance of your bar chart. Figure 4-1 shows the output of this example.

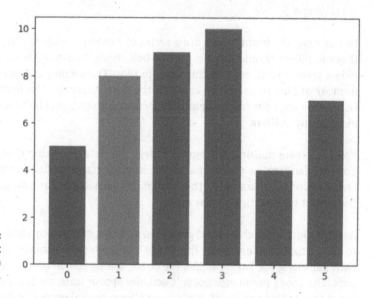

FIGURE 4-1:
Bar charts make it easier to perform comparisons.

TIP

This chapter helps you get started using Matplotlib to create a variety of chart and graph types. Of course, more examples are better, so you can also find some more advanced examples on the Matplotlib site at `https://matplotlib.org/stable/gallery/index.html`. Some of the examples, such as those that demonstrate animation techniques, become quite advanced, but with practice you can use any of them to improve your own charts and graphs.

Showing distributions using histograms

Histograms categorize data by breaking it into *bins*, where each bin contains a subset of the data range. A histogram then displays the number of items in each bin so that you can see the distribution of data and the progression of data from bin to bin. In most cases, you see a curve of some type, such as a bell curve. The following example shows how to create a histogram with randomized data:

```
import numpy as np
import matplotlib.pyplot as plt
%matplotlib inline
```

```
x = 20 * np.random.randn(10000)

plt.hist(x, 25, range=(-50, 50), histtype='stepfilled',
         align='mid', color='g', label='Test Data')
plt.legend()
plt.title('Step Filled Histogram')
plt.show()
```

In this case, the input values are a series of random numbers. The distribution of these numbers should show a type of bell curve. As a minimum, you must provide a series of values, x in this case, to plot. The second argument contains the number of bins to use when creating the data intervals. The default value is 10. Using the range parameter helps you focus the histogram on the relevant data and exclude any outliers.

You can create multiple histogram types. The default setting creates a bar chart. You can also create a stacked bar chart, stepped graph, or filled stepped graph (the type shown in the example). In addition, it's possible to control the orientation of the output with vertical as the default.

As with most other charts and graphs in this chapter, you can add special features to the output. For example, the align parameter determines the alignment of each bar along the baseline. Use the color parameter to control the colors of the bars. The label parameter doesn't actually appear unless you also create a legend (as shown in this example). Figure 4-2 shows typical output from this example.

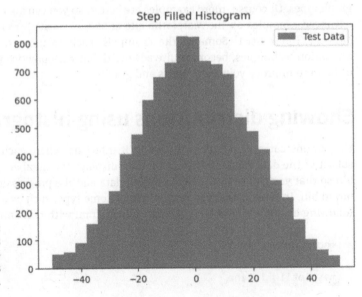

FIGURE 4-2: Histograms let you see distributions of numbers.

REMEMBER

Random data varies call by call. Every time you run the example, you see slightly different results because the random-generation process differs.

Depicting groups using boxplots

Boxplots provide a means of depicting groups of numbers through their *quartiles* (three points dividing a group into four equal parts). A boxplot may also have lines, called *whiskers*, indicating data outside the upper and lower quartiles. The spacing shown within a boxplot helps indicate the skew and dispersion of the data. The following example shows how to create a boxplot with randomized data:

```
import numpy as np
import matplotlib.pyplot as plt
%matplotlib inline

spread = 100 * np.random.rand(100)
center = np.ones(50) * 50
flier_high = 100 * np.random.rand(10) + 100
flier_low = -100 * np.random.rand(10)
data = np.concatenate((spread, center,
                       flier_high, flier_low))

plt.boxplot(data, sym='gx', widths=.75, notch=True)
plt.show()
```

To create a usable dataset, you need to combine several different number-generation techniques, as shown at the beginning of the example. Here's how these techniques work:

>> spread: Contains a set of random numbers between 0 and 100

>> center: Provides 50 values directly in the center of the range of 50

>> flier_high: Simulates outliers between 100 and 200

>> flier_low: Simulates outliers between 0 and -100

The code combines all these values into a single dataset using concatenate(). Being randomly generated with specific characteristics (such as a large number of points in the middle), the output will show specific characteristics but will work fine for the example.

The call to boxplot() requires only data as input. All other parameters have default settings. In this case, the code sets the presentation of outliers to green Xs by setting the sym parameter. You use widths to modify the size of the box (made extra-large in this case to make the box easier to see). Finally, you can create a square box or a box with a notch using the notch parameter (which normally defaults to False). Figure 4-3 shows typical output from this example.

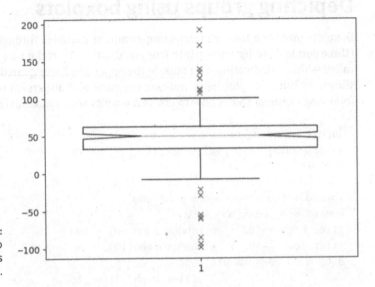

FIGURE 4-3:
Use boxplots to present groups of numbers.

The box shows the three data points as the box, with the red line in the middle being the median. The two black horizontal lines connected to the box by whiskers show the upper and lower limits (for four quartiles). The outliers appear above and below the upper and lower limit lines as green Xs.

Seeing data patterns using scatterplots

Scatterplots show clusters of data rather than trends (as with line graphs) or discrete values (as with bar charts). The purpose of a scatterplot is to help you see multidimensional data patterns. The following example shows how to create a scatterplot using randomized data:

```
import numpy as np
import matplotlib.pyplot as plt
%matplotlib inline

x1 = 5 * np.random.rand(40)
x2 = 5 * np.random.rand(40) + 25
```

```
x3 = 25 * np.random.rand(20)
x = np.concatenate((x1, x2, x3))
y1 = 5 * np.random.rand(40)
y2 = 5 * np.random.rand(40) + 25
y3 = 25 * np.random.rand(20)
y = np.concatenate((y1, y2, y3))

plt.scatter(x, y, s=[100], marker='^', c='m')
plt.show()
```

The example begins by generating random x and y coordinates. For each x coordinate, you must have a corresponding y coordinate. It's possible to create a scatterplot using just the x and y coordinates.

You can dress up a scatterplot in a number of ways. In this case, the s parameter determines the size of each data point. The marker parameter determines the data point shape. You use the c parameter to define the colors for all the data points, or you can define a separate color for individual data points. Figure 4-4 shows the output from this example.

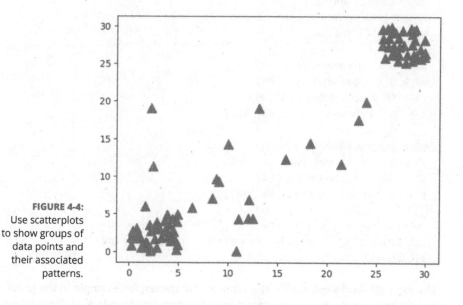

FIGURE 4-4: Use scatterplots to show groups of data points and their associated patterns.

Creating Advanced Scatterplots

Scatterplots are especially important for data science because they can show data patterns that aren't obvious when viewed in other ways. You can see data groupings with relative ease and help the viewer understand when data belongs to a particular group. You can also show overlaps between groups and even demonstrate when certain data is outside the expected range. Showing these various kinds of relationships in the data is an advanced technique that you need to know in order to make the best use of Matplotlib. The following sections demonstrate how to perform these advanced techniques on the scatterplot you created earlier in the chapter.

Depicting groups

Color is the third axis when working with a scatterplot. Using color lets you highlight groups so that others can see them with greater ease. The following example shows how you can use color to show groups within a scatterplot:

```
import numpy as np
import matplotlib.pyplot as plt
%matplotlib inline

x1 = 5 * np.random.rand(50)
x2 = 5 * np.random.rand(50) + 25
x3 = 30 * np.random.rand(25)
x = np.concatenate((x1, x2, x3))

y1 = 5 * np.random.rand(50)
y2 = 5 * np.random.rand(50) + 25
y3 = 30 * np.random.rand(25)
y = np.concatenate((y1, y2, y3))

color_array = ['b'] * 50 + ['g'] * 50 + ['r'] * 25
plt.scatter(x, y, s=[50], marker='D', c=color_array)
plt.show()
```

The example works essentially the same as the scatterplot example in the previous section, except that this example uses an array for the colors. Unfortunately, if you're seeing this in the printed book, the differences between the shades of gray in Figure 4-5 will be hard to see. However, the first group is blue, followed by green for the second group. Any outliers appear in red.

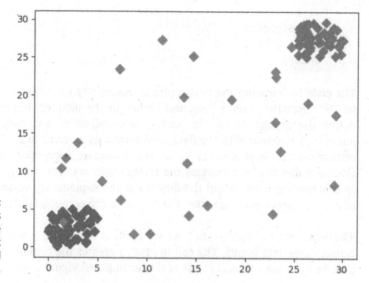

FIGURE 4-5:
Color arrays
can make the
scatterplot
groups stand
out better.

Showing correlations

In some cases, you need to know the general direction that your data is taking when looking at a scatterplot. Even if you create a clear depiction of the groups, the actual direction that the data is taking as a whole may not be clear. In this case, you add a trendline to the output. Here's an example of adding a trendline to a scatterplot that includes groups whose data points aren't as clearly separated as in the scatterplot shown previously in Figure 4-5:

```python
import numpy as np
import matplotlib.pyplot as plt
import matplotlib.pylab as plb
%matplotlib inline


x1 = 15 * np.random.rand(50)
x2 = 15 * np.random.rand(50) + 15
x3 = 30 * np.random.rand(25)
x = np.concatenate((x1, x2, x3))


y1 = 15 * np.random.rand(50)
y2 = 15 * np.random.rand(50) + 15
y3 = 30 * np.random.rand(25)
y = np.concatenate((y1, y2, y3))


color_array = ['b'] * 50 + ['g'] * 50 + ['r'] * 25
plt.scatter(x, y, s=[90], marker='*', c=color_array)
z = np.polyfit(x, y, 1)
```

```
p = np.poly1d(z)
plb.plot(x, p(x), 'm-')
plt.show()
```

The code for creating the scatterplot is essentially the same as in the example in the "Depicting groups" section earlier in the chapter, but the plot doesn't define the groups as clearly. Adding a trendline means calling the NumPy `polyfit()` function with the data, which returns a vector of coefficients, p, that minimizes the least-squares error. (Least-square regression is a method for finding a line that summarizes the relationship between two variables, x and y in this case, at least within the domain of the explanatory variable x. The third `polyfit()` parameter expresses the degree of the polynomial fit.)

The vector output of `polyfit()` is used as input to `poly1d()`, which calculates the actual y axis data points. The call to `plot()` creates the trendline on the scatterplot. You can see a typical result of this example in Figure 4-6.

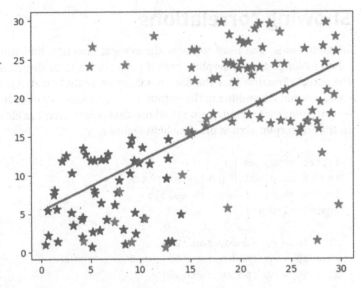

FIGURE 4-6:
Scatterplot trendlines can show you the general data direction.

Plotting Time Series

Nothing is truly static. When you view most data, you see an instant of time — a snapshot of how the data appeared at one particular moment. Of course, such views are both common and useful. However, sometimes you need to view data as it moves through time — to see it as it changes. Only by viewing the data as it changes can you expect to understand the underlying forces that shape it. The following sections describe how to work with data on a time-related basis.

Representing time on axes

Many times, you need to present data over time. The data could come in many forms, but generally, you have some type of time tick (one unit of time), followed by one or more features that describe what happens during that particular tick. The following example shows a simple set of days and sales on those days for a particular item in whole (integer) amounts.

```
import pandas as pd
import matplotlib.pyplot as plt
import datetime as dt
%matplotlib inline

start_date = dt.datetime(2023, 7, 29)
end_date = dt.datetime(2023, 8, 7)
daterange = pd.date_range(start_date, end_date)
sales = (np.random.rand(
    len(daterange)) * 50).astype(int)
df = pd.DataFrame(sales, index=daterange,
                  columns=['Sales'])
print(df)
```

The example begins by specifying the `start_date` and `end_date`, then using them to create `daterange`, the range of dates used for the output. It then creates a series of random values to use as data points and places them in `sales`. The number of values must match the length for `daterange`, and normally, you'd rely on actual data. The next step is to create a `DataFrame` to hold the information using `daterange` as an `index` and the values in `sales` as the data. So, what you end up with is a table of dates and associated values similar to this (the data values you see will vary):

```
            Sales
2023-07-29     14
2023-07-30     47
2023-07-31     17
2023-08-01      4
2023-08-02     38
2023-08-03     18
2023-08-04      0
2023-08-05     25
2023-08-06      9
2023-08-07      2
```

Now that you have some properly formatted data to use, it's time to create a plot. The following code shows a typical method of plotting data in the DataFrame format shown previously:

```
df.loc['Jul 30 2023':'Aug 05 2023'].plot()
plt.ylim(0, 50)
plt.xlabel('Sales Date')
plt.ylabel('Sale Value')
plt.title('Plotting Time')
plt.show()
```

Using df.loc accesses rows and columns in a DataFrame using labels, which are dates in string format in this case. So, the resulting plot won't show all of the data in df; it will instead show just the data from 'Jul 30 2023' to 'Aug 05 2023'. The call to plot() creates a line graph containing the requested data. The rest of the code provides various formatting and labeling features for the plot, which is then displayed using plt.show(). Figure 4-7 shows the result.

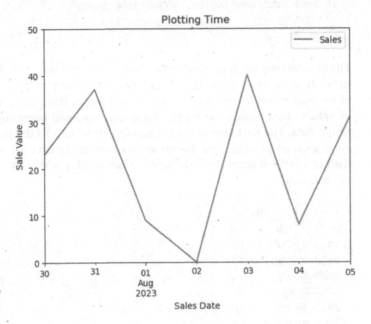

FIGURE 4-7: Use line graphs to show the flow of data over time.

Plotting trends over time

As with any other data presentation, sometimes you really can't see what direction the data is headed in without help. The following example starts with the plot from the previous section and adds a trendline to it:

```python
import numpy as np
import pandas as pd
import matplotlib.pyplot as plt
import datetime as dt
%matplotlib inline

start_date = dt.datetime(2023, 7, 29)
end_date = dt.datetime(2023, 8, 7)
daterange = pd.date_range(start_date, end_date)
sales = (np.random.rand(
    len(daterange)) * 50).astype(int)
df = pd.DataFrame(sales, index=daterange,
                  columns=['Sales'])

lr_coef = np.polyfit(range(0, len(df)), df['Sales'], 1)
lr_func = np.poly1d(lr_coef)
trend = lr_func(range(0, len(df)))
df['trend'] = trend
df.loc['Jul 30 2023':'Aug 05 2023'].plot()

plt.xlabel('Sales Date')
plt.ylabel('Sale Value')
plt.title('Plotting Time')
plt.legend(['Sales', 'Trend'])
plt.show()
```

REMEMBER

The "Showing correlations" section earlier in this chapter, shows how most people add a trendline to their graph. In fact, this is the approach that you often see used online. You'll also notice that a lot of people have trouble using this approach in some situations. This example takes a slightly different approach by adding the trendline directly to the DataFrame. If you print df after the call to df['trend'] = trend, you see trendline data similar to the values shown here:

	Sales	trend
2023-07-29	41	28.181818
2023-07-30	6	26.896970
2023-07-31	14	25.612121
2023-08-01	29	24.327273

```
2023-08-02     46   23.042424
2023-08-03     14   21.757576
2023-08-04     33   20.472727
2023-08-05      6   19.187879
2023-08-06     28   17.903030
2023-08-07      7   16.618182
```

Using this approach makes it ultimately easier to plot the data. You call `plot()` only once and avoid relying on the `matplotlib.pylab` function shown in the example in the "Showing correlations" section.

When you plot the initial data, the call to `plot()` automatically generates a legend for you. Matplotlib doesn't automatically add the trendline, so you must also create a new legend for the plot. Figure 4-8 shows typical output from this example using randomly generated data.

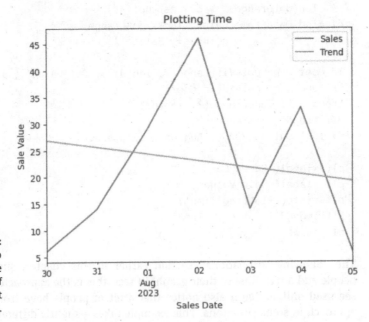

FIGURE 4-8:
Add a trendline to show the average direction of change in a chart or graph.

Plotting Geographical Data

Knowing where data comes from or how it applies to a specific place can be important. For example, if you want to know where food shortages have occurred and plan how to deal with them, you need to match the data you have to geographical locations. The same holds true for predicting where future sales will occur.

You may find that you need to use existing data to determine where to put new stores. Otherwise, you could put a store in a location that won't receive much in the way of sales, and the effort will lose money rather than make it. The following sections describe how to work with Cartopy (`https://pypi.org/project/Cartopy`) to interact with geographical data.

WARNING

You must shut the Notebook environment down before you make any changes, or else conda will complain that some files are in use. To shut the Notebook environment down, close and halt the kernel for any Notebook files you have open and then click Quit in the Jupyter page or press Ctrl+C in the Notebook terminal window. Wait a few seconds to give the files time to close properly before you attempt to do anything.

Using an environment in Notebook

Some of the packages you install also have a tendency to change your Notebook environment by installing other packages that may not work well with your baseline setup. Consequently, you see problems with code that functioned earlier. Normally, these problems consist mostly of warning messages, such as deprecation warnings.

In some cases, however, the changed packages can also tweak the output you obtain from code. Perhaps a newer package uses an updated algorithm or interacts with the code differently. When you have a package, such as Cartopy that makes changes to the overall baseline configuration, and you want to maintain your current configuration, you need to set up an environment for it. An environment keeps your baseline configuration intact but also allows the new package to create the environment it needs to execute properly. The following steps help you create the Cartopy environment used for this chapter:

1. **Open an Anaconda Prompt.**

   Notice that the prompt shows the location of your folder on your system but that it's preceded by (base). The (base) indicator tells you you're in your baseline environment — the one you want to preserve.

2. **Type** conda create -n Cartopy python=3.10 anaconda=2023.03 **and press Enter.**

   This action creates a new Cartopy environment. This new environment will use Python 3.10 and Anaconda 2023.03-1. You get precisely the same baseline as you've been using so far.

3. **Type** y **and press Enter when asked if you want to proceed.**

The installation process begins. This process can take a while to complete, especially when the software needs to download packages from online, so you need to be patient.

4. **Type** conda activate Cartopy **and press Enter.**

You have now changed over to the Cartopy environment. Notice that the prompt no longer says (base); it says (Cartopy) instead.

5. **Type** conda install -c conda-forge cartopy **and press Enter to install your copy of Cartopy.**

6. **Type** y **and press Enter when asked if you want to proceed.**

The installation process begins.

7. **(Optional) After the installation, make sure you're in your Notebooks directory using a command such as** cd \Users\John\Anaconda Projects **(for Windows developers).**

8. **Type** Jupyter Notebook **and press Enter.**

You see Notebook start, but it uses the Cartopy environment rather than the (base) environment. This copy of Notebook works precisely the same as any other copy of Notebook that you've used. The only difference is the environment in which it operates.

REMEMBER

This same technique works for any special package that you want to install. You should reserve it for packages that you don't intend to use every day. For example, this book uses Cartopy for just one example, so creating an environment for it is appropriate.

After you have finished using the Cartopy environment, press Ctrl+C to stop the server, type **conda deactivate** at the prompt, and press Enter. You see the prompt change back to (base).

Using Cartopy to plot geographic data

Now that you have a good installation of Cartopy, you can do something with it. To start with, you need to import all the required packages:

```
import numpy as np
import matplotlib.pyplot as plt
import matplotlib.ticker as mticker
import cartopy.crs as ccrs
```

```
import cartopy
from cartopy.mpl.gridliner import \
    LONGITUDE_FORMATTER, LATITUDE_FORMATTER
%matplotlib inline
```

These various packages let you download the map, format it, and add points of interest to it. The following example shows how to draw a map and place pointers to specific locations on it:

```
austin = (-97.75, 30.25)
hawaii = (-157.8, 21.3)
washington = (-77.01, 38.90)
chicago = (-87.68, 41.83)
losangeles = (-118.25, 34.05)

ax = plt.axes(projection=ccrs.Mercator(
    central_longitude=-110))
ax.coastlines()
ax.set_extent([-60, -160, 50, 10],
              crs=ccrs.PlateCarree())

ax.add_feature(cartopy.feature.OCEAN, zorder=0,
               facecolor='aqua')
ax.add_feature(cartopy.feature.LAND, zorder=0,
               edgecolor='black', facecolor='lightgray')
ax.add_feature(cartopy.feature.LAKES, zorder=0,
               edgecolor='black', facecolor='lightblue')
ax.add_feature(cartopy.feature.BORDERS, zorder=0,
               edgecolor='gray')

x, y = list(zip(*[austin, hawaii, washington,
                  chicago, losangeles]))

gl = ax.gridlines(
    crs=ccrs.PlateCarree(), draw_labels=True,
    linewidth=2, color='gray', alpha=0.5,
    linestyle='--')
gl.xlabels_top = False
gl.left_labels = False
gl.xlocator = mticker.FixedLocator(list(x))
gl.ylocator = mticker.FixedLocator(list(y))
gl.xformatter = LONGITUDE_FORMATTER
gl.yformatter = LATITUDE_FORMATTER
```

```
ax.plot(x, y, 'ro', markersize=6,
        transform=ccrs.Geodetic())

plt.title("Mercator Projection")
plt.show()
```

The example begins by defining the longitude and latitude for various cities. It then creates the basic map. The `projection` parameter defines the basic map appearance. You can find a listing of projection types at https://scitools. org.uk/cartopy/docs/v0.15/crs/projections.html. The `central_longitude` parameter defines where the map is centered. To see the coastlines of the various countries, you use the `coastlines()` method. This example doesn't look at the whole world, so it uses the `set_extent()` method to crop the map to size.

The example uses the `add_feature()` to add features to the basic map. You can color the features in various ways to provide a distinctive look. The features are documented more fully at https://scitools.org.uk/cartopy/docs/v0.14/ matplotlib/feature_interface.html.

In this case, the example creates x and y coordinates using the previously stored longitude and latitude values. As part of displaying the coordinates, the map also creates gridlines to show their longitude and latitude with the `gridlines()` method. The resulting object, `gl`, allows you to modify the grid characteristics. The documentation at https://scitools.org.uk/cartopy/docs/v0.13/ matplotlib/gridliner.html tells you more about working with gridlines.

The code then plots these locations on the map in a contrasting color so that you can easily see them. The final step is to display the map, as shown in Figure 4-9.

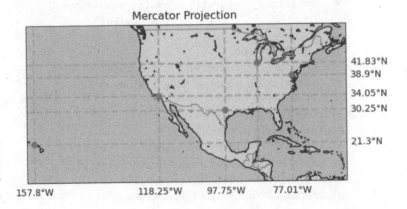

FIGURE 4-9: Maps can illustrate data in ways other graphics can't.

Visualizing Graphs

A *graph* (in the network sense of the word) is a depiction of data showing the connections between data points (called *nodes*) using lines (called *edges*). The purpose is to show that some data points relate to others, but not all the data points that appear on the graph. Think about a map of a subway system. Each station connects to other stations, but no single station connects to all the stations in the subway system. Graphs are a popular data science topic because of their use in social media analysis. When performing social media analysis, you depict and analyze networks of relationships, such as friends or business connections, from social hubs such as Facebook, Google+, Twitter, or LinkedIn.

REMEMBER

The two common depictions of graphs are *undirected*, where the graph simply shows lines between data elements, and *directed*, where arrows added to the line show that data flows in a particular direction. For example, consider a depiction of a water system. The water would flow in just one direction in most cases, so you could use a directed graph to depict not only the connections between sources and targets for the water but also to show water direction by using arrows. The following sections help you understand the two types of graphs better and show you how to create them.

Developing undirected graphs

As previously stated, an undirected graph simply shows connections between nodes. The output doesn't provide a direction from one node to the next. For example, when establishing connectivity between web pages, no direction is implied. The following example shows how to create an undirected graph:

```
import networkx as nx
import matplotlib.pyplot as plt
%matplotlib inline
G = nx.Graph()
H = nx.Graph()
G.add_node(1)
G.add_nodes_from([2, 3])
G.add_nodes_from(range(4, 7))
H.add_node(7)
G.add_nodes_from(H)

G.add_edge(1, 2)
G.add_edge(1, 1)
G.add_edges_from([(2,3), (3,6), (4,6), (5,6)])
```

```
H.add_edges_from([(4,7), (5,7), (6,7)])
G.add_edges_from(H.edges())

nx.draw_networkx(G, node_color='yellow')
plt.show()
```

This example builds the graph using a number of techniques. It begins by importing the Networkx package. To create a new undirected graph, the code calls the `Graph()` constructor, which can take a number of input arguments to use as attributes. However, you can build a perfectly usable graph without using attributes, which is what this example does.

The easiest way to add a node is to call `add_node()` with a node number. You can also add a list, dictionary, or `range()` of nodes using `add_nodes_from()`. In fact, you can import nodes from other graphs if you want.

REMEMBER

Even though the nodes used in the example rely on numbers, you don't have to use numbers for your nodes. A node can use a single letter, a string, or even a date. Nodes do have some restrictions. For example, you can't create a node using a Boolean value.

Nodes don't have any connectivity at the outset. You must define connections (edges) between them. To add a single edge, you call `add_edge()` with the numbers of the nodes that you want to add. As with nodes, you can use `add_edges_from()` to create more than one edge using a list, dictionary, or another graph as input. Figure 4-10 shows the output from this example. (Your output may differ slightly but should have the same connections.)

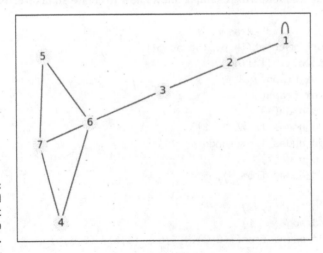

FIGURE 4-10:
Undirected graphs connect nodes to form patterns.

Developing directed graphs

You use directed graphs when you need to show a direction, say from a start point to an end point. When you get a map that shows you how to get from one specific point to another, the starting node and ending node are marked as such, and the lines between these nodes (and all the intermediate nodes) show direction.

TIP

Your graphs need not be boring. You can dress them up in all sorts of ways so that the viewer gains additional information in different ways. For example, you can create custom labels, use specific colors for certain nodes, or rely on color to help people see the meaning behind your graphs. You can also change edge line weight and use other techniques to mark a specific path between nodes as the better one to choose. The following example shows many (but not nearly all) the ways in which you can dress up a directed graph and make it more interesting:

```python
import networkx as nx
import matplotlib.pyplot as plt
%matplotlib inline

G = nx.DiGraph()

G.add_node(1)
G.add_nodes_from([2, 3])
G.add_nodes_from(range(4, 9))

G.add_edge(1, 2)
G.add_edges_from([(1,4), (4,5), (2,3), (3,6),
                  (5,6), (6,7), (7,8)])

colors = ['r', 'g', 'g', 'g', 'g', 'm', 'm', 'r']
labels = {1:'Start', 2:'2', 3:'3', 4:'4',
          5:'5', 6:'6', 7:'7', 8:'End'}
sizes = [800, 300, 300, 300, 300, 600, 300, 800]

nx.draw_networkx(
    G, node_color=colors, node_shape='D',
    labels=labels, node_size=sizes, font_color='w')
plt.show()
```

The example begins by creating a directional graph using the DiGraph() constructor. You should note that the NetworkX package also supports MultiGraph() and MultiDiGraph() graph types. You can see a listing of all the graph types at https://networkx.org/documentation/stable/reference/classes/index.html.

Adding nodes is much like working with an undirected graph. You can add single nodes using add_node( ) and multiple nodes using add_nodes_from( ). The order of nodes in the call is important. The flow from one node to another is from left to right in the list supplied to the call.

Adding edges is much the same as working with an undirected graph, too. You can use add_edge( ) to add a single edge or add_edges_from( ) to add multiple edges at one time. However, the order of the node numbers is important. The flow goes from the left node to the right node in each pair.

This example adds special node colors, labels, shape (only one shape is used), and sizes to the output. You still call on draw_networkx( ) to perform the task. However, adding the parameters shown changes the appearance of the graph. Figure 4-11 shows the output from this example.

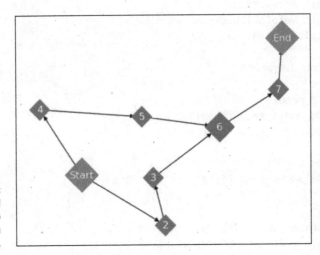

FIGURE 4-11:
Use directed graphs to show direction between nodes.

Index

About the Authors

Jack Hyman is the founder of HyerTek, a Washington, DC-based technology consulting and training services firm specializing in cloud computing, business intelligence, learning management, and enterprise application advisory needs for federal, state, and private sector organizations in the United States and Canada. He is an enterprise technology expert with over 20 years of digital and cloud transformation experience, collaborative computing, usability engineering, blockchain, and systems integration. During his extensive IT career, Jack has led U.S. federal government agencies and global enterprises through multiyear technology transformation projects. Before founding HyerTek, Jack worked for Oracle and IBM. He has authored many books, provided peer-review guidance for scholarly journals, and developed training courseware with an emphasis on Microsoft technologies. Since 2004, he has served as an adjunct faculty member at George Washington University, American University, and the University of the Cumberlands. Hyman holds a PhD in Information Systems from Nova Southeastern University.

Luca Massaron is a data scientist and a marketing research director specializing in multivariate statistical analysis, machine learning, and customer insight, with more than a decade of experience in solving real-world problems and generating value for stakeholders by applying reasoning, statistics, data mining, and algorithms. From being a pioneer of web audience analysis in Italy to achieving the rank of top ten Kaggler on kaggle.com, he has always been passionate about everything regarding data and analysis and about demonstrating the potentiality of data-driven knowledge discovery to both experts and nonexperts. Favoring simplicity over unnecessary sophistication, he believes that a lot can be achieved in data science by understanding and practicing its essentials.

Paul McFedries has been a technical writer for 30 years (no, that is not a typo). He has been messing around with spreadsheet software since installing Lotus 1-2-3 on an IBM PC clone in 1986. He has written more than 100 books (nope, not a typo) that have sold more than four million copies worldwide (again, not a typo). Paul's books include the Wiley titles *Excel All-in-One For Dummies*, *Excel Data Analysis For Dummies*, *Teach Yourself VISUALLY Excel*, and *Teach Yourself VISUALLY Windows 11*. Paul invites everyone to drop by his personal website (https://paulmcfedries. com) and to follow him on Twitter (@paulmcf) and Facebook (www.facebook.com/ PaulMcFedries/).

John Paul Mueller is a freelance author and technical editor. He has writing in his blood, having produced 124 books and more than 600 articles to date. The topics range from networking to artificial intelligence and from database management to heads-down programming. Some of his current books include discussions of data science, data security, machine learning, and algorithms. His technical editing skills have helped more than 70 authors refine the content of their manuscripts. John has provided technical editing services to various magazines, performed various kinds of consulting, and written certification exams. Be sure to read John's blog at `http://blog.johnmuellerbooks.com/`. You can reach John on the internet at `John@JohnMuellerBooks.com`. John also has a website at `http://www.johnmuellerbooks.com/`. Be sure to follow John on Amazon at `https://www.amazon.com/John-Mueller/e/B000AQ77KK/`.

Lillian Pierson is a CEO and data leader who supports data professionals in evolving into world-class leaders and entrepreneurs. To date, she's helped educate over 1.3 million data professionals on AI and data science.

The author of six data-oriented books from Wiley Publishing as well as eight data courses on LinkedIn Learning, Lillian has supported a wide variety of organizations across the globe, from the United Nations and *National Geographic* to Ericsson and Saudi Aramco and everything in between.

A licensed professional engineer in good standing, Lillian has been a technical consultant since 2007 and a data business mentor since 2018. She occasionally volunteers her expertise in global summits and forums on data privacy and ethics.

Dr. Jonathan Reichental is the founder of Human Future, a global business and technology advisory, investment, and education firm. His previous roles have included senior software engineering manager and director of technology innovation, and he has served as chief information officer (CIO) at both O'Reilly Media and the City of Palo Alto, California.

In 2013, he was recognized as one of the 25 doers, dreamers, and drivers in government in America. In 2016, he was named a top influential CIO in the United States, and in 2017, he was named one of the top 100 CIOs in the world. He has also won a Best CIO in Silicon Valley award and a national IT leadership prize.

Reichental is a recognized global thought leader, keynote speaker, and business and government adviser on a number of emerging trends, including urban innovation, smart cities, sustainability, blockchain technology, data governance, the fourth industrial revolution, digital transformation, and many more.

He is an adjunct professor in the School of Management at the University of San Francisco and instructs at several other universities. Reichental regularly creates online educational video courses for LinkedIn Learning, which include a highly successful series on data governance.

Reichental has written several books, including *Smart Cities for Dummies, Exploring Smart Cities Activity Book for Kids,* and *Exploring Cities Bedtime Rhymes.*

You can learn more about his work at `www.reichental.com`, and follow him on LinkedIn and Twitter.

Joseph Schmuller is a veteran of over 25 years in the field of information technology. He is the author of several books on computing, including *Statistical Analysis with R For Dummies*, *R Projects For Dummies*, and all five editions of *Statistical Analysis with Excel For Dummies* (all from Wiley), and the three editions of *Teach Yourself UML in 24 Hours* (SAMS). He has created and delivered online coursework on statistics and Excel for LinkedIn Learning. Over 100,000 people around the world have taken these courses.

For seven years, Joseph was the editor-in-chief of *PC AI* magazine, and he has written numerous articles on advanced technology.

A former member of the American Statistical Association, he has taught statistics at the undergraduate and graduate levels. He holds a BS from Brooklyn College, an MA from the University of Missouri-Kansas City, and a PhD from the University of Wisconsin, all in psychology.

He and his family live in Jacksonville, Florida, where he works on the Digital Cloud & Enterprise Architecture Team at Availity.

Alan Simon is the managing principal of Thinking Helmet, Inc., a boutique consulting firm that specializes in enterprise data management, business intelligence, and analytics. Alan began his technology career in 1979 while still in college, working on a prehistoric data warehouse hosted on an antiquated UNIVAC mainframe computer. From that moment, he was hooked on data management and data-driven insights. For more than 40 years, Alan has been at the forefront of disciplines such as data warehousing, business intelligence, big data and data lakes, and modern analytics. In addition to working through his own firm, over the years, Alan has held global, national, and regional business intelligence and data warehousing practice leadership positions at leading consultancies and software firms. He has built both brand-new practices and turnaround situations into top-tier organizations, often working side by side with his consultants on critical client engagements.

Alan is especially known for being a "trusted adviser" to clients, helping them navigate through the hype and hidden traps when bringing emerging data technologies and architectures into their enterprises. His client work focuses on assessment, strategy, architecture, and road-map engagements for data lakes, data warehousing, business intelligence and analytics, and enterprise-scale systems, as well as rescuing and reviving problematic programs and projects.

Alan has also taught college and university courses since the early 1980s to both undergraduate and graduate students. He has authored more than 30 business and technology books dating back to the mid-1980s, including the first edition of *Data Warehousing For Dummies* (Wiley).

From 1982 to 1986, Alan was a United States Air Force officer, where he wrote software for the nation's nuclear missile attack alert system.

His "other other job" besides consulting and teaching is writing historical novels and contemporary fiction, including (so far) one title that appeared on *USA Today's* bestseller list.

Allen G. Taylor is a 40-year veteran of the computer industry and the author of more than 40 books, including *SQL For Dummies, Crystal Reports 2008 For Dummies, Database Development For Dummies, Access 2003 Power Programming with VBA,* and *SQL Weekend Crash Course.* He lectures internationally on databases, networks, innovation, astronomy, and entrepreneurship, as well as health and wellness. He also teaches database development through a leading online education provider. For the latest news on Allen's activities, check out his online courses (at pioneer-academy1.teachable.com) and his blog (at www.allengtaylor.com). You can contact Allen at allen.taylor@ieee.org.

Publisher's Acknowledgments

Executive Editor: Steve Hayes
Compilation Editor: Colleen Diamond
Project Editor: Colleen Diamond
Copy Editor: Colleen Diamond
Senior Managing Editor: Kristie Pyles

Production Editor: Tamilmani Varadharaj
Cover Image: © DC Studio/Shutterstock

Leverage the power

Dummies is the global leader in the reference category and one of the most trusted and highly regarded brands in the world. No longer just focused on books, customers now have access to the dummies content they need in the format they want. Together we'll craft a solution that engages your customers, stands out from the competition, and helps you meet your goals.

Advertising & Sponsorships

Connect with an engaged audience on a powerful multimedia site, and position your message alongside expert how-to content. Dummies.com is a one-stop shop for free, online information and know-how curated by a team of experts.

- Targeted ads
- Video
- Email Marketing
- Microsites
- Sweepstakes sponsorship

20 MILLION PAGE VIEWS EVERY SINGLE MONTH

15 MILLION UNIQUE VISITORS PER MONTH

43% OF ALL VISITORS ACCESS THE SITE VIA THEIR MOBILE DEVICES

700,000 NEWSLETTER SUBSCRIPTIONS TO THE INBOXES OF

300,000 UNIQUE INDIVIDUALS EVERY WEEK

# of dummies

Custom Publishing

Reach a global audience in any language by creating a solution that will differentiate you from competitors, amplify your message, and encourage customers to make a buying decision.

- Apps
- Books
- eBooks
- Video
- Audio
- Webinars

Brand Licensing & Content

Leverage the strength of the world's most popular reference brand to reach new audiences and channels of distribution.

For more information, visit **dummies.com/biz**

PERSONAL ENRICHMENT

Staying Sharp	**Facebook**	**Guitar**	**Investing**	**Beekeeping**	**Digital Photography**
9781119187790	9781119179030	9781119293354	9781119293347	9781119310068	9781119235606
USA $26.00	USA $21.99	USA $24.99	USA $22.99	USA $22.99	USA $24.99
CAN $31.99	CAN $25.99	CAN $29.99	CAN $27.99	CAN $27.99	CAN $29.99
UK £19.99	UK £16.99	UK £17.99	UK £16.99	UK £16.99	UK £17.99

Meditation	**Pregnancy**	**Samsung Galaxy S7**	**iPhone**	**Crocheting**	**Nutrition**
9781119251163	9781119235491	9781119279952	9781119283133	9781119287117	9781119130246
USA $24.99	USA $26.99	USA $24.99	USA $24.99	USA $24.99	USA $22.99
CAN $29.99	CAN $31.99	CAN $29.99	CAN $29.99	CAN $29.99	CAN $27.99
UK £17.99	UK £19.99	UK £17.99	UK £17.99	UK £16.99	UK £16.99

PROFESSIONAL DEVELOPMENT

Windows 10	**AutoCAD**	**Excel 2016**	**QuickBooks 2017**	**macOS Sierra**	**LinkedIn**	**Windows 10**
9781119311041	9781119255796	9781119293439	9781119281467	9781119280651	9781119251132	9781119310563
USA $24.99	USA $39.99	USA $26.99	USA $26.99	USA $29.99	USA $24.99	USA $34.00
CAN $29.99	CAN $47.99	CAN $31.99	CAN $31.99	CAN $35.99	CAN $29.99	CAN $41.99
UK £17.99	UK £27.99	UK £19.99	UK £19.99	UK £21.99	UK £17.99	UK £24.99

SharePoint 2016	**Fundamental Analysis**	**Networking**	**Office 2016**	**Office 365**	**Salesforce.com**	**Coding**
9781119181705	9781119263593	9781119257769	9781119293477	9781119265313	9781119239314	9781119293323
USA $29.99	USA $26.99	USA $29.99	USA $26.99	USA $24.99	USA $29.99	USA $29.99
CAN $35.99	CAN $31.99	CAN $35.99	CAN $31.99	CAN $29.99	CAN $35.99	CAN $35.99
UK £21.99	UK £19.99	UK £21.99	UK £19.99	UK £17.99	UK £21.99	UK £21.99